THE ARCHITECT & THE AMERICAN COUNTRY HOUSE
1890–1940

The ARCHITECT &
the American Country House
1890–1940

Mark Alan Hewitt

Architectural photographs by Richard Cheek

Yale University Press   New Haven & London

Published with assistance from the Graham Foundation for Advanced
Studies in the Fine Arts.

Designed by Ken Botnick.
Set in Garamond #3 type by Highwood Typographic Services,
Hamden, Connecticut.
Title page lettering by Anita Karl.
Printed in Hong Kong by Everbest Printing Company.

Library of Congress Cataloging-in-Publication Data
Hewitt, Mark A.
The architect and the American country house, 1890–1940 / Mark
Alan Hewitt; architectural photographs by Richard Cheek.
p. cm.
Includes bibliographical references.
ISBN 0-300-04740-1 (alk. paper)
1. Country homes—United States. 2. Architects and patrons—United
States. 3. United States—Social life and customs—20th century.
I. Cheek, Richard. II. Title.
NA7561.H4 1990
728.8'0973—dc20
89-77575
    CIP

The paper in this book meets the guidelines for permanence and
durability of the Committee on Production Guidelines for Book
Longevity of the Council on Library Resources.

10 9 8 7 6 5 4 3 2 1

Frontispiece: **The Hill-Stead.** Farmington, Connecticut. Greek revival
porch of office wing added in 1907. (Richard Cheek.)

To Lynn and Sarah

Contents

Preface

This book was written out of my personal interest in a relatively little-known group of American domestic designers who were trained at the turn of the century, during my grandfather's time. After five years of research and writing, it has become something of an obsession, one architect's tribute to colleagues of a generation twice removed.

I first became aware of these architects as a student of Vincent Scully, the great American architectural historian, and was further introduced to their achievements during my graduate studies in architecture at the University of Pennsylvania. Many of my fellow students, especially those under the influence of Robert Venturi's ideas, felt the lingering presence of the old Philadelphia school; trips to Chestnut Hill, Haverford, and the Main Line convinced us of the extraordinary quality of their work. It is no coincidence that my book takes up where Scully's *Shingle Style* leaves off and stops short of the generation of modernist designers who were to loom so large in my training—the teachers of my teachers. So I have done what many architects are prone to do: renounce my fathers to embrace a previous generation.

Because I am an architect, the biases of my research and ideas are skewed toward design and architectural practice. I have endeavored in this book to answer questions that seem to be not only historically important, such as how architects thought and worked, how they got their commissions, and who their patrons were, but also of interest to the practicing architect today. It is an accident of fate that while I have been writing this book I have also been designing (with my wife and partner) a large country house on the site of one of the great Long Island estates of the 1920s. As we have dealt with the myriad problems that face any designer, I have read with interest such humorous chronicles as *Mr. Blandings Builds His Dream House* and *The Honeywood File* and dug deeply into the accounts of country house building during the early twentieth century. Needless to say, the resonances and ironies connecting our experience and that of past architects have been painful and funny. Some of the lessons learned from straddling the fence as historian and architect have contributed to making this book a little more interesting—and will make our next residential designs a good deal better. If other architects find some of those same lessons in these pages, I shall have accomplished one of my purposes.

This is also a work of architectural history and theory, and I suspect it will be judged more critically from that point of view as a frankly revisionist work. That is also intended; my views of the importance of eclectic and classical theory and the unfortunate denigration of their contributions to American architecture are house is a distinct type that emerged during the late 1880s as a reaction to Queen Anne cottages and larger estate models. It flourished for some fifty years within a cohesive taste culture of architects, critics, and patrons. I hope to show the breadth and aesthetic vitality of this American house type as a reflection of the vision and creativity of the architects and patrons who created it.

Writing a survey of this kind is hardly a single-handed enterprise. I was gratified when I began the task that a number of interested parties came to my aid and encouraged my efforts. The list of debts quickly grew. So let me begin with a general thank you to all who contributed their thoughts, courtesies, and material to this book.

I was fortunate to have the support of a number of scholars and friends who were extremely generous with their time. Foremost among those who donated research and criticism was Stephen Fox of Houston and the Anchorage Foundation, who not only encouraged me in my darker moments but offered detailed comments on two drafts of the manuscript. Stephen also suggested a number of research directions that were extremely useful. Also high on the list is Richard Cheek, my collaborator in the photography, whose ideas, bibliographic skills, and general knowledge of the subject were invaluable. Indeed, I would not have come to a number of important points without our long discussions on the form and content of the book. And of course the book would be only half as good without his wonderful pictures. His work deserves to be seen as art on a level with that of the great photographers of the early twentieth century, and I am glad that we can present it as such here.

Keith Morgan read later drafts of the manuscript and was extremely generous with time and suggestions as to how to improve the writing and content. I am grateful for his efforts on my behalf and for his excellent contributions to the subject of the country house in publications cited throughout the text. Without his research on Charles Platt this study would not have been possible.

I am likewise indebted to David Gebhard, who read the first draft, for his pioneering work on California architects and on the work of traditionalist designers in general. He encouraged me to pursue my study under the framework of eclectic theory and practice and was very helpful in suggesting directions for research. He and Lauren Bricker also guided me through the superb architectural archives at the University of California at Santa Barbara, from which a number of photographs were culled. Robert A. M. Stern, my colleague while at Columbia University, also read an early draft of the manuscript and was always on hand with criticisms. His knowledge of architects and houses, particularly in the New York area, was invaluable.

Others who gave early advice and support were Alfred Branam, Jr., David DeLong, Gavin Townsend, and John Deming. Mr. Branam's suggestions on photo collections, tours of Philadelphia houses, and research on Horace Trumbauer all contributed greatly to this book. I thank him for all of his help. Gavin Townsend's

excellent dissertation on Tudor houses greatly influenced my thoughts; he also read an early draft and gave helpful comments. John Deming was a valuable source for information on Philadelphia, and David DeLong read early chapters of the book.

A number of people shared archival material and led me to research sources. Katherine Warwick, director of the Hill-Stead Museum, opened her entire archive and house to Richard Cheek and me, allowing us to unveil some of its marvelous history, both here and in an article for *Antiques.* She was a collaborator, host, and researcher. David Warren, director of the Bayou Bend Museum, was kind in sending photos and providing information on that superb house. Janet Parks and the staff of the Avery Archives were patient, knowledgeable, and helpful during the many visits I paid them and expedited photo orders at several key times. Herbert Mitchell, the librarian in charge of archival acquisitions at Avery, led me to several important photo collections in his treasure trove. Angela Giral, head librarian at Avery, graciously gave permission for publication of the material there. The staff of the Long Island Studies Collection, Nassau County Museums at Hofstra University, provided enormous help in locating photos from the Mattie Edwards Hewitt collection. Scott Marshall, assistant director of the Edith Wharton Restoration, provided extensive data on Lenox and The Mount. Steven M. Bedford graciously shared his research on John Russell Pope. To all, a hearty thanks.

For special photo permissions and access to houses, I wish to thank Mr. Paul Mellon, Marc Appleton, the late Mrs. Medora Bass, Mr. and Mrs. Fuller J. Callaway, Jr., Donald McTernan of the National Parks Service and the Vanderbilt Mansion National Historic Site, Villa Banfi Wines, Inc., Susan Poulsen-Crough of the Wingstead Foundation, the S. C. Johnson Company, Charles Montooth of the Taliesin Fellowship, the Trustees of the Hill-Stead Museum in Farmington, Connecticut, the Parks Department of the City of Beverly Hills, California, the Biltmore Company, SOKA University in Tokyo and Calabasas, California, the Nassau County Museum at Muttontown, Virginia House and the Virginia Museum in Richmond, the Atlanta Historical Society and Swan House, Bayou Bend Museum and the Museum of Fine Arts, Houston, Koch and Wilson Architects of New Orleans.

My thanks also to people who helped with various things along the way: Allan Greenberg, Michael Adams, Dale Flynt, Anne Trowbridge, Marc and Mary Appleton, Stanley Taraila, Earle Shettleworth, Ellie Reichlin, Dana Geel, Gladys O'Neal, Dan Bluestone, Dana Cuff, Kevin Daly, the late Dolores Kaup, Jim and Mary Vaughan, Ned Kaufman, Frank G. Matero, Shirley Driks, Peter Papademetriou, John Ferguson, Gary Hammond, William B. O'Neal, John Zukowsky, Sabra Clark, Robert Bruegmann, Scott Burrell, James Pahlau, Richard Wynchley, Ford Peatross, Dini Pickering, Harry Mariani, Carmen Joseph Tintle, Father Philip of St. Josaphat's Monastery and the Ukranian Order of St. Basil the Great, Karl Jensen, Julius T. Sadler, Jr., Lauren Weiss Bricker, Deborah Nevins, Lila Stillson, Betsy Cheek, Denis J. Lesieur, Mr. and Mrs. James Black, Eric Kimura, Beverly King, Sandra Tatman, Sam Wilson, Jr., Louise R. Johnson, Julia Converse, Jean Wolf, Elizabeth Bede, Edward J. Smits, Cynthia Parker, John and Beth Werwaiss, Samuel G. White, Bayard Whittemore, and George E. Thomas.

I am particularly grateful to the three research assistants who stuck with me during the early, middle, and late stages of this project. Cindy Oettchen, on board during the planning stages at Rice University in 1985, did a splendid job of finding initial sources, surveying periodicals, and drafting biographies of the architects. Michael Gotkin took over at Columbia in the summer of 1987 and was a workhorse in researching and drafting architect biographies, as well as in locating a number of key sources. Last and hardly least was Jim Hennessy, who photocopied material in a hot library, read drafts, combed Avery Library for periodicals, and mainly provided moral support when it was most needed during the summer of 1988.

To Carter Manny of the Graham Foundation I owe an extraordinary debt of gratitude, not only for giving me the grant that started this project but for his patience and support during its long gestation. Like many Graham authors, I believe that this philanthropic organization is one of the most important perpetuators of significant architectural research in the United States. In a period of economic hard times for the arts, it has been a beacon.

Finally, I wish to express my deepest gratitude to Judy Metro, my tireless and patient editor at Yale University Press, for all of her labors on my behalf, and to Ken Botnick, the designer, and Karen Gangel, manuscript editor.

Chaos then confronts us, in that there is no single architectural following, but legion; and in that fact lies the honour of our art, for neither is society one, or even at one with itself. Architecture is nothing unless it is intimately expressive, and if utterly different things clamour for voicing, different also must be their architectural manifestation.

—RALPH ADAMS CRAM

Rich Men and Their Houses

1

Unfortunately, almost every city gentleman who comes into possession—whether by purchase or otherwise—of a plain country house, from which some honest well-to-do farmer has just decamped, puzzles his brain first of all, to know how he shall make a "fine thing" of it.

—DONALD G. MITCHELL

ငၣ BILTMORE AND OAK SPRING

During Christmas of 1895, near the small town of Asheville, North Carolina, George Washington Vanderbilt toasted the opening of Biltmore, his 255-room country house, with a party hosted by his mother, Mrs. William H. Vanderbilt. It was a celebration marked by the sad irony that the architect of this great French Renaissance–style mansion, Richard Morris Hunt, had died the previous July, and that the landscape architect, Frederick Law Olmsted, was ailing and would in three years be committed to a mental institution.[1] For even as the toast was raised, the American scene that gave rise to Biltmore was changing.

Hunt, Olmsted, and Vanderbilt created at the Biltmore estate an oddly articulate testament to the uncertain culture of post–Civil War America. The enormous house, conceived in 1889 and finished six years later, seemed to close out one era and begin another, opening the doors on an American Renaissance, yet clinging to certain Victorian values. Reflecting the extraordinary wealth of the Vanderbilt family, the material and financial resources used to build it were massive: "vast brackets, as it were, to the very face of Nature," according to Henry James, who saw the estate in 1905. The house was a "castle of enchantment" in the wilderness, stand-ing out from it like a "patch of old brocade . . . [against] the woof of the native homespun."[2] At once a palace, dairy farm, forest preserve, resort cottage, model utopian enterprise, and collector's menagerie, Biltmore epitomized the multifaceted nature of wealthy men's houses at the end of the Victorian era. It was created by the most eminent architect and landscape architect in the nation, for a scion of one of its most prominent families. The largest and most celebrated house of its time, it summarized a series of palatial domestic demonstrations that defined the aspirations of America's emerging modern plutocracy.

Biltmore remains unequaled in size and grandeur, a monument to an age of excess. It is America's greatest country house, as defined by the English: the aristocratic seat of a gentleman land-owner, from which he administers his estate lands. Yet it differs profoundly from any English examples. Both wealth and political power are vested in the country houses of the British Isles, but this is not so in America, even at Biltmore. Vanderbilt's estate yielded income from its dairy, agriculture, and forestry enterprises, but the house was far more a symbol of culture and taste than a source of capital. Observers of that era would have called it a stately home. Biltmore was the most compelling example of the grand, semipublic country house designed to celebrate the achievements

1 Richard Morris Hunt. **Biltmore** house (1892–95), Asheville, North Carolina. Stair tower and entrance pavilion of east front. (Richard Cheek.)

I

2 Richard Morris Hunt. **Biltmore** house. West facade shortly after completion, from French Broad River. (Biltmore Company.)

3 The creators of **Biltmore**: George Washington Vanderbilt (center), Richard Morris Hunt, and Frederick Law Olmsted, among associates in Biltmore Forest during construction, c. 1892. (Biltmore Company.)

of the capitalist oligarchy of which its builder was a leading figure. Its conspicuous symbolism was of leisure and wealth, not of political dominance.

The patron of Biltmore, George Washington Vanderbilt (1862–1914), was a member of the third (monied) generation of one of America's richest families—a grandchild of the famous Commodore Vanderbilt and a son of William Henry Vanderbilt, the railroad and shipping tycoon. Unlike his better-known brothers,[3] he was a philanthropist, not a true-blue American capitalist. Bookish and too reticent to be a public figure, he turned away from business toward cultural pursuits, the most important being the construction of his house, which took over half his inheritance (said to be over $6 million), costing some $45,000 per day at the peak of construction. He collected an outstanding library, housed in one of Biltmore's most impressive rooms, and was a major donor to the New York Public Library.[4] He was not unlike the English builder of Harlaxton Manor (1831–44) in Lincolnshire, Gregory Gregory, a gentleman "rich, but not all that rich," who devoted his entire adult life to the construction of a fantasy house, half Elizabethan and half baroque, that would be a perfect embodiment of himself.[5] Vanderbilt was an American Victorian dilettante. His house was the center of a little universe of his own making, representative of both his personal tastes and his utopian ideals.

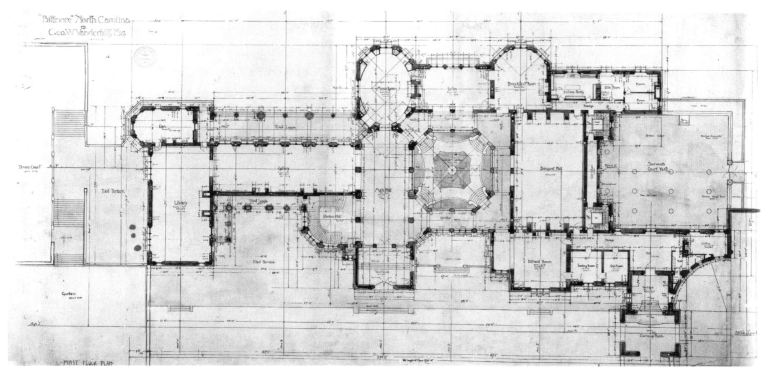

4 **Biltmore** house. First floor plan by Richard Morris Hunt, from the original working drawings. (Biltmore Company.)

5 **Biltmore** estate. Plan of home grounds. Office of Frederick Law Olmsted, c. 1889. (Biltmore Company.)

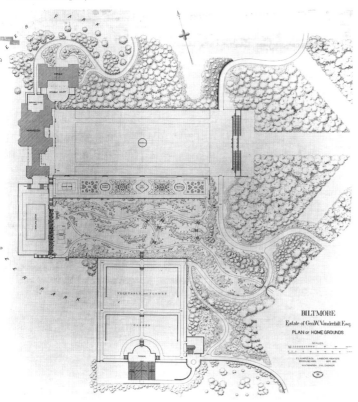

As a model for his new stately home, Vanderbilt chose the country houses of the French Renaissance. He had initially wanted merely a large frame summer cottage, not unlike the one designed by Hunt for his brother William on Long Island (Idle Hour, at Oakdale, 1876–78). Early on, however, Hunt convinced Vanderbilt to visit the great châteaux of France, which the architect had come to know during his days at the Ecole des Beaux-Arts. Using material collected on the trip, Hunt incorporated details from Blois, Fontainebleau, and other French palaces into the design. His great staircase, with its elaborate floral bronze ornament and chandelier, as well as the elaborately carved dormers outside, synthesized his favorite motifs from the François I period he loved so well. Yet something of the American cottage remains in Biltmore's plan and room arrangement. Comparing it to Waddesdon Manor (1874–89), built by the French Beaux-Arts architect G. H. Destailleur for Baron Ferdinand de Rothschild in Buckinghamshire, one senses the difference between an American house and a European one. Waddesdon had one formal reception room after another filled with exquisite furniture and art—an enfilade of riches. Biltmore had a family dining room and a lounging room, disposed around what could have been the palm court of a hotel. It had grand rooms too, like the huge banquet hall, but Hunt arranged them with an openness and informality that almost belied his own Beaux-Arts training. The interiors ranged in character from rich, European, and cosmopolitan pastiches to comfortable and slightly passé Victorian confections. Hunt gave his client both a palace and a summer cottage, a synthesis that left anomalies barely under the surface. In 1890 a reporter for the *New*

6 **Biltmore** house. View of east front from the esplanade at dawn. (Richard Cheek.)

7 G. H. Destailleur. **Waddesdon Manor** (1874–89), Buckinghamshire, England. (Girouard, *The Victorian Country House.*)

8 *opposite* **Biltmore** house. Dormers on the roof of the central entry pavilion. (Richard Cheek.)

York Sun found the building so large and prepossessing as to be mistaken for a hotel—the only type of building known to most Americans that was comparable to the size and lavishness of Biltmore.[6]

Like a proper English country house, Biltmore had its landscape gardens, formal areas, and agricultural trappings. The estate, modeled by the brilliant hand of Olmsted, had an approach road that was one of the masterpieces of nineteenth-century landscape design in America. Driving the gently curving road in a carriage was like taking a trip through an idealized American arcadia; forests, glades, and meadows unfolded magically at every turn. Olmsted took great pains in laying out and constructing the road so that each vista would look uncontrived and would take maximum advantage of the existing topography and natural features. He carefully distinguished the naturalistic outer landscape of the forested areas from the formal terraces surrounding the house, as if to place brackets around Hunt's building. Thus, in the end, Biltmore's park was no more an English country park than the house was a French château. Like Hunt, Olmsted was a profoundly original artist who adapted the traditions of English gardening to the American landscape.

Biltmore's vast expanse not only was beautiful but served a useful scientific purpose as well. Vanderbilt's major philanthropic enterprise at the estate was the creation of a great forest preserve and the nation's first school of forestry, presided over in its early years by Gifford Pinchot. By making his estate a semipublic venture, Vanderbilt made a beneficent gesture in the spirit of private noblesse oblige. Cultivation, planting, and management of the forest areas first envisioned by Olmsted were carefully stewarded by Pinchot and his successors. The compass of the Biltmore estate was immense—some 125,000 acres before the largest portion of it was deeded to the federal government to form the Pisgah National Forest. Today it seems a picturesque North Carolina wilderness, similar in character to the Great Smoky Mountains National Park to the north. In fact it is the result of extensive, careful reforestation, the same kind of meticulous grooming of the landscape so characteristic of English and German estates.

That the Biltmore forests, hills, lakes, and its two rivers appear untouched, and that the enormous house fails somehow to dominate even its prominent site, testify to the powerful fact that it is an American place, made by American artists. The country, still hostile, engulfs it. Its urbanity and elegance are grafts from another time and place. Its European airs are ultimately perfunctory—merely cultural foils necessary to a nation entering the arena of world powers and approaching a new century. As an American country house, Biltmore was an idealistic connection to the past and to the many cultures that had created a new nation. Constructed with the forces of technical ingenuity and managerial skill that characterized American business during the Gilded Age, Biltmore proclaimed its greatness by the sheer scale of its conception and execution. In Henry James' words, it was a "vast Carolinian demonstration, . . . an affirmation of resources?—made with great emphasis indeed, but in a clear and exemplary way; so that if large wealth represented some of them, an idea, a fine cluster of ideas, a will, a purpose, a patience, an intelligence, a store of knowledge, immediately workable things, represented the others."[7]

Several hundred miles north of Asheville, in the rolling hills of Virginia, west of Washington, D.C., a country house vastly different in character stands overlooking pristine pastures used today for grazing horses. The Brick House at Oak Spring was built in 1940 for Paul Mellon,[8] one of the most esteemed philanthropists of his generation. Oak Spring is smaller than the stables alone at Biltmore and far less pretentious, despite the fact that its owner had one hundred times the resources of Vanderbilt. Even its name suggests understatement and reserve. It sits quietly in the landscape, almost hidden from view by the grove of mature oaks that the architect and client took pains to save when it was built. Aside from a splendid collection of paintings, it has no European airs.

Described by its architect, the patrician New Yorker William Adams Delano, as a "design in a free Georgian manner,"[9] the house is taken today for a rather close copy, at larger scale, of William Buckland's elegant Hammond-Harwood House in Annapolis (1773–74). That is what the client wanted—a trim Colonial Revival house of sturdy brick. He had studied briefly at St. John's College in 1939–40 and had admired the Hammond house, along with several other Annapolis mansions. Delano was hired because of his connection with the Mellon family and his reputation as a Colonial Revival specialist.[10]

As one of the masterpieces of eighteenth-century American architecture, the Hammond-Harwood and other houses of the colonial period came to represent a proud cultural independence from Europe and a rediscovery of the virtues of Early American art. Close on the heels of a great war, a boom, and a crash and on the eve of a greater conflagration, this was an American house made to evoke simple ideals of patriotism and pride of place. Even in the heady years of a machine epoch, when modernism surfaced in the arts of Europe and America, and the Century of Progress provided streamlined visions of the future, Americans of means found their domestic ideals vested in their own past. Both colonial Williamsburg and the City of Tomorrow existed as powerful embodiments of American culture in the 1930s.[11] The Brick House, also soon to become an anomaly, closed out another era, beginning in fin de siècle America, in which a host of cultural and social contradictions were submerged. The house was simple, "modern," and restrained, yet also deeply nostalgic—one of the last vestiges of the Colonial Revival that had gripped America since the 1880s. Its plan was tightly formal, its rooms sparingly decorated and carefully proportioned, its exterior brick surfaces taut and planar, enlivened by areas of carved wood. The overall impression is one of tasteful reticence, a fitting tribute to its patron.

Paul Mellon, like Vanderbilt, was heir to one of America's largest industrial fortunes—the Pittsburgh banking and aluminum empire built by his father in the early years of the century.[12] And, like his predecessor, he chose philanthropy over the expansion of his fortune, supporting many cultural institutions under the aegis of the Andrew W. Mellon Foundation, among other charities. A

9 William Adams Delano. **Brick House** at Oak Spring (1940), estate of Paul Mellon, Upperville, Virginia. (Author.)

10 Oak Spring. Garden facade. (Author.)

pillar of the arts in America for forty years, former chairman of the Board of Trustees of the National Gallery of Art, founder of the Paul Mellon Center for British Art at Yale University, and a distinguished collector, Mellon was renowned for his philanthropic activities, which overshadowed all private trappings of wealth. His house did not need to speak for him, as Biltmore did for George Vanderbilt. Even his passion for horses took on a cultural dimension—his personal collection of horse paintings by George Stubbs is one of the finest in the world. Oak Spring was meant to be a large, pretty Virginia farm. Its owner wanted only the quiet, solid authority of a Georgian house. By 1940, public beneficence and the private domain were to be distinctly separate.

Mellon's country house spoke in reserved, assured tones about an America more sure of its cultural virtues, yet still sentimentally attached to the past. Though it had many of the same features as Biltmore—agriculture, leisure pursuits, elegant collections of art and antiques, and vast landholdings—Oak Spring manifested itself as a very private domain that could sustain a life in comfort,

without grand and ostentatious gestures. It was a house, not a hotel or palace. Though still within the genre of a wealthy man's domicile, it was meant as a repudiation of many of the values associated with the robber baron generation of which Mellon's father was a part.

Biltmore and Oak Spring serve as apt symbols of their era and appropriate brackets to the story of the American country estate from the late nineteenth century to the eve of World War II. During this half century of economic expansion—when millionaires proliferated—thousands of large houses were built in quasirural and suburban areas, in remote landscapes, and in resort enclaves, where a life on the land could be enjoyed, with attendant leisure activities. In the midst of America's greatest commercial and industrial growth, the persistent English ideal of the manor and the country gentleman remained a mark of social and cultural status, just as it had in the Victorian era in England. As *House and Garden* commented in June 1904: "Our country is to become one of beautiful homes and gardens, where a busy man of the twentieth century can get away from the storm and stress of active business or professional life, and renew his wasted strength and energy only where it can be truly renewed, in 'God's own Out of Doors.'"[13] As we now know, the optimism of that prediction was only partially realized, for the American country house is full of contradictions—concerning definition, ambivalence between city and country life, class and ethnic boundaries, the shifting, caste-like structure of upper-class society, the meaning of architectural styles, the role of architect and patron in the creation of estates. Even the formal qualities of the house as an architectural type often seem to defy classification. The houses of George Vanderbilt and Paul Mellon are rife with these ambiguities.

Biltmore and Oak Spring are symptoms of a cultural phenomenon that swept the United States during its most important period of capitalist consolidation—what one might call the domestic eclecticism of the American plutocracy. Their patrons were members of a social class that dominated American business and philanthropy, a class that provided ideals of domestic life that have never been entirely relinquished.[14] Their architects were key figures in a large and successful group of historically inspired designers who controlled house design for the middle and upper classes from the late nineteenth century until the eve of World War II. Like Hunt and Vanderbilt, Mellon and Delano shared values, taste, and social position; architect and client were part of the same taste culture, as Herbert Gans has defined it—that is, a culture with definable characteristics and particular aesthetic preferences.[15] Indeed, both the architects and the wealthy patrons who created the modern country estates were governed by a conservative aesthetic code that produced the predictable house styles familiar to many Americans, from the comfortable Tudor mansion to the reserved Georgian or sunny Spanish Colonial.

This golden age of country estate building can be traced through a survey of the many popular and professional publications that sprang up around the turn of the century. *House and Garden, Country Life in America, American Homes and Gardens, The House Beautiful, Arts and Decoration, Antiques,* and *Town and Coun-*

11 **Biltmore** estate. Approach road designed by Frederick Law Olmsted. (Richard Cheek.)

try, among other publications, were founded as a reflection of the significant market of upper- and middle-class readers aspiring to a landed life.[16] After reaching a peak in popularity in the 1920s, several folded during the depression, while others changed their orientation to reflect a reordering of society and a change in domestic values prior to World War II. The major architectural journals devoted significant coverage to the country house beginning around 1905, with the *Architectural Record* and *Architectural Forum* devoting a yearly number to the subject throughout the 1910s and 1920s. Numerous articles singled out the American country house as a building type for which this country was becoming particularly renowned, and praised domestic architects for their innovation, artistic sensibilities, and design skill.[17] Moreover, a new subculture of professional architectural writers specializing in domestic architecture emerged to follow house design. Their views will appear often in this book. Finally, numerous books were published that documented photographically the country house movement, such as the *American Country Houses of To-Day* series (1912–35), published by the Architectural Book Publishing Company of New York. One finds a rich and evocative documentary history of the culture of the country estate in these sources.

Following that tradition, this book is a study of the architecture of America's modern country houses. Its emphasis is on the meaning they conveyed in their time, the ideas that guided their architects, the social and economic forces that spawned their construction, and the circumstances of their making—architectural practice, patronage, building technics, design theory, landscape history, and material culture. In order to begin to understand the complex and often contradictory aspects of the turn-of-the-century country house, it is first necessary to understand the society that spawned it as a domestic institution. For this we shall turn to the economic and social conditions that provided patrons like Paul Mellon and George Vanderbilt with their wealth and that defined their place in America's democratic melting pot during the later years of the last century.

12 **Biltmore** house. View of west front from ponds near the French Broad River. (Richard Cheek.)

The boom in country estate building that occurred at the turn of
the century could only have been sustained by an increase in
wealth and an expansion of America's upper class. Following the
Civil War, between 1870 and 1900, the national wealth rose from
$30,400 million to $126,700 million. By 1914 it had doubled
again, reaching $254,200 million.[18] This extraordinary capital-
ist expansion was controlled by a select but growing group of
industrial entrepreneurs, the "captains of industry," who owned
some 50 percent of the nation's wealth by 1910—approximately
40,000 families, according to figures from the Bureau of the
Census, or less than 1 percent of the population (9 percent owned
over 71 percent of the capital). The number of millionaires
increased dramatically from the middle of the century—when
Pierre Lorillard, William Backhouse Astor, and Alexander Tun-
ney Stewart were among the richest men in America, with fortunes of around $10, 20, and 50 million, respectively—to its end,
when Andrew Carnegie had an annual income of between $15 and
30 million. In 1892, the *New York Times* listed 4,027 men as millionaires, whereas *Forum* magazine estimated that there were 120
men in the country with fortunes in excess of $10 million.[19] The
number of ultrawealthy grew in 1922 to an astounding sixty-seven
men with annual incomes of $1 million or over, with four taxable
incomes of more than $5 million. Of the ten richest men in the
world at that time, six were Americans.[20] The economic consolidation of wealth into the hands of this capitalist oligarchy formed
the foundation for the structure of America's modern plutocracy.

The 1890s were a watershed for the captains of business. What
began as a crash following the panic of 1893 became an economic
miracle created out of business consolidation. As Ferdinand
Lundberg and Gustavus Myers, two of the first analysts of America's modern fortunes, have made clear, the mammoth power of
the industrial trusts synthesized the nineteenth-century merchant, manufacturing, banking, and railroad wealth into a new
agglomeration of capital at the end of the century. Ownership of
the trusts was vested in a small number of powerful family
dynasties—what Lundberg has called "America's Sixty Families"
—which through intermarriage, political control, stock, banking, and commodities manipulation, and land ownership gained a
dominant hand in the U.S. economy.[21] By 1937, when Lundberg's
book appeared, the top sixty families had fortunes estimated
between $100 million and $2.5 billion. As they ascended to the
top of the economic pyramid, the new American dynasties also
changed the social structure of the Protestant establishment, placing themselves in positions of authority to insure caste solidarity.
They were the lords of a system that J. W. Ghent, at the turn of the
century, called "Our Benevolent Feudalism."[22]

Most of the patrons of the great American country estates are
related in some way to this extended business oligarchy. Standing
at its apex, the Vanderbilts and Rockefellers, who intermarried or
did business with a large group of second-tier plutocrats, constructed several dozen of the most important houses of the era.

13 Edward T. Stotesbury sitting for a portrait bust with the artist Hugo Gari
Wagner, Palm Beach, c. 1920. (Historical Society of Palm Beach County.)

Wealth derived from Standard Oil, the largest of the trusts, built
such famous estates as Henry Flagler's Whitehall in Palm Beach,
Florida, Rockefeller's Kykuit in Pocantico on the Hudson, New
York, the Harkness estate in Madison, New Jersey, and Dosoris
Park, the one-thousand-acre compound of the Pratt family on the
North Shore of Long Island. Nearby, J. P. Morgan and his partners
bought much of the picturesque coastline near Glen Cove and
built an enclave of large houses there. Not to be outdone, John
Edward Aldred (a utilities millionaire) and a series of partners purchased the entire village of Lattingtown, tore it down, and created
a private town and club for themselves. Other somewhat mega-
lomaniacal house builders, famous for their exploits, were William Randolph Hearst, E. T. Stotesbury, Andrew Carnegie, and
Marshall Field III.[23]

To assimilate themselves into the established genteel society of
America's upper class in the 1870s and 1880s, the families of the
new capitalist moguls adopted several institutions that would
allow penetration into elite circles and eventually insure social
control. Each was a kind of club. The Social Register, an elite listing of the most prominent American families, was first published
in 1887, around the time when New York established itself as the
center of America's high society, eclipsing Boston and Philadelphia. The poles of metropolitan and rural caste definition were
established by the urban gentlemen's (or ladies') club and the
country club. Although the former were common throughout the
nineteenth century, the first country club was established in
Brookline, Massachusetts, in 1882, and one of the first exclusive
club-centered suburbs at Tuxedo Park, New York, in 1886. These
were followed not long after by exclusive golf links at St. Andrews
in Yonkers, New York, and at Shinnecock Hills in Southampton,
Long Island, among others established from 1890 to 1900. Social
commentators in that time and ours have been quick to point out
that country clubs were first and foremost social instruments and
only secondarily dedicated to sport and leisure pursuits.[24] They
existed to draw lines between ethnic, class, economic, and social
groups, and quickly became registers of social prominence in
themselves. Henry James called them "complete product[s] of the

social soil and air which alone have made [them] possible" and "inimitable, invaluable accents[s] of American authority."[25] Indeed, country clubs and the institutions surrounding them — the country day school, summer resort, elite university, exclusive suburban enclave — were the most important barometers of power and prestige in elite circles during the era of capitalist consolidation. Their numbers paralleled the proliferation of country estates — by 1929 there were 4,500 country clubs in the nation.[26]

The historian E. Digby Baltzell has maintained that the country club and its satellite expressions of rural gentility were the manifestations of a "social defense of caste" that split the United States of the 1880s into a wealthy and intellectual elite class and an ethnic lower and middle class, primarily composed of immigrants, working ethnic minorities, and former slaves. An increasing desire for distinction and social exclusivity among old-stock (and newly wealthy) Americans gave rise to numerous ancestral associations during this same period. Baltzell mentions the Sons of the Revolution (1883), the Colonial Dames (1890), the Daughters of the American Revolution (1890), Society of Mayflower Descendants (1894), and the Baronial Order of Runnymede (1897), among approximately thirty-five associations founded between 1890 and 1900.[27] By establishing such pedigrees and associations with the founding of the country, old-stock Americans could claim a kind of superiority over the waves of upwardly mobile immigrants coming through Ellis Island at the turn of the century and thereafter.

America's modern country estates can only be understood within the framework of the capitalist oligarchy and the institutions that insured its exclusivity. Whether standing alone or as extensions of country clubs, elite suburban enclaves, summer resort communities, or even privately owned islands and villages, the country houses of the upper class extended the social protection of caste to the domestic realm. Just as English country houses are properly considered physical manifestations of aristocratic

power and the structure of the peerage dating from the medieval droit du seigneur, America's estates follow an equally intricate but more opaque social structure based upon clublike associations. As Ferdinand Lundberg observed, rich men's houses were disposed around the armature of the family dynasty, the social club, the seasons of travel, cultural events and marriages, the place of business, and, not least, for avoidance of the tax collector.[28] Because domestic life did not have a fixed center for most of the plutocracy, houses were built where the right kind of society could be found. In fact, houses and clubs were reciprocal components in the social life of the corporate oligarch. (Henry James thought the two surprisingly similar in their lack of distinction between public and private spaces: the "diffused vagueness of separation between apartments, between hall and room, between one room and another, between the one you are in and the one you are not in, between place of passage and place of privacy, is a provocation to despair which the public institution shares impartially with the luxurious home.")[29] This helps to explain why it is so difficult to develop an unambiguous definition of the modern American country house: many had no sense of domestic comfort, no fixed relationship to landscape and place, no firmly defined program, not even a dominant style. As an observer of country houses remarked in 1907, "A style of a dwelling-house is the ripe product of a complete and definite social growth, whereas in our own country social forms remain undeveloped and ambiguous."[30]

Indeed, the houses Americans built in the country had historically resisted social and typological codification. The manorial seats of eighteenth-century tobacco or cotton plantations in the South were true "power houses," like those discussed by Mark Girouard in England. They were producers of wealth, marks of social status, and even came to define townships and counties. Yet they vanished with the eclipse of their society and economy during the Civil War. Merchants, bankers, and early industrialists built various types of leisure country seats during the early and middle years of the nineteenth century, but these houses and their estates were sporadic and diverse in their architectural expression. Many supported agricultural enterprises for moral and economic edification, such as the estates of the Du Ponts in the Brandywine Valley.

14 Golfers at the Onwentsia Club, Lake Forest, Illinois, c. 1914. (Chicago Historical Society.)

Some, such as Eleutherian Mills, stood as "the house upon the hill" watching over industries and workers with a patrician dominance. The most coherent and influential country house type of the nineteenth century was the gentleman's villa espoused by A. J. Downing after 1850. Seen in the Hudson Valley and far afield, the picturesque and artistic estates of this kind were the first to dissociate themselves from agriculture and to treat the country as an arcadian retreat. Yet even this country house tradition was short-lived; by the 1880s the "villa" came to have the same pejorative connotations as the "brownstone" town house. With America's rapid fluctuations in wealth and social stratification, new ideals emerged with each passing generation.

It is not difficult to explain the explosion in the number of country estates after 1890. Never before had so much capital been available to such a large number of Americans for the pursuit of leisure. By 1910, there were 15,190 families with incomes of more than $50,000—an amount defining an urban-industrial upper class capable of having country houses.[31] According to statistics in 1919, such an income would allow for a house and land worth $100,000 and for yearly operating costs of $7,500—rather lavish by standards of the time, when an adequate middle-class house could be purchased for $6,000. Building a house or set of houses in picturesque environs, for the pleasure of sports, gardening, social intercourse, or for the architecture and decoration itself, was merely one manifestation of a frenzy of consumption first chronicled by Thorstein Veblen in *Theory of the Leisure Class* (1899). Upper-class Americans were buying more, traveling more, and living better than nearly anyone else on earth at that time. With discretionary capital available for collecting art, buying elaborate clothes, traveling to Europe for exposure to such cultural centers as Paris, London, and Vienna, paying servants and gardeners, and exploring other leisure pursuits, the mogul capitalists were becoming increasingly cosmopolitan in their tastes. Upper-class families were in a position to redefine their domestic culture with the greater sophistication gained by travel and select acquisitions. Moreover, this new plutocracy began to acquire land on a grand scale during the late nineteenth century—and land was the oldest standard of wealth and status.

As Veblen first established, the key factor separating the country estates of the 1880s and 1890s from previous examples was the purchase of land merely for leisure pursuits, for the pride of possessing a piece of natural beauty, or for the symbolic effect of social status.[32] It was a commodity to be consumed. The landscape was no longer seen as an economic resource but had become a social symbol—of a bygone genteel tradition, of a natural world untrammeled by industrialization, of an aristocratic way of life born in Europe, of an America fading in the collective memory with the passing century, an arcadia ripe for domestic cultivation. Though many nineteenth-century gentlemen's villas were primarily devoted to "artistic" rural life and similiar leisure pursuits, they maintained a symbolic connection to the agrarian landscape.[33] During the 1890s this rural America was changing profoundly, becoming domesticated to an unprecedented degree by subdivision, speculation, and estate building. It was a badge of

status for the modern proprietor of the country estate to own vast acreage without the necessity of deriving a penny of income from his land (though he may have made a substantial fortune in land speculation elsewhere). By placing coveted land in private hands, he could insulate his family from the middle class, who were also building in the country and frequenting resorts. Estate holdings during the 1890s could amount to hundreds or even thousands of acres and often claimed the most beautiful and distinctive rural, exurban, and resort settings. Hardly a more monumental example of Veblen's theory of conspicuous consumption exists than these landholdings.

Paradoxically, the defining characteristics of the modern American country house were its association with leisure and social clubs and its dissociation from income-producing property. Properly speaking, most country houses were built to sustain facets of country life passed down from the Anglo-Saxon tradition: gentlemanly farming, breeding horses and livestock, gardening, equestrian pursuits, hunting and fishing, perhaps sailing and yachting, and the "modern" sports of tennis and golf. Cultivation of these domestic pursuits (with varying degrees of seriousness) was seen as salubrious, morally uplifting, and socially correct. What, then, was a country house? For our purposes, we may begin with the definition proposed by Fiske Kimball in 1919:

By the "country house" in America we understand no such single, well-established form as the traditional country house in England, fixed by centuries of almost unalterable custom, with a life of its own which has been described as "the perfection of human society." Even in England today the great house yields in importance to the new and smaller types which the rise of the middle classes has strewn over the country and on the fringes of the city, and with [which] the variety is infinite, from the dwellings of the further suburbs to the distant, self-sustaining estate. Yet the common characteristic of all is clear enough—a site free of the arid blocks and circumscribed "lots" of the city, where one may enjoy the informality of nature out-of-doors.[34]

The key factor in Kimball's definition is a concept of everyday life with nature, which is unequivocally antiurban. Though a mistrust of urban life has a long history in American culture, the reality of the city and its ills were never more apparent than in 1901. During that year Americans living in rural areas still outnumbered those living in urban areas, according to the U.S. census, by 60 percent to 40 percent (45,835,000 to 30,160,000).[35] By 1920 statistics would verify the fact that the land of farm and frontier had been replaced by a nation of cities: the urban to rural ratio tipped the other way, 51 percent to 49 percent. Even as the cities grew in size, power, and economic might, the U.S. population was beginning to shift toward the urban fringes. In 1910 New York's suburbs had almost two million residents, Boston's almost a million. Twenty-six percent of the population of America's "metropolitan districts and adjacent territories"—that is, central cities and suburbs within ten miles of their borders—was already in the adjacent areas.[36]

The reasons for this first flight of the affluent from urban centers, beginning in the 1880s, are generally linked to the waves of immigration that brought America's ethnic working classes to the cities—both Europeans and southern blacks—as well as to the economics of home ownership and ready transportation outward to the "borderlands."[37] The great capitalists were wed to the cities, both economically and socially, yet wished to preserve the aura of country living. Concerned with maintaining their exclusive social standing, wealthy families increasingly chose life outside the city among members of their social caste or kept seasonal houses in town, country, resort, and European locations. One or more of these houses might be called a country house, a definition more nostalgic than real.[38]

America's captains of industry were a peripatetic lot. Once a fortune had been made and the Social Register breached, one had to participate in the shifting venues of the social season—the places depending upon the choice of friends and the desired level of status within the upper class. (There were, of course, ethnic, religious, and family divisions as well.) Newport was the most prestigious enclave of summer houses but later received competition from such towns as Bar Harbor, Maine, Lenox, Massachusetts (the inland Newport), and Lake Geneva, Wisconsin (the Newport of the Midwest). Building a house in such areas established one's family among a social elite. Although most summer colonies initially began with hotels and rustic cottages, many later became crowded with palatial homes and even self-consciously agrarian country houses.

The impetus behind constructing these houses was often more symbolic than typologically correct. They served as places of sporadic or seasonal residence rather than as permanent family seats—one might call them serial houses. Incessant travel—around the United States, Europe, the Far East, and even South America—was a condition of existence for many of America's wealthiest families at the turn of the century. After the fall opera season in New York, a family might winter in Florida or Georgia, return to the Hudson River or Newport for the spring, sail for Europe in the early summer, and finally return to New York via Bar Harbor or Newport. A major motivation for seasonal decamping from city to country to summer or winter resorts was the ritual of courtship and marriage. Having a house in which to entertain prospective sons- or daughters-in-law improved the prospects of social climbing through intermarriage, the most effective means of consolidating social prestige and power. This perpetual motion of the upper classes profoundly influenced domestic culture—as society moved in its seasons, so did the family.

Another attraction to the country was the tenacious belief that nature was a necessary moral tonic. During the Progressive Era, Americans continued to cling to what Peter T. Schmitt has called the arcadian myth, as evinced by "back to nature" movements, suburban developments, and other cultural attachments to rural life. Writers on American life feared the coming urbanization and its effect on the domestic environment. Scouting, conservation and nature clubs, city park movements, camp and resort compounds, and an entire literary culture flourished around the ideal of living with nature.[39] "Foremost of the social conditions affecting the country house," Fiske Kimball argued, was the "great wave of renewed love of the out-of-door life and of nature which swept over America in the last years of the nineteenth century and the opening years of the twentieth."[40]

In an article in *Scribner's Magazine* of 1890, the patrician architect Bruce Price lamented the disintegration of the country and its society (circa 1800), which he found "intelligent, refined, and almost chivalric in its intercourse," condemned the cities and the "race for wealth," and called for new homes "scattered apart or grouped together, upon the hills, in valleys, and along the streams that wander through them to the ocean, or perched upon the bluffs and beaches."[41] He was speaking of suburban country houses within commuting distance of major cities, such as his many Shingle Style "cottages" in Tuxedo Park, New York. Another writer could remark that the "American country house [was] hardly yet to be found" and that the true example "should 'possess the country'—that is, have a good degree of retirement... lack of conventionalism [and] quiet simplicity.... Its first principle is that is should fit the place where it stands."[42] Following such apologists for the country house as Donald G. Mitchell and Andrew Jackson Downing in the Victorian era, turn-of-the-century writers encouraged a sentimental return to the landscape of rural America.[43] There was a clear sense of lost innocence, gentility, and beauty in these voices—the country as many Americans knew it in the nineteenth century was being erased by change.

Country pursuits were an affirmation of gentility for wealthy Americans. The freedom to cultivate a garden or steward a farm was now a luxury made possible by urban industrial wealth. Many of the new moguls had begun their lives on farms and looked to rural life as a lost ideal. A review of the literature of the period suggests that widely held concepts of family, domesticity, comfort, sociability, and leisure were all associated with country life, even as late as the 1920s.[44]

The ideal of recapturing a lost country life coalesced in fin de siècle America around the country estate and the country club—two patently artificial institutions reserved only for the privileged class. The trappings of an elite rural gentility were best expressed in the specialized periodicals of the era, the best being *Country Life in America* and *House and Garden*. In their editorial policies, contents, and yearly program, these periodicals spelled out the requisite ingredients of country life; expected social and behavioral rituals were superbly rendered in their pages. The monthly issues, or numbers, marked the seasons: fall house building and hunting; winter socials, costume balls, and Christmas nostalgia; spring gardening, flower shows, nature and conservation; summer sports—sailing, golf, tennis—and other fashionable leisure pursuits. Using theatrical pomp and Vivaldian tones, the colorful covers remind us of the rituals of society, especially in the country. With the marriage and courtship season ever present, patrician young faces and fashionable figures decorated many of the articles, just as they do in *Town and Country* today. Architecture, fashion, decoration, and connoisseurship were treated as the necessary elements of genteel, aristocratic existence. As threats to that life became more real, the artifice sustaining a nostalgic return to the country intensified.

There is vivid social history in the pages of these periodicals, one too extensive to be explored here. Rather, our concern must be with the houses and estates that provided the background to that life. To sum up the eclectic characteristics, the "cluster of ideas" that attended the wealthy man's country estate at the end of the nineteenth century, we may observe that:

1   Country estates were designed to be appreciated primarily as manifestations of wealth and leisure.

2   The estate property was most often delineated to capture and claim the most coveted areas of the rural and resort landscape, to domesticate and privatize parts of the country that had hitherto been reserved for agriculture or left in a natural state.

3   Estates were built in proximity to social centers—around resort areas, country clubs, exurban districts close to places of business, in family or caste enclaves, or garden suburbs. Socially, the estate was an extension of other caste-protective mechanisms.

4   Symbolically, the country house was associated with models drawn from other aristocratic, genteel, or rural societies, whether European or indigenous.

5   The house and estate were programmed to support various leisure diversions, sporting pursuits, and other manifestations of rural gentility.

The urban wealth that grew from the consolidation of industrial trusts after the panic of 1893 and the adoption of the gold standard established a new American aristocracy and made possible a new, elite country life. Only with the passing of this oligarchy during the depression and World War II did the country estate decline. Yet as a type, the new country estates defy precise classification—partially because of the fluidity and ambiguities of society itself.[45] Herbert David Croly, one of the premier architectural critics and political thinkers of the Progressive Era, recognized the fragile and paradoxical nature of the country estate better than any other writer of his time. His work provides the most complete and persuasive interpretation of the institution of the country estate and the peculiarly American social conditions that created it.

HERBERT CROLY AND
THE CRITICAL VIEW OF THE COUNTRY ESTATE

During the past fifteen or twenty years there have been built in the United States a large number of expensive and magnificent private dwellings. These houses have had their predecessors, of course, but hardly any precursors. They are as different in size and magnificence from the earlier types of American residence as the contemporary skyscraper is from the old five-story brick office. And since they are a comparatively new fact in American domestic architecture, it may be inferred that they are the expression of similarly new facts in American economic and social development.

—Desmond and Croly, 1903

There were thirty periodicals in 1900 devoted exclusively to architectural subjects, a sharp decrease from the forty-six of ten years earlier.[46] This surprising statistic gives some measure of the importance of the media in fin de siècle culture, especially among architects and patrons. Add to this the spate of popular periodicals devoted to country life, gardening, women's domestic issues, and nature, and the total would at least double. Upper-class Americans could find inspiration for their domestic predilections in the splendid photographs, stories, and art that graced these journals. Because of their enormous popularity and significance, turn-of-the-century periodicals offer us a lucid window on the culture of the country estate.

Architectural publishing reached its zenith of diversity and creativity during the eclectic era, largely as a response to a public that discussed and understood design. The modern architectural critic emerged during this period as a spokesperson for popular values and tastes, as opposed to the later avant-garde, intellectual critic, who railed against the status quo. The distinctions between high-brow producers of art and middle-brow consumers were not so pronounced as they are today; architect, patron, and critic were more often than not on the same side of an issue.

Critics began writing about architecture regularly during the 1870s in popular magazines such as the *Century, Harper's,* and *Lippincott's.* Marianna Griswold van Rensselaer and Montgomery Schuyler, two renowned architectural writers of this period, devoted a substantial proportion of their criticism to domestic architecture. Both made their reputations as journalists. Architects were also writing criticism and were encouraged to add their voices. Bruce Price, Russell Sturgis, Ralph Adams Cram, and A. D. F. Hamlin contributed often to the journals as both critics and apologists for the needs of their profession. By the turn of the century, a potent, persuasive, and influential group of critics was operating to observe and sustain the culture of domestic eclecticism. None, however, offered the combination of intellectual gifts, education, and point of view of Herbert Croly.

Croly, whom Thomas Bender has called "the precursor of the modern literary intellectual in New York,"[47] was born on January 23, 1869. He could hardly have been better trained to enter his profession. His father, David Goodman Croly (1829–91), was the editor of the *New York World* and an intellectual of controversial philosophical and social views. His mother, Jane Cunningham Croly (1829–1901), was perhaps the best-known woman journalist in America, an early feminist and a contributor to many popular magazines in the late nineteenth century. Both parents were liberal thinkers with broad-ranging interests and views, a trait imparted to their child. When he entered Harvard as a "special student" in 1886, Croly had already been exposed through his father to such sophisticated ideas as the positivism of Auguste Comte and was ready to enter the intellectual ferment of the nation's leading university. Though socially ill at ease and shy, Croly had his father's intellectual support to bolster him. He took courses with such luminaries as Josiah Royce, William James, George Santayana, and George Herbert Palmer, all of whom taught under the firm leadership of President Charles William

Eliot. Indeed, father and son were so close in temperament and communication that Herbert's education was largely shadowed and directed by his father. This paternal dominance may have contributed to Herbert's academic and social difficulties, such that the young man left the university in 1888 to serve at his sick father's side, only to witness his death a year later. Reentering in 1892, Herbert lasted only an additional year before a breakdown forced him to end his education without a degree.[48]

Shaken by his father's death but determined to continue the spirit of his work as an analyst of social and political structures, he spent the years prior to 1900 traveling and seeking direction as a writer. Characteristically, he returned to work at a magazine that was an extension of family associations. His father bequeathed him a part interest in the *Real Estate Record and Guide,* a trade journal devoted to news of building and real estate business in New York City. The *Architectural Record* had become an offshoot of this periodical in 1891.[49] From its inception it provided a balance of literary and pictorial coverage of both American and European architecture, distinguishing itself from its major competitors, *American Architect and Building News* and the earlier *American Builder,* by its commitment to criticism and feature articles rather than to simple coverage of major buildings.[50] When he joined the editorial staff in 1900, Croly affirmed the catholic policies of this new journal, while also embarking on a series of critical writings that used architecture as a vehicle for studying American society as a whole.

Although the young journalist was assigned to cover major building activity in New York City, an urban environment he knew well, and to travel to other cities for coverage of expositions and large buildings, he was given rather free rein to pursue subjects of his own interest. He contributed at least one major article per year during the decade, wrote book reviews and unsigned editorials, and was influential in determining the content and policy of *Record* during its formative years. In surveying the approximately fifty articles he wrote before 1913, when he left the editorial staff, two subjects stand out: urbanism and, especially, domestic architecture. As a direct outgrowth of these articles, he published two books: *Stately Homes in America: From Colonial Times to the Present Day* in 1903, with *Record*'s managing editor, Harry W. Desmond, as coauthor, and *Houses for Town or Country* in 1907 under the pseudonym William Herbert. (Croly often published under pseudonyms, the most ubiquitous being A. C. David or Arthur C. David.) As a whole, this body of writing represents the most comprehensive study of American domestic architecture of its time.

Croly believed that the house was the key building block and root manifestation of American individualism—a tenet so often identified with Jefferson and Wright that it is surprising to note that he differed profoundly with both these great agrarian-democratic architects. He began writing about American houses, especially the "palaces" of capitalist moguls, almost immediately upon joining *Record*. Croly saw his role as critic in terms of the analysis, interpretation, and improvement of society at large. He approached his architectural writing with a specific purpose and program in mind: to study the social, economic, aesthetic, and technical factors that influenced the design of houses. He related housing forms and types to current social conditions, while also citing the key traits of the work of major architects. Unlike many of his contemporaries, he seldom dwelt on characteristics of eclectic styles but chose to look at the reasons behind a particular design—including function, technology, symbolism, and individual character. Though untrained in design or construction, he had an eye for proportion and authored major essays on modern materials and technology. A strong believer in national characteristics, Croly would have seen himself as quintessentially American in his method and point of view.[51]

Croly's major competitor as a specialist in domestic architecture was Barr Ferree, a journalist, teacher, and critic associated with *Scientific American Building Monthly,* whose *American Estates and Gardens* of 1904 spoke favorably of the development of palatial houses and gardens.[52] Ferree's position was wed to the capitalist bourgeoisie itself and evidenced a belief in the leadership of an enlightened elite. As editor of the magazine *American Homes and Gardens,* he seldom criticized the taste of home owners in his profiles of houses and was less attuned to the abilities of individual architects than Croly. Another writer who followed the emergence of the large country estate was the architect Joy Wheeler Dow, who in 1902 began a series of articles in *Architects' and Builders' Magazine,* entitled "American Renaissance: A Review of Domestic Architecture," which was later published as a book.[53] Dow's rather bumptious and hyperbolic writing seems to reflect the values of the time but is hardly on a par with the work of the more intellectual architects and professional journalists. On the far left of Croly was Thorstein Veblen, the midwestern economist, whose *Theory of the Leisure Class* savagely attacked the capitalist moguls for their tendencies toward consumptive display, their predatory business practices, and their cultivation of anachronistic behavior based on European aristocratic society.[54] Croly was thus writing in an atmosphere of intense interest in the domestic habits and tastes of wealthy Americans, a renaissance of criticism that paralleled the new architectural developments.

He was the only architectural critic of his time, however, to advance a comprehensive approach that tied the architectural characteristics of houses to new social conditions, thus extending some of the ideas of Veblen and helping to explain eclecticism. He began with a simple theory: that the attitude of the individual toward his domicile and the characteristics of domestic architecture in a given time period were embodiments of a man's perceived relationship to society as a whole.[55] All of his writings on domestic architecture were based on this idea.

Recognizing that the late-nineteenth-century captain of industry was the personification of American social and economic ideals, Croly looked carefully at these "Rich Men and Their Houses" in 1902.[56] His witty, brilliantly incisive essay in *Record*

HOUSE BEAUTIFUL

COUNTRY HOUSE NUMBER
35 CTS · APRIL 1924 · $3.00 A YR

Vol. II No. 2

JUNE, 1902

PRICE, 25 CENTS
$3 A YEAR

COUNTRY LIFE IN AMERICA

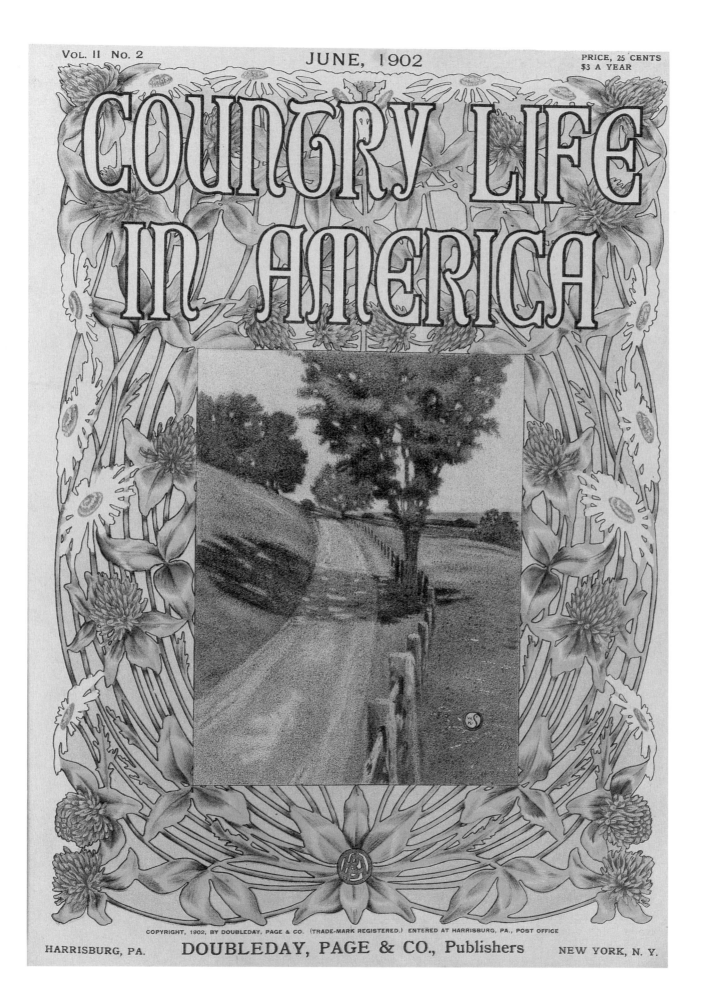

HARRISBURG, PA.   DOUBLEDAY, PAGE & CO., Publishers   NEW YORK, N. Y.

17 Delano and Aldrich. **Oheka** (c. 1917–30s), Otto Kahn estate, Huntington, Long Island. Aerial view. (Long Island Studies Institute, Nassau County Museums.)

was only a precursor to the lengthier treatment of the houses of wealthy Americans in *Stately Homes* a year later. His argument went something like this: during the post–Civil War period, thirty years before the turn of the century, a new American capitalist had emerged, one whom Croly considered different from any previous wealthy, self-made man. "The great American millionaire," as he was called, had amassed fortunes far surpassing any in history, simply for the pleasure of making money—so much money that new ways had to be invented for spending the excess. Only a generation old, these families and their fortunes had not yet solidified in American society; they were still striving to define their political, cultural, and class status in the democracy. Ingenuity and extraordinary success in commerce and manufacturing were the only secure virtues of this new capitalist plutocracy. Socially and culturally the new millionaire and his wife were bound to tradition and the safest, most conservative values. Their social mobility left them adrift, searching for a stable role. Like Silas Lapham, the protagonist of a novel by William Dean Howells, the self-made capitalist had both envy and contempt for such aristocracy as existed in the United States during the indus-

trial boom. He needed the trappings of society not for himself but for his family. Croly understood his position implicitly:

He does not try to cover up his sense of his own newness merely by vulgar ostentation, or as he perhaps would in an older and aristocratic country, by an attempt to buy his way into society. What society he wants, he has; for the rest he prefers to remain a business man. But he does wish to emancipate his children and his fellow countrymen from the reproach of being raw and new; and consequently he tries in every way to bring to bear upon them historical and traditional influences. He wants them to acquire and to realize more of a past than a few hundred years on a new continent can afford; and he wants to make that past something to be seen and felt. So he distributes enormous sums of money for educational purposes; he and his family are frequently abroad; he often becomes an ambitious collector of pictures and "objets d'art;" and particularly in all aesthetic matters, he wants things with a European reputation.[57]

Croly then discussed the architectural manifestations of these traits, with considerable criticism of the shallowness of the decorator's mentality, the overwhelming palatial quality of many museumlike houses, and their lack of domestic grace. He pointed out that with this new class of millionaire had emerged a new type of house, grand in character and semipublic in purpose, which he distinguished from similar European aristocratic models. "The

European house was built for a member of a class even when the class to which the man belonged occupied a socially inferior position," he later stressed, "whereas the American house is built for an individual."[58] The primary symbolic function of the rich man's house was the expression of individual character and economic achievement. "Well to do Americans are apt to differ from one another more widely than well to do Englishmen or well to do Frenchmen in habits of life and in the vicissitudes of their personal history and their aesthetic likes and dislikes; and the absence of any authoritative standards of taste or accepted traditions of form bestow on these personal peculiarities a sanctity to which they are frequently not entitled on their merits."[59] Hence the wide range of eclectic styles in American houses was a product of democratic individualism and the need to establish differences in identity.

Croly called these new palaces stately homes, in reference to their importance as status symbols. His book on the subject can really be called the first social history of American domestic architecture. Though rather sparse on architectural analysis, *Stately Homes* attempted to provide a framework for a history of the American home grounded in the country's political and economic structure. Colonial houses, though they borrowed stylistically from "decadent, insular and English" forms, were also mirrors of society—"genuine, because [they were] simply and faithfully accepted."[60] What followed during three-quarters of the nineteenth century was "the Transitional Dwelling," implying a middle period leading to house forms that were truly expressive of the national character and life. In this critique of the narrow individualism of the pioneer period (corresponding roughly to the opening up of the West and the thesis of Frederick Jackson Turner) Croly found most large nineteenth-century houses expedient, practical, indiscriminate, and ultimately vulgar (a word he repeated many times), but nevertheless the necessary product of economic and social conditions the democratic spirit had wrought. He went to great length analyzing the aesthetic failings of this architecture, which could finally be attributed to the implacable conservatism of the nouveaux riches and of democracy itself. The emergence of eclecticism after 1825 and the concomitant envy and appropriation of European culture were symptomatic of a lack of self-confidence, independence, enterprise, or originality.[61] Here Croly seemed to side both with Veblen and with proponents of a distinctly American architecture, but his argument abruptly swerved from this side of the dialectic.

Paradoxically, Croly maintained that out of this plethora of stylistic choices would emerge a "greater modern" American dwelling that was both "grammatical and idiomatic."[62] This house would be American by its relationship to unique social and contextual conditions but would continue to be grounded in European stylistic languages. The appearance of this "modern" residence after 1885 was attributable to cosmopolitan education and tastes, the influence of H. H. Richardson, Richard Morris Hunt, and French culture, the growth of such cities as New York, and finally the overwhelming existence of wealth. The latter half of *Stately Homes* was devoted to a description of the characteristics of the "Greater Modern Residence," then in the midst of its formative period.

The houses that Desmond and Croly illustrated as examples of this new stately home were rather indiscriminately chosen, though broadly representative of their time. Lavishness, ostentation, and grandeur were much in evidence, in spite of the authors' criticism. The great fortunes were represented—all four of the Vanderbilt brothers, Flagler, Phipps, J. P. Morgan, Astor, Gould, and Mackay, even California barons like Huntington and Crocker—reinforcing the view that patrons were far more important than architects in the emergence of this new house type. In fact, architects' names were seldom mentioned in the text and can only be found inconspicuously printed below each plate. Nearly every major town house and estate built between 1885 and 1900 was documented in photographs, including such grand country houses as Biltmore, Whitehall, The Breakers, Harbour Hill, Blairsden, and Georgian Court.[63] The visual evidence not only suggests the overwhelming conspicuous consumption and "anarchy of meaningless architectural imitation" implicit in the conservative tastes of Croly's great American millionaire but offers little to support a thesis that American domestic architecture was improving or finding its own path. What are we to make of Croly's optimism and the contradictions in his critical position?

The young journalist provided an answer to that serious question in a series of subsequent articles in *Record*. Yet his ideas were implicitly articulated even in *Stately Homes*. He believed that it was the architect's role to raise the standard of design in America, and the critic's place to give the best architects a platform from which to advance their ideas. What is unusual to the current observer is Croly's position that reform in aesthetic standards could be achieved through a purposeful collaboration among architects, critics, and patrons. Intellectuals and artists were coequals, not merely complementary forces. Collaboration was to be achieved through friendship and social intercourse among a diverse group of leaders in various fields—an enlightened community of educated artists and intellectuals. Not surprisingly, Herbert Croly was a key figure in such a community.

Croly's social circle centered on the summer artists' colony at Cornish, New Hampshire. The cottagers there included the architect Charles Adams Platt; artists Thomas Dewing, Kenyon Cox, Maxfield Parrish, and George Brush; Louis and Ellen Biddle Shipman (the playwright and the influential landscape gardener who were the Crolys' closest friends); and the diplomat Willard Straight (of whom he wrote a biography).[64] The ideas of these generally well-born, highly educated leaders in their respective fields were cross-fertilized in the atmosphere of the landed life at Cornish and disseminated in literature and art. Croly, like many in the colony, had a house designed in 1897 by Charles Platt, who would himself become the nation's most respected architect of the modern house and garden during the years before World War I. Ellen Shipman, who like Platt would first learn her art at Cornish, became one of the leading garden designers of her time. Dorothy and Willard Straight would later underwrite Croly's progressive magazine, the *New Republic*.

The Cornish colony was also a kind of arcadian experiment in house and garden design, with Platt as its leading light.[65] It is no

18 Carrère and Hastings. **Blairsden** (1898), C. Ledyard Blair country house, Bernardsville, New Jersey. (Ferree, *American Estates and Gardens.*)

19 **Blairsden.** Garden axis looking from the house toward the river valleys near Bernardsville. (Richard Cheek, from *Architectural Record,* 1903.)

20 J. Edward Kiern. Lawrence C. Phipps house (1901–03), Pittsburgh, Pennsylvania. (Desmond and Croly, *Stately Homes in America.*)

21 Charles A. Platt's own country house (1890), at Cornish, New Hampshire. (Richard Cheek, for *Antiques.*)

surprise to find that Croly championed his friend's architecture in one of his first monographs in *Record* in 1904, just about the time that the architect was hitting his stride with major commissions.[66] Platt's work was to Croly the beginning of a new approach to the American country house, one that united architecture and landscape, cut loose from palatial ostentatiousness, and provided a graceful, practical domestic environment for the American of wealth and refinement—who would now be mature enough to accept a more understated domicile.

As Keith Morgan has pointed out in his study of Platt's architecture, Croly's friend precisely fit the mold of the new progressive professional who would lead the country into "national fulfillment" in the twentieth century.[67] By confronting the problem of the American house and garden on its own terms, developing an enlightened clientele who appreciated his work, and pursuing the integrity of his artistic ideals, Platt was the epitome of the socially engaged artist. Just as Croly was to model his analysis of American politics and society in *The Promise of American Life* on his earlier studies of the American stately home and its capitalist patrons, he found in Platt the model for a new group of national leaders, which he described in the final chapter of that book.[68]

It is clear from the second group of Croly's writings on domestic architecture that he looked to Platt and a new generation of architects to transform the house and elevate the taste of wealthy patrons. He carefully chose talented and similarly disposed architects for criticism. After Platt, he introduced the early domestic work of John Russell Pope in a piece entitled "The New Use of Old Forms," which directly addressed the question of the creative versus doctrinaire adaptation of historical sources. After traveling to the Midwest around 1905, he wrote sympathetically, though not without criticism, of the large houses of Howard Van Doren Shaw. He saw and commented upon Frank Lloyd Wright's work as well.[69] A journey to California brought the regionalist eclectic houses of Myron Hunt and Elmer Grey to his attention. Finally, in 1912 he was one of the first critics to recognize the importance of Harrie T. Lindeberg, a specialist in the romantic country house.[70]

All of these architects had one thing in common: they were striving to "naturalize European traditions" in their search for an appropriate American house, rather than look for a radical break with historical styles. To Croly, this was the kind of evolutionary architectural development that would build upon established norms rather than try to insert new forms into the canon. In their work, Croly found a refreshing advance from the grander, Beaux-

Arts-inspired houses of Richard Morris Hunt, McKim, Mead and White, and Carrère and Hastings, toward houses more representative of the American way of life. Yet he was not prepared to accept the visionary and iconoclastic work of Wright—domestic architecture was too much bound up with the conservative tendencies of democratic America to be ready for such a reformulation of ideas.

In fact, Croly confronted the midwestern proponents of the new architecture in a head-to-head debate in *Record*—initially in a controversial article of 1904 entitled "The Architecture of Ideas."[71] His target was the Prairie School architect George Washington Maher, whom Croly believed ignored the real conditions of society and clients' needs in producing a kind of art for art's sake. He admitted that Frank Lloyd Wright was "the most creatively original" of a new group of free-spirited Chicago architects, of whom he singled out Richard Garden for praise and Maher for condemnation. Maher responded in 1907 with a piece in *Record* that blamed "eastern publications" for an unfair view of the new movement toward an "indigenous art." He wrote: "If we constantly copy the architecture of past ages, jotting down every proportion, every detail with no attempt to vitalize any portion of it from life's great inspiration, we dishonor the past by plagiarizing it and the work then produced must necessarily be meaningless as genuine works of art."[72] A new age was at hand, according to the author, in which architecture would outgrow its need for past styles, break free of Europe, and reach a higher state of being. America would invent its indigenous art fresh from these new conditions.

Croly answered Maher with a lengthy and persuasive article in the same issue of the journal and published along with it an extensive sampling of Maher's domestic work in Chicago, which he criticized as an architecture of mere "temperamental" expression. America had an already established indigenous architecture, derived from European models, he argued. Socially and intellectually the country had "never been independent either of Europe or of the past, as Mr. Maher's argument implies." It was this architecture that needed to be acknowledged and used as a source: "A new America can only be slowly and cautiously constructed out of the materials afforded by the American past and present." Once again, Croly's view found the middle ground, building on established norms, just as his mechanisms for reform in politics did in *The Promise of American Life*. "American architecture," he vigorously asserted, "will improve just in proportion as the American architect ceases to adopt either on one side or the other, the position of an extremist."[73]

What clearly angered Croly about Maher, and perhaps about Wright as well, were his imperious aesthetic elitism and his refusal to acknowledge the practical and socially bound aspects of house design as important. He also, quite perceptively, found Maher's work overzealous in striving for new forms, almost to the point of incoherence. Maher's bizarre and overblown house for Harry Rubens in Glencoe, Illinois, provided ample fodder for a thoroughgoing negative critique in the most spurning tone.

The factor distinguishing architects like Platt, Pope, and Shaw from Maher was a balance between social convention, "local pro-

priety," and "personal expression." All looked first to European architecture as a source—Platt found his inspiration in Italian villas and gardens, Pope in Roman and Palladian classicism, Shaw in the work of English Edwardian architects like Lutyens and Voysey. They responded to the conditions of their locale and clientele in adapting both European and American Colonial models and were careful to learn the rules of whatever idiom was chosen. What gave their architecture the stamp of quality, propriety, and "style" (probably the most semantically complex word of its day) was the degree to which each architect made the work his own, expressing his artistic personality in subtle ways through the eclectic source. For Pope, classicism was a means of personal expression as well as a system of rules. Achieving style—the ineffable quality of rightness of form and personal distinction—was the highest form of architectural achievement for both architect and client.

By 1909, when he published his first summary assessment of the reform movement, "New Phases of American Domestic Architecture," Croly saw a distinct shift in values from the era of the stately home and an increase in the influence of architects, in fulfillment of his hopes of six years before. Though "consummate domestic design" had not yet been fully achieved, wealthy men were building fewer palaces and tended to "bring a much more liberal group of ideas" to their houses. Most important, the authority and reputation of individual architects was being recognized nationally, pointing to the kind of change in taste and awareness of architectural quality that Croly prescribed in his early writings.[74] When he left the *Architectural Record* as a full editor in 1913, Croly was confident that the eclectic architects he championed would govern domestic design for the immediate future. Yet just as his prescriptions for progressive government in *The Promise of American Life* failed to take hold in the postwar foreign and domestic policy of the Wilson administration, there were cracks in the foundations of eclectic practice that would become evident as the century wore on.

Nevertheless, we have in the writings of Herbert Croly a crucial interpretation of the social and architectural factors that produced the modern American country estate. Croly observed several things in his analysis of "Rich Men and Their Houses" that help to fill out the definition of domestic eclecticism as a culture. First, he saw that the large estate of the late 1880s and 1890s was a different type of country house than the previous agrarian manor houses, plantations, cottages, and gentlemen's villas of the nineteenth century. New social and economic conditions supporting the rise of the mogul capitalist had spawned this domestic institution. He recognized that the historical associations evoked by eclectic styles were necessary to the nouveau riche patrons of these houses, who had no long-standing family history or land to establish cultural and social identity or authority. The new country house served that purpose, perhaps above all others. Furthermore, and equally important, he understood acutely the situation that architects, as artists, faced in designing houses for this kind of patron. He realized that the eclectic architect was a collaborator in the making of artistic houses and gardens, not the sole arbiter of taste, style, and architectural convention. An architect's personal stamp could be read in subtle ways by a discerning critic or layman; but Croly recognized the futility of attempting to interpret the work of such masters as Charles Platt and Harrie Lindeberg as trailblazing innovators or romantic individualists. They were participants in a significant culture in which artistic progress was measured in small, intricate, and detailed steps built on an established source or tradition.

Like William Dean Howells, the fiction writer who most closely mirrored his prose style, Croly stood firmly in the middle of his literary and artistic culture, observing and attempting to mold it from within. Croly established the critical tone that would guide a significant group of architectural writers prior to the depression—a gentleman's rhetoric that easily and gracefully fit the eclectic architecture it evaluated. He clearly and succinctly analyzed the architecture of the modern country estate during its golden age. He will serve as our guide as we attempt to do much the same thing from a different vantage point.

22 **Box Hill,** Stanford White's own country house at Saint James, Long Island
(original house, 1832; altered 1892 and after). (Richard Cheek.)

Gentlemen Architects

2

No other artist comes into such direct personal contact with his patron. None other has such a need to understand what they *want, as what he wants himself. No other is so dependent for a chance to do his best, upon his powers to influence their judgment, to control their wishes, to fall in with and yet guide and elevate their senses. Tact— which means a keen insight into their minds and a perfect control of one's own mind and tongue—is desirable in every relationship of life, but absolutely essential if one would succeed in architecture.*

—MARIANNA GRISWOLD VAN RENSSELAER

৩ AN ARCHITECTURAL GENEALOGY

Mrs. van Rensselaer, an astute critic of society as well as architecture, might have been describing any of the successful architects of the rich man's house. Charles Platt fit the description. According to his son Geoffrey, he was a "calm, humorous, and sympathetic person . . . who dressed meticulously in his own style"; in spite of his "strong presence" he nevertheless made his listeners feel important and "never imposed his convictions on anyone unless it was appropriate."[1] So too did the slightly younger William Adams Delano, who epitomized the elegant, witty, well-educated society architect. The same could be said of Howard Shaw, a somewhat shy and retiring gentleman to outsiders. His small but important circle of wealthy clients found him a sympathetic, intensely committed artist and devoted professional who gave them the understanding that only an insider could offer in designing a house. Exemplary of the generation of architects between the wars, Mott Schmidt and William Lawrence Bottomley of New York displayed the same reserved qualities. They were gentlemen in the old-fashioned sense, masters of tact. Quiet, solid, and predictable, they understood the tastes and aesthetic preferences of their clients as only social equals could.

The large group of American architects known for the eclectic country house can best be understood as a kind of genealogy. The biographical data in the appendixes of this book suggest significant connections between succeeding generations of architects working before World War II. With their similar backgrounds of education, apprenticeship, mentor-protégé successions, and the patronage of influential society families, these architects became part of a broad network of influence. There were three generations represented within this group, each of which had different attitudes toward the design of country estates. The first generation, and the model for succeeding ones, consisted of architects who flourished from the 1880s until about 1900; the second group, having trained with the first, began practicing at the turn of the century; the third flourished in the years following World War I. In number and influence, these generations conform to an expanding family tree. Such an analogy allows us to consider the architect in parallel with the patrons, whose families and wealth were also increasing with each generation.

The roots of this many-branched genealogy lie in the patriarchal influence of one man, Richard Morris Hunt (1827–95). Not only was he America's first Beaux-Arts-trained architect, but he ran the first atelier in the United States. An influential member of the American Institute of Architects (AIA), he established himself among New York's Four Hundred as a society architect par excellence with his celebrated house for William K. Vanderbilt on Fifth Avenue and 52nd Street in 1882.[2] Joy Wheeler Dow attributed to Hunt the emergence of the European-inspired stately home as an ideal for country estates during the late 1880s.[3] Hunt was at the very center of a profound change in the structure of America's capitalist aristocracy—the hegemony of New York's new money over the ancien régime of Boston and Philadelphia. Hunt's clientele for his large resort and country houses was drawn almost entirely from this sphere.[4] In developing the pretentious, grand, and palatial models he chose for The Breakers, Marble House, and eventually Biltmore, Hunt was implicitly creating a style for a sophisticated New York patronage. New York became the apex of the patronage tree and therefore the center of the domestic culture that supported eclectic designers. Most of the leading architects of the first and second generations were based in New York.

Hunt also created a role model for the society architect. Along with such well-connected New York architects as Bruce Price and George B. Post, Hunt established himself as a social equal of his patrons—through membership in the same clubs, churches, and cultural institutions. By his leadership, social position, and example, Hunt helped to assure that the architect would no longer be considered a "piece of business or social machinery to be lugged in when . . . a house is to be built," as Herbert Croly put it.[5] A photograph from the famous costume ball given by James Hazen Hyde at Sherry's around the turn of the century shows Stanford White and Francis Hoppin amid a group of New York socialites, clearly demonstrating the new prominence that architects had achieved through Hunt's example. This status was hard won in a country where commercial interests tended to overwhelm pretensions toward art and businessmen tended to equate architects with builders and tradesmen. Contemporaries such as Stanford White and Charles McKim gave Hunt credit for establishing the architect as both a professional and an artist; he was "a pathfinder and icebreaker" for his fellow designers.[6]

23 Fancy dress ball at Sherry's, c. 1900. Stanford White (center), Francis L. V. Hoppin (seated at left), and Adele Sloane Burden (holding open fan). (Wecter, *The Saga of American Society*.)

Yet despite his hard-won social and professional status, the architect could not fully dictate the stylistic and aesthetic parameters of domestic design. He was generally still at the mercy of his patrons. In discussing the treatment of the architect in popular fiction—specifically in Edith Wharton's *Sanctuary*, Robert Grant's *Unleavened Bread*, and Robert Herrick's *The Common Lot*—Herbert Croly examined the architect's changing role in American society at the turn of the century.[7] Grant's novel of 1900 portrays the architect as a pawn in a scheme of a woman reformer, Selma White, to turn her sleepy midwestern town of Benham into a bustling eastern-style commercial center. Her Beaux-Arts-trained architect, Wilbur Littleton, is portrayed as a sensitive, gaunt, and earnest young artist, possessed of "nervous energy" and "poetic impulses," which set him apart from the midwestern social milieu and lead Selma to take him as her first husband.[8] Eventually he is driven to his death by her manipulations and by the artistic compromises forced upon him. Croly was disturbed by this kind of portrayal, suggesting that the architect needed more social authority to establish an artistic credibility with businessmen.

Other books cast him in slightly better light. In *The Rise of Silas Lapham*, by William Dean Howells (William Rutherford Mead's brother-in-law and himself the father of an architect), both Charles McKim and Stanford White are parodied in the persona of Lapham's architect, Mr. Seymour. A confident and authoritative artist, Seymour persuades his conservative client to build a Colonial Revival house rather than the dark Victorian brownstone with a French roof he initially wants. In the end, Lapham is delighted with his somewhat anomalous brick facade, in spite of delays and cost overruns. A less than sophisticated aesthetic observer, he can't tell whether he is fifty years behind the times or ten years ahead.[9] As the image of the architect changed, his influence increased, and his social visibility gave him more authority in matters of taste. In this novel he has clearly arrived. During the climactic scene in which the Laphams dine with their old gentry rivals, the Coreys, at their Beacon Hill house, Mr. Seymour is a guest and a pivotal figure in the conversation. Both the "nobs" and the "swells" seem to hang on his every word, as he skillfully analyzes the qualities of his new house for Lapham and compares it to the one at which he is dining. As he triumphs in covering over the differences, social and architectural, between the two domiciles, Mr. Corey, the Boston Brahmin, concludes: "You architects and the musicians are the true and only artistic creators. All the rest of us, sculptors, painters, novelists, and tailors, deal with forms that we have before us; we try to imitate, we try to represent. But you two sorts of artists create form. If you represent, you fail. Somehow or other you do evolve the camel out of your inner consciousness."[10]

The hero of Herrick's *The Common Lot*, who wishes he had Hunt's inherited wealth and social connections, struggles to make a career in both commercial work and high society circles in Chicago, only to find himself done in by the unscrupulous practices of a builder from whom he had gotten an early break. Despite his desire to rise to the top, he remains in the middle. The novels of this period make it clear that the architect had gained a great deal of social respectability but had not yet achieved the power to control taste.

If any firm was able to command that kind of power, it was McKim, Mead and White, who inherited Hunt's mantle and some of his clientele in the 1890s. Though the partners trained with H. H. Richardson, they came to associate themselves more with Hunt and the New York chain of patronage than with old Boston and the waning influence of Richardson. As the first large and multifaceted architectural office in the United States, this partnership did much to establish educational, personal, and professional ideals for academically trained designers.[11] Charles McKim, who is frequently mentioned in memoirs as the father of a movement, was another patriarchal figure in the genealogy. "It would be hard to imagine Mr. McKim without his vast knowledge of scholarly detail which under his deft hand carries on the style where the Italian masters left off," Howard Shaw said in a speech to the AIA.[12] Thomas Hastings found McKim to have "perhaps more of the true sense of beauty than any of his predecessors in American Art."[13] John Russell Pope, another of his protégés, said, "I believe him to have been by far the finest architectural influence we have had in a hundred years."[14] The flamboyant Stanford White occupied a similar, if more legendary, position with his colleagues and was one of the great socialites of his day.

The office of McKim, Mead and White in New York became the training ground for a group of early-twentieth-century American architects who had a profound impact on the country's domestic and urban environments. Many of the leading domestic specialists who trained at the office imparted in turn these same high standards of American architectural practice to others. Moreover, the patrons of the firm, like those of Hunt, represented the top of the social and business ladders.[15] From 1895 to 1905 many of the most prestigious country houses were designed by this preeminent firm. However, when White was murdered in 1906 and McKim died in 1909, the chain of patronage was broken, and a significant shift occurred in domestic practice. It is not surprising that several former clients turned to architects who had apprenticed with the firm. Harrie Lindeberg, James Brite, Henry Bacon, and John Russell Pope all seized the opportunity to open practices in the wake of their mentors' deaths.

Consider the case of two of the most successful designers who trained with McKim, Mead and White. John Merven Carrère (1858–1911) and Thomas Hastings (1860–1929) began their independent partnership in 1885. Both were from wealthy, established families whose connections gave the young architects a brilliant start and propelled them to almost instant prominence. Carrère, the son of a well-traveled coffee merchant, was born in Rio de Janeiro and traced his French ancestry back to the Revolution of 1789, when his family fled to Baltimore. Hastings, the sixth male descendant to bear the name, could claim prestigious New England ancestry: settlers of the Massachusetts Bay Colony in 1634, a cleric grandfather who wrote the hymn "Rock of Ages," among other tunes, and a father who was one of New York's most distinguished clergymen — the president of the Union Theological Seminary and Presbyterian pastor to many of the city's most prominent business leaders. Both received excellent cultural and academic educations, Hastings by tutor and Carrère in Swiss schools, and were naturally drawn to each other when attending the Ecole des Beaux-Arts in Paris in the early 1880s.[16]

Both were draftsmen at McKim, Mead and White from 1883 to 1885, when Hastings' family connections afforded the two the extraordinary opportunity to design for Henry Morrison Flagler the lavish Ponce de Leon Hotel in St. Augustine, as part of his resort developments in Florida.[17] Flagler was a family friend and a member of the father's congregation in New York. The smashing success of their debut building presaged an association that would produce such acclaimed public edifices as the New York Public Library, won by competition in 1897, and the House and Senate Office Buildings in Washington, D.C. (1905–09). As a rule, however, the firm obtained its commissions for both domestic and public projects not by competition but through strong social and professional liaisons. As with the buildings done for Flagler, domestic and public commissions of Carrère and Hastings were often intimately connected. Their many country estates differed little in grandeur and style from some of their classical public buildings. The personalities of the partners and the social sphere in which they moved say much about the new status of the architect and the importance of influential patrons in establishing a practice.

Carrère, who served as the business and professional partner in the firm until his tragic death in 1911 in a taxicab accident, was a hard-driving personality who could push a project along, as he did in the case of the library on Fifth Avenue. His "strict, nervous stature," lacking humor and outward charm, was in stark contrast to the "generous, affectionate, sunny-natured" persona of his partner. Hastings, the more artistically gifted of the two, was a deft draftsman and sketcher with "a penchant for drawing ornament" and naturally handled most of the design in the office. He was a cool, logical, lucid, and unemotional designer in the best tradition of a Beaux-Arts-trained architect. His planning and use of precedent reflected his French taste and training and his intense commitment to history and tradition.[18]

Hastings' strong but understated personality went hand in hand with his patrician upbringing and aptly fit his social sphere. Like many successful men of his class, he managed to balance leisure and professional pursuits with a kind of carefree dexterity. An equestrian, he preferred summer social gatherings and country life at his Westbury, Long Island, home, Bagatelle (1908), to New York gentlemen's clubs, the opera, or other urban diversions. He also built a horse farm and country house in the fashionable enclave of Aiken, South Carolina. Significantly, both homes were rather modest in comparison to much of the work of the firm. His marriage in 1900 to the daughter of E. C. Benedict, for whom he designed his first major country house, Indian Harbour, in 1895–96, grew out of an important social and professional liaison. Hastings, a frequent guest on Benedict's impressive yacht, *Oneida,* was listed on the log thirty-five times between 1890 and 1917. It is clear from the other names in the log that the architect developed close associations with current and future clients, such as Ledyard

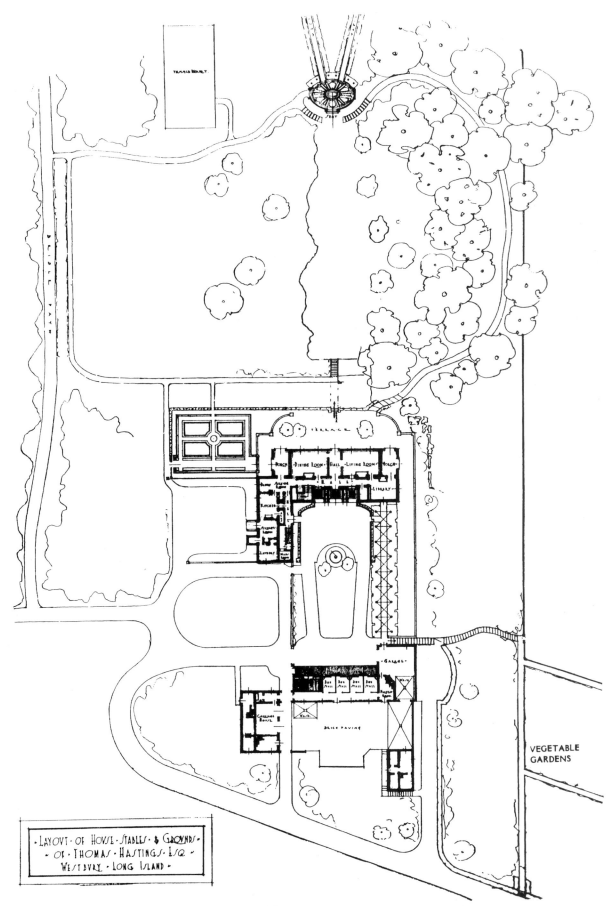

24 Thomas Hastings. **Bagatelle** (second version of 1908), architect's own house, Westbury, Long Island. Plan. (*American Country Houses of To-Day*, 1915.)

VEGETABLE
GARDENS

·LAYOVT·OF·HOVSE·STABLES·&·GROVNDS·
·OF·THOMAS·HASTINGS·ESQ·
·WESTBVRY·LONG ISLAND·

25 **Bagatelle.** View of court. (*American Country Houses of To-Day,* 1915.)

Blair, on board his father-in-law's yacht.[19] This nonchalant maritime sport was really serious business—an extension of Benedict's lavish seaside estate in Greenwich, Connecticut, which served as a showcase for Hastings' considerable gifts as an architect. It is also indicative of the gentlemanly mingling of artists, professionals, and businessmen typical of that day.

Hastings displayed his talents in over a dozen of the most elegant of America's country houses between the mid-1890s and the 1920s, including Blairsden, Bellefontaine, and Whitehall. He became known as the leading exponent of the modern French stately home. When a wealthy man such as Alfred I. Du Pont wanted a French house, he naturally turned to Hastings. Thus in 1910 he designed the grand Nemours estate in the Brandywine Valley and in 1916–17 was retained to do Templeton, in Brookville, Long Island. His firm, in an unusual and important commission, won a competition in 1909 to design Arden, one of the largest post-1900 houses, for financial tycoon E. H. Harriman (who had just completed his extraordinary consolidation of the railroads and was then on top of the financial world). The two other architects invited to compete were no less than Edwin Lutyens and Bertram Goodhue, both far more familiar with the client's preferred idiom, English Tudor. Looking at the three designs, it is difficult to assess why the winning scheme was chosen, because it was a thinly disguised French courtyard type in English dress, whereas the other two were brilliant and expansive essays. Perhaps when one considers Hastings' powerful social standing, the result is easier to comprehend. He was the quintessential gentleman architect of his day, moving easily within the highest social circles. At times the authority of his personality acted as a substitute for persuasive design, and this was fully acceptable to some clients. The artistic and charismatic sides of the man were inseparable—a trait typical of the successful society architect. Hastings stood in the shadow of Hunt and McKim; an architect was now a man to be listened to, a man with the same respect as a financier.

The chain of succession within this architect-patron network proceeded into the next generation through Hastings' mentorship of William Adams Delano, whom we shall consider below. It is clear that Delano modeled himself after Hastings' example—in his education, manners, social connections, clubs, academic philosophy, and even the design of his small country estate in Muttontown, Long Island. Hastings was Delano's patron, or atelier master, in French parlance, just as McKim had been Hastings'. Some of Delano and Aldrich's early clients were naturally among the social network established by the mentor firm.

During the last decades of the nineteenth century the American architect rose from the "unleavened bread" of his previous milieu

INDIAN HARBOUR, Conn.
property of E.C.Benedict Esq

CARRÈRE & HASTINGS.ARTES.
44&46 Broadway N.Y.

26 Carrère and Hastings. **Indian Harbour** (1895–96), E. C. Benedict house,
Greenwich, Connecticut. Site plan. (Richard Cheek, from *T-Square Annual.*)

27 Carrère and Hastings. Murray F. Guggenheim house (c. 1903), Elberon, New Jersey. (Richard Cheek, from *Architectural Record,* 1903.)

to a new social position. Julius Gregory summarized the situation this way in 1930: "The architect is still looked upon as the man who makes a house look beautiful—and up to date—and, to some extent, as one who gives it as much of an air of social distinction or correctness as possible. But just how does an architect make a house artistic? Only by being business-like. That is the point."[20] Gentleman, artist, and businessman in equal measure, the architect won his client's esteem and trust by solidarity and understanding. How the architect came by his skills as a designer, socialite, and manager is the next subject to consider, and a crucial one in understanding how he thought and worked.

TRAINING AND PRACTICE

There were very few men to be found in the club at this hour. The dingy library, buzzing like a beehive at noon with young men, was empty now except for a stranger who was whiling away his time before a dinner engagement. Most of the men that the architect met at this club were, like himself, younger members of the professions, struggling upward in the crowded ranks of law, medicine, architecture. Others were employed in brokers' offices, or engaged in general business. Some of them had been his classmates in Cornell, or in the technological school, and these had welcomed him with a little dinner on his return from Paris.

— Robert Herrick

Advances in education played a large part in establishing architects as esteemed social leaders. The architects of McKim's generation developed the system of architectural education we know today—the collegiate professional degree program. Practicing around the time of the founding of the nation's first schools of architecture, at the Massachusetts Institute of Technology (MIT) (1865), Cornell (1871), and the University of Illinois (1873),[21] they created planning committees, educational institutions such as the Beaux-Arts Institute of Design[22] and the American Academy in Rome and were responsible for the first professional licensing of architects in the United States.[23] Among their number were the first influential architectural educators in the country, including William Robert Ware of MIT, A. D. F. Hamlin of

Columbia, Herbert Langford Warren of Harvard, and John Van Pelt of Cornell. By their authority these figures transformed the profession in America from one based primarily on apprenticeship to a modern, academically centered system. This system of professional education provided the basis for a consistent set of standards in practice and design theory.[24]

To a young man with talent, a good Anglo-Saxon name, and a family of means, acquiring the education to become an architect was a relatively straightforward matter in the first decades of this century. Because professional training was institutionalized in the last quarter of the nineteenth century through collegiate programs and licensing, a large and productive second generation of formally trained architects emerged. The pattern of training became codified and the path to a successful career was clear enough that more young men, and eventually young women, from the middle class upward, could securely choose architecure as a career. One hundred of the most important architects working between 1890 and 1940 can be divided into three groups: those born between 1850 and 1870; those born from 1870 to 1880, and those born in 1880 and after (see appendix). A comparison of education and apprenticeship among the three generations reveals some significant facts.

First, the often-cited influence of the Ecole des Beaux-Arts on eclectic architects can be verified by noting that the majority were exposed to atelier and *concours* (competition) instruction in Paris, if only briefly. Other statistics indicate that the number of Americans attending the Ecole program rose from 10 in the 1860s to 110 in the 1890s and peaked shortly after 1900. Moreover the leading American architectural schools—MIT, Columbia (1881), Pennsylvania (1874), Cornell, and New York's Beaux-Arts Institute (1894)—offered programs heavily indebted to teaching methods at the Ecole. Although none of the three initial collegiate programs had Paris-trained faculty, all eight of the leading schools had acquired studio masters from the Beaux-Arts by 1908.[25]

The typical educational path for the gentleman architect was, like that of his bourgeois French counterpart, a fairly lengthy one. A Frenchman might spend ten years at the Ecole, especially if he had the opportunity to become a *pensionnaire* at the French Academy in Rome by winning the *Grand Prix de Rome* in the arduous annual competition (he was limited only by the cut-off age of thirty). A few Americans of Hastings' generation spent up to five years in Paris before embarking upon a three- to five-year apprenticeship with an established American firm, usually in New York, Boston, or Philadelphia. But the more typical route for a well-heeled young designer was first to obtain a liberal education at an elite college such as Yale, Haverford, Columbia, or Harvard, where he might meet his future clients, and then to head for Paris; or, should he fail the difficult entrance examinations, he might receive his initial Beaux-Arts training at home and then do an abbreviated grand tour. The next step was nearly always to secure a position as a draftsman or designer in a prestigious firm, which not only provided atelier-style tutelage in both aesthetic and technical matters but also got a young architect started in the network of referrals that to this day contributes heavily to his success or failure.

As the survey shows, McKim's firm was a leading training ground for the older generation, Carrère and Hastings for the younger, although it was not uncommon for architects trained in New York and Paris to look for apprenticeship in the cities in which they chose to settle. Donn Barber of New Haven had perhaps the most gold-plated of educations: Yale College, Columbia School of Architecture, the Ecole, and an apprenticeship with Carrère and Hastings. On the other end of the spectrum, Lewis Hobart of San Francisco began with a Berkeley education, won the Rome Prize to the newly founded Academy, and rounded out his education with a stint at New York's Beaux-Arts Institute of Design, before heading back to California to begin his practice.

A significant number of architects beginning their practices before 1900 received their tutelage in design through the apprentice system, at the hand of a master practitioner, but that number diminished rapidly after 1900. Designers brought up in Philadelphia and Boston, where English customs were more entrenched than in New York, sometimes went to London for training or were exposed to the British custom of a longer studio apprenticeship. One such designer was Frank Miles Day of Philadelphia (1861–1918), considered one of the most literate architects of his time.[26] Educated at home by his English-born father, Charles Day, he distinguished himself as a scholar at the University of Pennsylvania, graduating in 1883, then went on to study abroad for three years at the South Kensington School of Art (Lutyens' alma mater) and the Royal Academy of Art in London. He worked for the Edwardian architect Basil Champneys, as well as at the Philadelphia office of Addison Hutton, before founding his own firm in 1887.[27] Like Hastings, Day moved in a relatively close-knit social world of literate, Anglophile Philadelphians for whom the advancement of such country pastimes as the hunt was a passion supported by a refined but rustic architectural ethos. Like his New York contemporaries, he became one of the mentors for a later generation of eclectic masters.

Hence, there were two basic educational patterns, one French-influenced, the other English, one based on classical principles, the other on romantic, picturesque, and Ruskinian ones. The education of the eclectic architect played a crucial part in forming his eventual philosophy of design—especially his attitude to history and tradition. In principle the two schools agreed on the necessity

for free and creative use of the historical source or type. As Thomas Hastings warned: "Now that photographs and illustrated books are so accessible to the student, copying or adaptation is a greater temptation than ever before. It destroys progress in art. . . . [We must not] comprise more than we compose."[28] What distinguished them was their approach to the fundamentals of formal composition, not toward the use of historical sources. A classicist designed "by the axes" in a strict formal system based on symmetries; the picturesque designer used his feeling for massing, texture, and volume in a perspectival mode of composition. As Julien Gaudet wrote, "Symmetry is that regularity [of form] which one must apprehend in a single sweep of the eye. Symmetry is intelligent regularity. . . . I love the picturesque, it is what pleases me most when I enter a village, but one does not compose that way."[29]

The academic classical method was the more formally codified of the two and exerted far greater influence. Eclectic architects worked with a knowledge of historical sources that was ingrained in them as students, when they learned to draw and study precedents as a part of a highly structured, pedagogical program used at both the Ecole and its American imitators.[30] Structurally, the program had three components: the atelier, the academy, and the concours system. The first two were linked by the third. Students received their training in design at the hand of a patron who was a practicing architect and their education in technical, theoretical, and historical subjects from lecturers at the school itself. Students progressed through the three stages of their education—from second class to first class and finally (for the best) to pensionnaire at the French Academy in Rome—by competing in monthly competitions, which were judged by faculty and academicians. Much has been written about the so-called Beaux-Arts system, citing both its evils and its miraculous formulas for design. Its major advantage was simple—it offered the student a clear exposition of a mode of design thinking, called simply the art of composition.

Precise, decisive thinking was taught through the sketch, or *esquisse,* made in only nine hours without the aid of criticism or source books. Through the sketch, which by the rules of the problem had to be used as the basis for a final design, the young architect was required to commit himself (*prendre parti*), thus making clear, expedient thinking essential. Rational understanding of space and mass came about after exhaustive analytical drawing of cast ornament, the human figure, and various floral and natural forms—that is, through limitation in the process of representation itself. Both repetition and imitation were key concepts in the academic classical method of design.

Understanding the principles of geometry as a tool for understanding form was of even greater importance. According to the doctrine of *dessin géometral,* the student was first taught to understand an object or building by cutting it apart along the cardinal axes and unveiling its inner structure. In buildings, the plan was the key analytical and design tool. "All good composition begins with a thorough study of the plan," Hastings stressed; "the silhouette or outline of the whole structure is really projected on the plane of this drawing."[31]

As he advanced in skill, the student would study qualities of

28 Julian Francis Abele. "A Residence." One-day esquisse problem, architecture
program, University of Pennsylvania, c. 1901. (*University of Pennsylvania Biennial
Review,* 1902.)

mass and modeling through skiagraphic, or light and shadow, rendering. As an advanced tool of representation, academic wash rendering allowed the young architect to depict vividly the effects of light falling on any surface or material. Shadows were worked out mathematically, allowing for both incident and reflected light in subtle gradations. Finally, the fundamental pedagogical vehicle of the concours gave students a variety of problems, arranged in increasing difficulty and judged in an atmosphere similar to that of the professional competitions they would later encounter.[32]

After acquiring the analytical and descriptive means to undertake a problem, the student was instructed in stylistic principles (from Gothic, French Renaissance, or any other traditional style—not just classical variants) and asked to locate, select, and reinterpret examples from history to solve modern building problems. John Harbeson stressed the importance of choosing the right sources in two chapters of his excellent Beaux-Arts textbook, *The Study of Architectural Design* (1927). He underlined the necessity of having a repertoire of sources at hand when undertaking a design problem:

The study of design—of proportion—resolves itself into a study of tradition; the study, in essence, of the worthy efforts of the past, the unworthy being passed by where there is such a quantity of material. To this the designer has added his contribution when his design is made to suit new conditions, new methods of construction, new aesthetic requirements. So to study the proportions of the elements, we study the proportions used by the masters for those elements, from actual examples, if possible, or from books or photographs.[33]

He clearly favored a form of typological adaptation: the study of current and past examples of particular building types as analogies to a modern building of a similar type—essentially codifying the method used so effectively by McKim, Mead and White in their mature buildings. For McKim's followers, precedents were the cornerstones of creative innovation.

Harbeson's recommended library became a canon for nearly all eclectic architects of these two generations. It was composed primarily of the folio editions of drawings made for the use of Ecole students and architects, from Letarouilly's measured drawings published in *Edifices de Rome moderne* (considered the office bible at McKim, Mead and White) to the lavish folios of Hector Despouy's Prix de Rome collections and the German documentations of Italian architecture in photographs and drawings, such as Stegmann and Geymüller's *Architecture of the Renaissance in Tuscany*.[34] These tomes, with their precise and beautiful drawings and photos of details, were the inspiration for many architect-historians documenting American, Spanish, and English architecture for dissemination to revival specialists in the 1910s and 1920s. The eclectic's library was adjunct and fodder to his imagination. His creativity was measured not in degree of originality, but in what he added to tradition.

Books were not a substitute, however, for direct exposure to the great monuments of Western architecture, which were measured and sketched firsthand during the grand tour. Many American architects remembered their European tours as the capstone of their educations abroad; years later they took out their sketchbooks to use as inspiration for new designs. As the camera came into general use, photographs often augmented sketches. In 1877, McKim, White, and several other architects made a famous sketching trip to familiarize themselves with Colonial buildings in New England, documenting their work in the *New York Sketch Book of Architecture*. Arthur Little, another early exponent of the use of Colonial precedents, kept an extraordinary set of scrapbooks that recorded old American houses side by side with the work of his firm. The details and particular design features used were noted in the margins for reference on later work. John Russell Pope used his own hand-camera photographs of various English buildings not only for his own reference but as a means of instructing builders in antique techniques, such as brickwork and half-timbering.

After leaving school and completing the grand tour and an apprenticeship, the young architect faced the problem of finding initial clients. For many successful domestic architects, especially those of the generation following 1876, having a mentor was the key to a career. The patronage chain that influenced McKim, Mead and White was repeated elsewhere in the country. One sign of this nepotism within the two generations was a tendency of wealthy families to stay with an almost predictable group of closely "related" architects in building and remodeling their estates. As Henry James once remarked of Philadelphia's old society: "It would find itself happy enough only if it could remain closed enough."[35]

The consistency of philosophy among architects during this important half-century comes from a sharing of education, social background, and professional experience. As Herbert Croly observed in 1911, "The majority of contemporary designers have been profoundly influenced by the example and counsel of some of their eminent predecessors, and influences derived from this source have probably been more powerful and more prevalent than those derived from any single direction."[36] Architects of the second or third generation practicing in Minneapolis, Denver, Kansas City, or Spokane were closely connected to those in New York and Philadelphia, having often trained in the East. And even if provincial architects of the postwar period did not go to New York or Europe, they benefited from increased dissemination of work in the media, especially in professional and popular journals. In spite of America's vastness, diversity of landscape, and cultural variety, the eclectic architect worked in a homogeneous professional milieu.

The sharing of aesthetic and professional ideals among architects was facilitated by the institution of the architectural club— yet another manifestation of gentlemanly conduct. Such organizations proliferated in the 1880s, often as alternatives to the more professionally oriented American Institute of Architects; many were far more influential and vital. New York had the largest and most active organization, the Architectural League, founded in 1881 with eighteen members. Not limited to architects, the membership deliberately included artists and craftsmen to "recognize the essential alliance of the decorative arts." The league

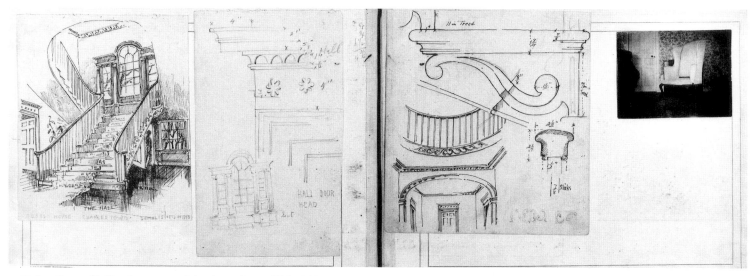

29 Herbert Browne (?). Sketches, measured drawings, photos of Colonial house details combined in a typical office scrapbook. (Little and Browne Scrapbooks, vol. 3, Avery Architectural Archives.)

sponsored a yearly exhibition of the work of members, modeled after various showings in European institutions such as the Royal Academy in London. It also awarded medals for excellence in design—Charles Platt received the Gold Medal in 1912 for his country house oeuvre. By 1920 its membership included nearly all of New York's eminent designers.[37]

Philadelphia's T-Square Club, founded in emulation of the league by Frank Miles Day, William L. Price, and Wilson Eyre in 1883, seemed grounded more in the English Arts and Crafts movement than in the pretentious French pomp associated with New York. A number of English architects were regular exhibitors. It too sponsored yearly shows and issued a splendid printed yearbook reproducing the best designs by architects, artists, and craftsmen. Contests for travel sketches and renderings, as well as members' photographs, were part of the exhibitions. Issues discussed in meetings were recorded in short papers.[38]

Other cities founded clubs modeled on these institutions, some publishing members' work in periodicals sponsored by the club. In 1900 there were major clubs under the aegis of the Architectural League of America in Boston (established in 1889), Chicago (1885), New York, Philadelphia, Cleveland (1894), Detroit (1895), and Pittsburgh (1896), along with the Society of Beaux Arts Architects, a national organization. The largest organizations were New York's Architectural League, with 405 members, the Boston Architectural Club, with 188 members, Philadelphia's T-Square, with 156 members, and the Chicago Architectural Club, also with 156.[39] Architects were also well represented in more patrician social organizations, such as New York's Century Association, Players Club, Metropolitan Club, and Union League, and generally maintained memberships in country clubs. Harrie Lindeberg's commission to design the prestigious Onwentsia Club in Lake Forest helped further his patronage in Chicago, and William Adams Delano designed a number of important club buildings in New York.

Greater professional and business organization among archi-

tects brought increased exposure to media sources and advertising—contractors, tradesmen, craftspeople, manufacturers, and retailers sought out architects as sponsors and advertised by drawing upon the notoriety of projects, designers, and clients. Advertising brochures and books, such as those put out by leading country house builders to promote their work, were beautifully designed and evocative in their own right: quality, craftsmanship, and artfulness spread into many corners of country house culture.[40] There were even "scholarly" builders, like Virginia's Herbert A. Clairborne, Sr. (1886–1957), whose firm, Clairborne and Taylor, was a favorite of Bottomley's in Richmond; in addition Clairborne was the nation's leading expert on eighteenth-century brickwork and a distinguished antiquarian in other respects.[41] Samuel Yellin (1885–1940), the Philadelphia ironwork craftsman and collector, played so large a role in the design of wrought and cast metal elements in many buildings, public and domestic, that in 1920 he was given a medal for his achievements by the AIA.[42]

This was also a period in which both the art and the technical scope of architectural drawing reached an extraordinarily high level. Draftsmanship was taught as a skill, ensuring a uniform standard of technical drawing within the profession. Not only was academic wash rendering used to present projects, but a school of specialist architectural renderers emerged at the turn of the century to answer the need for more elaborate drawings—among the best of these were Jules Guérin, Schell Lewis, Chester B. Price, Harvey Ellis, and Otto Eggers. Architectural clubs sponsored competitions for sketching, rendering, and presentation drawings, which clearly showed the care architects put into their graphic representation. Craftsmanship in drawing often translated into meticulous detailing in the actual building, as the fine working drawings produced by the better firms demonstrated. Country houses, of course, required enormous amounts of good detail work.[43]

The consistency of outlook within these two generations was also reflected in the way they ran their practices. Many Paris-trained architects followed the lead of Hunt by structuring their

Residence for Mr. Frank Bigelow,
Fox Point, Wis.
Elmer Grey, Architect,

View from the road.

offices like an atelier, with a single patron, an assistant, or *massier,* and a handful of draftsmen as apprentices. In addition, the hierarchical business organization, increasingly influential in the twentieth century, provided a model in which specialization of tasks facilitated efficiency and maximized profits. The larger and more diverse the practice, the greater the need for such organization. At the top were the partners, perhaps one a designer and the other a businessman or manager; the rest of the staff included several senior architects, perhaps an engineer, a rendering specialist, and the draftsmen necessary to produce working drawings. Most residential specialists did not require extensive staffs, because the partner or partners were able to control directly all stages of the design and construction process.[44]

Finally, the office environment reinforced the eclectic philosophy and played up the image of the architect as cultured antiquarian as well as professional. Early eclecticists such as Hunt cultivated the artistic image by decorating their offices like a Paris atelier. In 1916, William Adams Delano, who as a young man lived in a fine Greek Revival town house at 12 Washington Square North, remodeled an old stable in Murray Hill into a town house for his second "ideal architect's office." [45] Wilson Eyre also used a Georgian town house on Spruce Street as his home and office—the facade of which evinced the unpretentiousness of Quaker simplicity, according to one critic. Inside, Eyre's home and office had the idiosyncratic aura of a collector's menagerie, much like the famous terrace house of John Soane in London.[46] Such individuality reinforced the image of Eyre as an artist-architect. Other architects were more businesslike. Dwight James Baum's Riverdale studio was designed in an English vein to resemble one of his

30 *top* Elmer Grey. "Residence for Mr. Frank Bigelow, Fox Point, Wis.," sketch c. 1900. (Architectural Drawing Collection, University Art Museum, Santa Barbara, California.)

opposite
31 Schell Lewis. Charcoal study of a doorway for a country house. Office of Charles Platt. (*Architecture,* 1915.)

well-known houses. The interior was divided into artistic and professional realms: the drafting room was Spartan; special rooms were provided for contractors and engineering staff. But Baum's private office, where he met clients, was a cozy replica of an Early American parlor, complete with teakettle in the fireplace, musket on the mantel, and a copy of Stuart's *George Washington* hanging above on the pine-paneled wall. Within these surroundings, a prospective client could imagine himself in his own "home sweet home," while Baum made his pitch.

In keeping with the importance of books, the library was often the centerpiece of the architect's office and might be decorated with plaster casts, tapestries, antique furniture, and art objects to inspire and educate draftsmen. The small building Mellor and Meigs designed to house their Philadelphia office was a masterpiece of this serene, history-laden genre. What they called the Big Room of the office was a kind of studio, library, and reception room. The high-vaulted space was inspired by English Edwardian architecture but managed to synthesize elements of many cultures—Italian, Spanish, American. This shrine to architectural history, with its Renaissance-like hearth, inspired architects to conjure up spirits of the past.

32 Office of Mellor, Meigs and Howe, Philadelphia, Pennsylvania. Street facade. (Athenaeum of Philadelphia.)

33 *right* Office of Mellor, Meigs and Howe. "Big Room." (Athenaeum of Philadelphia.)

ECLECTICISM AND THE FUNCTION OF SOURCES

In the design of many American country houses the issue of copying from historical sources is commonly misunderstood. It is not unusual to hear docents and tour guides in a turn-of-the-century house describe a room or even an entire building as a replica of a European palace from some identifiable period—a Louis XVI château, a sixteenth-century Venetian palazzo, or a Tudor manor house. True enough, there are many examples of period houses that are closely based on popular models, such as Mount Vernon, Compton Wynyates, or the Petit Trianon. Sometimes the attributions have a basis, but more often they are used to give the stamp of authority or to impress the tourist by the connoisseurship of the owner and the historical aura that something old naturally conjures up. Moreover, the charge of mere replication is also used as a means of denigrating the work of eclectic designers—it takes no talent to reproduce a work of architecture from a book. As the above exposition of the architect's education and practice has made clear, none of these architects would have seen his residential work as copying. Even a detailed analysis of some of the most derivative houses seldom reveals the consistent, archaeological use of a single source.

There is additionally the problem of pejorative connotations of *eclectic,* a misleading and complex term. Architects at the turn of the century disliked it because it smacked of things Victorian, of a chaotic and unprincipled period in America's recent past. As Joy Wheeler Dow wrote in 1904: "That term 'eclectic style,' which so frequently crops out in treatises upon architecture, were you to follow it up, would be found to signify, as a rule, merely American nonsense and aberration."[47] Currently, however, we use *eclectic* to describe art whose sources are diverse and people whose taste is pluralistic and catholic—though this is not its original meaning. The term is derived from the Greek *eklektos,* meaning chosen or

picked out,[48] a definition that more accurately suggests the philosophy of architects at the turn of the century—that of choosing and transforming architectural details from history under the rubric of a style or idiom.

Just how did the architect and patron work out the design of a house, and how were historical sources used? To understand fully the theories, values, and methods of the eclecticist, one must examine the issue of imitation in design and the significance of historical models. In analyzing the use of sources there is an important difference between typological adaptation—that is, the formal and symbolic continuity of building types in a canon—and the "quoting" or reinterpretation of specific motifs, models, and details. In addition, it is essential to recognize the difference between the architect's view of the function of sources and that of the patron; they were not always in accord.

To an eclectic architect the choice of a source was in itself a creative act, a means of identifying with an ideal or credo, a profession of who he was and what he aspired to. When he "quoted" from the work of a great master, such as Palladio or Thomas Jefferson, he did so in homage. When he used a particular historic house as a model, he acknowledged the universality of the ideas and functional innovations in it and offered his variation as a perpetuation of a classic formula. When he was asked by a client to design in a particular style or to use a particular paradigm, he usually did his best to avoid strict replication. Historical sources were foils, not ends in themselves. As Wilson Eyre said, "Do not copy.

34 *top* Private office of Dwight James Baum. (*The Work of Dwight James Baum.*)

35 Office of Dwight James Baum, Riverdale, New York. Plan. (*The Work of Dwight James Baum.*)

. . . If you know only a little, you reproduce; if you know a great deal, you adapt, combine in fact, originate, for no imagination, however vivid, can conceive a thing that is not a combination of what he has seen."[49]

There were essentially four ways in which an architect might approach his sources: (1) typological analogy, (2) genre application, (3) scholarly quotation, and (4) pastiche of new and old fragments. The most important methodologically was the use of formal and historical types in analogous modern situations. McKim, Mead and White were the masters of typological adaptation in their many institutional buildings—the use of a Florentine palazzo as a model for the University Club, for instance. In houses, the use of a formal type, such as the plan for an eighteenth-century center hall, was also an analogue of past and present. Functionally, the plan was chosen to solve a program and provide constructional and climatic advantages. Yet as a connection with similar houses in its locale, it was a way of bowing to tradition. As we have already seen, an academic architect was educated to recognize analogies in historical types and to choose the correct models for adaptation and transformation. This selective approach is one of the central theoretical imperatives of early-twentieth-century eclecticism.

The second approach to sources, which might be called genre architecture, referred to generic ways of designing that architects understood intuitively (see chapter 3). For architects familiar with the stylistic terms, a client need only request work in an English vein or a Tudor vein. The best early example of this approach is Richard Morris Hunt's adaptation of the François I style. Each architect developed his own interpretation of a particular idiom and worked freely from that understanding. No rigid formal, decorative, or stylistic rules were applied, merely a set of qualities that might vary from house to house. Not surprisingly, architects who drew well tended to use the genre approach to greater advantage than those who did not. Wilson Eyre's Tudor work was very different from that of Horace Trumbauer—the major distinctions were in their means of planning and the flare with which they applied the idiom. Yet a client would not have questioned the authority of either architect's essays.

In contrast to the intuitive use of sources, many architects saw themselves as scholars, publishing measured drawings and studies of both American and European architecture for use in the drafting room. Fiske Kimball is perhaps the most distinguished example of the scholar-architect, but he was hardly the only member of his generation to write books on architectural history. Much important research on American buildings was done by architects between 1880 and 1940, not simply out of historical curiosity but to perpetuate the traditions of building in this country. Although knowledge of sources was not proof of artistic sensibility, it did give the stamp of authenticity to residential work, especially within regional building traditions. Use of functional and ornamental details, as literal quotations in an otherwise originally designed house, was one means of giving a building style in the general sense. Quotation of details from well-known American houses was also a means of symbolizing American values and patriotic virtues. When patrons insisted on exact replication of motifs, such as doorways, the clever architect usually managed to alter the design with enough subtlety to satisfy both his client and himself. The Georgian houses of Mott Schmidt and William Lawrence Bottomley during the late 1920s and 1930s provide ample proof that research on Early American domestic architecture spurred more exacting Colonial Revival work; in addition, as connoisseurship rose among clients, architects established their individuality through more sophisticated variations in detail. Being a scholarly architect did not necessarily imply a lack of creativity. As Thomas Hastings said, "Restraint is not bondage; it makes perfect freedom and progress possible. . . . Restraint does not destroy, but promotes originality, guiding and stimulating it."[50]

It is tempting to view the fourth approach, that of pastiche or assemblage of architectural fragments from actual buildings, as a method requiring no skill or originality whatsoever. Julia Morgan, the designer of San Simeon, William Randolph Hearst's famous country house in California, would not have seen it that way, however. Though much of the material in that vast historical pile was salvaged or removed from European buildings, Morgan was required to act as artist, scholar, scene designer, and decorator in her synthesis of architectural elements. The building she designed had no precedent in architecture, yet evoked the historical auras of the various fragments Hearst had collected. Like many eclectic designers, she was equally willing to work with fragments or from scratch. Working within the restrictions imposed by the preexisting elements created an artistic challenge.

Although architects accepted historical sources and idioms as the linguistic system that governed their art, they were nonetheless beholden to clients who held a different view of the function of style. To a patron, styles often had literary, associational, and theatrical aura. The collections of historical objects that symbolized a patron's position and taste often required dramatic backdrops. Consider, for instance, the following instructions to Stanford White from Katherine Mackay:

Will you treat my Library in the following two ways:

1st. Renaissance. Plaster ceiling to look like old marble—marble window and door trims, marble mantelpiece. Walls covered with that red stuff of Baumgarten's. The two best tapestries hung on the two panels where the bookcases now are. No brackets. Lights introduced into candelabra showing on the floor. The two other tapestries used as portieres into hall and drawing room. No furniture.

2nd. Louis XV: Boiserie to ceiling: French walnut: unpolished finish: no gold: tapestries framed in panels. Large French mantelpiece: Brackets at door, over mantel and at either side of large windows. Tapestry curtains at all windows. My other two tapestries used as portieres. No color in room. Plaster ceiling with cupids.

Please make me two *colored* drawings for these, very carefully and *think* about it, as I want the room fine, when I do it.[51]

36 Genre work: Wilson Eyre's **Rye House** (1909), *top*, compared with **Little Thakeham** (1902) by Edwin Lutyens. (Author)

37 Scholarly quoting: the often-cited gabled grouping of **Compton Wynyates,** Warwickshire, England, *left,* compared with **Bonniecrest,** John Russell Pope's Stuart Duncan house (1912–14) in Newport, Rhode Island. (J. R. Pope, *American Architect,* 1924)

To a woman like Katherine Mackay, one of the richest of her day, having a room designed to fit two very expensive tapestries, a vessel in which to display treasures acquired abroad, was far more important than having an architecturally distinctive space. Obviously, Mr. White had not given her the right thing on his first try and had little choice but to make another stab at it. Period styles reflected the works of art produced during the time—architecture, collecting, and connoisseurship were intimately connected. Buying a Renaissance painting or chair necessitated building a Renaissance room in which to display it. An architect was often required to create a setting—what Edith Wharton called a mise-en-scène—for collected objects or for a way of life that mimicked the European aristocracy. Historical elements, motifs, and decorative features were signs of cultural legitimacy. Therefore, rooms or buildings created in a particular style had to be scenographically exact.

Why did architects go along with this patent theatricality? For one thing, many of them had a similar liking for the art treasures they were "framing" with their buildings and rooms. Stanford White accompanied the Mackays and other patrons on antique- and art-buying trips to Europe, as did William Lawrence Bottomley and George Washington Smith. For another, they enjoyed the challenge of designing properly within an idiom, of studying the sources to create an authentic surround for objects. Most

important, they often had little choice but to go along with the idiosyncratic demands of wealthy clients. Nothing in the writings of eclectic architects suggests that source replication was anything but a game; the design of even the most opulent and historically derivative house had little to do with scholarly exactitude.

This, then, was the framework within which a domestic architect worked. There was a commonly understood schema of principles that critics, patrons, and architects believed made a good house—qualities of style and decorum derived in part from nineteenth-century theories of architecture, among them the picturesque, Ruskinian, High Victorian associational, and Beaux-Arts classical tenets that scholars have examined in detail elsewhere.[52] To summarize these principles, we may observe that the criteria for measuring houses were: (1) grammatical coherence or a sense of being idiomatic; (2) a certain integrity of constructional, stylistic, and compositional expression, resulting in a unified, comprehensible design; (3) a distinct quality of uniqueness, character, or personality akin to human individuality; (4) beauty, as defined by either classical or romantic aesthetics; (5) a fitness of purpose, appropriateness to a way of life, sense of place, and decorum (or proper degree of pretension) in ornament or decoration; and (6) an adherence to a set of less easily definable criteria such as honesty, charm, simplicity, and style. Most of these principles have a history in eighteenth- and nineteenth-century architectural theory, yet their particular combination and balance in American architecture gives a distinct character to turn-of-the-century eclecticism.

The second generation of domestic specialists may be divided into two groups, based on their education and philosophy of design: the classicists, who remained committed to their Beaux-Arts principles in some measure, and the romanticists, who cultivated rustic, medieval, Art and Crafts, and English ideals in the design of houses. The leading designers of country estates practicing after 1900 were required to work in all of the popular styles, but many developed predilections for a particular idiom, especially during the 1920s, when regional eclectic movements proliferated.

In terms of success, influence, and number of commissions, the most important classicists of the second generation were John Russell Pope, Horace Trumbauer, and William Adams Delano. Each of these architects executed major estates, built fifty or more large houses, and was known nationally among wealthy patrons. They were also capable of working in romantic styles and used picturesque idioms in major commissions. Each benefited from a mentorship succession—Pope from McKim's influence, Delano from Thomas Hastings', and Trumbauer from the Hewitt brothers'. In philosophy they can be contrasted with the leaders of the romantic school: Wilson Eyre of Philadelphia (a member of the first generation who had a long career), Harrie T. Lindeberg of New York, and Howard Van Doren Shaw of Chicago. Like the first group, these designers were fully capable of designing formal houses. (Within this category, two influential architects who made most of their reputation in work outside the residential field, Ralph Adams Cram and his erstwhile partner Bertram Grosvenor Goodhue, should also be mentioned.)[53] And like the first three, each of these architects was launched through either a mentorship or an inherited social position. A comparison of the early careers and patronage of these six leaders reveals important similarities in the pattern of practice.

After Thomas Hastings, the first of these architects to achieve prominence as a classical specialist in the stately home was the Philadelphian Horace Trumbauer (1868–1938). Trumbauer's suc-

38 Horace Trumbauer. **Whitemarsh Hall,** Edward T. Stotesbury estate (1916–19), Chestnut Hill, Pennsylvania. (Mattie Edwards Hewitt, collection of Alfred Branam, Jr.)

39 Horace Trumbauer. **Lynnewood Hall,** Peter A. B. Widener house (1898), Ashbourne, Pennsylvania. (Ferree, *American Estates and Gardens.*)

40 Horace Trumbauer. **Ardrossan,** Robert L. Montgomery house (1909), Villanova, Pennsylvania. (*American Country Houses of To-Day,* 1913).

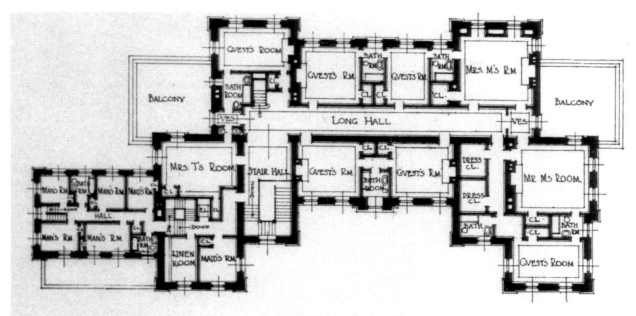

SECOND FLOOR PLAN

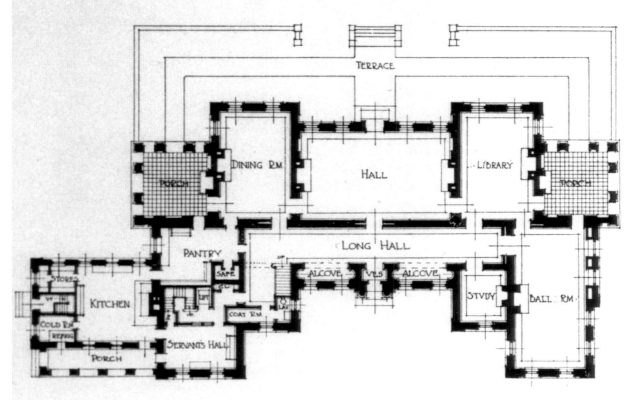

FIRST FLOOR PLAN

COVNTRY RESIDENCE
FOR
MR·ROBERT L MONTGOMERY
VILLA NOVA PA

41 **Ardrossan,** first and second floor plans. (*American Country Houses of To-Day,* 1913.)

cess is unusual because he rose to the status of a society architect with neither a social pedigree nor a gentleman's education. As George Thomas has pointed out, he carved a niche for himself out of the patronage of nouveaux riches in Philadelphia who were ignored by the old Episcopalian or Quaker oligarchy and its sanctioned architects. His early clients were wealthy Jews, Methodists, and Catholics building outside the enclaves of old Philadelphia society, away from Rittenhouse and the Main Line, in places like Elkins Park and North Philadelphia. At sixteen he began an apprenticeship in the office of G. W. and W. D. Hewitt, and at twenty-two opened his own practice. His first large house, a Gothic castle known as Grey Towers (1892–94), designed for sugar magnate W. D. Harrison, was hardly indicative of the penchant for French classicism that became his trademark in the late 1890s. He designed first in the fashionable late-Victorian and Tudor styles used so effectively by the Hewitts, showing an ability to assimilate an idiom quickly and to produce convincing designs in it.

Trumbauer succeeded, however, not by conforming to the Anglo-Tudor styles that were popular with the old gentry but by initiating flashy new idioms that were associated with New York's captains of industry. Harrison introduced him to two of Philadelphia's most successful nouveaux riches moguls, Peter A. B. Widener and William L. Elkins, whose loyal patronage launched his practice. Widener and Elkins, owners of a railroad-trolley system and investors in real estate, were rapidly developing streetcar subdivisions around the city. The intermarriage of these two families provided the architect with a long string of related clients. Trumbauer's first grand classical houses were the Widener residence, Lynnewood Hall in Elkins Park (1899–1901), and the Elkins residence (1896–1900). They were designed to make an immediate impact—to turn heads in Philadelphia—and they succeeded brilliantly. These pompous classical houses, located in a suburb built by new money, were deliberately reminiscent of the showy Newport houses the Vanderbilts were building. Trumbauer picked up the mode of Hastings and Hunt so effectively that his work came to the attention of the *Architectural Record* in 1904. Ralph Adams Cram, in an extensive review of Trumbauer's work, observed its similarity with that of the more sophisticated architects in New York; with this acclaim his career was launched.[54]

Deliberately eschewing the romantic eccentricity that was peculiar to Philadelphia, the young architect successfully established his identity outside the traditions of his milieu. Trumbauer appears to have broken through social barriers with talent, luck, and good business sense. As his new-money clients brought him publicity, he eventually began to be recognized by establishment patrons. His practice flourished after the turn of the century and was one of the most lucrative of the domestic specialist firms.

He became known as an architect who could give a client anything desired—any style, any size, on any schedule. If his work lacked the kind of personal expression that critics considered essential for success, it was nevertheless remarkably consistent and appropriate to the setting. An efficient office organization was the key to his ability to please wealthy patrons—Trumbauer appar-

ently relied on talented associate designers to execute his ideas, while he spent much of his time developing and cultivating new clientele. He took on the first black graduate of the University of Pennsylvania architecture program, Julian F. Abele, as an associate in 1902. The younger designer ran the office from 1908 until Trumbauer's death in 1938. Trumbauer's office designed several of the grandest estates of the eclectic era. Whitemarsh Hall (1916–19), the estate of the stockbroker E. T. Stotesbury in Chestnut Hill, Pennsylvania, was his largest and most monumental design. A classical design inspired by English precedents, it represented the apotheosis of opulence and grandeur in its time. Ardrossan, the house designed in 1909 for the venerable estate of Robert Montgomery in Villanova, Pennsylvania, was more understated but stately, nonetheless. Success with wealthy patrons, however, did not translate into recognition among his peers. Trumbauer was shunned for many years by the architectural establishment in Philadelphia, who thought him opportunistic and flashy. He was not admitted to the AIA until 1931, at the end of his career. Yet he was able to garner many of the most prestigious commissions in Philadelphia through connections with the patrons behind the new economic development. His career, however, contrasts sharply with the patronage succession followed by most architects within an established society.[55]

John Russell Pope (1874–1937), considered the dean of New York's later corps of eclectic masters, and the man with the largest claim to McKim's Bramante-inspired classical leanings, followed a more typical path to success as a society architect. Though known primarily for his extensive public and monumental work in Washington, D.C., Pope was also a major residential designer. He acquired his knowledge of academic classicism at City College of New York (1892) and Columbia University (1894) and received the first fellowship to the newly founded American Academy in Rome through McKim's direct intercession, as well as to the Ecole (Atelier Deglane, 1897). After his return he assisted McKim in teaching courses at Columbia[56] and worked for Bruce Price until 1903, when he established his own practice as a residential specialist.[57] Because Pope was the son of an artist and had no immediate society connections, he clearly benefited from Price's patronage network as well as from the professional mentorship of McKim.

John Russell Pope's major country houses were designed largely in the first half of his thirty-five-year career, before his public work assumed preeminence. He inherited a number of clients from the McKim, Mead and White network, such as the diplomat Henry White (a friend of McKim's) and members of the Vanderbilt family. The McKim influence is also apparent in the models he used for his early country houses. The consummate academic, he was able to canonize the elements of each stylistic idiom in producing houses that magnificently capture their archetypes: the picturesque Tudor in his estates for Allan Lehman and Clarence Lewis (Skylands Farm, 1924); the Georgian in houses for James Swan Frick (Baltimore, 1914), Andrew V. Stout (Red Bank, New Jersey, 1918–19), Thomas Frothingham (Far Hills, New Jersey, 1919–21), and especially Marshall Field III (Caumsett, on the

42 John Russell Pope. **Skylands Farm** (1924), Clarence McKenzie Lewis house, Ringwood, New Jersey. (Samuel Gottscho, Library of Congress.)

43 John Russell Pope. Ogden Mills House (1913–15), Woodbury, Long Island. Garden elevation. (Richard Cheek, from *Monograph of the Work of John Russell Pope.*)

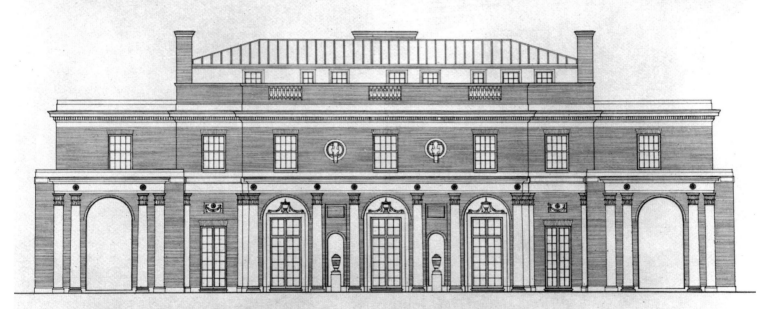

Garden Elevation

Residence of Ogden L. Mills, Woodbury, L.I.

North Shore of Long Island); and even a gentler clapboard Colonial in his farm for Robert J. Collier (Wickatunk, New Jersey, b. 1911), a variation on White's The Orchard. Pope took the genres established by McKim and White in their free eclectic experiments and turned them into models for a slightly younger group of New Yorkers in their increasingly specialized practices.

Pope's work set a pattern for residential architects, in which the client retained the architect to design both town house and country house, requiring knowledge of formal, urban house planning as well as picturesque country idioms. In this respect Pope was the acknowledged master. His ability to switch from strict French or Georgian classicism to lyrical and romantic Tudor was considered nearly unique among architects of his generation. This somewhat schizoid quality in his residential work has been overshadowed, however, by the severe nature of his public buildings. Croly emphasized Pope's talent in lamenting the situation prevalent among his contemporaries in eclecticism: architects might "become correct in several different styles, but rarely if ever [did] they become fluent and forcible." One need only see Pope's magnificent house for Stuart Duncan, Bonniecrest (1912–14), on Ocean Drive in Newport, to recognize the architect's deep feeling for pleasing composition.[58] Pope's architecture was precise, urbane, and meticulously finished. His trademark was suavity, even in romantic houses. In articles for *Record* in 1905 and 1911, Croly pointed out the subtle personal differences that separated a rising star like Pope from his contemporaries. Probably the most exacting and proportionally elegant planner of his generation, Pope was admired most for the grammatical consistency of his work, if not always for the warmth and charm of it. His elegant Georgian town houses and country estates marked him as a master of the Colonial Revival, and his work as a monumental classicist spurred Joseph Hudnut of Harvard to call him "the last of the Romans."[59] Eclecticism did not prevent him from becoming one of the most fluent and forcible stylists of his generation.

For William Adams Delano, who began his practice the same year as Pope, becoming a gentleman architect was as easy as joining the Century Association. Thomas Hastings put him up for membership, and his name did the rest. He made a career the old-fashioned way — by birthright greased with hard work. Delano was the grandson of Dr. William Adams, parson of Madison Square Presbyterian Church (a building designed by McKim, Mead and White), and a direct descendant of Henry Adams of the Boston clan. His father, Eugene Delano, was a businessman with Brown Brothers Company, and of Huguenot descent. He grew up in Philadelphia, was schooled at Lawrenceville, and attended college at Yale. Delano liked to point out that he received his Yale diploma from Timothy Dwight in 1895, one hundred years after his great grandfather, John Adams, received his Yale degree from Dwight's grandfather.[60] He rounded out his education by attending the architectural program at Columbia, apprenticing with Carrère and Hastings, and attending the Ecole under Victor Laloux.

Like Hastings, Delano and his partner, Chester Aldrich, were blessed with an early patron who brought them one of their most

44 John Russell Pope. Robert J. Collier house (b. 1911), Wickatunk, New Jersey. (Richard Cheek, from *Monograph of the Work of John Russell Pope*.)

45 Ogden Mills house. (Samuel Gottscho, Avery Architectural Archives.)

46 Delano and Aldrich. **Oak Knoll** (1922), Bertram Work house, Oyster Bay, Long Island. Entry front and forecourt. Rendering by Chester B. Price. (*Portraits of Ten Country Houses.*)

important commissions. While on his grand tour with Arthur Brown, Jr., in 1903, Delano met Henry Walters through his Yale classmate Cornelius Vanderbilt IV, aboard the yacht *The North Star,* anchored in Venice. Delano accompanied the Baltimore millionaire on art-buying excursions in Italy, and when he returned to New York that year to start his practice with Aldrich, a phone call came from Walters. "I want to build a gallery in Baltimore for all the treasures my father and I have collected, and I am going to give you boys a chance, provided you do what I tell you," Delano recalled Walters telling him in a subsequent lunch meeting.[61] Thus the small firm began their practice with no less than the impressive Walters Art Gallery (finished in 1910) and quickly added houses for Willard Straight (1914) and John D. Rockefeller, Jr. (1907), to the list of early commissions.

Like most creative eclectic architects, the firm adapted a set of models for their houses from historical types, but Delano and Aldrich were particularly adept at matching the type to the client. According to the purpose of the house, the temperament of the patron, and the character of the site, the architects chose among four major models for their country houses: an English stucco, a formal Georgian block with dependencies, a classical villa based on Italian and Beaux-Arts precedents, and a modest version of a Colonial Revival house. Each was tailored to a particular group of patrons, and each was a consciously abstract rendering of its historical paradigm.

Delano and Aldrich established themselves as purveyors of understatement—their trademark was a kind of eclectic minimalism. As William Lawrence Bottomley wrote in praising their work: "Both in the plans and the elevations [of Delano and Aldrich buildings], whether of a facade or the side of a room, one feels a fine relationship of parts. From the point of view of decoration, there is a small amount of ornament, very telling because [it is] well placed and brought into strong accent by contrast with simple planes and wide wall spaces. The beautiful, high, narrow proportions of their doors and windows are another note of distinction drawn from the eighteenth century tradition."[62] This abstraction and restraint can be appreciated in such houses as the classical block for Bertram G. Work, president of the Goodrich Rubber Company, one of the most costly and ostentatiously elegant of their many large houses, begun in 1916 in Oyster Bay, Long Island. Synthesizing such sources as the popular Petit Trianon (a building that inspired the creation of dozens of American country houses in its image) and Thomas Jefferson's pavilions at the University of Virginia, Delano stripped away all but the essential classical detail to produce a compact, prismatic building set amid vast axial gardens—a kind of French garden pavilion. Royal Cortissoz called the forecourt "one of the happiest strokes I know in the architecture of to-day. . . . This is an austere design in more respects than one, a house with a spare, very dignified facade, rising on the north above a lordly straight terrace. Yet it is not academic or cold. The wonderfully manipulated levels, the trees and the turf, take care of that, to say nothing of the graceful propor-

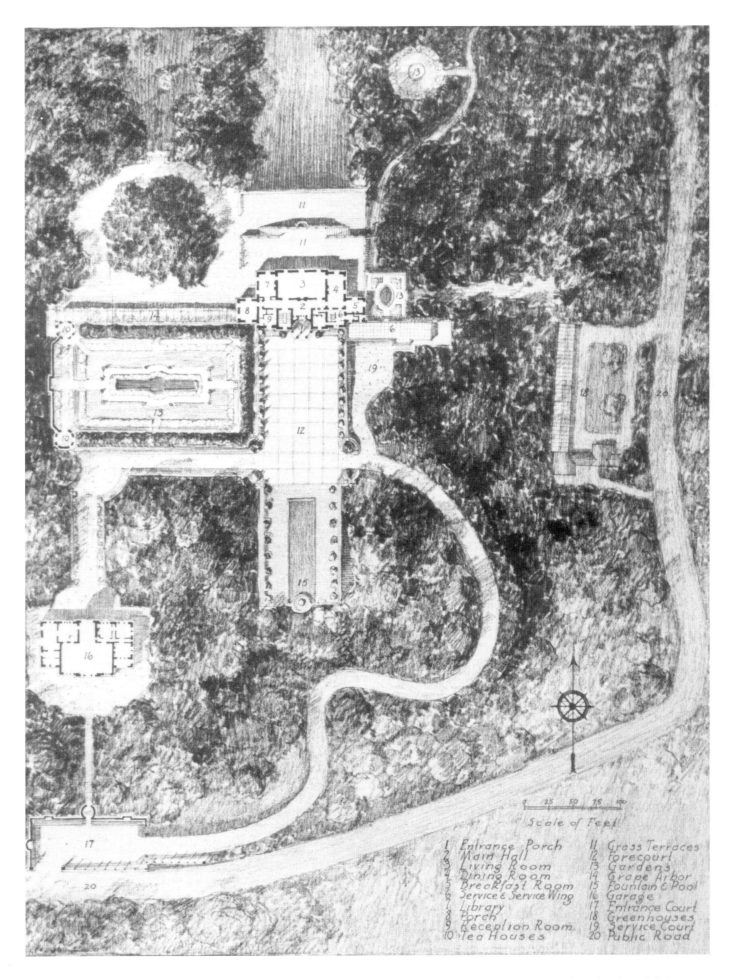

47 Delano and Aldrich. **Oak Knoll.** Site plan. Rendering by Chester B. Price.
(*Portraits of Ten Country Houses.*)

1 Entrance Porch   11 Grass Terraces
2 Main Hall   12 Forecourt
3 Living Room   13 Gardens
4 Dining Room   14 Grape Arbor
5 Breakfast Room   15 Fountain & Pool
6 Service & Service Wing   16 Garage
7 Library   17 Entrance Court
8 Porch   18 Greenhouses
9 Reception Room   19 Service Court
10 Tea Houses   20 Public Road

48 Delano and Aldrich. **Oheka** (c. 1917–30s), Otto Kahn house, Huntington, Long Island. (Long Island Studies Institute, Nassau County Museums.)

tions everywhere and the relief judiciously afforded by daintily grilled balconies."[63]

Like Platt, Delano took great care in the linkages between house and garden, making the most of formal and informal contrasts. But not all of his austere exercises in French classicism turned out so happily. His great château for Otto Kahn, Oheka, begun in 1915 but not completed until well into the depression, was one of the largest private houses ever built in America. In most respects Oheka was also an aesthetic failure, for its details were insufficient to control the vast scale of its rooms and facades. Delano's recollections of the great New York financier and his house—"it grew and grew in size as his self-importance grew"—were indicative of the poor chemistry between architect and client.[64]

When that chemistry worked, as it did on most occasions, Delano and Aldrich fashioned houses of understated elegance that perfectly embodied the ideals of their patrons. Delano's first clients were a group of mutual friends he had met in college or while summering on Long Island. Many were members of the clubs Delano designed: the Knickerbocker Club (1914), Brook Association (c. 1915), and new Colony Club (1924), each done in his characteristic abstracted Georgian. Lawyers in the group included the Winthrop brothers, Bronson and Egerton, and Victor Morawetz. Cornelius Vanderbilt introduced Delano to the Whitneys, Harry

Payne, and Gertrude Vanderbilt, who became major patrons. Mrs. Whitney's cousin, Adele Sloane Burden, followed, to become another major client. Delano also built two houses in Mount Kisco for his Yale classmate Robert Brewster. As one reads his memoirs, the associations seem the inevitable consequence of warm friendships. When Delano built these houses for friends, it was as if he were designing for himself. The clubbish comradery from which he benefited in his career and the affinity in taste between architect and patron were essential features of eclectic practice in the 1920s. Delano was perhaps the most representative and prolific society architect of his time, having designed over one hundred country houses.[55]

As successful and well-published architects working in the residential field, Delano, Pope, and Trumbauer exerted considerable influence on a third generation of eclecticists in smaller cities around the nation. The practices of these three leaders were built on the foundation of key patrons who offered them large and prestigious commissions early in their careers. In their maturity, they were sought out by clients from diverse social circles and cities far from New York and Philadelphia. They were known as designers who could handle the formal idioms associated with classicism—Georgian, Colonial Revival, Modern French, or Palladian. When clients wanted something with rustic charm, informality, or a medieval flavor, however, they turned to one of the established romantic designers.

"He is a poet, a dreamer of dreams," observed a fellow architect of Wilson Eyre, Jr. (1858–1944), the hero of the romantic school.

A handsome and self-consciously artistic man, Eyre had the looks of Rudolph Valentino and the poetic idealism of William Morris. "He is a polished Bohemian, a man of the world; a charming after dinner companion who can sing Italian opera or describe the quiet life with exquisite charm. In his manner he is thoughtful and reserved, and really known only to his intimates, though there is a personal magnetism about him, so that those who work under him are ever loyal to him."[66] Born in Florence and educated in Europe, Canada, and Rhode Island, Eyre was among the most cosmopolitan architects of his day. He personified the aesthetic affectations and anachronisms of romantic country life in a manner more akin to English architects like E. Guy Dawber and W. R. Lethaby than to American practitioners.

Eyre achieved his notoriety early and was in some respects spoiled by youthful success. He entered an apprenticeship in Philadelphia with the Englishman James Peacock Sims as a very young man and was sent to MIT to learn the profession. When his master died in 1882, he was forced to leave the architecture program after only one year to take on the practice. His clients were thus inherited from Sims' well-established patronage network. "I was a mere boy. . . . I was insufficiently trained, and tried to be original at the expense of everything technical," he remembered.[67] Endowed with superb drawing ability, Eyre produced several brilliant

Queen Anne or Shingle Style houses in the 1880s that have been cited by Vincent Scully, who unfortunately focused on early works that the architect later disclaimed. In many respects Eyre had two careers; from the free and complex designs of his youthful period he eventually turned to a style reminiscent of the work of English architects, such as Ernest Newton or C. E. Mallows.[68] He became one of the most original and convincing exponents of this English romantic school; half-timbered stone and stucco houses with interlocking, picturesque plans mark his later style. Unfortunately, his evocative freehand drawings of these houses are all that we have to measure much of his later career, because many of his buildings are no longer standing. Prior to World War I, he was considered one of the leading domestic architects in the nation, and his work exerted a major influence on a generation of Philadelphia architects.

Eyre was the epitome of the picturesque country house architect, who let his drawing hand and intuitive grasp of massing and texture control the direction of a design. He is said to have designed in freehand sketches, testing alternatives with numerous perspective views, which he could quickly lay out without mechanical aids. His drawing style was itself romantic—he

49 Wilson Eyre. **Ashford,** country house for Frank Squier, Riverside, near Greenwich, Connecticut. Preliminary design sketch (c. 1898). (*Architectural Annual,* 1900.)

Country House
for
Mr Frank Squier
at Riverside. Conn
Wilson Eyre Jr
Architect
Phila

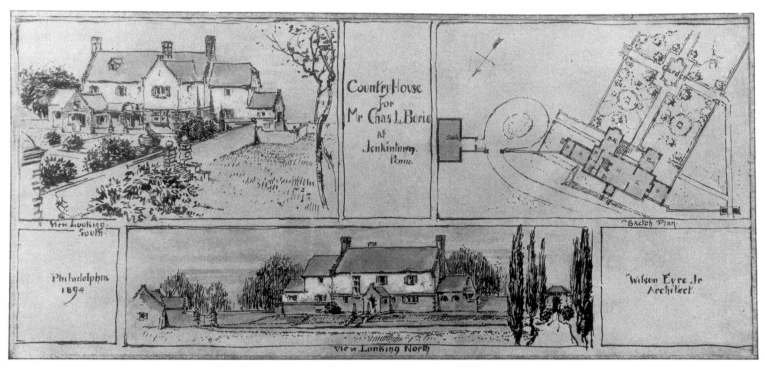

50 Wilson Eyre. Country house for Charles L. Borie, Jenkintown, Pennsylvania.
  Preliminary study (1894). (*Architectural Annual,* 1900.)

worked in Shavian ink textures, charcoal, impressionistic Conte crayon, or free watercolor. "Even the roughest, quickest studies you should keep as brilliantly rendered as possible," he admonished his students. "You then, perforce, try and keep the standard of your design on a level with the charm of its expression."[69] Critics saw this emotional and pictorial freedom as the essence of his architecture, and found much to fault as well as to praise in his sometimes undisciplined handling of elements. A Wilson Eyre house always had a sense of movement and assymetrical massing that was meant to surprise and charm. His houses fit their sites in the way that many Edwardian houses do—they were to be appreciated as great overgrown cottages in an old garden, full of rustic texture and color, mellow with the patina of age.

John Harbeson, writing a tribute to Eyre and his work, cited his "idealism, his innate gentility, and his unerring instinct in matters of taste. . . . His individuality had a pervading influence on the [architectural] profession in Philadelphia." He pointed to Eyre's country house work as his best, stressing that Eyre was an adaptor of English, American, and Italian forms for the modern house. He saw in Eyre the origins of the craftsmanlike instincts of the Philadelphia school:

He was absorbingly preoccupied with textures—textures achieved by every day materials used in countless ways; varying the bonding and the mortar width in stone and brickwork, adze dressing of timber, roughness in plaster surfaces. He was continuously interested in craftsmanship, and full of ingenuity in obtaining good work with the craftsmen at hand. "There is no use in giving a man modern tools and telling him to do a bad job" (to get character)—"give him primitive tools, and tell him to do the best job he can."[70]

Typical of his stucco, English-influenced work are Rye House, the residence of Isabel D. Curtis in Litchfield, Connecticut (1909), and Allgates, the Horatio Gates Lloyd house in Haverford, Pennsylvania (1911). An active exponent of the Colonial Revival, he worked in both Pennsylvania stone and clapboard vernacular in many houses. The most influential were perhaps Ashford (1898–1900), the house for Frank Squires in Greenwich, Connecticut, and Mohican Cottage (1901), for William Bixby in Lake George, New York. He also designed a number of country houses in the fashionable seaside watering holes on Long Island. In 1912 he took on John Gilbert McIlvaine as a partner, and the two maintained the practice through the 1920s. His largest estates were probably Fairacres for John W. Pepper (see chapter 5) and Hunting Hill Farm (1916–24) for Walter Jeffords in Media, Pennsylvania.

Eyre's charm helped him cultivate a large and socially prominent set of Philadelphia clients who remained with him throughout his career. Major patrons included the Biddle, Pepper, Drexel, Strawbridge, Clothier, and Dulles families of Philadelphia, the Detroit tycoon Charles Langdon Freer, and the elite of New York and Connecticut. He was so successful at one point that he opened a branch office in New York. In spite of a varied practice, he considered himself to be primarily a residential architect. Unfortunately, his influence outside of Philadelphia waned quickly in the post–World War I years, and he died a forgotten man.

The Arts and Crafts architecture of England also had a profound effect on Harrie T. Lindeberg (1880–1959). A residential specialist who designed very little except country or suburban houses, he operated one of the most successful such offices in the United States. Like Pope and Platt, he set up a practice in New York, beginning in 1905. He had been a draftsman with McKim, Mead and White for six years, after having trained at the National Academy of Design in New York from around 1889–1901. When Stan-

54 Harrie T. Lindeberg. Harry Knight house (1927), St. Louis, Missouri. (Samuel Gottscho, Avery Architectural Archives.)

55 Harrie T. Lindeberg. Frederick Patterson house (1925), Dayton, Ohio. Entry gable. (Samuel Gottscho, Avery Architectural Archives.)

Chicago's leading eclectic domestic architect of the turn of the century, Howard Van Doren Shaw, was also a devoted Anglophile and a great admirer of Lutyens, whose work he had studied first-hand. Shaw had a gentleman's education, a conservative upbringing, and the sort of architectural taste that made him anathema to Chicago's progressive Prairie School designers. The *Architectural Record* called him "the most conservative of the rebels, and the most rebellious of the conservatives."[83] The son of a wealthy Chicago drygoods merchant of Scottish Presbyterian stock, he had a privileged education at Chicago's Harvard School (1887), Yale College (class of 1890), and the architecture department at MIT (1891–92). In 1893 he traveled through England, Italy, and Spain, sketching and observing. His notebooks include his own firsthand photos and sketches of Lutyens' Surrey houses.[84] He was able to set up his own practice at the age of twenty-four, receiving early commissions from Edward Ryerson, the president of Ryerson Steel and a Yale graduate, as well as from other society figures.

In keeping with his closeness to the wealthy elite, Shaw's clients seemed to have a rather deterministic effect on his work.[85] "I never can see, for instance, anything in Howard Shaw's residences but that which he decided to give his clients," Thomas Tallmadge wrote in his eulogy.[86] Even critics of the time cited the "miscellaneous" and uneven quality of his houses, owing perhaps to his willingness to provide conservative clients too much of what they wanted.[87] He was, in a curious way, struggling against his milieu—one sees in his work many uncertain dichotomies between his lack of pretension, love of handcrafts, and tendency toward soft and rustic forms and the tasteful expectations of his wealthy clients, who often wanted classical houses. "Born, brought up and living in a community and among a circle of friends where the best that breeding, education and wealth can produce, was his pleasant portion in life, and vulgarity in his work would have been inexcusable," said Tallmadge.[88]

Shaw's artistic predilections clearly showed in work inspired by English Arts and Crafts, in which he demonstrated a lithe freedom of composition and a likable softness of line. His own house, Ragdale (1897), in Lake Forest, is one of the finest American variations on the tri-gable theme of such houses as Lutyens' Homewood and the stucco work of C. F. A. Voysey. Shaw and his wife built an outdoor amphitheater called Ragdale Ring on the grounds (modeled after the garden theater at the Villa Gori near Siena), where in the tradition of Morris and his circle they would perform amateur productions of plays and musical entertainments. Frances Shaw recalled her husband's joy during these events:

He made colored masts and forked gonfalons and a circuit of orange lanterns easy to install. He practised lighting effects of moon light in the deep glade and sunsets from the wings. We had dancers and stringed instruments, and he worked on the settings, and I worked on the pantomimes or dramatizing of the plays, and when the day dawned fine and auspicious, it was the very happiest time we ever had at Ragdale. That— and the Harvest Moon Bonfires in the Ragdale meadow, and the cider-making every autumn in the Ragdale orchard.[89]

Shaw, a vigorous promoter of the pleasures of country life in the English tradition, made every effort in his architecture to demonstrate his pastoral convictions.

His major country houses in Lake Forest included those for business leaders Hugh McBirney (1908), E. L. Ryerson (1906), Finley Barrell (1912), the Swift family, and Thomas E. Donnelley (1911). These houses, though they contained sections of great interest and even some formal innovation, were clearly not fully formed. One of his largest estates, the complex for A. H. Marks near Akron, Ohio (1914), a brick palace for one of the eccentric chemists of the rubber companies, showed a confusion and architectural pretension that was avoided in more romantic compositions. Combining classical, Tudor, and picturesque motifs, these houses never quite succeeded in finding the kind of balanced, coherent formula that Lindeberg achieved. Significantly, it is in his summer houses that he seemed to let loose and boldly show his compositional flair. (See chapter 6.) He also found a successful balance of elements in the charming village center designed in 1917 at Lake Forest, known as Market Square.

Shaw's death, at age 57, took a promising architect, slow to reach maturity, from the American scene before he reached full stride.[90] He would undoubtedly have given Chicago more houses that attempted to bridge the gulf between the progressive work of Wright and the conservative eclectic work of many eastern firms. His personal reticence and modesty—traits that gave his residences a placid grace and delicacy of detail—seemed also to prevent him from fulfilling his promise. And, like a Salieri to Wright's Mozart, he saw in a friendly rival the genius he wished for in full flower.

Shaw, Lindeberg, and Eyre were touched by modern English architecture in much the same way that Hastings and Trumbauer were influenced by France—they translated the ideals of romantic country house design to America and introduced new forms to the traditions in which they worked. They were seen by critics as important artists because they went beyond the general stylistic idioms they favored to establish a distinctive personality in their houses. Colleagues recognized a work by Eyre or Shaw immediately by their signature motifs and characteristics, whereas a lesser and more doctrinaire firm might produce work with no flair or distinction. This quality, above all others, separated the work of the leaders from that of the followers in eclectic practice.

These innovative architects also supplied influential models for the country house, which became standard modern country house types. Inevitably, replication of successful motifs, plan types, and even popular designs introduced by a respected architect like Pope or Lindeberg diminished the freshness of the prototype. This too was indicative of their status as formers of the traditions that sustained the eclectic country house until the eve of World War II. Yet as significant as the work of Pope, Trumbauer, Delano, Eyre, Lindeberg, and Shaw was to the development of this American house type, none achieved the influence of Charles Platt.

56 Howard Van Doren Shaw. **Ragdale,** the architect's own country house (1897), Lake Forest, Illinois. Exterior view and plans. (Richard Cheek, from *Architectural Review*, 1904.)

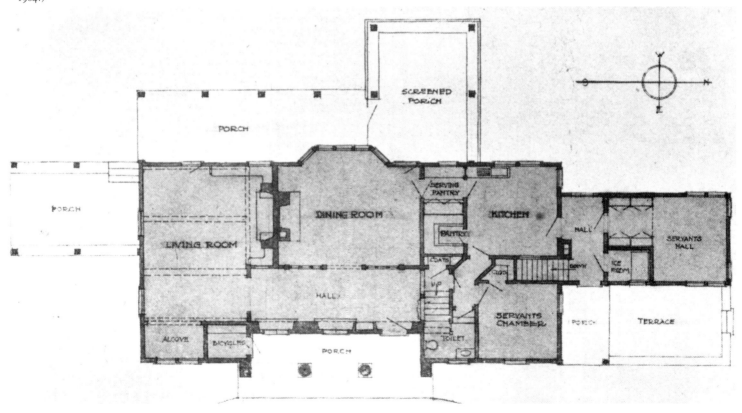

57 *top* Howard Van Doren Shaw. Hugh J. McBirney house (1908), Lake Forest, Illinois. Entrance detail. (Richard Cheek, from *American Country Houses of To-Day,* 1915.)

58 Howard Van Doren Shaw. Finley Barrell house (1912), Lake Forest, Illinois. Garden. (Richard Cheek, from *American Country Houses of To-Day,* 1915.)

59 *opposite* Howard Van Doren Shaw. A. H. Marks house (1914), Akron, Ohio. Plan. (*Architectural Record,* 1913.)

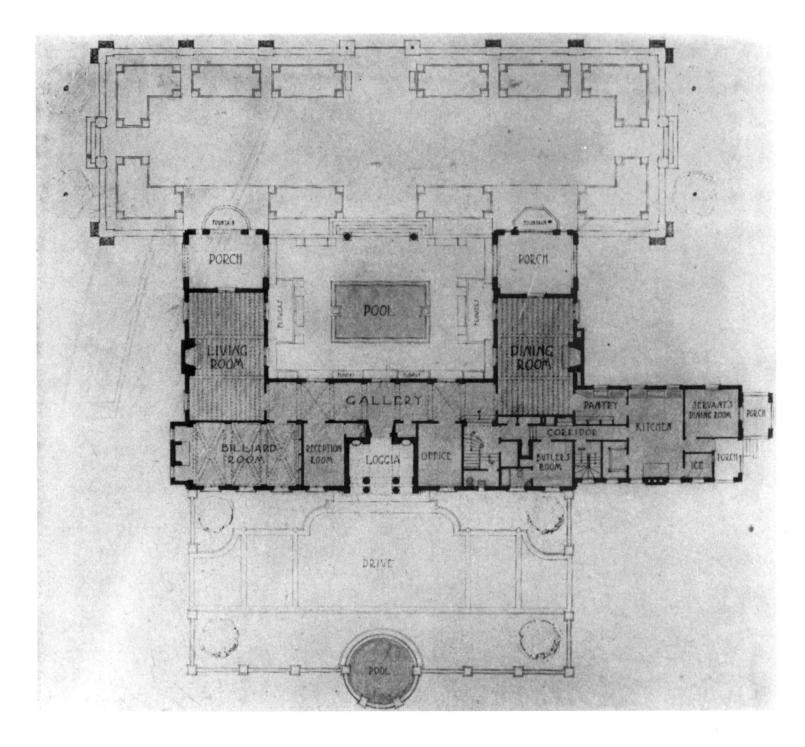

CHARLES PLATT AS REFORMER

Charles Adams Platt, the man Herbert Croly extolled as the epitome of the new progressive architect at the turn of the century, occupies a central position in the culture of domestic eclecticism. Platt, the most important country house designer of his time, stands out from all of the leaders of individual schools, such as Wright, Hastings, and Eyre, as a reformer, the inventor of new models for the house and garden, and a fundamental influence on the succeeding generation of architects. No domestic architect in America during the early twentieth century escaped his influence. He was also the leader of a significant group of American garden

designers who created the tradition of the country house and garden ensemble. Though his work now seems conventional, in its time it was a revolutionary step in adapting house and garden types to the domestic needs of wealthy and middle-class Americans. One of the difficulties in assessing Platt's contribution lies in the typicality of his work, its deliberate plainness and lack of drama. Even his life was one of calm predictability and uneventful success. It is fitting that we conclude this set of architectural portraits with this ultimate antihero, this subtle, creative eclecticist.

Born into a wealthy Connecticut–New York family, Platt did not enter the architectural profession from an established gateway. He began his adult career as a landscape painter and etcher and had

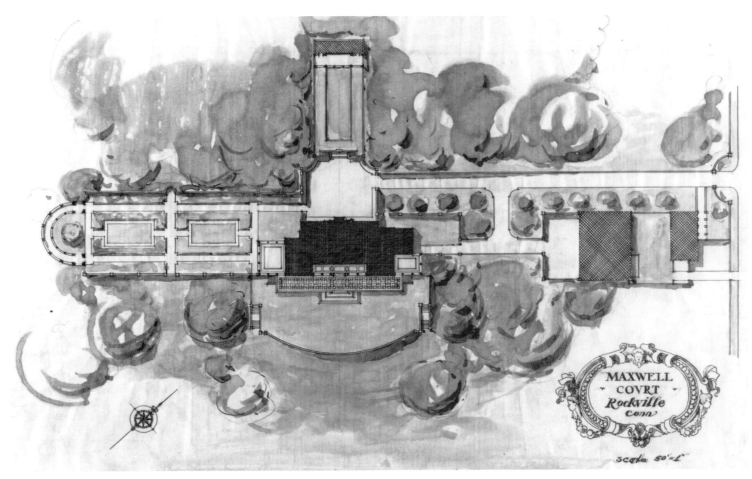

60 Charles Platt. **Maxwell Court** (1901–03), Francis T. Maxwell house, Rockville, Connecticut. Site plan. (*Monograph of the Work of Charles A. Platt.*)

61 **Maxwell Court.** View of garden front. (Richard Cheek, from Baker, *American Country Homes and Their Gardens.*)

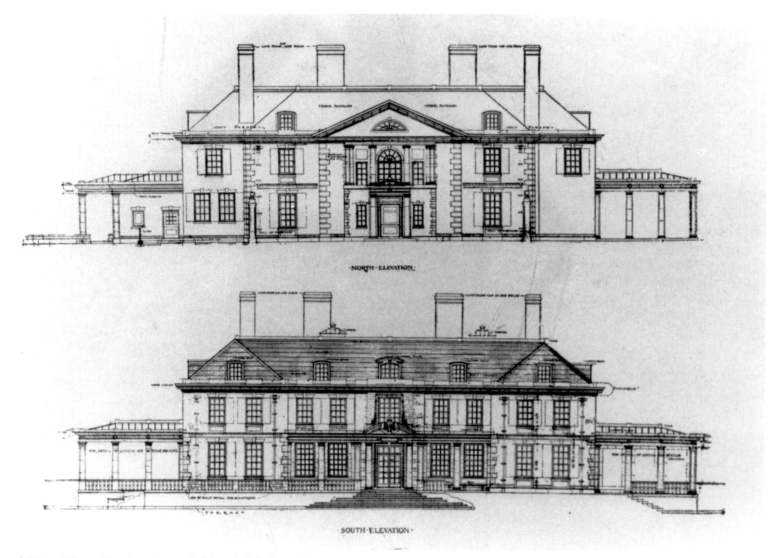

·NORTH·ELEVATION·

·SOUTH·ELEVATION·

62 **Maxwell Court.** Elevations. (*Monograph of the Work of Charles A. Platt.*)

some success at his art. He studied painting in Paris and lived in Europe from 1882 to 1887. In this respect he was something of a fresh wind, an outsider in the genealogy of eclectic architects. Without the doctrine of a Beaux-Arts architectural education he was free to approach the problems of house and garden design with a clean slate.

His architectural career began at Cornish, where after his first visit in 1889 he summered with the Crolys and other members of the artistic and intellectual group centered there. He designed houses for himself (1890) and the Crolys (1897), as well as creating a large U-shaped classical house, High Court (1891), for the philanthropist Annie Lazarus.[91] All three were modest, comfortable, and restrained by the standards of the time and were beautifully sited to take advantage of the countryside. By first dabbling in architecture, he learned the pragmatic, constructive, and formal aspects of the profession without indoctrination in any theory or philosophy of design. The utopian atmosphere at this New Hampshire retreat encouraged experimentation that was to pay off in later domestic commissions.

His career as a major garden designer began in 1892, when he went on a tour of Italy with his brother, William Barnes Platt, an aspiring landscape architect who had studied with Olmsted. In 1894 they published a book on the Italian garden, one of the first of its kind in English. Using what he had learned empirically in Europe, Platt designed two major gardens in Massachusetts: Faulkner Farm, on the estate of Charles F. Sprague in Brookline (1897–98),[92] and The Weld (1901) for Larz Anderson. Both were immediately hailed as innovative solutions to the problem of adapting the formal garden to the American landscape and became the most published works of landscape architecture of their day. In a profession still dominated by Olmstedian principles, Platt's application of classical pergolas, axial relationships, and villa garden elements was striking, even blasphemous. Yet his classicism, both in garden design and architecture, was tempered by a strong sense of pragmatism and an innate feeling for the textures, forms, and materials of nature — what Herbert Croly called classic quality with a picturesque idea. In this way his work was a bridge between that of the Beaux-Arts designers and the English-inspired romantic architects — and was perceived as such even in his own time.

63 **Maxwell Court.** Side garden room, looking toward house. (Richard Cheek, from Baker, *American Country Homes and Their Gardens.*)

The fact that Platt approached the design of houses from the point of view of the landscape and garden, that he began his designs from the outside in, is fundamental to understanding his work. As he said in an interview in 1931, "The essential truth in country house architecture . . . is that house and gardens together form one single design. They cannot be separated. They must be taken as a whole. That principle has been impressed upon me from the first, mainly, I suppose, through my beginning professional work as a landscape painter."[93] Hence, when one talks about a Platt country house, one is really talking about a house and garden as a whole, and it is this concept that revolutionized the domestic architecture of the turn of the century. Though Carrère and Hastings were credited as the first firm to plan estates as integrated formal conceptions, Platt was the architect most responsible for this new way of looking at the house in the landscape. After experimenting with this concept in modest houses throughout the 1890s, he began receiving large commissions, designing his most important country houses between 1900 and 1917.[94] It is a testament to his rapid rise to prominence that when his monograph appeared in 1913 he was hailed by critics as the most eminent of the country's domestic architects.[95]

Maxwell Court (1901–03), the Francis T. Maxwell house and garden in Rockville, Connecticut, was one of the first mature examples of Platt's work and offers a succinct statement of the difference between the graceful, commodious house Croly described as appropriate to the modern gentleman and those he decried as overopulent and institutional. As he said in discussing Platt's refreshing new classicism, "Some architects have used the classic forms in order to obtain at any cost a grandiose and stately effect." Platt avoided such "promiscuous forms" by selectively choosing types for study and use.[96]

The house is located on an ample plot within the Maxwell family estate near the town in which they owned and operated textile mills (Platt's connection to the family came through his mother's family, the Cheneys of Manchester, also mill owners). Platt ordered the site economically, unostentatiously, and with deference to the landscape. Sited below the crest of a hill overlooking the town, the house and gardens stretched laterally across the slope, punctuated with major and minor axes in the manner of Italian villa gardens that Platt had seen and admired. The south front, articulated by a ground floor loggia, faced out on a large terrace lawn, while to the west an axial flower garden was cleverly interlocked with the living room's extensive porch. Each garden space had a specific relationship to a part of the house, thus connecting building and landscape directly and providing a variety of areas for outdoor living. This compartmentalization of the

64 Charles Platt. **Timberline** (1907), Bryn Mawr, Pennsylvania. Rendering by Schell
Lewis. (Avery Architectural Archives.)

grounds and gardens, using direct linkages to rooms in the house,
is an essential feature of all of Platt's country houses.

Even in the representation of his house and garden designs,
Platt precisely depicted his intentions. The typical presentation
drawings of his work (made for his book) were of two kinds: intricate, small-scale (1/16") plans and elevations of the house, in line
and poché, and beautifully rendered ink-wash site plans, showing
the house as a dark block amid a three-dimensional depiction of
garden spaces. In this way, the house was a neutral but distinct
element in the plot plan, allowing the reader to see how each garden space interacted with it.

This technique, borrowed from renderings of gardens in Italian
villas, can be seen in the plot plan of Maxwell Court. As Keith
Morgan has pointed out, this design is reminiscent of the Villa
Gamberaia at Settignano, near Florence, which Platt had probably seen while touring Italy. Learning from the treatment of loggias in the Tuscan villa, Platt incorporated porch elements into all
four fronts of the house but subtly integrated them in plan and
massing so as not to compromise the formality or axiality of the
block. Rather than be rigid about the symmetries in the plan,
Platt often slid servants' rooms, kitchens, and other service spaces
into unused areas of the block. Whereas a Beaux-Arts-trained
architect might have felt compelled to add new ceremonial rooms
to fill out a formal plan diagram, Platt and his followers were far
more pragmatic, while preserving a classical feeling in the overall

concept of a house. This sense of accommodation in both the interior and the garden layout provided much of the richness in Platt's
work. He seldom felt the need to embroider or be inventive spatially or geometrically; his intent was, rather, to gain gracious living space and aesthetic interest through subtle restatement and
refinement of time-honored models.[97]

Without turning away from European classicism—indeed by
synthesizing the essential formal and decorative aspects of a
number of historical country house types—Platt achieved the
kind of creative adaptation all eclectic architects strove for. In this
way, his work was a subtle manifestation of reform in domestic
taste. He showed that a boxlike villa following generic Palladian
or even Colonial Revival types, when properly integrated with the
garden spaces, made a perfectly pragmatic and elegant model for
the modern American country house. Recognizing that Americans were as fond of outdoor living as the Italians, though less syb-
aritic, and as enamored of a compact, orderly home as the English,
he fused the best of both traditions. And although his new country
houses were inherently bound by classical principles of order, they
did not adopt the more pompous and monumental attributes of
the typical rich man's palace. Herbert Croly summed up Platt's
innovation by citing his houses for their combination of appropriate modesty, solidity, and grace with an overriding sense of whole-
ness: "The peculiar value then of [his] work consists of this union
of completeness of form with propriety of effect."[98]

Platt's successful development of the generic concept of the villa
was exemplified in such key works as Timberline (1907), for W.

Hinckle Smith, in Bryn Mawr, Pennsylvania; Box Hill (1914–15), for A. Drexel Paul, in Radnor, Pennsylvania; Eastover (1906), for George Palmer, in New London, Connecticut; and Woodston (1904–08), for Marshall P. Slade, in Mount Kisco, New York.[99] Upon publication in leading journals, his architectural plans exerted a powerful influence on domestic design and were used repeatedly as inspiration by younger colleagues and peers alike. Such major architects as Howard Shaw, Mott Schmidt, Harrie Lindeberg, and Neel Reid acknowledged his fundamental influence. His colleagues recognized that he had accomplished what all eclectic architects strove for—the subtle transformation of histori-cal models as a solution to modern building problems. In this way Platt was the quintessential architect with eclectic principles, a master of tradition and subtle individuality. As he said, "An artist should not consciously attempt to do something original. . . . He uses all the knowledge that he has been able to obtain through education and observation and practice. If he applies all this knowledge in solving his problem the individual elements of the problem itself will help to make the result original. His own individuality will do the rest."[100] There can be no better summation of the eclectic architect's creed, and no better exemplar of it than Charles Adams Platt.

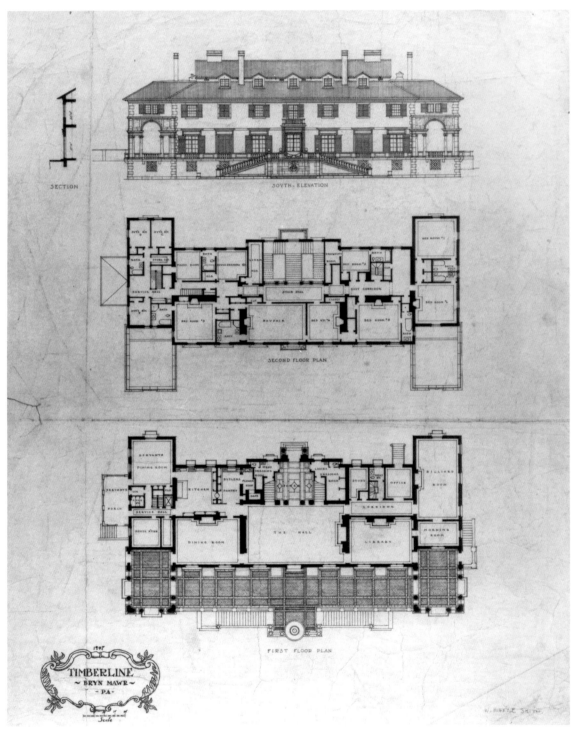

65 **Timberline**. Plans and elevations. (Avery Architectural Archives.)

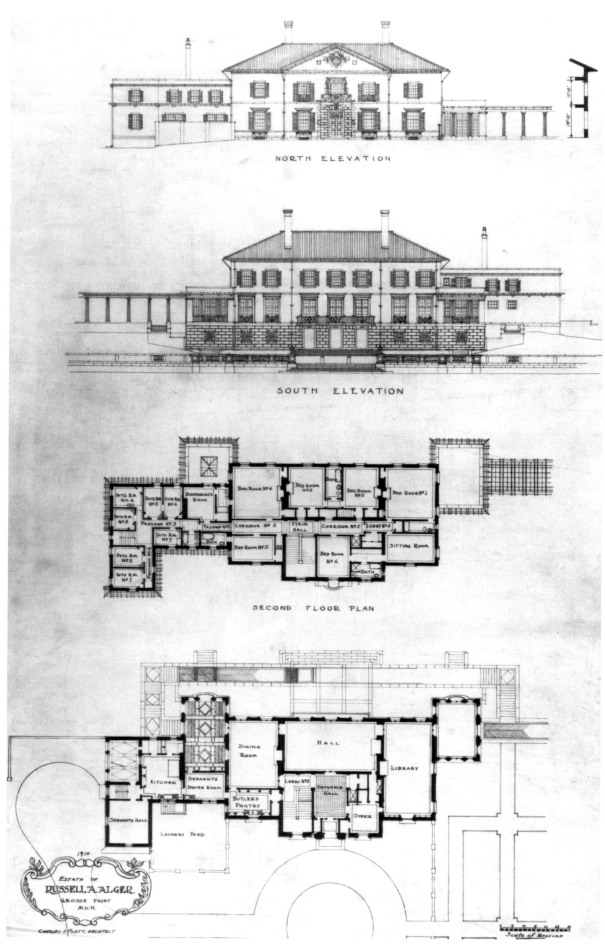

NORTH ELEVATION

SOUTH ELEVATION

SECOND FLOOR PLAN

66 Charles Platt. **The Moorings** (1908–10), Russell Alger house, Grosse Pointe,
Michigan. Plans and elevation. (Avery Architectural Archives.)

The Architecture of Country Houses
Style and Typology

3

Then, around 1900, something went click in our architectural mentality. We stood up and, so to speak, wiped the perspiration of vain effort from our brow, gazed around upon the classic and accepted standards of domestic architecture, and decided they were good. . . . Against the restless memory of Henry Hobson Richardson we weighed our plumbing, our automobiles, our typewriters, yes, even our phonographs . . . and felt that even if we had not revolutionized architecture we had contributed our quota to the health, comfort, and amelioration of life, a contribution the extent of which is the value sign of any civilization.

—AUGUSTA OWEN PATTERSON

ॐ THE FRAMEWORK OF FORM AND MEANING

Charles Platt and his contemporaries were leading a quiet revolution in domestic architecture. By the turn of the century they had created a distinctly American form of country estate by adapting traditional models to solve the needs of the modern American capitalist. The so-called modern country houses in the literature of the period were usually dressed in a familiar historical costume but in fact had few of the characteristics of European aristocratic seats.[1] These houses were distinctive in their planning formulas, new room types and activities for them, new stylistic features, and new approaches toward landscape and site planning. And they were products of the social conditions fostered by the rise of the capitalist oligarchy. My purpose is to examine this type as it matured in the early decades of this century and waned during the depression.

We can best understand the development of the modern American country house from a twofold perspective: the analysis of formal and programmatic types, overlaid and contrasted with the iconography of style. By looking at both style and type, the complex relationship between form and meaning can be analyzed.

Most sources of the period organized taxonomies in terms of style, not type. No subject elicited more disagreement or comment among critics than the question of an appropriate American style for the modern country house: Should a new indigenous type be invented or should European styles be used? Every architect had an opinion on the subject of style. Bertram Goodhue reluctantly accepted the phenomenon of eclecticism in 1905, writing that "it is probable that we shall never again have a distinctive style" for American houses.[2] Frank Miles Day argued that style was a relatively minor consideration in achieving "a right and reasonable and beautiful solution of the problem of building."[3] Conversely, Horace Mann thought it crucial to the success of the country house: "Style is by definition a component part of architectural expression and every building cannot avoid showing this element of personality, even if a definite attempt were made to conceal it."[4] Few writings on domestic architecture could avoid discussion of the question. Yet the word itself has acquired so many conflicting associations and definitions in this century that it is difficult to assess its meaning. It is therefore essential to establish some operative definitions.

The word "style," from the Greek *style* (for inscribing stylus), had two primary connotations for the architectural observer of 1900. As Professor A. D. F. Hamlin stated, one was related to

67 Horace Trumbauer. **The Elms** (1899–1901), E. J. Berwind house, Newport, Rhode Island. Oblique view of garden facade, with statue. (Richard Cheek.)

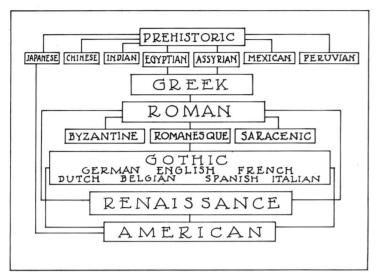

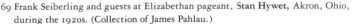

68 Manifest Destiny in Architectural Style. "Diagram Showing the Development of
Architecture from the Prehistoric to the American." (Robinson, *Domestic
Architecture.*)

quality and expression in building, the other to the history of
architecture: "Style is quality; the 'historic styles' are phases of
development. Style is character expressive of definite conceptions,
as of grandeur, gaiety, or solemnity. An historic style is the particular phase, the characteristic manner of design, which prevails at a
given time and place. It is not the result of mere accident or
caprice, but of intellectual, moral, social, religious, and even
political conditions."[5]

Russell Sturgis, in his *Dictionary of Architecture and Building*
(1901–02), elaborated on the first definition as "character; the sum
of many peculiarities, as when it is said that a building is 'in a
spirited style.'"[6] Thus defined, style was closely associated with
human qualities, in either the temperament and artistic personality of the architect or the persona of the owner; houses were seen
to reveal the personal qualities of their makers or inhabitants.
Properly designed, they portrayed human character as precisely as
a suit of clothes. The house of a cultured gentleman and his family
evinced social decorum, suggested class values, and established
links to other members of a social group. This associational refer-
ent has a long tradition in Victorian architecture, dating back to
the writings of John Claudius Loudon and Andrew Jackson
Downing.[7]

Reading criticism of domestic architecture in popular and professional journals of the early twentieth century is a little like reading the society page—taste is described largely in anthropomorphic terms. A house might be described as "sincere,"
"charming," "masculine," "suave," "demure," "plain-talking,"
and so on—all of which are vague attributes, for how can one
rationally determine the sincerity of a building? An analysis of
style-related jargon, however, reveals some interesting connotations. Then, as now, houses with style were perceived as more
desirable, as if the moral fiber of the building was just as important as that of the owner. In 1916 Henry Hodgman Saylor cited the
criterion of the house defining the occupant as the most important

factor in his choice of the "Best Twelve Country Houses in America."[8] Other critics sought strains of the architect in the house—
his artistic *maniera.* It is clear that the definition of style as a form
of character or artistic distinction was an extremely important
consideration in architectural criticism of this period.

Sturgis identified the second more familiar concept of style
with "a peculiar type of building, or ornament, or the like, consti-
tuting a strongly marked and easily distinguished category or
epoch in the history of art." According to this definition, both the
typological and ornamental characteristics of buildings of distinct
epochs and cultures were considered. In fact, there was some confusion over whether historical types or ornamental elements com-
prised the essential definition of style in this sense of the word.
Was symbolism or form the most important factor in defining the
Elizabethan house, for instance?

The meanings associated with historical epochs, clearly important to the builders of country houses, came to life in reincarnated
styles as a kind of social theater. Proponents often compared modern living to a bygone era with which they identified. Augusta
Patterson, for instance, was struck by the popularity of old
English scenes: "When we see a good example [of an Elizabethan
country house] we also mentally visualize Henry VII chasing one
of his numerous wives through the shrubbery, or Queen Elizabeth
being coy with Leicester. . . . Think of Elizabethan and you think
of a pageant."[9] Frank Seiberling, the tire mogul, had just such a
pageant in mind when he built Stan Hywet, his Tudor house in
Akron, where he played host to costumed entertainments as part
of the ritual of life. A critic writing in 1921 could have been
describing Seiberling or any number of his contemporaries: "A
man should not build a house in the medieval spirit, or one in the
style of royal France unless, in the first case he leads a highly colored, individual life, of picturesque conception, or in the second
case, one of extreme elegance and sophistication."[10] To both architect and patron, historical symbolism and the legitimacy of its
expression were crucial to the character of a house.

Historical styles also supported social ideologies. Critics saw
Tudor, Dutch Colonial, Georgian and other styles as representa-

69 Frank Seiberling and guests at Elizabethan pageant, **Stan Hywet**, Akron, Ohio,
during the 1920s. (Collection of James Pahlau.)

tive of specific values, often associated with their original cultural milieu but sometimes related to immediate political and social propaganda. One of the dominant issues of the day was the preservation of Anglo-Saxon patrimony in the American population in the face of waves of immigration. Colonial Revival and English styles served as professions of nationalism and ethnic purity. The message explicit in having a certain style of house was apparent to both peers and society at large—the domicile was the raiment of one's values, social position, heritage, name, and personal taste.

Yet some observers began to question the use of the term *style* to signify both decorative vocabularies and building types. As Matlack Price wrote in 1927, "I have never held with the popular habit of using the term 'style' to designate 'type.' Style is a matter for scholarly reproduction, whereas our houses, seldom attempting scholarly accuracy in their renderings of European precedent, are adaptations, and, as such, should fairly and properly be called 'types.'"[11] Price understood how architects combined the symbolic trappings of historical idioms with certain typological features to generate hybrid forms. Thus the Spanish house signified the synthesis of several historical house types from Andalusia, California, Mexico, and so on, as well as the use of details borrowed from a broad range of Hispanic precedents. The hybrids worked because they were tailored to particular climatic conditions and sanctioned by local tradition.

In 1912, at the height of the country house boom, a small book of essays from *House and Garden* appeared that summed up the opinions and values of the time. Edited by the redoubtable Henry Hodgman Saylor, a self-proclaimed authority on the country house, *Architectural Style for Country Houses* was meant as a definitive compilation of the "merits and characteristics" of the most popular "types of [country house] architecture."[12] Saylor asked specialists in particular architectural idioms to join in a literary debate over which styles or types were most appropriate for modern America. In the individual essays architects and critics attempted to relate a specific idiom to American values and to cite its functional advantages for modern life. They also played heavily on personality, character, and patriotic virtues: "For a gentleman of taste, for a lady of discernment," argued Frank Wallis, "Colonial is the only fitting environment. . . . We can see human qualities sticking out of it everywhere. . . . That type of house represents dignity, education, cultivation, and home, as no other style devised by man can do."[13] J. Lovell Little, writing for "the English plaster house" (meaning a generic English Arts and Crafts style), argued that the Colonial style was symbolic of an aristocratic era, not a modern democratic one, and emphasized the advantages of a more informal house.[14] Other articles praised the Swiss chalet, Italian adaptations, Tudor houses, the Spanish Mission type, half-timbered styles, Dutch Colonials, and Prairie School houses—referred to as "A Style for the Western Plains."

Arguments ran from the impassioned to the spurious, playing on patriotism, snobbery, practicality, and character. Because the English looked for beauty without effort, appreciated the countryside, and understood the quality of home better than any other nationality, the all-brick Tudor house was without question the most esteemed model. Architecture suited a people as personally as clothing suited an individual, Allen Jackson wrote, admonishing Anglo-Saxon Americans to embrace the half-timbered medieval architecture of their forebears. Aymar Embury II maintained that because the Dutch Colonial style was not at all Dutch but purely an American invention, it was the only indigenous and truly national architecture ever created on American shores. Ergo, the style to use was "Dutch or nothing." More radical and modern were the arguments for Prairie School houses, in which the site, individuality of the owner, and relative importance of the house were the ingredients of style, not materials or personal attributes. Architects created style through a "synthesis of formal principles," Hugh Garden proclaimed in the best Wrightian tone. There was even an argument for stylelessness, put forth by Bertha H. Smith, an advocate of the protomodernist work of Irving Gill in southern California.

Which style-monger won the debate? It hardly matters, though some of the authors admitted that Wallis' plea for the Colonial was very persuasive. The range of opinions and the plurality of idioms indicated that in 1912 Americans were defining their domestic ideals according to the values associated with various architectural styles: the homegrown Colonial suggesting elegance yet simple virtue; the English Tudor, with its venerable aura of age and coziness; the prairie bungalow, evocative of pioneering independence, and the Spanish Colonial, symbolizing exotic and dreamy escapism. Saylor's interesting little book provides a barometer for taste in the eclectic era, when style was a powerful symbol of status, personal character, and class distinction. Values, meaning, and taste could be read in the facade of a house, in the decor of the rooms, in the arrangement of the garden, even in an eave or baluster. Additionally, the concept of style was associated with functional, climatic, regional, and compositional issues. In fact, an entire system of eclectic architectural theory could be formed around the single concept of style.

THE SYMBOLIC UNIVERSE: STYLES AND THEIR MEANINGS

Choice of a historical style was the most significant decision to be made by owner and architect alike. Augusta Owen Patterson, the witty editor of *Town and Country* magazine, provided a similar index of popular house idioms in *American Homes of To-day,* published in 1924. By then there were six major styles favored by the upper class—three European classical (French, English, and Italian), two picturesque (Elizabethan and modern), and America's own Colonial. As she pointed out, Americans came to their conservative domestic preferences after a good deal of casting about in the late nineteenth century and seemed content to adapt models from the past for their modern houses, though the models chosen by architects and patrons were hardly indiscriminate. One can best appreciate the major idioms as genre scenes, defined by patterns of living, entertaining, and decoration. The periodicals and books of the era indicate that four broad categories achieved widespread acceptance with patrons and architects: Modern French or Beaux-Arts, Tudor, Colonial Revival, and Mediterranean.

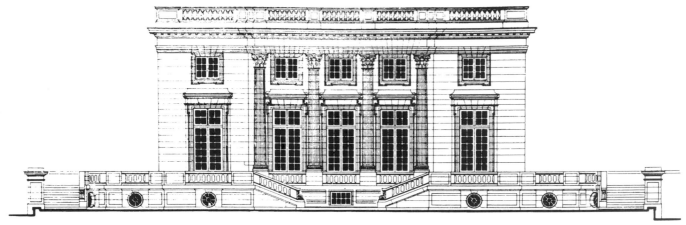

WEST ELEVATION.

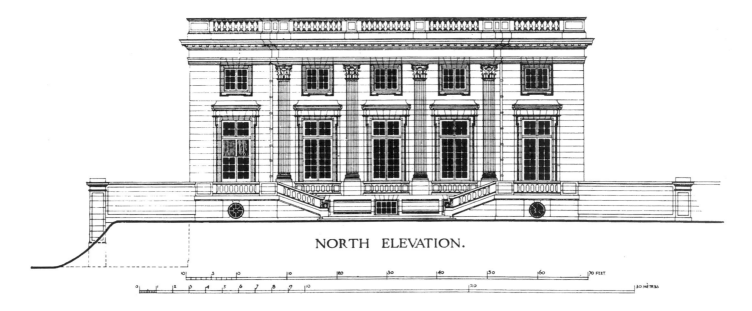

NORTH ELEVATION.

Classical Opulence: The Modern French Influence

Between 1890 and World War I, the most opulent models for American country houses came from France. Though not all architects shared Richard Morris Hunt's Francophile ideals, nearly all had to come to terms with the invasion of Modern French influence by way of the Beaux-Arts. Paris of the *belle époque* was a center of decorative and fine arts, fashion, and high culture, the city in which elite standards of taste were established. It was a must on the grand tour and a haven for collectors. Inevitably, wealthy Americans endeavored to create French settings for their paintings, furnishings, and other treasures. During the late 1880s both patrons and architects were attracted to French classicism as a new approach for estates and gardens with formal, aristocratic pretensions. So pervasive was the French influence that in 1899 the American Institute of Architects devoted its convention proceedings to the impact of the Beaux-Arts on the architectural profession.

What came to be called Modern French or Parisian Renaissance models for the country house, which today would be labeled Beaux-Arts, represented a blending of sources from châteaux of

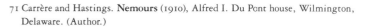

70 Ange-Jacques Gabriel. **Le Petit Trianon,** Versailles, France. North and west elevations. (*Year Book of the Boston Architectural Club,* 1913.)

71 Carrère and Hastings. **Nemours** (1910), Alfred I. Du Pont house, Wilmington, Delaware. (Author.)

72 Horace Trumbauer. **The Elms** (1899–1901), Edward J. Berwind house, Newport, Rhode Island. Garden front. (Richard Cheek.)

the sixteenth to the eighteenth centuries. Architects used decoration and major architectural elements (roofs, aediculae, pediments, window and door surrounds, and so on) from Renaissance, baroque and neoclassical houses to impart a rich flavor to the French-American country house. The most popular decorative styles were Louis XIV, XV, and XVI—either directly imported from Parisian decorators or competently interpreted by such American Francophiles as Ogden Codman, Horace Trumbauer, or Carrère and Hastings.

For the leading architects, designing in a French classical mode was more a compositional than a decorative method. "The right way to adapt a French chateau for an American house," wrote Joy Wheeler Dow in 1904, "is really to make believe to restore one, pretending for the nonce that one is M. Pierre Lescot, M. Claude Perrault, or M. Gabriel, and that the king or some grand seigneur of the realm has commanded one's services for the purpose."[15] But the archaeological approach was not as popular among architects and clients as Dow made out. There were three primary strategies of French classical design. The first involved the adaptation of models from the great French *palais, hôtels,* and *châteaux,* some-

times incorporating specific requests from a client who had visited the Loire or the Ile de France. A second approach was to begin with a particular historical style, which was then hybridized to suit the clients, the site, and the scope, as Richard Morris Hunt did so brilliantly at Biltmore. But the most interesting strategy for adapting French as well as English formal houses was to follow the strict rules of classicism as taught at the Ecole, thus producing buildings with no direct source but with a strong connection to the Beaux-Arts buildings the architect had admired in his student days in Paris. In debating the applicability of Parisian Renaissance architecture to the American scene in 1899, Ralph Adams Cram reinforced the sentiment toward the use of classical essence rather than of style: "On the one side we shall put the principles of modern classicism—these are the lasting qualities; on the other side we shall put the style itself—this is the accident, the matter without vitality or comment. In a word, the motive is good, the style bad."[16] Although architects tended to side with Cram, clients sought the trappings of style for symbolic reasons. To have a French classical house in 1900 was to be at once contemporary yet connected to a grand tradition.

The marks of the Modern French country house were usually ostentation, opulence, and strict formality. Perhaps the best example of this kind of house is The Elms (1899–1901), the mansion and garden of Edward J. Berwind[17] in Newport, designed by

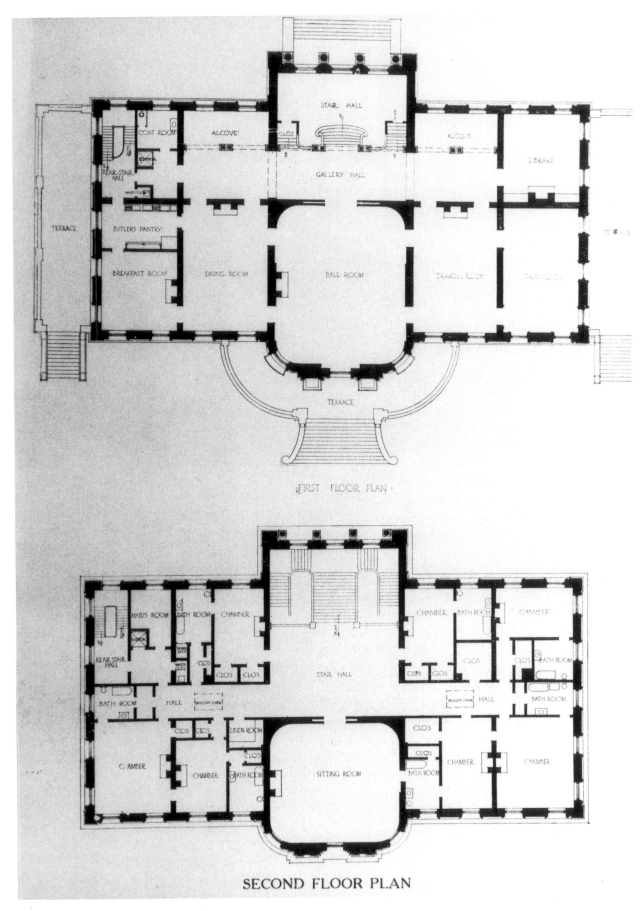

STAIR HALL

COAT ROOM   ALCOVE   CLOS   ALCOVE   LIBRARY

REAR STAIR HALL   GALLERY HALL

TERRACE   BUTLERS PANTRY   TERRACE

BREAKFAST ROOM   DINING ROOM   BALL ROOM   DRAWING ROOM   PALM ROOM

TERRACE

· FIRST · FLOOR · PLAN ·

MAIDS ROOM   BATH ROOM   CHAMBER   CHAMBER   BATH ROOM   CHAMBER

REAR STAIR HALL   CLOS   CLOS   STAIR HALL   CLOS   CLOS   CLOS   BATH ROOM

BATH ROOM   HALL   HALL   BATH ROOM

CLOS   CLOS   LINEN ROOM   CLOS   CLOS

CHAMBER   CLOS   CHAMBER

CHAMBER   CHAMBER   BATH ROOM   SITTING ROOM   BATH ROOM   CHAMBER   CHAMBER

SECOND FLOOR PLAN

73 **The Elms.** Plan. (*American Country Houses of To-Day*, 1912.)

74 **The Elms.** Stair hall. (Richard Cheek.)

Horace Trumbauer. Adapted from the Château d'Agnes at Asnières, near Paris, The Elms combined rational organization with richness of detail in a manner that suggested the best work of Hastings but also showed Trumbauer's chilly classical touch to its best advantage. A telling aspect of the plan is the placement of a ballroom at the center, with other rooms dedicated to entertaining arranged in a constellation around it, not unlike the formal cruciform plans of the French baroque château. Sitting majestically on Bellevue Avenue, the mansion was little more than an overblown suburban villa for the display of wealth and opulence.[18] Its sophisticated setting within fine formal gardens made a very urbane and monumental statement on Newport's old main street, among older cottages and such stately edifices as Rosecliff and Marble House. Here was the style worked to its best advantage, designed to impress and to provide the backdrop for entertaining in the mode of the great fêtes of the 1890s. Modern French was one major style that was not supported by overt ethnic and moral associations. It was predominantly a collector's idiom among patrons, and a badge of allegiance to classicism among architects. After an initial period of experimentation during the 1890s, under the influence of Richard Morris Hunt and Thomas Hastings, a number of Beaux-Arts-trained architects, such as John Russell Pope, selected English Georgian for classical or formal work.

The major criticisms of the French classical house were functional and social. Americans, even those with airs of nobility, found it difficult to live in such overbearingly formal houses, and the elaborateness of such surroundings was too hard to sustain. After World War I the French classical mode declined in popularity: "There are probably fewer houses going up today on the French model than any other," wrote Patterson in 1924, a trend she attributed to "a previous generation [that] went in for its French chateaux, both Renaissance and neo-classic, too generously."[19] Herbert Langford Warren maintained that "the most successful and characteristic developments in American architecture, the commercial building and the country house, do not depend in the least on direct French influence."[20] Even Paul Philippe Cret (1876–1945), the eminent French-American academic architect, never designed a French classical house. (His three major domestic commissions were executed in Provincial, Italian, and Tudor idioms.)[21] Infatuation with French classical styles dissipated, to be replaced by interest in the picturesque idiom known popularly as French or Norman Provincial, which was very much closer to the English vernacular.[22] Nevertheless, the French taste was seductive for those wishing a connection to the belle époque. As Edith Wharton said in 1905, through one of her characters, these sorts of houses were founded on "the desire to imply that one has been to Europe, and has a standard," and that in "America every marble house with gilt furniture is thought to be a copy of the *Trianon*."[23]

75 Willis Polk. **Uplands** (1912–17), Charles Templeton Crocker house, Hillsborough, California. (Moulin Studios, San Francisco.)

76 Achille Duchène, Willis Polk, and others. **The Carolands** (1913–25), Frances Carolan and Harriet Pullman house, Hillsborough, California. (Moulin Studios, San Francisco.)

The Romance of Tudor

Throughout the nineteenth century English architectural ideals and styles crossed the Atlantic, including varieties of the Gothic Revival, Old English, and Queen Anne movements. Because of the close ties of many Americans with their Anglo-Saxon ancestors, there were constant parallels in domestic taste between the two countries. During the 1880s, however, a new genre of English-inspired house began to capture the imagination of architects and wealthy patrons—one with the romantic associations of medieval manors, yeomen, and squires, at the very origin of England's domestic traditions. Sometimes termed Elizabethan, Jacobean, half-timber, Old English, or Jacobethan, what came to be called the Tudor style quickly caught on among wealthy country estate builders. At its peak of popularity around 1910, almost 30 percent of the country houses being published in the leading journals could be grouped under this heading, making the Tudor house a close second to the Colonial in popularity.[24]

Tudor usually referred to archaeologically and historically inspired interpretations of the domestic architecture of fifteenth- and early-sixteenth-century England, and sometimes to houses of simple, rustic design and construction influenced by the English village and farm. Also within the English category was the work of Edwardian Arts and Crafts architects as translated for American social conditions. Of course, English architects such as Voysey, Gimson, and Baillie-Scott were all distilling early English architectural motifs and techniques in their work; medievalism and adherence to vernacular craft and building techniques were essential parts of their design philosophy. It was sometimes difficult to distinguish a house in the more modern English Arts and Crafts idioms from one in a more "correct" and historical vein. As the varieties were mixed, the American Tudor house gradually attained a stylistic life of its own, free from any English associations, and found its way into suburban plan books and mail-order catalogues.

Gavin Townsend has observed in his excellent study of this idiom that Americans seemed to find similar reasons for their attachment to both Tudor- and Colonial-style houses. Both satisfied a yearning for the simple life of the farmstead, both evoked ideals of sound craftsmanship and comfortable domesticity, both seemed well adapted to the American landscape, and both were quintessentially Anglo-Saxon and therefore embodied the white Anglo-Saxon Protestant ethos.[25] In fact, a picturesque house in the ancient Tudor style could be more bucolic than even the simplest Colonial house. Wilson Eyre found "the epitome of home" in the style and argued convincingly that American architects ought properly to look to Britain rather than to France for models and inspiration for the country house.[26] Allen Jackson argued that Tudor or half-timbered styles were inherently more flexible in their plans and more truthfully expressed their rooms on the outside than could any classic or Colonial house dependent upon symmetry and uniformity in elevation. "If the *entente cordiale* is lacking in the Georgian work between the plan and its elevations, it is, on the other hand, in this very matter that the strength of the true English work of the Tudor period lies, for the rambling timbered or plastered houses of this time, by wholly ignoring symmetry, gain at the very outset an immense freedom." Another advantage to the style was its fitness in natural settings, its rusticity and primitive charm. Jackson stressed the organic analogy in discussing the siting of Tudor houses: "They are offsprings of the soil, with their brick and mortar from the fields, and rough-hewn timbers dragged from the forest. As a tree lacks symmetry but possesses perfect balance, so do they."[27]

From the social point of view, Americans seeking ancestral and historical pedigrees were immediately attracted to the Tudor style. Redolent of the literate, landed aristocracy of England, of Shakespeare and the old universities, Tudor signified the authority of history and learning. Literary and antiquarian gentlemen embraced Tudor as a means of expressing their interest in collecting books, their search for genealogical lines, or their passion for things English, medieval, or historical. It also eventually became a trademark of financiers—as the epithet "stockbroker's Tudor" that has come down to us vividly demonstrates. Probably the most

77 **Synyards** (late fifteenth century), Otham, Kent, England. (Lloyd, *A History of the English House.*)

78 Ernest Newton. "House No. 13—Entrance front," from Newton, *A Book of Country Houses,* 1903. (Richard Cheek.)

79 Trowbridge and Ackerman. **Killenworth** (1913), George D. Pratt house, Lattingtown, Long Island. (Mattie Edwards Hewitt, Long Island Studies Institute, Nassau County Museums.)

elaborate and elegant stockbroker's estate was that of Clarence McKenzie Lewis, built in 1924 in the Ramapo Mountains of northern New Jersey. John Russell Pope assembled a number of late English medieval features into its multigabled masses and deftly linked the rambling wings to fine gardens by Vitale and Geifferts. In the end, however, it was the American's longing for his ancestral land and his romantic view of its domestic values that made Tudor so enduring: "Those soft, beautiful [English] houses which affect us by their perfect repose and harmony," Jackson rhapsodized, "their feeling of rest and simplicity—no stress or striving here, only peace and quiet. Nowhere are there such *homes* as these."[28]

When examining English influences on the country house, it is impossible to separate fully the more progressive Arts and Crafts designs, which were coming to America in magazines such as *The Studio,* from Tudor- and medieval-inspired domestic work. American architects like Wilson Eyre and Howard Shaw were fully aware of the latest Free Style and modern English work. Such free-thinking architects as William L. Price and George W. Maher

80 Dwight James Baum. **Lawridge** (1921), Robert J. Law house, Port Chester, New
York. (Samuel Gottscho, Avery Architectural Archives.)

81 **Killenworth.** Strapwork in hall. (Mattie Edwards Hewitt, Long Island Studies
Institute, Nassau County Museums.)

were strong advocates of the social and artistic tenets of the Arts
and Crafts. Chicago's progressive Robert C. Spencer (1864–1958),
a friend and colleague of Wright, designed both conservative and
Prairie School suburban houses that could loosely be called
Tudor—that is, they used half-timbering and gable motifs from
the derivative idiom. Wright too used the style.[29] In spite of the
clear influence of Arts and Crafts on American design at the turn
of the century, the most successful architects working did not
fully adopt the social, aesthetic, and moral precepts of the movement, possibly because their wealthy clients were conservative
capitalists with little sympathy for the socialist ideals of the movement as it existed in England. It is thus not appropriate to speak of
a separate Arts and Crafts mode for American country houses.[30]

The larger influence of English domestic architecture came
through the abstraction and hybridization of historical and vernacular elements. Following the 1880s and 1890s, during which
time historical models were openly copied, architects began to use
the English Tudor style more generically. Harrie Lindeberg,
Bertram Goodhue, and Wilson Eyre, among other architects, saw
the picturesque mode used by their British colleagues as inspiration for a modern house type that used the textures and rustic
materials of the ancient house in refreshing American variations.
The first attempts at transformation appeared in such houses as
Ormston (1913–18), designed by Goodhue, in Lattingtown,
Long Island, and Killenworth (1913), designed by Trowbridge
and Ackerman for George D. Pratt, also on Long Island. But it
was in Philadelphia (see chapter 6) that the English romantic
influence found its most fecund home. Wilson Eyre's stucco, half-
timber, and stone houses paved the way for such firms as Mellor,
Meigs and Howe; Robert McGoodwin; and Edmund Gilchrist,
who produced numerous romantic houses based loosely on
English models. In the late 1920s the style had become crisp and

82 Roger Bullard. **Villa Banfi,** originally **Rynwood** (1927–29), Samuel Agar Salvage
house, Glen Head, Long Island. Gable of living room wing from side garden.
(Mattie Edwards Hewitt, Long Island Studies Institute, Nassau County Museums.)

austere, almost akin to art deco, as can be seen in Roger Bullard's
widely admired Rynwood (1927–29), at Glen Head, Long Island,
or Harrie Lindeberg's brilliant house (1925) for Frederick Patterson, president of National Cash Register, in Dayton. These later
essays exemplify the best of American variations on the Tudor
genre.

Tudor was the most popular alternative to classical and formal
idioms during the heyday of country house building. One finds
good examples throughout the nation, including the West Coast,
where such eclecticists as H. Roy Kelley, Gordon B. Kaufmann,
Marston and Van Pelt, Willis Polk, John Hudson Thomas, and
Ernest Coxhead successfully interpreted the style.

83 Harrie T. Lindeberg. Frederick Patterson house (1925), Dayton, Ohio. (Samuel
Gottscho, Avery Architectural Archives.)

84 Charles Schneider. **Stan Hywet** (1911–15), Frank Seiberling house, Akron, Ohio.
(Collection of James Pahlau.)

85 **Villa Banfi/Rynwood.** View of garden front from lawn. (Richard Cheek.)

86 Gordon B. Kaufmann. **Greystone** (1925–28), E. L. Doheny house, Beverly Hills, California. Concrete Tudor. (Richard Cheek.)

87 Bertram Grosvenor Goodhue. **Ormston** (1913–18), J. E. Aldred house,
Lattingtown, Long Island. (Richard Cheek.)

The Colonial Revival

For many critics during the eclectic era, the search for an appropriate national style led not to European idioms but to the indigenous
architecture of eighteenth-century America. What better way to
emulate the life of a landed gentleman than to live in a plantation
or manor house designed after the hallowed landmarks of the colonial period? And what more natural domestic model to use for the
modern country house? As the *Architectural Record* stated in 1912:
"This country can name but four characteristically national types
of house, four types that belong with any historic sanction, and
these are the Spanish Mission, the Southern Colonial, the Dutch
Colonial, and the Georgian Colonial."[31] Nationalism and patriotism created a movement that had a profound effect on all aspects
of American culture from 1876 to 1940—the Colonial Revival.

According to William Rhoads' pioneering research on the subject, Americans' interest in their past culture, especially their
early domestic architecture, began to emerge in the late 1850s,
when the first study of colonial architecture in New England
appeared. The movement did not take hold, however, until Americans began to sense their own expanding power and place in the
world. The Colonial Revival grew out of an uncertain, late-
nineteenth-century America in need of symbols. At the Centennial Exposition in Philadelphia, which opened on May 10, 1876,
with the starting of the seven-hundred-ton Corliss steam engine,
there was little to suggest that Americans had produced a distinctive art or culture to match that of Europe. Visitors to the fair
viewed impressive American products and know-how—in direct
competition to the achievements of Europe—and were clearly
stimulated by national pride tinged with cultural envy. Signs of an
awakening interest in the early history of the nation were evident
in literature and art by the 1880s.[32] The movement gained

88 Colonial Revival precedents from an architect's scrapbook. (Little and Browne Scrapbooks, vol. 3, Avery Architectural Archives.)

momentum as the new century neared and became a powerful cultural force throughout the 1920s and 1930s, as research on the arts of the colonies and the early republic increased. Through popularizers such as Wallace Nutting, scholars such as Sydney Fiske Kimball, and prestigious advocates such as Franklin Delano Roosevelt (who loved the Dutch Colonial of his native Hudson Valley), the Colonial became a kind of national style. As early as 1886 Marianna van Rensselaer cited longevity, history, and tradition as key reasons for building in Colonial idioms: "Our colonial work has stood longer than any other, and is identified with whatever historic associations we can call our own; and it is all so analogous as to offer an instance of the flourishing on our soil of something that may be called a coherent, comprehensible, all-pervading style."[33]

Rhoads has suggested that the popularity and longevity of the Colonial Revival can be attributed to a number of factors. First, patriotism and the representation of the Colonial as the ancestral style made it attractive to both old society and Americans who wished to continue the traditions of their forebears. Before 1900 organizations based on ancestral lineage, such as the Daughters of the American Revolution and the Society of the Cincinnati, were founded for the study and appreciation of family heritage, with clear implications for the "protection of caste."[34] A Boston architect, Robert D. Andrews, even maintained in 1904 that these societies, which were often quartered in neo-Colonial buildings, were largely responsible for the rise in popularity of the Georgian style in domestic architecture.[35] The issue of class was also stressed by Joseph Everett Chandler in 1916: "There seems to be no doubt that this style is the best which is adaptable to the needs of the better class of our people, that class generously sprinkled through all those divisions of society which range from the very poor (with good taste), through the ranks of the rather well-to-do, to the very wealthy class (still with good taste). This 'better class' fortunately seems to be growing in that sense which is a far greater blessing than the mere ability to make money."[36] His remarks underline the ethnic, moral, and cultural bias of the period toward "old stock"—Americans of Scotch-Irish or Anglo-Saxon ancestry.

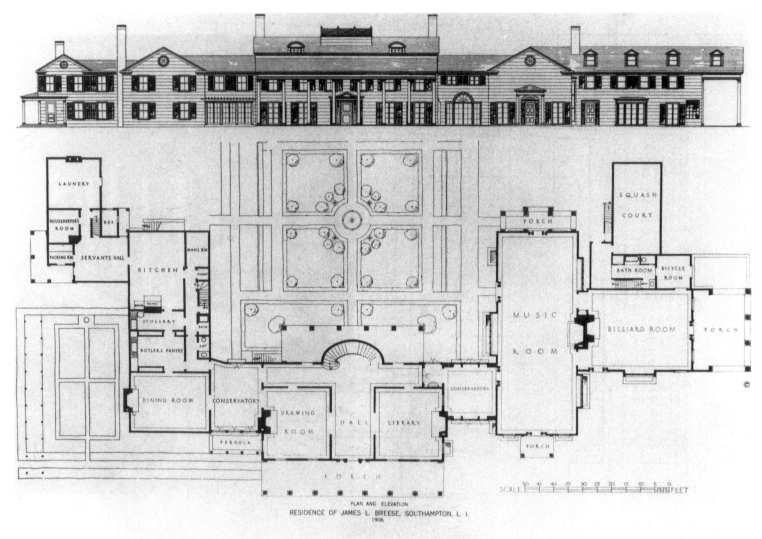

PLAN AND ELEVATION
RESIDENCE OF JAMES L. BREESE, SOUTHAMPTON, L. I.
1906

The Colonial Revival was also part of a larger phenomenon in which classical architecture and antiquity were the highest forms of artistic achievement, a view clearly influenced by architects and artists trained at the Ecole des Beaux-Arts. American Renaissance architects such as McKim saw no discrepancy between the use of high classical sources from ancient Rome and the Italian Renaissance for some buildings and the more homegrown classicism of eighteenth-century American buildings for others. Motifs from both were often combined during the freer, early period of academic eclecticism, producing buildings of considerable beauty and interest. Indeed, during the 1890s and 1900s, the definition of Colonial was broad enough to include almost any house with features of English Georgian, English neoclassical, Federal, Greek Revival, or vernacular architecture of the colonies.[37] As Ralph Adams Cram remarked in 1913: "Apart from the Classical trend, which includes many variants, from the roman villa through a kind of Palladian Anglicism to the suave well-being of the latest French Louis, there are of course the two models which most insistently suggest themselves to us in this land and generation, and these two are 'Colonial' (or its antetype English Georgian) and the immortal predecessor thereof, the standard type developed in England during the reign of the Tudors."[38]

89 McKim, Mead and White. **The Orchard** (1898–1907), James L. Breese house, Southampton, Long Island. Plan and elevation. (*Monograph of the Work of McKim, Mead and White.*)

90 Robert Rodes McGoodwin. W. W. Harper house (1912), Chestnut Hill, Pennsylvania. (*American Country Houses of To-Day,* 1915.)

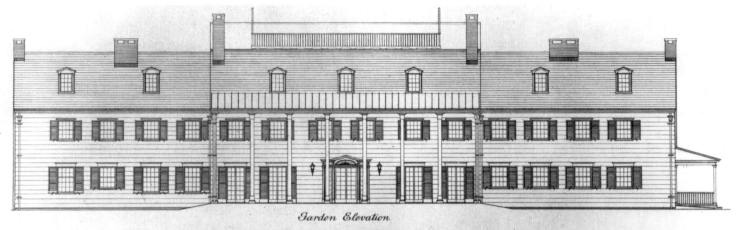

Garden Elevation

Residence of Robert J. Collier. Wicatunk. N.J.

Garden Elevation of the

Residence of John Sloan. Far Hills. N.J.

91 *top* John Russell Pope. Robert J. Collier house (b. 1911), Wicatunk, New Jersey. Garden elevation. (Richard Cheek, from *The Architecture of John Russell Pope*.)

92 John Russell Pope. Thomas Frothingham–John Sloan house (1919–21), Far Hills, New Jersey. Elevation. (Richard Cheek, from *Monograph of the Work of John Russell Pope*.)

93 *opposite* William Lawrence Bottomley. **Milburne** (1934), Walter S. Robertson house, Richmond, Virginia. (Richard Cheek.)

The models used for Colonial Revival country houses follow a pattern of scholarly research, publication, and popularization of Early American house types, beginning with such influential sources as Ware and Keefe's *The Georgian Period* in the early 1890s.[39] The two most ubiquitous early types were the Mount Vernon paradigm and the generic brick Georgian block, or block with dependencies, borrowed from Virginia and Maryland houses. Following World War I, when such scholars as Fiske Kimball documented the variety and richness of America's early domestic architecture, the range of models became more regionalized (see chapter 6) and the sources more varied and rich—Dutch Colonial, Greek Revival, New England, Pennsylvania, and Louisiana idioms gained popularity. But even before the war more houses were being built following Early American models than in any other style, including English Tudor, a trend that continued throughout the 1930s.[40]

The essential attractions of the Colonial styles were, once again, sentimental and visual. Yet the imagery of homegrown styles was more vivid, more palpable, and more laden with direct nostalgia.

Builders of Colonial Revival houses, envisioning a vanishing early America, longed to live as their grandparents had. As Augusta Patterson put it:

Back of everything in the modern architects' and builders' mind, aside from question of detail and the essential two story porch, is a picture of a graceful, sweeping, well-proportioned white clapboarded farm house in some picturesque relation to the surrounding landscape, on a hillock top, in an apple orchard, surrounded by pines, or with a brook running through the front yard. A Colonial house to be successful must be a picture as well as a building. . . . The modern Colonial is not a copy of original models. It is an entirely sophisticated, an entirely glorified, twentieth century adaptation of a mental idea.[41]

315

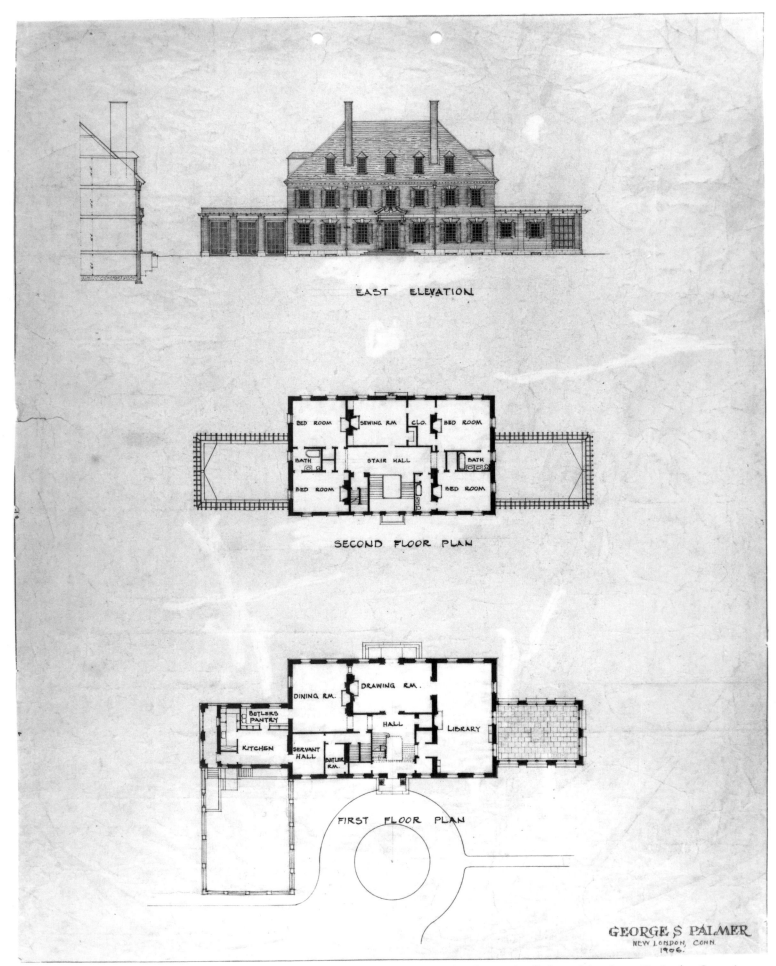

EAST ELEVATION

SECOND FLOOR PLAN

FIRST FLOOR PLAN

GEORGE S PALMER
NEW LONDON, CONN.
1906.

94 Charles Platt. **Eastover** (1906), George Palmer house, New London, Connecticut.
(Avery Architectural Archives.)

95 J. C. Schweinfurth. **Hacienda del Pozo de Verona** (1898), Phoebe Apperson Hearst house, Pleasanton, California. (Ferree, *American Estates and Gardens.*)

Mediterranean and Hispanic Idioms

The logical extension of American interest in colonial domestic architecture during the eclectic era was the investigation of Spanish influence early in the nation's history. The vitality, longevity, and breadth of Hispanic revivalism in American architecture are extraordinary, not only in such states as California, Texas, and Florida, where climate and history merited continuity with building traditions implanted during colonization, but in all regions of the United States. What came to be called Mediterranean styles played a crucial part in the development of regional types for the country estate, especially during the 1920s. Like the English imprint in the colonies, the Hispanic influence was diverse, ranging from pure adaptations of Spanish Provincial, Portuguese, Italian, and Moorish house types, to domestic architecture inspired by the Spanish missions and haciendas, New Mexico adobes, Territorial work (that is, the architectural styles that prevailed when New Mexico was still a territory), regional Mexican architecture, and Caribbean styles. The same romanticism that moved patrons to dream of living in the domains of François I, Henry VIII, or George Washington also brought them to the doorstep of El Greco.

One finds the roots of the Spanish Colonial Revival in California during the 1880s, when writers such as Helen Hunt Jackson and Charles Fletcher Lummis began to extol the frontier simplicity of early Hispanic settlement. Jackson's *Ramona* (1884), one of the best-selling novels of its time, brought national attention to a state known previously only for its gold rush and frontier booms.[42] Jackson also wrote a descriptive text for *Glimpses of California and the Missions* in 1883, a book that emphasized the sublime, exotic, and romantic aspects of the architecture of the colonial period. Postfrontier California began to reinvent its history and physical identity through this idealization of its colonial past.

The first return of an architectural style became known as Mis-

sion Revival, after the almost legendary exploits of Father Junipero Serra and his Franciscans in the colonization of California. "Besides being in wonderful accord with California landscape and climate, the Mission style always recalls the heroic work of our early missionaries," wrote a critic in 1924.[43] The imagery of the mission churches and cloisters began appearing in many building types from the late 1880s until well into the new century. Herbert Croly, writing for *Architect and Engineer* in 1906, cited the advantages of the style: "Rudimentary as these buildings were and simple to the verge of attenuation, they reached, both by what they avoided, and by what they effected the essentials of good domestic architecture."[44] In keeping with its qualities of modesty and practicality, the Mission image generally had more influence on Arts and Crafts houses for the middle class than on large country dwellings. There is, nonetheless, a major example of a country estate inspired by this movement, the Burrage mansion (1899–1901) in Redlands, by the Boston architect Charles Brigham, with its literal application of the two-towered church facade and heavy religious imagery. In 1898, the eccentric Phoebe Apperson Hearst built the huge, fortresslike Hacienda del Pozo de Verona with architect J. C. Schweinfurth in Pleasanton. Though extensively published as a Hispanic house, it had only the barest stylistic and typological resemblance to its supposed model, a large house for a wealthy Mexican landowner.[45] Before World War I the more common country house type for the California climate was a vague Italian classical villa, seen in the Platt-inspired James D. Phelan estate, Villa Montalvo (c. 1914), near Los Gatos—hence the more general appellation Mediterranean.[46]

During the late nineteenth century the literary revival of Hispanicism was attended by a resort and leisure movement that brought scores of wealthy easterners to the West Coast for vacations. Many stayed on, either for their health or from sheer love of the exotic beauty and perfect climate that California could offer.[47] One of the greatest appeals of Spanish Colonial architecture was its sense of the exotic, the novel, its marked contrast from the cultural focus of the East. This intense difference—in climate, way of

96 Bertram Grosvenor Goodhue. **Dias Felices** (1915–18), Henry Dater house, Montecito, California. Oblique view of terrace with mountains in the distance. (From a color slide of the 1920s taken by Peter Cooper Bryce. Collection of Marc Appleton.)

life and work ethic, concept of the house and its setting — seemed to draw many non-Hispanic Americans to a domestic tradition far from their own. Resort entrepreneurs in Florida also played on the Spanish heritage in their buildings, as in Henry Flagler's famous Ponce de Leon and Alcazar hotels, eventually developing a Mediterranean tradition in domestic architecture in what was to be called the American Riviera.[48]

After World War I, two factors promoted a second wave of interest in Hispanic architecture among wealthy patrons: the gardening movement, with its emphasis on outdoor living, and a trend toward simplicity among the builders of country houses. As Rexford Newcomb, a key scholar and promoter of the Spanish influence, observed: "The salient message of all Mediterranean architecture is its reaction to climate, its essential sunniness, its emphasis of light and shade. This quality is apparent in its every line, be it plan, elevation, roof, or decoration."[49] The emergence of the modern California garden at such estates as Arcady in Montecito fostered the idea that the whitewashed houses of Spain made the best backdrop for the colorful, sun-loving flora indigenous to a "Mediterranean" climate. "The Spanish house," wrote R. W. Sexton, "is primarily designed as one in which the occupant may enjoy outdoor life to the utmost, providing a maximum of light, air and sunshine, while affording at the same time a desirable privacy."[50] The patio done as an inner courtyard also appealed to many patrons, who increasingly desired a more private existence, in contrast to the extremely public, showy nature of earlier stately homes. Moreover, as tastes swung toward greater conservatism in the display of wealth, it became socially acceptable, indeed desirable, to live more simply. The Spanish house, with its informal plan organized around the outdoors, came to represent the epitome of the carefree, yet still proper, way of life.

Architects were initially attracted to Spanish for its exoticism, its formal simplicity contrasted with small areas of rich, complex ornament, and its regional associations. Bertram Goodhue, mentioned as one of the most creative free eclectic masters, was converted to California life early in the century, eventually designing many important buildings in Hispanic idioms. His greatest impact on the Mediterranean revival is generally thought to be the buildings designed for the San Diego Panama-Pacific Exposition of 1913, one of several fairs celebrating the completion of the canal. He also designed several of the most influential early Spanish houses in the Santa Barbara area (see chapter 6). By looking directly to Spain and not at colonial buildings, he helped focus attention on the complex sources of Hispano-American architecture. This stimulated the study and drawing of buildings from both the Spanish and colonial cultures, as the spate of publications after World War I demonstrates.[51] As interest in Hispanic architecture intensified among architects during the 1920s, the Spanish Colonial house came to be increasingly associated with its functional and environmental features, eventually being touted as a rather "modern" model of the efficient dwelling in warm climates. In the resort colony of Santa Barbara, Reginald D. Johnson designed several important estates that helped set the tone for Spanish design. Among the largest were the John J. Mitchell estate, "El Mirador," built during the 1920s for the former Lolita Armour of Chicago, the John Percival Jefferson estate (1921) at Montecito, and the Harold Stuart Chase estate (1924) at Hope Ranch. In the Chase house Johnson cleverly adapted plans for the typical English-influenced country house to simple Spanish motifs on the outside. As Johnson later wrote of his attraction to Hispanic sources, "When I first went to California [in 1910], I

97 Reginald D. Johnson. Harold Stuart Chase house (1924), Hope Ranch, California.
Entrance front. (Richard Cheek, from Staats, *California Architecture in Santa
Barbara.*)

98 Reginald D. Johnson. John Percival Jefferson house (1921), Montecito, California.
(Richard Cheek, from Staats, *California Architecture in Santa Barbara.*)

wanted to take the various styles of the past, particularly of Spain and Italy, and to adapt them to a semi-tropical climate. We have now, in California, three types of country house architecture. These are the houses that are based on the Spanish, on the Italian renaissance, and on the houses that were built by the first American settlers who came to California before '49. Each type has individuality and is adapted to the climate."[52]

A sudden surge in Spanish building occurred in California, Texas, New Mexico, and Florida during the 1920s, because of both the influx of wealthy patrons commissioning resort homes and the rise of a new generation of eclectic architects with interest and expertise in Hispanic styles.[53] Addison Mizener conjured a Mediterranean mythology in his exotic Palm Beach and Boca Raton houses, often combining features of Spanish, Italian, and even French Romanesque decoration in wildly eclectic pastiches. Other members of the Palm Beach school included the talented Maurice Fatio, Marion Syms Wyeth, and John Volk. In Texas the leaders of the Mexican-American revival were Atlee and Robert Ayres (see chapter 6), while similar regionalist movements flourished in New Mexico.

The symbolism behind the popular styles of country houses served to reinforce class values, to reflect life-styles, hobbies, and passions, and to suggest ideologies among architects. Americans wanted an aura of history, a sense of permanence, a palpable connection to the Old World. The symbolic universe of the country house provided the milieu for their dreams of the good life. In part 2 of this book I shall examine the social forces that underlined the domestic ideals of the plutocracy and shaped the rise and fall of certain styles. In most cases one observes a general development, a flourishing, and then a decline, similar to many formal patterns in art history. Experiments in free adaptation came first, followed by a more scholarly and archaeological correction, followed in turn by a paring down of ornamentation and typological characteristics toward a more abstract reading of the style.

Yet it is essential to underline the *representational* nature of eclectic styles. In contrast to types, which were canons of social or architectural forms, eclectic idioms depicted ideas, pictures, historical or ornamental languages, and characteristic moods. The genres of the country house were about imagery and romance—which is not to say that they were excluded from the fundamental substance of architecture. Indeed, eclectic architects believed wholeheartedly in the power of images to communicate meaning and feeling. These images, however, hide the important formal and social changes that created the modern country house, and these can only be read through an analysis of the plan, room use, and the daily functions of the household.

99 *top* Atlee and Robert Ayres. Marian Koogler McNay and Donald T. Atkinson estate (1929), San Antonio, Texas. View of stair hall. (Architectural Drawings Collection, University of Texas at Austin.)

100 *center* McNay estate. Oblique view of entrance front. (Architectural Drawings Collection, University of Texas at Austin.)

101 *bottom* Addison Mizener. **Casa Bendita** (1921), John S. Phipps house, Palm Beach, Florida. Courtyard and tower. (Historical Society of Palm Beach County.)

102 **Casa Bendita.** Interior of living room. (Historical Society of Palm Beach
County.)

THE SOCIAL ARMATURE: ROOMS AND THEIR USES

*When we speak of the well planned house just what do we mean?
Surely it is not an unattainable ideal, but it is one which is difficult to
define. No house is well-planned unless the unavoidable daily tasks
may be carried out in it with the least possible irritation and monotony.
But the well-planned house should be more than a tool to make life
easy. It should stimulate those human faculties which make for cultural
and racial progress. Thus, we might say in a few words that the ideal
home is one where the vexations that make the human spirit mean and
ugly are reduced to a minimum, and those influences which make the
human spirit large and beautiful increased.*

— Arthur C. Holden

When analyzing the design of the ideal house plan, it is prudent to
look both at formal attributes, which are largely determined by
architectural composition, and at the house plan as a diagram of
the complex structure of family life. As the critic R. W. Sexton
wrote, "The individuality of the people is injected into the plan
more readily than through any other detail. . . . The problem
which confronts the architect in this country is to adapt the plan,
as well as the design [of the historical model], to conditions prevailing here, and it is in this process of adaptation that the type is
evolved."[54] One of the great challenges in analyzing domestic
architecture of any kind is sorting out these social and architectural influences.

The typical program of the country house, which was in flux
during the latter half of the nineteenth century, settled into a canonical formula between 1900 and 1910.[55] During these years the
domestic ideals of the American family were radically transformed
by notions of the simple life and a sense of modernity.[56] The elaborate moral codes and social rituals of the Victorian household were
under siege in the popular literature. Critics and reformers called
for such changes as a reduction in the number of specialized rooms
reserved for formal behavior, for example, the second parlor or
reception room, a rationalization of plan forms, a new compositional aesthetic based on honesty and balanced proportion, and a
general simplification of decor. The new progressive home contrasted with both the complex aestheticism of the Victorian home
of the 1850s and 1860s and the subtler spatial order of the Queen
Anne or Shingle Styles of the 1880s. The rich man's country house

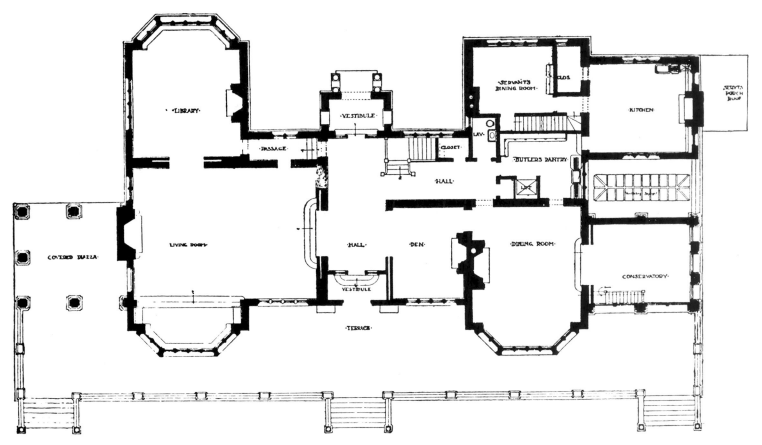

103 Herbert Croly. Ideal country house plan. (Richard Cheek, from *Houses for Town or Country,* 1907.)

absorbed some of the larger cultural forces going on in domestic architecture, not quite renouncing the Victorian gentleman's house of English derivation,[57] but certainly remaking it in an American way. As Sexton observed, the most significant innovations occurred in the house plan and site plan, which were transformed by changes in taste, the family, and architectural ideas taking shape at the turn of the century.

We see an ideal modern country house plan illustrated in Herbert Croly's book *Houses for Town or Country* (1907).[58] The basic components are familiar: a living room, a "plain and businesslike" center hall with stair hall, and a dining room form the formal ground floor suite. Attached to it is the requisite service wing containing butler's pantry, kitchen, servants' dining hall, and other utilitarian rooms. Around the formal suite are rooms dedicated to leisure and outdoor living: a small den, located off the dining room, for family gatherings; along the south side, a covered piazza (or porch), a veranda, and a conservatory; and a library with a private passage, serving as a retreat and study for the master of the house. Upstairs are ample bedrooms with accompanying bathroom suites, and a set of servants' rooms that are spartan but adequate. In its program, this country house differs very little from the kinds of houses Americans inhabit today—it is a modern dwelling in all essential respects.[59]

How radically different it is, however, from American country

houses of the 1850s or 1880s. The plan of "A Large Country House" by Andrew Jackson Downing (1850) shows the same basic **H** form and English derivation as the Croly plan, but its rooms function very differently, according to formulas established for gentlemen's houses of the Victorian era. One enters a stair hall not unlike those of nineteenth-century town houses. To the left is a hall, probably containing heirlooms of baronial splendor, the antecedents of which are still medieval and English. Instead of a living room there is a drawing room (sometimes a parlor), which functions as the most formal entertaining and reception space in the house. Behind it is the library, still the master's private domain and business office. Its opposite number, as a frame to the drawing room, is the boudoir for the ladies, a charming misnomer (for which Americans are famous). The verandas, though connected to all the major ground floor rooms, are built onto the house rather than into it, a symptom of the reluctance of the picturesque designer to let the outdoors into the formal areas. The house is a picture set in the landscape; the landscape a picture to be seen from within the house, but the integration of the two has not yet been achieved. The service wing is not directly connected to the dining room, indicating the explicit segregation of servants and masters.

There is an implicit formality of address and function in this room layout that is not seen in the Croly plan—a direct result of changes in the way Americans carried on their daily lives at the turn of the century.[60] The Victorian gentleman's house addressed itself to the segregation of the sexes, the concealment of servants from masters, the ritual of reception into the house, and the chore-

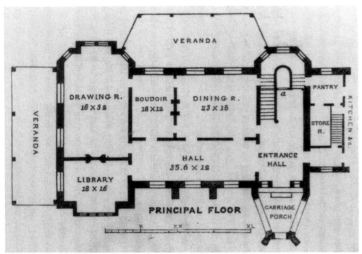

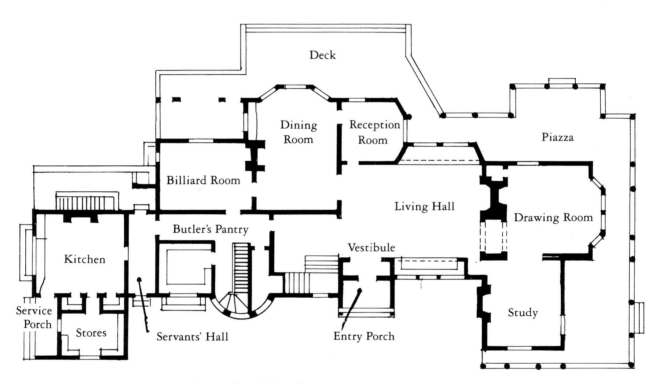

104 *top* Andrew Jackson Downing. "Design 29: A Large Country House," 1850. Plan and perspective view. (Downing, *The Architecture of Country Houses.*)

105 McKim, Mead and White. Victor Newcomb house (1880–81), Elberon, New Jersey. Ground floor plan. (Author.)

ography of formal behavior associated with strict social mores. Many newly wealthy Americans were questioning the behavior of this period. A new, more open house type reflected a life-style based on leisure and greater informality. This influence is best perceived in the transitional houses associated with resort life in the 1880s. Americans with leisure time learned how to socialize in a new way during summer sojourns, and their summer houses reflected this. Two great innovations are evident in these quintessentially American dwellings: the more open plan of the ground floor associated with the "living hall," first developed here by H. H. Richardson, and the increased importance of porches as exten-

sions of the living spaces on this floor. Both were to leave their mark on the modern country house.

The development of the living hall in the 1870s and 1880s as the locus of all activities in the summer house is critical. What began as an enlargement of a stair hall, with overtones of the English great hall of medieval times (and those of Norman Shaw in England), gradually became a multiuse room filled with furniture, objets d'art, and a large hearth—the center of houses such as McKim, Mead and White's important house for Victor Newcomb (1880–81) in Elberon, New Jersey. American architects took the concept of spatial interpenetration between hall and adjoining formal rooms (parlors, dining room, and library) further than their English Queen Anne counterparts had. Mrs. van Rensselaer remarked on this interrelationship during the 1880s:

106 McKim, Mead and White. **Naumkeag** (1885–88), Joseph Hodges Choate house,
Stockbridge, Massachusetts. Living hall, toward stair and dining room.
(Richard Cheek.)

Now in homes of every size the tendency is to make the hall at once beautiful and useful, the most conspicuous feature in the architectural effect
and the most delightful living room of all; not a living-room like the
others [the parlors or drawing rooms], but one with a distinct purpose
and therefore a distinct expression of its own . . . a room which in its uses
shall stand midway between the piazzas on the one hand and the
drawing-rooms and libraries on the other; perfectly comfortable to live
in when the hour means idleness, easy of access from all points outside
and in, largely, open to breeze and view, yet with a generous hearthstone
where we may find a rally-point in days of cold and rain; in short, a spa-
cious yet cozy and informal lounging-place for times when we cannot
lounge on our beloved piazzas.[61]

The popularity of the living hall waned, however, during the
1890s, partially as a tangent of the passing of the Shingle Style,
partially because it was impractical to have a circulation space also
be a major living area. Its functions were combined with those of
the parlor or drawing room, usually the showpiece and largest
room in a formal house, to produce the modern "living room"—
popular in the United States by the turn of the century.[62] This left
the hall, as before, only for stairs and circulation (though we shall
see that the living hall concept held on in some formal homes into
the early twentieth century). The search for comfort and the need
for an informal gathering place for the family led to modifications
in traditional room use, and eventually to this distillation of several rooms into one large multiuse space. As Charles Hooper
observed in his manual on the country house in 1905, "Of the evo-

107 Delano and Aldrich. **Oak Knoll,** Bertram Work house, Oyster Bay, Long Island. Drawing room or living room. (Mattie Edwards Hewitt, Long Island Studies Institute, Nassau County Museums.)

lutions of the various rooms of the modern country house from the feudal 'hall,' . . . it may be said that they arrived at the same destination in the course of time only to be shuffled up and misused by the modern American."[63]

The emergence of the modern living room is a telltale of a tendency toward merging the functions of the ground floor rooms into one unified family suite, with space less differentiated according to sex, degree of formality, or purpose. In contrast to the drawing room, where formal dress and behavior were required, the living room was a place for various family activities. (It is interesting to note that the term *drawing room manners* entered American colloquial usage as a pejorative during this time.) A living room could be the setting for dancing, cards, reception of guests, conversation after dinner, or informal leisure gatherings of the family alone. Wilson Eyre, in a discussion of the program of the country house in 1908, illuminates the new importance of the living room and its incorporation of the functions of the living hall, reception room, or library. Eyre knew the advantages of the living hall— he was a key proponent of it in his early work—but also realized its drawbacks. He suggests that "the living hall with a stairway leading to it is a picturesque feature but not very practical because the stairway, thus much enclosed, is a source of drafts and makes a traffic way of your living place. If your means are limited and you cannot afford a large stairway hall it is far better to have a small one and make a large comfortable living room." The key word here is *comfortable,* a term not applied to the drawing room. A living room could be both impressive in its decor and informal enough for regular family use.[64]

During the period from 1890 to 1915, one finds either a living room or a drawing room illustrated in most country house plans; after World War I the living room predominated, even in rather formal houses. There was always a formal dining room, always an entry space and a stair hall, and nearly always a library or den. Meals were still the major focal point of social intercourse, and the

dining room had to provide the proper setting for an elegant repast. Many were decorated in a Tudor style, with heraldic associations to the hunt. At this time the library also began to take on a more diverse function, and the den became a popular male domain. Charles Hooper attributes the evolution of the den to a downgrading of the gentleman's smoking room and portrays the library as both a book room and a retreat for master or family.

Of course, the size and degree of pretense in the design of the house, influenced by its stylistic models, have great bearing on the program. The more palatial and aristocratic the model, the more the tendency to have formal rooms such as ballrooms, boudoirs, salons, great halls, trophy rooms, and painting galleries. Rustic houses, however, tended to support more leisurely, outdoor-oriented spaces—gun rooms, garden rooms, conservatories, and the like. And because the country house served various functions, the secondary rooms in the program reflected the interests of the individual patron. Wealthy Americans tended to be eclectic in their choice of rooms for a house, and rather freewheeling in their "period" decoration of these rooms. Use of a range of styles for the decor of various formal rooms remained a characteristic of the country house into the 1920s.

108 **Oak Knoll.** Stair hall. (Mattie Edwards Hewitt, Long Island Studies Institute, Nassau County Museums.)

109 Peabody and Stearns. **Elm Court** (1886), William Douglas Sloane house, Lenox, Massachusetts. Ballroom. (Edward Hale Lincoln, Lenox Library Association.)

110 Harrie T. Lindeberg. Frederick Patterson house (1925), Dayton, Ohio. Trophy room or den in the basement. (Samuel Gottscho, Avery Architectural Archives.)

In spite of the influence of English country life in America, the living room affirms that the American house functioned very differently from its English counterpart. The most characteristically American space was the porch, veranda, or piazza, a feature almost never found in English country houses. One of the most ingenious adaptations of American architects was the incorpora-

tion of a porch into every stylistic model used for modern country houses (a loggia might suffice in certain classical variants). Porches linked the main rooms of the house with the gardens but also provided a buffer between nature and the private interior world. Wilson Eyre described their purpose aptly: "The living rooms in the house face the southern exposure and this is called the garden front, in our climate the verandahs or porches are on this exposure and would very appropriately, therefore, look out upon the terrace and pleasure garden."[65] Then as now, Americans lived outdoors in the spring and summer, and the porch allowed any indoor activity—eating, reading, or conversation—to spill into the outdoors. Sleeping porches were also quite popular around 1900, when the healthful qualities of sea or mountain air were seen as invigorating tonics or cures for certain ailments.[66]

The activities of sleeping, bathing, and other hygiene were also being reshaped in the modern house. A key distinction cited by Herbert Croly between the palatial houses of the late-nineteenth century and those of 1907 was the scaling down of bedroom suites. No longer was the bedroom a large apartment in the European mode. "And, by the way, has not the *boudoir* gone out?" he stressed. "It does seem to the writer . . . that the *boudoir* is not as well recognized a part of the lady's private domain as it was in England forty years ago, and in America then and thereafter in houses of much more than common extent and splendor . . . the bedroom grows more and more like unto a pleasant private sitting-room as the modern refinements have sway."[67] As people

111 *top* Frederick Patterson house. Conservatory. (Samuel Gottscho, Avery Architectural Archives.)

112 *center* Cross and Cross. **Bayberryland,** Charles Sabin house (c. 1920), Southampton, Long Island. Porch with trestle table and wicker furniture. (Mattie Edwards Hewitt, Long Island Studies Institute, Nassau County Museums.)

113 *bottom* Charles McCann house (1925), Oyster Bay, Long Island. Bathroom designed by Thedlow Associates. (Mattie Edwards Hewitt, Long Island Studies Institute, Nassau County Museums.)

spent less time in the upstairs domain and more time outdoors or in the main living areas, bedrooms were treated more functionally, with refinements tailored toward comfort rather than show. From the 1880s until World War I there were also significant changes in bathing and hygiene fostered by technology.[68] The widespread introduction of indoor plumbing and advances in toilet design made the bathroom a prominent feature of the bedroom floor, challenging architects to design interlocking bedroom and bath suites efficiently. Charles Platt was one of the first country house architects to graciously link bedrooms with private closets and bathrooms. Leading manufacturers such as J. L. Mott, Crane, and American Standard introduced a wide array of well-designed fittings and porcelain fixtures, making America the best plumbed nation in the world. As Americans developed a taste for these new modern wonders, the bathroom grew in size, reaching its most lavish dimensions and decor during the 1920s and 1930s.

By the turn of the century a distinct and modern social armature had emerged to govern the "society of rooms" in the country house. Within it was the now-familiar triangle of living-dining-kitchen facilities on the public floor, with modern bedroom suites above, trimmed to less lavish dimensions and fitted out with modern plumbing and hygienic gadgets. This basic layout held sway, with some important alterations, for forty years. The key factors influencing its transformation were the automobile, the economics of home building, and, most important, the introduction of new service technologies. But the architectural treatment of the service wing, which was radically transformed in the early decades of the century, reflects the peculiar attitudes of Americans toward mechanical conveniences, efficiency of labor and material, and class ambiguity.

From 1885 to 1905, when the elaborate stately home flourished as a domestic ideal, wealthy Americans depended on servants and employees to run the estate. According to David Phillips in *The Reign of Gilt,* a millionaire's household required a housekeeper, a butler, four parlor- and chambermaids, a French laundress, a "linen woman," someone to pack and unpack guests' luggage, and some "Irish girls" to do the polishing and cleaning. Four footmen and two other workers were under the butler's command. Depending upon the number of carriages and automobiles to be cared for, a coachman and chauffeur were required, with appropriate staffs. In the kitchen, the head chef directed a sous-chef and two scullions. There was the personal valet or maid for each family member and guest, as well as the private secretaries of the master and mistress of the house. Nannies, nursemaids, governesses, and tutors for the children rounded out the staff of a great house. Then, of course, the servants had to be tended to by their own four servants. For a large city or country residence the total staff could reach forty, requiring a rather substantial service wing by American standards.[69]

American dependence on servants was never as great; nor was society as conditioned to their presence, as in Europe. As a rule, the staff was considerably smaller in American households than in European ones. Herbert Croly emphasized this in 1903, attributing it to the fact that "the expense of domestic labor in this coun-

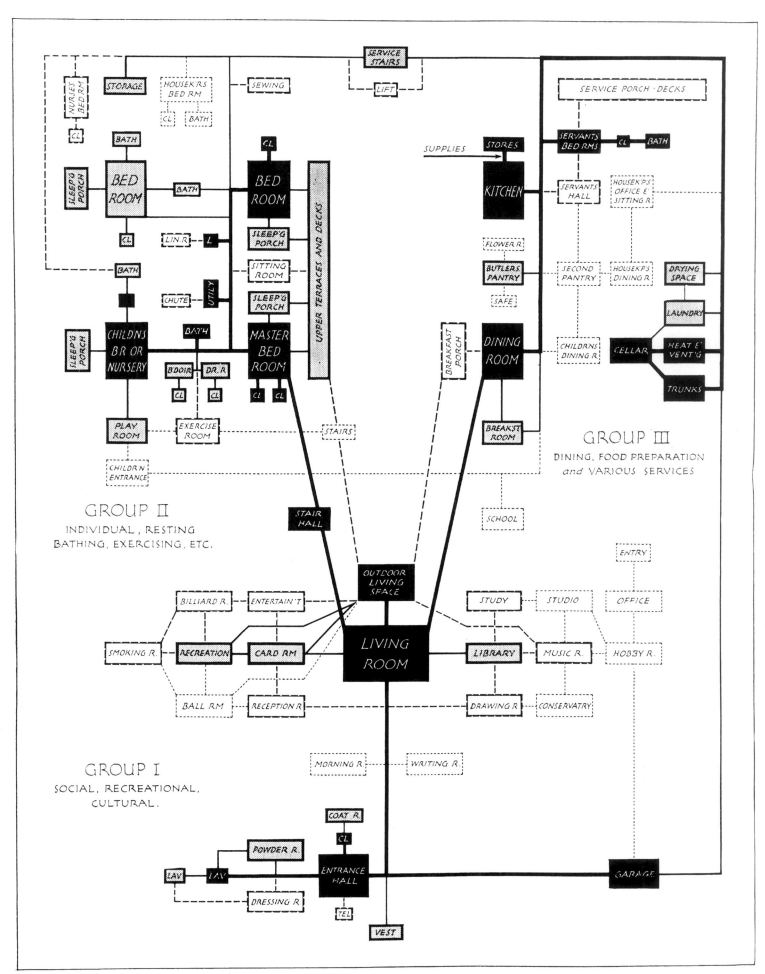

114 Country house adjacency diagram. (Richard Cheek, from *Architectural Forum*, 1933.)

try is a consideration even to millionaires, and this necessity of economizing service has in all grades of American dwellings done much to keep the houses compact and their internal arrangement convenient."[70] In comparison to England, where through a centuries-old tradition the household structure was bound up with servants, and where such labor was conventionally cheap, American families depended on servants primarily from a labor-economy standpoint. With ever-increasing labor costs after 1900, even the privileged were compelled to streamline their needs for domestics in the manner that Croly described.[71] Indeed, service areas of the modern American country house continuously diminished in size from 1900 onward. Statistical data support this: in 1880 the percentage of Americans gainfully employed as domestics was 8.4, whereas in 1920 the number was only 4.5.[72]

In addition, the negative social stigma associated with servants in America was a long-standing corollary of democracy and equality. Many native-born American women considered domestic service an embarrassing necessity. They nonetheless complained constantly of the shortage of good servants, and it became fashionable for upper-class families to bring domestics from abroad, a trend facilitated by massive immigration. American employers tended to attribute certain characteristics to nationality—the French maid or Irish cleaning woman—whereas foreign employees presumably did not share the American's prejudiced views of the servant-master relationship, held over from colonial times. Like the attempt to invent domestic tradition among American gentry, the relationship between domestics and the families they served never became codified in the mold of European aristocratic society. In the North, servants became less important in running the household, though they were not done away with altogether. Below the Mason-Dixon line the serving tradition held on a bit longer, with racial segregation and separate servants' quarters a by-product of the waning culture of the Old South. As a commentator in *Arts and Decoration* lamented in 1920, "One of the problems today is how to find wealth enough to allow of indulgence in the labor saving devices we all need so much, now that the housemaid and the once common maid-of-all-work seem as extinct as the great auk and dinasaurus."[73]

Because of the servant problem, both architects and patrons struggled to minimize the effect of service areas on the house and estate. They did so largely at the expense of servant comfort and amenities. As an expert in domestic service wrote in 1920: "I can safely say that in the majority of homes today the service wing does not measure up to the rest of the house."[74] In the age of the stately home, the servants' wing occupied a substantial percentage of the square footage of the house (perhaps as high as 30 percent), whereas following the war service areas were reduced considerably. Biltmore's wing was nearly as long and tall as the main block of the house but was cleverly screened by trees and by a change in level. The Mackay house used one dependency for services, again screening it with trees and providing a separate access drive. Whereas these houses could support up to fifty servants' bedrooms, the house of the 1920s could run efficiently with less than ten servants.

The functional areas of the large service wing were centered on

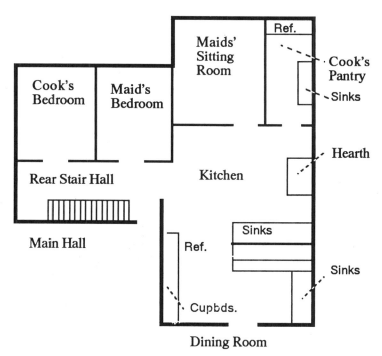

115 An ideal service wing, from *Country Life in America*. (Author, linecut.)

the main level, often including the kitchen suite (pantries and storage rooms, cold room, laundries, and so on), butler's pantry near the dining room, silver and china rooms, and the housekeeper's office. Sometimes the hub of the servants' quarters, the servants' dining room, would also be located in this area, where one could pass the long hours of waiting between duties. If such a room was not provided, the kitchen would suffice. (But as an expert observer made clear, not having a dining room could lead to problems: "Many girls have told me that they have left housework because their men friends hated to sit in the kitchens and go out the back door.")[75] On the bedroom floor, a linen room, chambers for personal servants, and another room for butler and housekeeper would be placed. Sleeping and washing accommodations were handled the least effectively in the servants' wing. Often the unused areas of attics and basements became the crowded dormitories for lower-echelon domestics, subjecting them to poor ventilation and inadequate furnishings and sanitation.[76]

From both a formal and functional standpoint, service wings were treated simply and tended to follow one of three formulas: (1) the service ell or attached wing with service court, generally containing a kitchen, servants' dining hall, butler's pantry, and service porch; (2) the integral service area, tucked into a corner of the block plan, generally in formal or classical houses in which wings would compromise the architectural idea or symmetry; and (3) the basement service zone, facilitated by the use of dumbwaiters, speaking tubes, and elevators. Even in relatively large houses of pre–World War I, these wings were tightly planned and efficiently organized to minimize their architectural effect. After the war, country house owners often cut the live-in staffs to a minimum: a butler, two or three chambermaids, a chauffeur, and a small garden staff might suffice on smaller estates. Servant accommodations could then be trimmed commensurately.

116 Frederick Patterson house. Service court with servants' porch. (Samuel Gottscho, Avery Architectural Archives.)

117 "The House of Comforts," James Spear Co. Advertisement. (Author, from *T-Square Annual*, 1909.)

118 "American Standard Porcelain Enamel Baths and Plumbing Goods Are the Most Sanitary Made." Advertisement. (Author, from the *T-Square Annual*, 1909.)

Americans' penchant for labor-saving inventions was not lost on the country house, and the effect of new technologies on the servant problem was considerable. Gas cooking stoves were available to the wealthy by the middle of the nineteenth century and were in common use by its end; the first "modern" washing machine was patented in 1869; four makes of carpet sweepers were introduced as early as 1860. Appliances were electrified in the 1880s and 1890s, and in 1904 the invention of an electrical plug increased the usefulness and mobility of machines. Electric lights, irons, sewing machines, vacuum cleaners, and finally, in the 1920s, the refrigerator cut household chores and reduced the number of required servants. The individual yearly consumption of electricity in the nation averaged 378 kilowatt hours in 1924, increasing dramatically to 631 kilowatt hours a decade later. The number of refrigerators also increased significantly, from 65,000 in the mid-1920s to over seven million in 1934. As these advances were incorporated into the household, the kitchen and laundry areas of the country house became better organized, smaller, and more efficient.[77] A kitchen from around 1910 used a large, heavy, chimneyed gas or coal stove as its center and had little storage or work space on the walls; the modern kitchen of the 1920s, however, was full of cabinets and hygienic appliances, indicating just how profound were the technological changes in the country house.[78] The effects of these innovations were most apparent following World War 1, when necessity and invention neatly coincided. And the automobile came on the scene as a major mode of transportation and leisure, bringing with it the second most profound change in the country house—what J. B. Jackson has called "the domestication of the garage."[79]

During the first decade of the century most wealthy Americans owned automobiles—which were considered expensive consumer items and as such were used primarily as leisure diversions. Motoring was a popular upper-class sport. Like many of their friends, Edith Wharton and Henry James enjoyed the adventure of short vehicular excursions from Lenox, Massachusetts, and the slight

119 Frederick W. Vanderbilt estate, Hyde Park, New York. Garage and carriage house. (Richard Cheek.)

120 **Stan Hywet,** Akron, Ohio. Kitchen of the 1920s. (Collection of James Pahlau.)

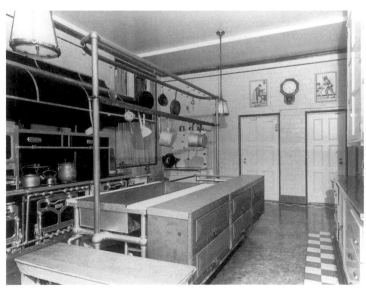

feeling of danger while riding in the horseless carriage caused considerable titillation. Horses were a good deal more reliable. Given the competition between the horse and the car, it is not surprising that both were given similar architectural accommodations. Since grooms and trainers lived in the stable block, so should the chauffeur reside with his steeds—the gleaming Packards, Pierce Arrows, and Daimler Benzes. Stable buildings and garages occupied the same service quadrant of many estates and often sported identical decoration. Aesthetically, it was crucial that they be kept away from of the main house.

But the era of the auto as second cousin to the horse was short-lived. Americans, far more than Europeans, began to look upon their cars as necessary mechanical conveniences, and eventually as extensions of themselves. When the Model T exploded on the American scene, it arrived not as a household guest but as a member of the family. Its presence was felt not only in middle-class dwellings but in the country house. For although wealthy Americans could afford to keep their motorcars out of sight, they did not want them out of mind. Country house plans of the immediate postwar years began to incorporate a garage wing into the service court. During the 1920s the garage became an integral part of the

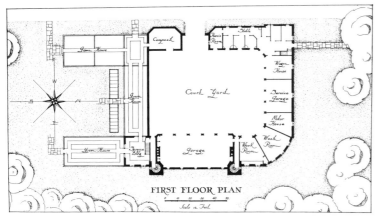

FIRST FLOOR PLAN

121 Harrie T. Lindeberg. **Glencraig** (1926), Middletown, Rhode Island. Garage and stable buildings. Ground floor plan. (Richard Cheek, from *Domestic Architecture of H. T. Lindeberg.*)

house, often taking up an entire wing of its own. This increasing domestication of the automobile was also occurring in middle-class suburban houses. It changed the layout of the house and the site plan, since both a formal forecourt for cars as well as a service court for vehicles had to be provided, along with adequate parking for guests. The service entrance was increasingly designed for convenient vehicular access.

Aside from the incorporation of the garage, the most important change in the country house of the 1920s and 1930s was its simplification and reduction in size. A good architect could squeeze more into the plan and with the help of new mechanical systems produce a more efficient domestic plant. The program changed very little but was often reduced to a minimum number of spaces. Aside from the expected eating, living, and service areas, additional special rooms would include, according to an *Architectural Forum* checklist of 1928, a morning room for the mistress and library for the master, along with rooms for entertainment, children, and diversions.[80] Such conveniences as the powder room, cloak room, and upstairs dressing room were common by this time. Bathrooms and kitchens were taking a more prominent role, though hardly the central one they occupy today.

In little more than half a century the program and service zones of the country house were transformed from a highly ordered, hierarchical organism based on Victorian values and social organization to a less formal, more flexible engine that depended not on human labor but on mechanical devices. American architects and other reformers who saw the house as a machine for living were eventually drawn to a new ideal—the modernist villa. Advocates of new social mores, family relationships, and patterns of daily life (such as Katharine Morrow Ford; see chapter 7) began to espouse the virtues of modernism, especially as practiced by European immigrant architects. Because formal behavior was no longer an expected social mode, critics argued, and because Americans were discovering the sun and leisurely living, the house should naturally reflect these trends by being opened up. The free plan was a perfect manifestation of this. A landmark article in *Fortune* magazine in 1935 made modernism an officially sanctioned artistic posture for the business elite, stressing the practicality of the new

"workable house" and pointing out that the machine was just then becoming domesticated (as it had not been a decade before). "Modernism in America will be full of gadgets," the writers insisted, "because modernism in America will be the gadget's child."[81] It is perfectly consistent with the eclectic architect's method that historical types too would absorb and accommodate changes in behavior, social structure, and mechanical inventions. An examination of the plan types chosen by architects and of the means of construction used in the country house shows how the modern country house lived up to its name despite its historical costume.

HOUSE AND ESTATE PLAN TYPES

The program of activities and service functions of the modern country house took form in a limited number of plan types, each selected to reflect a social and compositional mode. This is where type and style converged, as architects adapted traditional house forms to the requirements of modern life. Not only did the house plan change dramatically during the 1890s, but American architects and landscape designers began to redefine the house in relation to its site, introducing a range of new models for the estate and its gardens.

The four most significant types of house plan were: (1) the formal block or articulated block plan; (2) the block with dependencies plan; (3) the courtyard plan; and (4) the modern picturesque plan. Beaux-Arts-trained architects tended to favor the first three forms, while romantic architects preferred the freedom of the latter. Because these planning models had already proven themselves by tradition to be suitable to the program and architectural problems of the country house, it was simply a matter of transformation rather than of redefinition for the domestic architect to make them fit the requirements of twentieth-century life.

All four of these basic formal types are distinctive and significant in relation to aesthetic preferences and changing domestic ideals. None was popular during the Victorian era, when individuality and variety were contingent on the complexity of the plan, massing, and ornamental articulation. In stark contrast to both gentlemen's villas and Shingle Style summer cottages, the hallmark of the modern country house plan is its rational form and general regularity. *Simplification* was the word used most to describe the new attitude to house planning. Beaux-Arts-trained architects were taught to value concise arrangement of spaces, tight disposition of program elements, and simple proportions.

Not surprisingly, the outstanding examples of formal block planning are found in the work of classical masters such as Pope, Platt, and Delano. When using the compact, pavilion form, architects usually wished to set off the house as a strong mass in the landscape, emphasizing its idealized form standing in space. Circulation and room organization generally followed one of three formulas: (1) a simple center hall, with or without a stair in the hall itself; (2) a transverse hall or "double-pile" arrangement (two ranges of rooms bisected by a hall); and (3) compartmentalized, room to room circulation. The axial, hierarchical arrangement of

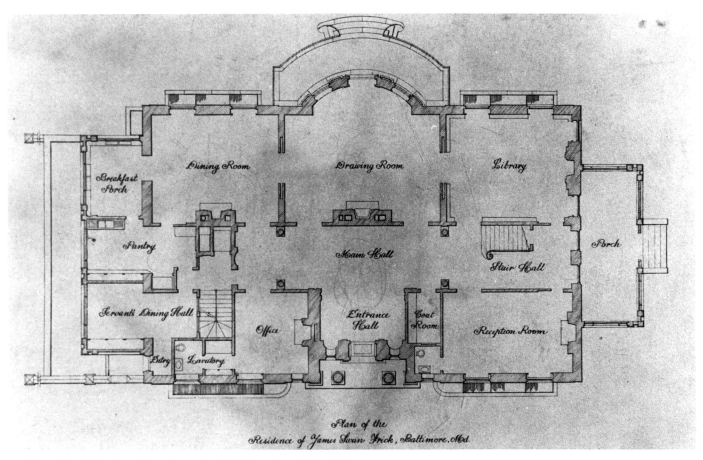

Plan of the
Residence of James Swan Frick, Baltimore, Md.

122a Formal block: John Russell Pope. James Swan Frick house (1914), Roland Park,
Maryland. (*Monograph of the Work of John Russell Pope.*)

122b Formal block: Charles A. Platt. **Gwynn** (1911), Cleveland, Ohio. (Avery
Architectural Archives.)

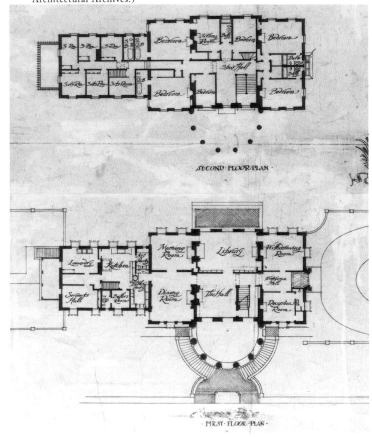

· SECOND · FLOOR · PLAN ·

· FIRST · FLOOR · PLAN ·

rooms in the block plan made for a sense of grace, pomp, and order often associated with eighteenth-century manners. A comparison of five examples, by Charles Platt, John Russell Pope, Neel Reid, Dwight James Baum, and Mott Schmidt, shows how flexible the block plan could be in the hands of a good planner, and how the later classical and Colonial Revival house accommodated its service functions. Classical architects were clearly challenged by the difficulty of achieving formal perfection in the block form while still incorporating the often complex needs of the modern country house program.

The block-with-dependencies type offered more flexibility yet provided the panache and elegance associated with classical houses. Problems caused by servant wings and garages could be solved by using one or both of the outbuildings for services. One can see the potential of this model in a comparison of examples by Pope, Delano and Aldrich, John Staub, and Mott Schmidt. It is useful to note the differences between early and late examples: Pope and Delano have little concern for a direct correspondence to eighteenth-century plans, whereas Schmidt and Staub use specific Early American models. In Pope's Sloan house the large right dependency is given over to a living room with three exposures. A more formal set of rooms — hall, dining, and drawing — are kept within the block. Delano uses a deep main block in his Burden house to accommodate all of the major formal rooms as well as

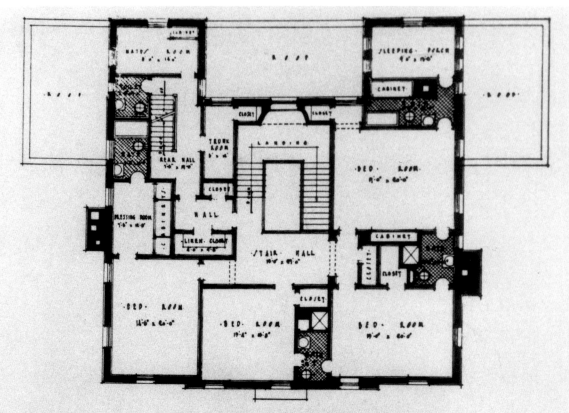

·SECOND· FLOOR· PLAN·

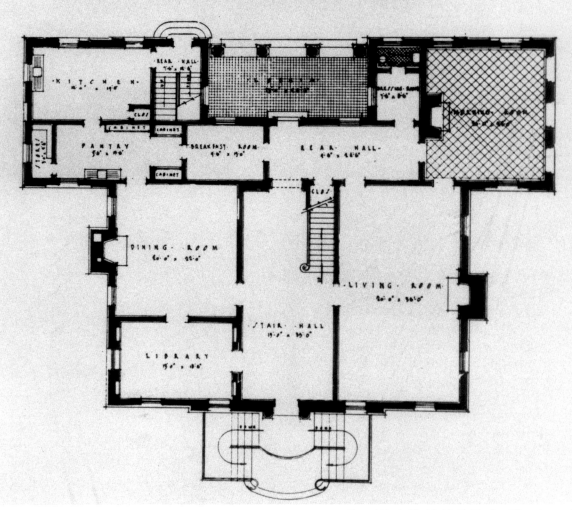

122c Formal block: Neel Reid. R. Vaughan Nixon house, Atlanta, Georgia. (*The Architecture of Neel Reid.*)

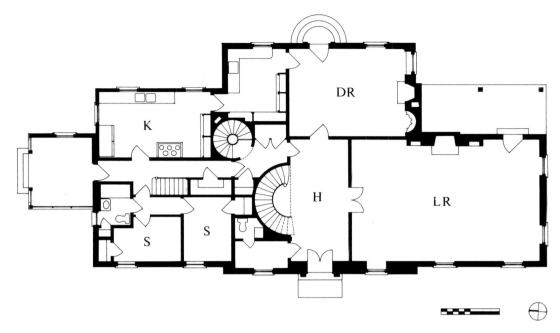

122d Formal block: Mott B. Schmidt. Jeremiah Clarke house (1933), Old
    Brookville, Long Island. (Author, after working drawing.)

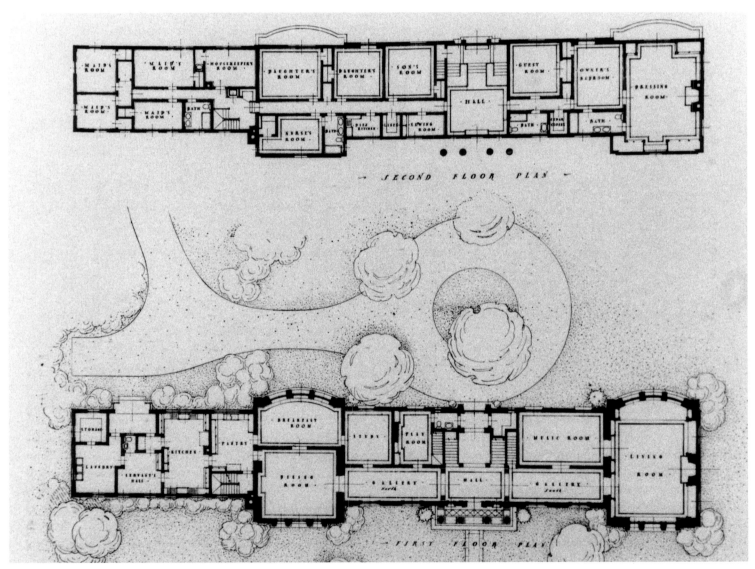

122e Formal block: Dwight James Baum. William Hoffman house (1920s),
    Riverdale-on-Hudson, New York. (*The Work of Dwight James Baum.*)

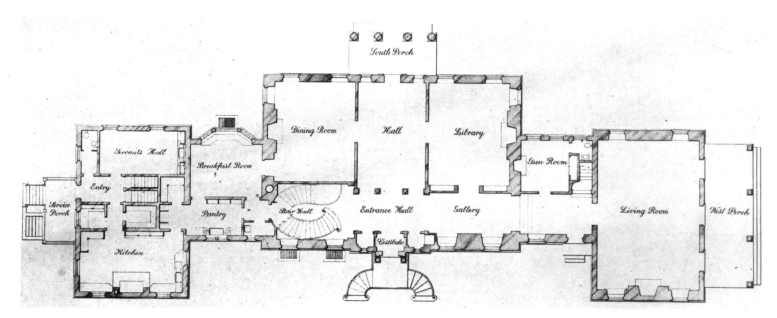

123a Block with dependencies: John Russell Pope. Thomas Frothingham house
(1919–21), Far Hills, New Jersey. (Richard Cheek, from *Monograph of the Work of
John Russell Pope*.)

123b Block with dependencies: Delano and Aldrich. **Woodside** (1916), James A.
Burden house, Syosset, New York. (*Architectural Review*, 1917.)

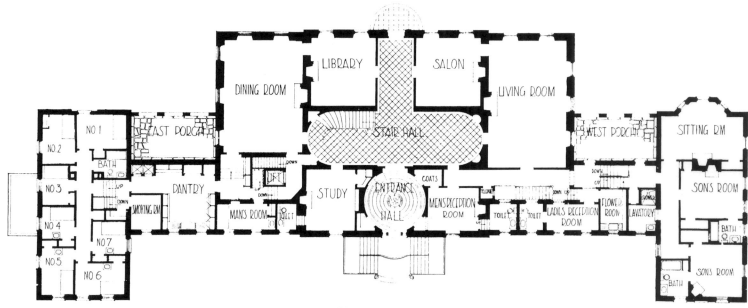

FIRST FLOOR PLAN

some key services, all organized around a cross-axial hall and stair
system. Mott Schmidt, an efficient and pragmatic planner, disregards the classical and Palladian precepts behind the model to
squeeze services into the left side of the main block. Too much
pragmatism and too many services nearly always spoiled a classical house plan.

The asymmetry of the picturesque plan permitted a far greater
range of solutions to the service room-formal room dichotomy.
Augusta Patterson, who coined the term *modern picturesque*, distinguished the style from Elizabethan or Tudor as well as from earlier
Shingle Style plans, citing its derivation from English models:

First and foremost it is conscientiously asymmetrical, the type which our
English cousins call the sun-trap house. There is usually one basic wing
from which a number of others radiate, each one figured out to get the
morning, the noon, and setting sun, or a glimpse across a certain
meadow, or over Peconic Bay. As a subsidiary aid to this principle of
planning, the house is usually erected on sloping ground with two or
three levels so that as one circumnavigates its walls every few yards bring
a different angle of vision, a new series of pictures. Just as in its prototype
cottage there is always a sense of the structure being low lying and well
tied down to the ground, one has a feeling of driving down into its forecourt rather than ascending to stately distances and spectacular views.
The Modern Picturesque type must be intimate or it fails.[82]

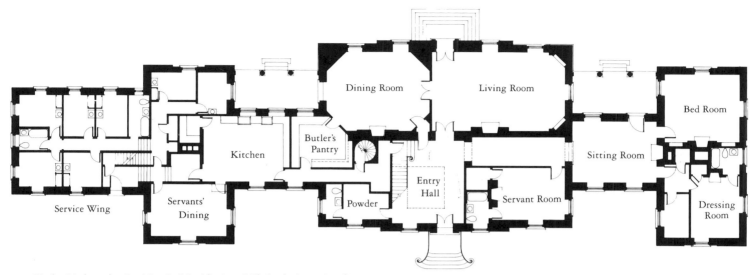

123c Block with dependencies: Mott B. Schmidt. Sergei Obolensky house (1926), Rhinebeck, New York. (Author, after working drawing.)

123d Block with dependencies: John F. Staub. **Bayou Bend** (1929), Houston, Texas. (Author, after working drawing, courtesy of the Museum of Fine Arts, Houston.)

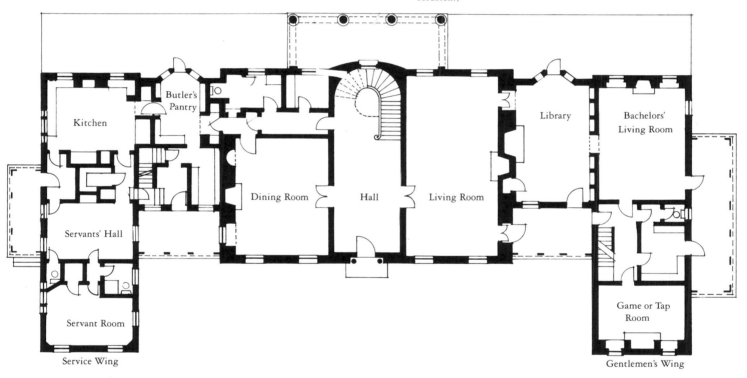

In examining this type further, three varieties of picturesque composition are evident: interlocking, additive, and holistic. The first, which really grew out of the Shingle Style and was exemplified in the best work of Eyre and the Philadelphians, applied the lessons of Queen Anne planning developed by Norman Shaw. In this method of composition, rooms and their volumes are interlocked with adjoining spaces to form a complex, puzzlelike order, given unity by an overriding figure like a U, L, or butterfly form. This can be seen in Wilson Eyre's house for H. Gates Lloyd, a spectacular composition of interlocking interior and exterior spaces, both on the ground and second floor. The living room alone, with its own living porch and loggia, has five distinct nooks or spaces. In the second variation, the additive or accretive plan, volumetric units are assembled as in more ancient houses, where each piece retains its constructional integrity and is attached to another directly, without overlap. Many Mediterranean houses were made this way to suggest their affinity with their sources, although they were generally not built as bearing-wall masonry structures. Some simple romantic English and French Provincial houses also consciously employed this planning method to reinforce their rustic character, as we see in Robert McGoodwin's house for Staunton Peck. The third method, favored by Lindeberg, called for the

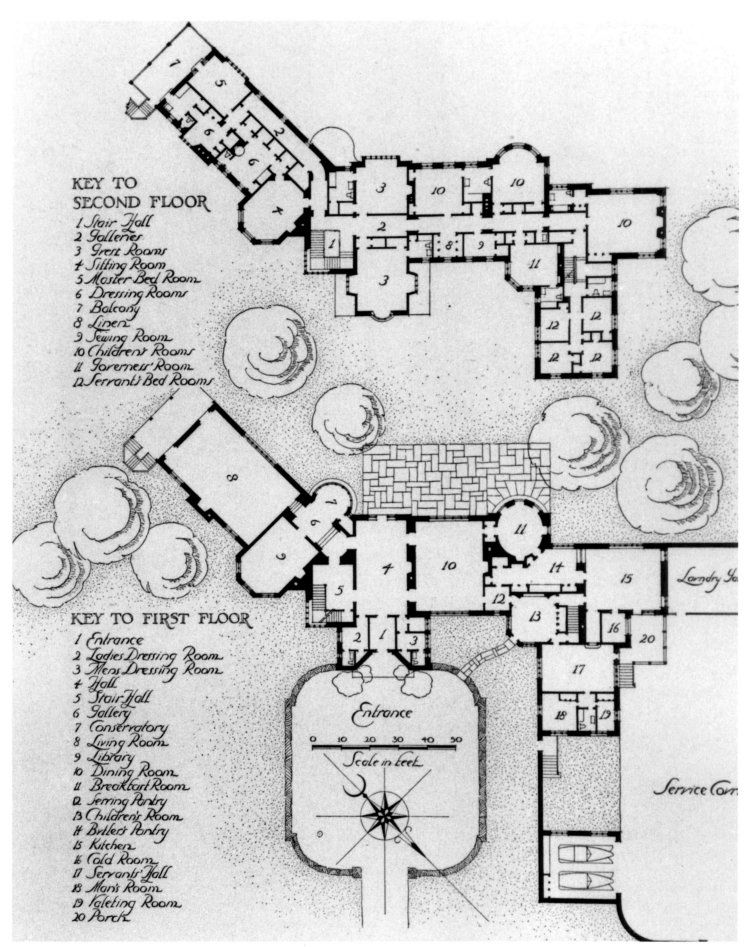

KEY TO
SECOND FLOOR

1 Stair Hall
2 Galleries
3 Guest Rooms
4 Sitting Room
5 Master Bed Room
6 Dressing Rooms
7 Balcony
8 Linen
9 Sewing Room
10 Children's Rooms
11 Governess' Room
12 Servant's Bed Rooms

KEY TO FIRST FLOOR

1 Entrance
2 Ladies Dressing Room
3 Men's Dressing Room
4 Hall
5 Stair Hall
6 Gallery
7 Conservatory
8 Living Room
9 Library
10 Dining Room
11 Breakfast Room
12 Serving Pantry
13 Children's Room
14 Butler's Pantry
15 Kitchen
16 Cold Room
17 Servants' Hall
18 Man's Room
19 Valeting Room
20 Porch

Entrance

0 10 20 30 40 50

Scale in Feet

Laundry Ya...

Service Corr...

124a Modern picturesque: Harrie T. Lindeberg. Frederick Patterson house (1925),
Dayton, Ohio. (*Domestic Architecture of H. T. Lindeberg.*)

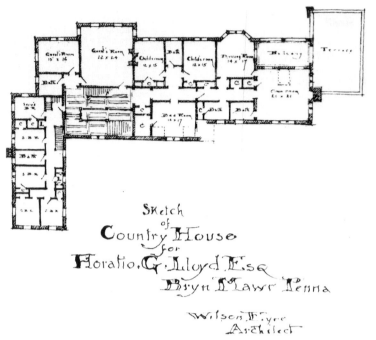

Sketch
of
Country House
for
Horatio. G. Lloyd Esq
Bryn Mawr Penna

Wilson Eyre
Architect

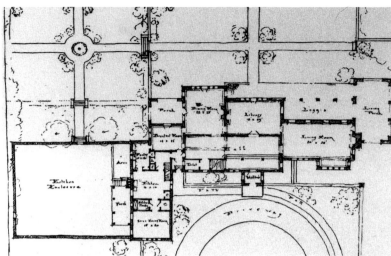

124b Modern picturesque: Wilson Eyre. Horatio G. Lloyd house (1911), Haverford, Pennsylvania. (*American Country Houses of To-Day,* 1912.)

124c Modern picturesque: Frank J. Forster. Guiseppe Cosulich house (1928), Fieldston, New York. (*Architectural Forum,* 1928.)

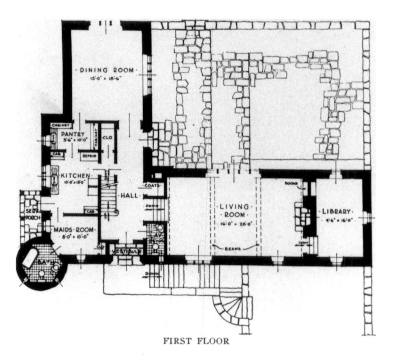

FIRST FLOOR

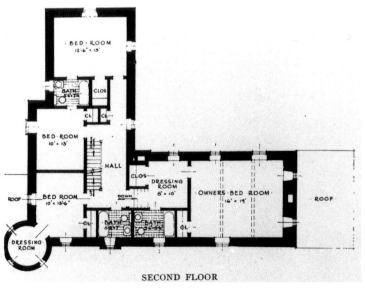

SECOND FLOOR

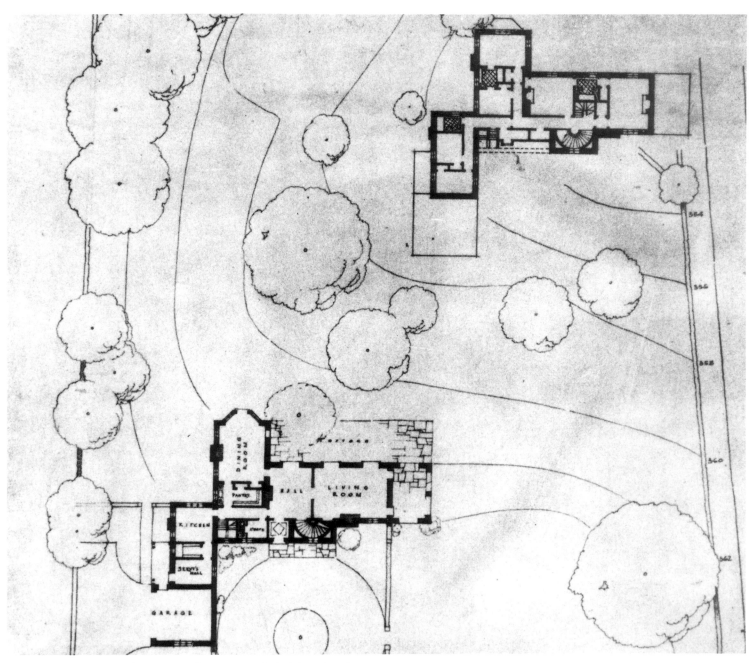

124d Modern picturesque: Robert R. McGoodwin. Staunton B. Peck house (1924), Chestnut Hill, Pennsylvania. (*The Work of Robert Rodes McGoodwin.*)

treatment of the entire house as a sculptural form, most often united by the massing of the roof and chimneys. The Patterson house by Lindeberg brilliantly demonstrates the way rooms could be used to form a complex massing envelope: the projecting entry, living, library, conservatory, and breakfast rooms each contribute a unique feature to the exterior of this extraordinary house. The plan, in effect, was subservient to an overarching concept in exterior articulation.

Modern picturesque houses were endlessly varied but nonetheless united in their qualities of responsiveness to site, irregularity, and variety of outline; as implied in the name, they possessed a multiplicity of "faces" from every point of view. Each appendage and wing added to the interest of the massing. Generally the pic-

turesque plan disposed the major elements of the house into two or three connecting wings, located to accommodate topography, orientation, and service access. Use of an impressive, medieval-like entry hall as a center is common to this type, reflecting its English roots. We see it in the Patterson, Lloyd, and Peck houses, though less as an organizing space than as a progression of rooms. Frank Forster's smaller house is more typical of the later picturesque plan: two cocked wings, a hingelike stair tower, an oriel, and a turret give an air of provincial rusticity to a simple diagram. The smaller picturesque houses of the 1920s, like the examples shown here by McGoodwin and Forster, deftly accommodate a garage and smaller service wing into the main body of the house, but the planning principles are the same.

The least indigenous plan type, the courtyard, can be considered an entirely new and modern formal model for the American

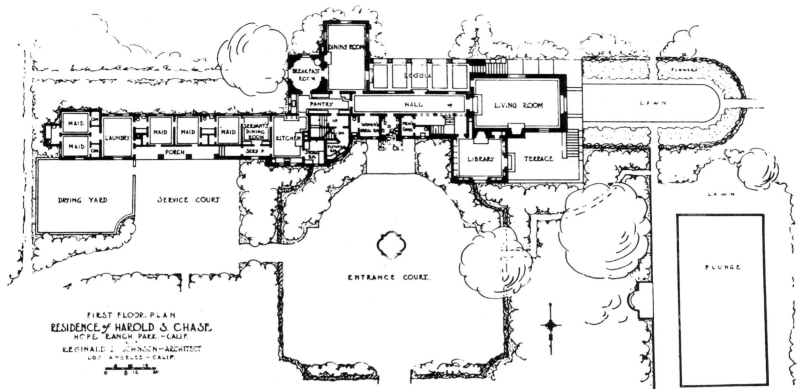

FIRST FLOOR PLAN
RESIDENCE of HAROLD S. CHASE
HOPE RANCH PARK - CALIF.
REGINALD D. JOHNSON - ARCHITECT
LOS ANGELES - CALIF.

124e Modern picturesque: Reginald Johnson. Harold Chase house (1924), Santa Barbara, California. (Richard Cheek, from Staats, *California Architecture in Santa Barbara*.)

house, if one considers only examples on the East Coast. Platt, Hunt, and Hastings all experimented with the disposition of rooms around either an exterior or interior spatial locus. For Hunt and Hastings the court was an organizational armature, the equivalent of the *cour d'honneur* (literally, court of honor, referring to a central courtyard) in a French plan. One sees this principle at work in such diverse works as The Breakers and Hastings' Arden House. This was the only plan type in which the major motif was a negative space. Furthermore, when the court was linked to a great garden sequence, as it often was in classical houses, this model provided a potent theme for the design of the house and grounds.

In mission- and adobe-inspired houses built in the West and Southwest, the courtyard took on a very different, if equally important, role: it became the primary circulation and living space, the American equivalent of the Hispanic patio. Regionalists of the 1920s experimented successfully with the patio concept in major country houses (see chapter 6). Our comparative plate shows examples by Atlee B. Ayres, Charles Platt, Bertram Goodhue, Morgan, Walls and Clements, and Howard Shaw. Three are Spanish types, one Italian, and one English, demonstrating the flexibility of the courtyard model. Howard Shaw used the courtyard in romantic ways, following English precedents; there is still something of the castle yard in it. Charles Platt's Villa Turicum in Lake Forest followed the Italian *cortile* (courtyard) precedent in organizing the entire house around a square courtyard, stepping down a hillside toward Lake Michigan to form a garden sequence. The three Spanish-influenced plans illustrate how the patio could serve as an organizing locus for the entire house.

A comparison of historical plan paradigms with the examples shown here reveals that the modern American house program exerted considerable force on the traditional models, often altering their character in a fundamental way. When the model could not incorporate social functions adequately, it was usually criticized and discarded, as happened with the French court of honor type. Porches and other peculiarly American features *were* accommodated. Most good architects saw a challenge in fitting modern programs and mechanical systems into historical types. In the best examples of this adaptation process, it is possible to see an entirely new type evolving out of the old: the modern center-hall Colonial plan is one example, the California Spanish patio type another, the English picturesque plan a third.

The fundamental unit in the traditional house plan is still the room, not amorphous space. Despite the openness of the American plan, there is never any question of the spatial distinction between one room and the next. Rooms were imbued with new uses and activities at the turn of the century. They served as vessels for decorative scenes. But the most important innovations in room use and planning occurred in the integration of interior and exterior spaces—there were as many outdoor rooms as indoor ones. A good plan began with the site, with circulation and logical disposition of key formal rooms, and worked to enhance the rituals and daily activities that went on in each area of the house and surroundings. A country house always had several faces to present, each set off by a different garden space. The first was the formal front entry, which might be approached obliquely for surprise effect (as in most English houses) or axially (as in many French châteaux). In the automobile age the entry usually had a circular drive or forecourt for guests arriving by car. If a house had a major prospect or view, the second face was usually the expansive garden front, designed to afford the major rooms access to these landscape pictures. Usually there was another, more intimate space relating to an enclosed garden—a kind of private counterpart to the previous countenance. Finally, there was the all-important service court or yard, usually screened from views. Significantly, most service wings also had their own porch—the domestics had as much right to the outdoors as the patrons. Architects often remarked on the importance of designing the service yard well in order for the house to function smoothly.[83] A good house and garden plan always made the most of the character of each face of the house, manipulating solar orientation, views, and relationships to natural features of the site.

This attention to the design of house and site together was one of the major innovations in the modern country house. The ideas that spawned the renaissance of garden planning were first put forth in Marianna Griswold van Rensselaer's *Art Out of Doors: Hints on Good Taste in Gardening,* published in 1893 as a book but first written for periodicals. Mrs. van Rensselaer advocated a new awareness of the artful, painterly qualities of garden design—"the art which creates beautiful compositions upon the surface of the ground"—in the best aesthetic tradition.[84] Her formula for artful success in garden design was really to find a middle ground between the outer landscape and the architectural qualities of the house, precisely what Charles Platt achieved. The major theme of Mrs. van Rensselaer's book and of the house and garden ideal was

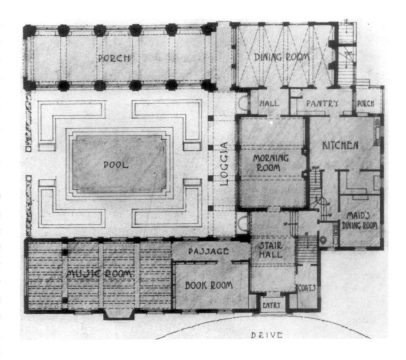

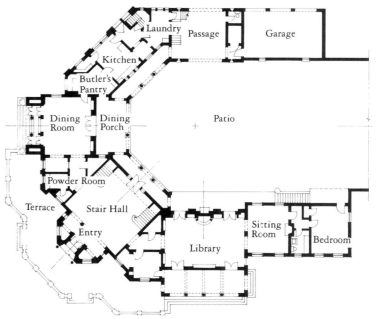

Courtyard plans:

125a Charles A. Platt. **Villa Turicum** (1911), Lake Forest, Illinois. (*Monograph of the Work of Charles A. Platt.*)

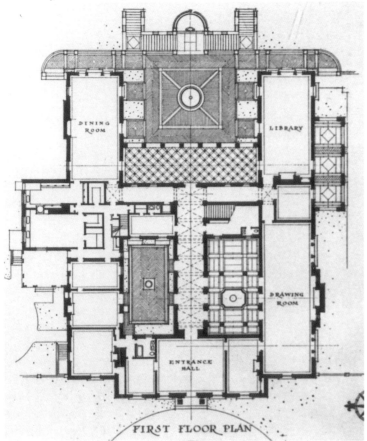

FIRST FLOOR PLAN

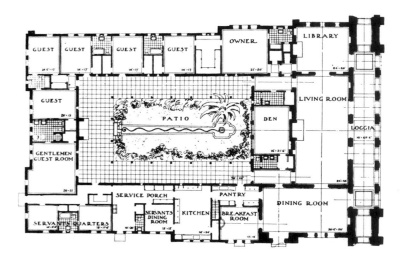

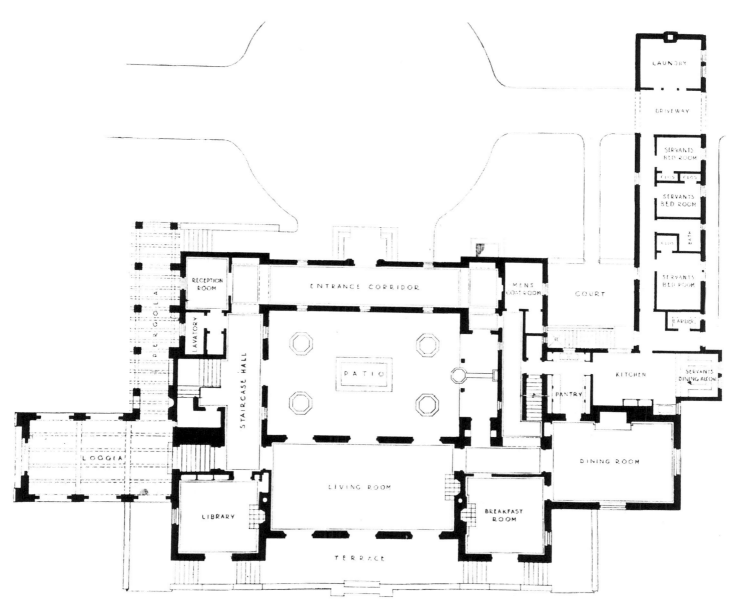

125e Bertram G. Goodhue. Henry Dater House (1913–18), Montecito, California.
(Richard Cheek, from *Bertram Grosvenor Goodhue*.)

opposite
125b *top* Howard Van Doren Shaw. Norman Scott house (1910), Lake Forest, Illinois.
(*Architectural Record,* 1913.)
125c *center* Atlee and Robert Ayres. McNay house (1929), San Antonio, Texas.
(Author, after working drawing, courtesy of the University of Texas at Austin.)
125d *bottom* Morgan Walls and Clements. Guasti house (c. 1928), Guasti, California.
(*Architectural Forum,* 1928.)

the total integration of house and garden, something that mattered little to Olmsted. In the new country place, the garden would become an extension of the rooms of the house, and the house an open and reciprocal vessel for nature's beauties. The garden was to be a place of use, cultivation, and pictorial prospect. It should have "rooms" relating to recreation, entertainment, relaxation, and service. The salubrious contact with soil, sun, and flora was tacitly accepted, and gardening was seen as an important if not essential hobby for the cultured woman. And everywhere the garden should suggest the sublime artifice of humankind in accord with nature, reminding the owners of their place and privilege. Each prospect from the house and toward it should represent a carefully made picture, displaying the artistry of the maker and culture of the patron.

The ways in which these ideas were assimilated into estate planning can be seen in a selection of plot plans from the 1890s to 1925. As Mrs. van Rensselaer made clear, the distinction between formal and picturesque garden design became blurred as designers included many traditions in their work. In relating the house to the site, there are several approaches: (1) the house and its architectural elements are completely dominant, as in Carrère and Hastings' plan for Indian Harbour (1896); (2) the house occupies its own precinct, including its garden rooms, and the rest of the site is organized in a balanced relationship to it, as in the plan of Rynwood (1927–29) by Roger Bullard and Ellen Shipman; (3) the

126a Site plan: Ellen Shipman and Roger Bullard. **Rynwood** (1927–29), Glen Head,
Long Island. (*Yearbook of the Architectural League of New York.*)

house is placed in a picturesque relationship to the natural site but
is otherwise allowed to float free of the surround, as at Pope's Bonniecrest (1914) on the Ocean Drive in Newport; (4) the house is
placed as a villa block within a tightly axial and compartmentalized overall landscape, as a foil—the favorite approach of Platt;
and (5) the house is clearly subservient to an overriding landscape
plan, reinforcing but not defining the site layout, as at Mellor,
Meigs and Howe's Newbold farmstead (1919). As Augusta Patterson said, "There are . . . two ways of looking at gardens, from the
house outward or from surrounding nature inward—as an extension of the house architecturally into the landscape, or as a breaking of the landscape in waves of more and more conscious cultivation toward the house. The garden is, of course, the liaison
between the house and nature; which of these two elements should
be the more important constitutes the difference in the two
schools of garden design [the Italian and the English]."[85]

All of these plans emphasize domesticating the area around the
house—either for leisure pursuits, garden cultivation, agriculture, or, in the case of walled gardens, as extensions of the rooms.
The garden room became a necessary element in the new ensemble, most often opening out from one or more of the formal rooms
in the house. Both Platt and Carrère and Hastings, two of the
most influential site planners, made use of the garden room in
their major commissions. Walled or box-enclosed spaces were
often attached to the living room, drawing room, morning room,
dining room, or a conservatory-solarium. The enclosed or open
porches that graced nearly all American country houses served as
intermediary spaces between these outdoor architectural pieces
and the rest of the house. Pergolas, garden structures, terraces,
and a variety of follies extended the architecture of the house outward and further defined the domesticated landscape. That particularly American concern for the "health, comfort, and amelioration of life" was expressed in commodious rooms and ample
garden spaces and affirmed by "those influences which make the
human spirit large and beautiful."

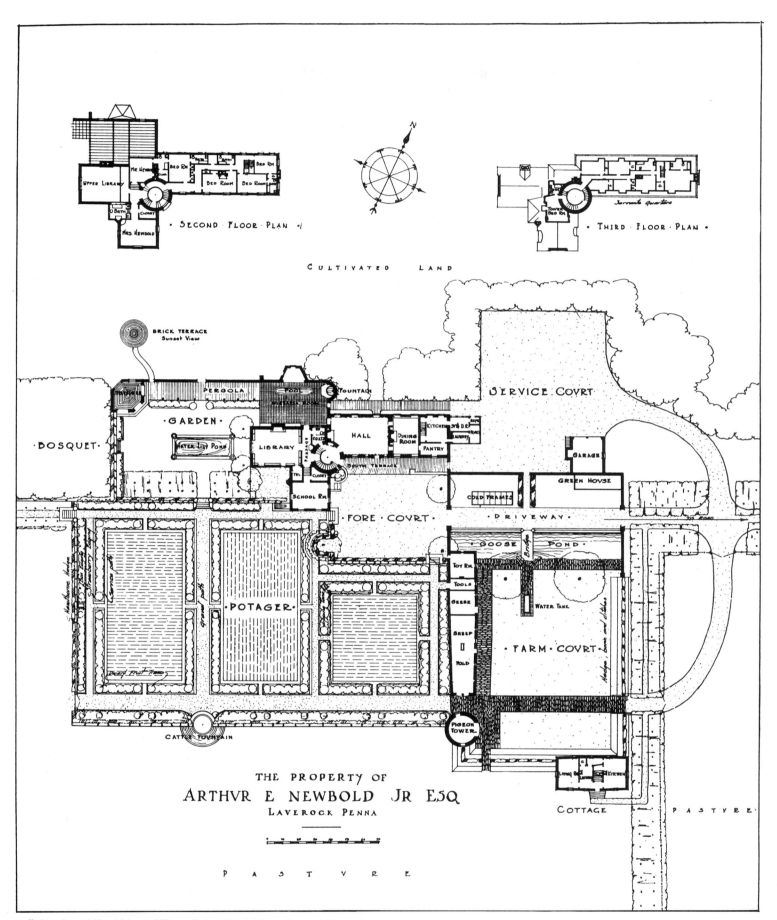

· THIRD · FLOOR · PLAN ·

CULTIVATED LAND

BRICK TERRACE
Sunset View

PERGOLA

SERVICE · COVRT

GARDEN ·

BOSQUET ·

POOL

FOUNTAIN

WATER LILY POND

LIBRARY

HALL

DINING ROOM

KITCHEN

PANTRY

GARAGE

GREEN HOVSE

SCHOOL RM

COLD FRAMES

FORE · COVRT

DRIVEWAY ·

GOOSE POND

TOY RM

TOOLS

GEESE

SHEEP

FOLD

WATER TANK

FARM · COVRT

POTAGER

CATTLE FOUNTAIN

PIGEON TOWER

THE PROPERTY OF
ARTHVR E NEWBOLD JR ESQ
LAVEROCK PENNA

COTTAGE

PASTVRE

PASTVRE

126b Site plan: Mellor, Meigs and Howe. Arthur Newbold farm (b. 1919), Laverock,
Pennsylvania. (*Monograph of the Work of Mellor, Meigs and Howe.*)

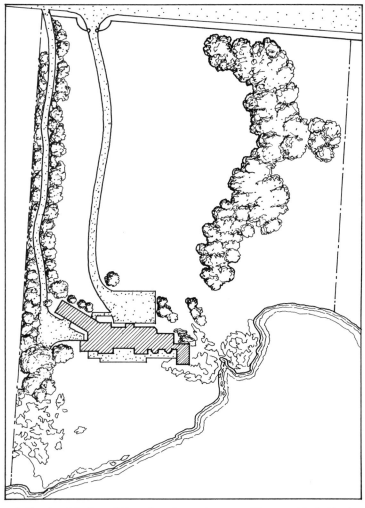

126c Site plan: John Russell Pope. **Bonniecrest** (1912–14), Newport, Rhode Island. (Author, after Samuel Howe.)

CONSTRUCTING THE COUNTRY HOUSE:
MODERN TECHNOLOGY FOR ANTIQUE EFFECT

All eclectic country houses were technologically modern buildings. With the exception of some eccentrically romantic clients and architects who pursued anachronistic building techniques exclusively, most large houses built in this era were made with the most technically sophisticated materials, mechanical systems, and construction possible. This was a time when construction practices and building technics in the United States were being radically altered by such new materials as reinforced concrete and modern structural steel, as well as by dozens of products and finishes designed to offer miracle durability, ease of application, and minimum expense. This was also a time of extraordinary craftsmanship and ingenuity in the building trades, a period of fine ornamental stonework, metalwork, brick masonry, woodwork, and plasterwork. Machines made the manufacture of ornamental details in such materials as terra cotta a relatively cheap alternative to labor-intensive practices, to the benefit of all buildings. While some commentators looked askance at the use of new

materials to simulate old, most agreed that modern construction for antique effect was the convention of the day. Eclecticism was a condition not only of society but of architectural production.

Building a fireproof, half-timbered house, a maintenance-free stucco one, or an adobe of earthquake-proof reinforced concrete was seen as a necessary advance made possible by new technologies. The paradox of antiquarianism served by the machine created a lingering debate among architects, but few designers and clients could completely resist the advantages offered by new materials and methods of construction—resistance to dreaded fires being the most powerful incentive to build with modern methods. During the early twentieth century the American building industry experimented with a variety of techniques and materials, targeted mostly at industrial and commercial building but applicable to house construction as well. Two of the most promising fireproof systems, it was thought, were reinforced concrete and hollow tile, made of terra cotta. Both offered clear advantages over wood, long the dominant building material for American houses, and were less expensive than brick or stone.

The use of new masonry products in residential construction during the early twentieth century has often been associated with the concrete block experiments of Frank Lloyd Wright, yet this technology was far more widespread. Hollow terra cotta tile, extruded from clay and baked to form units of three to twelve inches in modular sizes, emerged in the late nineteenth century as a product to fireproof steel construction. Inventors saw the potential for structural use of these masonry units, especially in flooring systems made by bonding the serrated tiles together with common mortar, and expanded their use in wall construction to produce whole systems. The leading manufacturer of these tiles, NATCO, was located in Perth Amboy, New Jersey. Advocates of tile construction pointed out that it offered enormous flexibility, both for structure and infill, and was cost effective at around eighteen to twenty cents a cubic foot. It could be covered easily with stucco or even faced with brick and stone and was also made in a textured facing style. Its disadvantage, and eventual downfall, was its resistance to water and to freeze-thaw cycles. Yet from 1900 to 1930 hollow tile remained a popular construction system for houses. Most of the leading residential architects experimented with it as a building material. William Adams Delano used it in his own house in Muttontown as well as in such major commissions as the Whitney studio and the Bronson Winthrop house; all were covered with stucco and concealed their construction method with ornamental articulation. The Thomas Kerr house in White Plains, by Albro and Lindeberg, and the award-winning Murray F. Guggenheim estate in New Jersey, by Carrère and Hastings, were built of hollow tile. Howard Van Doren Shaw also found uses for this material in his residential work.[86] Because hollow tile was most often faced with stucco or other masonry materials, it is difficult to assess whether a house is constructed of it.

It has also been common for historians to associate the use of reinforced concrete with modernist or protomodernist buildings of the first quarter century without recognizing that the material was used widely for traditional residential construction as well.

127 Country house construction: *top,* concrete—Henry E. Huntington house (1906), San Marino, California. (Architectural Drawing Collection, University Art Museum, Santa Barbara, California.); *bottom,* masonry block—Caspar Morris house (1916), Haverford, Pennsylvania. (Athenaeum of Philadelphia.)

Oswald C. Herring, in *Concrete and Stucco Houses* (1912), argued that "the greatest artistic success with the use of [concrete and stucco] has been achieved so far in country houses, the gardens and outbuildings."[87] It is fair to say that concrete construction was considered the most exciting and promising advance in residential building at the turn of the century. Many large houses in a variety of eclectic styles were built using concrete for structure, walls, and even cast decorative elements. The inexpensive production of Portland Cement, patented in the United States as early as 1871, and the introduction of new labor, design, and production methods made concrete an economical material even for small-scale buildings. Several major reinforcing systems were introduced between 1900 and 1910 for use in framing large buildings.[88] The use of stucco, cast stone (a fine concrete using ground stone as aggregate), and reinforced concrete (structural poured concrete strengthened with steel bars to resist tension) became ubiquitous in residential construction after the turn of the century.

Charles Platt's Gwinn (1907), the classical villa on the shores of Lake Erie in Cleveland, is constructed largely of poured, reinforced concrete and cast stone. Julia Morgan's San Simeon, begun in 1919, consists of an entirely reinforced concrete structural system of floor slabs, walls, and trusses. It is astounding that the vast building complex was built without the aid of mechanized devices for mixing, moving, and pouring the concrete.[89] Villa Vizcaya was fabricated largely of concrete, with trim executed in various stones, especially the local coral and fossil limestone. Yet scale made little difference in deciding whether to use concrete. Howard Shaw's small Bartlett house in Lake Geneva used concrete extensively for walls, which were then covered with stucco. Irving Gill's celebrated Dodge house in Los Angeles employed his tilt-up system of construction. Surely the most unusual and romantic concrete country house was Henry Chapman Mercer's Fonthill (1908–10), designed for himself near Doylestown, Pennsylvania, and built using only earthwork forms. The organic and primitive quality of the construction is evident in the plan—few rooms are rectilinear. Mercer's Arts and Crafts philosophy, so well manifested in his Moravian Tile works near the house, carried over into the way he used this most modern of building materials. Like a good follower of William Morris, he left the concrete surface exposed to show the way it was constructed.[90]

128a "Cabot's Quilts" insulation from Samuel Cabot, Boston, 1901–02.

128a-d Advertisements from *T-Square Annual.* Antique products and modern technology for the country house. (Author.)

The competition between these emerging building methods and materials and existing technologies was fierce during the first thirty years of the century. The wood industry fought back with its own advertising, academic, and propaganda materials and eventually won out. A number of very large country houses were built of structural steel clad in masonry, as for example the Georgian house of James A. Burden by Delano and Aldrich.[91] There was probably more variety in the building trades during this period than at any other time in U.S. history. Not only did the plethora of stylistic idioms demand products such as windows, millwork, tiles for floors and roofs, and various finishes that could replicate those of the historical model, but manufacturers actively developed new products to solve functional and technical requirements of the country house.

Two ready examples of technology conforming to eclecticism are found in the introduction to residential building of metal casement windows and asbestos roofing shingles. (Products using asbestos were considered miraculous technical advances and were extremely popular with the building industry.) Both of the these advances offered economy and durability, which made them alternatives to wood windows or roof slates. The manufacturers nevertheless designed their products to approximate closely the look of the older items so as to ensure their use in traditional as well as modern construction. In many product lines one finds the manufacturer producing variants in each popular residential style, from lighting fixtures and hardware to such unlikely things as stucco. Of course, not all architects ignored the intrinsic features of a new material, and many worked with manufacturers to design products that made the most of the advantages offered by new technologies. The range of choice in building materials—an eclecticism in its own right—offered the designer an exciting dilemma: whether to choose a new material or a time-tested and antique one.

For the Ruskinian advocate of handicrafts and old-time methods, the choice was an obvious moral imperative. Restora-

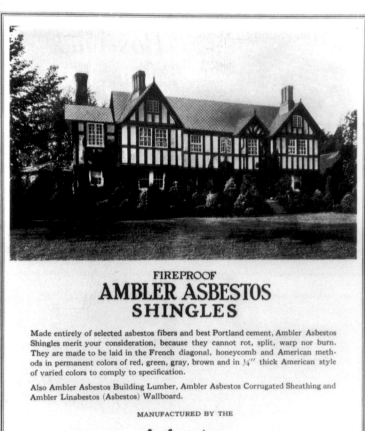

128b Ambler asbestos shingles for the half-timber house, 1909.

tionists and antiquarians were aided by the fact that craftsmen from both Europe and the United States were readily available to execute fine wrought iron work, plasterwork, wood carving, stone dressing and carving, stained glass—nearly any technique desired. Sometimes the authentic look of age could only be achieved by using old materials and elements, and dealers in architectural salvage and antiques were happy to oblige. Architects often went to Europe on buying trips to procure necessary elements—Addison Mizener went once a year to Spain and Italy; Frank Forster scoured the countryside of France; William Randolph Hearst plundered all of Europe. Mizener, John Byers, and Henry Mercer researched traditional tile-making techniques, built kilns and factories, and ended up marketing the antique clay products they initially used for their own works.

Half-timbering with aged oak was used on many Tudor houses, two of the most elaborate being Bonniecrest and Stan Hywet, in which the traditional plastering, pegging, and construction methods were employed to the letter. Pope's office even scoured the East Coast for old bricks to be used at Bonniecrest, to achieve the instant patina of age.[92] Nevertheless, the choices in brick— modern stamped or wire-cut, or antique handmade—were enormous.[93] Masons capable of laying bricks in sophisticated corbeled patterns with difficult jointing and striking techniques could be found at a price. One can find not only good replicas of eighteenth-century colonial brickwork during the 1920s and 1930s but also excellent approximations of Jacobean masonry, especially in chimneys, based on drawings in scholarly pattern books.[94] Hand-planed mortise and tenon millwork was not uncommon in Colonial Revival buildings. Adobe construction techniques, using a battered wall and uneven mud finish, which were traditionally the province of women laborers, were employed by John Gaw Meem on some buildings in Santa Fe. The craftswomen were still practicing their art during the 1920s. John Byers, who spoke fluent Spanish, learned the traditional adobe-making techniques of the Mexicans by interviewing craftsmen and writing oral histories of the process, like a folklorist. Thus, the range of craftsmanship corresponded to the demand for high-quality, antiquarian work. And the eclectic architect made it his business to understand the methods he was employing—involvement with handicraft was a philosophical as well as practical issue.

New materials gave the architect even more choices. Building insulation made of asbestos and synthetic fibers, asphalt shingles for roofs, new glazing and facing methods in the manufacture of clay products such as brick and terra cotta, linoleum and synthetic tiles for floors, new paint compounds, methods for treating wood against water and pests, and improvements in the fabrication of metalwork were only some of the innovations that came into use

128c "Colonial" sconces from Lawrence Gas Fixture, 1909.

during the early twentieth century. Manufacturers touted the functional characteristics of their products but were always careful to also cite their sentimental, style-related values as well, as a perusal of trade catalogues and advertisements in periodicals and club yearbooks makes clear.

How did architect and client deal with the variety and complexity of trades, materials, and technologies in the country house? Some architects, such as Mizener, managed the construction process themselves, but more often the client entrusted the job to a general contractor. Large construction businesses sprang up in the late nineteenth century as the demand for monumental and high-rise commercial buildings increased. During the era of the stately home, some large houses were built by big commercial companies, such as Norcross Brothers, the favorite builder of both H. H. Richardson and McKim, Mead and White. Specialty residential builders, such as the Elliot C. Brown Company of New York, the E. W. Howell Company of Babylon, Long Island, and the R. C. Ballinger Company of Philadelphia, met the need for quality construction for country house clients.[95] A third alternative, favored by clients with an interest in building, was to hire a trusted foreman or local builder and to manage the process oneself. Alfred Atmore Pope circumvented McKim, Mead and White by doing this in the construction of the Hill-Stead in 1899, using his daughter Theodate as supervisor. Alfred I. Du Pont had no faith in the contractors proposed by Carrère and Hastings and instead hired a local Brandywine Valley builder to handle Nemours, trusting the man so implicitly as to require no contract or invoices.

It took an enormous amount of careful coordination and planning to manage the typical multiyear process of building a house from excavations to the final finishing and painting. And it took a considerable amount of labor, especially before the advent of extensive mechanization using cranes and earth movers. A good case in point is the construction of Frederick Vanderbilt's house in Hyde Park (see chapter 4). John B. Clermont, superintendent of building for Norcross Brothers, the Worcester, Massachusetts, firm who did the work, provided an oral history of the building process to the National Parks Service in 1954. Norcross handled the work for a typical 3 percent fee over and above all labor and materials, amounting to around $20,000 for the house and guest house. Clermont was on the job from August 4, 1895, when work was begun on the Pavilion and Old Langdon Mansion, to March 27, 1899, when virtually all work was complete on the new mansion. As superintendent, he managed all of the work crews, suppliers, and subcontractors during the four-year process. As in any modern construction, contracts were let based on proposals solicited from subcontractors for various phases of the work, with some labor and materials handled directly by the Norcross firm and its crews.[96]

Because the only limits on craftsmanship and material quality were cost and availability of labor, the most elaborate and labor-intensive houses were constructed largely before the curtailing of the great fortunes and the changes in labor and material economy brought on by the income tax (1913), antitrust laws, and unions.

128d Face brick in Jacobean molds from Cox, Janeway and Co., 1901–02.

Building costs fluctuated during the 1890s and 1900s but rose continuously through the postwar years into the 1920s, nearly doubling between 1914 and 1920 alone. In 1908 a leading book on residential architecture indicated that a small frame house could be had for under $1,000, a good-sized brick house in a large city for $6,000 to $15,000, and a grand stone house for $200,000 to $400,000.[97] Square foot costs in the years around World War I were, according to one source, about $2 to $5 for a simple house of frame construction. The minimum price for "a two-story frame Colonial house of good quality" was $5,000.[98] *Architectural Forum*'s country house number of 1928 confirms that costs for residential construction had risen appreciably, to around $5 to $10 per square foot and up. The average suburban country houses presented in its survey cost between $35,000 and $75,000.[99] New technologies during the 1920s made certain effects achievable at a lower cost, but architects were inevitably forced to deal with a simplification in materials and craftsmanship brought on by economic factors as well as by taste.

It is ironic that this sophisticated, modern construction practice should have served the effect of historical authenticity, age, romantic rusticity, old-time craftsmanship, and sentimental virtue. Architects of the progressive schools railed against such "dishonest" representation in building construction, yet clients and eclectic architects were content to have the best of both worlds. Innovative and clever use of new materials was not limited to more overtly avant-garde and experimental architects. Often new details for achieving a particular aesthetic effect became canonical, living on to become part of the building vernacular. Yet it is unfortunate that many fine millwork, window, roofing, flashing, and masonry details, invented, tested, and proven in residential construction by eclectic architects, were jettisoned when modernism transformed the building industry after World War II. The modern American country house solved its functional problems with an efficiency that often belied the sentimental values proudly displayed on its surface.

The dichotomy between style and type in the American house is a persistent and crucial factor in residential design in the early twentieth century, not only in country houses but in suburban and pattern-book dwellings. Because the adaptation process was driven by different attitudes among architects and clients, some buildings achieved only a superficial dressing up, using ornament and stylistic trappings, while others were true transformations of a typological model. Most critics and designers agreed, however, that the best houses, those that truly answered the needs of modern American families and were derived from a thorough understanding of historical types, did produce new variations in the canon of traditional house models. These variations were distinctly American in several respects: first, they were based on a program and social framework that had evolved during the late nineteenth century out of peculiarly American domestic patterns; second, plans were developed according to the American desire for informality, outdoor living, hygiene, efficiency, and comfort; third, American architects had developed their own theories of eclectic transformation out of academic classical and picturesque composition; and fourth, new materials, mechanical contrivances, construction methods, and structural systems had fundamentally altered the building of houses in the modern era.

Stately Homes
The Aristocratic Model of Domestic Culture

4

The assimilation of plutocracy into aristocracy has been the vital problem of Society in America since its beginnings, but particularly since the rise of the great industrial fortunes. It has been imperative somehow to translate richesse permet *into* noblesse oblige.

—DIXON WECTER

The first model for the new American country house was fittingly called the stately home by many commentators in the late 1890s.[1] It was patently aristocratic, a building type derived from European dynasties. Stateliness connoted the lofty and regal qualities associated with homes of the privileged class. Even in a reputedly classless society, expression of dominion through wealth was essential. The capitalist entrepreneurs who had built a successful manufacturing, industrial, and service economy felt the necessity of creating not only cultural institutions in their images but also a new domestic institution to signal their prominence in the nation and the world. Since the palace, country house, and landed life were regarded as the highest symbols of aristocratic society, it was perhaps inevitable that America's plutocracy would seek to emulate these institutions.

Emulation of the aristocracy manifested itself in some obvious ways—if America could not have Debret's and the peerage, it did have the Social Register. One of the most popular subjects for satire at the turn of the century was the seasonal journey of wealthy American families to Europe, with marriageable daughters in tow, in search of titled (often poor) nobility. In addition, many society women imitated the dress and manners of favorite queens, countesses, and other historical figures, not only at formal occasions but in all aspects of their daily lives. But more important than dress were the art and decorative objects collected during trips to England and the Continent. The conspicuous presence of coveted artworks in the stately home attested to one's wealth. Collecting—with or without proper connoisseurship—was the most ubiquitous aristocratic affectation taken up by the capitalist moguls.

As early as the late 1860s, the retail magnate A. T. Stewart had surrounded himself with the opulent treasures of European artistic culture in his New York mansion. He seemed to collect art as zealously as he purchased merchandise for his famous department store in the Ladies Mile.[2] The ideal of the city house as an "airy pleasure hall" designed "for the display of festal assemblage" (as Edith Wharton put it)[3] was an early invention of the Gilded Age, which spread to country houses almost as a matter of course. Even in the 1890s the motivation behind this culture of display was much discussed. As Wharton's friend Paul Bourget, the French novelist, then maintained, Americans seemed to feel the need to be surrounded by things that had an aura of stability and time, while they scrambled for a dollar and climbed the social ladder.

129 Frederick W. Vanderbilt house, Hyde Park, New York. Den or library. (Richard Cheek.)

130 Charles Dana Gibson. "Studies in Expression." *Life,* May 5, 1904. The formal dinner in city or country. (Cabinet of American Illustration, Library of Congress.)

Russell Lynes later argued in *The Tastemakers* that the transience and fluidity of American society caused the wealthy to reach for symbols of high culture and to emulate indiscriminately the habits and customs of European dynasties and merchant princes.[4] And of course Thorstein Veblen pounced on these habits in his *Theory of the Leisure Class.* Building a palatial home decorated with objects of European aristocratic culture established a sense of class superiority and created a historical aura for the self-made capitalist. It solidified his place in the shifting social structure of late-nineteenth-century America, a country searching for order.

Stately homes of that period were programmed for formal social codes and daily routines that were partially inherited from early "genteel" behavior and partially borrowed from European manners. The ancien régime of American society continued to resent the European aristocracy, but in the late nineteenth century a newly traveled and cultured group began to warm toward continental manners. This produced an odd hybrid of social conventions. Charles Dana Gibson, the famous magazine illustrator, satirized these patterns of behavior in a number of his best cartoons. Grand dinners followed by cigars and bridge, oppressively large and opulent rooms, and various subtleties of sexual behavior were among the subjects wonderfully captured in his unique drawings. Life in the stately home, with its theatrical and ritualistic overtones, begged for social commentary.

Edith Wharton was not the only writer to take aim at her upper class milieu (Henry James also liked the subject), but she was certainly the most observant of manners per se. She set many of her novels and stories against the backdrop of rigid social mores and cast her major characters in opposition to them. Her sophisticated appreciation for architecture, gardens, and interior design is no coincidence, for she recognized that domestic architecture painted a potent and exacting picture of social customs, fantasies, and self-image.[5] The accuracy of Wharton's depiction of fin de siècle manners is apparent in a comparison of one of her greatest characters, Lily Bart, with a woman of almost equal romantic willfulness,

Florence Adele Sloane (1873–1960). From the diaries Miss Sloane kept during her courtships in the 1890s and the strikingly parallel events in Wharton's *The House of Mirth,* one can appreciate the ballet of social liaisons, house parties, travel, formal events, and fantasies for which the stately home was the mise-en-scène.

If Lily Bart was ultimately destroyed by the society trappings she so desperately coveted, Sloane achieved success on the terms set by her peers, marrying James A. Burden, Jr., scion of the Troy iron dynasty, in 1895. Her recollections of her romantic adventures and whirlwind social life are remarkable not only for who she was and whom she knew, but for the intensity with which she undertook her ingenue role. Adele Sloane was the daughter of the New York merchant William Douglas Sloane and Emily Vanderbilt Sloane (White)—whose mother was Frederick Vanderbilt's sister. She thus moved in the highest social circles of her time, frequenting the country houses of her Vanderbilt relatives, such as Biltmore and the Elliot F. Shepard house in Scarborough on the Hudson, and savoring life at Elm Court, her family's enormous cottage in Lenox.[6] She enjoyed the company of her uncle George Vanderbilt and was present during the construction of Biltmore in 1893, when she briefly fell in love with Gifford Pinchot, only one of the illustrious beaux in her life.[7] She was also courted by Harry Payne Whitney, who eventually married her cousin, Gertrude Vanderbilt, but remained a lifelong friend.

For both Lily and Adele, specific locales elicited vivid emotional responses, perhaps because their families traveled so much. The settings presented in both the novel and the diary are familiar ones. For Lily, the Bry's fancy dress ball in New York, the voyage of the yacht *Sabrina* to Europe, Monte Carlo's casinos, Newport, Bar Harbor, and especially Mrs. Trevor's country house on the Hudson, Bellomont (a play on The Mount), all had distinctly different meanings and flavors.[8] In her diary Sloane recorded stays at Versailles, various country houses, the Adirondacks, and finally her own estate, Woodside, in Syosset, Long Island (which would eventually have a house designed by Delano). Wharton used the country as Shakespeare did in *Midsummer Night's Dream,* as a liberating setting for romance and discovery of emotional truths. Adele Sloane felt the same about Elm Court, writing in June 1893: "This

131 Charles Dana Gibson. "Mrs. Julie Poole's Housewarming." *Life,* January 2, 1902. (Cabinet of American Illustration, Library of Congress.)

132 Peabody and Stearns. **Elm Court** (1886–1900), William Douglas Sloane house, Lenox, Massachusetts. The country home of Adele Sloane during her girlhood. (Desmond and Croly, *Stately Homes in America*.)

afternoon I have been down alone in our little house in the woods [Cozy Cot, the playhouse]. It was so quiet there and so perfect. I felt almost as if I were hundreds of miles away from anyone. There was not a sound excepting the low, moaning sigh which the wind makes through the pines. The birds did not sing, for the sky was heavy with clouds, and every now and then a far away rumble of thunder was heard. . . . I am quite happy in the country again; it is very beautiful now."9 Both women seemed to feel that the strictures of society were loosened during sojourns in the country, especially amid the gardens and natural areas of the estates. Lily Bart experienced her most important catharsis with Mr. Selden on just such a day as Adele Sloane described, away from the rest of the house party, where she had been stifled by bridge games and formal dinners. One practical advantage of country stays was the decreased supervision by chaperones, which gave young couples rare chances for romantic encounters.

There were also the worlds of sporting, cultural, and social events. In the country that meant riding, walking, gardening, fishing and shooting, archery (a popular sport eclipsed by tennis in the twentieth century), sailing, carriage jaunts, and the like. Later golf and tennis were added to the list, when country clubs were built as ornaments or anchors to these enclaves. Motoring and aviation were also fashionable in the early years of the twentieth century; articles in *Country Life in America* helped to popularize these mechanized intrusions into the natural environment as suitable upper-class diversions.

Every event was choreographed as an episode in a pageant, with attendant pomp and ceremony. Society photographers and eventually newspaper columnists recorded the proceedings. Perhaps the most characteristic piece of social theater was the costume ball. This age-old aristocratic custom, which Americans made over, was indicative of society's aspirations toward European behavior and manners. In *The House of Mirth,* the climactic scene of a fancy dress ball at the Bly's New York mansion focused on the popular tableau vivant, based on the paintings of old masters. This party custom required the young ladies in attendance to create exact liv-

133 Mr. and Mrs. Finley Barrell as frontier Americans, at a costume ball, 1914. (Chicago Historical Society.)

ing pictures of Titian, Reynolds, Goya, and Veronese in front of painted backdrops—something Lily Bart was rather good at. The photo collections of professionals hired to document these occasions make for entertaining moments, with otherwise serious practitioners of the Protestant work ethic appearing silly and slightly ill-at-ease in the garb of cowboys, Persian sultans, or powdered and bewigged marquises. This element of life in the stately home was both serious social posturing and good fun. As Wharton remarked about the Bly's house: "The air of improvisation was in fact strikingly present: so recent, so rapidly-evoked was the whole mise-en-scène that one had to touch the marble columns to learn they were not of cardboard, to seat one's self in one of the damask-and-gold arm-chairs to be sure it was not painted against a wall."[10] Wharton was describing a made-up world that was very real among members of America's social elite. Lily Bart and Adele Sloane shared the same *tableau vivant*. Sloane's family photo albums presented her as a fresh, attractive girl at numerous costumed occasions, dressed as a Japanese geisha (on her honeymoon), a Turkish woman, and a Renaissance courtier, among other characters. Dressing up for photographers and friends was analogous to dressing up one's houses, or making camps in Japanese style, or having Chinese tea houses, emphatically illustrating the home as social theater. Life in the American stately home was as much an elaborate fiction as a comfortable reality.

VANDERBILT MANSION, HYDE PARK

A wonderful case study of a home built expressly for the aristocratic life is the Vanderbilt estate at Hyde Park, New York, now a National Historic Site. The children of William Henry Vanderbilt were the most prolific home builders of their time. After seeing such monuments to opulence as The Breakers and Marble House, one is tempted to associate the entire clan with conspicuous consumption and overbearingly rich taste. However, Frederick and Louise Vanderbilt's intentions in creating the Hyde Park estate were hardly the same as those of their well-known kin. That their house ended up looking as it did gives credence to the assumption that at certain levels of society in the 1890s it was impossible to avoid a regal life.

Frederick William Vanderbilt (1856–1938), brother of George Washington, Cornelius II, and William Kissam I, was perhaps the least-noticed member of his prominent family.[11] Like his brother George, he was quiet and seemingly unambitious and received a relatively modest $10 million inheritance, while his two elder brothers more or less split a $200 million estate. But Frederick made the most of his Yale education as well as his capital. At his death he was worth more than $78 million, even after founding Vanderbilt University and donating generously to Yale and Columbia. He avoided publicity during his lifetime, preferring to live and work quietly, attempting to embody the spirit of noblesse oblige that his family's position mandated. Servants told of a man so shy that he hid from passersby in his own garden at Hyde Park. Even his marriage in 1878 to Louise Holmes Anthony, who divorced her first husband, Arthur Torrance, in 1877, was kept secret for nearly a year.[12]

Their country house at Hyde Park, New York, was designed by McKim, Mead and White and constructed from 1896 to 1899. The house alone cost about $660,000[13] and was tastefully elegant—though it hardly stood up to the elaborate displays of his siblings. It is significant that the controlled and concise Charles McKim was in charge of the commission. These Vanderbilts might have wished for a more modest accommodation but undoubtedly felt compelled to build a house befitting members of

their social sphere. Moreover, because of their relatively sedate life-style, the seasonal routine of the Frederick Vanderbilts (who had no children) gives a truer picture of country life in the 1890s than the often sensational doings of their peers and relatives.[14]

These Vanderbilts lived graciously, without making a spectacle of their lives. At Hyde Park they enjoyed a life rooted in the genteel agrarian tradition, in which the pleasures of yachting and gentlemanly farming could be pursued. Frederick was renowned in Dutchess County for his garden produce, Belgian horses, and purebred Jersey cattle. He pursued his avocations as vigorously as his business and philanthropic interests. An avid sailor and motor yachtsman, and a member of the Hudson River Yacht Club, he built the *Rainbow*, the America's Cup defender in 1934, and sailed extensively each season. He even had a brush with disaster when his largest vessel, *The Warrior*, sank after striking a reef off the coast of Colombia in 1914. Louise was known as a colorful woman, whose interests ranged from astrology to social history. She had a particular fascination with the lives of powerful women, such as Marie Antoinette and Josephine (of whom she read fifteen biographies). Nevertheless, she too was a serious philanthropist and became a legend around Hyde Park for her generosity to local people. A Christian Scientist, she died in Paris of an apparent throat infection in 1926.[15]

In choosing to build at Hyde Park, the Vanderbilts joined an illustrious series of owners of the famous estate, including Dr. Samuel Bard (the original owner, during the Revolution), John Jacob Astor I, and the noted horticulturist Dr. David Hosack.[16] Frederick thus entered a tradition of conservative, gracious wealth rather than of opulence. Like his neighbors, James Roosevelt, Ogden Mills, and Levi P. Morton, he valued life on the majestic and historic Hudson River. Though his house was as up-to-date in the classical mode as any Newport cottage, it was also beholden to the building that preceded it, the Langdon mansion of 1847, utilizing its footprint and basic lines. In fact, Vanderbilt had planned simply to renovate the older house, as their neighbors the Mills

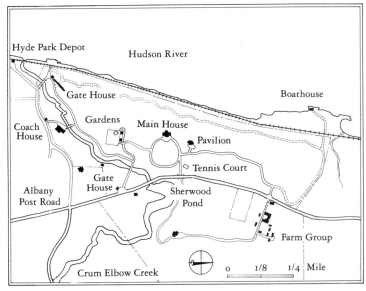

134 Map of Hyde Park estate, Roosevelt-Vanderbilt National Historic Site. (Author, after National Parks Service map.)

135 *opposite* McKim, Mead and White. Frederick W. Vanderbilt house (1896–99), Hyde Park, New York. Entrance portico. (Richard Cheek.)

136 Vanderbilt house. View from south lawn, showing riverfront portico. (Richard Cheek.)

had done. In 1896, however, Mead discovered that the building was structurally unsound and had to revise the plans.[17] The final classical design owes much not only to the former house but also to nearby Montgomery Place (1804–06, 1841–44), by A. J. Davis and others, one of the most distinguished villas on the Hudson. Both buildings are simple blocks articulated by pilasters and feature a semicircular portico on the river side. It is a tribute to Vanderbilt's character that McKim, Mead and White produced for him one of their most ingenious, compact, richly appointed, and distinguished houses. Though grand, it was not vast; though splendid, not overwrought.[18] If it lacked the balance and elegance of Marble House, it was more American by its sturdy and rough classicism.

Life on the Vanderbilt estate was marked by a blend of formality and rural gentility appropriately captured by the Corinthian facades of the house and the verdant park surrounding it. The picturesque landscape, redesigned by James Greenleaf, featured specimen trees, barns, a carriage house, stone bridges, a wildly rushing cascade, and steeply sloping banks overlooking the Hudson—the perfect counterpoint to the stateliness of the house. The working farm produced meat and produce, while the gardens and greenhouses provided flowers for the table. The family had horses and several carriages, but automobiles became the major source of transportation after 1910. During the 1920s there were six vehicles on hand: a Cadillac, Rolls Royce, Minerva, Simplex, Packard, and a big Renault.

The Vanderbilts generally spent the spring, early summer, and part of the fall in Hyde Park, making it nearly a permanent home in a highly peripatetic era. Visiting the great circuit of "serial houses" owned by the family was traditional during the decades before World War I. Frederick had houses in Newport (Rough Point, designed by Peabody and Stearns), Bar Harbor (Cornfield), Palm Beach, and New York City (for the opera and social season from mid-November to January). The family also had a retreat in the Adirondacks, called Japanese Camp, on Upper St. Regis Lake, which was built by fifteen Japanese wood craftsmen brought over specially for the job. The Vanderbilts usually spent part of the midsummer traveling in Europe. The Hyde Park house was opened on October 1 and closed after the Thanksgiving holidays, though the family often came back for a town Christmas party. It was opened again in April and closed in June.[19]

Though guests were invited for indefinite stays, the weekend house party was the major vehicle for formal entertaining. After arriving and being shown their rooms, guests were prescribed a walk around the grounds. Dinner, served at 7:30 or 8:00, was a formal and elaborately staged ritual, the focus of the weekend's activities. Like scene changes, each course was attended by a change of flowers, linens, and other table decor. After a dinner of several courses, the men enjoyed cigars and brandy while the women "withdrew." If a dance had not been planned, cards were the usual order. Guests retired late—to a room done in eighteenth-century French decor—slept late, and were served breakfast in bed. The vigorous could take a round of golf, sail a bit on the river, or just stroll. A fairly elaborate Sunday lunch was served between 1:15 and 2:00. And so the routine went—for frequent guests it must occasionally have had the numbing aura of many scenes in the fiction of Henry James or Edith Wharton.

The rooms served as perfect stage sets for these weekend rituals, made possible by an army of servants behind the scenes. Each room functioned as a setting for a part of the schedule of entertaining and daily life during the Hyde Park season. Following Robert Kerr's prescription for mid-Victorian country houses (*The Gentleman's House,* 1864), there were male and female domains—although the Vanderbilts hardly went to the lengths of some English nouveaux riches in segregating their servants from themselves.[20] The staff numbered sixty-two, with seventeen house servants. These included three butlers, four chambermaids, three laundry women, two female cooks, a kitchen girl, and one parlor maid.

The hierarchy of ground-floor formal rooms was articulated in McKim's concise, classical plan. Equal emphasis was given to the dining room and living room (or drawing room), at either end of the transverse axis (the names were used interchangeably by Croly

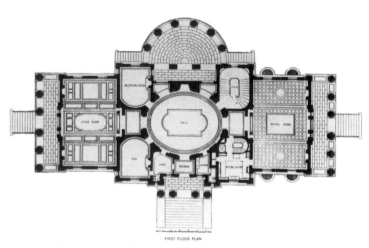

137 Vanderbilt house. First floor plan and entry elevation, east. (*Monograph of the Work of McKim, Mead and White.*)

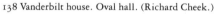

138 Vanderbilt house. Oval hall. (Richard Cheek.)

139 Vanderbilt house. Dining room. (Richard Cheek.)

in 1903, when the living room was a relatively new concept). The drawing room was the same size as the dining room and was used for such formal events as Saturday evening dances. These were the major set pieces. But the center of both circulation and the "society of rooms" was the oval hall, rising two stories, to which McKim nevertheless gave a relatively warm and comfortable scale. It was smartly decorated with Doric pilasters and a range of colored marbles. Paradoxically, this space functioned similarly to a Shingle Style living hall. Though formal, the room was furnished with tall palms, animal skin rugs, and comfortable couches. As a former butler remembered, "After a game of golf, for instance, guests would come in and sit down and fall asleep in front of that big fire."[21] On the short axis of the oval one passed from the entry front to the semicircular portico facing the river. The long axis

represented the formal route from dinner to withdrawing in the European manner. Four subsidiary rooms completed the corners of the plan: Mr. Vanderbilt's library and study, the Gold Room or reception room (a female domain), a grand stair hall, somewhat in the vein of Biltmore, and a servants' stair with butler's pantry, providing access to the downstairs service areas. Locating the service areas, including the kitchen, in the basement was expedient, because a service wing would have seriously compromised the plan. Thus a classical, cross-axial scheme aptly accommodated the social needs of the house and the constraints of the river site.

The plan, though seemingly rigid, offered a welcome flexibility of function. The dining room was the setting for luncheons and formal dinners, each elaborately and artistically planned by Mrs. Vanderbilt. Both a small family table and a large banquet table were kept in the thirty-by-fifty-foot room, which featured heavy

140 Vanderbilt house. Mrs. Vanderbilt's bedroom. (Richard Cheek.)

paneling, French tapestries, and two stone Renaissance mantelpieces. The Gold Room was used for small teas, sherry before dinner, card playing, and conversation. The most formally decorated of the smaller spaces, it was also the least used room on the ground floor. Vanderbilt carried on his business affairs from the study, an extraordinarily carved fantasy in Santo Domingo mahogany, decorated with Italian and Flemish flintlock pistols and containing the owner's four-hundred-volume collection. The library served additionally as the family living room, tea room, occasional dining room, and even as a correspondence room for Mrs. Vanderbilt. The daunting scale of the formal spaces undoubtedly encouraged the couple to stay in cozier areas. The Vanderbilts thus adapted a socially required plan to their everyday needs and patterns of living.

The house was nevertheless a theatrical place, meant to be appreciated for its evocations of past splendors and its royal pretensions. Its interiors, by Georges Glaezner and Ogden Codman, Jr., were period set pieces, filled with fine reproduction furnishings, made by leading French craftsmen of the time.[22] According to the butler, however, Mr. Vanderbilt lacked a collector's zeal and treated objects with indifference.[23] Mrs. Vanderbilt's bedroom, one of the most extraordinary rooms in the house, was a replica of a queen's Louis XV chambre-boudoir, complete with a rail for the morning levee, so that she could literally live out her admiration for the grand ladies of eighteenth-century France. The dramatic and comedic ceremonies of the Vanderbilt estate call to mind French farces, Restoration comedies, Viennese operettas, and other theater pieces associated with the manners of the ruling class.

Among American country houses, there was no better embodiment of this aristocratic ritualism than McKim, Mead and White's widely praised estate for Clarence Mackay, Harbour Hill (1899–1902), at Roslyn, Long Island. One of the most famous country houses of its time, it gained further notoriety in 1924, when the Duke of Wales visited but failed to attend a party given in his honor. It was fitting that this project be handled by the flamboyant Stanford White, since it was probably the most opulent of all the houses designed by the firm. Harbour Hill was an unusual McKim, Mead and White design for its close adaptation of seventeenth-century French models, specifically François Mansart's Château de Maisons-Laffitte (1642–46). This 648-acre estate, built for a modern-day monarch and her spectacularly rich husband, contained splendid European collections and supported a life that Louis XVI might have envied.

To appreciate the pomp and grandeur of Harbour Hill, one must first understand its primary patron, the vivacious and indefatigable Katherine Duer Mackay. The daughter of a prominent New York attorney, Mrs. Mackay was a textbook example of the new society woman involved in philanthropic, community, and social pursuits—a founder of the Equal Franchise Society for women's voting rights as well as a member of the Colony Club, where the group met. She was also notoriously overbearing and regal. Barr Ferree surmised her character from one visit to Harbour Hill: "Opposite the doorway [of the boudoir] is a canopied couch, over which hangs a rich ermine robe—a truly royal throne

141 **Harbour Hill**. Aerial view in the 1930s, showing gardens by Jacques Gréber. (Collection of Alfred Branam, Jr.)

for the queen that rules there."[24] And rule she did, over her husband and her architect. She pushed White relentlessly and was not in the least timid about making suggestions, demanding in her first letter, "Express me as soon as you get this, some books about and drawings of Louis XIV chateaux. Very severe style preferred." Later, in a letter of July 27, 1899, she wrote concerning the program: "The style of the full front view of Maisons-Laffitte comes nearest to what I mean. And even that has the windows too ornate

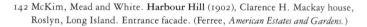

142 McKim, Mead and White. **Harbour Hill** (1902), Clarence H. Mackay house, Roslyn, Long Island. Entrance facade. (Ferree, *American Estates and Gardens.*)

143 **Harbour Hill**. Mrs. Mackay's boudoir. (Ferree, *American Estates and Gardens.*)

to suit us."[25] Sending along her own plan sketch ensured that White would not misunderstand her detailed instructions. By such overt manipulations she got precisely what she wanted from the most temperamental and charismatic architect of the time.

She paid for such extravagances with the vast fortunes of her husband, Clarence Hungerford Mackay, and his father, John William Mackay. The elder Mackay had acquired his first riches during the California Gold Rush, with the Virginia City Bonanza Mine. His millions were then invested with the Commercial Cable and the Postal Telegraph companies, of which his son became vice president in 1894 and which later merged with International Telephone and Telegraph. When the elder Mackay died in 1902, he left his son and daughter-in-law not only the planned Roslyn house and estate but several hundred million dollars in assets.[26] According to office records of McKim, Mead and White, the eventual cost of the house and outbuildings was $781,483, every penny of which worried the parsimonious Clarence, who had "a horror of extras."[27] Some estimates indicate that Mr. and Mrs. Mackay spent an additional $5 million on furnishings, art, and decoration before the house was completed in 1906. The elaborate gardens, by Guy Lowell and Jacques Gréber, took another twenty years.

Designing a home for the Mackays was hardly a simple matter, even for an architect known for his boundless ego and his ability to get what he wanted from clients. The usually swashbuckling White was required in this commission to function somewhat as an academic, educating his clients in matters of stylistic consistency, introducing them to such books as Claude Sauvageot's *Palais, châteaux, hôtels et maisons de France du XVe au XVIIIe siècle* (1867), traveling to Italy in 1903 to buy antiques, and attempting to channel Mrs. Mackay's narrow requirements and headstrong stylistic demands into a building that would have unity and integ-

rity as well as pomp. If, in spite of its sumptuousness and splendor, Harbour Hill had an overblown and lifeless quality not usually associated with an architect known for his lively, delicate hand in detailing and overall joie de vivre, it may have been because he labored with two extremely difficult clients.

For her part, Katherine Mackay fulfilled her role as a grande dame of the Mauve Decade, desiring to build an elaborate showcase for her expansive style of life. In this she surpassed even such fictional characters as Mrs. Phillips in Herrick's *The Common Lot,* who charmed her architect into designing a French palace in otherwise staid Lake Forest. Mrs. Mackay surrounded herself with symbols of aristocratic culture. In her own suite, arranged not quite correctly as a French *appartement,* the sitting room was regal, the bathroom cozy, rich, and cluttered, the anteroom somewhat prim — "decked with the thousand and one articles . . . which every great lady finds comforting to existence," as Ferree put it.[28] Her early letters to White described each room in detail: "I want on my floor (over the ground floor) on the north side over the library my suite. Consisting of a dressing and bathroom combined opening into a bedroom which opens into a sitting room, which is to be the corner room facing water view. Next to my bathroom I wish another room as large as it for dresses." Her husband's needs came second — "Also: over the hall facing the water a suite for Clarie the same as mine, his study opening into my boudoir."[29] She lived as a modern queen with liberal social ideas, and the contradictory sides of her public and private lives were clearly on view in her house.

White, the notorious bon vivant, relished his role in searching out the expensive objects and materials used in the interiors. Alternately charmed by Katherine Mackay and repelled by her arrogance, he played his part cautiously but effectively. His dealings with her husband were not always happy. The correspondence shows that he frequently locked horns with Clarence Mackay over the cost of many elements of the decoration, sometimes with

144 **Harbour Hill.** Stair hall. (Ferree, *American Estates and Gardens.*)

American home it had to have a porch). In the circulation, neither the traditional cross-axial nor the English circuit configuration was followed—one was forced to pass through the main hall or its balcony corridors to reach any of the public areas of the mansion. There was a lack of grace in the way a guest had to weave through the house, as if the client had insisted on queer configurations that the architect could not resolve.

At the center of the house was a huge double-story great hall, sixteenth-century English in inspiration but formally derived from Beaux-Arts houses like The Breakers and Ochre Court. Such an impressive space, though hardly domestic in scale, became de rigueur in the largest and most pretentious stately homes. White placed a salon to the left, as part of the women's realm, while the men's billiard room was situated in a corner, as if to symbolize the cool separation of his clients, who were married but hardly connected. Two treasure-filled rooms were placed on the garden side of the house: the Italian Renaissance–inspired Stone Room, which framed tapestries and religious paintings by Verrocchio, Bellini, Botticelli, Perugino, and Raphael's *Garden of Gethsemane;* and across from it the heavy, paneled dining room, which like the main hall boasted an elaborate strapwork ceiling (dining rooms were often done in English Tudor). The salon, which we have already heard described by the client, was another treasure chest.

Harbour Hill's odd, inefficient, and not terribly gracious plan was concealed behind a massive, disciplined exterior of limestone and steeply pitched mansard towers. The "very severe style" specified by Mrs. Mackay had been concisely achieved. Only in the entry door and dormer details did White show a little of his flair for ornamental invention, though even these were probably

absurdly comical results. In a letter of November 3, 1902, his client wrote: "In regard to the remaining moose heads which you strongly advise me to buy . . . you seem to forget the main point, viz: the price. I know that this is a very small matter to you, and that you do not like to burden yourself with too many figures, but I look upon it in an entirely different aspect."[30] Later, on February 24, 1903, Mackay became even more exasperated with his architect's willingness to spend his money: "I will tell you right here that I would not think of paying such an absurd price as 100,000 francs for any mantelpiece, unless I had the income of a Carnegie or a Rockefeller!"[31] Clarence Mackay (who did have the income of a Carnegie or a Rockefeller) wanted a palatial estate that would symbolize his family's extraordinary financial success but was not always willing to pay for it.[32] His wife, like the Duchess of Marlborough, made certain that the coffers never remained closed for long.[33]

As a work of architecture, Harbour Hill in no way vanquished Maisons. The house was far less classically disciplined than Mansart would have condoned. But White was a pragmatist, with a considerable array of conflicting goals to fulfill. In plan, he struggled hard but in vain to balance elements symmetrically: the stair hall with an oddly placed billiard room, the vast service wing with a strange "glass enclosed piazza" and porch (and note that as an

145 **Harbour Hill.** White drawing room or salon. (Ferree, *American Estates and Gardens.*)

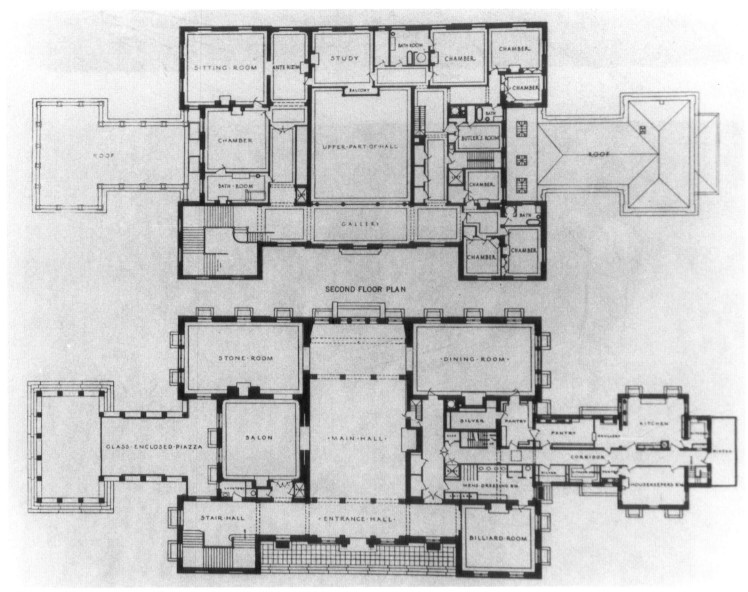

SECOND FLOOR PLAN

146 **Harbour Hill.** First and second floor plans. (*Monograph of the Work of McKim, Mead and White.*)

147 **Harbour Hill.** Stables designed by Warren and Wetmore. (Ferree, *American Estates and Gardens.*)

adapted from Sauvageot's book. White's design seemed to summarize the semipublic, stately, and impersonal qualities that clients like the Mackays demanded in their houses. Even the gardens were monumental. The formal terrace, which stretched from the enclosed loggia, formed an axis almost as impressive as that at Biltmore. The estate had a complete dairy, extensive stables, ten miles of bridle trails, dog kennels, an elaborate barn, a working farm, and a palatial carriage house. No English country house of the twentieth century could boast such extraordinary trappings.

Taken as a whole, Harbour Hill was impressive in every way that counted among members of America's capitalist aristocracy. Part museum, part social club and ballroom, part park for sports and gardening, part office for Mrs. Mackay, the house could no longer be considered a comfortable home in the country. It was an institution.

148 Carrère and Hastings. **Bellefontaine** (1896–98), Giraud Foster house, Lenox,
Massachusetts. Portico. (Edward Hale Lincoln, Lenox Library Association.)

BELLEFONTAINE: THE COTTAGE AS CHÂTEAU

An idiosyncratic and equally stately country house fitted with
even more comforts was Bellefontaine (1896–98), the estate of
Giraud Foster in the bucolic summer colony of Lenox, Massachusetts.[34] Designed by Carrère and Hastings, Foster's house
offers an example of the Beaux-Arts approach to a country house
done in French taste.[35] It is also indicative of the tendency among
the wealthy to disregard conventional architectural types—in this
case, the rustic summer cottage—when stateliness was desired.

Though not the largest of the Lenox cottages, Bellefontaine was
the most architecturally commanding and distinguished, precisely portraying the baronial demeanor of its owner, who was for
many years the leading citizen of Lenox as well as a great society
figure. He was, among other things, senior warden of the neighboring Trinity Church and manager of the Lenox Library. Foster's
Scottish grandfather, Andrew Foster, had arrived in America in
the early 1800s with both substantial wealth and a social pedigree.

By the time his grandson married Jane Van Nest, also from old
stock, the family had established itself among the Lenox cottagers, all of whom perpetuated the genteel tradition. Giraud Foster could rightly claim to be a modern-day country squire and
lived his life among the elite of New York, Palm Beach, and Lenox
as a kind of Beau Nash. He considered Bellefontaine to be not
merely a summer home but a country seat.

Carrère and Hastings were at the height of their career when
they were commissioned almost concurrently to design houses for
the Van Nest sisters—Jane's sibling being Mrs. Richard Gam-
brill, for whom they did Vernon Court, in Newport. Although
Bellefontaine was often compared to eighteenth-century châteaux
and garden buildings, especially the Grand Trianon, it owed its
form to no historical example. Its brilliant site plan used the tricks
of Beaux-Arts training to the fullest, setting the main rooms of
the house perpendicular to a grand garden axis stretching north
and south from both fronts. Even the rendering of the plan, in
academic wash on a vertical rectangular sheet, as published in
American Architect and Building News, purposely suggested the
concours style.

Carrère and Hastings planned the house and gardens "by the axes," as their Ecole masters would have dictated. One approached the house from the west, or flank, cross axis, proceeding from a grand gate house down an *allée,* and entered through a small side garden and loggia. The strict, formally conceived plan of the house formed a simple U, with a courtyard to the north and a grand hexastyle portico to the south. The three main rooms, a dining room, living room, and salon, were located along the south front, their enfilade ingeniously in line with the garden-entry axis. A transverse hall provided circulation on the courtyard side. The grand conceit of the house, however, was its remarkable series of axial garden vistas, which could only be appreciated after entering the building. On the south side, the more formal front, stepped terraces opened onto a panorama of the countryside. The Italian gardens, which governed the north portion of the site, were probably the estate's most distinctive feature. They were defined by a huge, dense outdoor room, suggesting the Boboli amphitheater as well as other mannerist gardens. On the major axis, as finally planned, was a lily channel leading to a verdant grotto, which formed the foil to the garden cortile of the house several hundred feet away. Like Platt, Hastings found inspiration in the traditions of the Italian garden, here fusing them with Beaux-Arts

149 **Bellefontaine.** Site plan. (*American Architect and Building News,* 1899.)

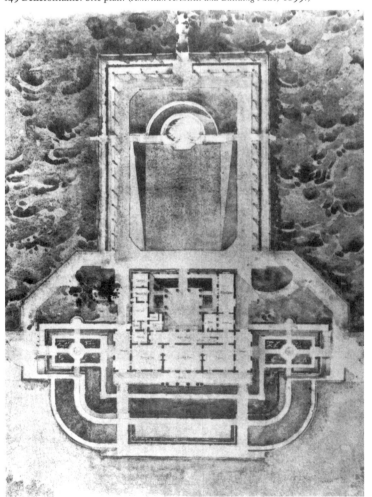

150 *top* **Bellefontaine.** Garden court. (Edward Hale Lincoln, Lenox Library Association.)

151 **Bellefontaine.** North side. (*American Architect and Buildings News,* 1899.)

precision and rational planning. (The firm was, according to the *Architectural Record,* the first American office to offer complete landscape, interior, and architectural services to wealthy clients.) The Italian theme extended to the vast *selvaggio* (wild) gardens, where visitors would unexpectedly come upon statuary, *grotteschi* (such as satyrs), and temples in the forest. The estate is reputed to have contained some eighteen hundred pieces of garden sculpture.[36]

Bellefontaine was appropriately grand in its massing and its fine gardens, but Hastings' experiments with a patchwork of brick and locally quarried Lee marble and haphazard use of quoins and stone trim diminished its presence considerably. Like Blairsden, the house was overly rich and uncertain in articulation, a fault remedied somewhat in later works of Carrère and Hastings. Its interiors were carried out with consistency and grace, along eighteenth-century French lines, effectively combining the rustic garden conceits with stately elegance. The living room and two garden loggias reflect the preference of the owner for comfort as well as pomp. Bellefontaine represented the disciplined, logical, and potentially innovative qualities of the Modern French style as well as any house of its time. Yet its self-consciously European gardens and formal air seemed out of place among the rolling hills of the Berkshires, where beautiful fountains paled beside forest streams.

152 **Bellefontaine.** Dining room. (Edward Hale Lincoln, Lenox Library Association.)

153 **Bellefontaine.** Giraud Foster in the loggia. (Lenox Library Association.)

THE ROAD TO THE POOR HOUSE

Like Bellefontaine, the stately Tudor home of Henry William Poor (1844–1915) struck a somewhat dissonant chord with residents of the exclusive country enclave at Tuxedo Park, New York.[37] Perched blithely on the tallest hilltop in this beautiful and isolated lakeside community, the house even today has a somewhat arrogant and alien presence. No less a portrait of its owner than Harbour Hill, this distinguished Jacobean summer house was built for a man who thought himself king of Tuxedo, just as to many he seemed king of Wall Street. When he bought the mountaintop near the property of the colony's founder, Pierre Lorillard, Poor was undaunted by the fact that the site might not support a large house. "Mr. Poor promptly argued that, if there were not room at the top, he would make room by building up his mountain until he had space sufficient and to spare," Barr Ferree recalled. "So the outer corner of the flower garden is supported by a high wall, giving him as much space as he desired on the summit, and a corner of the globe that he has made his very own."[38]

Poor's megalomania extended to his conquests on Wall Street, where he made room for himself at the top of the financial world. His father, Henry Varnum Poor, was a lawyer and perhaps the nation's leading authority on railroads and their financial mechanisms. During the important consolidation of the country's many rail lines during the late nineteenth century, his handbooks provided invaluable information to investors and businessmen. The elder Poor established a securities firm to handle railroad issues and made a fortune, which he handed to his son. In keeping with his father's penchant for information dissemination, Henry William established the investor's guide, *Poor's Handbook of Investment Securities,* and made $5 million by shrewdly playing the market during the 1890s.[39] In a rags to riches to rags cycle, he then expended much of his capital on two houses, an art collection, and a library of English books and manuscripts (several thousand volumes), one of the finest of its day. Stanford White lavishly

remodeled a town house on Lexington Avenue for him in 1899, relieving Poor of over $100,000 in the process. Poor then had T. Henry Randall (1862–1905) design a country house, which was finished by 1902 at an undetermined cost. What was left of his fortune was lost in the panic of 1907. He died eight years later, over $2 million in debt.[40]

On the road to ruin, Poor created what Gavin Townsend has called "the supreme example of an American Jacobean structure." Its basic motives were a series of rounded Flemish gables, inspired by English houses such as Aston Hall (1618–35) in Warwickshire, which were also popular in many English Victorian country houses.[41] Randall studied his sources avidly, detailing the brickwork (alternating glazed clinkers and stretchers in English bond), corbeled chimneys, carved limestone, stone cross mullions, and leaded light windows to emulate precisely English examples. The plan was a modified U, forming an entry court, with a set of three projecting gables massed on the garden front. Even the garden terrace, though incongruous on its precipitous site, was meant to recall seventeenth-century examples. Both Poor and Randall seemed to revel in the aura of historical settings. (Poor was himself an "ardent student, and throughout his life kept up his reading in Greek and Latin and his studies in Sanskrit, Hebrew, Icelandic and Russian," according to his biographers.)[42] Architect and client strove to capture to the letter the qualities of the Elizabethan prodigy houses, with their complex heraldic details, strapwork, classical pieces, and grotesques. The elaborate carved stonework over the front door, the several extraordinary mantelpieces, and the decor of the major rooms testified to this zealous commitment to authenticity. Stanford White supplied some of the door frames and interior decoration from collecting trips abroad, but the majority of the work was reproduced from historical examples.

The main hall was designed to evoke the famous Long Gallery at Haddon Hall in Derbyshire, with a geometric strapwork ceiling in plaster and superb oak paneling. The staircase was modeled on that of Blickling Hall in Norfolk, another popular source. All of the formal rooms—a drawing room hung with tapestries, a paneled dining room, and the all-important library—opened off

154 T. Henry Randall. Henry William Poor house (1902), Tuxedo Park, New York. Facade from gardens. (H. H. Sibman, Avery Architectural Archives, photo albums from the personal collection of Henry Poor.)

155 Poor house. View from driveway. (H. H. Sibman, Avery Architectural Archives.)

156 Poor house. Garden terrace. (H. H. Sibman, Avery Architectural Archives.)

of the hall. From the library, Poor's private domain, one could step out to a loggia, facing west and overlooking the lake and the Ramapo Mountains. As in Mrs. Mackay's boudoir, the dark walls of the library, lined with leather volumes, seemed to suggest the inner secret of Poor's character, just as the furnishings and decor proclaimed a public portrait of the man who had briefly conquered Wall Street. On the floor below, a masculine smoking room filled with sporting objects bespoke the leisurely, informal side of Henry Poor—"most suggestive of the strenuous outdoor life," according to Ferree.[43]

Yet as venerable as the Poor house might seem, its presence offended one of the most unique landscape settings in America. As a critic wrote in the *Architectural Record* in 1907, "A Jacobean dwelling tends to look very much better on a comparatively flat site, and it needs, also, the assistance of vines and many trees before it can properly take its place in the countryside. [Unless so situated] its outline and masses seem to be an excrescence on the countryside—as anyone may see by looking at the appearance of Mr. Henry W. Poor's house at Tuxedo from the other side of the valley. . . . It looks as if it were perched insecurely on its site, and as if at any moment it might spread its wings and fly away."[44] With Poor's fleeting fortune, his treasures did just that, while the shell of his dream remained on the mountaintop.

left

157 *top* Poor house. Gallery. (H. H. Sibman, Avery Architectural Archives.)

158 *center* Poor house. Porch or loggia overlooking Tuxedo Lake. (H. H. Sibman, Avery Architectural Archives.)

right

159 *top* Poor house. Smoke room. (H. H. Sibman, Avery Architectural Archives.)

160 Poor house. Library. (H. H. Sibman, Avery Architectural Archives.)

161 *bottom* Poor house. Dining room. (H. H. Sibman, Avery Architectural Archives.)

162 Myron Hunt and Elmer Grey. Henry E. Huntington house (1906–11), San Marino, California. (Architectural Drawing Collection, University Art Museum, Santa Barbara, California.)

VILLA VIZCAYA AND THE HOUSE AS HOBBY HORSE

If the rituals of life during this era were theatrical, so were the everyday objects of that life. Stately homes were like museums, reliquaries full of instant heirlooms. They were places of invented culture and fabricated history, realizations of the fantasy worlds to which capitalist parvenus such as Henry Poor aspired. Collecting affected many wealthy Americans like a drug, causing them to spend huge amounts of money not only for art and art objects but for mansions in which to display them.

Many of these homes have now become public museums. Good examples of such treasure houses include the Isabella Stewart Gardner Museum in Boston and the Morgan Library and Frick Collection in New York. Lodged firmly in the American consciousness is the home of Citizen Kane—William Randolph Hearst's great ranch at San Simeon in California, the surprisingly artful agglomeration of European pieces that Julia Morgan composed between 1919 and 1947.[45] To the American public the Enchanted Hill was the apotheosis of the collector's fantasy, the culture baron's personal museum gone wild. Today it remains a popular tourist attraction in California. Yet Hearst's Spanish castle on the hill was but one of many personal monuments to art in the nation, built by wealthy patrons whose collecting defined their later lives.

Another important collector of the period was real estate and transit millionaire Henry E. Huntington of Los Angeles. His great San Marino estate, with its classical Mediterranean house designed by Myron Hunt and Elmer Grey, was built largely as a frame for a library. When begun in 1906, the building was considered an epic enterprise for the Pasadena colony; constructed of reinforced concrete, it required an entire studio of local carvers to

execute the intricate interior decoration designed by White, Allom and Co. of London. Porter Garnett called it "the most 'palatial' residence in California," praising Hunt's ability to reconcile the cold and formulaic aspects of the classical house with the spectacular variety and warmth of the locale, flora, climate, and vernacular traditions.[46] Yet nothing but a palatial house would have been fitting for Huntington's spectacular collection of books. With his extraordinary wealth and acumen as a bibliophile (and through the efforts of intelligent agents), over decades he acquired one of the world's finest private libraries, eventually housed in a special building designed by Hunt in 1920.[47] In the original plan of his house, however, the library was given a preeminent location. The entire estate, with its lavish gardens, was an ornamental surround to the treasured manuscripts within.

The country house as museum could also become the "collected object" in itself, as in the cases of Hearst and Alexander Welbourne Weddell (1876–1948) of Richmond, Virginia, who chose to import and reconstruct an entire house. Weddell was not only one of Richmond's most active civic and cultural leaders, but also a key patriot of the New Deal. A forty-year career diplomat, he served as Franklin D. Roosevelt's ambassador to Argentina from 1933 through 1939, then as ambassador to Spain until 1942. He was a self-made man who studied many cultures and traveled widely. Like many Americans, he prized his Anglo-Saxon heritage. Thus, when Warwick Priory, the sixteenth-century English house begun in 1125 for the first Earl of Warwick, was to be demolished in 1925, Weddell seized the opportunity to purchase it. Then, amid protest from local Britons and the press, he shipped the house stone by stone to Richmond, where it was re-erected as the core of his new country estate on the James River. Although he believed this to be an act of preservation, the English did not, satirizing him in a *Country Life* editorial in April of 1926:

163 Huntington house. Plan. (Architectural Drawing Collection, University Art Museum, Santa Barbara, California.)

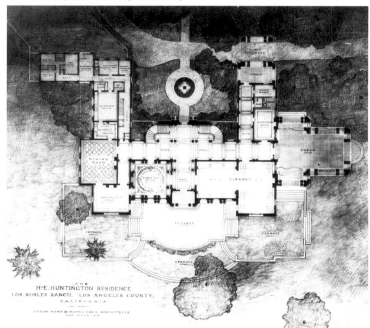

Of old when Orpheus harped and sang
The woods with heavenly music rang
And rapt trees left the woody bed
And followed wheresoer he led.

Today the more ingenious Yank
Need only let his dollars clank
And straight the houses here grow frantic
And bound across the broad Atlantic.

Weddell commissioned architect Henry Grant Morse (1876–1934) and landscape architect Charles F. Gilette to add a terraced garden and a wing, said to be an exact copy of George Washington's ancestral English home, Sulgrave Manor. (During the mid-1920s, this house was painstakingly restored, with considerable American support, by Reginald Blomfield.) He later asked William Lawrence Bottomley to design a large porch using a set of Spanish Renaissance columns he had imported. Weddell, who prized both his house and his collection of European antiques, objects, and pictures, published a lavish book on the entire collection in 1947 before donating most of it to the Virginia Historical Society. Virginia House, as the estate was paradoxically titled, symbolized the highminded and passionate collector, the man reaching for a lost but noble ancestry through a building.[48]

The endeavors of Weddell, Hearst, and others to assemble and reconstruct fragments of buildings or entire structures were part of a broader cultural theme—the house as hobby horse. Shortly after receiving an enormous inheritance in 1923 and briefly trying his hand at breeding sheep, Henry Francis Du Pont began his now-legendary collection of Early American furniture, decorative arts, and period rooms. He chose to house these treasures in his country house, which quickly took on the look of a museum. Du Pont's decorative arts collection was not his only passion; he was also

164 Henry Grant Morse, restoration architect. **Virginia House** (1925), Alexander Welbourne Weddell house, Richmond, Virginia. (Author.)

trained as a horticulturist and created one of the great gardens in the country. Clive Aslet has traced the scandalous escapades of Andrew Carnegie, William Waldorf Astor, and Hearst in England—at Skibo Castle, Hever Castle, and St. Donat's, respectively—in remodeling some of Britain's finest medieval buildings as sumptuous, stately homes abroad.[49] Millionaires seemed to want these impressive old houses for several reasons. As in Weddell's case, it was often to reclaim an ancestral pedigree. There was also the lure of consumption and collecting itself, undoubtably the motive for such culture barons as J. P. Morgan, Henry Huntington, and the eccentric Hearst. Many wealthy collectors were driven to leave a great gift or legacy in the form of a building and its treasures—hence the adage "To be great one must build great."

No American house exemplifies the power of personal fantasy better than James Deering's Villa Vizcaya. This popular Florida landmark was created between 1912 and 1916 through the unique artistic collaboration of four men. Born in 1859 to William Deering, founder of Deering Harvester Company, James wanted to be a painter but in 1902 found himself instead the largest manufacturer of farm machinery in the country. He had studied in Paris for a season and was encouraged by no less than John Singer Sargent to pursue an artistic career. Though fate intervened to prevent that, he was able to have it both ways when he retired from International Harvester a multimillionaire in 1910. Because he suffered from pernicious anemia, Deering sought a warm climate for his winter residence. His parents had wintered at Coconut Grove since 1901, and he came to love the south coast of Florida, eventually purchasing 180 acres of waterfront forest land, called a hammock, south of Miami. Resolved to build both a collection and a house dedicated to art, he called on the New York decorator and tastemaker Elsie de Wolfe for advice and through her found his alter ego, Paul Chalfin.

Elite and well educated, Chalfin (1873–1959) was also trained as a painter, studying in the prestigious atelier of J. L. Gérôme in Paris. Like Deering he went in many directions with his career, teaching design at Columbia's School of Architecture in 1909–10, then dabbling in architecture, decorating, and lecturing on art. He was hired by Deering as an art consultant but came to be something of a major domo and artistic director. He accompanied his modern-day prince on trips abroad for six years to acquire objects and paintings for the great Florida house, not always buying first-rate works. As the collection grew, so did the scope of the endeavor; Chalfin's authority eventually extended far beyond matters of collecting. It was he who chose the model for the house, Longhena's Venetian baroque Villa Rezzonico in Bassano del Grappa (1670). According to James T. Maher, he also picked and directed the architect who would realize the "basic fantasy" he and Deering were striving to achieve.[50] The New York architect F. Burrall Hoffman, Jr., who apprenticed with Carrère and Hastings, was placed in charge of technical and architectural matters, while the landscape architect Diego Suarez (1888–1974) designed the elaborate formal gardens that contribute so much to Vizcaya's magic.[51]

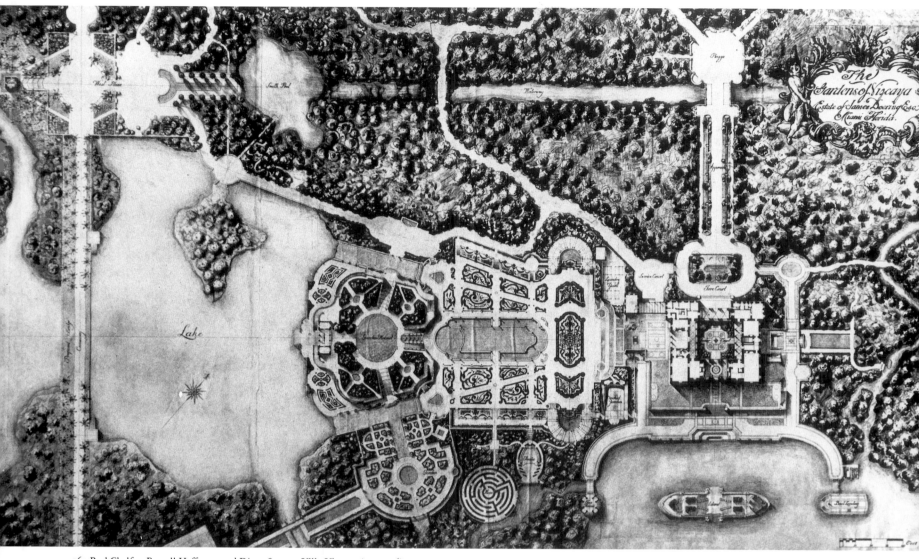

165 Paul Chalfin, Burrall Hoffman, and Diego Suarez. **Villa Vizcaya** (1912–16),
James Deering estate, Miami, Florida. Site plan. (*Architectural Review,* 1917.)

Chalfin was acutely aware of his role as a kind of *bricoleur,* or Jack of all trades, and reveled in it. The project quickly became as much his hobby horse as Deering's. He recognized the sentimentality, the pseudoauthenticity, the insubstantiality, and the patently theatrical qualities of what he was producing. "Great building and garden projects," he wrote in 1917, "are essentially not of the aspiring periods of art. They succeed and serve leisure; they enhance individuals and dynasties; they embody the turning of strong wills upon pleasures too large for a man or a generation to appropriate; they call into collision elements as fundamental as dawn, distances, and the seasons. They are demanded, and remain, as monuments to avowed dreams of pleasure and *bien-etre."* He was able, through the whim and wealth of Deering, and the talents of his collaborators, to write a great *Don Quixote* on the landscape of the Florida coast. Though aware of the fakery of this artistic conjuring, Chalfin believed that at Vizcaya he had created something "up to now unachieved in the new world, . . . a house and garden that date from a proud and vigorous past."[52]

Like a stage designer with an art historian's sense of structure, Chalfin gave the house and gardens an iconographic program, a story to tell. The story began with the name Vizcaya itself, evoking the Spanish port of Biscay, for which Florida's Biscayne Bay was named. Vizcaya was also a Basque province, and one of Columbus' vessels in his second voyage was christened the Vizcaino. Thus the link between Old and New Worlds. The four sides of the villa, arranged by Hoffman in a cortile plan, represented different civilizations: facing the bay was the fifteenth-century architecture of Columbus' time; facing north, the robust sixteenth-century mannerism of Michelangelo; overlooking the formal gardens to the south, the seventeenth-century richness and pomp of Louis XIV; and greeting the visitor at the entrance, the eighteenth century "of Madame Pompadour."[53] Each facade had a stage-set quality. Most impressive were the extraordinary waterfront terrace, looking out on a Roman barque carved out of coral stone, and the gardens radiating to the south. Here Suarez synthesized planning and decorative motifs from Italian baroque gardens, such as those of Isola Bella in Lago Maggiore, French eighteenth-century formal gardens containing elaborate parterres, and the hillside villas of

167 **Villa Vizcaya.** Formal garden axis looking toward house. (Richard Cheek.)

166 *left* **Villa Vizcaya.** View from stone barge on Biscayne Bay. (Richard Cheek.)

Tuscany, which he had studied firsthand with Arthur Acton. Part of his genius lay in the adaptation of these sources to a tropical and maritime setting—water from the bay was cleverly incorporated to interact with the terraces, and the plants were painstakingly chosen and tested for their ability to withstand the climate and pests of south Florida. Each historical epoch was further enhanced by such contrivances as a system of canals (reminding the visitor more of the Venetian scenes in the film *Top Hat* than of the Canal Grande), a splendid frescoed grotto pool on the north side, and an eighteenth-century casino at the far end of the main garden. Yet Suarez, like Chalfin, conceived of his creation as both an encyclopedia of great garden art and a series of backdrops for paintings. As Chalfin wrote in 1917: "While you reflect on the means which have succeeded in creating this vision of beauty; while you regard the silent palace, mirroring the whiteness of its walls, towers, terraces in the clear water, as a Venetian palace would be mirrored in the lagoon, it is not difficult to image a Longhi figure, clad in somber drapery."[54] Indeed, costumed historical figures, like tableaux vivants, seem to beg to inhabit the rooms and gardens of this unique place. Not surprisingly, Vizcaya is one of the most popular film-making locations in the United States.

Translating the multifarious art references, these three-dimensional canvases, into a buildable reality was Hoffman's task, and he met the challenge deftly. Devising a massive concrete superstructure and a composite concrete and coral stone system for the house, he stewarded a building campaign that was one of the largest of its day—employing an army of workers from Miami for two and one half years. Many materials were imported, such as the handmade roof tiles from Cuba. Technical details were handled with the same vision as the decoration: the house had a sophisticated private telephone system, the most up-to-date kitchen equipment, and many other mechanical advances.[55]

What Chalfin described as an Italian fortress plan was really a rational Beaux-Arts courtyard scheme, with all of the major formal rooms following en suite in a clockwise direction around the open cortile. As in many museums, the visitor could proceed from room to room, encountering a different art historical theme, genre, or period in each. Vizcaya not only makes a good museum, but its period rooms offer a splendid array of decorative styles. This was precisely Chalfin's intention in creating his set pieces, beginning with sixteenth-century Venetian decor and ending with neoclassical taste and French *Directoire*. In between, one traversed a Renaissance hall that would have pleased the Gonzaga or the nobles of Ferrara, the "frivolous sort of grandeur" of a rococo music room, a Marie Antoinette room, a library inspired by Robert Adam, a delightful vaulted loggia, and the climactic "Tea Room" facing the south garden, which Chalfin described as enchanted: "Its high walls are spaced with rhapsodic painted architecture, in such cool colors, such grays and rusty darks, such apricot pinks and watery greens and marbly whites—its faintly tinged flood of sunlight gathered in the magical crystal vase at the center of the pattern of the floor." Intense and hyperbolic, Chalfin's description fits not only this room but all the rooms he designed. Though one is tempted to touch the marbles and antique drapery

to test their reality, Chalfin made certain that historical authenticity augmented the sensual qualities of his settings. He bragged that "hardly a modern door exists throughout it; not one new fireplace; hardly a piece of contemporaneous furniture has found a place in any of its rooms; nor a single commercial lighting fixture; not a material has been purchased from a dealer's stock, not a fringe, not a tassel."[56]

Vizcaya was a collage of both images and antiquities—for example, the baroque fountain brought from Bassano di Sutri, near Viterbo, which represented the traditions of the Italian gardens of Vignola at Caprarola and Bagnaia. Throughout the estate antique remnants spelled out a myth, although there were occasional works by modern artists, such as the barge fountain carved by A. Stirling Calder. The interiors contained sublime fakery and architectural decoration so deftly integrated as to make one distrust the reality of it all, while still surrendering to the illusion, as in a film. As a connoisseur, artist, and collector of images, Chalfin successfully assembled pieces of the past into a rare composition. When compared to Julia Morgan's extraordinary and inventive efforts at synthesis at San Simeon, Chalfin's fantasy is the more convincing, suggesting that creative vision was more important to the house as hobby horse than architectural integrity.

As if to complete the mise-en-scène, Vizcaya opened its doors on Christmas of 1916, with a pageant arranged by Chalfin. As Deering stepped off his yacht onto the terrace, the lights of his villa came on in sequence, a line of servants emerged from the loggia, and two cannons fired a salute. The evening's festivities were topped off by a masquerade ball peopled by Italian gypsies. Some twenty-one years after the opening of Biltmore, it was a scene even Edith Wharton could not have anticipated.

Stately homes like Vizcaya, Bellefontaine, and Harbour Hill were built as monuments to the self.[57] As such, they were primarily the inventions of headstrong moguls rather than of their Beaux-Arts architects. Hunt, McKim, Hastings, Trumbauer, and Codman contributed to and abetted this grand vision, but in the end architects were merely handmaidens to larger social forces. Perhaps partially for this reason, their considerable artistic achievements have been devalued in the criticisms of society's excesses during the Mauve Decade.

Jackson Lears' observations on the identity crisis within this generation of American gentry and intellectual elite offer a cogent interpretation of the reasons behind this culture of display. By creating opulent demonstrations of wealth and assuming the airs of European nobility, capitalist moguls simultaneously proclaimed their modern achievements and retreated into anachronism, into a kind of "evasive banality."[58] The theatrical fantasy of these houses could only be sustained by men and women striving to define themselves in a world of shifting values and class distinctions. Desmond and Croly astutely recognized the paradox of the stately home: "They are magnificent, spectacular, impressive, and rather impersonal. They were inhabited by people who lived public lives, and to whom the exclusiveness of the Anglo-Saxon home [that is, English country house] did not appeal. Finally, they were

168 **Villa Vizcaya.** Loggia. (Richard Cheek.)

designed by architects who were primarily interested in the more formal and architectural qualities of their buildings. In short, they are the types of that sort of semi-public domestic architecture which modern conditions have hitherto favored in this country."[59] It is fitting that many of these grand estates have now become museums.

Obsessions with house building and collecting were sometimes driven by money alone, as the magnitude of financial achievement was translated into lavish edifices and gardens. Intense desire to re-create past splendors, to outdo the Neros, Louis, and Marlboroughs, to relive experiences abroad, to rewrite family history, or simply to bring a dream to life also contributed to the ideal.

But the central idea behind these palaces was the institutionalization of the individual: the captains of industry, realizing the fleeting nature of recognition within their enterprises, wanted permanent monuments to their names. The country house, made of stone or brick, provided just that. Its roots lay in English feudal systems of land ownership, political power, and social hierarchies. These edifices of conspicuous consumption and cultural display were intended also as vehicles of education, idealism, and propaganda for the Horatio Alger myth. Their implicit message was: "This dream can be yours." Unfortunately, as Henry James and Edith Wharton observed, even hollow palaces of stone could crumble if a society did not institutionalize the wealth and patrimony behind them. Unlike England, America tended to resist such edification.

170 **Villa Vizcaya.** Sunken grotto in formal gardens. (Richard Cheek.)

169 *left* **Villa Vizcaya.** Tea room. (Richard Cheek.)

171 McKim, Mead and White, with Theodate Pope. **The Hill-Stead** (1898–1902),
Alfred Atmore Pope house, Farmington, Connecticut. North front from fields.
(Richard Cheek.)

Country Places
The House and Garden Movement

5

We would preach the sermon of the out of doors, where men are free. We would lead the way to the place where there is room, and where there are sweet, fresh winds. . . . We shall endeavor to portray the artistic in rural life.

—COUNTRY LIFE IN AMERICA

The second major model for country houses among the plutocracy followed the English country life movement at the turn of the century. The landscape historian Norman Newton has called this the era of the country place, reflecting the proliferation of major estates and gardens built between 1890 and 1930.[1] What were popularly called country places were small estates (of perhaps ten to fifty acres) grouped in enclaves, often around a country club. Many were built on onetime farmlands bought for their scenic beauty and proximity to urban centers.[2] These houses were used mostly as retreats for short sojourns from the city but sometimes became primary residences when patrons became attached to the picturesque environs. They were places of pastoral leisure, houses in which the garden played a dominant role in both the architecture and the style of life.

As in the stately home, it is important to understand not only the physical manifestations but also the social conventions of this model. It was not simply that well-to-do Americans wanted to dress in tweeds, breed dogs, cows, and sheep, become amateur horticulturists, take up golf, and cultivate the casual pursuits of the English smart set. Many Americans took a more robust atti-

tude toward making nature part of their lives. As Peter Schmitt has observed in his book *Back to Nature,* "The pursuit of country happiness was a recognized part of the city dweller's dream life by the 1890's. . . . [Urban Americans] insisted on defining 'country living' as the highest expression of cultured society. . . . More and more [of them] convinced themselves that they were naturists, claiming closer friends among the woodchucks and warblers than among their country neighbors, and taking as their standard the gospel of the holy earth."[3] The genteel tradition of the gentleman's farm with its leisurely pace was a persistent ideal among upper-class Americans. So powerful was the lure of the outdoors that many progressive and well-to-do Americans proselytized extensively for a back-to-the-land movement.

Frances Kinsley Hutchinson, the Chicago socialite and wife of the civic-minded patron of the arts, Charles Lawrence Hutchinson, recorded the naturalist sentiments of the period with greater zeal than any other writer of her time. In her trilogy, *Wychwood: The History of An Idea,* she waxed rhapsodic on the joys of gardening, wildlife watching, farming, and other country pursuits at their estate on Lake Geneva, Wisconsin. Their Tudor house was designed by the venerable Boston firm of Shepley, Rutan and Coolidge and built from 1902 through 1905. The simple linear plan of the building and its slightly bumptious half-timbered idiom hardly made great architecture,[4] but the surrounding rustic gardens and lakeside setting were magical. Both Charles Sprague Sargent and the Olmsted Brothers firm were involved in their planning. As the name suggested, Wychwood was a numenous, spellbound garden, filled with the sounds of wildlife and the smells and colors of native flora. In its heyday the house was almost hidden by overgrown plants.

Mrs. Hutchinson's memoir, like other testimonials to the country life—many of which were published by Doubleday Page[5]—admonished Americans to find solace in nature. "For joyful recreation, for healthful exercise, for novel experiences, for the development of individuality, the possibilities of the woodland home are infinite," Mrs. Hutchinson informed her readers. Describing her home in winter, she wrote: "Now is the country divine! In a cloudless sky without a breath of wind the sun rises, a globe of fire. On this our sober, tangible, prosaic earth, this rich tangle of white-dropped branches, this iridescent expanse of unsullied purity!"[6] Frances Hutchinson saw herself not only as a poet of the outdoors but also as a champion of the urban American's right to country life: "One comforting thought to that mass of people who have always lived in the city is, that they will enjoy each phase of country life much more than the old rural inhabitants."[7] Her almost transcendentalist ideals—literally to make Wychwood a life's work—were extreme but by no means unusual for women of her station.[8] What began as a summer cottage became a year-round obsession.

Other wealthy summer cottagers, such as Louise de Koven Bowen of Chicago, privately published romantic memoirs of their rural existence. Her cottage, Baymeath, designed by Andrews, Jacques and Rantoul and built at Hulls Cove in Bar Harbor in 1894–95, was an attractive but not distinguished variation on Mount Vernon. It was noted for its pretty site and lush summer garden.[9] Mrs. Bowen, who summered at Bar Harbor for over fifty years, was a leading suffragette, social activist, and philanthropist, with none of the aristocratic pretensions of some of her New York contemporaries. She joined Jane Addams in the cause of Hull House in 1893 and lectured extensively on social issues. Progressive in her avocations as well, her house and style of life in Maine were marked more by a love of the place and its intrinsic beauties than by the social standing acquired there.

Choosing a site on Frenchman's Bay, which she said reminded her of the Bay of Naples, Mrs. Bowen settled on the simple Scottish name Baymeath: "It was on the bay, and meath being the Scotch word for meadow, the name seemed not only simple but appropriate." Simplicity was her professed creed. "Our idea about the house was that it should be a farm house, rather low, and, in order not to keep too many gardeners, its long grass was to come to the front door. But we had a very clever architect, Herbert Jacques . . . who knew what we ought to have."[10] A graceful Colonial Revival edifice, not a humble farmhouse, was the architect's prescription. The finished house was enormous, with large porches, two dining rooms, eleven bedrooms, and eight maids' rooms. Its large outdoor swimming pool was a novelty. And any hope of having only a small gardening staff was dashed by ambitious planting schemes. However expansive and lavish, Baymeath reflected the desire for a life of simple pleasures. Summer there was the high point of the year for the Bowen family.

Ida M. Tarbell, the New York journalist famed for her muckraking history of Standard Oil, kept a farm in Easton Corners, Connecticut. "Frankly, I return to the city to make money to support my farm. Some day I hope that the plan on which I am working will bring me to the point where I shall feel justified in breaking with the town altogether and retiring to the comforting and quieting companionship of the real country," she admitted to an interviewer from *Country Life In America* in 1915. The interviewer, upon seeing her subject engaged in feeding the pets and making jelly all day, found it "difficult to associate this placid, smiling housewife with the wielder of the trenchant pen that has brought to book so many malefactors."[11]

These prominent women were hardly alone among America's social and intellectual elite wishing to retire to the country. Probably the most famous and intellectual advocate of the country place was Edith Wharton. Deliberately turning away from the pomp and frivolity of her family's Newport home, she used the profits from her first successful novels to build The Mount, her country estate at Lenox, Massachusetts.[12] Her architects, Hoppin and Koen, looked to Belton House (Lincolnshire), a seventeenth-century English country house then thought to be by Wren, as a model for her stucco "cottage," designed in 1901 and occupied by 1902.[13] Wharton helped to design the interiors herself, making The Mount a testament to the decorating ideas that she and Ogden Codman had espoused during the 1890s.[14] She sited the building not only to encompass a set of terrace gardens and a small amphitheater but to capture an expansive view of the Berkshire hills from the drawing room. For several years Wharton lived and entertained at her country house, taking in her literary friends and devoting herself to writing. As she recalled in her autobiography, "I should have preferred to live all the year round at the Mount. There, every summer, I gathered about me my own group of intimates, of whom the number was slowly growing." These included Henry James, Bernard Berenson, Bayard Cutting, Walter Berry, and Stanford White. Only her estrangement from her husband,

172 Shepley, Rutan and Coolidge. **Wychwood** (1902–05), Mr. and Mrs. Charles Hutchinson house, Lake Geneva, Wisconsin. View from lake showing wild garden planted by Frances Hutchinson. (Hutchinson, *Wychwood.*)

173 Hoppin and Koen. **The Mount** (1901–02), Edith Wharton house, Lenox, Massachusetts. (Richard Cheek.)

Teddy, who managed the estate, caused her to leave Lenox for Europe, never to return.[15]

By raising simple life in picturesque places to the level of art and high moral purpose, advocates of country life sanctioned a new culture for the country house. The makers of country places saw their dwellings more as aesthetic environments in which to enjoy the out-of-doors than as grand edifices of cultural display. They purposely set themselves apart from the palace builders. As a critic remarked of Wychwood upon first seeing Lake Geneva in 1905: "Across the lake, sticking out like a sore thumb, is visible a summer home, a large three-story stone building, Renaissance in design, entirely out of keeping with the landscape. Soon we came upon the entrance gate to Wychwood, the Hutchinson estate; at once the keynote of the place is struck. The gate is so simple that one almost feels as though the stones of the road have come together of themselves, rather than by the hand of an architect."[16] In the new country place, it was nature's own artifice that governed design.

The various back to nature movements that emerged in fin de siècle America had a far-reaching impact on the domestic scene. The influences of nature, the garden, and country activities were most intense in the years around 1900; it is no coincidence that the most important house and garden periodicals were founded at that time, that the first professional association for landscape architects was established in 1899, and that Charles Platt emerged as a major architect of the time. The movement toward simplification, ease, and informality in domestic architecture is readily observed in the country houses published in journals after 1900.[17] New attitudes

toward a genteel life in harmony with nature were manifest in the architecture of houses, gardens, and the estate environment, causing many wealthy Americans to forsake the stately ideal for the bucolic.

The models chosen for country places reflected a desire to emulate the life of an English country gentleman—whether historical or contemporary. Many estates were built to look and work like farms and farmsteads, despite the fact that their owners had only a recreational interest in raising crops and livestock. Affecting the trappings of agriculture professed one's gentility. A second popular estate type was the rustic country retreat, intended to unite the patron with the natural environment. There are numerous exam-

174 McKim, Mead and White. **Beacon Rock** (1888–91), E. D. Morgan house, Newport, Rhode Island. (Detroit Photographic Company collection, Library of Congress.)

175 Shepley, Rutan and Coolidge. **Hilldene** (1905), Robert Todd Lincoln house, Manchester, Vermont. (Author.)

ples of larger country houses that were built for more than seasonal use because of an owner's love of a particular spot. Robert Todd Lincoln's Hilldene (1905) in Manchester, Vermont, designed by Shepley, Rutan and Coolidge, was occupied for seven months of the year, though it was called a summer house. Houses originally designed for sporting activities, such as riding, golf, sailing, fishing, or shooting, were sometimes enlarged and embellished to become year-round estates. Indeed, any of the popular activities of country life could serve as an excuse for building a large house.

Among American gentlemen, the favorite country diversions were sports. One of the era's leading sportsmen was Robert J. Collier (1876–1918), the New York publisher of *Collier's Weekly.* A vigorous patriot and fiery advocate of truth-telling journalism, Collier balanced his concern for various causes with a staggering schedule of country sports. He was a squash champion at Georgetown, an expert polo player ("his ranking was never below America's top four"), a master of the hunt, keen on cross-country riding, golf, and auto racing, and one of the first Americans to take up flying as a hobby.[18] His years at Oxford taught him that a gentleman should neglect neither the mind nor the body; appropriately he became a noted collector of rare books. These avocations all needed a proper backdrop, so Collier hired John Russell Pope to design him the most up-to-date country place in New Jersey, which was begun at Wickatunk before World War I. A splendid Mount Vernon–type Colonial Revival crowned the two-hundred-acre complex of stables, guest quarters (for fifty), polo fields, and hunting grounds. Augusta Patterson called it "one of the most perfect and most extensive Colonial developments in the coun-

try."[19] It was a fitting surround for the man who saved Abraham Lincoln's birthplace and erected a shrine to' him in Kentucky. (Unfortunately, Collier died soon after the buildings were completed.) He was representative of a type of American gentleman who emerged during the early twentieth century, the progressive sportsman in the mold of Teddy Roosevelt.

I trace in this chapter the major types of pastoral country estates, including the colonial farmstead, English-influenced garden estate, artist's retreat, gentleman's enclave, utopian architectural compound, and seaside farming estate. What ties these together is a general interest in the cultivation of the land itself, in its domestication and artful stewardship. They are testaments to the extraordinary gardening and land-conservation movement that swept America during the first quarter of this century. Finding the "artistic" in rural life was the ultimate goal for this group of patrons and architects.

THE HILL-STEAD: A COLONIAL REVIVAL FARM

Farmington, Connecticut, is one of the most charming historic villages in the state. Despite its proximity to bustling Hartford, it retains much of the quaint colonial feeling that persuaded Theodate Pope (1867–1946) to attend Miss Porter's School one hundred years ago and eventually to settle in the town. The house that she and her parents built there, now a splendid museum, contributes so much to what makes Farmington unique that it is difficult to imagine the place without it.[20] The peculiar and special character of the Hill-Stead begins with its sense of belonging in Farmington, amid white clapboard houses and narrow village lanes. It extends to a feeling, common to every visitor, that the house is a vivid portrait of its three patrons: a daughter with a vision of what architecture ought to be, a father with a passion for color and paintings, and a mother tied to the conventions of society in nineteenth-century Cleveland. Because the house stands basically intact, as Mrs. Theodate Pope Riddle left it in her will in 1946, the Hill-Stead gives a palpable sense of how the Pope and Riddle families lived.[21] It is one of the few houses of the period that has been completely preserved for the enjoyment of the public, making it perhaps the finest Colonial Revival house, and museum, in the United States.

Despite its seemingly artless and simple qualities, the Hill-Stead was formed out of a rather complex set of intentions and circumstances. Here was a modern American house represented as a colonial survival, a farm built in the old way. Yet it was also a country house, built for the leisure pursuits of a rich man during an era of palatial constructions. It was designed to contain a collection of French impressionist paintings that was one of the earliest and most important of its day in America.[22] Pope began to acquire works by Whistler, Manet, Degas, Monet, and Cassatt in the 1880s. They were hung not in richly appointed galleries but in comfortable rooms designed for living and entertaining. The clapboard exterior of the house concealed a fireproof brick construction and a number of technological innovations that were advanced for the time. The anomalies of the Hill-Stead go far deeper than meet the eye. It is one of the earliest American country houses that can genuinely be called Colonial Revival and is thought to have been designed by the architects who popularized Early American styles. Yet even this assessment conceals the true picture of this remarkable house.

To understand why Alfred Atmore Pope built a farm and not a palace for his French paintings, as many of his contemporaries might have done, one must look at the man himself and at his eccentric and forward-thinking daughter. Pope was born of sturdy Quaker stock in the village of North Vassalboro, Maine, in 1842. His temperament and career recall the character of Silas Lapham, the hero of William Dean Howells' famous novel. The fictitious Lapham was a New Englander very sure of his paint company but uncertain where his wealth was leading his family. Similarly, Alfred Pope was a dogged and serious businessman possessed of an almost compulsive practicality. He made his fortune with the Cleveland Malleable Iron Company, which he joined in 1869.[23] His letters give us a taste of his down-to-earth sense of virtue and hard work, as well as his modest delight in high culture and society — a society he and his wife entered by virtue of their new class and wealth. He married Ada Brooks of Ohio in 1866; it was she who helped him make his place among the elite of Euclid Avenue, where they built a Queen Anne house (at number 949, near the Rockefellers) and entertained lavishly. Their daughter, Effie Brooks Pope, was born in 1867. It was expected that she would have the education, social finishing, and "coming out" expected of a girl of her station.

When young Miss Pope insisted upon changing her name to Theodate — meaning "gift of God" — upon her graduation from Cleveland's Mittleburger School in 1886, her parents were made painfully aware that she would not take the path of social convention. To call the young woman odd by the standards of her time would be an understatement. She was a headstrong girl with definite ideas about her future; her diaries record dreams of having a farmhouse, taking in poor children, and developing an "ideal eductional system" — hardly the common concerns of a debutante. Theodate Pope had a difficult and unhappy childhood, spent constantly struggling against her mother's wishes and being intimidated by her example as a popular hostess. She was shy and plump, awkward in social situations, and found the manners and behavior of a Victorian woman stuffy and artificial. She rebelled by pursuing interests far from those accepted for women of her day. Her practical bent was more in keeping with her father's character, so it is no surprise that the two were very close. Because of her difficulties in fulfilling her expected role as a marriageable girl, she was sent to Miss Porter's School from 1886 to 1888, an event that was to influence her life profoundly.

Farmington was for Pope the antithesis of her "brown decades" milieu on Euclid Avenue. There she led a simple, unpretentious life amid small white houses and rolling farmland — "real life," as she remembered it, for the first time in her experience. Her coming-out party in 1889 was a disaster, which finally convinced her parents to stop "trying to fit me into their pattern." She was thereupon given permission to live in Farmington. In 1890 she restored an eighteenth-century house (the O'Rourkery), added to it, and set up a tea shop for the girls at Miss Porter's. "For a year I cooked every meal. Through the night I frequently struck matches to see my watch in order to be up at six o'clock to build the kitchen fire," she later recalled. "The experience was all so deliciously new to me that I felt I had stepped over a frame into a picture."[24]

For eight years she remained in her picture-perfect cottage, gradually developing her ideas for her parents' estate and planning a career in architecture. Though the source of her training is not certain, she apparently corresponded with and was tutored by members of the fine arts faculty at Princeton, which at that time did not have a formal architectural program.[25] Her determination to become an architect was unstoppable, despite the sex biases and professional impediments she would face as a woman. Convincing her father to build a house that she would help to design was the first step.

The story of the planning and construction of the Hill-Stead began in August 1898, when Alfred and Ada Pope set sail for Southampton on a European tour. (Both they and their daughter were experienced travelers, having first visited the Continent in 1888.) Some time earlier Theodate had convinced them to purchase land in Farmington in order to build a country house that would serve as their major residence after retirement. They chose a site to the east of the village, to be assembled out of several parcels of land — eventually to comprise some 250 acres. Harris Whittemore, the scion of a Naugatuck manufacturing family, a business associate of Alfred, and former fiancé of Theodate, was entrusted to make the purchases. Theodate received a cable on August 3

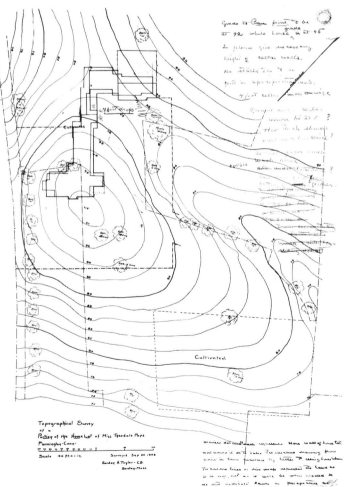

177 **The Hill-Stead.** Plot plan with notes by Theodate Pope, c. 1898. (McKim, Mead and White collection, courtesy of The New-York Historical Society, New York City.)

from her father: "Be sure to act freely about buying in Farmington, your judgment and Harris's will be mine without question."[26] He also instructed his daughter to commission McKim, Mead and White to act as architects for the house. The firm was the obvious choice because Stanford White had recently designed a Colonial Revival country house in Naugatuck for John H. Whittemore to contain paintings acquired in Europe. But this architect-client relationship was to be a highly unusual one for the famous firm. Alfred Pope gave his daughter a free reign to make the new estate according to her own ideas. The architects, according to her father, should be used as consultants to her: "I would advise your giving to McKim Mead & White . . . *your* plan . . . to get them to assist in deciding on location. . . . I think you should have the pick of your house place."[27] A triangle formed in the early stages of planning, with Theodate at the apex, acting as conduit between her father and the firm. The arrangement was not without its problems.

Theodate's initial letter to McKim, Mead and White, not dated but written in August or early September, is indicative of her particular ideas and rather authoritative attitude toward the men hired to design her father's house.[28] In it she describes the site, gives a specific program, and indicates precisely what she will expect from the firm in terms of drawings. She is not only curt and presumptuous but seems determined to establish her own expertise at the outset. Such a letter must have warned experienced architects that they would have an unusually meddlesome client; this would also explain why they did not assign a partner to handle the design.[29]

Theodate Pope met with the architects in late September, as land was being bought and arrangements made to begin construction as soon as drawings could be prepared. There was a good deal of urgency to the process. In October Egerton Swartwout, the associate in charge, made a site visit, and preliminary plans were prepared for a thorough critique by Miss Pope. She made her detailed criticisms to the architects in writing and demanded that her instructions be followed to the letter, even to the point of having her changes drawn on the plans during an office visit.[30]

In November 1898, the Popes returned from Europe and met with Theodate and the architects in New York to view for the first time the plans for their country place. Her letter of November 3 to Swartwout in preparation for this meeting requesting a "pretty

drawing" for their benefit has the tone of a nervous artist awaiting judgment. Working drawings for the house were in preparation during January and February of 1899. The initial plans and elevations dated February 2, 1899, are preserved in the New York Historical Society. It is worthwhile to consider the proposed design and how it related to other Colonial Revival houses of the time.

For some fifteen years before they worked on the Pope house, McKim, Mead and White had been champions of the use of Early American house models for the modern country house. Charles McKim, in his notes to inaugurate the *New York Sketch Book of Architecture,* an early source of photographs of colonial architecture begun in 1874, contested the prevailing view that old American houses were ugly: "To our mind there is greater charm to be found about the front-door step of one of these old houses, more homeliness than in most of the ambitious dwellings of the present day. They are always reasonable, simple in outline, and frequently show great beauty of detail. Nor is it a small merit that many of them have stood up for a hundred and fifty years, while a few of the survivors can count over two hundred."[31] As has been noted above, the firm was among the leaders in the development of

178 **The Hill-Stead.** Entrance drive and porte cochere. (Richard Cheek.)

models for the Colonial Revival house. Moreover, the partners had as early as 1877 made trips to New England to document and study Early American houses. They were, therefore, hardly untutored in the styles and details that might be used on a commission such as the Popes'. Stanford White bought an 1832 Greek Revival house in Saint James, Long Island, and in 1892 began to remodel it extensively to create Box Hill, his own country place.[32] Both White and McKim, however, were firm believers in an undoctrinaire, creative adaptation of plans and details from historical models and tended to produce designs showing their academic training and high-style predilections. Around 1900, the firm worked on several Colonial houses concurrently with the Hill-Stead; these show how the adaptive process worked.

The most important of these was The Orchard (1898–1907), the James L. Breese estate in Southampton, Long Island (see. fig. 89). Breese, a wealthy stockbroker, had purchased an eighteenth-century Long Island house and had it moved to a site in town as the locus of a large summer residence. McKim devised a scheme that used the old house as one wing of a long, classically axial plan. The one-room-deep wings formed a large forecourt and rear garden indebted to French academic design. The main front of the house was designed with a deliberate nod to Mount Vernon, although the use of Doric columns was very different from the original, which used posts. This two-story porch was considered the epitome of Southern Colonial design and began to appear on numerous Colonial Revival houses around this time. The Breese house is often credited with popularizing the Mount Vernon image and was certainly one of the most extensively published houses of its day. Yet the colonial flavor of The Orchard was only skin deep. Many other aspects of the house, including Stanford White's lavish, eclectic interiors, had little to do with any supposed Colonial precedent. Breese, as a wealthy, fashionable gentleman of his day, wanted a palatial house in rustic eighteenth-century American dress, and that is what he got.

How does the Hill-Stead compare to this almost exactly contemporaneous design, for which we have clear evidence of the participation of both McKim and White? The first thing we notice in the Hill-Stead is the absence of any grand, large-scale gestures that might indicate a wealthy man's house, or indeed the hand of an architect wishing to show his own artistic stamp. This includes, of course, the curious absence of the two-story porch that now graces the west front of the Hill-Stead. The drawings show a rather large farmhouse, with appendages growing from it as if time had added them—in a very undesigned way. It is doubtful that a trained architect, such as White, would have allowed such an informal, somewhat piecemeal design to leave the office under his imprimatur. The second thing that belies the involvement of a partner is the plan itself. Unlike either the Shingle Style plans the firm developed during the 1870s and 1880s or their classical and academic plans of the 1890s, this is an additive composition with some peculiar elements to it. The main block, which faces west as Theodate and her father had planned, suggests a common center hall arrangement, yet because the house was to have two fronts, perpendicular to each other, certain compromises had

179 **The Hill-Stead.** Front elevation, *left,* and first floor plan. McKim, Mead and White, working drawings dated February 1899. (Courtesy of The New-York Historical Society, New York City.)

to be made. The dining room, placed at the very center of the plan so that several rooms connect to it, is the key to the diagram: it is the hinge about which the whole house turns. Theodate's letters talk of a large dining room for her mother's entertaining and specify this central arrangement; one suspects, therefore, the architects adopted this feature at her request. There is also the oddity of the coach entrance to the house leading directly into a porch and hallway leading to the dining room. Nothing in the work of McKim, Mead and White suggests that they would have favored such an unusual, asymmetrical room arrangement as that of the dining room, L-shaped drawing room, stair hall, and service wing at the Hill-Stead. Finally, the way in which the barn was attached to the house to the east seems more in keeping with farmsteads than with traditional country house service courts. This too was at Theodate's insistence. She had the barn designed by a man in Farmington and sent the plans to the architects. Thus, there are several rather uncharacteristic aspects to the design of this house, which point directly to Miss Pope's ideas rather than to those of her architects.

The working drawings were hurriedly completed, amid a storm of complaints from the Popes, during the early months of 1899. The architects struggled to keep control of the process, only to be repeatedly rebuffed by Theodate or her father, who insisted on using their own contractors and tradesmen and constantly meddled in design details. The clients and architects had a falling-out, yet McKim, Mead and White insisted on completing the commission. Construction continued on the house throughout 1900 and into early 1901, but there are scant records of how the remaining aspects of the building and decorating were handled. On May 30, 1901, the Popes gave their first dinner, by gaslight, as new residents.

The story does not end here, however. Because both Alfred and his daughter loved to tinker, they continued to make changes in the house and landscape over the next several years. The most significant was the addition, sometime between 1901 and 1902, of the Mount Vernon porch.[33] This element, for which the house is now renowned, probably came at Alfred's insistence, somewhat in repudiation of his daughter's intention to have an unpretentious farmlike ensemble. The absence of a large, unifying element on the west facade would have been obvious to an architect wishing to

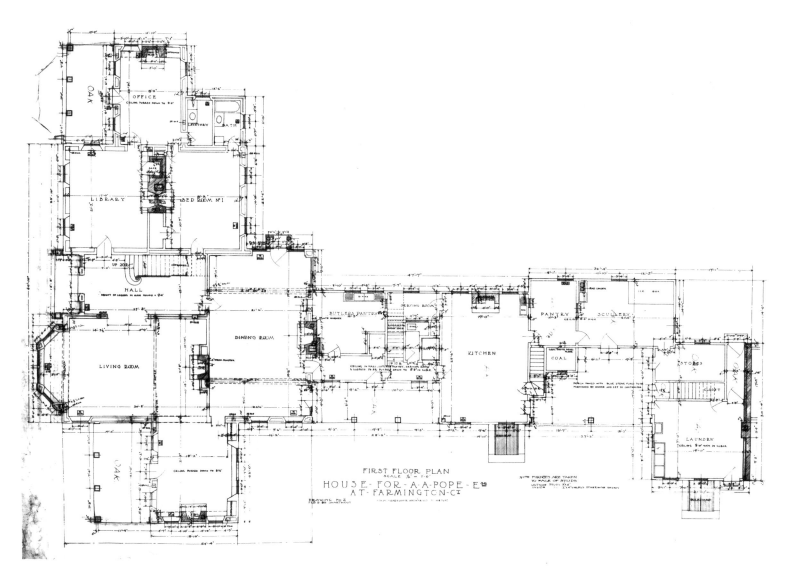

FIRST FLOOR PLAN
SCALE ⅛" = 1'-0"
HOUSE · FOR · A · A · POPE · ESQ
AT · FARMINGTON · CT

balance and bring together the disparate pieces of the house. (Theodate had the architects prepare their initial perspective of the house from an oblique angle on the south approach, showing this facade.) The lawn and garden, which were developed symmetrically from the west front, made it imperative that a larger gesture be made, and the two-story porch solved the problem with ease. When the library was expanded to the north in 1907, this flaw would have appeared even more acute. McKim, Mead and White did the work on these alterations, including minor changes to the porte cochere and service porch. Other buildings on the estate, altered or added over the years, were handled by Theodate Pope as part of her architectural practice.

Thus, the making of this American country place was very much a collaboration—among architects, patrons, and craftsmen—albeit an unusual one for so renowned a firm as McKim, Mead and White. The experimental and piecemeal nature of the design and construction illuminates not only the true character of the Hill-Stead but its allure and personality as a work of art.

The house is perfectly sited, placed on a plateau in a way that could only be revealed by days of walking the land and studying its qualities. Theodate Pope understood her landscape deeply; her genius must have envisioned the entry drive, which rolls down a

furrow and up again to bring the visitor to an opening between the west front and a group of trees, revealing a spectacular view of the countryside to the north. The great porch projects obliquely, framing an expansive prospect of rolling hills. Only then does the drive turn gracefully toward a charming porte cochere on the south. At this point one notices the farmyard ahead and a subtle, sunken garden on axis with the doorway. That garden, made with the help of Theodate's friend and colleague Beatrix Jones Farrand, is one of the special glories of the Hill-Stead that has reemerged only in recent years.

Each side of the house is designed with a distinct purpose. The north front is stoic, protective, as it must be to withstand the winter temperatures and winds. To the east are the workshops, barns, and farm buildings, made of stone and clapboards, with a kind of Arts and Crafts sensibility that charms easily. The kitchen garden and two service porches are screened from the visitor's eye. The entrance facade to the south recalls certain Queen Anne houses, not only in the United States but in England, with large multi-paned windows and fine millwork detailing. Everywhere the details depict careful study and application of principles known to early carpenters and builders—another manifestation of Theodate Pope's understanding of the tradition in which her work would

180 **The Hill-Stead.** Dining room. (Richard Cheek.)

181 **The Hill-Stead.** Stair hall. (Richard Cheek.)

182 **The Hill-Stead**. Living room. (Richard Cheek.)

stand. There are many more surprises upon entering the house—most immediately, the colors and idiosyncratic decor of the interiors. A subtle brown-gold scheme pervades the downstairs rooms, allowing the pastel hues of the paintings to come forth as vividly as possible. In an era marked by heavy, opulent decoration this would have seemed extremely fresh. Also astonishing to an architect are the openness and practicality of the plan, which on paper looks somewhat unresolved. The overall impression is one of unity, of a picture that Theodate and her father had firmly in mind. The unique color palette can only have come from a thorough study of the paintings. The controlling impulse was to present a slightly more elegant version of the New England houses they admired. We see this in the ashlar-block wallpapered hall, reminiscent of the 1830s, the old-fashioned, dull yellow graining of much of the woodwork, the stair newel and balustrade, and the general informality of the rooms. Two elements are in counterpoint to the Colonial Revival tenor of the interior: the paintings, and the smattering of Victorian or Queen Anne furniture and fittings, which presumably came from the Cleveland house. These

can only have been installed to satisfy Mrs. Pope's taste. The house achieves its personality from the coexistence of three intentions: Theodate's, to create an old Farmington house; Alfred's, to make a setting for his collection; and Ada's, to have a home like the one on Euclid Avenue.

The Hill-Stead fit its place and purpose in a way that sets it apart from other grand estates containing art collections. The Popes clearly wished to live in the mode of their early New England ancestors yet to have a level of comfort and culture in keeping with their wealth and achievement. Through their daughter's vision, and with the help of architects who understood their intentions, they created an outstanding country house in the colonial tradition. When he visited the Hill-Stead in 1910, Henry James saw the unique qualities of this "new house on a hilltop," qualities that seemed to transcend both the image of Mount Vernon and the environs of Farmington. The surprising mixture of "tastes" gave the house its individuality, he thought. The Hill-Stead achieved its unusual artfulness by mixing its metaphors, standing out like a quatrain of poetry in a body of prose. "It made everything else shrivel and fade: it was like the sudden trill of a nightengale, lord of the hushed evening."34

In 1887, five years after beginning his practice in Philadelphia, Wilson Eyre began work on the fifty-acre estate of John W. Pepper in Jenkintown, Pennsylvania. It would become for him not simply a job but an ongoing obsession through which he would refine his ideals for the American country house and garden. His alterations to the estate were to continue over twenty-five years, making it a barometer for his changing tastes and architectural ideas.[35] Because of Eyre's influence on other Philadelphia architects, it is possible to see Fairacres as the quintessential romantic country house of the Anglophile school in the Delaware Valley. In its early incarnations, the house straddled the formal traits associated with Queen Anne and early Tudor houses. Later, in its 1904 version, it manifested the more sophisticated variations on English themes that Eyre developed after his trip to England in 1895.[36]

Fairacres could only have been designed for a patron who shared his architect's view of the appropriateness of Elizabethan styles for the country house. John W. Pepper was a noted collector of antique English furniture and a member of one of Philadelphia's most prosperous landed families. The patriarch, Henry Pepper, born Johan Heinrich Pfeffer (1739) in Strasbourg, Germany, came to America in 1774. He built up a large brewing business in Philadelphia, leaving a large estate to his son George on his death in 1808. George Pepper (1779–1861) acquired significant real estate in and around the city. Perhaps the richest man in Philadelphia at the time of his death, he divided his estate among his children and grandchildren.[37] Among these heirs were Senator George Wharton Pepper (born in 1867), one of the city's most famous attorneys, and his cousin John Worrell Pepper (1852–1918), head of one of nine Pepper family units listed in the Social Register in 1940. The Peppers were leaders in civic affairs, donors to the University of Pennsylvania, and prominent members of Philadelphia's Episcopalian community.[38] Wilson Eyre stewarded the design of James Peacock Sims' St. Paul's Church in Chestnut Hill, bringing him into contact with this prosperous and influential family during the 1880s.

Eyre's first residential commissions, such as Anglecot (1883), the Shingle Style house for Charles A. Potter in Philadelphia, and the half-timbered house (1885) for Richard L. Ashhurst at Overbrook Station, were based on the premise of a linear plan topped with an expressive multigabled roof. Eyre was fond of interlocking and overlapping masses—porches that moved in and out of the main mass of the building, small gestural turrets and dormers, and sliding roof planes. When he designed the Pepper residence he used the same formula, in which the house stood as a dynamic object unto itself. Fairacres was conceived as a half-timbered volume resting on a base of closely laid schist, the famous local building stone that gives Philadelphia houses their unique texture. Even the juxtaposition of the two wall systems was rather picturesque and slightly haphazard. Commentators praised much about the first Fairacres but still found it an immature and flawed design.[39] The qualities that made it a plausible Queen Anne house became problems when the formal garden was added.[40]

183 Wilson Eyre. **Fairacres,** first version (1887), John W. Pepper house, Jenkintown, Pennsylvania. (*Architectural Record,* 1903.)

When Eyre undertook the planning of the extensive gardens, greenhouses, and outbuildings on the Pepper estate in 1893, these flaws became more apparent. Because the gabled projections and other elements of the house obeyed no larger order, the architect found it difficult to relate the building to the gardens in any but the most perfunctory way. (Shingle Style cottages, though often intimately related to the land, were almost never surrounded by elaborate gardens.) To the southeast of the house, Eyre designed a walled garden on several levels, containing extensive boxwood work, somewhat after the manner of English Renaissance terraces. Included were two greenhouses, an English summer house, or gazebo, in one corner, a fountain sequence, pergolas, and an enclosing row of Lombardy poplars. Its axial and rectangular layout was in sharp contrast to the picturesque qualities of the original house. As a critic remarked in the *Architectural Record* upon seeing the estate, "Seated upon a broad bench at the foot of the three columns [at the termination of the axial garden sequence] the visitor looks back toward the house and is surprised to notice that the garden has no formal connection to the house, unless a straight walk and coincident axes may be called such."[41]

Fortuitously, however, Wilson Eyre decided to make a three-week "sketching trip" to England in 1895. His impressions, recorded after the journey, indicate that he was profoundly influenced by what he saw there. For despite his early admiration for English houses, he had not yet seen country houses and gardens in their natural settings. He made it a point to see examples of centuries past as well as new work, visiting Haddon Hall, Chatsworth, Warwick Castle, and the towns of Oxford, Chester, Tewkesbury, Warwick, Litchfield, Worcester, Liverpool, and London. He saw examples of the modern work of Richard Norman Shaw, Ernest Newton, Harold Peto, and his partner, Ernest George, and regretted not having seen Philip Webb's houses—"as I understand that he is considered by many English architects as one of the best and most individual men in the profession." Eyre was struck most by the consistency of English domestic traditions, the way houses and gardens worked together, the way roofs were used to express the character of the house, the "homelike" qualities that each possessed, concluding that

184 Eyre's design for the garden at **Fairacres**, 1898. (Avery Architectural Archives.)

185 **Fairacres.** Garden. (*International Studio*, 1910.)

no idea can be gained, except from personal study of the completeness and fitness of the country houses and farm houses and of their surroundings, their "flocks of gables," the grouping and composition which through the most careful study arrives at the entirely unstudied and almost haphazard effect, and above all the impression produced that the building belongs to the spot upon which it is built and to no other. This is what makes the English domestic work better, to my mind, than any I have seen and so well worthy of study, especially by our American architects.[42]

After his trip to England, Eyre's appreciation for the variety and historical breadth of the English country house and its situation was increased immeasurably. His work began to evince the characteristics of modern English country houses more directly, and he

186 Wilson Eyre. Design for a country house in the modern English manner, 1901. (Avery Architectural Archives.)

187 Wilson Eyre's sketches of the second **Fairacres**, c. 1902. (Avery Architectural Archives.)

became a tireless advocate for integrated house and garden planning. It was also around this time that the T-Square Club began featuring the work of such major English domestic architects as Newton, Guy Dawber, and George and Peto. Eyre's love of things English was also reflected in his collaboration with Frank Miles Day in founding *House and Garden* in 1901, which in its early issues featured photos and sketches of the vernacular buildings, gardens, and landscapes of the English countryside. Undoubtably some of these were made on Eyre's trip.

All of these images and influences converged when John W. Pepper asked Eyre to enlarge his house in 1901 or 1902. According to Henry Saylor, the architect "drew up plans for a rather elaborate scheme of alterations. 'Just how much of the old house is there in this new scheme?' was the question asked by Mr. Pepper when the sketches were completed. 'So little that it would be better to neglect it altogether and build afresh,' was Mr. Eyre's reply. And it was done."43 The result was a second, larger Fairacres, finished in 1904, which was designed to attach to the existing garden.

This house, disposed so that its major rooms would take advantage of the terrace, became a prototype for several important later country houses by Eyre, in which he jettisoned the half-timbered image in favor of a stronger, more abstract massing in either stucco or stone facing. Each was to employ a two-story block with gabled appendages projecting toward the garden to form a U, with a loggia also on the garden side. (A number of English houses of the era employ this basic formula, though in rather different ways.) In the plan of Fairacres, Eyre worked out the scheme for these more sophisticated houses, a diagram in which each face of the house interlocked with gardens, forecourt, or service courts to take maximum advantage of the site. In the tradition of English houses, the architect designed a distinct service or entry court with a projecting porte cochere. Upon entering the house, the visitor immediately noticed the lateral disposition of rooms to right and left. From any of the formal rooms, the garden was visible through large windows, a separate picture for every space. At Fairacres the two-story, Tudor great hall was the most prominent room. Directly ahead was an unusual Adamesque reception room, designed to contain a suite of porcelain and furniture. The library,

with its notable inglenook, was freer and more in the Queen Anne mode, and the paneled dining room was filled with heavy English oak pieces. All of the main rooms had access to the terrace, and the library, or living room, had its own porch, reflecting Eyre's new-found concern for planning the house to fit the site.

The massing and articulation of the new house were more disciplined and straightforward than in the first version, though the new Fairacres employed the same vocabulary. Eyre cleverly interlocked a half-timbered block on the garden side comprising three asymmetrical gables with a more austere stone-faced block on the entry side. The garden axis was absorbed into a small loggia, framed by two rustic stone columns—a motif that was to become one of Eyre's signature pieces. He used this same basic approach in his houses for H. Gates Lloyd in nearby Haverford, built of stucco, and for Isabel Curtis in Litchfield, Connecticut, among other works of the first decade of the century. His experiments at Fairacres resulted in clearer, more succinct houses. Eyre was able to solve for himself the problem of achieving a romantically free composition within the constraints of basically formal site planning, something that Lutyens achieved with even greater facility and genius in his contemporaneous works in England.

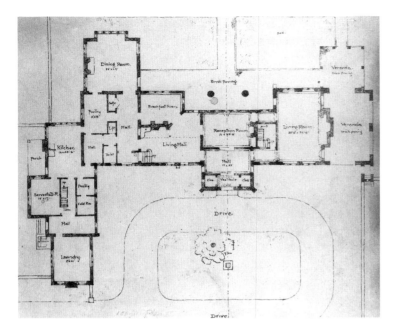

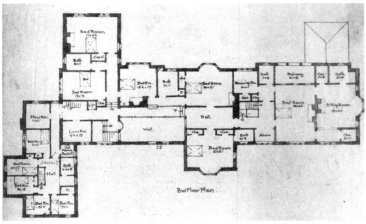

188 *above* Wilson Eyre's preliminary plans of the second **Fairacres**, c. 1902. (Avery Architectural Archives.)

189 *top* Wilson Eyre, second **Fairacres** (1904). Axial view from garden. (*International Studio,* 1910.)

190 *center* **Fairacres**, second version. Library or living room. (*International Studio,* 1910.)

191 *bottom* **Fairacres**, second version. Hall. (*International Studio,* 1910.)

Fairacres was the most published and admired of Eyre's large houses, honored by its appearance in England's *The Studio,* as well as in the American *Country Life* series entitled the "Best Twelve Country Houses in America."[44] Critics found it the epitome of a country estate in the English genre. As at the Hill-Stead, the patron and designer seemed intent upon molding a place where country life could be cultivated, like a garden, over many years.

Despite Eyre's experiments in Philadelphia, Charles Platt was widely considered the creator of the country place ideal—the architect who brought house and garden together. Sylvania, built from 1904 to 1909 at Barrytown, New York, near Rhinebeck on the Hudson, is one of his lesser-known but archetypal works.[45] In it we find not only the spirit of architectural reform that Platt initiated in his villas and Colonial houses, but a story of intellectual renewal for its client, John Chapman, one of the leading political radicals of the Progressive Era. Sylvania rings with the literary images of an antique villa, but its associations are more with the Hudson Valley retreats of Washington Irving and Frederick Church.

John Jay Chapman (1862–1933) was a literary critic and progressive reformer very much in the mold of Herbert Croly, Willard Straight, and Winston Churchill, three of Platt's leading clients. His life was one of intense early activism and creative energy, which was nearly destroyed by disillusionment and shattered idealism.[46] As one biographer put it, he "hurled himself with concentrated energy against his times," only to be rebuffed by the ineffectual results of his written critiques of politics, morals, and society.[47]

His ancestry, like that of Henry Adams, haunted him throughout his life. Though his father was a New York stockbroker, his clan was dominated by great American lawyers and abolitionists. John Jay, for whom young Chapman was named, was governor of New York and chief justice of the United States, and William Jay one of the most famous lawyers of the nineteenth century. Chapman's maternal grandfather, John Jay II, was a leader in antislavery causes and this tradition of social activism was instilled in the young man at an early age. After a gentleman's education at St. Paul's and Harvard (1884), he read law and was admitted to the New York Bar in 1889. His intellectual interests and political activism, however, drew him to social criticism. He published a series of savage parodistic pamphlets entitled *The Political Nursery* from 1897 to 1901, as well as two major works of political and moral thought, *Causes and Consequences* (1898) and *Practical Agitation* (1900). He also wrote works of literary criticism and biography. Chapman's writings were targeted at the political corruption and business machinery of the Gilded Age but were framed in a worldview shaped by his ancestors in the age of gentility during the early Republic. Like many members of the old gentry during his time, Chapman was appalled by the engines of economic and social change which were driving late nineteenth-century America. He wrote: "A civilization based upon commerce which is in all its parts corruptly managed will present a social life which is unintelligent and mediocre, made up of people afraid of each other, whose ideas are shop-worn, whose manners are self-conscious."[48] It was this kind of sentiment that not only drove Chapman to fight and be beaten by the New York political machine but also brought him to leave the city for a life more akin to that of his ancestors.

A decade of law practice in New York and a decade of political activism during the 1890s came to an end for Chapman with the death of his first wife, Minna Timmins, in childbirth. In 1898 he married Elizabeth Chanler, whose family owned Rokeby, a nineteenth-century Hudson River estate north of Rhinebeck. Unfortunately, he succumbed to nervous exhaustion, or neurasthenia (a common psychological ailment of the gentry during this period), just after the turn of the century following an unsuccessful political career. He and his wife left New York City in 1904 to build a new country home near Elizabeth's family on the Hudson.

Platt was therefore building within the great tradition of Hudson River country seats, for clients who valued genteel country living but wished to promote a vital new art as well. Like Olana, the house of Frederick Church near Hudson, the Chapman villa was an artistic and literary retreat. Here Chapman studied, wrote, entertained intellectual friends, and most of all renewed his flagging spirit in a setting rich with familiar customs. Platt approached the design by passing over the Victorian era for more historical sources. Reminding one the Villa Emo or Monticello adapted to the modern situation, Sylvania represents Platt at his compact, classical best. Here, as one critic put it, he "dared to be simple to the point of bareness," disarming the world of the stately home by achieving elegance without a trace of opulence.[49]

Sylvania was one of a series of the architect's first mature works in simplified, geometric, compact pavilion forms using the general concept of the villa (in its Italian sense)—a prismatic block interlocked with semiformal gardens. Here, as well as at Villasera (1903–06), Woodston (1904–08), and The Mallows (1905), Platt strove to find a formula for a classical house that was also restrained and appropriate as a foil to a country garden.[50] In these works he achieved a sophistication missing from Maxwell Court and earlier works, while retaining their charm and straightforwardness.

The plan is one of the most subtle and rational of Platt's solutions to the country house program. Because the house was approached axially and, like a typical Hudson villa, sat on a plateau overlooking the river, the entry and river fronts were given slightly different treatments—engaging the Ionic portico on the east side and letting it stand as a free porch on the west. (This is a feature found in a number of American Colonial houses.) The center of the house, in both social and architectural terms, was the drawing room, placed directly behind the west, or river, portico; the informality and comfort of its decor made it a living room to all intents and purposes. The Chapmans, being artistic, used the room for musical performances and readings. The stair, off a small transverse hall, was also unusually underplayed. More prepossessing was the library on the south side, a large room with its own porch. Fittingly, the second most prominent room in the house was dedicated to books and writing. Filling out the house were a morning room, streamlined servants' quarters, a dining room, and only six bedrooms. It is useful to note Platt's cleverness in placing the numerous bathrooms and service areas in between major rooms, always a trick in a modern classical block. His formula came close to being canonical for villa or block country houses and was copied by many architects of country as well as suburban houses. That is one reason why it looks so conventional to the modern eye.

192 Charles Platt. **Sylvania** (1904), John Jay Chapman house, Barrytown, New York.
Oblique view from southeast and plans. (Avery Architectural Archives.)

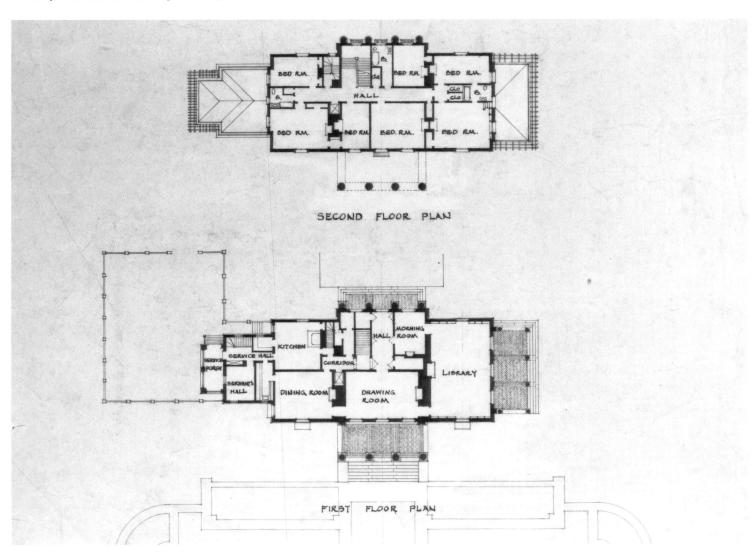

SECOND FLOOR PLAN

FIRST FLOOR PLAN

Critics of Platt's time were quick to recognize the subtle innovations achieved by an integrated country place like Sylvania. "The design of the house in its relation to the grounds is characterized by the simplicity, the economy and the distinction, which

is more than ever becoming the note of Mr. Platt's work," wrote a critic in the *Architectural Record* (September 1908). "The Chapman house fits its site, commands its view, and holds its own in the landscape, and it does all of these things without any suggestion that it is trying to be a little bigger and more impressive than it really is." Implicit in this point of view was the fact that by 1905 too many stately homes were being built merely to impress by their size, richness, and style. A classical house did not necessarily have to drip with French opulence. Boston's *Architectural Review* commented: "Aside from the perfection of its composition, only possible of attainment by the most careful study of every part of its complex detail, there is to be felt a certain freshness in the treatment of the ornament—a freshness and vitality not ordinarily to be associated with projects conceived in so long-dead a form of classic architecture; the same classic purity that is to be found in the later work of Palladio, for instance."[51]

Platt's design for the gardens, like that of the house, was consummately simple and articulate. Using only lawn terraces, carefully chosen and placed species of trees, and low shrubs, the architect achieved a balance of expression between architecture and planting. The plateau and view of the river were heightened by a formal terrace placed slightly below the grade of the west front, perceivable in its lozenge form from the porch but resembling an informal grouping of low shrubs from the river below. The great approach axis, extending through the house, was further articulated after crossing this terrace by a piece of lawn, leading the eye down to two stands of mature trees framing the view to the Hudson. Without elaborate materials and devices, this garden achieved the ideal of dignity and refinement so critical to the new country place. It also succeeded with its patron, who reentered public life in 1912, after almost ten years as a Hudson River gentleman.

194 **Sylvania.** West front. (*Architectural Review,* 1908.)

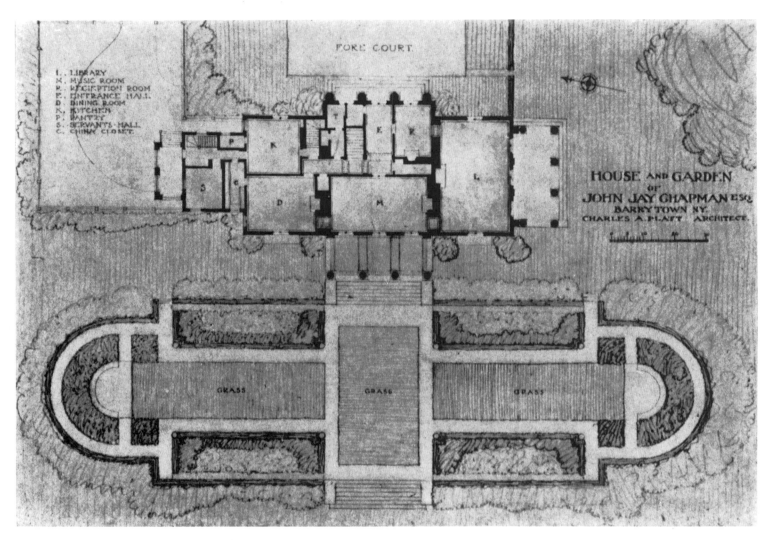

Legend on plan:
L . LIBRARY
M . MUSIC ROOM
R . RECEPTION ROOM
E . ENTRANCE HALL
D . DINING ROOM
K . KITCHEN
P . PANTRY
S . SERVANTS-HALL
C . CHINA CLOSET

FORE COURT.

GRASS   GRASS   GRASS

HOUSE AND GARDEN
OF
JOHN JAY CHAPMAN ESQ.
BARRYTOWN NY.
CHARLES A. PLATT   ARCHITECT.

195 **Sylvania.** Site plan. (*Architectural Review,* 1908.)

THE HOUSE IN THE WOODS: A SUMMER STUDIO

Like Charles Platt, Howard Shaw saw his country house practice blossom around 1905, when he began a series of large residences for many of the Middle West's most important businessmen. Shaw's clients were conservative, self-made men, generally from the second generation of Chicago's upper class. Adolphus Clay Bartlett, one of the elder statesmen of the city's business elite, was a notable exception.[52] Bartlett made his fortune in wholesale hardware merchandising and was active in city politics, serving on the Board of Education for many years.[53] He hired Shaw to design both a city house and a summer place. The House in the Woods (1905–07), Bartlett's summer residence at Lake Geneva, was really planned around the needs of Bartlett's son Frederick, who was a painter. Shaw and the younger Bartlett, who were good friends, created a bucolic haven very much in the manner of Platt. It was cited by *Country Life* as one of America's twelve best country houses in 1916, was profiled in 1915 by Samuel Howe in *American*

Country Houses of To-Day, and was featured in *Ladies Home Journal* in 1909.[54]

Whereas Sylvania was an expansive, outward-looking pavilion, dedicated to view, Shaw's house for Bartlett was aptly named for its inward-oriented nature. It was set within a dense forest, so that "shade and shadow as well as the whisper and majestic movements of the trees enter day and night into the scene and form a part of it." It was indeed a house secreted and retired, "a veritable nook in the woods," as Samuel Howe commented in 1915.[55] Howe also remarked that the house—two houses really—was patently theatrical. Shaw designed the courtyard expressly as a performance center, much like the amphitheater at Ragdale, his own house. The House in the Woods also owed certain of its rustic qualities to nearby Wychwood—clearly one element of Lake Geneva society dedicated itself to naturalism with missionary zeal. Here was a modern evocation of Serlio's rustic scene, a theater of the pastoral.

Lake Geneva had long been one of the most fashionable watering holes of the Chicago-Milwaukee area, since it was just over the borders of Wisconsin and Illinois in the eastern part of the state. It attracted not only Midwestern architects and clients but some Easterners as well. Among the notables with estates along the

196 Howard Van Doren Shaw. **The House in the Woods** (1905–07), A. C. Bartlett
house, Lake Geneva, Wisconsin. Lake front facade. (*Country Life in America,*
1916.)

198 **The House in the Woods.** Plan. (*Country Life in America,* 1916.)

197 **The House in the Woods.** Gallery with painted decoration. (*Country Life in
America,* 1916.)

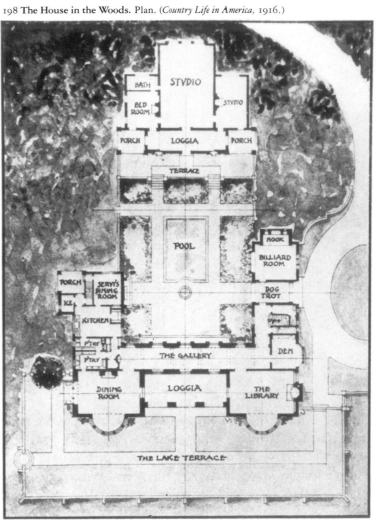

lakeshore were the Wrigleys and Schwinns. The earliest large houses, such as Northwoodside (1876) and William LeBaron Jenny's Blacktoft (1881), reflected the Chalet Style and Queen Anne influences of their times. Many of the largest houses were built between 1895 and World War I on slender tracts of lakeshore frontage off Snake Road, to the west of the town of Lake Geneva.[56] During these years the Lake Geneva enclave came to be known as "The Newport of the Midwest."

Bartlett and Shaw chose to locate their country place in the western area of Snake Road, near the stately Georgian Wadsworth Hall (1905) by Shepley, Rutan and Coolidge. The house was a mature, self-assured work, using two of Shaw's favorite devices: the courtyard plan (seen in the Norman Scott and A. H. Marks houses, among others) and the gently projecting bow windows on the formal south front (visible in many of Shaw's works). The courtyard worked to great advantage in uniting the larger L-shaped wing of the elder Bartlett with the studio pavilion built for Frederick and his family on the upper-level terrace. Shaw's models, in addition to Platt's severe, plain exteriors, were undoubtably the Queen Anne courtyard plans of his great namesake in Britain, such as Cragsyde and Leyswood. As a good English architect would have essayed, Shaw managed to use sev-

eral symmetrical plan groupings, disposed on the axis of the pool, without suggesting any overt symmetries in the overall perception of the house. And since one approached through a gateway on the flank, even the relative symmetry of the south front remained hidden. Only after passing through axially did one finally see the lake. But the architect saved his most convincing composition for the courtyard itself—a miniature Italian water garden facing a kind of stage.

Like Sylvania, The House in the Woods was a place of work, entertainment, and recreation that took full advantage of the beauty of its surroundings and the particular charm of the locale. Shaw, along with the garden designer Jens Jensen, was later to work nearby on Villa Hortensia for the Swift family. Shaw's Lake Geneva houses were built for exponents of artistic country life, allowing them a degree of freedom from convention and aesthetic simplicity that some wealthy clients might have found hard to accept. But they were also traditional, conventional houses that did not proclaim their modernity, choosing to let it show in subtle ways. Shaw chose dignity through plain and modest expression, Platt through evocation of the classical tradition. Both houses epitomized the ideal of the early country place and helped define it for architects and clients building in the 1910s and 1920s.

199 **The House in the Woods.** Studio and courtyard theatre. (*Country Life in America,* 1916.)

200 William Adams Delano. Architect's own house (1910), Muttontown, Long Island. Garden front as altered. (Richard Cheek.)

MUTTONTOWN AND THE GENTLEMAN'S WEEKEND BOX

One of the first firms to pick up on the ideas of Platt in the prewar years was Delano and Aldrich. Beginning their practice at around the same time as Lindeberg and Pope (in 1903), they received several prestigious commissions during 1907–14, which rapidly established them as specialists in the new country house and garden concept. In 1915, when Samuel Howe published his apology for unified house and site design in the third volume of *American Country Houses of To-Day,* they shared the honor (with Lindeberg, Shaw, Pope, and Platt) of being represented by more than five commissions. Their most important early experiments were undertaken on Long Island, where Delano received the opportunity to create a house for himself in conjunction with several larger commissions, as a kind of theme and variations.[57]

These were the houses of the Muttontown enclave, the 450-acre tract of the Winthrop brothers, New York attorneys and ancestors of the Puritan clan. Like other groups of houses built on the North Shore, the Muttontown houses belonged to a circle of mutual friends who enjoyed the same leisure activities. Delano became a member of this social set when he was invited to purchase a ten-acre parcel of land in the enclave. He quickly joined the Winthrops' influential circle of friends and developed a patronage chain out of this congenial country setting. Eventually Delano designed over fifty houses on Long Island.

The first Delano house was designed for the prominent attorney Bronson Winthrop (1863–1944), who in 1903 had purchased an old farm tract inland from Oyster Bay. He had intended to live in the existing farmhouse, but after one summer of roughing it he commissioned Delano to design a more elegant residence. He wanted mainly a weekend retreat from New York, where he could keep horses, raise livestock, and be near the fashionable Meadow Brook Hunt Club and the various golf clubs then being built on the North Shore (also the haunt of his clients). The estate could be used as a getaway any time of the year, for a day or a month, since the Long Island Railroad was nearby. Delano and Aldrich made their reputation by designing what might be called a gentleman's weekend box for their New York clients.

The design Delano proposed for Bronson Winthrop in 1909 was an abstractly conceived U-plan house with a vaguely English character. Located one hundred feet above sea level on a slight rise, it had views of Oyster Bay and Long Island Sound. Taking a cue from Charles Platt, Delano took pains to relate each major interior space on the ground floor to a major garden area or porch. What might have been a strictly axial, formally defined house and garden plan in an earlier Beaux-Arts architect's design became slightly idiosyncratic and picturesque in the hands of Delano. Samuel Howe called it "mellow of tone." A great maple-enclosed grass terrace to the west was balanced by the stable block, shifted off the axis of the house, to the east, while a tiny tea house was located to cap the major cross axis running through the center of the house. The impressive view of the south elevation was

201 Delano and Aldrich. Bronson Winthrop house (1909), Muttontown, Long Island. Garden front. (Avery Architectural Archives.)

202 Bronson Winthrop house. Entrance. (Avery Architectural Archives.)

Scale of Feet

1 Living Rooms
2 Library
3 Dining Room
4 Kitchen & Service
5 Porches
6 Entrance Court
7 Service Court
8 Garage & Stables
9 Tea House
10 Grass Terrace
11 Swimming Pool
12 Tennis Court
13 Apple Orchard
14 Vegetable Garden

203 Bronson Winthrop house. Site plan. Rendering by Chester Price. (*Portraits of Ten Country Houses.*)

grounded by a great lawn, framed by huge trees, as seen in Chester Price's evocative rendering.[58] As a lively and unorthodox twist, the swimming pool was placed in a hollow at an oblique angle to the house, creating, as Royal Cortissoz put it, "a little embowered paradise." This delightfully graceful estate influenced several later designs by the firm, sometimes dressed in a slightly different style on the exterior.[59]

The Winthrop house, though an austere and rather abstract rendering of English domestic styles, was really fresh and innovative for its time. The architects tended to favor this very simple treatment in many of their weekend houses on Long Island. Delano remembered in 1953 the precepts he followed in his early work, ideas that he clearly considered revolutionary at the time: "In those days, many of our architects were still designing buildings where the facades were 'borrowed' from well-known European models and too often over-ornamented. My training at the Ecole under the wise guidance of Victor Laloux had taught me the value of a simple, well-organized plan and elevation expressive of what the interior contained; so I was in revolt against the prevailing habit of designing the facade first and then squeezing the interior into the shell; furthermore, it seemed to me that we had enough indigenous examples of simple, well-proportioned buildings in our own country to guide us."[60]

Following that philosophy, he employed the same, straightforward approach in his own house, a hollow tile, brick, and stucco L-shaped dwelling reminiscent of the vernacular-inspired houses of Voysey, Baillie Scott, and Lutyens in England. Deliberately primitive in character, sporting timber king-post dormers and porches, the house cultivated the well-worn, overgrown look of an old cottage. The plan had the same basic but artful organization that Bronson Winthrop's had, on a smaller scale, and the same integral relationship to the gardens. Here the rooms and their corresponding exterior spaces were interlocked in a subtle interplay of shifted axes. Royal Cortissoz pinned down the essence of the strategy in these terms: "The thing that has struck me most forcibly . . . has been the grasp and the tact with which Delano and Aldrich see their problem as a whole, in mass, and make the land about the

205 Delano house. Garden front with pergola, as originally designed. (Avery Architectural Archives.)

house seem neither a preparation for it nor an extension of its character, but an indispensable member of one carefully pondered scheme."[61]

The scheme for the gardens was a clever overlay of formal and informal spaces, including a rose garden, teahouse, greenhouse and gardener's cottage, service group, tennis court, flower garden, and orchard with axial walk. As in the Winthrop site plan, Delano placed a great circular grass bowl in a dynamic, oblique relationship to the other garden spaces. As one traversed the axial or curving paths from one garden to the next, the experiential and pictorial logic of plan became clear. Though this was one of Delano's most complex site layouts, it retained the balanced and unified concept that Cortissoz saw as the essence of his style. According to Beatrix Farrand's records, she was also involved in advising Delano on the planting of this small estate.[62] She shared his penchant for creating garden rooms in contrasting geometries and plant materials, as is evident in her wonderful work at Dumbarton Oaks.

Both the Winthrop and Delano houses demonstrated a key characteristic not only of Delano and Aldrich but also of some of their contemporaries — the critical importance of the gardens and site plan. Living outdoors was the great attraction of country life in America. American houses in the mid-nineteenth century had begun to make porches an essential element of the plan, but in the early twentieth century eclectic designers began to experiment with more expansive conceptions of outdoor living, no better demonstrated than in these splendid Long Island estates. Delano clearly relished a quasi-agrarian style of life on the land, among his patrician neighbors. The Muttontown enclave became his retreat, a bucolic oasis of rejuvenation, and the most exclusive of his many club affiliations.[63] The style he employed here was a distinct and original one, used for a number of other gentlemen's weekend boxes. Foremost among these were the Vincent Astor house in Port Washington (1922), the W. G. Borland house in Mount Kisco (1910), the George Whitney house in Westbury (c. 1920), and the C. B. Alexander house in Bernardsville, New Jersey (c. 1914). The use of hollow tile faced with either stucco or whitewashed brick emphasized their planar surfaces. Their massing was consummately simple, their garden spaces pleasant and roomlike.

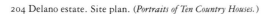

204 Delano estate. Site plan. (*Portraits of Ten Country Houses.*)

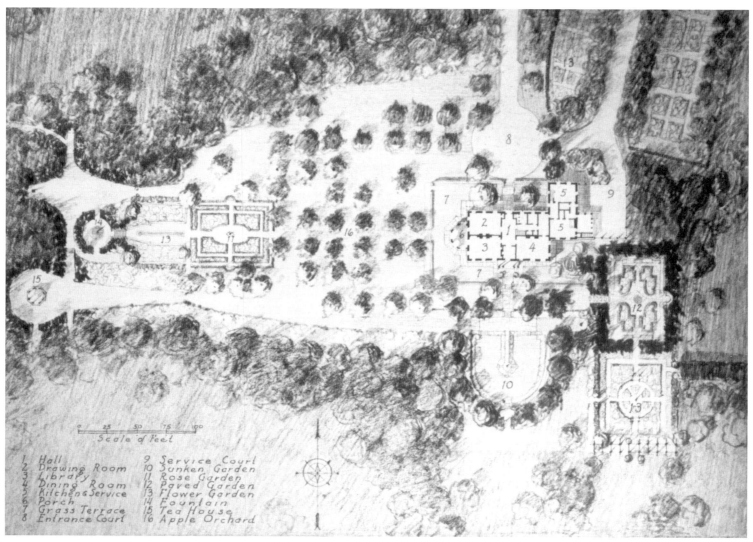

206 Delano and Aldrich. Egerton Winthrop house (1914), Muttontown, Long Island. Site plan. Rendering by Chester Price. (*Portraits of Ten Country Houses.*)

207 Egerton Winthrop house. South front. Rendering by Chester Price. (*Portraits of Ten Country Houses.*)

The last of the early designs was the Colonial Revival house (c. 1914) of Egerton Winthrop, Jr.[64] Though more formal in conception, and clearly influenced by the burgeoning interest in eighteenth-century American architecture and decorative arts, this house and garden manifested the same shifting dichotomy between the picturesque and the axial as the two earlier estates. Its center hall plan, eighteenth-century interior decoration, American antiques, and prominent cupola evoked the colonial spirit but were hardly archaeological in intent, as some work of the 1920s would become. A caption in *Town and Country* cautioned the viewer not to mistake this house for "a picture of old Virginia" and praised the estate as being "singularly free from any affectation or enrichment that could well be escaped." The reviewer, again Samuel Howe, stressed the same unified qualities in the house, site plan, and plantings that he had found so attractive in the two other Muttontown places: "The architect, painter-like, has here remembered the value of so repeating certain plants, shrubs and trees as to form a link-like connection running through the various decorative shapings of the property, unifying and holding everything together." The design worked as a single conception, both visually and experientially.[65]

209 Egerton Winthrop estate. Stables. (Richard Cheek.)

The early Muttontown houses brought Delano and Aldrich several commissions nearby that, though done in different styles, exhibited the same bucolic attitudes as the Winthrop and Delano places. One was built (c. 1915) in East Norwich for the diplomat Lloyd Griscom, whose wife was a cousin of Bronson Winthrop. Though similar in plan to the other houses, Delano gave it a slightly more colonial feeling. Griscom loved his life there, eventually taking up watercolor painting after his retirement from the foreign service. The last in the series were done for Victor Morawetz, another prominent New York lawyer, and for Benjamin and Alexandra Moore, also of New York. Here Delano went to a more formal classical block but stuck close to the formulas for site planning and small house design used so successfully in his early works.

The country life and leisure movement that spawned Muttontown and other such enclaves on Long Island suggested to wealthy Americans that they could have modest country places among members of their class and interest group. Around World War I a number of architects and patrons turned to these new country place types as a tonic to the stately home. But it was Delano and Aldrich who were best able, through talent and social connections, to realize this dream of a small, well-fitted arcadian retreat.

208 *left* Delano and Aldrich. **Chelsea** (c. 1924), Benjamin and Alexandra Moore house, Muttontown, Long Island. View of courtyard and moat. (Richard Cheek.)

FORTRESS AND FARMSTEAD: WRIGHT'S SHINING BROW

It may seem strange that I have made little mention of Frank Lloyd Wright, the architect most readily associated with innovations in American domestic architecture, with nature and the concept of the organic, with an answer to the dilemma of machine art and craft, and with the relationship between the house and the American landscape. Yet when one considers the oeuvre of this supreme individualist and rebel in American art, a great many paradoxes emerge in considering his relationship to the country house.[66]

First, although Wright designed and built hundreds of houses, only a small fraction qualify as large country houses; most were in fact dwellings for middle-income Americans in settings just outside the city. Wright's great typological inventions, the Progressive Era prairie house and the Usonian house of the depression years, were aimed directly at the dream of middle America for a little piece of turf and garden, close to the urban center. As Broadacre City would later demonstrate, he was the suburban architect par excellence. His houses were meant to be seen as antitheses to the complex and overwrought late Victorian country houses so prevalent in his formative years. Ever the prophet and preacher, his didactic watchwords were designed to undermine the architecture of his day; he spoke of "breaking out of the box," striving for "simplicity inviolate," eliminating all "period," creating houses with eaves stretching to embrace the land, leaving the better part of the site connected with the "life of the house," doing away with the basement, and so on. Organic architecture set itself apart from the conventions of its milieu.[67] Or at least it did so in principle.

In his early career Wright also carefully set *himself* apart from conservative Chicago society, maintaining that only enlightened clients like Frederick C. Robie and Avery Coonley (whose brother built a house with Shaw) had the vision to patronize him and appreciate his work.[68] Only later, when commissions were scarce and his ideals tempered, did he unabashedly embrace such capitalist entrepreneurs as Edgar Kaufmann, Aline Barnsdall, and Herbert F. Johnson—for whom he built lavish residences.

Yet as much as Wright railed against architectural conventions during his long life, he also mirrored and assimilated those conventions in his work, transforming them through a rare synthetic genius. During the Oak Park years he was clearly aware of the work of Howard Shaw (whom he counted a friend while heavily criticizing his houses), Robert C. Spencer, Harrie Lindeberg, and other romantic architects from whose works he greatly profited. Paradoxically, he was a friend of both the English Arts and Crafts architect C. R. Ashbee and the Welsh traditionalist Clough Williams-Ellis. He admired in print the country house work of Edwin Lutyens as well. Moreover, although he may have disdained the opulence and elitism associated with the country house, he consciously chose that ideal when, in 1911, he left constricted, suburban Oak Park with Mamah Borthwick Cheney, retreating to his fortress-cum-farmstead, Taliesin, on his mother's property near Spring Green, Wisconsin.[69] Taliesin East, Wright's most personal prairie house, was also a country estate, complete with servants' quarters, stables, farm buildings, a service court for automobiles, and gates to keep out the curious. Eventually comprising three thousand acres, the rural landscape around his house was carefully molded to conform to his own vision of a midwestern arcadia.[70] Although stylistically conceived to coincide with Wright's theories for an organic architecture and spatially conceived to demonstrate open planning[71] and dynamic formal relationships, the house differs little from many progressive country houses of its day in its program and even its basic relationship to garden spaces. Its major distinction is Wright's handling of the space itself—both architectural and landscape.

Wright could, on one hand, associate himself with wealth and elitism, since he was by this time a relatively successful professional, while, on the other, profess to embrace the simple values of a Wisconsin farmstead. He had designed large suburban houses, such as those for Darwin Martin in Buffalo (1904) and Avery Coonley in Riverside, Illinois (1908), but had also competed in 1907–08 with Charles Platt for the prestigious country house of Harold F. McCormick in Lake Forest, bitterly losing the commission. By 1911, when he returned from exile in Europe, he had enough experience with upper-class taste and styles of life to know what a wealthy gentleman ought to have in his country estate. As Walter Creese has pointed out, he also knew that other prominent artists and architects were retreating to their own utopian worlds, away from the storm of the city. Taliesin was in many respects a synthesis of the Coonley, the Martin, and especially the McCormick projects. It was also fully in tune with the country places that many urbane and wealthy Americans were building.

In both the McCormick and Coonley houses Wright had studied the problem of working with sloping terrain, using parts of the house as bridging, terracing, ground-hugging, nestling, or

towerlike elements to create contrast and to engage the hillsides. By utilizing sliding and overlapping roof forms to give horizontal continuity to the massing, he was free to open up the plan at points of access and along axial paths, through loggias and balconies, using the characteristic continuous casements to provide visual openness from within. In each composition, the point of arrival was a courtyard or series of courtyards, which gave access to the various sections of the house. It is important to note that the great vistas and prospects toward the lake or landscape in these projects were reserved for the key interior spaces, as if to make them secret and private. Although Wright respected the land, he was clearly concerned that his audience focus on the architecture, as the approaches to each house make apparent. At the vast McCormick project, Wright also made use of the motif of water, through fountains, pools, and a stream that ran down a ravine to the lake. The water was both natural and formally architectural, flowing in a rocky stream and shimmering in geometric pools. In Wright's work, nature played a complex role—as foil, adversary, soothing balm, intransigent force to be tamed, or serene order to be obeyed. His natural house was in many ways metanatural. His success at creating such masterworks as Fallingwater and Taliesin lay in his ability to both engage and battle the topography, the four elements, the flora, and the earth itself.[72]

At Taliesin he lost the battle several times yet continued to struggle. There were three versions of this famous house, not counting the present one, left in 1959 at Wright's death. The first, built in 1911[73] and destroyed in the famous fire of August 1914 (when Mamah Cheney and six others were murdered by a servant), was Wright's own small country house, nestled on the "shining brow" of a hill overlooking the Wisconsin River, within sight of his first building on the family property, the Romeo and Juliet tower of 1896, and near the Hillside Home School (1901).[74] A miniature of the Coonley house, its major conceit was the way it wrapped around the hillside, allowing the crest of the land to create a dramatic, mounded hillside garden courtyard, the symbolic locus of the place. At its center was a great tree, its trunk cupped reverently by a rock garden. The Wright residence, separated from the rest of the buildings by a loggia, commanded the great views, from the corner of the living room at the northeast. A row of service structures was attached to the residence, extending out along the hillside. The building grasped the land the way a hand cups a mound of sand. Wright's choreographed approach to the house was also indicative of his view of the country place as a dialectic between architecture and nature. The visitor approached from below, past a waterfall with a striking view of the house, then completely encircled the hill in a great spiral motion (a pattern Wright would favor in several other mountainside projects), eventually arriving at the elbow of the house and courtyard, facing the loggia, to again address nature. This route, which unfortunately has been lost, provides a telling picture of the architect's oscillation between building and landscape.

In Taliesin II (1914),[75] the conception was expanded to include the large studio wing to house Wright's apprentices and a lower service terrace, which gradually took the place of the original entry drive. To the original program for "a garden and a farm behind a workshop and a home," Wright and his final spouse, Olgivanna, added their utopian Taliesin Fellowship (founded in 1932), a Gurdjieff-influenced experiment in communal living that also served as Wright's architectural office until his death in 1959. It thus became less a country house, more a monastic institution. Taliesin II was destroyed by a lightning-induced fire in 1925, and extensively rebuilt over the years to reflect the architect's changing requirements and philosophies. These later additions weakened the power of the original design, and the house is now in need of extensive restoration.

Wright's ideas for the country house were formed in this great experiment and personal testament to the ideal of a "natural house." (Nevertheless, prairie houses were in many respects late Victorian buildings, especially in their programs.) In the war years, while in Los Angeles, he built another hilltop oasis and artistic compound for the theater enthusiast and oil millionairess Aline Barnsdall (the great Olive Hill theater complex, Barnsdall house, and ancillary buildings, designed from 1914–24). Hollyhock House, the grandest of his California concrete block, pre-Columbian-influenced residences, was clearly derivative of his other large prairie houses but also reflected the formal needs of a wealthy patron.[76] During his fallow period in the early depression years, he had time to reflect on the idea of modernity and the large house. He put his new thoughts into form only in the mid-1930s, when he designed several modernist country houses (see chapter 7).

ROMANTIC CLASSICISM: HARRIE LINDEBERG'S GLENCRAIG

Harrie Lindeberg was already an established domestic practitioner and master of the country house in 1926, when he completed one of his most eccentric and ambitious houses for Mr. and Mrs. Michael Van Beuren near Newport, Rhode Island. Glencraig (or Grey Craig, as it was sometimes called) was in most respects an atypical Lindeberg work, austere and formal; but upon closer examination its romanticism was apparent. Unlike other country places built to fulfill the dream of a landed life, this seaside estate placed unusual emphasis on certain agricultural pursuits.

Whereas the Winthrop brothers descended from Puritan roots and the Chapmans from old New York English gentry, Michael Van Beuren's ancestors were among the founders of New Amsterdam. The Van Beurens were one of the oldest and most esteemed Dutch families in New York, having descended from Jan Van Beuren, the city's first famous physician. After study at the University of Leyden, he came to the city to practice medicine in 1700 and spawned a great genealogy of physicians and businessmen. Five generations down the line was Michael Van Beuren's father, Frederick Theodore, Sr., who managed the properties of Spingler-Van Beuren estates in New York City. One of his sons, Theodore, Jr. (1876–1943), became a well-known New York surgeon, professor of anatomy, and dean of the Columbia College of Physicians. The elder Michael (1872–1951) received the same patrician upbringing and education, receiving a B.A. from Yale in 1896.

He chose a business career, joining the brokerage firm of Van Beuren, Martin and Jessup in the late 1890s and making his fortune there. He was never completely happy in New York and decided to move his family permanently to an estate he had bought near Newport in 1913. A gentleman of the old school, Van Beuren believed that raising flowers and purebred Guernsey cattle was more in keeping with his station than selling stock or operating a bus company in Puerto Rico (a business he plied successfully in the prewar years). The development of his avocations into full-time pursuits required a larger and more elaborate estate, to be designed by Lindeberg.

By the early 1920s, Van Beuren had become a leading citizen of Rhode Island and one of Newport's great clubmen,[77] but he did not want a Newport cottage or palace as his new country house. He was after something with a deeper attachment to the land and to his agrarian enterprise. His program included elaborate greenhouses for his flowers, a farm group for livestock, stables, and an imposing main house with a view of the ocean. Lindeberg had designed large country estates with farms, such as the Tracy Dows complex (1909) in Rhinebeck and the Ernest Fahnestock farm (1910) at Shrewsbury, New Jersey, but nothing quite so extensive as this seaside agrarian compound. The first problem to be solved was the landscape, and Lindeberg managed to effect a harmonious, peaceful relationship between the house and the sea. A

210 Harrie T. Lindeberg. **Glencraig** (1926), M. M. Van Beuren house, Newport, Rhode Island. Plan. (*The Domestic Architecture of H. T. Lindeberg.*)

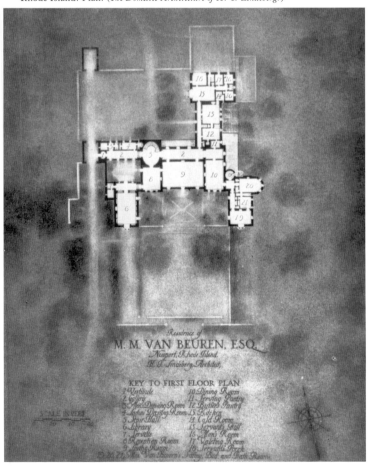

211 Frank Lloyd Wright. **Taliesin III**, architect's own country house, Spring Green, Wisconsin. View from ponds. (Richard Cheek.)

212 **Taliesin III.** (Richard Cheek.)

213 **Taliesin III.** View of roofs. (Richard Cheek.)

214 **Glencraig.** Grass terrace and waterfront facade. (Richard Cheek.)

215 **Glencraig.** Terrace front. (Samuel Gottscho, Library of Congress.)

grassy terrace led from the formal front down to the water, with no attempt to create a dominating castlelike mass on the coast. Lindeberg found a means of addressing each problem in the siting via a different device. The house had four distinct faces, yet the elevations disguised the true form of the plan. A block with dependencies from one view, it became a courtyard with a hidden garden from the entry and the setting for formal gardens on another side. Its true form was an **L**. As *Arts and Decoration* commented, "Planting . . . has been given its full stature as an element in the architectural plan. The nature of the country side is highly reminiscent of England in its repeated squares of meadow, its low dividing walls, and its gently rolling elevation. . . . The Van Beurens find their formal planting at the far side of their house, and nothing but the dipping slope of a plain lawn between themselves and the long view of Newport's seascape."78

Finding his inspiration in the site, Lindeberg then set about designing a house that was at once Georgian in some of its details and symmetrical massing as well as rustic in the way materials and forms were handled. Glencraig, a late work in a stripped or unornamented vein, was in many respects a summation of Lindeberg's architectural ideas. Its roof was almost a parody of the anthropomorphic hats of his earlier houses. The classical details were treated with a preciousness that almost belied their essence, yet such ornamental motifs as the elegant circular stair and wrought iron balusters showed that Lindeberg was a serious student of what Edwin Lutyens termed the high game of classicism. Abstract and

strangely planar, with almost no eaves or cornices, the main block of the house could have been overwhelmingly cold, had its surfaces not been treated with warm textures of closely laid, thin-coursed local stone and slates. Thus a classical block paradoxically appeared to grow up from the landscape in the expected vein of an Arts and Crafts house. The house succeeded in reconciling seemingly opposite ideals of the classical and romantic country place.

The quadrangle of stables, garages, and garden buildings, purposely given the same scale and roof pitch as the main house, pointed up this dichotomy by their unabashedly rustic quality. Indeed, the farm group is one of the most charming and beautiful buildings Lindeberg ever designed. In keeping with Van Beuren's attitude toward his estate, no expense was spared to make the accommodations for staff and animals as up-to-date as possible. The building suggested rustic English farm buildings, a romanticized icon of the kind of agrarian life Van Beuren wished to live. Like many of his fellow gentry during the early twentieth century, this gentleman seemed to wish he had lived a hundred or even two hundred years before the advent of the motorcar and the belching industrial metropolis. Although he profited from the industrial revolution, he did not consider himself a modern industrialist.

For the contemporary country gentleman, architects like Delano, Platt, and Lindeberg created a modern nostalgic estate, best exemplified by Glencraig. Lindeberg's synthesis of stout, rustic stone masses and vernacular textures with the strict proportions, massing, and detail of a Georgian house was the most original feature of this fine house—certainly one of his masterpieces.

216 **Glencraig.** Peacock gates and entry drive. (Samuel Gottscho, Library of Congress.)

217 **Glencraig.** Stairway. (Samuel Gottscho, Library of Congress.)

He was clearly drawn to this model, having used a tall hatlike roof on a block with dependencies for his own house at Locust Valley in 1927, and a variation of the formula at the large Dale Parker house at Sands Point in 1929. In his later years, he became increasingly fascinated with proportional formulas, developing what he called the module system of design in his monograph of 1940. Glencraig was a house that fulfilled every esthetic criterion of Modernism, according to its sympathetic critics. In this phase of his career Lindeberg was struggling to find an analogy to the vivid conceptions of his fellow architects involved with art deco skyscrapers. Here he attempted to strip away all but the essentials of style, much as Paul Cret did in his public buildings of the 1930s, yet remain authoritative and dignified in all crucial details. The degree of his success is still open to question, but there is no denying the intensity and conviction of his desire to find a fresh formula for the modern country house without forsaking his original romantic theories.

HILLWOOD, CAUMSETT, AND THE NORTH SHORE OF LONG ISLAND

The northwestern end of Long Island, known as the North Shore, is a series of peninsulas and inlets thirty miles long, extending from Little Neck Bay to Smithtown Bay. Between 1885 (when Theodore Roosevelt's Sagamore Hill made Oyster Bay and Cove Neck famous) and 1930, this striking, irregular shoreline was subdivided and developed as a series of estates. Prior to the depression, Long Island's Gold Coast had the largest concentration of country places in the United States. A unique rural environment easily accessible from New York, the North Shore developed not as a resort but as the most fashionable country club and estate area in America. Served by railroads and eventually highways from Manhattan, Long Island boasted numerous country estate types and models. It had leading country clubs and polo fields, yacht harbors, quaint villages—indeed, everything the modern gentleman and his family required. Mainly, however, it had the right kind of society.

Though country houses had graced this part of Long Island since the 1860s, the greatest concentration of development occurred during the 1910s and 1920s. One of the leaders of the flourishing garden culture was Marian Cruger Coffin, a pioneer landscape architect in the United States, who designed several of the finest gardens of this era on Long Island. Hillwood, occupying several hundred acres of rolling landscape in Wheatley Hills, was the largest and most compelling of her estate gardens. Designed and built between 1920 and 1922, it beautifully summed up the English gardening ideal during the era of the country place.

The owners of Hillwood not only had a good deal of money to spend on their new weekend estate but were perhaps the most powerful couple in the business world. Marjorie Merriweather Post, heiress of the Postum Cereal Company, wed Edward F. Hutton, the famed Wall Street stockbroker, in 1920 and divorced him in 1935. In between, they built Hillwood as well as two houses in

218 **Glencraig.** Close-up view of terrace and doorway. (Richard Cheek.)

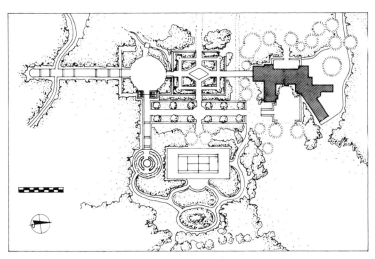

219 Marian Cruger Coffin, landscape architect. **Hillwood** (1920–22), E. F. Hutton and Marjorie Merriweather Post estate, Wheatley Hills, Long Island. Landscape plan. (Author, after Coffin's site plan in Clute, *Drafting Room Practice*.)

Palm Beach and created the General Foods Corporation. Among the smartest society couples of the Jazz Age, they clearly understood the requirements of a country house. They commissioned Charles M. Hart (1886–1968), a Beaux-Arts trained architect, to design a Tudorbethan residence, complete with horse farm and motoring house, and hired the up-and-coming Marian Coffin to do the gardens. She had in 1919 made a splash on Long Island with her design of Bayberryland, the Southampton estate of Charles Sabin, a colleague of Hutton's and chairman of the Board of Morgan Guarantee Trust. Through her familiarity with Gertrude Jekyll's ideas for the spraylike, native garden, Coffin had created variegated, colorful, and multi-textured seaside gardens around the English stucco house by Cross and Cross.[79]

In Wheatley Hills, Hart and Shape went to work designing a rambling, storybook Tudor with several gabled wings projecting asymmetrically from a central great hall.[80] Half-timbers, carved gargoyles, and diapered brickwork gave the house more than the usual hint of the medieval. Somewhat childlike and whimsical in character, the architecture of the house dictated the tone of the gardens but not their organization. The disorderly and quaint nature of the house challenged Coffin, who despite her admiration for English garden principles believed that any plan needed an axial armature or focus to give it coherence. She chose not to orient the plan around the great hall but to extend a north-south axis from the children's wing, planning the several garden rooms around an allée of magnolia trees reinforced by low boxwood. This dramatic axis terminated not orthogonally on a major feature of the house but diagonally at one of the oddly picturesque gables, creating a striking and unorthodox relationship.

The gardens at Hillwood have a playful and eclectic quality that seems to derive as much from their diverse purposes as from Coffin's theories. Included in the plan were a putting green, a small playhouse for Mrs. Post's daughter, Eleanor Riggs, a circular rose garden, a tennis court, a rustic rock garden with waterfall, and a formal topiary garden right out of *Alice in Wonderland*. Though each "room" had a distinct planting, shape, and feeling,

the overall effect was one of artful spaces for play and entertainment. The other dominant impression was of a colorfully illustrated children's story. This is not to say that the design suffered from any lack of seriousness, craft, or rigor, but that it conjured a new reality out of historical fantasy, like other creative eclectic works of its time.

Coffin's signature is apparent in the unorthodox combination of sources, plant materials, colors, and geometries. For instance, the rectangular topiary garden of precise, sculptural boxwood forms was framed by an impressionistic perennial border inspired by the work of Jekyll. As Jeanne Marie Teutonico has pointed out, such a garden was considered de rigueur for Tudor houses, although it would hardly have been treated with similar freedom in England.[81] Coffin was both gardener and architect, painter and sculptor, working to balance space, color, texture, and visual lines. Varied paving materials, intimate walled spaces, assorted garden sculpture, and subtle changes in level underscored the sense of surprise the visitor felt while meandering within. Architectural elements such as the sturdy piers of the rose arbor, the terminating double staircase, and the octagonal tower of Eleanor Riggs' house actively supported the plantings but did not compete. Coffin's genius consisted in making a romantically picturesque yet classically rigorous garden, a unified place appropriate to Long Island yet reminiscent of England. Her setting gave a rather undistinguished house an aura of the extraordinary.

220 **Hillwood.** Oblique path. (Mattie Edwards Hewitt, Long Island Studies Institute, Nassau County Museums.)

Hillwood is representative of the eclectic gardens that graced many Long Island estates during the country place era. There were, however, even grander attempts to capture country life, to emulate the domain that was the birthright of the English aristocracy. Between 1921 and 1928 Marshall Field III, the wealthy grandson of Chicago's great merchant prince, developed the most impressive estate of that area. Field and his first wife, Evelyn Marshall, moved to New York in 1921 to begin an investment banking firm.[82] They were familiar with the Peacock Point estate of Henry P. Davison, having rented Davison's Manhattan townhouse, and almost immediately acquired a two-thousand-acre site, the largest unbuilt property on the North Shore. Uniquely situated, with Long Island Sound to the north and Lloyd Harbor to the south, Caumsett was, in its raw state, a property of unparalleled beauty and history. Field initially asked John Russell Pope to develop a horse farm and residential compound, but the project quickly became one of the most ambitious estate building campaigns in Long Island's history.

In contrast to Otto Kahn, who approached the landscaping of his nearby Huntington estate with insensitivity, Field and Pope believed in enhancement through careful conservation. They left large portions of the wooded areas untouched, planted specimen trees, judiciously cleared farmland, and even restored a house of

Revolutionary War vintage as a gate lodge. With the exception of
the main house, the many buildings on the site were designed to
resemble the outbuildings of a large farm or the remnants of colonial structures. Field and Pope succeeded in beautifying the property, but with only minimal impact on the landscape. Not only
did Field wish the most sensitive and sophisticated land planning
for his Long Island estate, he also wanted a tightly run business
structure in its operation and architectural development. Pope's
office set up a large staff and management organization to handle
the job and stressed the success of their endeavor when the house
was published.[83] Like his grandfather, Field saw the world as a
great business organization and fitted his avocations—riding,
hunting, raising horses and livestock—into an efficient, depart-
mentalized world. For example, Field, who took as much pride in
the Guernseys and Ayrshires he produced as in his race horses,
hired an agricultural graduate of Cornell to run the farms because
of his expertise in cattle breeding. His gardener was English, and
the layout of the grounds was designed using precepts governing
larger English landscape gardens. Marian Coffin designed the
wild garden around the Winter Cottage, while Warren and Wetmore worked on planning the whole estate. He even kept a Scottish gamekeeper to breed pheasants and to train the best
Labradors. Field wanted the same kind of country life as Michael
Van Beuren, but on a scale one hundred times grander.

Caumsett (the Indian name for Lloyd Neck, where the estate
was located) had obvious roots in the distinguished colonial and
precolonial history of its locale.[84] It was thus a fitting monument

to the last phase of the Colonial Revival in America, as well as a
testament to the ideal of the country place as preserve, in which
nature and culture were deftly integrated. Field was brought up
and educated largely in England—at Eton and Cambridge—and
thus appreciated the ideals of the landed gentry even more
intensely than most of his American contemporaries.[85] And, like
Paul Mellon, Henry Du Pont, David Rockefeller, and other latter-
generation millionaires building in the 1920s, he sought understated and quietly elite manifestations of his culture and taste.

The program for the estate, which was dedicated to Field's
equestrian interests, included a Winter Cottage, three servants'
cottages, a stable for twenty polo ponies and their trainers; the
main residence (with fifteen bedrooms and ten servants' rooms); a
farm for breeding livestock; the gamekeeper's compound with
kennels, pheasant house, and cottage; indoor tennis courts; an
estate agent's cottage; a bathhouse; and a greenhouse and garden
buildings. The stables and farm were located in a group at the center of the property, with service buildings near the southern
entrance off Lloyd Harbor Road. The main house was beautifully
sited on a slight rise at the northeast corner, commanding views of
both the Sound and the rest of the estate. Field had a pond dug
near the shore to create the unusual view of two bodies of water
from the main terrace of the house.

Pope, the associated architects, and his staff applied a sure and
restrained hand to the design of all the buildings on the site. Of
particular note were the simple shingled bathhouse on the northern beach and the Winter Cottage, a secluded stone colonial at the
southwest corner of the property. The Georgian stable block, a
Palladian, pyramidal composition, was one of the handsomest and
most elaborate of its kind in the United States.[86]

226 **Caumsett.** Preliminary studies of main house by Otto Eggers. Garden entrance.
(*American Architect,* 1928.)

The vast main house, framed by huge trees, was a fitting culmination to Pope's series of Georgian houses with strict Beaux-Arts plans. As Augusta Patterson stressed in praising Caumsett, "A successful modern Georgian house must have an underlying strength, sturdiness, power, and even though this may seem a strange adjective to use, a hint of vivacity. The very worst thing you can call a Georgian house is to describe it as inoffensive. It must always interest."[87] In contrast to the austerity and proportional rigor of Pope's Stout house in Red Bank, New Jersey, or the slightly regency qualities of the Frick house in Baltimore, the Field house pushed the style to its limits of grandeur and monumentality. Centering the long facades on a set of pediments, Pope articulated the cornices, window surrounds, and other limestone elements as richly as the style allowed. The house can readily be seen as an eighteenth-century American Georgian house built on the scale and with the craftsmanship of English examples of the same period. In contrast to the radical rethinking of the classical language applied by Lutyens in such works as The Salutation, Gledstone Hall, and Heathcote, Pope demonstrated in his Georgian work a straightforward and typical quality that aimed for perfection without eccentricity. At Caumsett his success was limited to the exterior and a few of the main rooms, for the plan suffered from an overblown program, submerging the usually crisp and rigorous diagram that was a Pope trademark. Nevertheless, Pope achieved at Caumsett a balance of classical restraint and elegant detail that places it firmly within the pantheon of great American country houses.

Long Island's country places were probably the most elaborate and self-consciously artificial estates in the pastoral-genteel mode, and their New York owners the most urbane and fashion-conscious of America's wealthy business leaders. Yet even when astounding sums of money were spent on arcadian enclaves and ornamental farms, those patrons and architects committed to an ideal strove to work with architectural models that deferred to the landscape and fulfilled the dream of year-round existence in the country.

America's romantic country places sprang from an idealistic desire to commune with the land but also to possess it. The individualist impulse to retreat to the country seemed to some critics no less anachronistic than the wish for the aristocratic trappings of the stately home. Moreover, the craftsmanlike, antiquarian, and rustic house styles were no more attuned to the industrial world than were palaces. Threatened by higher land costs as the century progressed, and finally eclipsed by the garden suburb, the country place was just as short-lived a tradition as its forerunners. These superb homes and gardens stand as beautiful testaments, however, to a clear, if passing, vision.

During this period American architects and garden designers, spurred by the ideals of their patrons, made great strides in relating the house to the landscape. Frank Lloyd Wright was hardly the first to make a natural country house. As Samuel Howe wrote in 1915: "Probably the one word 'setting' has done more to revolutionize the architectural outlook than any other. It has, by its potency, recently forced its way into prominence and practical recognition. . . . An up-to-date, live and vigorous personality, who happens to be an architect, says to his client, 'We divide your money into two parts. We call one part the pudding, the other the sauce. The pudding is the house, whatever style you desire; the sauce is that which goes to make it palatable, the little piquancy, the perfume, the immeasurable romance and the big sweep of the thing, that is known as the setting.'"[88] Wilson Eyre, Howard Shaw, William Delano, Harrie Lindeberg, Marian Coffin, and John Russell Pope were fervent enough to insist on the importance of the setting. Their clients cared enough about the spirit of the place to pay for both pudding and sauce.

227 **Caumsett.** Aerial view. (*American Architect,* 1928.)

228 **Caumsett.** Floor plans. (Richard Cheek, from *Monograph of the Work of John Russell Pope.*)

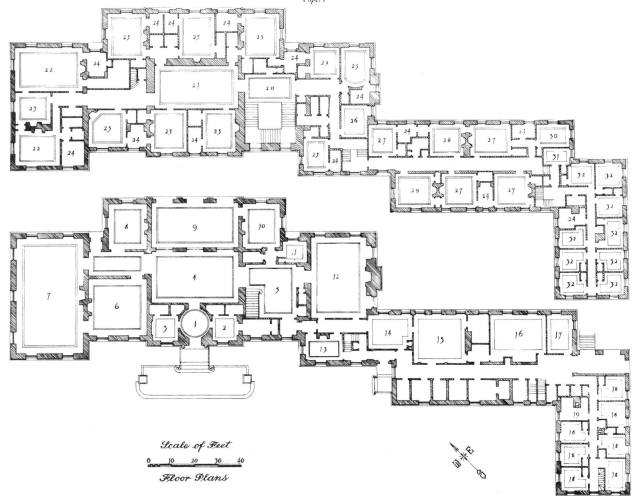

First Floor

1. Vestibule
2. Men's room
3. Ladies' room
4. Entrance hall
5. Stair hall
6. Library
7. Living room
8. Card room
9. Loggia
10. Gun room
11. Flower room
12. Dining room
13. Breakfast room
14. Butler's pantry
15. Kitchen
16. Servants' dining room
17. Servants' sitting room
18. Servants' bed rooms
19. Servants' bath

Second Floor

20. Stair hall
21. Main hall
22. Owner's bed rooms
23. Owner's sitting room
24. Bath rooms
25. Guest bed rooms
26. Linen room
27. Children's bed rooms
28. Children's sitting room
29. Day nursery
30. Governess' bed room
31. Sewing room
32. Servants' bed rooms

Scale of Feet

0   10   20   30   40

Floor Plans

229 **Caumsett.** Preliminary studies of main house by Otto Eggers. Main entrance.
(*American Architect*, 1928.)

230 **Caumsett.** Stables with horses and trainers in yard. (Samuel Gottscho, Avery Architectural Archives.)

231 **Caumsett.** Card room. (Samuel Gottscho, Library of Congress.)

232 Bertram Grosvenor Goodhue. Architect's own house (1904), Montecito,
California. (Richard Cheek, from *A Book of Architectural and Decorative Drawings by
Bertram Grosvenor Goodhue*.)

Regional Traditions
Indigenous Models for Domestic Culture

Is the effort of local architects to perpetuate ancient traditional forms a sound one? The answer is, emphatically, yes! . . . Architects who use old forms need do no violence to the ideals of contemporary architectural thoughts. On the contrary, the fundamental form of the time can best be expressed in a language native to the region.

—JOHN GAW MEEM

ꙮ FITTING IN:
INDIGENOUS TRADITIONS FOR THE JAZZ AGE

Following World War I, urban America expanded its cultural field of view—both outward to embrace a wider range of European influences and inward to recognize the achievements of Early American art. In domestic architecture this expansion resulted in a wider acceptance of eclectic idioms by the public. The most important additions to the canon of eclectic styles were not European but American, provided by the third generation of architects as they settled in the new urban centers and began to study vernacular buildings. Although there were local color movements in American architecture before the early 1920s, such as the Prairie School of the Midwest and the Californian school at the turn of the century, identification with indigenous American culture was the most widespread during the late 1920s and 1930s.[1]

Cultural historians recognize this period as the first in which writers, painters, composers, and other artists drew inspiration from specific regional cultures, the strongest of which were the Old South (reborn in the literature of Faulkner, Penn Warren, Wolfe, and others), the new Southwest, and California. The writers and artists espousing regionalism posited their cultures as distinct sociological, economic, and geographical entities.[2] No longer a homogeneous nation, America could celebrate its differences. This sense of difference is apparent in the popular literature dealing with domestic life and taste; many periodicals of the time began to focus on the diversity of America's decorative arts and architecture rather than on a nationalistic view of the Founding Fathers and the Colonial. This could only have happened through a greater awareness of the rich local traditions of American art and life. There are earmarks of this awareness throughout the cultural history of the 1920s and 1930s.

America canonized its own art during the Jazz Age. In 1924 the Metropolitan Museum of Art opened an American wing, the first institutional sanctioning of the country's indigenous culture. R. T. H. Halsey, the curator of the collection, proselytized for the acceptance of American art as high culture, to be studied as seriously as European art. The opening of this museum collection, along with those in Philadelphia and Boston, provided the impetus for a wave of personal collecting in America. The first issue of *Antiques* appeared in Boston in 1922, proclaiming itself guardian of the virtues of craftsmanship, steward of the achievements of America's past, and bible of the collector and connoisseur.[3] Buying American decorative arts became fashionable, patriotic, and a

195

good way to show one's bloodlines. Great collectors and connoisseurs, such as Henry Francis Du Pont, Wallace Nutting, Arthur Byne, Mildred Shapley, and Ima Hogg, were acutely attuned to local traditions in furniture, crafts, and the domestic arts.

Their sense of pride and identification with regional traditions was shared by new patrons who were migrating throughout the United States in search of economic opportunity. The 1920s was the decade of mobility, of the automobile, the tramway, and the train. The number of registered automobiles in the country increased tenfold between 1915 and 1929, from 2.3 million to 23 million. The smaller country house with its attached garage became the dominant domestic type for upper-middle-class Americans. Between 1922 and 1929 the rate of new home building in the United States reached an average of 883,000 units per year, an astounding figure by previous standards.[4] Building peaked in 1925. Most homes for the upper-income class were built in country enclaves or garden suburbs tailored to the car. Moreover, between 1910 and 1920 many American cities underwent their greatest growth by annexation—experiencing a 25 percent increase in population in suburban areas.

This extraordinary displacement of the population upset many Americans' sense of belonging. Not surprisingly, therefore, many embraced the traditions of their adopted regions more tenaciously than they had the old. By building a home in a regional idiom, with an architect who had established expertise in the style, the patron was able to identify more closely with the way of life and society in a new locale. The most ardent exponents of these historical revivals and reappraisals were often those who had come from elsewhere, finding economic or social opportunity in the new place. In the nineteenth century, Charles Fletcher Lummis and Helen Hunt Jackson, both Yankees, came to worship the Hispanic roots of colonial California, idealizing the past in their books.[5] Addison Mizener, seemingly born to be a vagabond and expatriate, found his fame and fortune in Florida after being a second-rate New York architect. Ernest Coxhead, Gordon Kaufmann, and James Osborne Craig made their way to California from England and Scotland to become leaders of architectural revivals there. These immigrants seemed to appreciate more intensely the qualities of their new regions, while sharing a common bias toward historical romanticism.

Regional migration brought a wider array of typological models into the canon of eclectic practice. American domestic architecture, even more than public and commercial building, was enriched by the new types and idioms culled from the diverse cultural patterns of the nation. The ranch house and Spanish courtyard house; New England saltbox; Virginia river plantation group; Mississippi River plantation house; Southwest adobe; Dutch Colonial farmhouse; and Pennsylvania stone farmhouse, among other domestic forms, supplied the impetus for variations on domestic eclecticism in the 1920s.[6] In the hands of the historically trained architect, these types became viable models for modern country and suburban houses. Historical studies and documentations of most of these house types appeared during the 1920s and 1930s.

In much the same way that architects of the school of McKim, Mead and White had designed by analogy, taking French châteaux, English country houses, and Italian villas as their inspiration for the new country house, regionalist architects applied ornamental and typological elements from American vernacular sources to new problems. The lessons learned from these home-grown examples were somewhat different, however, from those taken from high art sources. Many third-generation eclectics were drawn to their sources specifically because of associations with straightforward, economical, modern, and even functional building tenets. As John Gaw Meem, the Santa Fe architect, said, "The architecture of the southwest—the so-called Spanish Pueblo architecture of New Mexico—contains elements of traditional forms that have been in the writer's opinion, successfully used to solve a variety of modern problems."[7] Other regionalists felt the same way. The small efficient regional country house tended to be more abstractly conceived than previous eclectic houses. By understanding their sources, architects were able to move away from literal pastiche to a deeper transformation of models. Moreover, all regionalists were motivated by the powerful connections between style, building technics, materials, and the ethnic groups who used them in their buildings.

This perceived influence of locale on culture created its own spirit in architectural revivals all over the country. William Lawrence Bottomley's survey of the country house for the *Architectural Record* in 1920 was an implicit manifesto for these tendencies; in it he presented few examples by the established eastern architects of the previous generation, concentrating instead on small "provincial" houses and new firms. "Our architecture, like the population of the U.S. with its diversity of races," he wrote, "reflects types and styles from every land."[8] His introductory remarks suggested that such ethnic and stylistic diversity was in itself a zeitgeist for his era. His choice of the best country houses was unusually diverse and focused on new regional models.[9] All were relatively compact by the standards of fifteen years earlier and had integral garden spaces. All were specifically related to their local building traditions and were designed by architects qualified in the local idiom. As such, they were indicators of the new regionalist ideal that would dominate the domestic architecture of the 1920s and 1930s in America.

Interest in the indigenous architectural styles and building types from America's diverse geographic, ecological, and cultural areas, although fostered by local groups, was in large part a result of the eclectic architect's training. Most domestic specialists were capable of designing in any of the established period idioms that had been socially sanctioned during the previous thirty years. They had to be, since clients invariably had a period style in mind for a proposed house. The Beaux-Arts-trained architect was sensitive to his or her work fitting the place, whereas clients envisioned a house with some local color. This was the initial impetus for Colonial Revival work that was place- or culture-specific.

These flourishing regional movements were led by a talented, well-trained third generation of architects who had spread into new urban markets during the years following World War I. Many of these designers had trained with leading firms on the East Coast or in Chicago, taking the principles of eclectic practice with them to their new locales. Nearly every major city in the United States had its favorite domestic specialists during the 1920s and 1930s, and the pattern of patronage became localized, as wealthy clients recognized the talents of regional architects and increasingly chose them over national firms. Whereas before World War I a family like the Armours of Chicago hired Harrie Lindeberg to do a house in Lake Forest, thereafter they went to Chicago's own David Adler.

These architects took great pride and enthusiasm in the study of American buildings, another trait ingrained in them as students. As we have seen, among the pioneering scholars were Fiske Kimball, I. N. Phelps Stokes, John Mead Howells, Thomas Tileston Waterman, J. Frederick Kelley, Norman Isham, Arthur Shurcliff (a landscape architect), Albert Simons, Glenn Brown, Frank Wallis, and Rexford Newcomb. Many acquired their knowledge as restorationists, through documentation of the buildings in their charge. Their books remain among the most important sources of drawings on Early American buildings. Moreover, the studies they made for such landmark works as the *White Pine Series, Great Georgian Houses of America,* and the many books written about American towns and buildings during the 1920s and 1930s were indicative of their commitment to the examination of indigenous types as sources for new work. Russell Whitehead's editorship of the *White Pine Monographs* is a case in point.

Whitehead, already a noted architect and scholar by 1914, was engaged by two Midwest lumber manufacturers (the White Pine Bureau) to produce a series of pamphlets that would advertise their product and document outstanding examples, old and new, of America's wooden buildings. What began as an elaborate (though by no means unusual) trade catalogue became an important scholarly and architectural influence. The catalogues of current architectural booksellers confirm that nearly every architectural firm doing eclectic work subscribed to the monographs.[10] Whitehead and the architectural photographer Julian Buckly, along with other architects and historians, began by producing articles on colonial buildings, mainly New England houses, including meticulously measured drawings. In 1924, when the Weyerhauser lumber company began funding the series, Whitehead changed the focus to a specifically regionalist approach. Each monograph would henceforth concentrate on an entire town—not just in New England but in the South, and not featuring only buildings constructed of pine—in an attempt to document all aspects of building style, technics, history, and decorative arts. In 1932 *Pencil Points,* the architectural journal that would become *Progressive Architecture,* incorporated the monographs into its pages. The series lasted twenty-six years, ceasing publication in 1940.[11] Leading eclectic specialists such as Aymar Embury II, Frank Chouteau Brown, and Albert Simons took turns editing, receiving fifty dollars per volume. The drawings in the series were magnificently artful as well as precise, serving as models for the later work of the Historic American Buildings Survey, founded during the 1930s. They were also essential to the scholarly repro-

duction and craftsmanship that went into eclectic architecture of the 1920s. Perhaps most significant in the series were the periodic competitions for "white pine buildings" to solve modern problems. The entries for these events were heavily influenced by regional, Early American sources.

Another enterprise indicative of the spread of regional pride was *Southern Architecture Illustrated,* edited by Atlanta architect Lewis E. Crook and published in 1931. A compendium of the work of leading architects for Atlanta and the South (chosen by a committee picked by the local chapter of the American Institute of Architects), this book attempted to show the continuity of tradition from Early American sources to modern work, while also demonstrating conclusively the influence of such leaders as McKim, Platt, Lindeberg, and Pope on local practitioners. It began with illustrations of canonical Southern Colonial houses, such as Lower Brandon (1730) and the Hammond Harwood house (1773–74) in Annapolis. Dwight James Baum's introduction stressed the influence of these and other models on new work.[12] Local architectural clubs or branches of the American Institute of Architects in many cities published similar anthologies of domestic or public work in the 1920s and 1930s.[13] Unquestionably, publications such as these, along with the enormous proliferation of magazines targeted at upper- and middle-class readers, fostered the spread of eclecticism and strengthened its impact on the domestic architecture of America's smaller cities and towns. Where there were talented architects, clients with money to spend, and enthusiasm for building, country houses of considerable distinction were created, even during the worst years of the depression.

The regionalist ethos in domestic architecture is no better evinced than in the work of several schools of architects that flourished during the post–World War I era. Two of the most vital and creative were the English-influenced architects in Philadelphia and the extraordinary group of Colonial Revivalists working in Santa Barbara to create a New Spain. These two groups shared several traits that illuminate the nature of eclecticism as it developed during the 1920s and 1930s.

THE PHILADELPHIA SCHOOL

The most cohesive, long-lived, and distinctive of the regional schools of architecture flourished in Philadelphia from the 1880s until the depression. The character of Philadelphia, with its long-standing English leanings and distinct urbanistic coherence, was one reason for the longevity of the school. More important to the country house were the rural areas surrounding the city—the valleys of the Schuykill and Delaware rivers, the beautiful Brandywine area near Wilmington, and the Main Line suburbs that developed along the railroad lines—Chesnut Hill, Haverford, Villanova, Bryn Mawr, Ardmore, and Swarthmore are but a few of these charming communities. It was here, amid what seemed to be continuous vernacular building traditions dating as far back as the seventeenth century, that many twentieth-century Philadelphians chose to build country retreats. (There were numerous eighteenth- and nineteenth-century country houses already in these areas.) They found equally nostalgic architects to help them realize their dreams of a new country life. The Anglophile architects of Philadelphia were drawn to the simple buildings of rural Pennsylvania and Delaware as analogies to the village farmhouses of rural England. Combining the materials and basic massing of the early Pennsylvania houses with a sensibility borrowed from modern English work, the architects of this regional school made an identifiable new architecture, creating beautiful and compelling twentieth-century country houses.

One reason for the strong identity of the Philadelphia school lay in the conservatism of the city's patrons. Regardless of the source of their money, many wealthy Philadelphians insisted on identifying with their ancestors. The Biddles kept their farm, Andalusia, as a residence, making minor additions in the 1920s. In 1909 Robert C. Montgomery had Horace Trumbauer build him a larger, grander house in a seventeenth-century academic English style, on a vast Villanova estate of his ancestors, where he continued the life of the gentleman farmer. An island of pastoral charm, Ardrossan now occupies perhaps the largest private estate in the Philadelphia area. Walter Mellor and Arthur Meigs, both blue bloods, altered family farms as their first architectural commissions. These Philadelphia gentlemen seemed reluctant to give up the genteel life their ancestors had led.

Yet the apotheosis of this bucolic anachronism was the farm estate of financier Arthur Newbold in Laverock, Pennsylvania, remade around a Colonial Revival house by Mellor, Meigs and Howe between 1919 and 1931. It was above all a place where this new mogul could keep sheep, pigeons, ducks, geese, and all manner of ornamental farm animals. Fowl and livestock were conspicuous in most of the photographs of his country place, published in periodicals and in a monograph of 1925.[14] The Newbold farm was one of the most publicized domestic works of its time and became a kind of propaganda vehicle for the gentleman's farm as a paradigm for modern country life. The romantic view of the rural countryside seemed to strike a chord with conservative Philadelphians and was cultivated by an extraordinary group of likeminded architects after World War I. Any visitor to Chestnut Hill or the Main Line suburbs will sense even today the conservatism that upper-crust Philadelphians and their architects perpetuated — what one observer in the *Brickbuilder* called "picturesque, practical and straightforward, and rendered with an agreeable dash of personal individuality, and with that peculiar *friendliness* towards materials used that characterizes the works of the modern English architects."[15] Those unmistakably quaint materials — Wissahickon schist and white trim or rustic brick — were handled with the same reverence that such English Arts and Crafts masters as C. F. A. Voysey, Detmar Blow, Lutyens (in his Surrey vernacular days), Baillie Scott, and W. R. Lethaby brought to the construc-

233 Mellor, Meigs and Howe. Arthur Newbold farm (1919–31), Laverock, Pennsylvania. Aerial view. (Athenaeum of Philadelphia.)

tion of their vernacular romantic houses. Philadelphia's gentlemen architects brought a keen sensitivity for local color to their work in an area with a long agricultural tradition.

Their clients, often from families with old money and venerable patrimonies, were motivated by more than nostalgia. As we have seen in the ostracism that greeted Horace Trumbauer, Philadelphia society was a closed one in which a few sanctioned architectural firms dominated domestic practice. The gentry stayed in predictable, circumscribed city neighborhoods like the Rittenhouse area and chose equally exclusive country environments for their rural homes. By surrounding themselves, indeed insulating themselves, with nature, Philadelphians were among the first to flee the decaying city to create quasisuburban enclaves that evoked the life their ancestors had led or reflected their worldwide travels. They were clearly disturbed by twentieth-century urbanism, commercialism, and growth. In 1922 Owen Wister, in a tribute to his two friends Arthur Meigs and Walter Mellor, wrote:

The winds of change are blowing thick with dust. What is happening to life in the whirling obscurity? One thing conspicuously, the crowding of charm and beauty to the wall. For this commerce is responsible. Commerce juts up from the face of the world like a host of warts, huge lumps, long welts, mills, mean rows of houses; chimneys poke into the polluted sky. . . . What can be saved from the invasion of commercial ugliness? . . . Several things if we take thought; . . . but least unimpeded and most ready to our hand is the dwelling house, and no one has shown better than Mellor, Meigs and Howe how this may keep the expiring spark of beauty alive and clothe our domestic moments with some form of grace.[16]

For Philadelphia's gentry, the frontiers of Montgomery, Chester, and Bucks counties became the last haven of grace, while their city houses languished. Much of the charm found in the Main Line suburbs seems to have come from an energy sapped from the old city.

The cloistered nature of the city's gentry was mirrored in its professional associations. After the turn of the century Philadelphia's architectural community developed into one of the most closely knit circles of craftsmen, artists, and designers in the country. Its dominant figures were Wilson Eyre, Frank Miles Day, Walter Cope, and William Price. Its organ, the T-Square Club, was the epicenter of architectural ideas in Philadelphia during the eclectic era. From before the war into the late 1920s T-Square published its annual exhibition according to the principles of such English institutions as the Royal Academy and Art Workers' Guild, featuring the work of architects and artists in concert and publishing travel sketches, student projects, and articles on architectural history. It was an idealistic and insular group, full of the romantic views of architecture that were held by modern Ruskinians in England. The domestic work its members produced had a focus and stylistic coherence testifying to the hothouse atmosphere that must have prevailed in its meetings.

The firm of Mellor and Meigs, joined by George Howe in 1916, epitomized the ethos of Philadelphia's architectural culture.[17] Both partners were born in Philadelphia to wealthy parents.

234 Mellor and Meigs. Leonard T. Beale house (1912), St. Davids, Pennsylvania. (Athenaeum of Philadelphia.)

Headstrong and patrician, Arthur Ingersoll Meigs (1882–1956) attended Penn Charter and Princeton University, graduating in 1903. He served his apprenticeship with the venerable Theophilus Parsons Chandler, the founder of the School of Architecture at the University of Pennsylvania and the grandest gentleman architect of his day.[18] While working with Chandler he met Walter Mellor (1880–1940), who received a B.S. in mechanical engineering from Haverford College in 1901 and an architecture degree from the University of Pennsylvania in 1904. The two began their architectural partnership in 1906, and their families' social prominence brought them almost instant success. Like Delano, they were clubmen and designed buildings for the Pickering Hunt Club (1911), in Phoenixville, Pennsylvania, the Princeton Charter Club (1913), and several fraternity houses and eating clubs. Memberships in the Union League (Mellor), Philadelphia Club (Meigs), Radnor Hunt Club (Meigs), and Germantown Cricket Club (Mellor) rounded out the social sphere in which these quintessential gentlemen architects moved.[19]

Mellor and Meigs were traditionalists in life as in art, conforming to and perpetuating a distinctly Philadelphian mode. Their first houses showed the influence of Frank Miles Day and Wilson Eyre, who had experimented in the first years of the century with English vernacular styles. Mellor and Meigs' houses for William V. Alexander in 1910 and for Leonard T. Beale in 1912, both in St. David's, Pennsylvania, were marked by the advancing and receding gabled masses, quiltlike variety of materials and textures, and interlocking room configurations that Eyre had used so effectively in his work. But even in these early buildings the partners showed an uncanny ability to weave the textures and forms of the landscape into their houses, giving them an organic quality and variety that even Eyre's best works lacked. The storybook renderings they published were perfectly evocative of the house as an overgrown farm cottage, nestled into the countryside like the most secluded Cotswold villages.

During the war years the firm created several house and garden ensembles that rank among America's finest examples of modern domestic architecture. In addition to the Newbold farm, they designed Ropsley (1918), the Francis S. McIlhenny residence outside of Chestnut Hill, the Caspar W. Morris house (1916) in Haverford, and the Heatley C. Dulles house (1917, 1924–25) in Villa-

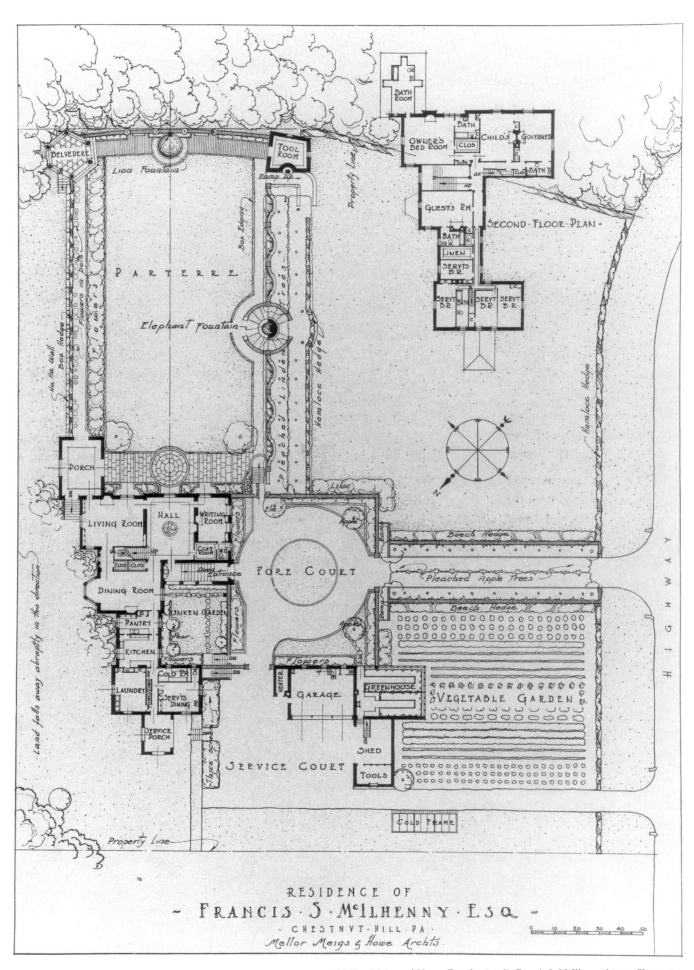

Within the site plan (labels):

SECOND·FLOOR·PLAN·

BATH ROOM · OWNER'S BED ROOM · BATH · CLOS · CHILD'S · GOVERNESS · BATH · GUEST'S RM · BATH · LINEN · SERV'TS B.R. · SERV'T B.R. · BATH · SERV'T B.R. · SERV'T B.R.

BELVEDERE · Lion Fountain · TOOL ROOM · Pump Up · Property Line
PARTERRE · Box Edging · Pleached Linden · Hemlock Hedge · Elephant Fountain · Flowers in Pots · Box Hedge · Ha Ha Wall
PORCH · Lilac · Elm · Apple · Beech Hedge · Hemlock Hedge · HIGHWAY
LIVING ROOM · HALL · WRITING ROOM · COAT ROOM · CLOS · CLOS · UP · FORE COURT · Pleached Apple Trees · Apple · Ramp
DINING ROOM · Dn · Entrance · Flowers · SUNKEN GARDEN · Pear · Flowers · Beech Hedge
PANTRY · KITCHEN · Cold Ro · VEGETABLE GARDEN
Flowers · HEATER · GARAGE · GREENHOUSE
LAUNDRY · SERV'TS DINING R · Flowers
SERVICE PORCH · Thick Screen · SHED · TOOLS
Land falls away abruptly in this direction
SERVICE COURT · COLD FRAME
Property Line

RESIDENCE OF
~ FRANCIS·S·McILHENNY·ESQ ~
·CHESTNUT·HILL·PA·
Mellor Meigs & Howe Archts

0 10 20 30 40 50

235 Mellor, Meigs and Howe. **Ropsley** (1918), Francis S. McIlhenny house, Chestnut Hill, Pennsylvania. Site plan. (*Monograph of the Work of Mellor, Meigs and Howe.*)

236 **Ropsley.** Aerial view from northwest. (Athenaeum of Philadelphia.)

nova. In each estate, planned on a relatively small parcel of land, the architects choreographed movement through the site and house as verdant and rustic progressions. The determining spaces and formal diagram were derived more from the site and enclosed garden areas than from the houses themselves, making the buildings, taken at face value, far less striking than the overall conception. In this respect interpretations of the firm's domestic work that have focused on only the buildings have missed a vital point. Like the work of Platt, any country house by Mellor and Meigs was really a complete site design, an ensemble of landscape and buildings determined by locale and topography. The McIlhenny house, for example, is comparable in its garden layout to Lutyens' masterpiece, Deanery Garden, built for Edward Hudson in 1901 with Gertrude Jekyl as garden designer. In each, the house defers to the garden and is planned along a series of ingeniously interlocking and crossing axes terminating on landscape features. Although there is something recognizably English in Ropsley's design, it is far more powerfully related to its specific locale than to any foreign model. In this respect it is a perfect example of a regional country house.

The client, Francis Salisbury McIlhenny,[20] was a prominent attorney, politician, and business leader. He wanted a small graceful estate surrounded by gardens, not a house with grand pretensions. Privacy, modesty, and an urbane coexistence with nature were his stipulations, and they were brilliantly realized by the architects. Ropsley was built, significantly, for a modest $59,650, by a family with enough wealth to have afforded a far grander house.[21] Meigs' own description of the problems faced in designing the ensemble gives the most accurate indication of the philosophy of the firm:

In the consideration of the problems involved in the design for the house of Mr. Francis S. McIlhenny two principal basic considerations were at once apparent. First, that the house was to be built upon a hill, and second, that the hill sloped towards the northeast and that the outlook was directly to the north. These two points formed the root and foundation of the whole design. Regarding the question of orientation, it was decided that the solution of the problem lay in planning the house in such a way that the principal rooms would look out to the southeast, and this necessitated the creation of the parterre at that point. By this arrangement the living room, the hall and the writing room, on the first floor, and the owner's bedroom and the other two principal bedrooms on the second floor, obtained this valuable exposure. The question of view, to a large extent, was subordinated, but, by the location of the dining room, the bay looks directly at the view, the living room has two windows facing it, and the porch is so placed that it commands both the parterre and the view In order to get the sun also into the dining room, the sunken garden was created, and while practical considerations make this a necessity, it brought about, as is almost universally the case, when such considerations are successfully handled, one of the pleasantest features of the design.

In fact, this process was followed throughout, and if the finished product has any merit at all, it is entirely due to the plan being born from its situation, and the elevations and outbuildings following as a logical sequence from the parti originally assumed. Of all the elements of design, this seems to me the most important.[22]

The plan of the house and garden did indeed follow logically from the orientation, views, and efficient management of a fairly compact site, but its artfulness went far deeper. Like Lutyens, Meigs deftly manipulated tableaux and axial vistas: from the street one first saw the modest entrance portal framed by a per-

237 **Ropsley.** Southeast elevation. (Athenaeum of Philadelphia.)

238 **Ropsley.** Lion fountain and tool room. (Athenaeum of Philadelphia.)

239 **Ropsley.** View from living room toward Belvedere. (Athenaeum of Philadelphia.)

spective allée through the forecourt; once inside, the sunken garden opened to the left; one moved into the hall off both its cross axis and the centerline of the house but quickly felt the strong presence of the great parterre; finally, views down the hill to the valley opened up subtly from the living room, dining room, and porch. Every room was connected to both key interior and exterior elements. In addition the plan was very compact, with only four major ground-floor rooms. Unlike Lutyens, however, Meigs eschewed any local symmetries or flirtations with a classical massing. One cannot describe the building as an eroded U-plan or a simple geometric solid with appendages. Each elevation and massing decision was fully dependent on a tightly controlled point of view, so that the unity of the design was subservient to local conditions. It is quite difficult to guess the overall plan and massing of

240 Mellor and Meigs. Caspar Morris house (1916), center, Haverford, Pennsylvania. Aerial view. (Athenaeum of Philadelphia.)

the house from one or even two sides. The McIlhenny house demonstrated Mellor, Meigs and Howe's essential contribution to modern picturesque planning and illustrated the key differences between American work of the 1920s and the English houses that influenced it.

What kept Mellor and Meigs firmly in the academic eclectic tradition, however, was not this ingenious, and somewhat modern, concern for siting but their care in studying, transforming, and using details. Brickwork patterns, stone joinery and moldings, window details, and timber framing in the best work of the firm can all be traced to a thorough study of past examples, whether from French and English vernacular architecture, the High Renaissance in Italy, or the local colonial architecture of Pennsylvania. (An early version of the McIlhenny house was designed in Tuscan villa style.) Like most good architects of their time, they used both their libraries and their travel sketchbooks as vital sources.

An even better example of this attention to materials and detail is the Caspar W. Morris house in Haverford. An English visitor entering the courtyard of this fine ten-acre estate upon its comple-

tion in 1916 would have felt uncannily at home. Like many Arts and Crafts houses in Britain, this house by Mellor and Meigs used the straightforward grouping of traditional farm buildings as a starting point for their richly textured and varied composition. Meant to appear venerable with age, as if each generation had added to it in different vernacular modes and materials, this American country place applied the lessons of modern English work to extraordinary effect. It is one of the masterpieces of Philadelphia architecture, equal in many respects to Lutyens' small country houses.[23]

Built on the Main Line for a member of one of Philadelphia's oldest and most esteemed families,[24] the Morris residence could be used year-round, since it was only thirty to forty-five minutes from the city. The natural features of the site—a spring and small stream (with spring house), an orchard, and a large sloping meadow—were to be respected and enhanced by the house, which was to be rustic, comfortable, and quaint. In typical fashion, Mellor and Meigs began with the site plan and let each major architectural gesture relate to a key aspect of it. One approached the house from the south, across the stream, turning at the spring house onto an axis defined by an allée of oaks and a high wall. This led the eye to the cupola of a small farmlike gate building in the dis-

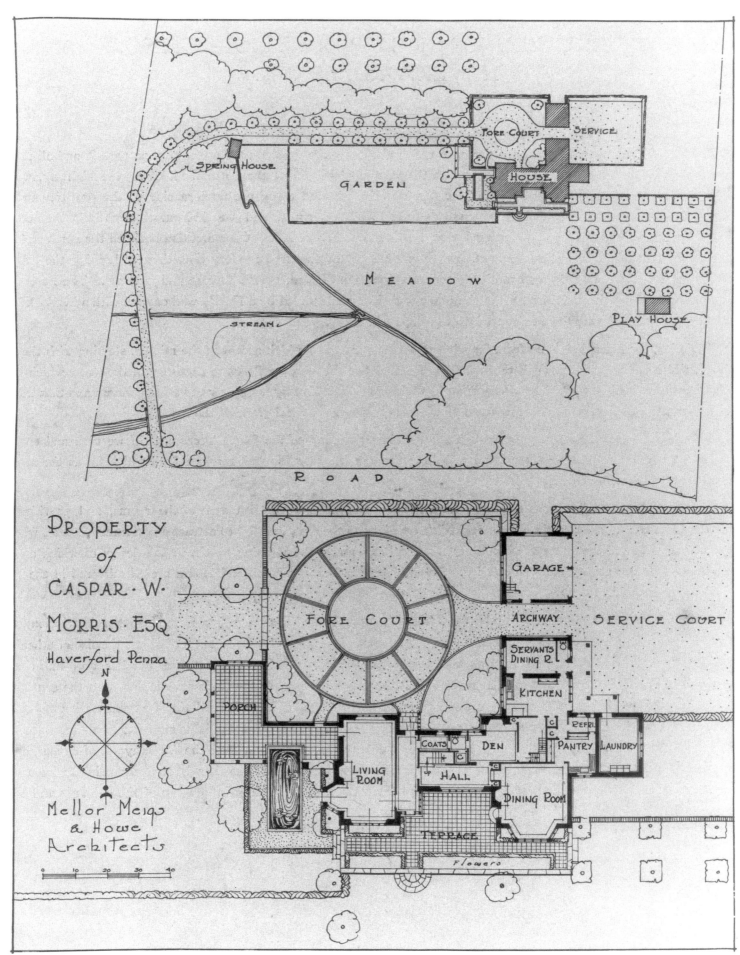

PROPERTY
of
CASPAR·W·
MORRIS·ESQ

Haverford Penna

N

Mellor Meigs
& Howe
Architects

0   10   20   30   40

FORE COURT   SERVICE

HOUSE

GARDEN

Spring House

MEADOW

STREAM

PLAY HOUSE

ROAD

GARAGE

FORE COURT   ARCHWAY   SERVICE COURT

SERVANTS
DINING R.

KITCHEN

PORCH

REFR.

PANTRY   LAUNDRY

COATS   DEN

LIVING
ROOM   HALL

DINING ROOM

TERRACE

Flowers

241 Morris house. Site plan. (*Monograph of the Work of Mellor, Meigs and Howe.*)

242 Morris house. View from west. (Athenaeum of Philadelphia.)

243 Morris house. Garden elevation and terrace. (Athenaeum of Philadelphia.)

244 Morris house. Forecourt. (Athenaeum of Philadelphia.)

tance. There were glimpses of the main house along the way, but upon entering the square forecourt in the summer one was surprised by the configuration of the prominent corner chimney and gable masses and the main entry at the southeast. As in many site plans of Mellor and Meigs, the house was placed to define two edges of a cross-axial demarcation, here made by the long garden wall, dividing north and south, and the garage wing, dividing entry court and service court east and west.

The architects concealed this basic cross configuration through several key diagonal gestures, the most important of which were the placement of the small den at the crook of the plan and the juxtaposition of the garden pool and porch on the southwest. Thus, though one moved orthogonally through the house, discovering wonders at each turn, the key views of the building from both garden and forecourt were meant to be oblique, in the best picturesque fashion. The corners of projecting masses and volumes were emphasized as they interlocked with other elements. A relatively simple house, with only a few formal rooms and the basic services, was made complex and unexpected by its conversations with the landscape and its brilliant massing.

Further, the house achieved a richness and material complexity through many ingenious tectonic features. The Morris house demonstrated Mellor and Meigs' consummate eye for detail and texture. The variety of materials—brick, oak timbering, yellow stucco, stone, and shingles—might have become chaotic in lesser hands. Yet each detail of this house—from the clever weathervane (ascending and descending cats) above the den chimney to the intricate molded bricks used in many of the window jambs, heads, and sills—contributed to a successful whole. The weaving of half-timbering, smooth stucco, and brick produced a house with an antique flavor without directly invoking Tudor or medieval precedents. These traits closely parallel the work of Lutyens in such houses as Greywalls, Gullane, Little Thakeham, Sussex, and Monkton, near Chichester. In comparing the Morris house to

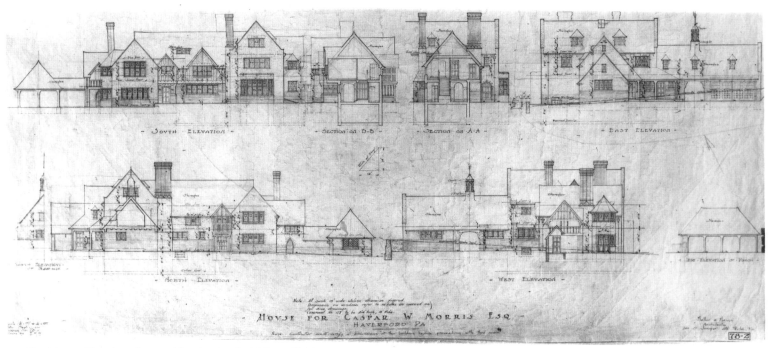

245 Morris house. Elevations, from working drawings by Mellor and Meigs. (Athenaeum of Philadelphia.)

246 Morris house. Terrace and pool. (Athenaeum of Philadelphia.)

these English houses, not only is cross-fertilization evident, but there is little question that these American architects were very much in step with their English brethren.

Mellor, Meigs and Howe were hardly the only local architects to employ a philosophy based on a reverence for indigenous building. The consistency of outlook perpetuated by members of the T-Square Club can be seen across the generations. William L. Price (1861–1916), the leader of the Arts and Crafts movement in Philadelphia, built several interesting large houses in a variety of styles. These range from the English, rather retrograde Woodmont (1892), for steel baron Allen Wood in Conshohocken, to the surprisingly modern concrete country house (1910) for Frank Van Camp in Indianapolis.[25] Charles Barton Keen (1868–1931), an alumnus of the architectural school at the University of Pennsylvania and an apprentice in Chandler's office, often turned to colonial vernacular sources. In 1912 he established himself as architect for R. J. Reynolds' tobacco empire in Winston-Salem, North Carolina, going on to design several noted country houses in the South. These buildings were as attuned to their locale as his northern works. Louis Duhring, F. Brognard Okie, and Carl Ziegler, like Mellor and Meigs, were specialists in Colonial Revival and Anglo-French pastoral styles. But the most important perpetuators of that tradition in the 1920s were Edmund B. Gilchrist (1885–1953) and Robert Rodes McGoodwin (1886–1967), who used the vocabulary of Eyre and Mellor, Meigs and Howe in the development of Chestnut Hill for Dr. George Woodward and built a number of distinguished smaller country houses in the Philadelphia area.

Their major country houses carried a romantic vocabulary and made the most of a pastoral vision. McGoodwin's early Mount Vernon prototypes, such as his residences for W. W. Harper (1912) and Barker Grummere (1911), and Gilchrist's Strawbridge house (1916) in Laverock or Awbury (1914) for William Kimber were atypical in size and pretension. As their careers progressed, both preferred a gentler, more informal style, manifested in such works as McGoodwin's English-influenced stone houses for Persifor Frazer III (1921) and Staunton B. Peck (1924), but especially in his ambitious estate for Samuel P. Rotan, Lane's End (1928). The landscape, the influence of the locale, and a preference for informal living induced McGoodwin and Gilchrist to design country places that were extensions of the Philadelphia school. Though not as talented or socially prominent as Mellor and Meigs, McGoodwin and Gilchrist were on a par with any regional designers of their time. Numerous country houses by these architects remain to be studied and appreciated.[26]

Even in its time, Philadelphia's storybook pastoral school was heavily criticized for its anachronistic attitude, which was stubbornly and fervently perpetuated by architects and clients with equal conviction. Lewis Mumford spoke of the "malady of the unreal," "homesickness for nature," and "the desire to cut loose from an environment in which the day is announced by the alarm clock, instead of the birds, and finished by the blare of the radio instead of the crickets and the katydids."[27] Sixty years later, instead of lamenting the "critical weakness" that Mumford saw in the modern picturesque—which, after all, accommodated cars, appliances, and radios along with *potagers* and pergolas—owners continue to covet and preserve this strong and persuasive architecture as a reconciliation of garden and machine.

GEORGE WASHINGTON SMITH
AND THE SPANISH HOUSE IN CALIFORNIA

In the twentieth century American architectural scene, there has been only one brief period of time and only one restricted geographic area in which there existed anything approaching a unanimity of architectural form. This was the period, from approximately 1920 to the early 1930's, when the Spanish Colonial or the Mediterranean Revival was virtually the accepted norm in southern California.

—David Gebhard

The most vital of America's regional schools was created during a century of mythmaking in southern California, beginning in the mid-nineteenth century and extending well into the twentieth. As the historian Kevin Starr has demonstrated, the Mission, Arts and Crafts, and Spanish Colonial Revival movements in the Golden State were the inventions of visionaries, artists, and progressive dreamers. The impulse to identify with Latin and Mediterranean cultures was in part a reflection of California's distinct climate and geography but more an idealistic desire to achieve beauty and prosperity in this paradise.[28] By embracing and idealizing its Spanish heritage, California created its own orientalism.

The state, which promoted itself as a great Edenic landscape, with every plot a potential garden, every tract a fertile farm, its mountains, seacoast, and deserts conserved as parks, was naturally rich with opportunities for country life. But California had also to live down the rapacious and uncouth image of its frontier past, in which art and aesthetic building had played little part.[29]

Even the large country estates of northern California, built by winegrowers and gold diggers in the last half of the nineteenth century, were hardly on a plane with eastern examples. Though the achievements of specialists, such as the Queen Anne and Mission styles of the Newsom brothers, were considerable, the earliest recognized artistic country houses were built after 1890, when architects newly arrived from the East were inspired to invent their own versions of the California dream.

James Waldron Gillespie's mountainside villa, El Fureidis (1902–03), designed by Bertram Grosvenor Goodhue in the late 1890s, was one of the first of these dream houses. Choosing the beautiful, sleepy coastal town of Montecito, near Santa Barbara, Gillespie set about creating a magical garden oasis. The name he chose for his house was not Spanish but Arabic, meaning place of delights. As a collector of exotic specimen trees as well as unusual fine and decorative art, he was at once the quintessential country house patron and California visionary.[30] Goodhue was likewise a master of make-believe, one of America's most gifted scenographic renderers. With this, his first major West Coast commission, the New York architect began an ongoing love affair with the historical imagery and landscape of the "land of sunshine." In 1904 he remodeled an adobe in Montecito for himself, which he used as a winter retreat.

Gillespie took Goodhue on a tour of Persian gardens to explore precedents for his new oriental country place. The two traveled over four hundred miles on horseback from the Caspian Sea to the Persian Gulf,[31] visiting, among other remarkable sights, the gardens of the Telegrapher's House in Shiraz, which Goodhue illustrated in his famed book of architectural drawings.[32] Upon his return, the architect did not try merely to replicate the images he had seen, as some of his contemporaries might have done, but instead used a freely synthetic approach in the design of the house and gardens.

The result was a curiously abstract and austere house in its massing and exterior detail. Recognizing that flora, not architectural surface ornament, could provide decoration for the building, Goodhue used large expanses of white wall articulated with the barest of classical elements to set off the exotic plants of the garden, a strategy that later architects would use to good effect in Santa Barbara. The plan of the house and gardens was also a hybrid of Beaux-Arts, vernacular, and Persian sources, linked by a complex series of shifted cross axes. The impressive hillside axis, forming the garden armature and drawn by a line of water, recalled both the Alhambra and the Villa Aldobrandini. The villa plan featured a large transverse courtyard, slightly off the center of the garden axis, entered at its upper corner—a brilliantly unorthodox move. Goodhue treated each wing somewhat autonomously, allowing it to absorb axes perpendicular to it without necessarily extending them through the plan, a device he would use again in later works. Inside, the rooms were generally spare, designed to highlight the owner's collections. The major set pieces were a gold-hued Persian room and a Turkish bath.[33]

The Gillespie house set a precedent for later essays in the California country house in several critical ways: first, by employing a

247 Bertram Goodhue. **El Fureidis** (1902–03), James W. Gillespie estate, Montecito, California. Main elevation overlooking garden terrace. (Frederick W. Martin, Architectural Drawing Collection, University Art Museum, Santa Barbara, California.)

Mediterranean, courtyard-type plan; second, by using simple, abstract massing and plain stucco surfaces to set off the shapes and colors of local flora; third, by emphasizing outdoor living spaces, such as roof terraces, garden courts, and loggias, as essential elements, taking full advantage of southern California's temperate climate; and fourth, by featuring a garden suited to the locale. This early attempt to find a paradigm for the California country dwelling was predicated on many Mediterranean and Eastern influences analogous to the Pacific Southwest region, setting the stage for more specific historical borrowing in the succeeding fifteen years.

Myron Hunt and Elmer Grey, two transplanted midwestern architects clearly influenced by Goodhue's ideas, assisted in the construction of El Fureidis.[34] Not only did they borrow his strategy in designing the Huntington estate on Los Robles Ranch in San Marino four years later, they also experimented with the courtyard type in several unrealized projects. In the Italian-inspired hillside villa (undated) for Lewis Bradbury in Duarte, California, Hunt used the shifted cross-axial plan with a dynamism similar to Goodhue's. Hunt tended to plan more statically, however, as evidenced in his project with H. C. Chambers, A House on the Edge of the Desert. His most successful work in this vein was the city house for Major J. H. H. Peshine in Santa Barbara in 1917, which used a linear configuration of rooms around a shallow patio, nestled in a mountainside setting. By this time the Spanish influence had begun to dominate.

The use of Spanish and Mission imagery from California's colonial days increased after the war in much the same way that Georgian, Tudor, and French Provincial styles did in the East. The most important locus for the development of the Spanish Colonial Revival was Santa Barbara. After the devastating earthquake of June 29, 1925, the city fathers, many of whom were transplanted easterners, endeavored to re-create the Spanish town, literally inventing a culture, phoenix-born from the disaster. By 1930 Santa Barbara had become an urbanistic "New Spain," complete with public, commercial, and religious structures, all done in vivid and creative revival idioms. The city was fortunate to have a stable of clever and committed artists and architects—such figures as Edwards, Plunkett and Howell, James Osborne Craig, Reginald Johnson of Pasadena, Soule, Murphy and Hastings, and Carleton Winslow of Los Angeles—who could translate Spanish influences into this new vision of the town. Their scenographic stucco and tile-surfaced buildings did not repudiate modern American life but conformed to the prevailing consumer-automobile culture. The rebuilt Santa Barbara contained gas stations, movie theaters, a shopping arcade called El Paseo (1921–23) that used fragments of older structures and, most impressive of all, a grand county courthouse (1929), whose storybook murals depicted the history of Spanish and American conquests in southern California.

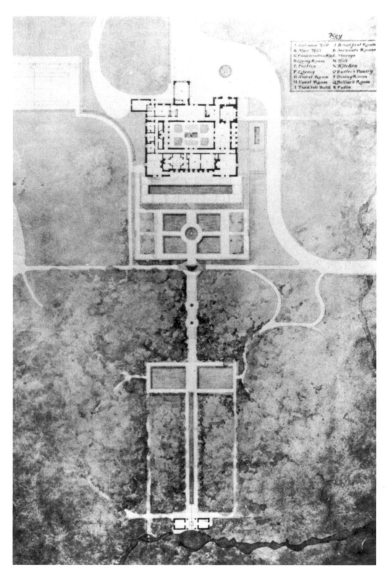

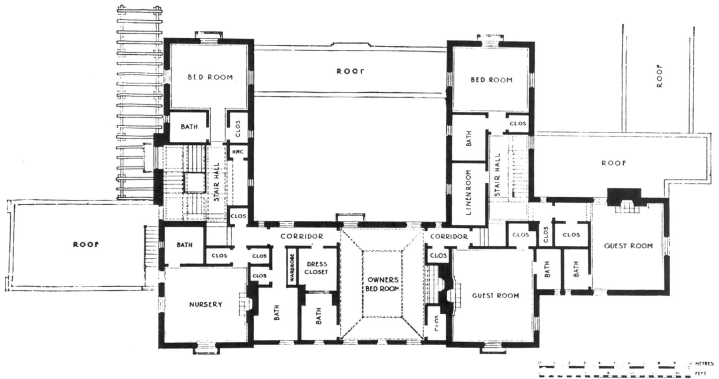

248 Bertram Goodhue. **El Fureidis.** Site plan. (Oliver, *Bertram Grosvenor Goodhue.*)

249 Bertram Goodhue house (1904), Montecito, California. Ground plan. (Richard Cheek, from *A Book of Architectural and Decorative Drawings by Bertram Grosvenor Goodhue.*)

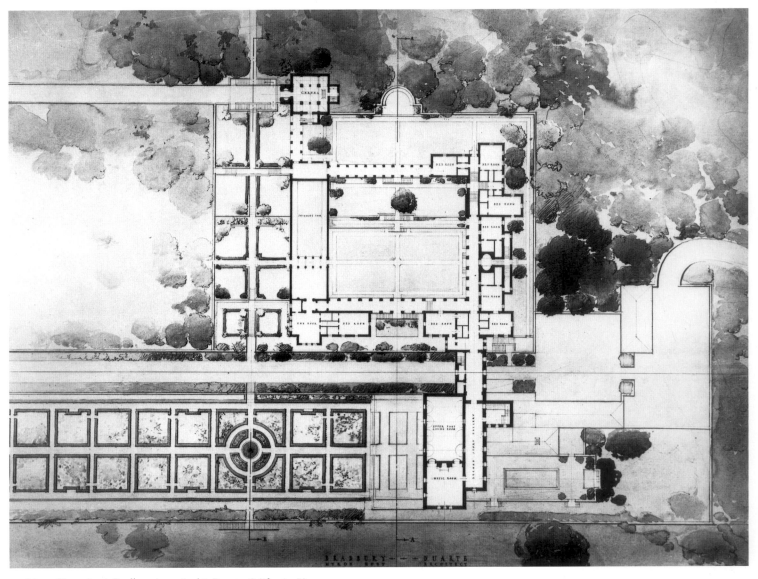

250 Myron Hunt. Lewis Bradbury house (n.d.), Duarte, California. Plan.
(Architectural Drawing Collection, University Art Museum, Santa Barbara,
California.)

Santa Barbara was already a popular upper-class winter resort in the late nineteenth century;[35] some easterners even decided to settle permanently in this lush environment, where the mountains met the sea.[36] In the 1920s, there was a small boom in house building, especially in the adjacent town of Montecito (the little woods), where in 1916–17 Bertram Goodhue designed an imposing Spanish country club. Not only did the dense, cool forest provide seclusion for the wealthy, as it does today, but Montecito became a showplace for California gardens. The great gardens of Francis T. Underhill and Charles Gibbs Adams at Arcady (1911–14), the Knapp estate, designed with Russell Ray and Carleton Winslow, extended the Hispano-Moorish imagery and layout of Goodhue's prototypical villa. Of the many talented designers working in Santa Barbara during its eclectic heyday, George Washington Smith stood above his peers as a genius whose work epitomized and extended the limits of the Mediterranean idiom. A regionalist in a deeper sense than either the rational Irving Gill of San Diego or the academic Carleton Winslow, Smith revealed

the *genius loci* of Montecito and explored the problems of the country house in the 1920s better than any architect of the Santa Barbara school.

Smith was born in the Centennial year in East Liberty, Pennsylvania—so it was not only his name that suggested a Yankee Doodle image. He was educated at elite schools—Lawrenceville and Harvard (1894–96), though he did not complete a degree in the architectural program. After working briefly in Philadelphia as an apprentice architect, he decided to give up the profession, finding that he could not support himself in the patrician manner of his upbringing. As a stockbroker he was easily able to achieve much more than a comfortable living, for he retired in 1912, at the age of thirty-six. He then decided to study painting at the Atelier Julien in Paris, where he became enamored of the landscapes of Paul Cézanne and the work of other avant-garde artists. At the outbreak of World War I, he and his family were forced to leave Europe, and in 1915, after a painting trip to Santa Barbara, they decided to settle there. He immediately built his celebrated studio-house in Montecito, Casa Dracaena (generally called the Craig Heberton house after its second owner), and began

251 George Washington Smith. Architect's own second house and studio (1920), Montecito, California. (Richard Cheek.)

to paint with the intention of selling his work in the upper-class colony.[37]

In the already Hispanic atmosphere of Montecito, Smith's tiny masterpiece of a studio made quite a stir. His paintings did not. He therefore began to practice architecture again, taking on a talented female graduate of the Berkeley architecture program, Lutah Maria Riggs, as an associate in 1921. As he recalled, "I soon found that people were not really as eager to buy my paintings, which I was laboring over, as they were to have a whitewashed house like mine. So I put away my brushes and have not yet had a moment to take them up again."[38] Although he designed several handsome public buildings in the 1920s, including the Lobero Theater (1922–24) and Santa Barbara Crematorium (1924–25), Smith's practice centered around residential projects, including some as far away as northern California and San Antonio, Texas. In spite of a career abbreviated by his premature death in 1930, he became one of the nation's most esteemed domestic architects.

The houses Smith and Riggs designed were always compact and intimate, even when a large program was involved. The major ideas and spaces were outdoors. A cool indoor room served as a respite from the gardens, patios, courtyards, and pergolas that formed the core of the Santa Barbara experience. Composing his designs with simple, one-room-deep, gabled wings, Smith used his architecture as a ground for outdoor spaces, the lively shapes and colors of flora, the spectacular views of the sea or surrounding hills. Like a landscape painter, he cast the planar and geometric forms of buildings in gentle opposition to the dominant rounded forms of the landscape and the natural textures of trees, flowers, and shrubs.[39] Even when using architectural ornament, generally taken strictly from Andalusian sources, Smith worked like a painter, incorporating colored tiles or iron grilles into the composition as accents. Moreover, the ornament was itself an abstraction of floral motifs.

Like the work of Mellor and Meigs, Smith's architecture was formally conceived as a reinforcement of garden spaces. Thus his house plans were often L-shapes, simple bars, or courtyard types designed to complete the larger site plan. One innovation Smith took directly from Spanish house forms was the composition of rooms without interior circulation, emphasizing instead outdoor spaces as places of movement. He was also a master of massing—chimney forms, deep window reveals, and subtle juxtapositions of roof pitches and wings provided an underlying strength to his designs that many of his contemporaries failed to achieve. His brilliant sketches and the equally accomplished renderings of Riggs showed an understanding of light, shade, and form that was both painterly and rigorously architectural. Though these drawings were evocative and scenographic, they showed an inherent command of forms in space that could almost be called modernist, as David Gebhard has pointed out.[40]

By the mid-1920s, Smith was well established as a leading domestic architect to California society. Small houses were his forte, as proven again by the second house he built for himself in Montecito in 1920. But it was not until 1922, when he received the commission for the George F. Steedman house, Casa del Herrero, in Montecito, that he executed a house and garden that competed with the great eastern and midwestern examples. It became a landmark in the development of the modern Spanish house in America.

Steedman (1871–1940), a St. Louis businessman and industrialist, was noted for his interest in architecture, endowing the Steedman Fellowship at Washington University and traveling extensively in Europe, especially Spain, to study buildings. He gave Smith carte blanche to design an authentic Andalusian house; as part of the arrangement, Steedman went to Spain on several occasions to do research in the region, to purchase antiques, and to take in the ambience of the architecture and gardens. Arthur Byne and Mildred Stapley, antiquarians and authors of many books on Spanish decorative arts, served as dealers and consultants to the Steedmans, even arranging for the manufacture of reproduction tiles for the house. Their largest purchase for the Steedmans was a complete fifteenth-century painted wood ceiling from El Convento de San Francisco near Naranco, Spain, which eventually graced the entrance hall. Smith worked as a creative eclecticist, cleverly integrating specific details into an elegantly simple whole, in both the gardens and the house.[41]

The entire enterprise was a collaboration: Smith worked with the massing and plan of the house, manipulating form and sketching in soft pencil or charcoal; the Steedmans chose favorite motifs and made suggestions on all aspects of the design. They had definite ideas, preferring the irregularity of Andalusian farmhouses to the formality of Italian models. Smith gave them both; the south facade was borrowed from a small Italian villa at San Casciano near Tuscany, whereas the massing was picturesque. Steedman engaged landscape architects to design gardens that were evocative of Spain, using native plants. Ralph Stevens created the initial design, which was later altered by both Lockwood de Forest, Jr., and Francis T. Underhill. During their twenty-year residency, George and Carrie Steedman also made contributions.[42]

The site was organized around two major axial gardens—one to the south, the other to the east. Service buildings were placed to the west, an entry court to the north. The southern gardens followed a rill from the house outward, first to a hemicircular terraced lawn flanked by parterres, then downhill along an allée

made of Eugenia hedges, opening up to a secluded garden room with fountains and tiled benches. Beyond a small wall was a cactus garden suggesting a primordial landscape. Surrounding these gardens were orchards. The gardens to the east followed a similar theme, through a series of connected outdoor rooms. Smith's scheme for the house complemented the garden design by connecting the west garden to a vaulted loggia enclosing a walled Spanish patio, which also served as an outdoor counterpart to the living room. A lawn spread laterally along the patio, which featured a richly detailed tile exedra at its center. Beyond this, on a lower level, was a *giardino segreto* (secret garden) of espaliered roses. The element of surprise is constantly at play as one traverses these spaces. As Smith pointed out, there was more influence from the Italian villa than from the sequential, mysterious, and secret gardens of the Spanish tradition in most Santa Barbara gardens.

The plan was composed as a compact bar, then jogged and eroded to allow the outdoors in. The interior spaces were exquisitely appointed with tilework, ironwork, and Spanish furniture. Of particular note are the small circular staircase, ornamented by tiles, and the equally intimate octagonal library adjoining a tiny outdoor space. The two largest rooms, filled with Spanish and European antiques, are the dining room and living room. Yet neither is large by the standards of most country houses. They are intensely appointed, causing the viewer to concentrate on the smallest details, the subtleties of material, light, and color. Smith tailored each room to the objects within, even creating special niches to display paintings or precious furniture. The Steedman house was a dense and compact architectural piece that became expansive and elaborate only in relation to the outdoors. In this, the work echoed his earlier training with the Philadelphia architects.

Smith's house for the Steedmans was one of the key works of eclectic design in its time, as its publication in the *Architectural Record* in 1926 made clear.[43] He later designed larger houses, such as the Italian villa–style mansion (1927–28) for Kirk Johnson, with its vast gardens by A. E. Hanson,[44] but never richer or more convincing ones. Smith was successful in part because he shared his clients' sentiments and was able to translate their dreams into physical form, stressing in an interview in 1930: "In spite of our foreign reputation of hard-fisted materialism we are so romantic and so sentimental that when we return from a European trip we cannot rest until we have created for ourselves a house in the manner of the country nearest our heart—a treasure house we might call it—to house our souvenirs of foreign travel—a background to live against, in all sincerity, until we outgrow it."[45] Casa del Herrero was just such a place.

Another was Smith's equally brilliant estate for Mr. and Mrs. Peter Cooper Bryce on the seacoast at Hope Ranch, known as Florestal (1925–26). Again, the architect worked closely with the client—the indefatigable Girly Bryce (the former Angelica Schuyler Brown of the Brown Brothers Harriman fortune)—who led him to other Spanish sources she had discovered in books and travels. Like the Steedmans, this eastern couple fell in love with the Hispanic orientalism of Santa Barbara and made it their per-

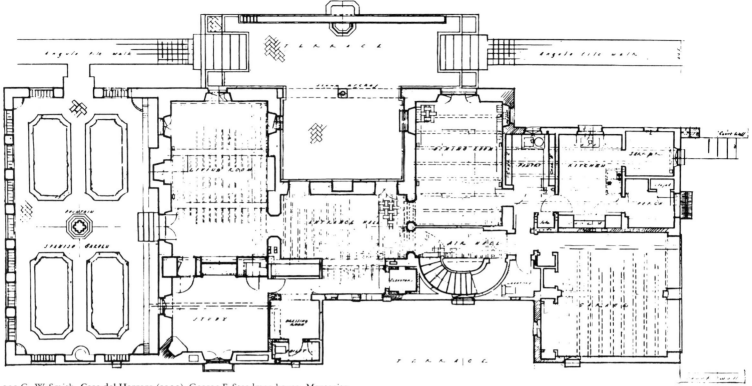

252 G. W. Smith. **Casa del Herrero** (1922), George F. Steedman house, Montecito, California. Plan and site plan. (Richard Cheek, from *Architectural Record,* 1926; author, after Streatfield, "The Garden at Casa del Herrero.")

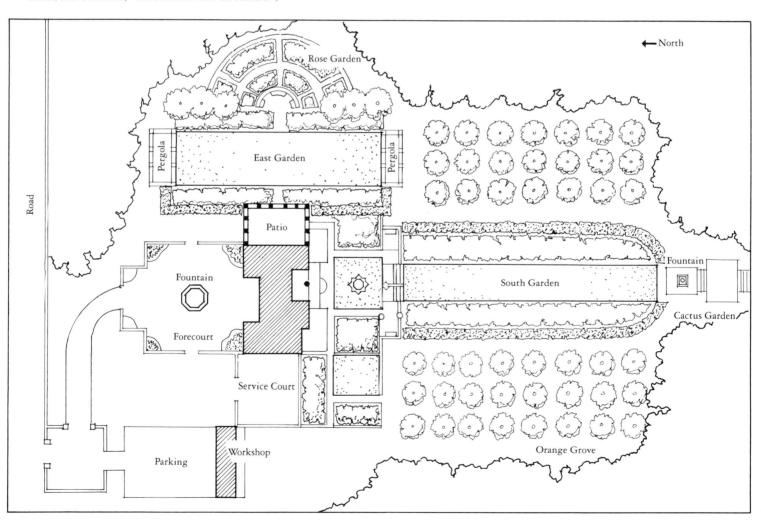

253 **Casa del Herrero.** South front. (Richard Cheek.)

254 **Casa del Herrero.** Loggia. (Richard Cheek.)

256 **Casa del Herrero.** Living room. (Richard Cheek.)

255 **Casa del Herrero.** Patio. (Richard Cheek.)

258 George Washington Smith. **Florestal** (1925–26), Peter Cooper Bryce house,
Hope Ranch, California. Aerial view. (Collection of Marc Appleton.)

manent home. Florestal, a much larger conception than Casa del Herrero, was tied to the seacoast but nevertheless focused on a courtyard theme.

The Bryces began spending winter holidays in California in 1917, staying in such splendid Spanish houses as Dias Felices, Bertram Goodhue's Montecito villa for Henry Dater, from 1921 to 1925 and Carleton Winslow's El Mirasol in 1917. They were familiar with the tradition of the country house, because Peter Bryce had spent part of his boyhood at Clayton, his father's Long Island estate (designed by Ogden Codman for Lloyd Bryce). They were also well traveled and cosmopolitan, having taken several European trips. Like the Steedmans, they toured Spain in search of inspiration for their California house, visiting, among other sites, the Alhambra, the Generalife, Barcelona, Majorca, Seville, Cordova, and Toledo. Mrs. Bryce wanted a patio to resemble the one she had visited at El Greco's house in Toledo, one of the familiar stops on a Spanish tour. Smith began the design in March 1925, working closely as always with his clients. Mrs. Bryce remembered the process as a collaboration. Her architect was rather untutored in specific details, and she was fully prepared to instruct him in how to get things right. An energetic student and artist in her own way, she planted her entire estate herself and had a hand in the design of the gardens. She wanted her house to be a spectacular place in which to live and entertain, not merely a

museum of old Spain. After two schemes the client and architect arrived at a unique solution to the site and program.

Smith's concept was to provide intimacy and urbanity through the use of three courts or patios, while also opening the house to excellent views of the mountains and ocean to the east and west. From the exterior the building looked very modest indeed, overgrown as it was with exotic flora and barely visible in its entirety. From within, however, it was a jewel that transported the visitor to Toledo or Salamanca; the tiny patios displayed small Moorish fountains, *rejas* (iron window grilles), elaborate tilework, and picturesque balconies entangled with flowering vines. The front court was public, accessible through wooden double doors; the rear court was private, accessible only from the master's suite. In between was a semipublic outdoor room occasionally used for dining. Above were marvelous rooftop terraces and pergolas that offered views of the ocean sunsets and lush hills. These were the same features used by Goodhue at the Gillespie house (at which the Bryces had been guests during their early visits to Santa Barbara), yet Smith made them friendlier and less classically austere. The major rooms were a large library, dedicated to Mr. Bryce's literary interests, and a formal dining room. Bryce, also an amateur photographer, had Smith design a darkroom for his printing work.

The house, which took approximately two years to design and build, was constructed on a heavily braced wood frame designed to resist earthquakes. Stucco facing covered the wood membranes,

257 **Casa del Herrero.** East garden access. (Richard Cheek.)

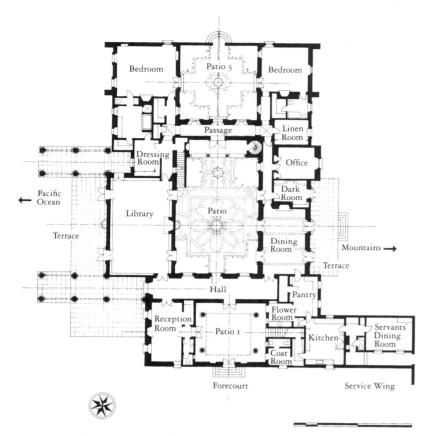

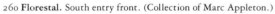

259 **Florestal.** Plan. (Collection of Marc Appleton, after George Washington Smith.)

262 **Florestal.** Arch in entry court, or first patio. (Collection of Marc Appleton.)

260 **Florestal.** South entry front. (Collection of Marc Appleton.)

261 **Florestal.** Central patio. (Collection of Marc Appleton.)

263 **Florestal.** Loggia in rear patio. (Collection of Marc Appleton.)

giving the look of massive masonry walls. Smith received a 12 percent commission for his work on this project. Local contractors, Snook and Kenyon, built the house for $183,963, some $20,000 over the original contract sum.[46] The clients moved in on January 1, 1927.

The gardens were linked only tangentially to the house, extending along a north-south axis. The meticulous grooming of the Steedmans, which required the services of landscape designers, was not for Mrs. Bryce. Her gardens were made with broader strokes. On the west facade of the building, Smith planned a terrace with a pergola extending from the main hall, leading to a view of the ocean. Mrs. Bryce emphasized this axis boldly by personally making a cut in the sand cliff to open the view. This terrace facing the sea was later (in 1934) balanced by a more intimate one on the east side of the house, facing the mountains. In the Bryce house, Smith made the most of the contrast between the introspection of the courts and the panorama of the seacoast and mountains. No less a masterpiece than Casa del Herrero, Florestal demonstrated another tenor in Smith's work within his Santa Barbara locale.

Smith and his contemporaries began a renaissance in domestic architecture in California that lasted through the depression and into the mid-century. So successful was it that California house styles and types appeared throughout the nation. Among Smith's leading competitors in the Spanish Colonial idiom was Wallace Neff (1895–1982), a native of California who became the architect to many Hollywood stars.[47] Whereas Smith was attracted to the Spanish house for its abstract simplicity, Neff liked the potential for geometric complexity in massing and in plan. He was inclined to experiment with circular turrets and hemicircular plans and to mold the stucco forms of his houses expressionistically. Far more playful than his fellow California eclectics, his work seemed to suit perfectly his theatrical clients. He remodeled Pickfair (1926–34) for Douglas Fairbanks, Jr., and Mary Pickford and designed two houses (1928 and 1937) for director King Vidor. His finest works, such as the Arthur Bourne house (1925) in San Marino or the Bryant Ranch complex (1927) in Santa Ana Canyon, were on a par with the best Spanish eclectic work of his time. They were also frankly modern, functional, and undoctrinaire, traits also found in the houses of other late eclectic architects, such as Roland E. Coate and John Byers.

Coate (1890–1958) graduated from Cornell in 1914, worked with the noted New York firm of Trowbridge and Ackerman, and moved to California to seek his dream in the early 1920s. He joined the English expatriate Gordon Kaufmann and the established Spanish specialist Reginald Johnson in a partnership in 1922, subsequently founding his own firm.[48] He became known as the leading exponent of the Monterey Revival, designing in the Anglo-Spanish idiom popularized by the colonial adobes of that town. His house in Montecito for Mrs. D. D. Cotton (1927) was perhaps the finest example, utilizing the familiar overhanging balconies and low-pitched tile roofs that characterized the style.[49] In plan, however, it was a dense, functional dwelling that could easily have pleased Walter Gropius, had the roofs been flat and the

ornament removed. Coate was also capable of working in any of the other popular idioms.

Southern California's eclectic regionalists, like their earlier counterparts in northern California,[50] created a domestic tradition that produced lasting typological innovations and fleeting stylistic trends. The vividness and theatricality of work of the 1920s and early 1930s seemed to dissipate after World War II, however, to be replaced by cultural consensus and loss of conviction. Younger architects lacked the training and verve; clients lacked the vision and capital. The decorative vitality of these original buildings was indeed integral to their success, as proven by the aesthetic standards they continue to set today and by the failure of current hackneyed versions to achieve anything approaching the same beauty and quality.

THE RANCH AND ADOBE: SYMBOLS OF THE SOUTHWEST

Two factors promoted regionalism: the commitment of architects to indigenous types and the identification of patrons with local traditions. The ranches and adobe houses of the Southwest are perfect examples of such regionalism. Leisurely living in the sun-baked climate of the coasts, mountains, and deserts of the West became the declared ethos in such regional periodicals as *Arizona Highways* and *Sunset Magazine*. The ranch house joined the bungalow and Spanish courtyard house as types identified with this life-style. With all rooms on one level, stretching out to embrace the landscape and shading its outdoor patios with wide eaves and loggias, the western ranch eventually outstripped the other two types in popularity. In Texas, the working ranch house was adopted by wealthy oilmen and businessmen during the 1920s as a diversion from city life. Many bought large ranches as leisure houses for fall and winter weekends, holidays, or as seasonal family homes. During the 1920s and 1930s magazines such as *House and Garden* treated the ranch life-style as just another variation on American country living.

Wealthy city dwellers of the western and southwestern states built ranch-type country retreats against dramatic mountain, desert, and plateau landscapes. Among Roland Coate's most evocative and free-wheeling designs was the quasi-Monterey-style ranch house (1934) for F. W. Cowlishaw in Nogales, amid the Santa Cruz Mountains of southern Arizona, its wings cocked and spreading lazily into the desert. A romantic country house in the best regional tradition, the Cowlishaw complex was at home in its western landscape yet comfortable in the modern world of swimming pools and appliances. Its entry court could easily accommodate either the horse or the automobile, as publicity photos suggested.

Wallace Neff's modern Spanish ranch (1929) in Calabasas, for King Gillette, head of the razor company,[51] was equally comfortable while blending splendidly with the rolling brown hills near Malibu, north of Los Angeles. Here Neff used his typically informal planning strategy for the main house, which was organized around a motor court and a formal patio. Neff anchored the plan to

264 *top left* Roland Coate. D. D. Cotton house (1927), Montecito, California. (Architectural Drawing Collection, University Art Museum, Santa Barbara, California.)

265 *top right* Roland Coate, F. W. Cowlishaw house (1934), Nogales, Arizona. Courtyard. (Architectural Drawing Collection, University Art Museum, Santa Barbara, California.)

266 Cowlishaw ranch. (Architectural Drawing Collection, University Art Museum, Santa Barbara, California.)

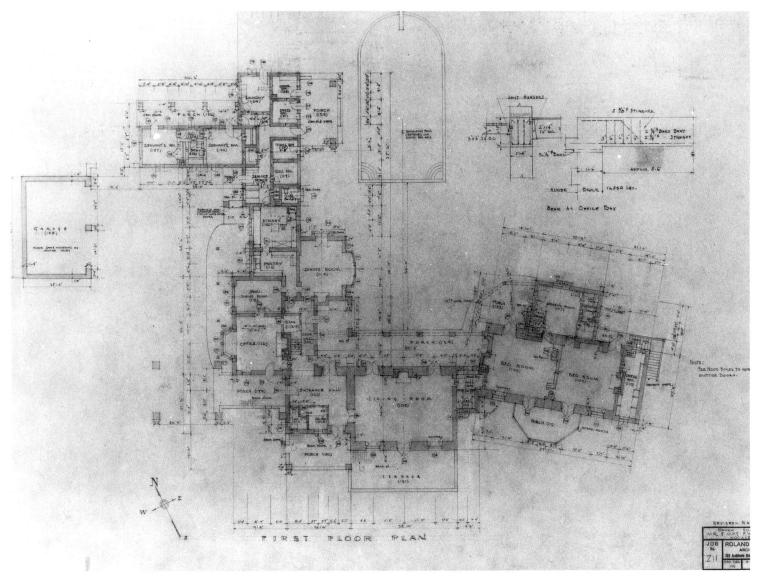

267 Cowlishaw house. Plan. (Architectural Drawing Collection, University Art Museum, Santa Barbara, California.)

its hillside site with a tower at the center. A free-standing arcade and a small patio, looking somewhat truncated in relation to the rest of the building, framed views of the hills. A critic remarked of the place: "One can bask in the sun in this little garden room with no thought of the morrow, and enjoy to the full the beautiful view of the surrounding mountains."[52] On the large property were a stable block and service buildings, each appropriately rustic. Riding quarter horses in the foothills on weekends was the California equivalent of eastern country life.

A ranch could be comfortable and polished, like the Cowlishaw house, or rugged and rustic, like the extraordinary Kemper Campbell ranch (1929, 1934–35) by John Byers, in Victorville, California. In this overtly frontier house, only horse, saddle, and bedroll were welcome. Byers (1875–1966) had been experimenting with authentic, primitive, mud brick construction for almost ten years before beginning this dude ranch in the desert foothills near Barstow. He located the house on the crest of a hill with views in all directions, but especially toward the Apple Valley at the edge of

the Mohave Desert. The scenery was splashed with the tinted colors of the nearby Calico Mountains. The mud brick created an organic relationship between house and landscape that both Byers and his client appreciated.[53]

Byers built the ranch for Kemper Campbell, an Oxford-educated businessman from Los Angeles who died in action as a pilot in 1943. Campbell purchased an eighteen-hundred-acre tract that had been a working ranch (the North Verde Ranch, owned by John Brown) for the use of his friends, who enjoyed trail riding and duck hunting on weekends. After his death the house was enlarged, to accommodate more guests, and run as a profit-making resort by his heirs, Mr. and Mrs. Raymond De Blassis, during the 1950s and 1960s.[54]

Aesthetically the Campbell ranch made the most of primitive and regionally appropriate adobe and wood construction. Byers was a specialist in this technique, having opened his own kiln for tile making in 1919, after studying the regional building traditions of the Hispanic colonies. A romantic vagabond somewhat in the mold of Addison Mizener, he began his career as an electrical engineer, spent time teaching English in Uruguay, and eventually headed the romance language department at Santa Monica High

268 Wallace Neff. King C. Gillette ranch (1929), Calabasas, California. (Richard Cheek, courtesy of SOKA University.)

School. After a chance encounter with Mexican craftsmen, however, he became so fascinated by the traditional building methods that he gave up his teaching position and set up his own business, advertising himself as a "manufacturer of Mexican handmade floor and roof tiles" and a designer and contractor for "Spanish adobe houses," without any formal training in architecture. Working sporadically with a trained architect, Edla Muir, he eventually gained a license in 1926. By approaching architecture first from the craftsman's point of view, he was able to appreciate the functional, climatic, and constructional advantages that the traditional adobe afforded in a warm, dry region like southern California. As he wrote, "Adobe construction has a romantic and historical past as well as a useful future. . . . The long low simple lines, the play of light and shadow on walls, the soft colorful texture of the roof and the sincerity of design and composition of primitive adobe are almost impossible to improve upon architecturally."[55] In designing the Campbell ranch Byers employed such authentic construction details as handmade tiles, heavy timber post-and-beam portals, and mud brick walls seventeen to twenty inches thick. The adobes were made on the site in the traditional manner: the mud was mixed in a large mound, packed into a mold, sun dried for a week, and ricked.

The plan of the main house shows the influence of the construction method; rooms are made only as deep as the span of a timber *viga* (beam), and the spaces are arranged in an unsophisticated linear enfilade. The south side is protected by an attached porch running the length of the bedroom block. With its low-spreading roofs hugging the hillside (adobe walls were built to a maximum of ten feet to a story), surrounded by Joshua trees and cactus, the Campbell ranch made a picture as reminiscent of the old West as any John Ford might have invented for his archetypal films. Akin to romantic country houses in the East, these California ranches consciously related to their landscapes and regions and suggested an escape from urban living. More distinctive than the later suburban ranch house, they were at once precursors of a new ideal and remnants of a fading dream.

Many new immigrants to the southwestern states expressed a similar interest in adapting a house to the land and the climate. In Texas, New Mexico, and Arizona architects began studying vernacular building forms as precedents for domestic work. The Southwest produced a number of Spanish Colonial revivalists whose work rivaled that of their California colleagues. San Antonio's Atlee B. and Robert M. Ayres (father and son) were nationally recognized as leading domestic architects as well as experts on the architecture of colonial Mexico.[56] The elder Ayres (1874–1969) moved to Texas with his family in 1888, studied architec-

269 John Byers. Kemper Campbell ranch house (1934–35), Victorville, California. (Architectural Drawing Collection, University Art Museum, Santa Barbara, California.)

270 Campbell house. Plans. (Richard Cheek, from Wagner, *The Arts and Decoration Book of Successful Houses.*)

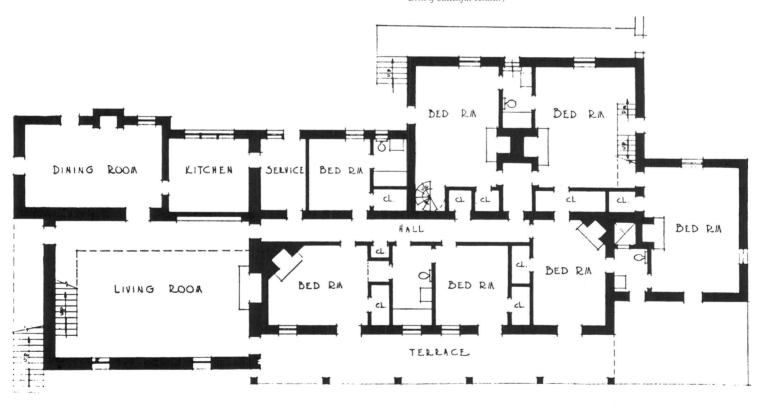

271 Atlee and Robert Ayres. Dr. and Mrs. Sam Roberts house (1929), Kansas City, Missouri. (Architectural Drawings Collection, University of Texas at Austin.)

272 Ayres and Ayres. McNay house. Courtyard. (Architectural Drawings Collection, University of Texas at Austin.)

ture in New York between 1890 and 1894, then worked in San Antonio and in Mexico City before establishing his own office in 1905, after the death of his first partner. He became an avid photographer, enthusiast, and amateur historian of regional vernacular architecture. His son, Robert (1898–1977), joined his practice in 1922. Influenced by the architecture of the colonial missions and old Spanish houses as well as by picturesque Arts and Crafts planning, the Ayres' houses were beautifully evocative of the past and well suited to the hot, arid climate of San Antonio. Loggias, patios, and upper-story balconies allowed for shade and ventilation. The firm favored a form of cranked plan in which tower forms acted as hinges to the several arms, usually enclosing a patio. Their style was first codified in the Thomas E. Hogg house (1924), but it was perfected in such works as the Dr. Sam Roberts house (1929) in Kansas City, Missouri, and the Carl D. Newton house (1928) in Olmos Park Estates.[57] The firm's best-known work, and their major country house, was the Marion Koogler (McNay) and Dr. Donald T. Atkinson estate (1929), now the McNay Art Museum, on the outskirts of San Antonio.[58]

John Gaw Meem, like Atlee Ayres, was an outsider who came to love the architecture and landscape of the Southwest—so much so as to become a preservationist and one of the founders of a revival in Santa Fe, New Mexico. Trained as a military man and civil engineer, Meem (born in Brazil in 1894) was forced to leave a career in international banking because of tuberculosis, for which he sought a cure at Sunmount Sanatorium in Santa Fe. While recuperating, he became friendly with not only his physician, a collector of traditional Southwest artifacts, but a group of regional enthusiasts, including the artist Carlos Vierra. Vierra not only

painted the adobes, pueblos, missions, and colonial structures of New Mexico but collected a multivolume album of photographs of vernacular and Spanish buildings. Meem took up architecture as his health improved, studying in Denver, and when he returned to Santa Fe resolved to develop a "new-old" style that would synthesize the traditional adobe architecture of the region—a rich combination of Spanish, Indian-Pueblo, and Territorial influences. As one of his early projects, he undertook the preservation of the town's ancient plaza (1930), an effort that would presage his lifelong involvement with conserving the character of old Santa Fe. Winning first prize in this competition brought him into contact with Cyrus McCormick, Jr., the Chicago millionaire and summer resident of the town, who was a primary sponsor.[59]

When McCormick wanted a country house built near Santa Fe, he asked Meem and Vierra to collaborate on the design. (The two men had also planned to produce a book on the traditional architecture of New Mexico, based on Vierra's albums. Though never published, it served as a source document for much of the architect's later work.) Vierra, with his vast knowledge of local building and decorative details of the old Santa Fe style, especially adobe and viga construction, was Meem's tutor in this project. Begun in 1929, the house was to be an authentic adobe in every respect, the focus of a hundred-acre ranch at Pojoaque. Like other eclectics, however, Meem saw his role as that of a creator of new architecture, simple and modern in its essential elements, which could serve as a ground for traditional decorative details, furniture, and even reused fragments. He chose a sprawling, spokelike plan to allow views of the mountains and river from all of the major rooms. Also essential to the building's success were its irregular outlines and battered walls, lying horizontal and close to the land but nevertheless very distinct from it. Meem attributed its aesthetic success to Vierra's eye, but the architectural concept

273 John Gaw Meem. Amelia Hollenback house (1932), Santa Fe, New Mexico. (Richard Cheek, from *American Architect*, 1934.)

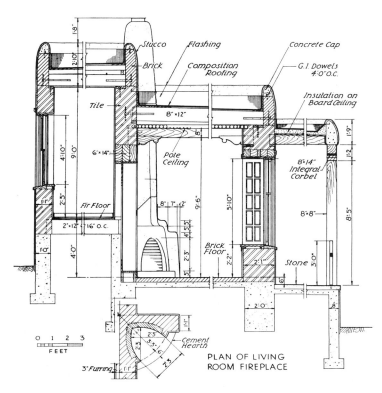

274 John Gaw Meem. Mary Vilura Conkey house (1928), Santa Fe, New Mexico. Portal section. (Richard Cheek, from *American Architect*, 1934.)

275 John Gaw Meem. **Las Acequias** (1931), Cyrus McCormick ranch, Nambé, New Mexico. Plan. (Author, after Bunting, *John Gaw Meem.*)

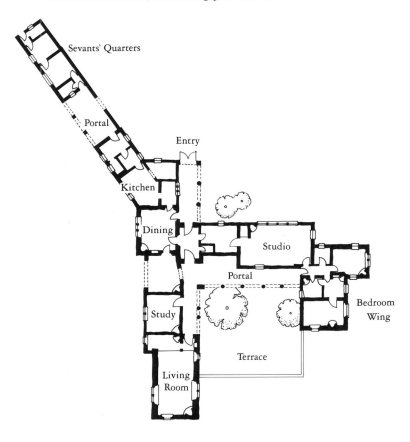

was his. Its traditional features included the lack of modern conveniences such as electricity and heating (which were originally planned but not executed), the use of local women as masons and plasterers for laying up the adobe fireplaces, the incorporation of over forty antique building fragments into its construction, and the insistence on using real mud brick construction. The McCormick house may be the purest example of a regionalist country house ever constructed in the modern era—a tribute to the almost religious zeal of its architects and patron.[60]

Meem's later buildings, including many smaller houses, exhibited a far less antiquarian style but nevertheless evoked the architectural heritage of New Mexico. Among these was an adobe he designed in the 1930s for Mrs. Amelia Hollenbeck near Santa Fe, which used the traditional portal, vigas, and pueblolike massing to brilliant effect.[61] He was also a founder of the Old Santa Fe Association, which like the landmark planning ordinance in Santa Barbara fostered the creation of a civic and architectural tradition for the town, based on regional building types and styles. As he stressed in his passionate writings on the architecture of New Mexico, the adobes made by Native Americans and early settlers belonged to the earth in ways that no other structures could. "They are the earliest expressions of the American Fundamental Form," he stressed in reference to Eliel Saarinen's theories; they are "almost automatically [in] harmony with the surroundings."[62] These "new-old" building forms were the natural models for a domestic type in the Southwest. The ranch and adobe houses that Meem, Ayres, Byers, Coate, and their contemporaries designed during the 1920s and 1930s are proof of the applicability of indigenous models to modern problems. Moreover, they demonstrated that Americans were adapting their domestic habits to the traditions of their new regions with a romantic zeal that paralleled that of country house builders of the previous generation.

SOUTHERN TRADITIONS

The increasing interest among America's social elite in indigenous decorative art and architecture during the 1920s was also evident in the cradles of English and French Colonial culture. Brought to life in literature and the popular imagination, the Old South had a romantic appeal for all Americans. Historians recognized Charleston, Williamsburg, New Orleans, Charlottesville, Natchez, and Savannah as unique repositories of American art and architecture. Major efforts to preserve the early houses of these cities were brought to the attention of both scholars and the public through publications. As Fiske Kimball, the leading historian of American Colonial houses, wrote in 1924: "It has been scarcely recognized that the South has also its own traditions, which offer an individual point of departure, not only in domestic, but also in monumental and religious architecture. Indeed, in the great area of the South there are not one but many local traditions."[63] Architects of the flourishing regional schools studied these diverse ways of building to good effect.

The most romanticized building type in the South was the plantation house—representing the legendary gentility and grace

276 Armstrong and Koch. **Shadows-on-the-Teche,** restoration and alterations (1922), New Iberia, Louisiana. (Koch and Wilson, Architects, New Orleans.)

of the antebellum period. The great southern houses that had escaped ravage during the Civil War became icons of domestic architecture. Mount Vernon and Monticello, landmarks in national preservation, were extremely influential models for restorations as well as for new houses.[64] As Richard Guy Wilson has pointed out, northerners were among the leaders of the resurgence of interest in these houses, especially during the 1920s. The Du Ponts bought Montpelier, the home of James Madison, in Orange, Virginia. Louis Hertle of Chicago purchased Gunston Hall, the famous home of George Mason, near Mount Vernon. The most notorious plantation restoration was done on Carter's Grove (1751–55, 1906) in Williamsburg, an effort that coincided with the Rockefeller campaign to create a village museum of colonial life. Purchased in the mid-1920s by T. Perceval Bisland, the house was restored by New York architect W. W. Tyree. The most egregious "colonial revivalizing" occurred on the magnificent woodwork of the hall, which was stripped of its white paint and stained. A second, more extensive architectural intervention occurred in 1928, when Mr. and Mrs. Archibald McRea purchased the building and commissioned Richmond architect W.

Duncan Lee to design additions and to alter some of its characteristic features.[65]

In writing about his work on Carter's Grove, Lee revealed a philosophy of creative adaptation shared by many contemporary eclectic regionalists — that of extending tradition rather than of scientifically restoring the past. Faced with the problem of making over an eighteenth-century river plantation house, in the form of a center block and two unattached dependencies, to fit the needs of a wealthy modern family, he was a little too pragmatic. "It began to look," he wrote of the three-year adaptation process, "as if we had bought four walls, a roof, and some lovely panelling, and somewhere under and between these we had to hide a lot of things that Burwell [the original owner] had got along without and never missed." Yet he was confident that his new work, done with an understanding of the classical vocabulary of eighteenth-century builders, would complement and enhance the old by its adherence to stylistic principles. "Where enlargements are absolutely necessary, a precedent of the period should be found and followed," he stressed. His "restoration plus" added new hyphens to fill out the areas between block and outbuildings and created several new formal rooms, as well as bathrooms and service areas.[66] As a creative eclecticist, Lee saw nothing wrong with this palimpsest upon an original colonial artifact. Also, he was clearly influenced in some of his new work by the Carter's Grove project, designing during the same years Grammercy Farm Estate, a splendid country place at Hot Springs, Virginia. This stone Colonial house had the basic outlines of the Williamsburg model.[67]

Lee and his clients clearly identified more with the image of the plantation than with its reality. The fiction and illusion of old southern houses fascinated the new rich of the Jazz Age. Redesdale, designed in 1925 for Mr. and Mrs. Leslie H. Reed by William Lawrence Bottomley, is one of a number of superb Richmond houses modeled after an eighteenth-century river plantation.[68] The client, an executive of the Imperial Tobacco Company, had purchased several farms on the James River near Richmond, with the intention of erecting an architecturally correct five-part Georgian house in which to entertain business colleagues. Having been impressed by Carter's Grove, Reed initially contacted Lee; eventually, however, the commission went to Bottomley (an honorary Virginian), who helped them create a vivid estate, full of scholarly quotations from old Virginia houses. Historians William O'Neal and Christopher Weeks have documented sources from Lower Brandon, Carter's Grove, Westover, and the Samuel Powel house in Philadelphia, whose parlor the clients had seen in the American wing of the Metropolitan Museum of Art.[69] Achieving an accurate rendering of the prototypes using modern methods required intense study and patience by client, architect, and builder. Though one of the best American examples of its kind, Redesdale is hardly unique. Interest in Virginia plantation models was high during the 1930s. Bottomley designed a number of fine houses throughout the state, as did William Adams Delano, in which patrons demanded scholarly details from eighteenth-century sources.[70] In New York enclaves Mott B. Schmidt and Dwight James Baum were also designing splendid five-part Georgian houses based on these sources.

There were also many native southerners who wished to connect with building traditions and the landscape itself; some had made their money in the South and wished to show their allegiance to the region by perpetuating its domestic culture. There is no better example of the New South meeting the Old than the Callaways and their modern plantation, Hills and Dales (1914–16), in La Grange, Georgia. Fuller E. Callaway, Sr., was a self-made millionaire who personified the Horatio Alger myth, starting with the proverbial five cents in his pocket and building a major textile company. His fortune made, Callaway and his wife bought the eighty-acre estate of Judge Blount and Sarah Coleman Ferrell, with its spectacular and unusual parterre formal gardens, in 1912. In doing so they consciously claimed the most important piece of land in La Grange—a plantation adjoining the town, which had become a kind of local institution. In the bargain they got one of the most unique pieces of landscape architecture in America. Mrs. Ferrell was a pioneer southern gardener who had from the 1840s through the 1880s cultivated a hillside Italian garden of boxwood and many exotic species of trees and shrubs.[71] The Italian terraces, as they were called, extended down six levels from a hilltop, along the axis of two circular fountains. Among Mrs. Ferrell's extraordi-

nary boxwood creations were parterres forming "God Is Love" (in a quaint expression of piety), an Italian water chain, a bunch of grapes, and a lyre. Many of the trees, shrubs, and flowering plants were unique to their locale. The Callaways deemed the Ferrells' unprepossessing Victorian villa unsuitable for their needs and had it pulled down. The new owners, setting themselves up as La Grange's manorial benefactors, then replaced the wooden manor house with a Palladian villa, restored the gardens, and expanded the estate to three thousand acres, adding various agricultural enterprises.[72]

To realize their dream of a new plantation they hired not a northern society architect but the rising Atlanta firm of Henze, Reid and Adler. Led by the talented J. Neel Reid, this firm was the leader in the city's architectural renaissance and designed many suburban houses in the exclusive Buckhead neighborhood of northwest Atlanta. After Reid's untimely death, Philip Trammell Shutze became the designer of the firm (and practiced into the 1970s). Both architects were bred and educated in Atlanta, had trained at the Ecole, and had apprenticed with leading New York firms before gaining the opportunity to build for wealthy southern clients in the 1910s and 1920s.[73] Indeed, prosperous Atlanta supported perhaps the most creative group of regionalist architects in the South during this period.

Reid, like his Chicago contemporary David Adler, was an even-handed, solid designer who worked in all the popular styles, his particular love being Italian villa and Colonial Revival idioms. His major domestic works were suburban country houses, modeled after those of Platt and Pope. Though small, they were always designed with a distinctive dash of elegance and a flair for decorative details. Had he lived beyond the age of forty-one, Reid might have developed into one of America's most remembered eclectic masters. Hills and Dales was his most elaborate and expansive commission, a country house that perpetuated the tradition of the southern plantation, while marrying other sophisticated sources.

Reid's design was an adaptation of several Platt prototypes, including Timberline, Sylvania, and the Russell Alger house in Detroit.[74] He described the house to Callaway as Georgian Italian, meaning a hybrid of classical sources from Palladio to James Gibbs. Using a classical block plan directly derived from Platt, Reid set a formal front facing the parterres to the south and ingeniously designed a hemicircular porch on the east side to extend the living room outdoors and to give the house a distinctive feature from the entrance drive. An unusual configuration for a seemingly symmetrical classical house, this double facade solved the problem of orienting to the existing axial gardens while also situating the house toward other views. In fact, one usually entered from the north side, under a less imposing porte cochere, and discovered the gardens from the house, rather than vice versa. A giant Ionic order, evocative of the villas of the Veneto and the imposing porticoes of many southern Greek Revival plantation houses, gave the entire block a stately and Italian character. Here Reid demonstrated that Platt's modification of classical planning, gardening, and decorative principles could be applied more freely to an unusual site. Although Hills and Dales was demonstrably

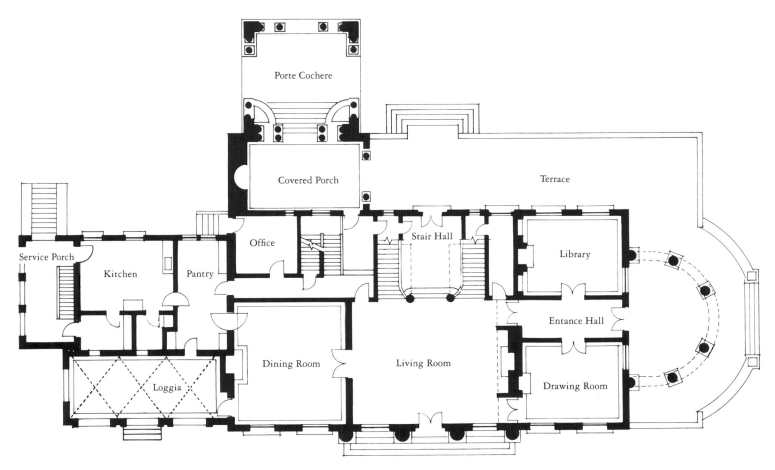

Porte Cochere

Covered Porch

Terrace

Office

Stair Hall

Library

Service Porch

Kitchen

Pantry

Entance Hall

Loggia

Dining Room

Living Room

Drawing Room

277 Hentz and Reid. **Hills and Dales** (1914–16), Fuller E. Callaway estate, La
    Grange, Georgia. Plan. (Author, after Grady, *The Architecture of Neel Reid in
    Georgia.*)

Italian Gardens

European in feeling, it was southern in the way it proudly commanded the hilltop and crowned the existing gardens with an
appropriately classical "big house."

The Callaways were serious about their new country life. They
added such supporting structures as a greenhouse, a separate
garage with chauffeur's apartment, a dog kennel, a new stable
block for Tennessee walking horses, and various farm buildings for
livestock and crop storage. As in many modern country houses,
agricultural production served the needs of the estate. Reid and
Mrs. Callaway altered the gardens in keeping with the Italian
theme by adding classical stone hermae, benches, and other sculptures. Local residents who were free to stroll the gardens, as part of
a tradition the Ferrells had begun, were puzzled at first by the
statues. The patron once overheard two men remark that if he had
gone to the trouble to erect so many effigies of himself around the
grounds, he ought to have picked a sculptor who could create a
better likeness: "Ain't none of 'em looks a bit like the old man!"[75]

In cities throughout the South, builders of suburban country
houses often adapted plantation house models. Pringle and Smith
of Tennessee designed a Natchez-style house for Scott Probosco in
Chattanooga during the late 1920s, which was featured in *Southern Architecture Illustrated*. Another regional house type, the Georgian block, was used by Dwight James Baum in his house for

Henry Clark Bridges in Tarboro, North Carolina. There were even
two modernist plantations. During the 1930s Henry Luce of Time
Incorporated had Edward Durell Stone design a modern version of
a plantation group in South Carolina, which affected the social
trappings of the traditional model (including a big house and slave
quarters). Mepkin Plantation, in Moncks Corner, shared with
Frank Lloyd Wright's Auderblass the distinction of avoiding historical stereotypes while attempting to embrace a deeper typological source. However, the range of inspiration taken by many
architects from southern models was never entirely doctrinaire.
For instance, the suburban houses that Reid, Shutze, and "Buck"
Crook designed in Atlanta ran the gamut of period styles, including some southern plantation and Louisiana idioms. One of the
qualities that distinguished them from other period houses was
their eccentricity, especially with regard to combining sources.
Shutze and Reid collaborated on the Calhoun-Thornwell house
(1919–22) in Atlanta, a rather bizarre variation on a Roman
baroque villa. If Atlantans seemed willing to cultivate a tinge of
flamboyance in their Jazz Age villas, Philip Shutze, a colorful and
outspoken architect who loved Italian and English classical work,
was their ideal counterpart. In his strangely wonderful Swan
House (1926–28) for Mr. and Mrs. Edward Inman, now part of
the museum complex of the Atlanta Historical Society in Buckhead, he produced the most colorful period revival house in
Atlanta. Shutze combined a host of English and Italian classical
sources in a tour de force of historical synthesis.[76]

278 William Lawrence Bottomley. **Redesdale,** Leslie Reed house (1925), Richmond, Virginia. (Richard Cheek.)

The hybrid nature of certain takeoffs on the plantation type can best be seen in Bayou Bend (1926), a house that reminds many Houstonians of nearby New Orleans. Though its colorful name evokes images of Tennessee Williams and the humid, mossy landscapes of east Texas, Ima Hogg's wonderful house in River Oaks has a straightforward appellation: it occupies a key site in the crook of Buffalo Bayou, the riverlike watershed that winds through the city. The property is located on the northern edge of Lazy Lane, where powerful and socially prominent Houstonians still make their homes. In social terms, it was intended to dominate bustling Houston, just as Hills and Dales had sleepy La Grange.

The architect of this modern country house was the talented John F. Staub, probably the most prolific and enduring domestic specialist in the South or Southwest. Born in Knoxville, Tennessee, in 1892, Staub attended the University of Tennessee and received a master's degree in architecture from the Massachusetts Institute of Technology in 1916. He spent his apprenticeship with Harrie Lindeberg in New York, where for six years he learned domestic design from one of the nation's masters. Lindeberg's work in Houston brought Staub to the growing oil and cotton capital and eventually led him to set up practice there in 1923. Staub quickly made his reputation in suburban design within the wealthy enclaves of Houston. He was the leading architect of houses in the private compounds of Shadyside and Broadacres, as well as in fashionable River Oaks, the eleven-hundred-acre tract developed during the 1920s by Will C. and Mike Hogg, sons of the former Texas governor, Stephen Hogg.[77] Staub designed the River Oaks Country Club as well as many eclectic residences in the area. The largest and most elaborate of these he built for the legendary Miss Ima Hogg (1882–1975), the sister of the founders and a renowned philanthropist.[78]

As the model for the plan, she chose Homewood (1803), the famous country seat in Baltimore, even going so far as to sketch a design for her architects to refine. Staub won the commission after a brief competition with Birdsall Briscoe. In keeping with regional traditions, he developed the house as a classical villa with pavilions, using motifs from New Orleans houses of the early nineteenth century. "I'd made up my mind that there was a certain type of house that belonged in this climate," Miss Hogg later recalled, "and I got some ideas from New Orleans because I thought they'd look pretty here. And then also I remembered [that in] Greece where they have brilliant sunlight [they] use pale pink."[79] Thinking pink, she and Staub studied the Louisiana models and made a special trip there to purchase traditional ironwork for use on the house. She had also by then begun her extraordinary collection of furniture and decorative arts, a hobby that resulted in the creation of the Bayou Bend Museum in 1958.

Yet in spite of the patron's wide array of mental images, Staub managed to design a house that is strong, unified, and abstract in its massing and plan. (Tongue in cheek, he dubbed the house Latin Colonial.) Like his mentor Lindeberg, he defined the house with taut, planar stucco surfaces and anchored its main block and dependencies with strong masses—an abstracted central pedi-

ment and two prominent chimneys as vertical accents. The entire composition is securely tied together with a thin cornice and a strictly proportioned grid of shuttered windows. In plan, Staub was relatively conservative, following well-established eclectic models to accommodate the unusual program of two bachelors and their eccentric sister.

Painted a pale pink with greenish brown shutters and decorated with elaborate wrought iron balconies, Bayou Bend evoked the urbanity of New Orleans and the gentility of southern life in the nineteenth century. The gardens of the estate, which connected to Houston's Buffalo Bayou on its northern boundary, were magnificently planted with azaleas and local flora. Ellen Biddle Shipman was initially hired to plan the gardens in the 1920s but contributed only to the east garden. Later, after establishing the basic outlines herself, Miss Hogg employed the local landscape firm of Fleming and Shepard and, finally, Ruth London to realize her ideas.[80] Today the gardens form a lush, dreamlike backdrop for Staub's splendid house, memorable as much for its exotic colors as for its bayou setting.

It is interesting to compare Staub's use of New Orleans sources with those of his contemporary Richard Koch in Louisiana. Bayou Bend is somewhat similar in type to Koch's country house (1936) for Donald Markel in Pass Christian, Mississippi. The Markel house, however, grafts French Colonial traits to a modern house plan, in much the same way that Staub borrowed features from nineteenth-century dwellings in the French Quarter. In other words, rather than attempting to copy a local type, these two houses merely incorporate regional features into a popular eclectic planning model. Koch knew a good deal about indigenous domestic traditions, having restored two of the South's most revered plantations: Oak Alley (1926), near Vacherie, for Andrew Stewart and Shadows on the Teche (1922), in New Iberia, for Weeks Hall. In neither case was he averse to some romantic and conjectural palimpsests. Like Duncan Lee, Koch was considering his work as part of an adaptation to modern needs. He designed a number of innovative regional houses during the 1930s, including the French-influenced weekend retreat for J. W. Reily, a coffee merchant, at Bayou Liberty in 1933 and 1937.[81]

Plantation models were taken up by southern architects and patrons for the same reasons that the ranch flourished as a country house type in the West: romantic and sentimental associations with the past, climatic and functional advantages, a sense of belonging to the region and landscape, and a desire among new patrons to be established in local society. None of the houses treated above can be seen as pure typological and stylistic replications, though architects such as Bottomley and Meem often hovered very close to the traditions they were perpetuating. Nor was the line between restoration and new work always securely drawn. The process of eclectic transformation was as complex in regional revivals as in earlier movements, and as effective as a background for American life.

During the 1920s the regional varieties of the country house supplemented but did not replace the established styles among

281 *top* **Hills and Dales.** Rear facade. (Richard Cheek.)

282 **Hills and Dales.** Dining room. (Richard Cheek.)

283 John Staub. **Bayou Bend** (1926), Ima, Stephen, and Will Hogg house, Houston, Texas. Entrance facade. (Museum of Fine Arts, Houston.)

284 **Bayou Bend.** Bayou garden facade. (Museum of Fine Arts, Houston.)

285 Armstrong and Koch. Donald Markel house (1936), Pass Christian, Mississippi. (Koch and Wilson, Architects, New Orleans.)

wealthy patrons. The examples cited in this chapter are indicative of a significant national trend toward identification with local cultures drawn from America's past, a trend that reached its height during the decades between the wars. Many other examples of sophisticated use of indigenous American house types can be cited. In the New York area, another Early American idiom to achieve widespread popularity during the post–World War I years was the Dutch Colonial with gambrel roof. Aymar Embury II, the architect and writer, became the champion of this style, adapting it for small suburban as well as country houses. Another exponent was Dwight James Baum, a successful and talented country house architect, who built a number of houses in the style in Riverdale and Fieldston. These two Hudson River communities in the Bronx developed a strong sense of local color through the houses Baum designed. A good example of his work is the stone and clapboard residence of Benjamin L. Winchell in Fieldston. Baum's monograph of 1927 is filled with excellent adaptations of Early American houses for suburban and country settings. As Matlack

Price wrote in praising his work, "Certainly the architect who is conscientiously true to his calling will exert his best persuasion to induce people to live in houses that are not only suitable to the family and its kind of life, but to the locality and its kind of life. No better example of the skilful versatility of the modern architect could be found than in the work of Mr. Baum."[82]

Professional opportunities for revival specialists abounded throughout the country in the 1920s. The most respected eclectic specialist in Minneapolis was Edwin Lundie, who brought a rugged, rustic style to his summer houses on Lake Minnetonka and White Bear Lake.[83] Benno Janssen, an Anglophile romantic-classicist, designed numerous country houses for the elite of Pittsburgh, in styles ranging from Lutyensesque English to abstracted French Provincial.[84] In the 1930s Jerome Robert Cerny of Chicago designed many suburban country houses in a Moderne style. In posh Greenwich, Connecticut, William F. Dominick turned out a group of elegant period houses in many romantic styles, tailored to the exacting demands of his cosmopolitan clientele.[85] In fact, nearly every major city, from Cleveland to St. Louis, Milwaukee to Dallas, had at least one talented residential specialist working

286 Armstrong and Koch. W. B. Reily house (1934), Lewisburg, Louisiana. (Koch and Wilson, Architects, New Orleans.)

during the housing boom that preceded the crash of 1929. These regional eclectics shared a way of thinking about domestic architecture derived from their academic training and were drawn to create houses that not only were attached to period idioms but also vividly evoked the special qualities of their locale, landscape, vernacular building, and early history.

It is important to recognize that for the traditionalist and the academically trained architect use of indigenous models was merely an extension of well-established theories and ideals. American house types became better models than European ones, as the nation began to appreciate their history and design. Fitting a house to its place was an imperative of domestic architects throughout the eclectic era, but it seemed to loom larger as Americans dispersed throughout the nation, discovering the rich variety of landscape and building traditions the nation had fostered over its history. Patrons embraced the life associated with plantations, ranches, and adobes for the same reasons that they had sought inspiration in European manners and pastoral ways of life. Much of the impetus behind regional revivals was still associational, although as experiments in indigenous living progressed, the commitment to local traditions became stronger. Unfortunately, the ideal of the regional country house was challenged during the 1930s by the advent of machine aesthetics, in which the icons were not only automobiles but toasters, biplanes, and refrigerators.

287 Armstrong and Koch. J. W. Reily game house (1937), Bayou Liberty, Louisiana. (Koch and Wilson, Architects, New Orleans.)

Modernist Experiments

7

We seem to have been following the wrong scent, to have lost our power of discrimination between the vital and the superficial, and to have bartered away our souls for mechanical inventions. To have ceased worshipping a God, either Christian or Pagan, and to be worshipping machinery instead!

—ARTHUR INGERSOLL MEIGS

Architecture suffers because, recognising it as an art, we ruin it by our respect, our insistence that art be "artistic." Car-building is not recognised as an art in the "artistic" sense, and the design of the twentieth-century vehicle is consequently unhampered by sentiment and artistic titivation. Yet a house and an automobile are built for purposes equally functional.

—FRANCIS R. S. YORKE

⌘ SENTIMENT VERSUS TECHNICS

At the Sixty-third Annual Convention of the American Institute of Architects held in Washington, D.C., in 1930, George Howe, C. Howard Walker, and several other noted American architects took the podium to debate the significance and influence of European "modernist" building—an issue that had begun to emerge in the late 1920s. As reported that year in *Architectural Forum*—one of the first American magazines to champion the new architecture—speakers on both sides were cautious and polite as they discussed whether International Style architecture belonged on these shores. In the same issue the journal presented two major country houses, each by an exponent of the competing ideologies: the Modern Tudor Rynwood in Glen Head, Long Island, designed by Roger Bullard for Samuel Salvage, with its splendid gardens by Ellen Shipman; and Square Shadows, in Whitemarsh, Pennsylvania, Howe and Lescaze's daring, modernist country house for William Stix Wasserman.[1] Between 1930 and 1940, *Forum* and other journals regularly, if infrequently, featured International Style houses. In mid-decade, Edward Durell Stone's sleek house for Richard Mandel, in Mt. Kisco, New York, was covered alongside the Wasserman house, finally completed in an altered version.[2] As

the decade progressed, it was clear that the winds of change were bringing new ideas that threatened to obscure tradition.

The presentation of these houses differed not only in the architectural languages employed but also in the terms and points of view used in their criticism. For nearly half a century, leading architectural critics had written about American domestic architecture from the standpoint of style, sentiment, comfort, tradition, and historical associations. Social and economic issues were important as well, especially in the writings of Croly. But artistic qualities in house design rested mostly in the architect's or client's personal stamp, in the creative interpretation of time-honored motifs, and in the ineffable pursuit of beauty or rightness of form. In the hierarchical, conservative, highly structured world of the haute bourgeoisie, correctness and decorum were essential. It was also imperative that the house embody and dramatize a sense of domesticity and comfort through familiar symbols and amenities—such icons as the hearth, the inglenook, the sheltering gable, and vertical chimney stacks. Critics recognized that the quality of home was as important as the architect's talent for formal invention. All these criteria had powerful sentimental associations.[3]

288 Frank Lloyd Wright. **Wingspread.** Wigwam interior. (Richard Cheek.)

241

The new architecture was criticized—analyzed, really—in an entirely different, more rational way. Building technics and social engineering, couched in terms of scientific research, concerned the architects and observers of the Neue Sachlichkeit (New Objectivity). The first important book in English to treat the modernist idiom in domestic architecture, F. R. S. Yorke's *The Modern House,* unequivocally set forth the agenda for the new villa in the country (although the author sheepishly admitted that mass housing, not the single-family house, would be the essential form of the future and command the attention of enlightened architects). Efficiency, fitness of purpose, technological innovations, and new means of production would determine the value of the modern house. As Yorke argued: "In this age of efficiency and machine-mindedness, it is unlikely that people will continue, for the sake of sentiment, to tolerate a manner of building that is obsolete." Maintaining that eventually the simplicity and manifest beauty of engineering forms would be appreciated by the public, Yorke took up the torch of his hero, Le Corbusier, showing ocean liners, biplanes, and objects of modern design in his book.[4] He devoted several chapters of the book to new building techniques and presented plates illustrating the houses of leading International Style architects, with details and terse descriptions of construction and materials but with little or no discussion of clients or aesthetic concerns, which were no longer considered relevant:

There is no aesthetic prescription, no aesthetic law for the typical form of an industrial product. There is only one law for it; that it shall be entirely appropriate to its purpose; give perfect service. The elegance is in the smooth, perfect performance; in the quality of the material. The modern architect does not force upon the house a symmetry or a geometric scheme if neither symmetry nor geometry is necessary to the purpose of his project. He does not cover it with decorations borrowed from the "styles" or with modernistic ornaments invented by catchpenny commercial fashion makers.[5]

Because modern engineering achievements and machines, as well as similarly conceived houses, needed no decoration and made no concessions to manners, social conventions, or domestic symbols, criticism of such architecture also dispensed with discussing such issues. Yorke's formula for critical presentation, really that of *L'Esprit Nouveau* and Le Corbusier, was soon taken up in America by his friend A. Lawrence Kocher, the influential editor of the *Architectural Record,* and by the editors of *Forum.* Even the graphic design in these books and journals was spare and purposeful. The modern house was presented and criticized on its own terms, with no bows to the irrelevancies of eclectic criticism as it existed up to the mid-1930s.

Although Yorke showed the work of U.S. architects Kocher and Frey, Howe and Lescaze, and Richard Neutra, it was not until 1940, when the journalists James and Katharine Morrow Ford published *The Modern House in America,* that the achievements of avant-garde domestic architects working in the late 1920s and 1930s were fully documented. The Fords adopted a technics-based method of exposition and a book design derived from both Yorke and a recent catalog of the Museum of Modern Art, but added a social dimension to their schema. "The essence of the new residential architecture," they wrote, "is revealed in its twofold purpose: to base its plan upon the organic life of the family to be housed, and to make a logical use of the products of invention."[6] A new social order for family life—more open, free, informal, and simple—would be reflected in the new American house, with its activity zones, reciprocity of indoor and outdoor space, and ample room for new technologies and gadgets. Implicit in this ideology were modernism's familiar call for a new society and political order and a criticism of bourgeois family values.

The authors preached and practiced the new life-style by living in a house designed by Walter Gropius, in Lincoln, Massachusetts. They championed the work of the European immigrant architects who had come to the United States during the late 1930s and before, admitting reluctantly that Frank Lloyd Wright was "the founder and Nestor of the new residential architecture" but failing to include any of his work in their book. Because relatively few modernist houses were constructed in the United States during the 1930s, it is fair to say that the Fords' book presented a comprehensive picture of its subject.[7] The authors included the work of Richard Neutra, Howe and Lescaze, Gregory Ain, Harwell Hamilton Harris, William Wilson Wurster, Pietro Belluschi, George Fred Keck, Rudolph Schindler, Raphael Sorriano, Edward Durell Stone, and Royal Barry Wills. The book was intended as a national survey, though the authors admitted that California architects seemed to be leading the way in the new work. Significantly, the society of southern California was relatively unconstrained by the social castes operating in the East and therefore seemed to support more avant-garde clients. Critical commentary was again heavily weighted toward describing new technologies, innovative activity zoning, and functional organization or discussing clever solutions to climate control and orientation. Appearing after the Museum of Modern Art exhibition of 1932, with the polemical catalog of Henry-Russell Hitchcock and Philip Johnson, and the publication of Yorke's book in 1934, *The Modern House in America* advanced the narrowly defined International Style idiom in domestic architecture and gave it further legitimacy.

There were other indications that the focus of criticism in residential design was changing. In 1933, *Architectural Forum* published one of the first articles to attempt a scientific functional analysis of the country house, complete with the now familiar "bubble," or adjacency diagram, showing the three major activity groups—social-recreational, dining-services-food preparation, and sleeping-hygiene—and mapping their ideal relationships. Dimensional rules of thumb and descriptions of each major room were also provided.[8] This article, which illustrated both modernist and traditional rooms, suggested two paradoxes: first, that there was a highly codified set of design paradigms for the country house by 1930; and second, that modern architects, by their objective and critical analysis, were attempting subtly to undermine these paradigms.

The extreme polarity between the two camps was not resolved during the years before World War II. "On every side the battle between the modernist and traditionalist waxes warm," confirmed an editorial in *Architecture* in 1928. "On the one hand there is strong impatience, mounting even to actual disgust, with the forms handed down to this generation from other times. . . . On the other hand there is the firm conviction that the accumulated beauty of civilization cannot be set aside by any upstart generation."[9] American eclectic architects, though interested in modernist work and ideas, were often skeptical about their applicability in the United States.[10] European architects working in this country, such as Neutra, Lescaze, and Gropius, maintained their ideological positions in the face of social conservatism and were only able to influence taste through avant-garde institutional support and academic platforms. Moreover, clients building modernist houses were largely outside the conservative social milieu— examples included intellectuals, political or social radicals, scientists, film stars, and artists. As such, the modernist villa did not seriously compete with traditional country and suburban house types during the 1930s, either in numbers or in real influence. The reasons for this are clear: shunning deep-rooted concerns about tradition, prescribed gentle relationships to landscape, familiar domestic symbols, and long-standing social norms governing room use, the modernist house did not have to address the sentimental issues important to wealthy clients. Magazines directed at upper-class readers remained rather cool about the new International Style.[11] Innovations in the new architecture were largely "sold" to the public by citing the technological advantages—more light and air, greater efficiency and convenience, new miracle materials, and so on.[12] But even then, these could be, and were, incorporated into the traditional house, as they were in the Austin house by Leigh French, Jr., near Hartford, in 1930.

American architects committed to the cause of modernism, such as George Howe, William W. Wurster, and of course Frank Lloyd Wright, made more concerted and positive efforts to find a middle ground during the 1930s. Howe was in a unique position to appreciate both sides of the dialectic, having practiced with leaders of both camps.[13] A fervent modernist, he nevertheless refused to forsake the lessons of his early training as a country house architect. As a formula for the modern American country house, his residential work of the 1930s was matched only by the great individualistic houses of Wright (with whom he disagreed in a famous debate in *T-Square* in 1932). In 1939 Howe remarked: "I think everybody agrees that comfort and convenience are the essentials of a modern house, but there *is* something else, and . . . that something is style. . . . I feel that the modern style *is* in the best American tradition, the tradition we are building and have been building from earliest colonial days, the tradition of willingness to try any reasonable experiment to attain the better life in the spiritual field."[14] Howe was right. Style, sentiment, and technics influenced both modernist and traditionalist house designs during the streamlined decade. For though the rhetoric was polemical, some American architects managed to incorporate the best aspects of technics and tradition into their forward-looking country houses.

FORWARD HOUSES AND MODERN VILLAS

The characteristic architecture of the thirties . . . will be Modern. . . . Modernism is not *an architectural style. Modernism is a basic idea.*
—Fortune

The Great Depression not only did much to dampen the vitality of regional eclectic movements in the United States but also took its toll on the development of modernism.[15] Between 1927, the date of Richard Neutra's seminal Lovell Health house in Los Angeles (acknowledged to be America's first important modernist house), and 1940, only about fifty major domestic works were built in the new style—less than a dozen on the East Coast.[16] When clients were scarce, architects invented work by producing hypothetical schemes and model houses for expositions or publication, such as Keck and Keck's futuristic house for the Century of Progress exposition in Chicago in 1933, Buckminster Fuller's Dymaxion house, and Kocher and Frey's Aluminaire house, first erected for a show at the Architectural League of New York in 1931. Each of these visionary works was demonstrative of new technologies and construction systems.

When clients had both the means and sophistication to build avant-garde houses, they did so with the intention of creating showpieces of the new art. Warren Shepard Matthews' Allvine house (1929) on Long Island, one of the first International Style houses constructed in the East, was built for a director of the Fox Film Corporation.[17] The interiors were among the early works of Donald Deskey, the important art deco designer. Edward Durell Stone's house (1935) for Richard Mandel, a modernist furniture designer (and partner of Deskey), wore its ideology proudly in conservative Westchester County.[18] Richard Neutra's sweeping country villa (1935) in Northridge, California, for Josef von Sternberg, the eccentric Hollywood director and actor, was a self-conscious demonstration of a new ethos, aptly reflecting the personality of its patron. Its imagery suggested speed and fast automobiles—one of Neutra's favorite metaphors. It boasted a lavish mirrored bathroom (without locks on the doors to prevent suicides), a walled enclosure for dogs, a moat alleged to be electrified, an overly long garage stall labeled "Rolls Royce," and a searchlight for special effects. The house was too idiosyncratic to become a model, in spite of the critics' praise.

Neutra's Windshield (1938), the John Nicholas Brown house on Fishers Island, New York, was less persuasive as a modernist icon but more attuned to the requirements of its wealthy client and his family. Its complex program included a music room, an art gallery, a large playroom, children's quarters in a large dormitory, and rooms for half a dozen servants. As such, it was properly a country house, built for clients who had resided in lavish traditional dwellings all their lives.[19] The family's only criticisms of the house were functional, not aesthetic. Aesthetically, the bathroom units designed by Buckminster Fuller were impressively futuristic; functionally, however, the large casement windows throughout the house leaked in the high winds that buffeted the island. Mrs. Brown found the house noisy, and the servants found it impossible

289 Edward Durell Stone. Richard Mandel house (1935), Mt. Kisco, New York.
Model. (*Architectural Forum,* 1934.)

290 Mandel house. (*Architectural Forum,* March 1934.)

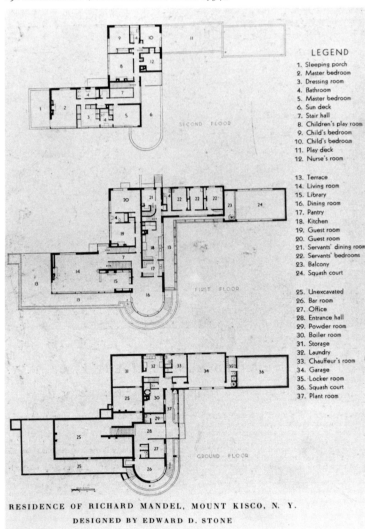

LEGEND

1. Sleeping porch
2. Master bedroom
3. Dressing room
4. Bathroom
5. Master bedroom
6. Sun deck
7. Stair hall
8. Children's play room
9. Child's bedroom
10. Child's bedroom
11. Play deck
12. Nurse's room

13. Terrace
14. Living room
15. Library
16. Dining room
17. Pantry
18. Kitchen
19. Guest room
20. Guest room
21. Servants' dining room
22. Servants' bedrooms
23. Balcony
24. Squash court

25. Unexcavated
26. Bar room
27. Office
28. Entrance hall
29. Powder room
30. Boiler room
31. Storage
32. Laundry
33. Chauffeur's room
34. Garage
35. Locker room
36. Squash court
37. Plant room

RESIDENCE OF RICHARD MANDEL, MOUNT KISCO, N. Y.
DESIGNED BY EDWARD D. STONE

to keep clean. Ironically, Windshield was heavily damaged in a hurricane during the year of its completion and was promptly nicknamed Won't Shield by its owners. In the final analysis the powerful modernistic aesthetic outweighed the functional concerns in these houses. Yet despite all the correct characteristics of an avant-garde house, Windshield looks rather labored, banal, and overburdened by its program when compared to Neutra's more visionary work.

In 1930 Lawrence Kocher and Gerhard Ziegler designed a country house in Connecticut for Rex Stout that overtly mimicked the color-plane polychromy of De Stijl architecture. Constructed of concrete and painted in a yellow, blue-grey, and black color scheme, the house had a raw, austere look that apparently did not bother the owner. Its organization, a U-plan around a garden court, provided for a zoned arrangement of garage, studio, formal entertaining, and service areas and articulated the program elements as interlocking rectangular solids. Kocher and Frey's Aluminaire house, also known as the K-F house, was purportedly designed to demonstrate rapid erection of lightweight wall systems using aluminum panels. An observer of current European architecture would have in 1931 noticed its clear debt to Le Corbusier, especially to his Maison Cook. The cubic block organization, *fenêtre en longueur* across the front, roof garden, *pilotis* (Le Corbusier's term for round concrete columns), biplane-style plan elements, and other features were laden with stylistic associations aimed directly at critics and other architects from the avant-garde. The architects claimed that the house could be erected in less than a week and that in huge quantities it would cost a mere twenty-five cents per square foot.[20] The Frederick V. Field house (1932), in West Hartford, Connecticut, another compact country house designed by Howe and Lescaze (but showing the latter's European biases), also demonstrated the influence of the new aesthetic—a

THE WEST
ELEVATION

291 Kocher and Ziegler. House in Connecticut (1930). West elevation and
   southwest view. (Yorke, *The Modern House.*)

292 House in Connecticut. Plan. (Yorke, *The Modern House.*)

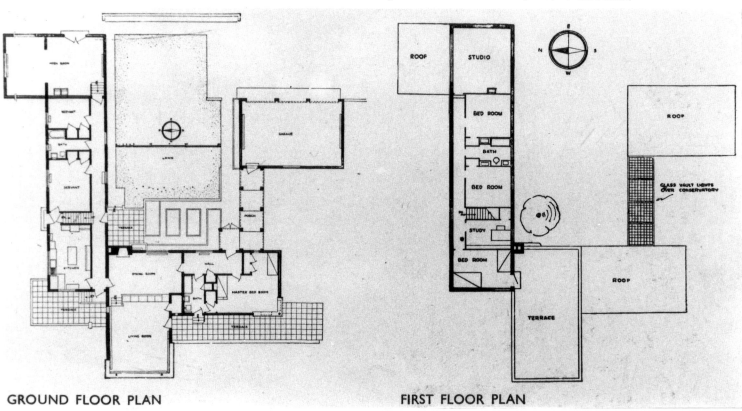

GROUND FLOOR PLAN   **FIRST FLOOR PLAN**

293 Kocher and Ziegler. **Aluminaire** house (1931), Westbury, Long Island. (Yorke, *The Modern House.*)

clear debt to French *purisme* and the work of Mallet-Stevens.[21] The program—really one large living-dining-library area below and an interlocking curved bedroom volume above—was bluntly described in Yorke: "Young couple. Simplify all household problems. No useless gadgets. Country house is to rest in, to enjoy sun, air and view, and to work in."[22] The clean, ascetic style of the house seemed fully in tune with the clients' intellectualism. Howe and Lescaze followed a similar T-shaped *parti* on a grander scale in their English country house (1933) at Totnes, Devonshire. Still tightly planned, this country villa had a more conventional program, with fully defined rooms, servants' quarters, and a slight formality, in keeping with English customs. The strict compartmentalization of the plan, while functionally necessary, compromised the spatial continuity and formal dynamism that were crucial to the modernist idiom.

Lescaze fully realized the ideal of a modern country house only in a hypothetical project—a telling fact in itself. In 1928 he published "The Future American Country House" (a proposal for a dwelling ten years in the future) in the *Architectural Record,* with appropriately insurgent rhetoric: "The present day house should be a tool of man, his implement which helps him to grow and live just as efficiently as his telephone, radio and other machines that help him conquer distances."[23] This house of the future would celebrate not only distance-conquering communications machines but also modern transportation advances. Placed at the intersection of a turnpike and an airport runway, the building announced itself as a point on a grid of lines representing travel in the new, shrinking world. Lescaze's controversial axonometric drawing showed a biplane being towed up to its integral hangar and an underpass leading to a large garage—clearly going Le Corbusier's (later) Villa Savoye one better. The hangar was to be equipped with gasoline faucets to remove gas and oil, while the house incorporated sponge rubber decking, exposed mechanical piping, air conditioning, and other futuristic elements of high technology.[24] Most emphatically polemical was Lescaze's insistence on doing away with the foremost symbol of traditional domesticity: "No fireplaces!"

If all of this new architectural rhetoric was meant to *épater la bourgeoisie,* it succeeded in assuring not only that few country houses were built in the new idiom but also that reaching a compromise between established domestic norms and the new architectural style would be difficult. Critics sanctioned the work of only those architects who were devoted to modernism and its antagonistic ideology, whereas the characteristics associated with modernism undoubtedly put off most wealthy and conservative clients. Nevertheless, clever and pragmatic American architects managed to attack the problem in several ways. Royal Barry Wills, trained as a construction engineer, applied the best techniques of functional planning to various traditional and modern styles. Wills consistently pointed to the commonsense advantages of more open planning and new building technologies but was careful to cite also some of the aesthetic disadvantages of the modernist idiom.[25] Though successful and popular with the public, he was for the most part disregarded by modernist critics. Raymond Hood, the master of the art deco skyscraper, chose to live in a simple, traditional house, but he designed several flamboyant country houses, with varying success. Some successful traditionalists, like Lindeberg and Staub, tried to find a domestic analogy to art deco, while also experimenting with an overtly modernist language in a few works in the 1930s. Others, like Reginald Johnson, became wholehearted converts. A few country houses of the era were designed to mitigate some of the ideological and formal strictures of European modernist design and to adapt its best attributes to the American situation.

One of the most eccentric of these transitional houses was Hood and Howells' large, pinwheel-plan villa (1930) for Captain Joseph M. Patterson in Ossining, New York. Like Lescaze's house of the future, this strange dwelling included such new-age advances as Bakelite finishes, a central rooftop observatory, and clocks that kept Western Union time, each connected to the power source with exposed conduits. Hood found Patterson a difficult client; when forced to place windows in a disordered pattern on the facades to satisfy his client's requirements, Hood painted the entire red brick surface of the house with art deco camouflage to disguise the problem. The Patterson house, criticized by Hitchcock and other avant-garde proponents, nevertheless had a unique,

294 Howe and Lescaze. Frederick V. Field house (1932), West Hartford, Connecticut.
View from the southwest. (Yorke, *The Modern House.*)

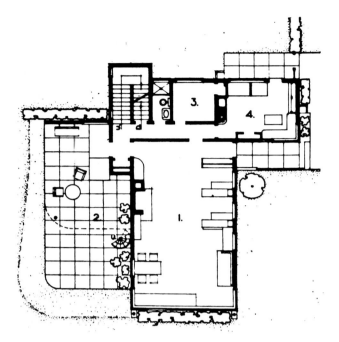

GROUND FLOOR PLAN.   1, living room;
2, terrace; 3, maid's bedroom; 4, kitchen.
The living room is 19 ft. × 33 ft.   Two desks
forming part of the built-in furniture provide
study space.

295 Field house. Ground floor plan. (Yorke, *The Modern House.*)

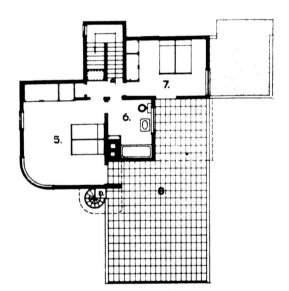

FIRST FLOOR PLAN.   5, bedroom; 6, bathroom; 7, bedroom; 8, sleeping porch and
terrace.

296 Field house. First floor plan. (Yorke, *The Modern House.*)

expressionistic whimsy not out of keeping with other eclectic houses of its time.[26]

Hood, along with Howard Walker, Harvey Wiley Corbett, and Ely Jacques Kahn, designed hypothetical country houses for an exhibition sponsored by R. H. Macy and Company and *Architectural Forum* in 1933. Entitled "The Forward House," the exhibition featured drawings and models that demonstrated new concepts of modern living, with an eye toward marketing modern home products available at the store. Hood's suburban villa was vertically organized in a T-plan to take advantage of terraces on the ground, second, and third floors, in keeping with the architect's belief that outdoor living was healthful and stimulating. "My own home for the past eight years has been a revelation to me of what can be done with the garden," he said, "and the house we are exhibiting is, to a great extent, the result of this experience."[27] The integration of house and garden, traditional fenestration, and simple massing gave the Forward House a conventional quality that was more palatable to the public. The architect's own traditional house (1925) in Stamford, Connecticut, as well as his art deco–Georgian Brooks house (1933) in Sands Point, New York, demonstrated a similar conventional bias toward the country house and garden, suggesting that he was not willing to apply the same radical architectural language of his commercial works to his domestic ones. He was not alone among successful art deco architects in believing that the streamlined aesthetic had its limits.

Nevertheless, Hood was not a domestic architect at heart. George Howe, on the other hand, had begun his career with an understanding of the traditions of the American pastoral country house and had come from a background that made him acutely aware of the dilemma faced by the modernist domestic architect. His reworking of Square Shadows, after the more overtly International Style scheme of William Lescaze, showed a struggle to resolve this problem of achieving domestic comfort and sentiment using modern materials, composition, and spatial concepts.

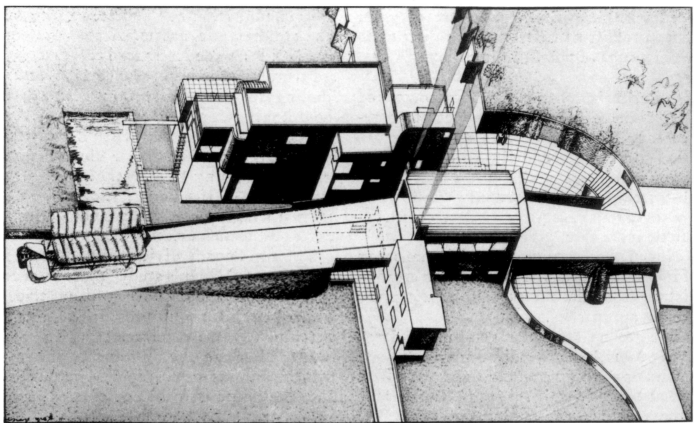

Lescaze, del.

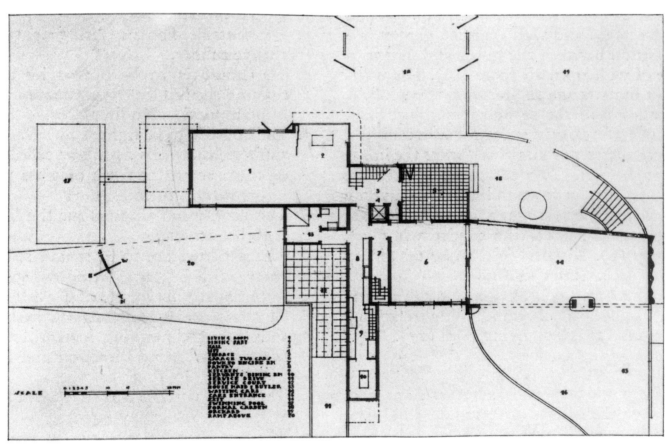

297 William Lescaze. A Future American Country House (1928). Sketch and plans.
(*Architectural Record*, 1928.)

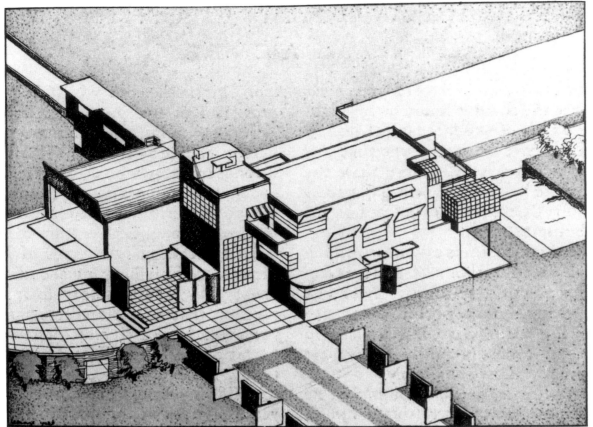

Lescaze, del.

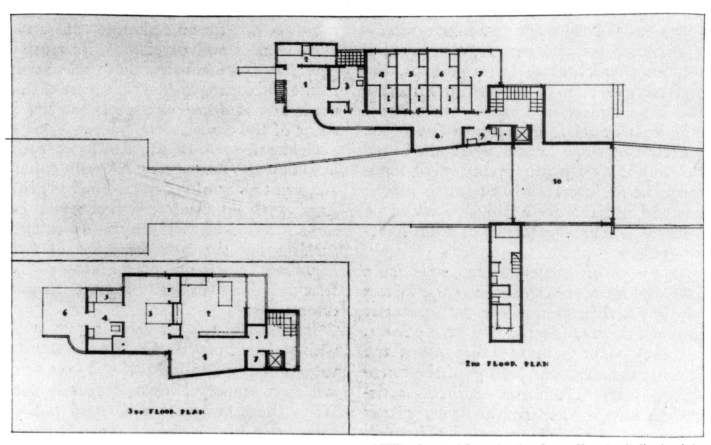

3RD FLOOR PLAN

2ND FLOOR PLAN

298 William Lescaze. A Future American Country House (1928). Sketch and plans.
(*Architectural Record*, 1928.)

299 Howe and Lescaze. **Square Shadows** (1932–34), William Stix Wasserman house, Whitemarsh, Pennsylvania. Rendering by William Lescaze of preliminary scheme, dated June 1929. (George Arents Research Library, Syracuse University.)

300 **Square Shadows.** Garden front. (*Fortune,* 1935.)

The commission for the Wasserman house began before 1929, while Howe was still with Mellor and Meigs. The first scheme, which was lost, was designed in a stripped Georgian style, perhaps not unlike Howe's house (1928) for George Tyler in Elkins Park, Pennsylvania. According to Wasserman, Howe and Lescaze presented a second, more Corbusian scheme to him in 1929, after forming their new partnership. (In fact, it was Wasserman, a Philadelphia stockbroker, who first introduced the two architects.) "I was presented with a concrete structure which resembled a modern factory," he remembered. "Some of the interiors replete with marble walls and stainless steel reminded me of a bank, while other rooms looked like a modern brothel."[28] The project was temporarily halted during the depression but then revived in 1932, after Howe and Lescaze had split their responsibilities for New York and Philadelphia commissions.

William Wasserman, like Richard Mandel, inherited a fortune from his father, who was chairman of Philadelphia's Artloom Rug Company. He traveled extensively as a young man, visiting the Soviet Union while selling bonds for a Philadelphia brokerage firm and getting a fair dose of European avant-garde culture. At thirty-four he started his own investment company, specializing in venture capital—a rather adventurous business endeavor in its time. Even during the depression his speculation on the monetary exchanges and in commodities futures netted him a sizeable fortune, which allowed him to continue with his country house project—eventually reprogrammed for his wife and four children. According to *Fortune,* which profiled him in 1935, he built a modernist house because: "(a) he and his wife came under the influence a few years ago of the Modernist architects Lescaze and Howe who convinced them of the logic of Modernism and . . . (b) his father-in-law had a habit of giving him excellent and very old Chinese primitives which fit into a Modern setting much more aptly than they do into any other."[29]

In contrast to his position in 1929, Wasserman did not want as severe a demonstration of the new aesthetic in the later scheme;

301 **Square Shadows.** Dining room interior. (*Fortune,* 1935.)

"SQUARE SHADOWS," HOME OF MR. AND MRS. WILLIAM STIX WASSERMAN, NEAR CHESTNUT HILL, 1934

Family Composition and Requirements. Mr. and Mrs. Wasserman and three children. Owners interested in politics, finance, and the arts. Musical and dance recitals frequently given. Active participants in country life and sports.

Plan. "The lines of human circulation on the plans are curvilinear axes of actual movement which replace the old rectangular axes of theoretical movement."

Construction. All bearing walls are of grey local rubble masonry. All curtain walls of light red Virginia brick. Air conditioning.

Interior. Much of the furniture, particularly that in dining rooms, designed by architect. Subtle use of color as background for Oriental painting, sculpture, and screens which decorate the principal rooms. Two dining rooms, one for the children and one for the parents and their guests, both served by a common pantry; when partition between is folded back the entire space becomes available for a large party.

Cost. Approximately $160,000.

Comments. "The use of the handrail of laminated wood as a beam supporting the semi-circular staircase is perhaps a novel structural device."

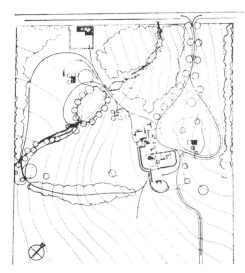

PLOT PLAN

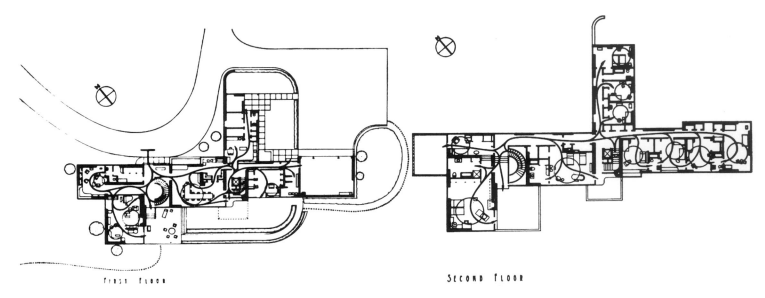

FIRST FLOOR

SECOND FLOOR

302 **Square Shadows.** Plot and floor plans. (Ford and Ford, *The Modern House in America.*)

nor was he prepared to pay for as lavish a program. Howe designed a scaled-down variation on the second parti, more linear in plan and marked by a concern for spatial continuity and a sense of curvilinear movement through each space. Thus, as shown in a flow diagram, one entered most rooms at the corner, breaking any box-like or axial characteristics. At the heart of the plan was an open, glassed-in stair hall with one of the world's first fully suspended spiral staircases, built of lightweight steel members. Here was the traditional symbol of grace and formal elegance, associated with ball gowns and grand entrances, now sleek and dematerialized. In the living room, broken at all of its corners, he designed a cleverly asymmetrical marble hearth—another traditional symbol made modern.[30] Howe, along with interior designer Jeanne de Lanux, carefully selected materials and colors to produce a rich, muted effect more in tune with contemporary French art deco than with the glaring primaries favored by Le Corbusier and his followers or de Stijl designers.

But Howe's most significant contribution to the modern country house lay in his application of traditional masonry materials—the brick and schist associated with the landscape of the Whitemarsh Valley—in concert with concrete, pipe columns, and steel sash windows. Howe articulated these materials with a structural logic related to their use and weight, rather than treating heavy and light materials as equal, abstract planes. Square Shadows proclaimed itself a new-age country house by its flat roofs, cubic massing, and self-consciously modern construction. It also related to the landscape and locale by its use of vernacular materials. As such, Howe was able to move beyond the aesthetic representations of technology to engage problems of landscape, place, and traditional domestic symbolism. Square Shadows, aptly named to suggest the bold, flat-roofed forms standing on the land, was perhaps the most important transitional American country house; with this solution he found a middle ground during a troubled decade in American architecture.

The small group of experimental country houses built in the United States during the late 1920s and 1930s was paralleled by a larger but still diminishing corpus of traditional buildings for clients who could somehow afford to build during the worst economic times in the century. By the end of the decade, changes in social norms and demographic and economic conditions signaled the end of the dream of the country house.

Perhaps only one American architect foresaw and came to terms with many of the problems of domesticity, individuality, transportation, and a new economic order in the 1930s. His was an idiosyncratic, free-spirited approach to the modern country dwelling, an approach that seemed to circumvent certain problems of the International Style. But it was also the statement of an ideologue, reformer, and cultural hero emerging from relative obscurity. It is fitting that Frank Lloyd Wright, America's greatest domestic architect, should have brought a final breath of life to the waning tradition of the country house.

FRANK LLOYD WRIGHT'S WINGSPREAD

Wright's two great country houses of the 1930s represented two poles in his solution to the problem of the modern country house—one a kind of future-oriented, mock International Style villa pulled down off its pilotis to engage a waterfall, the other a sweeping, rotorlike building that incorporated all the conservative trappings of the modern corporate mogul's estate. Although both were built for prominent business leaders of their respective cities—Edgar Kaufmann of Pittsburgh, the department store millionaire, and Herbert F. Johnson of Racine, Wisconsin, the wax magnate—they fulfilled different dreams and functions. Fallingwater was a true second home, a camplike dwelling in a nature preserve, whose raison d'être was to provide rest and the opportunity to commune with the land. (It was thus a fitting prototype for the later vacation house of mid-century.) The Kaufmanns had already built Latourelle (1924–25), a splendid neo-Norman suburban country house by Benno Janssen, in Fox Chapel, near Pittsburgh. Thus Wright was essentially able to give full rein to his artistic notions, creating what has been called the most famous twentieth-century house in the world, a building about which volumes of praise have been written.[31]

Wingspread, however, was another story—and a more important one in relation to the development of the country house. More than any other building of that decade, the Johnson house provided a machine-age analogy to the stately homes and country places built earlier in the century as symbols of self, records of achievement, and signs of culture. The key to this view of Wingspread lies in the persona of Herbert Fisk Johnson (1899–1978), whom Wright described as "a young prince of the Johnson line, who all his life long had had about everything he ever wanted."[32] The man who gave Wright the opportunity to build two of his masterworks, the Johnson Wax Company administration buildings (1936) and research tower (1944),[33] was one of the last of a breed of enlightened, progressive businessmen who ran family companies as models of American social ideals. A trained chemist who graduated from Cornell in 1922, he took over S. C. Johnson

and Son, Inc., upon his father's death in 1928, only a year before the great crash. During his father's time the company had grown from a small wood flooring business into a large manufacturer of floor wax and become the major employer in Racine. The family took pride in its civic beneficence, a tradition that "Hibbard the Johnson," as Wright called him in his *Autobiography,* perpetuated. The young executive bucked the lean years of the 1930s by introducing Glo-Coat, an extremely successful product, in 1932 and was apparently a quiet father figure to his employees, managing to avoid layoffs even during the hardest periods. His boldest gesture, and one that contributed much to the success and growth of the company, came in hiring Wright (then aged sixty-nine and at the low ebb of his career) to design the company's futuristic headquarters, which he chose to locate in a decaying area of the city as a beacon to future progress. Another popular public relations gesture was his sponsorship of the "Fibber Magee and Molly" radio program. His quiet, steadfast optimism and progressivist belief in private enterprise as a benefactor of the public good made him a rare and anachronistic figure in American business after his retirement in the 1950s.[34] It is easy to see why he and Wright, both late Victorians in their values, had such a fruitful collaboration.

Wingspread was a frank outgrowth of the headquarters buildings, with its Cherokee brick construction ("the best brickwork I have seen in my life," according to Wright), its sweeping lines, and the great bull-nosed hearth at its center. Johnson had divorced his first wife in 1934 (with whom he had a son and a daughter) and in 1936 married Jane Roach, who had two sons of her own. He asked Wright to plan a house for this newly formed family, a request that must have pleased the architect, who was used to unorthodox relationships. He recalled the first visit to the site: "One day [Johnson] had taken me out to see the tract of prairie (a small lake running its length) that he owned by the big lake (Michigan), and had for years been keeping as a kind of wild-fowl preserve. Some days after we had walked and talked about a house on that site and I had explained a zoned house to him, Hib brought me a little sketch plan he had himself penciled of the general outlines of a house zoned pretty much as his stands out there now on the prairie."[35] Unfortunately and tragically, his second wife died in 1938, before the house was completed. Wright responded poetically even to this event, believing that it was his duty to convince his patron and friend to proceed with the building of Wingspread in her spirit.

The program was maintained for a wealthy man's house (of fourteen thousand square feet), with four separate wings, or zones, each containing a separate domain for family members and sliding into the central communal space. This room, derivative of Wright's hearth-centered living rooms in his prairie house, contained a dining area, living area, library, and music area within one octagonal tentlike space, rising into a lookout perch in the hearth and engaged with a low balcony. It was thus both a modern, dynamically spatial conception and a traditional, centered form—an octagon suspended above a pinwheel of circulation. The effect was powerful, with the low, narrow hallways of each wing shooting into the expansive central volume. Wright also wanted it

303 **Wingspread.** Swimming pool. (Richard Cheek.)

draped with vines and plants, to bring the outdoors inside. The hybrid of modernist and traditional imagery was made more explicit by Wright's various names for his concept, known in the plan as the great hall or living room and by its owner as the wigwam—American and Old World terms colliding.

Wingspread had its roots in two worlds. Its zoned program pointed to strategies used in later suburban houses;[36] it had a master suite and a large playroom, a carport and a big blue outdoor swimming pool that said "modern house" in no uncertain terms; its multilevel living space had diverse uses; and there were clever built-in gadgets and conveniences everywhere, including a radiant-heated concrete floor. Johnson even insisted on such gimmicks as a diagonally oriented dining table that slid in and out of the kitchen with food, china, and settings in place. Yet it was also a rich man's country house, with expansive gardens and a large estate, a servants' wing, a formal circular driveway, and enough pomp to suggest social prominence. Wright clearly saw it that way: "What else than a house such as that one would be, could he buy with money or time that would yield him such large returns? This house I would build for him should be, definitely, 'capital' not only safe during this lifetime, but go on as true capital into the lives of his children—a joy meantime and a distinction. A proof of quality. What more capital use to make of 'capital'?"[37] This quintessential American architect understood the relationship between a rich man, his house, and his money.

Samuel Johnson, Hibbard's son, remembered the house as a great success with the children and father, though not with Irene Purcell, the third wife, who disagreed with Wright over redecorating. The wigwam fulfilled its purpose as a family meeting ground (not to mention a perfect arena for young boys playing war games), and the pool was a great novelty. The only functional flaws that made the building less than perfect were the persistently leaking skylights in the octagon, the problems resulting from putting five fireplaces in one large hearth, and a temperamental heating system.[38]

The house was interlocked with its knoll-like setting, next to a pond, in a manner typical of Wright. Appearing from some angles to hug the ground or burrow into it, Wingspread also had a breadth and expansiveness that reached out to the landscape unlike any other Wright building, seeming to take off like a bird or to float like a ship (a metaphor used by Henry-Russell Hitchcock). Wright's sweeping, horizontal perspective drawings made this clear. Only the anchoring tower at the center held it to the earth. Even the materials suggested this dichotomy of the modern

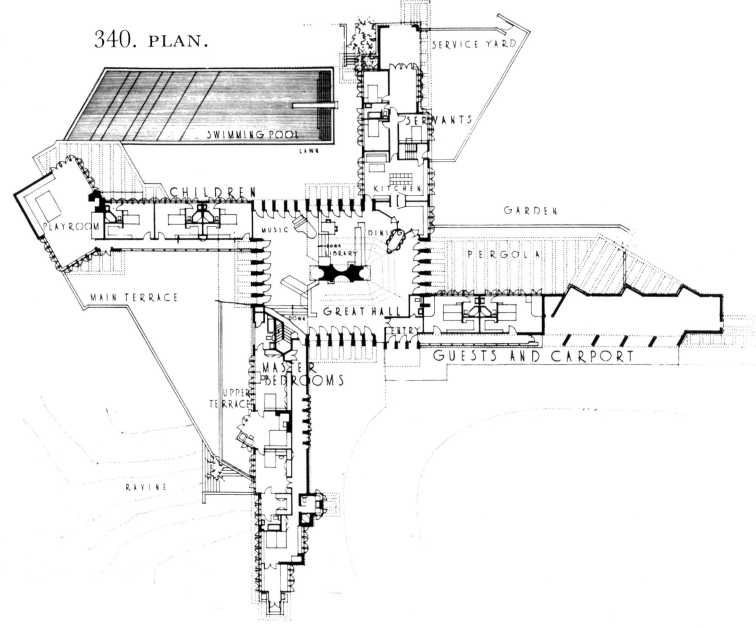

340. PLAN.

304 Frank Lloyd Wright. **Wingspread** (1937), Herbert F. Johnson house, Wind
Point, near Racine, Wisconsin. Plan. (Richard Cheek, from Hitchcock, *In the
Nature of Materials.*)

world of flight and the ancient one of fire, tents, and log houses;
cypress wood, metals, pink kasota stone, and Cherokee brick (laid
in a special joint pattern to emphasize the horizontal) gave it a
palette at once related to the land and alien to it. With these readings, among others, Wingspread proclaimed itself a potent solution to the new-age country house in the American landscape,
while also ending the tradition of the late-Victorian prairie house,
as Wright himself maintained.[39]

Was the ideal of the modernist country house a contradiction in
terms? Clearly for such architects as Wright and Howe it represented a critical problem to be solved, since Americans were reluctant to abandon their long-standing dream of a life on the land,
even in the face of a revolution in transportation, land use, and
urbanization. For European modernists, it may at first have

seemed trivial in relation to larger social and political issues, and
their visionary proposals suggested this. As such talented designers as Neutra began to understand American preferences and
the particular qualities of the locales in which they worked after
World War II, their designs achieved a more socially grounded
legitimacy, if also losing some of their aesthetic edge.[40] The modernist villa, though a vivid and cogent model for a few architects
and patrons during the 1930s, failed to capture the imagination of
the conservative society that had cultivated the country life ideal
for almost half a century, only to find it destroyed by a devastated
economy.

The many contradictions inherent in the concept of a country
house in a modern world were brought home by experiments in
placing a machine for living in an arcadian landscape. The con-
frontation between technical advances and sentimental symbols
produced glaring problems. Although Americans loved gadgets
and advances in home technology and were clever in the applica-

tion of new building methods and materials, they resisted stripping away the symbols of home, contrary to the hopes of critics. Modernist villas were often comfortable and (technical problems aside) quite functional but did not *look* that way to conservative clients. Perhaps more important was the initial attitude of the modernist toward the site and landscape. The Lovell house—constructed on a steep hillside and ingeniously engineered to terrace the site on extensive foundations—was essentially a confron-

tation with the topos, raising itself above the earth. Wright's answer to the landscape problem at Wingspread was more persuasive; but to clients used to a gentle, rustic house in a garden, it was equally harsh. Yet these frank and intellectually critical buildings were finally to become implicit indictments of an unsustainable dream. A cataclysmic war, followed by profound demographic and economic changes in the United States, finally put an end to the short-lived tradition of the modern country house.

305 **Wingspread.** Bedroom wing. (Samuel Gottscho, Library of Congress.)

306 **Wingspread.** Hearth. (Samuel Gottscho, Library of Congress.)

307 Charles Platt. **The Manor House,** J. T. Pratt estate, now Harrison Conference Center, Glen Cove, New York. (Richard Cheek.)

Domestic Eclecticism
A Summary

8

For a hundred years a large body of people have been trying to escape the age in which they live.
The leaders in this flight are precisely those who have extracted profit from steel mills and grain elevators and railroads
and urban land: they build Florentine palaces; they enshrine themselves in Tudor country houses; in the earlier,
cruder days they even went as far afield as P. T. Barnum, and strutted behind "Moorish" and "Iranian" facades.
The common mark of this architecture is that treasure lies in one age, the heart in another.
Up to the capacity of our tastes and incomes, the rest of us have followed in the footsteps of our financial overlords;
for whenever we can break loose from our anonymous cubicles, our standardized offices, our undifferentiated streets,
we abandon ourselves to Pure Romance.

—LEWIS MUMFORD

✂ PARADOXES OF THE MODERN COUNTRY HOUSE

If the preceding chapters have demonstrated the pervasiveness and cultural authority of eclecticism during the early twentieth century, among wealthy patrons as well as architects, this examination of the country estate has also underlined an inherent paradox. American domestic architecture during this important modern period tends to resist classification, perhaps manifesting the sweeping upheavals of the early twentieth century. Not only did the ideals of house owners fluctuate rapidly, but architects such as Wright continuously put forth new models that challenged the fragile existing norms. Moreover, the popular journals and architectural media helped to establish domestic ideals while simultaneously undermining them by documenting abrupt shifts in taste. Croly and his fellow critics, whose voices seemed clear at the turn of the century, were sounding hollow notes in the 1920s, as progressive ideals eroded. Economic and social changes were extremely precipitous during these years as well—capitalist entrepreneurs lost fortunes in the boom or bust cycles of war, depression, and further war. Families striving to institutionalize their wealth—the prerequisite of social position and the foundation of the country seat of old—often found it dissipating in the second generation. With such shifts in society and taste, how could any coherent tradition develop?

Eclecticism in one of its meanings points to variety, diversity, and cultural pluralism—familiar conditions in America's democratic melting pot. Yet the mere existence of such a patchwork does not explain the paradoxes at every level. Ostensibly, the architectural historian finds an enormous range of stylistic experimentation, a taxonomy that almost defies coherence. On closer examination, however, the typological characteristics of the house changed more gradually, with little variation in the plan and in social norms for room use. Although the theories that drove the architectural culture during the early twentieth century derive closely from those of the mid-nineteenth century, fin de siècle architects and critics resisted this eclectic and revivalist strain in American architecture, intent upon establishing an innovative attitude toward sources and history. They kept one foot in the traditional past and one in the technological future. By insisting upon their modernity yet arguing for a new architecture related to the classical tradition of the Renaissance, eclectic architects refused to acknowledge a polarity that has obsessed twentieth-century architectural critics—the disjunction between the idealized past and scientific progress. Were they treading an oxymoronic path?

This two-sidedness extends to the social realm as well. Americans of means seemed to want the security of deep-seated tradition as well as the freedom to explore new domestic ideals. These influences coexist rather than forming neat dichotomies; regionalist and vernacular culture, aristocratic behavior, the simple life of the agrarian past, a machine-age urbanism, sports and leisure activities as a basis for living, cultivation of the land, and the garden as the highest expression of gentility all blend together, further confusing the issue. Wealthy Americans, facing an unlimited array of domestic models, often chose several rather than one, an eclecticism in its own right. This is one major factor separating the last English country houses, which are parallel in some characteristics, from American ones. Although English architects and patrons had their own range of models, all were strictly indigenous and sanctioned by a centuries-old tradition.[1] English houses reflected a continuity of development, American ones an erratic attempt to satisfy current tastes. Americans seemed to reinvent constantly their domestic models and styles of life. The "unalterable custom" that critics like Croly hoped would gel among the social and intellectual leaders of the country never came about.

To bring this paradoxical subject into focus, let us reiterate two premises. First, there is an identifiable culture governing domestic taste during this period, defined by the generation of capitalist entrepreneurs—Croly's captains of industry—who dominated American society during the progressive and postprogressive decades. This class formed a closed culture that supported an equally closed elite of academically trained architects. These two groups, united from generation to generation through shared beliefs about living well and the importance of cultural traditions, formed the foundation that sustained domestic eclecticism. As long as the two were allied and their ideals coincided, the tradition of the eclectic country estate flourished, in spite of shifting economic and social conditions. Once the educational system for architects changed after World War II and the plutocracy was recast by a new economic order, neither group held the same power over domestic taste. Although this change does not fully explain the decline of the eclectic country house, which was driven more by economics than by taste, it does mark the boundaries of a distinct value system. This system of ideals, more than anything else, provides the historical armature for a study of the modern country estate.

Second, I have observed that these ideals fall into three major categories, based on the emulation of historical cultures or ruling classes (I have described these modes of living under the headings of the stately home, the country place, and the regional country house). The tendency for American patrons to look backward is a perplexing but understandable one. As Croly pointed out, with the erosion of class boundaries and the supplanting of the genteel agrarian society of the pre–Civil War generations, Americans cast about for models suitable to upper-class life. Culturally, the plutocracy lacked confidence in its tastes and manners, vainly attempting to copy those of European societies. Looking to the past was safe; pushing into the future was not. Americans were confident of their superiority in the realms of manufacturing and commerce, but culture had to be borrowed, adapted. The first models emulated were European, perhaps partially as a challenge, partially because Europe was a yardstick.[2] The stately home was a public monument that established the cultural authority associated with wealth. It was "an outward show of the fortunate life," according to Henry James. After a tour of the "ample villas, in their full dress," built by the new rich at the turn of the century, he was impressed only by their insubstantiality. They were "'installments,' they practically admitted, with no shade of embarrassment; 'expensive as we are, we have nothing to do with continuity, responsibility, transmission, and don't in the least care what becomes of us after we have served our present purpose.'"[3] When one visits these houses today, they appear to bear out James' analysis. Their hollowness echoes a fundamental lack of interest in the affairs of everyday life. (Considering how little they were lived in, this is hardly surprising.)

Criticism of the aristocratic treasure house, with its overt theatricality, helped to initiate the pastoral or genteel model, which architects such as Platt developed. Without fully renouncing associations with European high culture or classical sources, the promoters of the country place advanced a more domestic, private, and secure paradigm. The houses of Platt, Lindeberg, and Pope were gracious, workable environments but on a grander scale than most homes we know today.

The true authority of the country place, however, was invested in the land. Owning treasured areas of the American landscape evinced social and economic dominion more powerfully than did the building of palaces. As James aptly pointed out, privacy was "the highest luxury of all, the supremely expensive thing."[4] By appropriating vast tracts of land as private domains, the wealthy proclaimed their privilege. When giving it back to the public, as did the colonizers of Mount Desert Island and the heirs of George Vanderbilt, they also proclaimed their gentility, beneficence, and sense of noblesse oblige. During this period of urban growth the domestication of the landscape by estate building and suburban development was, in fact, one of the most significant transformations of the United States. Like the railroads, which have now disappeared from the public landscape, the country estate was a ubiquitous element in the consciousness of all Americans, celebrated on postcards and in popular photo books. City residents were well aware of where the rich lived, how much land they controlled, and where the boundaries of public access were set. And in spite of their coyness about publicity, rich men fully realized that their estates symbolized power in the minds of the proletariat.

Among wealthy women, the real tastemakers, gardening supplanted elaborate costumes and decoration as a mark of feminine gentility and culture. Men were also involved in the gardening movement, but on a lesser scale. For many patrons, creating within nature was a more personal profession of good taste than collecting objets d'art. (Mrs. Frances Hutchinson, for example, demonstrated her interest in high culture through her husband's leadership of the Art Institute of Chicago.) The country life movement of 1900 defined the pursuits of the new quasipastoral leisure life: sporting, gardening, and the artful transformation of domestic spaces with architectural greenery. Like many aspects of American culture, this movement was taken up by not only the rich but also the middle class, as attested to by the large circulation of magazines devoted to country living during this period. The impact of this movement on American life, manners, and the environment has not yet been fully explored or appreciated. Its influence on the country estate was profound, changing the way in which patrons and architects treated the house on its site. Never before in the history of American domestic architecture—not even in the heyday of the Downing villa and the picturesque movement—had the house so directly engaged its setting. As in the Italian villa, the architectural space of the dwelling was expanded to include the landscape, not merely to relate to it by contrast or to dominate it by grand gestures. A true American house and garden type was created by a group of talented architects and landscape architects who have largely been forgotten today.

Relating the house to its setting, a concept refined by the creative eclectic school, was also a tenet of the indigenous model in domestic culture. Nineteenth-century architects, fascinated by exotic architectural styles, sought to analyze and grasp their meanings for use in modern buildings. The same fascination seemed to capture architects who settled in new regions such as California and the Southwest. The fervor and seriousness with which this generation studied American architecture is evident in the extraordinary literature and documentary drawings produced from 1900 to 1940. Moreover, the regionalist ethos also captivated patrons. Embracing the native way of life was a profession of cultural inclusiveness. Georgia O'Keeffe and D. H. Lawrence, like Edith Wharton and Herbert Croly before them, sought an artistic country life. The Santa Fe colony was more remote, more avant-garde, more exiled than the Cornish settlement, but its impetus was the same. Communion with the wilderness or with the landscapes of a vanishing America was a statement of cultural authority in its own right. Rediscovery of America's natural beauty was not wholly new—the Hudson River School and the Yosemite Valley pioneer conservationists had led the way—nor was a pride in the achievements of early American builders, artists, artisans, and architects. The patriotic embrace of the colonial past was overwhelming in many movements of the 1920s, from historic preservation to antique collecting. During this decade indigenous traditions achieved real cultural sanction for the first time among the tastemakers. These traditions, too, were varied, eclectic, and hardly settled into a monolithic state.

Significantly, the regional models chosen for late country houses, such as the southwestern adobe, the plantation house, and the California ranch, lived on to become popular as suburban house types. From the 1940s through the 1960s William Wilson Wurster, Hugh May, and John Byers (among others) developed the ranch house into a potent model for informal living, or modern living as the magazines called it. By using the functionalist rationale—that ranches grew directly out of the solution of building problems related to climate, landscape, and ways of life—these architects were able to remove the negative associations that had destroyed other eclectic models when modernism surfaced as a theoretical imperative.[5]

When a handful of free-thinking architects suggested that the modernist language imported from Europe could be employed for the country house, a few forward-looking clients took up the challenge. Again the stability of an emerging tradition had been attacked almost as soon as it had achieved some measure of matur-

ity. On the whole the houses the avant-garde architects produced were either too conservative in their programs to be persuasive in the highly charged atmosphere of the 1930s, or too unrelated to the needs of the average wealthy American family to be widely accepted as a model by either patrons or other architects. Experiments in an open, technologically futuristic house that confronted nature in the manner of the Corbusian villa—by lifting itself away from the earth—were provocative, fresh, and problematic for America. Neutra, Schindler, and Howe (among others) struggled to find a formula for a house in the landscape that would address Americans' sentimental associations with the earth and their attachment to the individual home. Yet they did not come to a solution until after World War II. In this respect one might say that modernism never really challenged the conservative models for the country estate; one witnesses in the current revival of the country house a continuing interest in pitched roofs and old-fashioned details, not in streamlined, avant-garde design.

Thus, the three ideals that defined the culture of the modern country estate in the twentieth century were latent yet also specifically related to the needs of a modern capitalist class struggling to find an identity in a democracy. The styles that supported these ideals—diverse, sentimental associations with historical and regional architecture—were not simply the result of architects perusing sourcebooks in their libraries. They were directly attached to the sustenance of stately, aristocratic living, pastoral and genteel modes, or indigenous associations with American cultures. They made it possible to simultaneously express individual taste and achievement while also showing class solidarity. The popularity of certain styles during specific decades bears this out—the taste for Modern French during the 1890s, Tudor during the 1900s, generic Colonial peaking during the years after World War I and branching into numerous regional idioms during the 1920s and 1930s, and French Provincial, Cotswold, and Modern English during the 1920s. A general trend toward less complicated living patterns was reflected in the movement toward simpler and more abstract styles. This was also evident in the swing from public and palatial models in the early period to private, inward-looking, and reticent ones later on. The idioms and types that most directly addressed the ideals of a patron—of new wealth or old—were the ones chosen. Architects provided the models, the research, the expertise, the artistry, but patrons made the choices. This was fundamentally a patron's architecture.

This raises the large question of how to measure the achievements of the eclectic generation of domestic architects. Are we correct in considering these designers a footnote in the history of twentieth-century American architecture? Did their close association with, even dominance by, their clients rob their work of the integrity, individuality, and formal invention necessary to create genuine works of art? If I have fulfilled my intention, this book has demonstrated the diversity, the largeness of vision, and the scope of the achievements of these architects. Very little has been said of design innovation—with good reason. These eclectic architects did not advance the formal language of architecture as did Frank Lloyd Wright or Rudolph Schindler. That was not their purpose; eclectic theory placed little emphasis on pure formal invention. The emphasis was on the advancement of traditions, on subtle and personal transformations of sources and models. To the untutored eye, these transformations are all but invisible. A house by Harrie Lindeberg, considered surprising and fresh by the critics of his time, may look very much the same as one by an architect of lesser gifts because it has obeyed the strict conventions of an idiom. Once these conventions are appreciated, the "eyes which do not see," as Le Corbusier put it, may assess the extraordinary design qualities in these houses—qualities of texture, scale, massing, proportion, light and shade, spatial modeling—the very things that are present in all great architecture.

How, it may be asked, is the untutored person to achieve this understanding? Isn't this an architecture of scholarly elitism, of books and historical anachronism? Emphatically no. In its time, eclectic design was not a matter of elite knowledge but of popular critical understanding. History was alive in books and magazines, in films and popular culture. Patrons clearly knew how to judge a good house, just as did critics in the popular and professional media. The public appreciated the sentimental and historical associations that the styles affirmed—and understood their meanings. A number of domestic styles, such as Tudor and Georgian, flourished when applied to low- and middle-class housing, apartments, retail shopping villages, and public buildings. Indeed, the paradox of eclecticism extends to society itself, for there was a clear sharing of values and domestic tastes between middle- and upper-class Americans during this time. The system of values, so apparently closed and elite, was somehow assimilated into popular culture through the media. In this way, the elitism that might have attended the eclectic movement never came about. Moreover, many of the most successful country house architects were also involved in public housing, prison reform, urban planning, and conservation—hardly elitist pursuits.

The large school of creative domestic architects that this book has focused on clearly produced an extraordinary body of architectural work that profoundly influenced Americans' views of the ideal house and garden. The models they adapted (if not invented) out of a scholarly and creative knowledge of the past are still being used by home builders and architects today. The American family home was transformed by their ideas. Their gracious, efficient plans are as apt and functional today as half a century ago. Eclectic architects solved the problems of the servantless, mechanically controlled house long before the advent of smart house systems. They experimented with innovative and economical construction materials and methods—some of which were discarded, others generally accepted. They helped give us our ideal picture of the living room, porch, dining room, bedroom, and bathroom—all comfortable, graceful, and practical. With their talented colleagues in landscape design they formulated the model for a new American house and garden environment out of a synthesis of historical and indigenous sources.

These architects were as diverse in background and learning as the sources they employed, a condition that enriched the practice of architecture during the eclectic era. Because a designer had to be at various times a politician, gentleman, scholar, scene designer, craftsman, draughtsman, linguist, engineer, connois-

seur, and tactician, it is appropriate to find that America's domestic architects were all of these, and more. Charles Platt and George Washington Smith painted landscapes, John Byers taught languages, John Gaw Meem was a banker, Marian Coffin was a horticulturist, and Theodate Pope founded idealistic schools for boys and girls. Patrician and august gentlemen such as Thomas Hastings, Charles McKim, and Frank Miles Day staunchly played their roles as leaders, while bohemian and esthete colleagues such as Wilson Eyre, Wallace Neff, and Stanford White strutted society's stage like Tartuffes. Others, such as Julia Morgan, Howard Shaw, Mott Schmidt, and Frank Forster, worked quietly to create a large oeuvre almost unnoticed by anyone save their appreciative clients.

These excellent architects remained, as a rule, in the background, blending with the society they served. Though some taught architecture, few sought to proselytize or publicize the uniqueness of their ideas. The prototype of the trail-blazing individualist, the avant-garde propagandist, the master of public relations, which the architect of today continues to emulate, was far removed from the professional roles of these men and women. They worked within the confines of the social hierarchy and the wishes of their patrons, expecting that the art they produced would be recognized by sympathetic colleagues and critics. During the time this culture of eclecticism was nurtured, through the mid-1930s, the work reflected confidence and vigor. When the architectural press began to proclaim an entirely new ethos, however, many eclectic masters faded or had frustrated later careers. For Mott Schmidt, Frank Forster, and Wallace Neff, who continued to have clients, the conviction seemed to slip away in later work, as if a supporting armature had crumbled.

Full judgment of the work of this school of architects must await a greater critical assessment and chronological distance. This book is merely a starting point for the study of this important chapter in the history of twentieth-century domestic architecture. One can state with certainty that these architects created compelling domestic environments, beautiful compositions, and graceful houses that supported a society's needs. The ideals of the plutocracy, as romantic and distant as they seemed, were the foundation of a cultural authority for the individuals who had built the nation's economy. When considered as answers to the expression of these ideals, the country houses of the eclectic era achieve the same power and persuasiveness as those of the Victorian era in Britain, also long considered hackneyed and overwrought. The major architectural talents of the time, such as Platt, Mellor and Meigs, Lindeberg, Pope, and Smith, designed masterworks of the traditional country house that should be considered alongside the houses of Frank Lloyd Wright, Irving Gill, and Richard Neutra. Yet because they did not explore radical formal solutions to conservative domestic programs, because the plastic manipulation of space, mass, and structure was kept subservient to issues of comfort, sentiment, and historical association, these houses have regularly been excised from the history books. It is time that they again be regarded, as they were by critics in their day, as key examples of a building type that contributed uniquely to modern American architecture.

Epilogue

During the great fire of 1947 in Bar Harbor, a third of the 222 cottages on the island burned. That famous catastrophe is symbolic of the precipitous decline of the country house in America following World War II, when hundreds of great country places fell to the pressures of land subdivision, suburban growth, and disaster invited by neglect. Family fortunes not decimated by the depression frequently succumbed to the burden of death taxes. To raise capital, the large houses and valuable property—including beloved family seats—often had to be sold, sometimes for a fraction of their real or sentimental value. Once on the open market, unprotected from callous developers and insensitive institutions and generally too young to qualify for landmark status, many of America's greatest country houses fell, especially between the 1940s and the 1960s. Subdivision of suburban and resort estates obliterated the country places that had been a constituent element in the early twentieth-century landscape.

The examples are legion. Beatrix Farrand destroyed her own beloved Reef Point at Bar Harbor in the 1950s after failing to find an institution willing to take on the preservation of its great gardens. Following the death of Frances Hutchinson in 1932, Wychwood's great landscape and wildlife preserve by Olmsted and Olmsted was protectively deeded to the University of Chicago and used as a conference center. Unfortunately, the university sold the property into private hands in 1957, at the end of the twenty-five-year period stipulated in the Hutchinson will. Thereafter the Tudor house received a defacing alteration, and the land was allowed to deteriorate. The Mackay estate and mansion were early casualties of Long Island development in the 1940s; too large for anything but institutional use, the house was torn down after a short existence. Arthur Newbold's farm was even shorter-lived. This masterpiece by Mellor and Meigs, finished in 1931 and put on the market in the late 1940s, was suspiciously burned during its period of tender and sold for demolition. Only the swimming pool remains. John Russell Pope's vast Caumsett was given by Marshall Field's widow to the state of New York for use as a park during the 1950s. Robert Moses planned to construct a bridge across the Long Island Sound to Connecticut and to build a "North Shore Jones Beach" on the property, destroying all of the structures. Public outcry prevented this megalomania, but the buildings fared little better under "protection" as a state park. An unscrupulous warden allowed members of the staff to burn down a number of the wooden buildings, including a charming bath house on the Sound. Mrs. Field had already defaced the house by removing one wing. The state let the remaining house and the brick stable deteriorate. The buildings have only recently found reuse by Long Island educational institutions.

Whereas estates in suburban areas were prey to such bureaucratic pressures, those in far-off resort areas suffered from neglect and disuse. The Jekyll Island resort colony was literally abandoned after the start of World War II because of fear of attack and has only recently awakened as a park, under the aegis of the state of Georgia. Several of the houses at Dark Harbor in Maine's island resort haven were left to deteriorate until the new country real estate boom attracted owners interested in restoring them as hotels. One of the most heavily ravaged resort colonies was Lenox, which lost Shadowbrook to fire, Elm Court and Bellefontaine to ruin, and many other great cottages through disuse. Large houses, even in beautiful resort areas, were too expensive to maintain and became white elephants that small communities were hard-pressed to reuse and save. Many were first bought by institutions such as churches and schools, but these small, nonprofit organizations seldom had the funds for proper maintenance and often were eventually forced to sell. Edith Wharton's The Mount, for many years the dormitory of a girls' academy, suffered severe institutional wear and tear, which has hampered current attempts at restoration. A summer theater troupe, Shakespeare and Company, saved the building in the 1970s by using the grounds for its performances. The Edith Wharton Foundation, the present owner, which leases the grounds to the theater, is endeavoring to create a study center and museum in memory of the great novelist and to bring the estate back to its old glory. It faces a difficult future, operating only with private funds and small grants.

There have been even greater tragedies. Horace Trumbauer's Whitemarsh Hall, the E. T. Stotesbury estate, was lost solely because of insidious and planned neglect. For many years it was owned by a local company, which sold off pieces of the expansive estate to Chestnut Hill developers, creating a patchwork of tawdry subdivisions around a crumbling palace. After some years as an office building and a laboratory, with the owner unable or unwilling to find another use for the house, it languished. Vandalism went unchecked. The gardens became an overgrown forest; the sculptures were looted. Eventually the Gatsbyesque dream of Stotesbury dissolved in a wild tangle of flora, a ruined vision surrounded by the middle-class suburban boxes, like parasites around a carcass. Hardly a more biting symbol exists of one American dream supplanting another—Marble House engulfed by Levittown—with poignant and justified irony.

The rapid eclipse of the modern country house in America suggests that as a social and economic model it had little staying power. For a society constantly in flux, the waning of a powerful ideal in the face of war, depression, and economic leveling of classes is hardly surprising. What is surprising is the way in which Americans have carried on an ambivalent love-hate relationship with these large houses, canonizing them while their owners lived but allowing them to be destroyed afterward with callous forgetfulness. It may be that this is just another cruel by-product of American capitalism and its peculiar democratic society. However, there is more at stake in the destruction of this piece of the domestic fabric than a Veblenian interpretation will sustain. Already lacking a sense of the value of history and the positive lessons of even a short-lived domestic tradition, we lose something

further with the destruction of country houses—not only a trace of the individual soul of ownership, a symbol of self, but also a sense of how to live gracefully with the land. Holding on to the aesthetic and practical lessons provided by great houses is far more important than doting on the fads, foibles, and exploits of their owners, interesting as they may be. Although the institutional preservation of many country houses as house museums will never achieve the social sanction in America that it has in Britain, there is a clear need for conservation of historic landscapes, gardens, houses, and estate structures as intact ensembles. These artifacts not only are important as remembrances of things past but provide potent models for the future American house, lessons to live by.

Preservation of the early twentieth-century country house in its environment presents many daunting challenges and problems, most of which are economic. Private owners must often succumb to land development pressures, while public owners suffer under the burden of taxes and maintenance costs and face increasing competition for philanthropic funds. In a nation where government intervention is a philosophically suspect last resort, preservation must rely on private initiative and work in a semiregulated environment. The relatively weak and financially strapped National Trust for Historic Preservation, a semipublic organization, has been unable to actively seek out and accept estate properties, especially from this century. Its only modern historic houses are the small Usonian Pope-Leighey house, in Virginia, and Filoli, in Woodside, California (neither of which is a major example of its type nor a masterwork of its architect). Larger private preservation organizations, such as the Society for the Preservation of New England Antiquities in Boston, the Preservation Society of Newport, and the Massachusetts-based Trustees of Reservations, control more key properties than the Trust, including Naumkeag, Castle Hill, The Breakers, Marble House, and even Walter Gropius' house in Lincoln, Massachusetts. They also run, maintain, and interpret them rather well. But these are exceptional cases in the beleaguered arena of American preservation. Smaller foundations, such as the Western Pennsylvania Conservancy, which runs Fallingwater, or Historic Hudson Valley (previously Sleepy Hollow Restorations), have made positive contributions to the conservation of estate lands and houses, but they are too rare. Even less common are the self-sustaining house museums of which Biltmore and the Hill-Stead are primary examples. Moreover, since these estates are often far from cities with established landmark laws, public agencies, and preservation groups, they seldom benefit from legal and economic umbrellas. State-level intervention is the most practical geographical alternative, but state governments, with their tiny preservation offices and financially pressed parks departments, are nearly as impotent as small private foundations when it comes to restoring and maintaining large properties. A good example of their plight is New York's struggle to restore the Ogden Mills mansion by McKim, Mead and White, on the Hudson, which will require millions of dollars and years of work. It is clear that as more of these culturally significant country estates reach a stage where preservation is needed, new public and private organs and strategies will be required to ensure the conservation of a vital part of our heritage.

308 Horace Trumbauer. **Whitemarsh Hall,** E. T. Stotesbury estate, Chestnut Hill, Pennsylvania. (Mattie Edwards Hewitt, collection of Alfred Branam, Jr.)

Country house museums will remain a limited alternative in a society dedicated to progress and pragmatism. Reuse of country houses and their gardens presents a bigger and more pressing dilemma. Because a house so precisely mirrors its family's peculiarities, it is one of the most difficult building types to refit for other uses. As preservation wisdom dictates, the greater the similarity between new and old uses, the more successful the resulting adaptation. Large country houses have typically been converted into art museums, private hospitals, rest homes, religious retreats, convents, monasteries, conference centers, hotels, and, perhaps most ubiquitously, condominiums.

Ferncliffe, the Vincent Astor estate in Rhinebeck, New York, is now a rest home. Blairsden is a convent nestled in the hills near Bernardsville, New Jersey. Trumbauer's Shadow Lawn, the Hubert Parsons house, a frequent backdrop for television commercials, has for many years been a part of Monmouth College, near Long Branch, New Jersey. Bruce Price's The Turrets at Bar Harbor has also recently been incorporated as part of a college. Lindeberg's Foxhollow Farm is a private school. Several of the large cottages in Lenox have now been refitted as resort hotels, with varying success. Such institutional reuse offers a reasonable alternative to defacement or destruction but often severely compromises the scale and character of the original buildings and landscape.

Many large houses have been converted to business or educational conference centers. Their bucolic settings and combination of public and private accommodations are well suited to these programs and attractive to participants. The Harriman family gave its family seat, Arden House, to Columbia University in the 1940s; it has since served as a site for many meetings on international affairs, business, and government. Though not one of Carrère and Hastings' more successful designs, the house has worked well in its new use. Unfortunately, a series of renovations and poorly designed additions has detracted from the presence of the building on its spectacular hilltop site. Charles Platt's sprawling Manor House for J. T. Pratt, at Glen Cove, Long Island, is now a large private conference center. The site is still pretty, but Ellen Shipman's marvelous gardens are sorely missed. Frank Lloyd Wright's Wingspread has been preserved by the Johnson Foundation as a philanthropic conference facility, without guest accommodations, and serves as a model for other centers of its type. Beautifully maintained and sensitively refitted, it preserves the aura of a country home while also working well as a setting for small meetings.

The current real estate boom in condominium construction and conversion has had a large impact on country houses in areas with high land values. Developers have cashed in on the now-modified investment tax credits for conversions of historic structures, while reaping large profits on new housing units constructed on estate properties. Breaking up a large house into apartments requiring separate entrances, fire protection, complex services, and private yards is a difficult problem for architects. Few have handled it well. Moreover, placing of new units on garden sites may destroy views, focal planting, trees, and other key estate features.

Long Island awaits the completion of one of the most ambitious condominium conversion projects of recent vintage—the purported restoration of Oheka, Otto Kahn's massive 126-room mansion in Huntington. A proposed $12 million conversion by developer Gary Melius, which *Historic Preservation* magazine called "the luxurious alternative to the wrecker's ball," was to offer thirty-seven units costing between $500,000 and $750,000 each. The developer began the massive effort only to find his funds inadequate and placed the estate back on the market.[1] The fate of the building is again in doubt. Though the proliferation of condominium building in country, suburban, and resort areas is a trend that has had disturbing repercussions for the American landscape, it is a phenomenon that architects and preservationists concerned with the country house cannot ignore as a potential vehicle for reuse. Ironically, it appears that members of the upper middle class, who for several decades have survived in scaled-down versions of the great country houses, will find themselves permanent guests in the shells of some of these domestic fantasies, little Citizen Kanes in mini-Xanadus.

Preservation of the country house, like any form of conservation, is an affirmation of memory, a profession of pride in the past, and an acknowledgment of the continuity of traditions. If the American country house was indeed the last breath of an "architecture of escape," as Lewis Mumford argued in the heyday of Gatsby, then we must at least try to remember why our romanticism did not produce a domestic type that would last through all the shifts in American society, with its democratic indeterminacy. Mumford's indictment of the pseudoagrarian way of life, so boldly asserted in the Newbold farm, holds meaning for us today, as the monied tycoons of a new generation grab fitfully for domestic symbols of a bygone age. The 1920s and 1930s have become for many Americans as irresistibly romantic as the eras of Marie Antoinette and the Pilgrims were for the moguls of the eclectic era.[2] Do the young builders of today's country estates, which mimic those of the Jazz Age, understand why they long to escape from their own dull cubicles and faceless streets? Has America progressed from a time when an escape to a domestic arcadia was necessary? It hardly seems so. The extent to which the achievements as well as mistakes of an entire era have been covered over is borne out by watching history repeat itself. The irony is that our forebears did wish to make an integrated world in which romance coexisted with expedient and functional architecture. Preserving their houses, and some of the land on which they stood, reminds us of their achievements and teaches us how to do as well, if we are unable to do better.

Architects' Biographies

Note on sources: The following short biographies have been provided as a reference for the reader. The information is gathered either from monographs on the architects (which are listed in the bibliography) or, in most cases, from the following dictionaries of American architects: Placek, *The Macmillan Dictionary of Architects* (New York, 1982); Withey, *Biographical Dictionary of American Architects (Deceased)* (Los Angeles, 1956); Wodehouse, *American Architects* (vols. 3 and 4), Gale Research Series (Detroit, 1976–77); and Tatman and Moss, *Biographical Dictionary of Philadelphia Architects* (Boston, 1985).

Ackerman, Frederick Lee

New York   1878–1950

Born in Edmeston, New York, Ackerman studied architecture first at Cornell University, then for two years in Paris. From 1906 to 1921 he and Alexander Buell Trowbridge worked as the firm of Trowbridge and Ackerman. They were known in the New York area for their country houses, many of which won awards. Ackerman was also active in public housing and was a consultant for the New York Housing Authority, the Works Progress Administration Housing Division, and the Providence, Rhode Island, City Planning Commission. He was an architect of Sunnyside Gardens housing project in Queens, New York, and was a design consultant on the model town of Radburn, New Jersey. Ackerman also lectured on architecture at Cornell and Columbia universities. Trowbridge and Ackerman's best known country houses were probably the Truman Newberry house (c. 1914), at Grosse Pointe Farms, Michigan, and Killenworth (1913), the estate of George D. Pratt in Glen Cove, Long Island.

Adler, David

Chicago   1882–1949

Born in Milwaukee, Wisconsin, Adler studied architecture at Princeton University, graduat-

ing in 1904, and spent three semesters at the Polytechnikum in Munich, then traveled in Europe and studied for five years at the Ecole des Beaux-Arts in Paris. Working first for Howard Shaw, and later with Henry C. Dangler and then Robert Work, Adler established himself as one of the Midwest's premier architectural eclecticists during the late 1910s and the 1920s. His practice was devoted solely to residential work and country clubs, primarily in the wealthy enclaves of the North Shore of Chicago. He worked comfortably in many styles, and his finest houses are memorable for their graceful and meticulously detailed interiors. Adler was a fellow of the AIA and a member of the National Institute of Arts and Letters. His best works include the charming colonial William McCormick Blair house (1926) at Lake Bluff, Illinois; Castle Hill (1927), the mammoth Wrenaissance Crane estate at Ipswich, Massachusetts, for the faucet magnate; and the Pennsylvania-influenced Colonial Revival house (1931) for Kersey Coates Reed at Lake Forest, Illinois. His drawings can be found in the collection of the Burnham Library of Architecture at the Art Institute of Chicago.

Aldrich, Chester

New York City   1871–1940

Chester Holmes Aldrich, scion of the old Rhode Island family, was born in Providence and received his Bachelor of Philosophy degree from Columbia University in 1893. He studied at the Ecole (Atelier Daumer-Esquie) during the mid-1890s, and returned with his diploma in 1900. He began his association with William Delano during his tenure at Carrère and Hastings, establishing the firm of Delano and Aldrich in 1903. His family connection to the Rockefellers helped the new firm gain the prestigious commission for Kykuit (1907), the estate at Pocantico. Aldrich was active in Italy after World War I. He chose not to be an active partner during the last fifteen years of his life, preferring to live in Europe. He was appointed a trustee of the American Academy in Rome in

1926 and served as its director from 1935 until his death. He also taught architecture at Columbia University as an assistant to Thomas Hastings. Aldrich became a fellow of the National Academy of Design in 1939.

Andrews, Robert Day

Boston   1857–1928

Born in Hartford, Connecticut, Robert Andrews studied at MIT for two years and trained in the offices of several Boston architects. After a tour of Europe, he apprenticed with H. H. Richardson's office in Brookline, Massachusetts, and in 1885 established a partnership with Herbert Jacques (1857–1916) and Augustus Neal Rantoul (1864–1934). The firm of Andrews, Jacques and Rantoul, of which Andrews was senior partner, designed many urban and country residences as well as public structures, notably in Massachusetts and Colorado, including the east and west additions to the Massachusetts State House and buildings at Colorado College in Colorado Springs. Andrews was a cofounder of the Boston Architectural Club. He was noted for his work in Colonial Revival idioms and was active as a writer for Boston's *Architectural Review.*

Atterbury, Grosvenor

New York   1869–1956

Atterbury is known primarily for his work in low-cost housing, particularly for the innovative design of Forest Hills Gardens in Queens. Born in Detroit, he was educated at Yale and in Columbia's architectural school. Afterward he worked in the office of McKim, Mead and White. In 1895 he trained at the Atelier Blondel of the Ecole in Paris. He established himself as a noted restoration architect in America in the mid-1890s, working on the New York City Hall (1902–20) and designing the American Wing at the Metropolitan Museum (1924). His best known country house was designed in collaboration with England's George Crawley: Old Westbury house and gardens (1904), the estate of John S. Phipps. He also designed houses in eastern Long Island, including the Arthur B. Claflin house (1896–98) at Shinnecock Hills, and was the architect of the main wing of the Parrish Art Museum in Southampton.

Ayres, Atlee B.

San Antonio   1874–1969

Ayres, both alone and in partnership with his son Robert (*see* Ayres, Robert M.), was the preeminent builder of fine suburban and country houses in the San Antonio area from 1900 through the 1930s. Born in Ohio, Ayres moved to San Antonio with his parents at age fourteen. From 1890 to 1894 he studied architecture in New York City at the Metropolitan School of Art and the Art Students League. Ayres worked for various San Antonio architects during 1891–98, and worked for a short time with an American architect in Mexico City. In 1899 he established a partnership with C. A. Caughlin. He practiced alone from Coughlin's death in 1905 until he and Robert became partners in 1922. Atlee B. Ayres' fascination with Spanish and Mexican Colonial architecture is evident in his strong work in this idiom, often distinguishing his work from that of his son, who tended toward Beaux-Arts classicism. *Mexican Architecture,* by Atlee B. Ayres, published in 1926, was based on his research and photographs of the country's vernacular and colonial buildings.

Ayres, Robert M.

San Antonio   1898–1977

Born in San Antonio, Ayres was educated at Haverford School and received his architectural training at the University of Pennsylvania. He apprenticed with Murchison, Lamb and French in New York before returning to form a partnership with his father in 1922 (*see* Ayres, Atlee B.). Ayres began to handle major works of the firm in the late 1920s. For a description of some of the firm's country houses in Spanish styles, see chapter 6. Many of the Ayres drawings and records are in the drawings collection of the School of Architecture, University of Texas at Austin.

Barber, Donn

New Haven   1871–1925

Barber was one of Connecticut's premier beaux arts specialists, designing both large houses and public structures, notably the Connecticut State Supreme Court in Hartford (in association with E. T. Hapgood). Born in Washington, D.C., he received a Ph.D. from Yale in 1893, studied architecture at Columbia, and attended the Ecole des Beaux-Arts in Paris from 1894 to 1898. He worked for Carrère and Hastings, Cass Gilbert, and Lord and Hewlett, establishing his own office in New York City in 1900. He established the Atelier Donn Barber in New York and was instrumental in establishing the atelier system in America. From 1909 to 1910 he was president of the Society of Beaux Arts Architects and was also affiliated with the Architectural League of New York, the French Society of Beaux Arts Architects, and was an honorary member of the Royal Institute of British Architects. Barber also served as editor of the *Architectural Yearbook* in 1912, and of *New York Architect* magazine for four years.

Baum, Dwight James

New York City   1886–1939

Born in Little Falls, New York, Baum studied at Syracuse University (class of 1909) and later designed many of the structures on that campus. He began practice in 1915 in the pastoral Riverdale section of New York City and designed many of the notable homes there, as well as the charming Riverdale Country Club. He became a key advocate of Dutch Colonial, developing some of the best suburban house types in this popular idiom. Baum is also notable for his public structures, including the Young Men's Christian Association building on West 63rd Street in Manhattan and buildings for the 1939 New York World's Fair. He was one of the most successful businessmen among New York architects. He published articles on colonial architecture, and was a consultant architect for *Good Housekeeping* magazine. In 1930 Baum won the Bronze Medal of Award of the Better Homes of America Association for the best-designed small house built in America between 1926 and 1930, an award sponsored by former president Hoover and the AIA. In 1932 he received the Gold Medal of the Architectural League of New York. He was a member of the Architectural League of New York, the Beaux-Arts Institute of Design, and the American Federation of Arts. An uncharacteristic, eclectic house, which remains one of his best-known works, is Ca d'Zan (1926), the fanciful Venetian house of John Ringling of circus fame, in Sarasota, Florida.

Bosworth, William Welles

Boston   1869–1966

Bosworth's career is notable for his preservation activities abroad, as well as for his domestic work in architectural and landscape design. He seemed the quintessential dilettante architect of his time. Born in Marietta, Ohio, and educated at MIT (class of 1889), Bosworth worked for Frederick Law Olmsted and then for the noted educator William Robert Ware, with whom he toured Europe. He opened his own practice, then went back to Europe to study in London and at the Ecole des Beaux-Arts in Paris. On his return to America, he worked for Carrère and Hastings, then reopened his own office. In 1911 Bosworth contributed to the design of the granite house of J. D. Rockefeller, Sr., at Pocantico Hills, New York, the first structure of the Rockefeller family compound called Kykuit. He also designed the landscaping of the estate and later published a book, *The Gardens of Kykuit* (1919), with photographs and prose about the gardens. He was well known as a landscape designer, especially for the Kykuit gardens (1907) and the Samuel Untermeyer Estate gardens (1915), at Yonkers, New York. He also designed the house of J. D. Rockefeller, Jr., in Manhattan.

An avid classicist, Bosworth designed the American Telephone Building in New York City and the new campus of MIT in Cambridge, Massachusetts, in a rather archaeological mode. After World War I he directed the restoration of Rheims Cathedral, which had been damaged from shelling. He also administered the restoration of the palaces and gardens of Versailles and Fontainbleau, in ruin due to neglect during the war, with funds contributed by the Rockefeller family. After World War II he retired to France, where he was awarded the French Legion of Honor and the Cross of the Commander of the Order of Arts and Letters. Bosworth founded and served as president of the University Club of Paris.

Bottomley, William Lawrence

New York and Richmond   1883–1951

Born in New York City, Bottomley received his B.S. in Architecture from Columbia University in 1906 and pursued graduate work at Columbia, the Ecole des Beaux-Arts in Paris, and the American Academy in Rome. He apprenticed with Heinz and LaFarge and worked as a state architect in Albany. He began practice in New York in 1911, and from 1912 to 1919 was a partner in the firm of Hewitt and Bottomley. Bottomley designed many fine country houses on

Long Island, notably the J. Randolph Robinson house (1927–28) in Brookville. But it was through his patronage in Richmond, Virginia, that he became known as one of the foremost architects of country houses of the regionalist school. He received many awards, including a medal for apartment house design from the AIA in 1921. A frequent contributor to architectural journals, Bottomley was also the author of the book *Spanish Details* (1924) and the editor of *Great Georgian Houses of America* in two volumes (1933 and 1937). He helped to establish and direct the Architects Emergency Committee, which employed architects during the depression to document key Early American buildings, many of which were published in *Great Georgian Houses.* Bottomley's Richmond houses on Monument Avenue and in the fashionable Windsor Farms district are among the best Georgian domestic works of the 1920s and 1930s. They are well documented in O'Neal and Weeks, *The Work of William Lawrence Bottomley in Richmond.*

Briscoe, Birdsall Parmenas

Houston   1876–1971

Born in Harrisburg, Texas, Briscoe became one of Houston's best-known and most prolific domestic architects, working for the Hogg family and other prominent gentry during the oil boom. He was educated at Texas A and M and at San Antonio Academy. He began his practice in 1906 and remained active until 1950.

Brite and Bacon

James Brite, 1864–1942
Henry Bacon, 1866–1924
New York City

Perhaps the archetype of a firm spawned by the mentorship of McKim, Mead and White, Brite and Bacon opened their own offices in 1897, after both had spent some ten years with the firm. Henry Bacon was born in Watseka, Illinois, and studied architecture at the University of Illinois during 1884–85. He toured Europe on the Rotch Travelling Fellowship between 1889 and 1891 under McKim's sponsorship and returned to become the master's personal assistant. Brite was trained in Europe and in apprenticeship with the McKim firm. The Brite and Bacon partnership lasted until 1902, when each formed an independent practice. Bacon's most celebrated building is the Lincoln Memorial (1912–22), for which he received the AIA Gold Medal in 1923. His houses include

Chesterwood (1900), the estate of Daniel Chester French in Stockbridge, and the Donald MacRae house (1901) in Wilmington, North Carolina. Brite was the more successful in country house work, designing such large Tudor estates as The Braes (1912) for Herbert L. Pratt in Glen Cove, and Darlington (1904–07) for George Crocker in Ramapo Hills, New Jersey.

Brown, Arthur, Jr.

San Francisco   1874–1957

Brown is remembered as the Bay Area's most eminent classical architect. He designed homes, churches, and public structures in the San Francisco area, and the Interstate Commerce and Labor Department buildings in Washington, D.C. Brown was also one of three advisers on the remodeling of the U.S. Capitol. Born in Oakland, California, he was educated at the University of California College of Civil Engineering and at the Ecole des Beaux-Arts in Paris. He practiced in partnership with John Bakewell, Jr., from 1905 to 1927. Noted for designing the San Francisco City Hall and Coit Tower on Telegraph Hill, Brown also designed expositions, including the Panama Pacific Exhibition, the Chicago Century of Progress of 1933, and the Golden Gate International Exposition of 1939–40, of which he was architectural chairman. He designed the Hoover Library and other buildings at Stanford University. Brown taught architecture at Harvard University and the University of California. Abroad, he was a chevalier of the French Legion of Honor and in 1926 became a member of the Institut de France.

Brown, Frank Chouteau

Boston   1876–1947

Frank Chouteau Brown studied art and architecture in his native city of Minneapolis, in Boston, and while touring Europe. His career began at age twenty as a draftsman for Thomas C. Plant in Minneapolis. In 1902 he moved to Boston and joined James T. Kelly, who was known as a builder of fine homes. Later, in his own practice, Brown, too, specialized in residential work. He wrote frequently for architectural journals, on historic and contemporary architecture in New England and Europe. Many of his articles on old New England structures appeared in Russell F. Whitehead's *The Monograph Series: Records of Early American Architecture,* of which Brown was the associate editor. His books include *A Study of the Orders of*

Architecture (1925), *Letters and Lettering* (1921), and *Modern English Churches* (1923). Brown was editor of *Architectural Review* during 1907–19, and was on the editorial staff of *Old Time New England Magazine* during 1945–47. In 1934 he was appointed District Administrator in Massachusetts of the Historic American Buildings Survey, a Works Progress Administration project to record significant examples of historic American architecture.

Browne, Herbert W. C.

Boston   1860–1946

Born and educated in Boston, Herbert Browne attended classes at the Boston Museum of Fine Arts and later studied architecture in Paris and Florence. He returned to Boston and joined the firm of Jacques and Rantoul for training. In 1895 he went into partnership with Arthur Little and George H. Moore. When Moore withdrew, the firm became Little and Browne (*see* Little, Arthur). As one of Boston's specialists in Colonial Revival idioms and a leading restoration firm, Little and Browne designed many country estates and substantial city residences in New England. Browne's contribution is most evident in the planning of the Washington, D.C., house of Larz Anderson from 1902 to 1905. He remodeled the Harrison Grey Otis house, a historical federal home in Boston, for the Society for the Preservation of New England Antiquities, and was a member of the Society's board of trustees for fifteen years. He was a talented sketcher and watercolorist who exhibited his work frequently in his home city. Browne continued the firm name in practice after Little's death in 1925.

Bullard, Roger H.

New York and Connecticut   1884–1935

Bullard was born in New York City and studied architecture at Columbia University, graduating in 1907. He first worked for Grosvenor Atterbury, then in 1917 joined Philip Goodwin in the firm of Goodwin, Bullard and Woolsey. He established his own firm in 1921 and designed many Long Island estates and country clubs. Like his contemporaries Julius Gregory and Lewis Bowman, he favored an abstracted range of idioms based on English vernacular and French Provincial sources. His house for Samuel A. Salvage in Glen Head, Long Island, won the Gold Medal of Better Homes in America in 1933, and he received an Honorable Mention from the AIA in 1931 for an apartment building at 400 East 57th Street in New

York City. Bullard is notable as the designer of America's Little House, a model wood-frame home that stood at the corner of Park Avenue and 39th Street in Manhattan in the 1930s. Many of his best houses are on the south fork of eastern Long Island, in the Hamptons. These include the Salambier house (1924) in East Hampton.

Byers, John

Los Angeles   1875–1966

Byers was a romantic vagabond who turned to architecture late in life. Born in Grand Rapids, Michigan, he studied electrical engineering at the University of Michigan and at Harvard University. He taught romance languages in Uruguay and in San Rafael and Santa Monica, California. After a chance encounter with Mexican adobe craftsmen, he gave up teaching to become a contractor and businessman. He founded the John Byers Mexican Handmade Tile Company in 1919 and designed adobe houses in addition to producing adobe bricks and tiles used in their construction. He obtained his architectural license in 1926 and continued to practice, often in association with Elda Muir. His work consisted mostly of residential commissions in Santa Monica, Brentwood, and West Los Angeles. The later Byers house was usually a ground-hugging ranch type with overhanging eaves and an informal, comfortable feeling. Some of Byers' drawings are in the architectural drawings collection of the University Art Museum, University of California at Santa Barbara. See chapter 6 for a treatment of one of his major guest ranches.

Carrère, John Mervin

New York   1858–1911

Born in Rio de Janeiro, Carrère was educated in Europe and at age twenty entered the Ecole des Beaux-Arts in Paris. It was here that Carrère met Thomas Hastings, with whom he later formed the firm of Carrère and Hastings (*see* Hastings, Thomas), which designed some of the most renowned beaux arts country estates and public structures in America. Carrère was chief architect and chairman of the board of architects for the Pan American Exposition of Buffalo. He was a cofounder and served as president of the Society of Beaux Arts Architects, and helped to organize the New York Arts Commission and the Federation of Fine Arts. He also served as director and instructor at the American Academy in Rome. He died when

struck by a taxicab in 1911. See chapters 2 and 4 for a treatment of some of the firm's major works.

Clark, Cameron

New York, Connecticut, Virgin Islands   1887–1957

Clark had a varied career, notable for achievements in both urban planning and residential design. He was born in Holyoke, Massachusetts, and studied at MIT and at the American Academy in Rome. Most of his work was in New York and in Connecticut, but he also designed residences in Pennsylvania, New England, and St. Thomas, Virgin Islands. From 1943 to 1945 he was consulting architect to the Borough President of Manhattan and was a member of the Manhattan Advisory Planning Board. In Manhattan, he did design work for the East River and Harlem River Drives and the Battery Park Underpass. He was cochairman of the AIA Commission on Education of the New York chapter and was a member of the AIA Commission on Civic Design and Development. He was also active in planning commissions in Connecticut, especially in Fairfield County, where he served as chairman of the Post-War Planning Council. Clark designed model homes for *Good Housekeeping, Ladies Home Journal,* and *House Beautiful.* In 1938 he exhibited at the Architectural League of New York Exhibition and was commended for his handling of traditional Connecticut architecture. A noted Colonial Revivalist, Clark designed the Town Hall (1931) in Washington, Connecticut, and many clapboard New England residences of the smaller, postdepression type in northeast Connecticut.

Coate, Roland Ell

Pasadena   1890–1958

Coate was born in Richmond, Indiana, and received his architecture degree from Cornell University in 1914. After traveling in Europe, he worked for Trowbridge and Ackerman in New York from 1915 to 1919, then left for California. In 1922 he established a partnership with Reginald D. Johnson (*see* Johnson, Reginald) and Gordon B. Kaufmann (*see* Kaufmann, Gordon B.) in the firm of Johnson, Kaufmann and Coate. Coate established his own firm in 1925. He was largely responsible for the proliferation of eclectic houses in the Monterey revival style. His work in various idioms is notable for its clean lines, trim yet

informal planning, and general abstraction of detail. See chapter 6 for a treatment of two of Coate's typical works.

Codman, Ogden, Jr.

Boston   1863–1951

Though born in Boston, Codman received much of his early education in France and Germany. In 1882 he returned to America and studied architecture at MIT. After graduating in 1887, he apprenticed with his uncle, John Hubbard Sturgis. Codman established his own office in 1891, then two years later moved to New York, where he launched a successful career as a society architect and interior decorator of both city and country residences. He designed many of the elegant interiors and townhouses in Boston's Back Bay and New York's Upper East Side, as well as country estates in Long Island and Newport. He often designed in French eighteenth-century styles and, along with his acquaintances Edith Wharton and Elsie de Wolfe, was an important tastemaker around the turn of the century. In 1897 he coauthored *The Decoration of Houses* with Edith Wharton. Codman was also involved in historic preservation. Around 1903 he carried out restoration work to The Grange, his family's country home in Lincoln, Massachusetts. The measured drawings he made of many New England houses during his apprenticeship were later useful to restoration architects. Codman also had a notable collection of architectural books. After World War I he moved to France and remained there until his death, residing at his lavish classical villa, La Lecpolda, built during 1929–31. Among Codman's notable country houses are Clayton (1901), an English Georgian house for Lloyd Bryce in Roslyn, Long Island, and Hautbois (c. 1916–17), the French-style villa for Walter Maynard in Jericho. There are several collections of Codman papers and drawings: at the Metropolitan Museum of Art, New York; at the Avery Library, Columbia University; and at the Society for the Preservation of New England Antiquities, Boston.

Coffin, Marian Cruger

New York, Connecticut   1876–1957

Born in Geneva, New York, Coffin was among the first women to study landscape architecture at MIT, from which she graduated in 1904. A lifelong friend of Henry Francis Du Pont, she received several commissions due to his family's

.nfluence in Delaware. These commissions included advising Du Pont on the design of the grounds of his Winterthur estate and the landscaping of portions of the University of Delaware campus. Her career reached a peak of activity in the 1920s with the design of country estates and suburban gardens. As a member of the Horticultural Committee of the New York Botanical Garden, Coffin designed the Rose Garden and the Havemeyer Lilac Collection, and installed the Colonel Robert Montgomery Collection of Conifers there. In 1927 she moved to New Haven, Connecticut, and later transferred her practice there. In 1930 she received the Gold Medal of Honor from the Architectural League of New York for her design of the Edgar H. Bussick estate in Fairfield, Connecticut. Coffin wrote *Trees and Shrubs for Landscape Effects* in 1940, a book illustrated with examples of her designs. See chapter 5 for discussion of an example of Coffin's work. Archives of her work are at the Henry F. Du Pont Museum, Wilmington, Delaware; the Nassau County Museum of Fine Arts Archives, Roslyn, New York; and the Mattie Edwards Hewitt Archive, Long Island Studies Institute, Hofstra University, Hempstead, New York.

Cope and Stewardson

Walter Cope, 1860–1902
John Stewardson, 1858?–1896
Philadelphia

Cope and Stewardson was the patriarchal firm of the eclectic Philadelphia school, establishing its Anglophile and medieval principles. Noted for their association with the planning of the English-influenced campuses of Princeton University, Bryn Mawr College, and the University of Pennsylvania, the firm specialized in adaptations of Tudor and Jacobean architecture loosely known as Collegiate Gothic. Cope was born in Philadelphia and trained by apprenticeship with Addison Hutton and T. P. Chandler. He formed the partnership in 1885 with the Harvard-educated Stewardson (class of 1879), who had also attended the Ecole in Paris (1879–82). Respected for his knowledge of European architecture, Stewardson traveled and sketched on the continent in 1884 before beginning his practice. He died in a skating accident on the Schuylkill River during an outing with Wilson Eyre, and was mourned by much of the architectural establishment not only in Philadelphia but also on the East Coast. A well-known scholarship was named in his honor and is still awarded. The country house work of the firm was sporadic, but their list of patrons included many of the city's most prominent families.

Crook, Lewis Edmund, Jr.

Atlanta   1898–1967

Born in Meridian, Mississippi, Crook graduated from the Georgia Institute of Technology in 1919 and went to work for Hentz, Reid and Adler in Atlanta. He was Neel Reid's (*see* Reid, Joseph Neel) favorite draftsman and accompanied him on a sketching trip in Europe in 1922. In 1922, Crook established the firm of Ivey and Crook with Ernest Daniel Ivey. Ivey handled all phases of construction, while Crook was in charge of design. The firm specialized in residential design, but also completed many public structures including buildings at Emory University and, with other firms, the Clark Howell Housing Project for the Housing Authority of Atlanta. Crook wrote the foreword to *Southern Architecture Illustrated* (1931), a compilation of articles from *Southern Architect and Building News,* a journal to which Ivey and Crook were frequent contributors.

Day, Frank Miles

Philadelphia   1861–1918

Born and educated in Philadelphia, Day graduated from the University of Pennsylvania in 1883 as the class valedictorian. The son of English parents, he studied architecture in London at the South Kensington School of Art and the Royal Academy's School of Architecture. In 1885 he was awarded a prize by the Architectural Association of London. After traveling in Europe and working briefly for Basil Champneys, he returned to Philadelphia in 1886 and worked for George T. Pearson and Addison Hutton. The following year he opened his own firm; in 1893 he was joined by his older brother, Henry Kent Day. Charles Z. Klauder joined the firm in 1911, and after Henry Kent Day's retirement in 1912 the firm was known as Day and Klauder. Day had a distinguished career in collegiate work, including buildings at the University of Pennsylvania, University of Delaware, Penn State, Princeton, Cornell, and Yale. At the University of Pennsylvania he designed Franklin Field and, in association with Cope and Eyre, the University Museum. In 1918 he won the gold medal of the Philadelphia chapter of the AIA for his Princeton University dining halls. He was on the faculty of the University of Pennsylvania and the Pennsylvania Academy of Fine Arts, and was a visiting lecturer at Harvard and a trustee of the American Academy at Rome. Day was a frequent contributor to architectural journals and wrote the introduction to *American Country Houses of To-Day* (1912). Day's country house work around Philadelphia includes Abendruh (1892), for Charles Wallace Bergner; the Jacob Heil house (1906) in Wynnewood; and Cogslea (1902), for the artist Violet Oakley, in Mount Airy, later added to by Edmund Gilchrist.

Dean, Ruth Bramley

New York   1880–1932

Dean was born in Wilkes Barre, Pennsylvania, and studied at the University of Chicago. She then worked in both architecture and landscaping and established her own landscaping practice in 1913. The wife of the noted architect Aymar Embury II (*see* Embury, Aymar, II), she worked under her maiden name, independent of her husband. In 1929 she became the first woman recipient of the Architectural League of New York's Gold Medal of Honor in Landscape Architecture for three gardens she designed in Grosse Pointe, Michigan. Dean was a frequent contributor to journals, particularly *House and Garden,* as well as the author of *The Livable House: Its Garden* (1917).

De Forest, Lockwood

Santa Barbara   1896–1949

De Forest studied briefly at Harvard and at the University of California at Berkeley. He first worked with landscape architect Ralph Stevens in Santa Barbara, California. In the mid-1920s he opened his own landscape architecture practice and later designed buildings as well as gardens. He was one of the premier regionalist landscape architects of the southern California area.

Delano, William Adams

New York   1874–1960

Born in New York and reared in Philadelphia, Delano studied at Yale, Columbia, and the Ecole des Beaux-Arts in Paris. He met his future partner Chester Aldrich (*see* Aldrich, Chester) while apprenticing at Carrère and Hastings. The firm of Delano and Aldrich was established in 1903 and soon became one of the most successful architectural firms on the East Coast. Working in an austere classical revival styles as well as abstracted vernacular idioms,

Delano and Aldrich was known for its elegant interior finishes and refined estate planning. The firm designed many country estates for eastern society figures—probably more in the 1910s and 1920s than any other office in America. There were also city houses, schools, clubs, and monuments, including the Willard Straight house (now the International Center of Photography), the Nightingale School, and the Union Club, in New York City. The firm designed only one skyscraper, the Brown Building at 59 Wall Street in Manhattan (a commission that must have come from family connections—Delano's father was a prominent member of the investment firm). Delano taught architecture at Columbia University from 1903 to 1910. Later in his career he designed the first buildings for La Guardia Airport in New York. Delano was also responsible for renovations of the White House in Washington, D.C., during 1949–52. For a treatment of Delano's life and work see chapters 2 and 5.

Dominick, William F.

New York, Connecticut   1870–1945

Dominick was born and educated in Greenwich, Connecticut. After studying at Yale, he attended Columbia's School of Architecture during 1898–1901. Although he maintained his office in New York, his best-known works are in his hometown of Greenwich, and include Christ Church and several residences. In 1941 he received the AIA Award of Merit in the Small House Design Exhibit for his remodeling of the Arthur F. Brown home at Greenwich. His drawings are in the prints and drawings collection of the Library of Congress.

Duhring, Okie and Ziegler

Herman Louis Duhring, 1874–1953
R. Brognard Okie, 1875–1945
Carl L. Ziegler, 1878–1952
Philadelphia

Duhring grew up in Philadelphia and studied architecture at the University of Pennsylvania. He was the first recipient of the prestigious Stewardson Travelling Fellowship, in 1897. He worked for several firms and traveled in Europe before establishing his own office in Philadelphia in 1898. The following year he and two associates, R. Brognard Okie and Carl L. Ziegler, collaborated to form the firm of Duhring, Okie and Ziegler. Okie and Ziegler had also studied at the University of Pennsylvania. Although Okie resigned in 1918, Duhring and Ziegler continued together until 1924. The

firm concentrated on residential work in Philadelphia, with Duhring designing residences for Dr. George Woodward, the developer of St. Martins and Chestnut Hill in Philadelphia. Duhring and his partners were noted for their use of the Cotswold style mixed with the Pennsylvania farmhouse type—typical traits of the Philadelphia school. All three partners were recognized for their expertise in early regional architecture, and as restoration architects. Their patrons tended to be from the same conservative Delaware Valley society as those of their mentors, Eyre, Day, Cope, and Stewardson.

Embury, Aymar, II

New York   1880–1966

Embury is notable as an author and architectural critic in addition to having designed many residences and urban projects. Born in New York, he received his Civil Engineering degree from Princeton in 1900 and his master's degree in 1901. He later taught architecture at Princeton while establishing his career. Embury's designs for country houses were predominantly in regional revival styles, while his urban design projects were in bold, modernistic styles stressing engineering and materials. As an architectural consultant to the New York City Department of Parks, under Robert Moses, Embury created or collaborated on many civic structures including the Central Park Zoo, Randall Island Stadium, and the New York City Building at the 1939 New York World's Fair (now the Queens Museum in Flushing Meadow Park), as well as the first buildings on the Hofstra University Campus in Hempstead, Long Island. He also designed for the Triborough, Henry Hudson, and Whitestone bridges. His articles on country houses appeared frequently in journals, and his books include *One Hundred Country Houses* (1909), *The Dutch Colonial House* (1913), *Early American Churches* (1914), *The Livable House* (1917), and *The Aesthetics of Engineering Construction*. Embury was married to the noted landscape architect Ruth Dean (*see* Dean, Ruth Bramley).

Eyre, Wilson

Philadelphia   1858–1944

Eyre was born in Florence, Italy, and was reared in Newport, Rhode Island, and Lenoxville, Canada. He spent only one year of study at MIT and by age nineteen was working for James Peacock Sims in Philadelphia. He established his own practice in Philadelphia in

1882, and also lectured at the University of Pennsylvania during 1890–94. In 1912 he entered into partnership with John Gilbert McIlvaine, and the firm of Eyre and McIlvaine lasted until 1939. Eyre founded *House and Garden* magazine in 1901 as an extension of his interest in creating a country house and suburban lifestyle in accordance with his residential designs. He was a skilled draftsman and renderer. His drawings and designs, which frequently appeared in magazines, are evocative of his country living ideal and notable for their Arts and Crafts variations of eclectic revival styles. Eyre was an associate architect of the Museum of the University of Pennsylvania. He was active in the T-Square Club and the AIA, of which he became a fellow in 1893. For a discussion of Eyre's importance to the development of the romantic country house, see chapter 2. His documents are housed at the Avery Library, Columbia University; Burnham American Architectural Archives, Greenwich, Connecticut; and the University of Pennsylvania Architectural Archives.

Farrand, Beatrix Jones

New York, Connecticut   1872–1959

Beatrix Farrand was one of America's pioneer landscape architects and one of the great garden designers of her era. Born in New York City to Frederick R. Jones and Mary Cadwalader, she spent her girlhood with tutors and in travels. She was a niece of Edith Wharton, whom she came to know well. Farrand studied landscape in Berlin in 1893, but learned most of her gardening from Charles Sprague Sargent, the great Boston horticulturist. In 1895 she set up her own office in New York. With writer Wilhelm Miller, she was instrumental in promulgating English wild and native gardening ideals in the United States. Her country house work, with such architects as William Adams Delano, Theodate Pope, and Shepley, Rutan and Coolidge, was extensive, but little survives. Her best known extant garden, and certainly her masterpiece, is Dumbarton Oaks in Georgetown, Washington, D.C., begun in 1921 for Mr. and Mrs. Robert Woods Bliss.

Fatio, Maurice

New York, Palm Beach   1897–1943

Fatio was born in Geneva, Switzerland, on March 18, 1897. He graduated from Zurich Polytechnic in 1920. His father, an Italian-Swiss banker, later became an ambassador in the League of Nations. In 1921 Fatio came to

New York and established a partnership with William A. Treanor. Both architects had worked for Harrie Lindeberg. The firm of Treanor and Fatio designed many fine country houses on the East Coast. In 1925 Fatio opened the firm's Palm Beach office, while Treanor ran the office in New York. Fatio designed many villas and other structures in the wake of the Florida land boom. He was a deft socialite, a golfer, and a card player, and was popular at the Everglades, Seminole, and Bath and Tennis clubs in Palm Beach. His most notable nonresidential designs in Palm Beach are the library of the Society of Four Arts, the West Palm Beach Post Office, and the First National Bank building. During World War II, he had commissions in Santiago, Chile, and Rio de Janeiro, Brazil. Major commissions came from William J. McIneeny, Palm Beach (1928); Lucius P. Ordway, Palm Beach (1929); Mortimer Schiff, Ham Sandwich House (1929), Palm Beach; Harold S. Vanderbilt, Palm Beach (1930); Joseph P. Widener, Palm Beach (1930); Vadim Makaroff, Casa della Porta, The Reef (1936), Palm Beach. His documents are housed at the Historical Society of Palm Beach County, West Palm Beach, Florida. He was the author of *Treanor and Fatio, Architects* (1932) and *Recent Florida Work by Treanor and Fatio, Architects* (1938 and 1944).

Faville, William B.

San Francisco   1866–1947

Born in San Andreas, California, Faville became an architectural apprentice at the firm of Green and Wicks in Buffalo, New York, before attending a two-year course in architecture at MIT. In 1895 he went to work for McKim, Mead and White in New York, where he met his future partner, Walter D. Bliss of San Francisco. The firm of Bliss and Faville was established in San Francisco in 1898 and soon became one of the leading architectural firms of northern California. In addition to private residences, the firm designed many public structures, particularly in the San Francisco area, including the St. Francis Hotel, the Bank of California Building, the University Club, and the Oakland Public Library. The firm also assisted in the plans and buildings for the Pan-Pacific Exposition of 1913 in San Francisco. In 1925 the partnership ended and Faville continued in practice alone. He served as president of the AIA in 1922 and 1923.

Flagg, Ernest

New York   1857–1947

Ernest Flagg was born in Brooklyn. After abandoning formal education at age fifteen and working as an office boy in New York City, Flagg entered the second class at the Ecole des Beaux-Arts in Paris in August 1889. He studied in the atelier of Paul Blondel. There he met Walter B. Chambers, with whom he traveled and later formed an informal partnership. Flagg returned to New York in 1891 and won early recognition for his design of St. Luke's Hospital in Manhattan. His domestic architecture reflected the prevailing taste for Colonial styles. He used the popular Georgian mode for his town house (1906–07) at 109 East 40th Street, and Dutch Colonial for his country house, Stone Court (1897–99), on Staten Island. He also synthesized French and American neoclassicism in his Alfred Corning Clark House (1899–1900) on Riverside Drive in New York City. His only large country house is the Frederick G. Bourne house, The Towers (1904–06), Dark Island, Chippewa Bay, New York. His nonresidential work includes the plan and numerous buildings for the United States Naval Academy at Annapolis, Maryland; the classical Corcoran Gallery of Art in Washington, D.C.; and the Singer Building, one of the most famous early skyscrapers in Manhattan. During the last twenty-five years of his career, Flagg adapted his understanding of classical proportioning to problems of small house design. He presented his designs in a book entitled *Small Houses: Their Economic Design and Construction* (1922). However, his contribution to the development of larger country houses was not substantial. Flagg was a president and cofounder of the Society of Beaux Arts Architects, and was known with Thomas Hastings as one of the foremost exponents of Modern French design. He was elected to the AIA in 1911.

Flanders, Annette Hoyt

New York   1887–1946

Flanders was the landscape architect of numerous country estates and suburban lots, predominantly on the East Coast, but also in Texas, Hawaii, Canada, and France. Following her graduation from Smith College in 1910, she studied landscape architecture at the University of Illinois, engineering at Marquette University, and related subjects at the Sorbonne in Paris. She supplemented her education with trips to study vegetation in Europe and in North and South America. Flanders worked for the prominent landscape architecture firm of Vitale, Brinckerhoff and Geiffert before opening her own practice in New York in 1922. One of her most interesting projects was the restoration and replanting of Morven, a southern estate whose original gardens were attributed to Thomas Jefferson. In 1933 her modern garden at the Century of Progress Exposition in Chicago was judged the best individual garden exhibited. She also received the Gold Medal of Honor of the Architectural League of New York in 1936 for the French gardens on the Charles E. F. McCann estate in Oyster Bay, New York. A few years before her death, she moved her office to her native city of Milwaukee. Her major commissions include the estate of Vincent Astor, Long Island, New York and Morven, the estate of Charles A. Stone, near Charlottesville, Virginia.

Ford, O'Neil

San Antonio   1905–1982

Born in Pink Hill, Texas, Ford attended what is now North Texas State University at Denton. After completing an international correspondence school course in architecture, he worked in the office of David R. Williams in Dallas during 1926–32. Ford was interested in early Texas structures, indigenous materials, and the integration of crafts and architecture. He established his own practice in Dallas during 1932–34 and worked on many government projects. Joined by Arthur B. Swank, he moved his office to San Antonio, where, in 1938, he was hired to supervise the Works Progress Administration restoration of La Villita, an eighteenth-century neighborhood. That same year he entered into partnership with Jerry Rogers. The firm did much work on college campuses, notably the Little Chapel in the Woods at Texas Woman's University, Denton; Trinity University campus and buildings, San Antonio; and Skidmore College campus and buildings, Saratoga Springs, New York. Ford was a visiting professor at Harvard and the University of Texas at Austin, and was the recipient of many honors, including the Thomas Jefferson Award from the University of Virginia in 1967 and the Pitts Award from the Texas Society of Architects in 1978. He was made an honorary member of the Sociedad de Arquitectos Mexicanos in 1975.

Forster, Frank Joseph

New York   1886–1948

Born in New York City, Forster studied architecture through his travels in Europe and at Cooper Union, where he received his degree in 1908. He established his own practice in 1911 and specialized in country houses, for which he won the Silver Medal of the Architectural League of New York in 1927 and 1929, and an Honorable Mention in 1928. In 1933 he received the Better Homes in America Medal. His early designs were in an English picturesque mode, but after 1924 he turned almost exclusively to French Provincial. He was the nation's leading exponent of the rustic, farmhouse-like buildings that he had seen firsthand in the 1920s in the French countryside. Most of his houses were in suburban environs of Connecticut, Westchester County, and Pennsylvania. Forster was active in public housing and, as one of the winners of the 1935 Slum Clearance Competition, was appointed an architect for Harlem River houses in Manhattan. In 1931, he published *Country Houses,* an illustrated book on his work. Forster retired from New York in 1942 and continued to design houses in Killingworth, Connecticut.

French, Leigh H., Jr.

New York   1894–1946

French was born in Minneapolis and studied architecture at Columbia University and as a draftsman at various architectural firms. He began his practice after World War I, and became known as a designer of fine homes in various styles. He designed over 100 houses in Westchester County, New York, alone. In 1932 he originated The House That Grows for the years of the Great Depression, designed to be built in sections over a period of years. French collaborated with other architects in 1934 on housing for atomic energy experimenters in Oak Ridge, Tennessee. His interest in historical architecture is reflected in his books *Colonial Interiors* (1923), with photographs and measured drawings, and *The Smaller Houses and Gardens of Versailles from 1680–1815* (1926), published in collaboration with Harold Donaldson Eberlein. French's major works include houses for Mrs. Eleanor Patterson, Dayton, Ohio; Mr. J. Lippincott, Bethacres, Pennsylvania; and C. Everett Austin (in collaboration with Austin), Hartford, Connecticut (1930).

Gilchrist, Edmund Beaman

Philadelphia   1885–1953

Gilchrist, born in Germantown, Pennsylvania, spent one year of study at Drexel University, then took two years of electives at the University of Pennsylvania. After apprenticing with both Wilson Eyre and Horace Trumbauer in Philadelphia, Gilchrist opened his own practice in 1911. He designed numerous homes, clustered houses, and clubs in Philadelphia suburbs. He also designed notable nonresidential structures, including the Unitarian church in Germantown and, in 1924, the Free Library of Philadelphia. Gilchrist was involved in housing issues and in 1932 served on president Hoover's Conference on Home Building and Home Ownership. He was a member of the Community Planning Committee of the AIA during 1923–26, and of the Special Committee on the Economics of Site Planning and Housing of the AIA during 1934–35. In 1929 Gilchrist won the Chestnut Street Association Medal for his design of the Whitman's candy store in Philadelphia.

Gill, Irving John

San Diego   1870–1936

Born in Syracuse, New York, Gill trained in architecture under Louis Sullivan and stayed on as a draftsman until 1893. He moved to California for health reasons and, in 1895, founded a practice in San Diego. Gill worked independently except for the years 1898 to 1906, when he was in partnership with William S. Hebbard, and 1912, when he worked for Bertram G. Goodhue on the San Diego Exposition of 1915. Gill's practice was primarily domestic work in southern California, but he also designed many houses in the East, notably in Bar Harbor, Maine, and Newport, Rhode Island. Gill was an early modernist architect and his designs are distinguished for their use of reinforced concrete and hollow tile. He pioneered a system of tilt wall construction with concrete, and his interior innovations included drains in the floors and coved walls to floors. He also planned the gardens along with houses as integral "green rooms." Gill was active in low income housing through such works as Lewis Courts, built in 1910 in Sierra Madre, California. His nonresidential work includes the Christian Science church in San Diego, Scripps School in La Jolla, California, and Wilson Acton Hotel in La Jolla. After World War I his career declined. For a brief time before his death he maintained an office in

Los Angeles. Gill's most famous residential work was the concrete house (1914–16) for Walter Luther Dodge in Los Angeles, now destroyed, one of the landmarks of progressive design in California.

Gillette, Leon N.

New York   1878–1945

Gillette was born in Malden, Massachusetts, and had his initial training in architecture with the firm of Bertrand and Keith in Minneapolis. He received his Certificate in Architecture from the University of Pennsylvania in 1899, and studied at the Ecole des Beaux-Arts in Paris during 1901–03. After returning to the United States, Gillette worked in the office of Warren and Wetmore in New York until 1906, when he and A. Stewart Walker, a Harvard graduate, founded the firm of Walker and Gillette. The firm is best remembered for its commercial structures in the New York City area, most in a spectacular art deco style, but was also distinguished for residential work. Notable nonresidential works include 2 Wall Street (the First National Bank Building) and the Fuller Building (1928–29) in Manhattan, and Rye Playland in Rye, New York. In 1910 the firm won the AIA Medal for Apartment House Design. The firm's residential designs were recognized in 1922 with the Gold Medal of the Architectural League of New York, and in 1925 with the Gold Medal of the AIA. The best known of their country houses is Planting Fields (1919), the Tudor estate of financier William R. Coe (1869–1955) at Upper Brookville, Long Island, with its extensive Olmsted Brothers gardens. Walker and Gillette also designed the estates of H. H. Rogers (c. 1916) in Southampton, Henry P. Davison (c. 1920) in Lattingtown, and Francis L. Hines (c. 1918) in Glen Cove. Well connected in business and social circles, they designed the fashionable Creek Club in Locust Valley.

Greenleaf, James L.

New York   1857–1933

A leading landscape architect associated with McKim, Mead and White and their school, Greenleaf was trained as a civil engineer at Columbia University. In the late 1890s he began to work as a landscape architect, reworking the grounds of the Frederick W. Vanderbilt estate (*see* chapter 4) at Hyde Park. His estate work on Long Island included the widely admired gardens at Killenworth (1913) for

George Pratt, and the estates of George S. Brewster in Brookville and Mortimer Schiff in Oyster Bay.

Gregory, Julius

New York   1875–1955

Gregory, who was born in Sacramento, California, is notable for his many house designs for home magazines, in which he adapted new concepts to traditional styles. He attended the University of California at Berkeley and continued his studies abroad. He was architectural consultant for both *House and Garden* magazine, for whom he designed the Ideal House, and *House Beautiful* magazine, for whom he created the Pacesetter House. He also designed many churches in New York.

Hastings, Thomas

New York   1860–1929

Thomas Hastings was senior partner of Carrère and Hastings, one of the most successful firms designing Beaux-Arts-style structures in America. Born in New York City, he completed a two-year course in architecture at Columbia University and studied at the Ecole des Beaux-Arts in Paris, where he first met his future partner, John M. Carrère (*see* Carrère, John Mervin). In 1894 Hastings returned to New York where he worked as a draftsman for McKim, Mead and White. The following year he founded the firm of Carrère and Hastings. One of the firm's early benefactors was Henry Flagler, who commissioned the Ponce de Leon Hotel in St. Augustine, Florida. An early example of Spanish Revival style, the hotel garnered praise for the young firm. Carrère and Hastings designed many fine city and country houses, as well as churches and commercial and public structures—most notably the New York Public Library in Manhattan. Most of their residential work was in the New York area, and the firm was known for incorporating the gardens with the house as an ensemble. The firm won the Gold Medal of the AIA in 1903 for the Murray Guggenheim residence at Elberon, New Jersey. Hastings was honored with the Gold Medal of the Royal Institute of British Architects in 1922 and was a chevalier of the French Legion of Honor.

Hobart, Lewis P.

San Francisco   1873–1954

Born in St. Louis, Missouri, Hobart studied first at the University of California at Berkeley, then for a year at the American Academy in Rome, and finally, during 1900–02, at the Beaux-Arts Institute of Design in New York City. He began his practice in New York in 1904, but after two years moved his office to San Francisco. There he designed many municipal buildings, including the Museum of Natural History in Golden Gate Park and the University of California Hospital, as well as many large houses in Burlingame, Hillsborough, and San Mateo. He was also known for his fine architectural library, and as an enthusiast of Mexican archaeology.

Hoffman, Francis Burrall, Jr.

New York, Florida   1882–1980

Born in New Orleans, Louisiana, Hoffman graduated from Harvard University in 1903, then studied at the Ecole des Beaux-Arts in Paris, where he received honors. He left the Ecole in 1907 and returned to America to apprentice with Carrère and Hastings. In 1910 he began his practice in Manhattan, and later opened an office in Florida. Hoffman was distinguished for his design of theaters, private homes, and apartment buildings. He is best known as the architect of Vizcaya (1912–15), the estate of James Deering in Coconut Grove, Florida, in collaboration with Paul Chalfin. (See chapter 4).

Hood, Raymond Mathewson

New York   1881–1934

Hood is known for his distinctive skyscrapers in Manhattan and for his innovative use of color in decoration. Born in Pawtucket, Rhode Island, he attended Brown University and graduated from MIT in 1903. He worked for six months for Cram, Goodhue and Ferguson in New York, then left for the Ecole des Beaux-Arts in Paris, where he remained until 1911. He returned to the United States and worked for Henry Hornbostel in Pittsburgh, then in 1914 opened his own office in New York. He was later in association with Andre Fouilhoux, and then Frederick Godley, in the firm of Hood, Godley and Fouilhoux. Hood became famous in 1922 for his successful entry in the Chicago Tribune Building Competition, in association with John Mead Howells (*see* Howells, John Mead). He designed some of the most

important skyscrapers in Manhattan, including the RCA Building of Rockefeller Center and the American Radiator (now American Standard), Daily News, and McGraw-Hill buildings. He served as president of the Architectural League of New York. Hood's private house commissions were few, but his major works include houses for Capt. Joseph Patterson, Ossining, New York (1930); Raymond Hood, Stamford, Connecticut (1925); and William R. Morris, Greenwich, Connecticut.

Hopkins, Alfred

New York   1870–1941

Hopkins was born in Saratoga Springs, New York, and studied architecture at the Ecole des Beaux-Arts in Paris. In 1913 he opened the office of Alfred Hopkins and Associates in New York. He designed many country estates but was best known as a prison architect, notably for the Federal Penitentiary at Lewisburg, Pennsylvania. He was considered an authority on prisons, and in 1935 President Roosevelt appointed him a delegate to the International Prison Conference in Berlin. His diverse architectural interests are reflected in his books, which include *Planning for Sunshine and Fresh Air, Modern Farm Buildings, Banks and Bank Buildings,* and *Prisons and Prison Buildings.*

Hoppin, Francis L. V.

New York   1867–1941

Born in Providence, Rhode Island, Hoppin studied at Brown University, at MIT, and in Paris. He apprenticed at McKim, Mead and White in New York, where he met his future partner, Terrence A. Koen. The firm of Hoppin and Koen was launched in 1894, and was joined by Robert Palmer Huntington in 1904. The firm was known for its country houses in Newport, Rhode Island, and in the Hudson River Valley, as well as for several public structures in New York, notably the Police Headquarters of the city of New York in downtown Manhattan. Hoppin was a noted renderer and painter and, after Koen's death, retired from practice and turned to his watercolors. His major residential works include The Mount (1902), designed for Edith Wharton, Lenox, Massachusetts; Blithewood, the Capt. A. C. Zabriskie residence, Barrytown, New York; the Charles W. Cooper residence, Tuxedo, New York; and alterations to the home of Franklin Delano Roosevelt, Hyde Park, New York. Hoppin's documents are in the Avery Architectural Archives at Columbia University.

Howe, George

Philadelphia   1886–1955

Howe is notable for his varied career as architect, educator, and editor. Born in Worcester, Massachusetts, he grew up in France, Switzerland, and America. He graduated from Harvard in 1908, finished at the Ecole des Beaux-Arts in Paris in 1912, and began practicing in Philadelphia in 1913. He entered into many partnerships with prominent architects, beginning with Walter Mellor and Arthur Meigs. The firm of Mellor, Meigs and Howe (*see* Mellor, Walter, and Meigs, Arthur C.) lasted from 1920 to 1928 and was distinguished for many fine houses designed with interlocking interior and garden rooms in the Philadelphia area. During 1929–34 Howe was in partnership with the prominent Swiss architect William Lescaze (1896–1969). The firm of Howe and Lescaze designed one of the most important skyscrapers in America, the International Style Philadelphia Savings Fund Society Building (1931) in Philadelphia. Howe adopted the International Style, significantly modified by his innovations, for the country houses that he continued to design. In 1940 he formed a partnership with Louis Kahn, and from 1942 to 1945 Howe supervised construction of federal buildings. In 1945 he began a firm with Robert Montgomery Brown, and in 1950 was appointed Chairman of the Yale School of Architecture. Howe was a sponsor of *T-Square* and *Shelter* magazines and founded *Perspecta* magazine.

Howells, John Mead

New York   1868–1959

Born in Cambridge, Massachusetts, Howells, the only son of author William Dean Howells, graduated from Harvard University in 1891 and finished at the Ecole des Beaux-Arts in Paris in 1897. He was the architect of many important urban structures and country houses. In 1922 he collaborated with Raymond Hood (*see* Hood, Raymond Mathewson) on the winning design of the Chicago Tribune Building Competition. In partnership with I. N. Phelps Stokes, Howells designed the Panhellenic (now Beekman) Tower Hotel and St. Paul's Chapel of Columbia University, both in Manhattan. His knowledge of Early American architecture is evident in his designs for eclectic resort houses, and in his books, including *Lost Examples of Colonial Architecture* (1931), *Architectural Heritage of the Piscataqua* (1937), and *Architectural Heritage of the Merrimack*

(1941). He was a frequent contributor to architectural journals, and covered architecture for *Harper's* and *The Century* magazines. Howells was an active preservationist in Charleston, South Carolina, in Portsmouth, New Hampshire, and in Kittery, Maine, where he had a home. He served as president of the New York Society of Beaux Arts Architects. Among his works are the restoration of Stormfield house for Mark Twain in Redding, Connecticut. His partner, I. N. Phelps Stokes, built one of the most romantic Tudor houses in Greenwich, Connecticut.

Hunt, Joseph

New York   1870–1924

Joseph Hunt, a son of architect Richard Morris Hunt, was born in New York City. He graduated from Harvard University in 1892, studied architecture at Columbia University for two years, and continued at the Ecole des Beaux-Arts in Paris from 1896 to 1900. In 1901 Hunt entered into partnership with his older brother, Richard Hunt (*see* Hunt, Richard H.). The firm of Hunt and Hunt was notable for the design of significant structures in New York City and for several city and country houses. Joseph Hunt was also interested in city planning and spent several months in Jamashedput, India, planning buildings for the Tate Iron and Steel Plant. He served as director and president of the New York Municipal Arts Society and as secretary of the Federation of Fine Arts from 1904 to 1915.

Hunt, Myron

Chicago and Los Angeles   1868–1952

Born in Sunderland, Massachusetts, Myron Hunt, son of a nurseryman, received his architectural education at MIT. He graduated in 1893 and left to tour Europe. He then worked for Shepley, Rutan and Coolidge in Boston before opening his own practice in Chicago in 1898. Five years later he moved to Pasadena for health reasons. There he established a partnership with Elmer Grey that lasted until 1910, after which he was independent. Hunt designed the Rose Bowl and the Pasadena Public Library in Pasadena, and the Huntington residence (now Gallery and Library) in neighboring San Marino. He also designed the art galleries of La Jolla and Santa Barbara. In 1920 he went into partnership with H. C. Chambers, and in 1947 was joined by Lester Hibbard. Hunt served as president of the

Southern California Chapter of the AIA and in 1928 received the Pasadena Noble Prize Gold Medal. See chapter 5 for a brief treatment of Hunt's San Marino (1906–11), the Henry P. Huntington estate, Pasadena, California (now Huntington Gallery and Library), and chapter 6 for a discussion of his Spanish houses.

Hunt, Richard H.

New York   1862–1931

Born in Paris, Richard H. Hunt, a son of architect Richard Morris Hunt, studied at MIT and at the Ecole des Beaux-Arts in Paris. After training in draftsmanship with his father, Richard H. Hunt became his father's associate and practiced with him until 1896. In 1901 he began a partnership with his younger brother, Joseph (*see* Hunt, Joseph). The brothers continued to work for their father's clients, and designed Idle Hour (1899), the estate of William K. Vanderbilt at Oakdale, Long Island, to replace a house designed by Richard Morris Hunt which had burned. They designed Castle Gould (1909) at Port Washington for Howard Gould, and Beacon Towers (1917) for Mrs. O. H. P. Belmont in Sands Point. The firm of Hunt and Hunt also designed notable structures in New York City, including the East Wing of the Metropolitan Museum of Art, and buildings at Vanderbilt and Sewanee universities. Hunt and Hunt were perhaps the last purveyors of the stately, over-opulent styles that were predominant in the 1890s.

Janssen, Benno

Pittsburgh   1874–1964

Janssen studied architecture with the Boston firms of Shepley, Rutan and Coolidge and then Parker and Thomas. After two years in Paris, he moved to Pittsburgh, where he formed a partnership with Franklin Abbott. The firm of Janssen and Abbott designed the Pittsburgh Athletic Association Clubhouse in 1909. Janssen later went into partnership with William Y. Cocken. This firm, which lasted into the 1930s, designed the Mellon Institute for Industrial Research, Long Vue Country Club, and many fine country houses. Janssen generally used classical styles for public structures, and reserved the English Romantic style for his country houses and clubs. His residential work in the years following World War I resembles that of Harrie Lindeberg and Frank J. Forster.

Jensen, Jens

Chicago 1860–1951

Jensen was an important and individualistic landscape architect and educator in the Midwest. Born in Dybol, Denmark, he studied at Jutland Agricultural College and came to the United States at age twenty-four. By 1906 he had settled in Chicago and was the superintendent of many city parks. Jensen designed Columbus and Humboldt parks and the Garfield Park Conservatory for the city of Chicago. In 1920 he opened his own office and became known for his ecological, nonclassically designed gardens. He laid out the grounds of several country houses outside Chicago and in the resort area of Lake Geneva, Wisconsin, working on several occasions with Howard Shaw and Albert Kahn. One of his most notable nonresidential works is the Abraham Lincoln Memorial Gardens in Springfield, Illinois (1906). In 1935 Jensen moved to Ellison Bay, Wisconsin, where he established the Clearing School of Arts. Jensen's design philosophies were incorporated into his book *Siftings* (1939) and his essay *The Clearing* (1956). He was awarded the Gold Medal of the Massachusetts Horticultural Society. Jensen's major works include the estates of Edsel Ford (1920s) in Grosse Pointe Shores, Michigan, and Seal Harbor, Maine; the estate of Ogden Armour, Lake Forest, Illinois; the E. L. Ryerson house (1912), Lake Forest; and The Clearing (1919, 1935–47), the estate and school of Jens Jensen, Ellison Bay, Wisconsin.

Johnson, Reginald

Santa Barbara 1882–1952

After graduating from MIT, Johnson traveled in Europe and continued his studies in Paris. In 1912 he opened his office in Pasadena, California, and ten years later formed a partnership with Gordon B. Kaufmann (*see* Kaufmann, Gordon B.) and Roland Coate (*see* Coate, Roland Ell). The firm of Kaufmann, Johnson and Coate lasted until 1925, after which Johnson practiced alone. In the 1920s and early 1930s, Johnson was one of the chief proponents of Spanish and Mediterranean Revival. One of his most important early works is the Tod Ford residence (1916–17) in Pasadena. He designed several of the most influential Spanish houses in Santa Barbara during the 1920s (*see* chapter 3). Later in his career he renounced eclecticism for modernism—one of the few architects of his generation to do so. In the late 1930s and early 1940s he turned his attention to public housing.

Kahn, Albert

Detroit 1869–1942

Kahn is most famous as an influential industrial designer, but he was also the architect of several important country houses in the Detroit area. He was born in Westphalia, Germany, and came to the United States at age eleven. He soon got a job as office boy with an architect in Detroit and was later admitted free to the drawing school of sculptor Julius Melchers (father of painter Gari Melchers). Kahn apprenticed with architect George D. Mason and after a few years was given the task of designing factories. In 1890 he won a $500 scholarship from *American Architect Magazine,* which enabled him to study and travel in Europe for two years. Upon his return to Detroit, Kahn opened his own practice and was later joined in partnership by his brothers. He designed many factories, including war plants and naval bases, which garnered him an AIA medal for his significant contribution to the World War II effort. He also designed factories for the Soviet Union in its first Five-Year Plan. Kahn designed the most important structures in downtown Detroit, including the Detroit Free Press, Detroit News, Fisher, and General Motors buildings. He received many awards, among which were the Silver Medal from the Architectural League of New York for the Fisher Building in 1934; the Honor Award from the Detroit AIA for the Edsel Ford residence and the S. S. Kresge Administration Building; and a Gold Medal from the International Exposition of Arts and Sciences in Paris in 1927. Kahn was a chevalier of the French Legion of Honor.

Kaufmann, Gordon B.

Los Angeles 1888–1949

Born in London, Kaufmann attended the Whitgift School in Croyden, England, and at age twenty graduated from the Polytechnic Institute in London. He came to Los Angeles in 1914, and in 1920 began practice with Reginald Johnson (*see* Johnson, Reginald) and Roland Coate (*see* Coate, Roland Ell). The firm of Johnson, Kaufmann and Coate, which lasted until 1925, was known for fine residential work, most in Spanish Revival styles, and for some public buildings, notably St. Paul's Episcopal Cathedral in Los Angeles. Independently, Kaufmann designed many significant structures in the Los Angeles area, including the Los Angeles Times building and the Athenaeum and dormitories of Caltech in Pasadena. He was

the consulting architect for the massive Hoover Dam project during the 1930s.

Keen, Charles Barton

Philadelphia and North Carolina 1868–1931

Keen was born in Philadelphia and graduated with a B.S. in architecture from the University of Pennsylvania in 1889. For the next three years he attended night classes at the Pennsylvania Museum and the School of Industrial Art. He apprenticed first with T. P. Chandler and then with Frank Miles Day. In 1894 he opened a practice with Frank E. Mead in the firm of Keen and Mead of Philadelphia, which lasted until 1901. Keen worked with many developers in suburban Philadelphia, and also designed some estates on Long Island, New York. In 1912, a connection with the Reynolds family in North Carolina led to commissions there. He soon moved his home office to North Carolina and continued to design country houses.

Kitchell, Bruce Paxton

Palm Beach 1872–1942

Kitchell arrived in Palm Beach in 1919, and competed with Mizner, Wyeth and Fatio for villa commissions. He also designed commercial buildings and Works Progress Administration housing projects.

Koch, Richard

New Orleans 1889–1971

Koch was born to German immigrant parents in New Orleans and was educated at Tulane University (1910). He studied architecture at the Ecole des Beaux-Arts in Paris (Atelier Bernier) from 1911 to 1912. He began his apprenticeship in the office of Aymar Embury II, in New York City, later working for John Russell Pope and William Welles Bosworth. Returning to New Orleans in 1916, Koch joined with the well-connected Charles Armstrong to form Armstrong and Koch, a firm that continued until 1935. Koch worked alone between 1935 and 1955, then formed the firm of Richard Koch and Samuel Wilson, Jr., still one of the city's premier offices. While initially attracted to European classical models, Koch learned to appreciate the diverse regional idioms of Louisiana through preservation and documentation projects undertaken in the 1920s and 1930s. He supervised Historic American Buildings

Survey projects during the depression and was the restoration architect for such southern icons as Shadows On The Teche (1922) in New Iberia, Louisiana, and Oak Alley (1926) near Vacherie. Absorbing their influences, he began to design both country and city residences that synthesized the French, Spanish, and English idioms of New Orleans and the Mississippi Delta to create new models for regional living. He was instrumental in creating legislation for the Vieux Carré Commission, one of the first historic districts in the United States, during the late 1930s and served on the commission from 1944 to 1954. As a preservationist, he was responsible for several major restorations in New Orleans, including the Cabildo and the French Market, and served on the preservation committee of the AIA. In 1938 he won the Silver Medal from the Architectural League of New York for his regionalist work and was awarded a fellowship in the AIA for his contributions to the profession during the same year. Koch's major country houses include designs for J. W. Reily in Louisburg (1934) and Bayou Liberty, Louisiana (1933 and 1937); Mrs. John W. Gebert in New Iberia (1932); Donald Markel in Pass Christian, Mississippi (1936); and Pike Burden in Baton Rouge (1939).

Kocher, Lawrence

New York   1885–1969

In Kocher's activities as architect, educator, adviser, and author, he was both a leading preservationist and a modernist. Born in San Jose, California, he graduated from Stanford University in 1909. From 1912 to 1926 he taught at Pennsylvania State College, where he received his master's degree in 1916. He later studied architecture and architectural history at MIT and New York University. In 1926 he became the head of the McIntire School of Art and Architecture at the University of Virginia, and from 1928 to 1938 was the managing editor of *Architectural Record* magazine. Because of his expertise on Early American architecture, Kocher was appointed to the advisory committee of architects that guided the Williamsburg, Virginia, restoration, and he later served as chairman of the State Art Commission of Virginia. In partnership with Albert Frey, a pupil of Le Corbusier, Kocher built the famous Aluminaire House in Long Island, New York, in 1931. This cubist structure, surfaced with aluminum panels, was one of the first International Style homes in America. Kocher was supervising architect of the Washington Irving restoration in Tarrytown, New York, and

served as chairman of the AIA's Committee on Preservation of Historic Monuments and Scenery. His books and articles include "Architecture of Lancaster County" (1919); "Early Architecture of Pennsylvania" (1920–22); and *Colonial Williamsburg: Its Buildings and Gardens* (1949) and *Shadows in Silver* (1954), both written with Howard Dearstyle.

Lindeberg, Harrie Thomas

New York   1880–1959

Lindeberg was probably the most prolific and widely known domestic specialist of the eclectic era, designing almost nothing but country houses during his long career. His clients included wealthy business leaders from all corners of the nation—the Armours of Chicago, the Farrishes of Houston, the Pillsburys of Minneapolis, the Pattersons of Dayton, the Du Ponts of Delaware, and the Van Beurens of New York, among many. Still, little is known of his family or of his early life. Of Swedish ancestry, he was born in Bergen Point, New Jersey, on April 10, 1880. He is thought to have studied architecture at the National Academy of Design between 1898 and 1901. He worked for McKim, Mead and White from approximately 1901 to 1906, serving as an assistant on the influential James Breese house. In 1905 he joined with another McKim draftsman, Lewis Colt Albro (1876–1924), to form the firm of Albro and Lindeberg, which lasted until 1914. The firm's first commissions were substantial— a dormitory at Wesleyan University and the estate of National City Bank president James Stillman at Pocantico, New York. The Stillman house (1907) established Lindeberg's reputation as a leader of the romantic, English-influenced school of domestic architects, a position he held throughout the 1920s and 1930s. He also designed an influential Colonial Revival house, Foxhollow Farm (1907), for Tracy Dows near Rhinebeck, New York. As his career progressed he refined his design philosophy to incorporate art deco and even modernism. In his houses of the late 1920s he began to abstract and minimize the details of the typical medieval, Tudor, or Arts and Crafts house. Lindeberg's 1940 monograph included some "streamlined Moderne" country house designs. Honored by critics and colleagues during his middle years, he was almost forgotten by the time of his death. He married three times: to Eugenie Lee Quinn, who died within a year, in 1906; to Lucia Hull, with whom he would have three children, in 1914; and to Angeline Kreck James in 1937. He served as a flyer in

World War I, and designed the U.S. Embassy (1934) in Moscow. For treatments of characteristic works see chapters 2 and 5.

Litchfield, Electus Darwin

New York   1872–1952

Litchfield was born in New York, and he studied at Brooklyn Polytechnic Institute and Stevens Institute of Technology. He was associated with several architectural firms before 1926, when he established his own office. Although much of his work involved urban planning and civic buildings, Litchfield also designed many Colonial Revival houses, most of which are in Connecticut. Litchfield wrote about country houses for *Architectural Record* in 1915 and 1916. He was an architect of the Red Hook housing project in Queens, New York, and designed Yorkship Village, a World War I industrial town near Camden, New Jersey. Litchfield's further contributions in city planning included the founding of the New York Building Congress, membership in the Building Revision Commission of New York City, and directorship of the Citizens Housing and Planning Council. He designed public structures in several parts of the country, including the Denver Post Office and the National Armory in Washington, D.C. He served as president of the New York Municipal Arts Society.

Little, Arthur

Boston   1852–1925

Born in Boston, Little graduated from MIT in 1875, then studied and traveled in France. After returning to Boston he worked as a draftsman for Peabody and Stearns. In 1878 he opened an office with Herbert Browne (*see* Browne, Herbert W. C.). The firm of Little and Browne, of which Little was senior partner, was considered a pioneer in the Colonial Revival style; an example is the influential Cliffs house of 1879, in Manchester, Massachusetts. Most of the firm's commissions were for residences on Boston's North Shore, but some were for city houses, notably the E. W. Bliss residence in New York City and the Larz Anderson residence in Washington, D.C. Little was knowledgeable about colonial architecture and wrote *Early New England Interiors: Sketches in Salem, Marblehead, Portsmouth and Kittery* (1878). His major works include Cliffs house (1879), Manchester, Massachusetts; the estate of William S. Spaulding, Prides Crossing, Massachusetts; the estate of George Von Meyer, Hamilton, Massachusetts; and Faulkner Farm, Brookline, Massachusetts (later remodeled by Charles Platt). Little's documents are housed in the Avery Library of Columbia University, and the Library of the Society for the Preservation of New England Antiquities.

Lowell, Guy

Boston   1870–1927

Lowell was born in Boston. He graduated from Harvard in 1892, then studied architecture at MIT. He attended the Ecole des Beaux-Arts in Paris during 1895–99, where he studied architectural history, design, and landscape gardening. Upon returning to the United States, he established a practice in Boston. Lowell designed many public structures and school buildings in New England, including buildings at Phillips Academy in Andover, Massachusetts; Simmons College in Boston; Harvard University; and Brown University. His most famous design is the Museum of Fine Arts in Boston. He also designed several estates, including landscaped grounds, in Massachusetts and Long Island, New York. As a professor of landscape architecture at MIT, Lowell influenced a generation of landscape gardeners that rose to prominence in the 1920s and 1930s. He was one of the first American architects to publish a book on contemporary American gardens, *American Gardens* (1902). Lowell also wrote *Smaller Italian Villas and Farmhouses* (1916) in two volumes.

Maher, Gèorge Washington

Chicago   1864–1926

Maher was one of the leading members of the Prairie School in Chicago and is identified with the American Arts and Crafts movement as a furniture designer and architect. He served apprenticeships in Chicago with Bauer and Hill and later with James Lyman Silsbee, with whom Wright also worked. Maher also worked for Adler and Sullivan. In 1888 he opened his own office, specializing in rustic houses in the mode of Silsbee and H. H. Richardson. Near the end of the century he developed his own style, a variant on the decorative and spatial patterns developed by Wright, with some influence from Charles F. A. Voysey and other English designers. He formed a partnership with J. L. Cochran in 1893. His most elaborate houses were designed in the years between 1905 and World War I, culminating in Rock-

ledge (1912), the lavish summer house of pharmaceutical tycoon E. L. King, built over the Mississippi River in Homer, Minnesota.

Manning, Warren Henry

Boston   1860–1938

Born in Reading, Massachusetts, Manning studied landscape architecture by working in his father's nursery business and in Frederick Law Olmsted's office in Brookline. Once established on his own, he designed prolifically for a great variety of commissions. In addition to numerous private estates, Manning landscaped the campuses of Cornell, Johns Hopkins, and Princeton universities. He laid out the park systems of Duluth and Minneapolis, Minnesota, and Harrisburg, Pennsylvania, and consulted on Boston's park system and on Yellowstone and Glacier national parks. Manning was important as an educator and promoter of the fledgling field of American landscape architecture. He was one of the founders and directors of Harvard University's School of Landscape Architecture, and served as president of the American Association of Landscape Architects. He wrote *Thomas Jefferson as an Architect and a Designer of Landscapes* (1913).

McGoodwin, Robert Rodes

Philadelphia   1886–1967

McGoodwin was born in Bowling Green, Kentucky, and studied at the University of Pennsylvania, obtaining a B.S. (1907) and M.S. (1912) in architecture. He received the Brooke Gold Medal in Design from the University of Pennsylvania in 1907. McGoodwin studied at the Academy of Fine Arts, Philadelphia, and won the Cresson Travelling Scholarship in 1908, enabling him to attend the Atelier Duquesne in Paris during 1908–09 and to travel extensively in England, Belgium, France, Switzerland, and Italy. He also studied at the American Academy in Rome. McGoodwin was a designer for Horace Trumbauer from 1907 to 1908 and then went into partnership with Samuel D. Hawley until 1912. McGoodwin taught architecture at the University of Pennsylvania from 1911 to 1925.

Meem, John Gaw

Santa Fe   1894–1983

Meem was born in Relotas, Brazil. In 1910 he attended the Virginia Military Institute, study-

ing civil engineering. He went on to work for his uncle in New York on such projects as the New York City subway. After World War I, Meem returned to Brazil, but he became ill and in 1920 went to a sanitorium in Santa Fe, New Mexico, to recover. In 1922 Meem went to Denver to work for the architects Fisher and Fisher and attended night school at the Atelier Denver, a school affiliated with the Beaux-Arts Institute of Design in New York. Meem returned to Santa Fe in 1924, once again for health reasons. He was a partner in the firm of Meem and McCormick during 1924–29, in Meem, Holien and Buckley during 1956–59, and later worked by himself. Meem designed many residences and civic and school buildings in Colorado and New Mexico. He was also prominent in the early preservation movement in Santa Fe, working on the restoration of New Mexican mission churches and winning a competition for the revitalization of the old Santa Fe plaza. Meem helped found the Old Santa Fe Association, was chairman of the Santa Fe City Planning Commission from 1944 to 1945, and was instrumental in the adoption of the Historic Zoning Ordinance for Santa Fe in 1957. For a treatment of Meem's country house work in the adobe vernacular, see chapter 7.

Mellor and Meigs

Mellor, Walter 1880–1940
Meigs, Arthur C. 1882–1956
Philadelphia

Mellor and Meigs were both born in Philadelphia to wealthy parents. Meigs was connected to the old and influential Ingersoll family. His father, Arthur Vincent Meigs, was a physician. Mellor studied at Haverford and the University of Pennsylvania (1904). Meigs graduated from Princeton University, and worked in the office of Theophilus Chandler during 1903–05 and later for E. V. Seeler. In 1906 the firm of Mellor and Meigs was established and continued for thirty years. (George Howe joined as a third partner in 1916 and left in 1929.) In 1922 the firm received the annual Medal of Award from the Philadelphia chapter of the AIA for the Robert T. McCracken residence in Chesnut Hill; and in 1925 the Gold Medal Award from the New York Architects League for the Arthur E. Newbold estate in Laverock, Pennsylvania. After World War I the firm became the most convincing exponent of the pastoral, vernacular country house associated with the Philadelphia school. For a more extensive biographical treatment and a discussion of major works, see chapter 6.

Mizener, Addison

Palm Beach   1872–1933

This legendary Palm Beach architect and entre-preneur was born in northern California and traveled widely as a youth and young man, especially in South America, Spain, and China. After practicing first in San Francisco and then in New York, he moved to Florida in 1918 for health reasons. Under the patronage of Paris Singer, the sewing machine magnate, he foun-ded the Everglades Club as a rest home and hospital for war veterans. As Palm Beach became fashionable as a winter resort, Mizener took advantage of the Florida boom to found several companies in development and the building trades in order to further his architec-tural work. He typically managed a residential project from top to bottom, promising a com-pleted house within a year, and buying or man-ufacturing everything necessary for its construction and decoration. After his success in Palm Beach, he developed the resort town of Boca Raton beginning in 1925, only to see his fortune dashed in the land bust two years later. His career declined steadily up to his death in 1933. His books include *The Florida Architec-ture of Addison Mizener* (1928), with Ida M. Tar-bell, and *The Many Mizeners* (1932). Mizener's major commissions included El Mirasol (1919), for E. T. Stotesbury, Palm Beach; Casa Bendita (1921), for John S. Phipps, Palm Beach; El Sari-mento (1923), for J. Drexel Biddle, Palm Beach; and Villa Flora (1923), for Edward Shearson, Palm Beach. His documents are housed at the Historical Society of Palm Beach County, West Palm Beach, Florida.

Morgan, Julia

San Francisco   1872–1957

Morgan was born in San Francisco and attended the University of California at Berkeley, where she studied engineering. She was encouraged to pursue architecture by Bernard Maybeck and in 1896 went to the Ecole des Beaux-Arts in Paris. Morgan was the first woman accepted to the architecture division of the Ecole and later became the first licensed woman architect in California. After returning to the United States she collaborated with Maybeck on buildings at Berkeley, worked for John Galen Howard, and in 1903 received her first independent commis-sion for the design of the buildings of Mills College. She went on to design over seven hun-dred buildings, and is noted particularly for her Young Women's Christian Association buildings in California, Utah, and Hawaii, and for her designs for swimming pools. Morgan

worked for over twenty-five years for William Randolph Hearst, designing his estate (1919) in San Simeon as well as the elaborate "camp" complex at Wyntoon, near Mount Shasta.

Neff, Wallace

Los Angeles   1895–1982

Neff was born in La Mirada, California, and spent his early years on his grandfather's ranch. He was educated in Europe, including two years in Munich (1911–13) and a year in Geneva (1913–14), then studied for two years at MIT in the architecture program headed by Ralph Adams Cram. Neff became part of the firm of Neff and Edwards in Santa Barbara in 1919 and opened his own firm in Los Angeles in 1922. He was known as an architect to many Hollywood celebrities, including King Vidor, Douglas Fairbanks and Mary Pickford, Fred-erick March, Amelita Galli-Curci, Charles Chaplin, and Harpo Marx. His work, mainly in Spanish Colonial idioms, has a freedom and flair that pleased his theatrical clients, and he was a popular socialite with considerable per-sonal charm. He seemed to revel in the manip-ulation of plastic form that the Spanish idiom allowed. Neff received many awards from the AIA throughout his career, as well as an award from the Egyptian government for housing he designed in 1951. Late in his career he experi-mented with thin-shell concrete construction for low-cost housing. His finest works include the Arthur K. Bourne house (1925) in San Mar-ino, the Frances Marion and Fred Thomson house (1923–25) in Beverly Hills, and his own house (1928) in San Marino. For a treatment of other characteristic works, see chapter 7.

Peabody, Julian

New York   1881–1935

Peabody was born in New York City and attended Harvard University. After graduating in 1903, he continued his studies in Paris for three years until his return to New York, where he began work as a draftsman. In 1924 the firm of Peabody, Wilson and Brown was established. Peabody was responsible for such buildings as an apartment house at Broadway and 76th Street (1913) in Manhattan and the alterations to the Astor Hotel (1921–22) in New York, and for many large country estates. These include the Georgian Lathrop Brown house in South-ampton, the clapboard George Bacon house in Saint James, and work in Far Hills, New Jersey. The firm also designed a modernist beach house for the Brown family during the 1930s.

Platt, Charles Adams

New York   1861–1933

Platt was born in New York and studied at the National Academy of Design. He began his career as an artist, concentrating on landscape painting and etching. In 1882 Platt went to Europe for five years of study, and on returning to America joined a group of artists in the workshop of the sculptor St. Gaudens. In 1892, he exhibited his paintings in Europe and went on a study trip to document Italian villa gar-dens. With his brother he wrote an influential book on the subject, *Italian Gardens* (1894). He began to design houses for friends in Cornish, New Hampshire, during the 1890s. His first garden designs, the Weld and Faulkner Farms, were extensively published, launching his career in architecture. Between 1900 and 1920 Platt executed a distinguished group of country houses, for which he was awarded the Gold Medal of the Architectural League of New York. His monograph of this work, published in 1913, became the handbook for eclectic designers. Variations on his house designs can be seen in all parts of the United States. In 1916 Platt moved his architectural practice to New York City, and during the 1920s turned his attention to public commissions. He designed many apartment buildings and city homes, as well as such buildings as the Freer Art Gallery in Washington, D.C., the Leader News building in Cleveland, Ohio, and build-ings for Connecticut College, the University of Illinois, and Phillips Andover Academy. Platt retired in 1928 to become president of the American Academy in Rome. For a treatment of Platt's work and a more extensive biography, see chapter 2.

Polk, Willis Jefferson

San Francisco   1867–1924

Polk was born in Jacksonville, Illinois, and had one of the earliest architectural apprenticeships on record — beginning at age eight. He worked in his father's firm in Kansas City and for Henry Van Brunt, the distinguished St. Louis architect. By 1890 he had worked across the country for several other firms, eventually com-ing to New York and the office of Charles B. Atwood. His link to the Beaux-Arts, to San Francisco, and to McKim, Mead and White came through his employment with A. Page Brown. Polk moved with Brown to San Fran-cisco in 1889. While in Brown's office he met J. C. Schweinfurth and Ernest Coxhead. These architects became associated with a significant regional eclectic movement in the Bay Area at the turn of the century. Polk was perhaps the most versatile of these designers, working in crisp, classical styles and rustic, English idioms, and he is remembered for his proto-modern Hallidie Building (1918) and his grand Bourn House (1895–96). He formed the firm of Polk and Polk in 1892 and worked for ten years, then worked for Daniel Burnham from 1902 to 1905. He resumed his San Francisco practice on his own and designed a number of the finest eclectic estates, including Uplands (*see* chapter 3), Filoli, and The Bend (1898–99) for Charles Stetson Wheeler, one of the early rustic camps, which eventually became part of the Hearst complex near McCloud, California.

Pope, John Russell

New York   1874–1937

Pope was born in New York City. He attended the College of the City of New York and Columbia University, where he studied under William R. Ware. Pope won several scholar-ships and subsequently spent two years at the American Academy in Rome (he was among the first students to study there), then studied the Ecole des Beaux-Arts in Paris in 1900. After returning to New York he worked for Bruce Price, and met and was inspired by Charles McKim. Pope opened offices in New York in 1903 and designed many public struc-tures and homes in the United States and abroad. He did most of his country house work between 1904 and 1925, after which public buildings occupied his attention. His major monumental works include the Jefferson Memorial and the National Gallery in Wash-ington, D.C., and additions to the Tate Gallery and British Museum in London. He received honors from many organizations, including the AIA, the Institute of France, and the Royal Institute of British Architects. For further dis-cussion of Pope's country house work and career, see chapter 2.

Reid, Joseph Neel

Atlanta   1885–1926

Reid was born in Macon, Georgia, and received training while working in the office of Willis F. Denny. He also studied at Columbia University and at the ateliers of the Ecole des Beaux-Arts in Paris. He worked for the New York office of Murphy and Dana, then went back to Georgia in 1909 and opened the office of Normann, Hentz and Reid, which became the firm of Hentz, Reid and Adler in 1913. He specialized in public buildings and residential work where he coordinated interiors, gardens, and architec-ture. His death at age forty-one cut short a

brilliant career. For a discussion of Reid's mas-terpiece, Hills and Dales, see chapter 7.

Riddle, Theodate Pope

New York   1867–1946

Riddle was born in Salem, Ohio, and was one of the pioneering women in American architec-ture. The daughter of wealthy Cleveland busi-nessman Alfred Atwood Pope, she began her career as a dilettante, working with McKim, Mead and White on the design of her parents' country house in Farmington, Connecticut (*see* chapter 6). Although she received tutoring in architecture at Princeton during the 1890s, Theodate was largely self-taught. Establishing herself as an architect in Connecticut around 1905, she worked on the Charles O. Gates estate, Dormer House (1913–14), at Locust Val-ley, Long Island, and Westover School in Mid-dlebury, Connecticut (1907–09). Riddle also designed Avon Old Farms (1930) in Avon, Con-necticut, built with deliberately sagging roofs, and the John Perkins Chamberlain house in Middlebury. In 1916 she married John Wallace Riddle, a foreign service officer and ambassador to Russia and Argentina. That year she was cer-tified as an architect in New York State, and in 1918 she became a member of the AIA. She was appointed in 1919 as restoration and recon-struction architect for the Theodore Roosevelt Memorial in New York. Some of her letters and diaries are at the Hill-Stead Museum in Farmington.

Rogers, James Gamble

New York   1867–1947

Rogers was born in Kentucky. He studied first at Yale, then for five years at the Ecole des Beaux-Arts in Paris. Rogers returned to Amer-ica in 1897 and opened an office in Chicago, where he stayed for seven years. From 1904 to 1907 he was a partner of Herbert Hale of Bos-ton in the firm of Hale and Rogers, then worked alone from 1907 to 1923. In 1923 he opened the office of James Gamble Rogers, Inc. During the last year of his life he consulted with his son's firm. Rogers was not noted as a country house architect, though he did design major estates for his favorite patrons, including the Harkness family in Madison, New Jersey, and the Colt family in Garrison, New York.

Schmidt, Mott B.

New York   1889–1977

Schmidt was born in Middletown, New York. He studied architecture at the Pratt Institute, graduating in 1906. He spent four years abroad, then returned to the United States to establish his own firm in 1912. Through his association with Elsie de Wolfe, Schmidt obtained his first large commission as architect of several houses at Sutton Place in New York, including those for Anne Morgan (1920) and Mrs. W. K. Vanderbilt (1921). He made a spe-cialty of Colonial Revival styles, particulary redbrick Georgian. His work was nearly always crisp, restrained, and classical, as in the Robert Adam–inspired Vincent Astor house (1925), which now houses the Junior League of New York. Following World War II, when many of his contemporaries had died or retired, he con-tinued a flourishing eclectic practice in the suburban country house field. In 1966 he designed a two-story addition to Gracie Man-sion for the mayor of New York City in a Fed-eral idiom, which remains his best-known work. Schmidt's major country houses include Hudson Pines (1938) for Abby Rockefeller Mil-ton; Marienruh (1926) for the Astor family in Rhinebeck, New York; Rabbit Hill (1929) for William S. Lambie in Scarborough, New York; and Pook's Hill (1926) for himself in Bedford, New York. His house (1936) for C. Douglas Dillon at Far Hills is one of the most handsome late Georgian country houses in America. Schmidt's drawings are in the Avery Architec-tural Archives at Columbia University.

Schneider, Charles S.

Cleveland   1874–1932

Schneider was born and educated in Cleveland and trained in architecture at the firm of Mead and Garfield. He studied at the Ecole des Beaux-Arts in Paris, then began to work as a draftsman in 1901. He eventually worked with New York's esteemed George B. Post on the Statler Hotel in Cleveland, and in 1912 opened his own office. During the last twenty years of his life, Schneider designed several buildings in the Shaker Heights section of Cleveland, including the Plymouth Congregational Church, as well as school and civic buildings throughout the region. He became a fellow of the AIA in 1923. His best-known country house is the lavish Elizabethan manor Stan Hywet (1911–15) for tire mogul Frank A. Seiberling in Akron, Ohio.

Schutze, Phillip Trammell

Atlanta 1890–1982

Schutze was born in Columbus, Georgia. He studied architecture at the Georgia Institute of Technology with the aid of a scholarship, and graduated in 1912. In his spare time he worked for the Atlanta firm of Hentz and Reid. Schultze continued his studies at Columbia University and went on to Europe after winning the Prix de Rome in 1915. In 1920 he returned to America and worked in New York with F. Burrall Hoffman, Jr., architect of Villa Vizcaya in Miami, and with Mott Schmidt. Schutze left New York for Atlanta in 1923 and joined his old employers, now known as Hentz, Reid and Adler. He became a full partner in 1926. Among his notable domestic works are the Calhoun-Thornwell house (1919–22) in Atlanta, the Swan house (1926–28) for Mr. and Mrs. Edward Inman in Atlanta, and the English-Chambers house (1929). He designed several plantation-influenced country houses in the 1940s and 1950s in the South, and was among the last of the eclectic masters to practice.

Shaw, Howard Van Doren

Chicago 1869–1926

Shaw was born in Chicago to affluent parents. He attended Yale from 1887 to 1890, studied architecture at MIT, and traveled extensively in Europe and the Orient. He returned to Chicago in 1895 and worked in the office of Jenny and Mundie for two years, then established his own office in Chicago. Shaw was known for his houses and gardens on the North Shore and for his own home, Ragdale (1898) in Lake Forest, Illinois. His works include Donnelley's Printing House and the Lakeshore Country Club in Chicago; Market Square in Lake Forest, Illinois; and Memorial Hall (1925) in Racine, Wisconsin. See chapters 2 and 5 for a more complete treatment of his life and selected country house work.

Shipman, Ellen Biddle

New York 1870–1950

Shipman, who was born to wealthy Philadelphia parents as Ellen McGowen Biddle, graduated from Radcliffe College. Her knowledge of horticulture was acquired informally through the genteel pursuit of gardening with such friends as Maria Dewing. Shipman was in many respects a protégée of Charles Platt, with whom she and her husband, playwright Louis Shipman, spent summers in Cornish. The two

artists collaborated on several of his important gardens, notably The Manor House (1909) in Glen Cove for John T. Pratt. Shipman maintained a fierce independence and a feminist profile throughout her long career as a garden designer, maintaining that without women, the golden age of American landscape architecture would not have occurred. After establishing her career, she taught at the influential Lowthorpe School in Groton and at the Cambridge School of Architecture and Landscape Architecture—both restricted to women. Her landscape commissions were largely estate gardens; she distinguished herself with such works as Rynwood (1927) at Glen Cove, Long Island, for Samuel Salvage, and Longue Vue Gardens (late 1930s) near New Orleans for Edgar B. Stern. Her papers and drawings are collected at Cornell University.

Shurcliff, Arthur A.

Boston 1870–1957

Shurcliff was a landscape architect and town planner. He was born in Boston and educated at MIT (1894) and Harvard (1896). He helped to found the Harvard School of Landscape Architecture. Shurcliff was the senior partner of Shurcliff, Shurcliff and Merrill—the firm responsible for the planning of over forty communities, mostly in New England, and for redesigning the Boston Common in 1918 and the Esplanade (Storrow Memorial Embankment) along the Charles River Basin. Shurcliff also designed over fifty private estates and buildings for schools and colleges. His largest and best known garden is Castle Hill, the Crane estate in Ipswich, Massachusetts, planted during the late 1920s. He was a noted authority on Early American gardens, and was the landscape architect for the restoration of Colonial Williamsburg during 1929–33.

Smith, George Washington

Santa Barbara 1876–1930

Smith was born in East Liberty, Pennsylvania. He studied in Philadelphia at the Academy of Fine Arts and at Harvard. In 1912 Smith went to Europe for travel and study and remained there until the beginning of World War I. After returning to America, he opened an office in Montecito, California, and received his first commission in 1919. Smith specialized in residential work, adapting the Spanish style to California homes. For a treatment of his life and two major houses, see chapter 6.

Spencer, Robert C.

Chicago 1864–1953

Born in Milwaukee, Spencer graduated from the University of Wisconsin in 1886 with a degree in mechanical engineering. He studied architecture at MIT from 1886 to 1890, then traveled for three years in Europe. He returned to the United States in 1893, joining the firm of Shepley, Rutan and Coolidge at their branch office in Chicago. A year later Spencer opened his own firm, eventually establishing his office in the Schiller Building in downtown Chicago, next door to the office of Frank Lloyd Wright. Spencer specialized in designing Tudor and Tudor–prairie style houses, such as the H. W. Kelsey house (1898) in Wilmette, Illinois; the U. F. Orendorff house (1902) in Canton; the Adams house (1903) in Indianapolis; the August Magnus house (1905) in Winettka; the E. P. Wells house (1907) in Hinsdale; and the Susan Denckman-Hauberg house (1909–10) in Rock Island. Spencer's domestic work in Chicago provided a middle ground between Wright's abstracted geometric prairie houses and the Arts and Crafts influenced work of Howard Shaw.

Staub, John

Houston 1892–1981

Staub was born in Knoxville, Tennessee, and attended the University of Tennessee and MIT's architectural school, graduating with a master's degree in 1916. His apprenticeship was spent with Harrie T. Lindeberg in New York. It was Lindeberg's work in Houston that brought Staub to the Southwest and eventually led him to set up a practice there, in 1921. In 1923 Staub was asked by Kenneth Womack and William Stamps Farish to design the country club they were planning in what would become Houston's largest and best-known garden suburb, River Oaks. Staub soon became Houston's foremost domestic architect, designing approximately fifty buildings in the subdivision alone. An extremely capable planner, he made each formal, Georgian house work every bit as well as a picturesque French or English Arts and Crafts house. His most notable works include Ravenna (1934), a grand Palladian block with dependencies for Mr. and Mrs. Stephen Farish; the Mr. and Mrs. Harry Hanszen house (1930); the William J. Crabb house (1935), convincingly designed in the Spanish Colonial style; the "pure Louis XV" house (1931) of Robert J. Neal; the Beaux-Arts and Regency style house (1933) for Hugh Roy Cullen; and his Louisiana plantation style houses for Ray L. Dudley (1935) and Ernest Bel Fay

(1937). His practice with John Thomas Rather, Jr., from 1942 to 1971, produced one of the largest oeuvres of any eclectic specialists.

Swartwout, Edgerton

New York   1870–1943

Born in Fort Wayne, Indiana, Swartwout studied at Yale and worked for McKim, Mead and White. In 1900 he began a twenty-year partnership with Evarts Tracy. Swartwout received many awards from the AIA and the French Society of Beaux Arts Architects, among others. He wrote two books: *The Classic Orders of Architecture* (1918), and *Use of the Orders in Modern Architecture* (1920).

Trumbauer, Horace

Philadelphia   1868–1938

Trumbauer was born in Philadelphia and was educated in public schools. At age sixteen he apprenticed in the office of G. W. and W. D. Hewitt, where he worked until 1890, when he opened his own office. Trumbauer obtained early commissions through the Houstons, on whose estate the Hewitts had worked. In 1892 he designed Grey Towers for W. W. Harrison, and subsequent works included Lynnwood Hall for P. A. B. Widener and the Widener Memorial Library (1919) at Harvard. Although he generally preferred eighteenth-century French classicism, he designed in all styles. In 1902 he took on Julian Abele, the first black graduate of the University of Pennsylvania, as his chief designer. Trumbauer won first prize at the Third Pan-American Conference of Architects in 1927, and received an honorary M.A. from Harvard. See chapters 2 and 3 for discussions of Trumbauer's work and influence.

Volk, John

Palm Beach   1901–1984

Born in Graz, Austria, Volk came to the United States in 1909. He attended Columbia's architecture program and studied at the Ecole des Beaux-Arts in Paris. He later worked in New York for H. P. Knowles, then opened an office in Palm Beach in 1925. He followed Addison Mizener's Mediterranean idiom during the 1930s, and other styles, including modern, during the rest of his career. His clients included Horace Dodge, William Paley, Nicholas du Pont, George Storer, Herbert Pulitzer, and Matthew Mellon. Volk's work is represented in the collections of the Historical Society of Palm Beach County, West Palm Beach, Florida.

Williams, David

Dallas   1890–1962

Williams, one of the leading Texas regionalists, was born in Childress, Texas, on October 17, 1890. He was largely self-educated, pursuing correspondence courses until he entered the engineering school at the University of Texas at Austin, specializing in architecture, in 1912. From 1916 to 1921 he worked as an engineer and architect for American oil companies in Mexico. In 1921 he traveled to Europe, attending the New York School of Fine and Applied Arts in Paris and the American Academy in Rome. At age thirty-three he returned to America, first to New York and then to Dallas, where he opened his office in 1924. Major commissions included Greenway Parks (1923) in Dallas, a suburban park development; the Raworth Williams house (1926); the Ray McDowell house (1927), the first of his "indigenous" houses; the F. N. Drane house (1928–29), his most challenging commission; and the Elbert Williams house (1932), which gained national attention as an urbanized "ranch" house. In 1933 he entered government service and worked in various depression-era programs to create new housing. He continued to work for the government until after World War II. In 1960 he became a fellow of the AIA.

Wills, Royal Barry

Boston   1895–1962

Wills, designer of over 2,500 homes, was born in Melrose, Massachusetts. He graduated from MIT in 1918. After World War I he worked as a designer for a shipbuilder in Philadelphia, then as a construction engineer for Turner Construction Company, and in 1925 opened his own firm in Boston, specializing in Early American domestic design. In 1932 he received a Gold Medal from President Hoover for the best small home of the year, and continued to win acclaim for his work in housing. Wills wrote several books, including *Houses for Good Living* (1940), *Houses for Homemakers* (1945), and *Tree Houses* [for children] (1947). He became known for his homespun writing aimed at middle-class Americans as well as for his trim, functional adaptations of eclectic styles to modern suburban lots.

Winslow, Carleton Monroe

Los Angeles   1876–1946

Winslow was born in Maine, and studied at the Chicago Art Institute and in Paris. He came to California in 1911 and designed the U.S. building for the San Diego Panama-Pacific Exposition of 1915, in a Spanish Colonial style. He established offices in Los Angeles and Santa Barbara in 1917. Winslow specialized in churches and public buildings. His best-known Spanish design is Casa Dorinda, the William Bliss house in Santa Barbara.

Wurster, William Wilson

San Francisco   1895–1973

Wurster is best known as the founding dean of the College of Environmental Design at the University of California at Berkeley. Born in Stockton, California, Wurster studied architecture at Berkeley. He began his own practice in San Francisco in 1926. Among his noted early domestic works was the Gregory Ranch (1927) in Santa Cruz, an overtly regionalist country house. He continued his studies at Harvard and MIT, and from 1944 to 1950 was dean of architecture and planning at MIT. Wurster returned to California and served as chairman of the architecture department at Berkeley from 1950 to 1959, then as dean of the new College of Environmental Design from 1959 to 1963. He established the firm of Wurster, Bernardi and Emmons in 1945. The firm won several AIA awards and functioned very much as a team, designing such San Francisco landmarks as Ghirardelli Square and the Bank of America building.

Wyeth, Marion Syms

Florida   1889–1982

Wyeth was a member of the Palm Beach Mediterranean school associated with Addison Mizener. Born in New York, he graduated from Princeton University in 1910, studied at the Ecole des Beaux-Arts from 1910 to 1914, and spent a year in Rome with the Foreign Service. He returned to New York and apprenticed with Bertram Goodhue and Carrère and Hastings before serving in the Air Corps in World War I. After moving to Palm Beach in 1919, Wyeth quickly rose to prominence as a domestic specialist in the Palm Beach style. His society clients included E. F. Hutton, John S. Pillsbury, Franklin P. Smith, Clarence Geist, and Alexander McKinloch. One of his notable small commissions was the Dutch South African Village in Coral Gables, Florida. His documents are in the Historical Society of Palm Beach County, West Palm Beach, Florida.

Arthur Ingersoll Meigs
(Athenaeum of Philadelphia)

George Howe, 1926 (Earle Shettleworth,
MHPC*)

Grosvenor Atterbury (Earle
Shettleworth, MHPC)

Frederick L. Ackerman, 1921 (Earle
Shettleworth, MHPC)

John M. Carrère (Earle Shettleworth,
MHPC)

Thomas Hastings, 1899 (Earle
Shettleworth, MHPC)

Edmund B. Gilchrist, 1932 (Earle
Shettleworth, MHPC)

Ernest Flagg, 1899 (Earle Shettleworth,
MHPC)

Horace Trumbauer as a young man
(Collection of Alfred Branam, Jr.)

Robert C. Spencer (Earle Shettleworth,
MHPC)

Walter Cope, 1902 (Earle Shettleworth,
MHPC)

Richard Morris Hunt. Portrait bust
(Architectural Annual, 1900)

Charles Adams Platt (Brickbuilder,
1915)

Wilson Eyre (Architectural Annual,
1900)

Harrie T. Lindeberg. (Barnstone,
The Architecture of John F. Staub)

Donn Barber (Earle Shettleworth,
MHPC)

*Maine Historic Preservation Commission

Appendix
Three Generations of Architects

Architect	Date of birth	Education	Apprenticeship
Those Born Between 1850 and 1870			
Andrews, Robert	1857	MIT	H. H. Richardson
Atterbury, Grosvenor	1869	Yale, Columbia, Ecole des Beaux-Arts (EBA)	None
Bacon, Henry	1866	Univ. of Illinois	McKim, Mead & White (MMW)
Bosworth, William	1869	MIT, EBA	Carrère & Hastings
Brite, James	1864	Secondary	MMW
Browne, Herbert	1860	Boston Museum of Fine Arts	Jacques & Rantoul
Carrère, John M.	1858	EBA	MMW
Codman, Ogden	1863	MIT	John Hubbard Sturgis
Cope, Walter	1860	Secondary	Addison Hutton; Theophilus Chandler
Day, Frank Miles	1861	Univ. of Penn., London	B. Champneys; Hutton
Eyre, Wilson	1858	MIT	James Peacock Sims
Faville, William	1866	MIT	MMW; Green & Wicks
Flagg, Ernest	1857	EBA	None
Hastings, Thomas	1860	Columbia, EBA	MMW
Hoppin, Francis	1867	Brown, MIT, EBA	MMW
Howells, John M.	1868	Harvard, EBA	MMW
Hunt, Joseph	1870	Harvard, Columbia, EBA	R. M. Hunt
Hunt, Myron	1868	MIT, Europe	Shepley, Rutan & Coolidge (SRC)
Hunt, Richard H.	1862	MIT, EBA	R. M. Hunt
Keen, Charles B.	1868	Univ. of Penn. Museum	Chandler
Little, Arthur	1852	MIT	Peabody & Stearns
Platt, Charles	1861	Painting at EBA	None
Polk, Willis	1867	Secondary	A. Page Brown; H. Van Brunt
Pope, Theodate	1867	Princeton	MMW
Rogers, James	1867	Yale, EBA	Jenny & Mundie
Shaw, Howard	1869	Yale, MIT	Jenny & Mundie
Spencer, Robert	1864	Univ. of Wisconsin	SRC
Stewardson, John	1858?	EBA	Chandler
Swartwout, Egerton	1870	Yale	MMW
Trumbauer, Horace	1868	Secondary	Hewitt & Hewitt
Warren, Whitney	1864	Columbia, EBA	MMW
Those Born Between 1870 and 1880			
Ackerman, Frederick	1878	Cornell, EBA	None?
Aldrich, Chester	1871	Columbia, EBA	Carrère & Hastings
Ayres, Atlee	1874	Art Students' League of NY	Mexican firm
Barber, Donn	1871	Yale, Columbia, EBA	Carrère & Hastings
Briscoe, Birdsall	1876	Texas A & M	?
Brown, Arthur	1874	Univ. of Calif. Berkeley, EBA	?
Brown, Frank C.	1876	Secondary	Plant & Kelly
Byers, John	1875	Michigan, Harvard	None
Delano, William A.	1874	Yale, Columbia, EBA	Carrère & Hastings
Dominick, William	1870	Yale, Columbia	MMW

Architect	Date of birth	Education	Apprenticeship
During, Louis	1874	Univ. of Penn.	Furness & Evans
Embury, Aymar, II	1880	Princeton	?
Gill, Irving	1870	Secondary	Louis Sullivan
Gillette, Leon	1878	Univ. of Penn., EBA	Warren & Wetmore
Gregory, Julius	1875	Univ. of Calif. Berkeley	?
Hobart, L.	1873	Univ. of Calif. Berkeley, Rome, Beaux-Arts Inst.	?
Hopkins, Alfred	1870	EBA	?
Janssen, Benno	1874	EBA	SRC; Parker, Thomas & Rice
Lindeberg, Harrie	1880	National Acad. of Design, NY	MMW
Litchfield, Electus	1872	Stephens Inst. of Tech.	MMW?
Mizener, Addison	1872	Secondary	Arthur Brown
Morgan, Julia	1872	Univ. of Calif. Berkeley, EBA	J. G. Howard; Bernard Maybeck
Pope, John R.	1874	Columbia, EBA, American Acad. Rome	Bruce Price
Schneider, Charles	1874	EBA	G. B. Post; Mead & Garfield
Smith, G. W.	1876	Harvard, Penn. Acad. of Fine Arts	Philadelphia firms
Winslow, Carleton	1876	Art Inst. of Chicago	Bertram Goodhue

Those Born in 1880 and After

Architect	Date of birth	Education	Apprenticeship
Adler, David	1882	Princeton, Munich Polytechnic, EBA	Howard Shaw
Ayres, Robert	1898	Univ. of Penn.	Murchison, Lamb & French
Baum, Dwight J.	1886	Syracuse Univ.	?
Bottomley, W. L.	1883	Columbia, EBA	Heinz & LaFarge
Bullard, Roger	1884	Columbia	Grosvenor Atterbury
Clark, Cameron	1887	MIT, American Acad. in Rome	?
Coate, Roland	1890	Cornell	Trowbridge & Ackerman
Fatio, Maurice	1897	Zurich Polytechnic	Harrie Lindeberg
Ford, O'Neil	1905	None	David Williams
Forster, Frank	1886	Cooper Union	?
Gilchrist, Edmund	1885	Drexel Inst. of Tech., Univ. of Penn.	W. Eyre & H. Trumbauer
Hoffman, F. Burrall	1882	Harvard, EBA	Carrère & Hastings
Hood, Raymond	1881	MIT, EBA	Cram, Goodhue & Ferguson
Howe, George	1886	Harvard, EBA	Mellor & Meigs
Johnson, Reginald	1882	MIT, Paris	?
Kaufmann, Gordon	1888	London Polytechnic	?
Koch, Richard	1889	Tulane, EBA	Embury; Pope; Bosworth
Kocher, Lawrence	1885	Stanford, MIT, Penn. State, NYU	?
McGoodwin, Robert	1886	Univ. of Penn., EBA	Trumbauer
Meem, John	1894	Virginia Military Inst.	Denver firm
Meigs, Arthur	1882	Princeton	Chandler
Mellor, Walter	1880	Haverford, Univ. of Penn.	Chandler
Neff, Wallace	1895	MIT, Europe	None
Peabody, Julian	1881	Harvard, Paris	?
Reid, J. Neel	1887	Columbia, EBA	Murphy & Dana; Mott Schmidt
Schmidt, Mott	1889	Pratt Inst.	Not available
Schutze, Philip	1890	Georgia Inst. of Tech., Columbia, EBA	Henze & Reid
Staub, John	1892	Univ. of Tennessee, MIT	Harrie Lindeberg
Volk, John	1901	Columbia, EBA	H. P. Knowles
Williams, David	1890	Univ. of Texas, American Acad. Rome	?
Wills, Royal Barry	1895	MIT	Turner Construction
Wurster, William	1895	Univ. of Calif. Berkeley	Delano & Aldrich
Wyeth, Marion	1889	Princeton, EBA	Carrère & Hastings; Goodhue

Notes

Epigraph (p. v): Ralph Adams Cram, *The Ministry of Art,* 1914, 21–63; quoted in Leland Roth, *America Builds,* New York, Harper and Row, 1983, 459–460.

1   Rich Men and Their Houses

Epigraphs: Donald G. Mitchell, *Rural Studies, With Hints for Country Places,* New York, Scribner's, 1867, 44; Harry W. Desmond and Herbert Croly, *Stately Homes in America,* New York, D. Appleton, 1903, 3.

1. For information on the house, see Gerald Allen and Mark Hewitt, "Biltmore," *Via 6: Architecture and Visual Perception,* Journal of the Graduate School of Fine Arts, University of Pennsylvania, Cambridge, Mass., 1983, 130–141; Paul R. Baker, *Richard Morris Hunt,* Cambridge, MIT Press, 1980, 413–431; Nicholas Cooper, "Biltmore, North Carolina," *Country Life* 159 (1 January 1976): 18–21.

2. Henry James, *The American Scene,* ed. Leon Edel, Bloomington, University of Illinois Press, 1968, 395–402.

3. Cornelius (b. 1843), William Kissam (b. 1849), and Frederick William (b. 1855). In 1883 the two elder brothers took over the Vanderbilt railroad and shipping empire from their father, splitting control of the several companies. For a synopsis of their lives, see *National Cyclopedia of American Biography,* vol. 6, 211–213.

4. See *Dictionary of American Biography,* vol. 19, 174–175, for a detailed account of Vanderbilt's life. He lived in New York with his widowed mother until her death in 1898. On June 2 of that year he married Edith Stuyvesant Dresser who bore him one child, Cornelia.

5. Mark Girouard, *The Victorian Country House,* New Haven, Yale University Press, 1979, 92–93.

6. *New York Sun,* 29 June 1890; quoted in Laura Wood Roper, *FLO: A Biography,* Baltimore, Johns Hopkins University Press, 1973, 416, 530.

7. James, *The American Scene,* 396–397. Though the author does not mention Biltmore by name, it is clear that he is speaking of the house.

8. Born on 11 June 1907, to Pittsburgh financier and former Secretary of the Treasury Andrew W. Mellon. He married Mary Conover on 2 February 1935, and built the house for her. She died in October 1946. See *Who's Who in America,* 1972–73, vol. 2, 2153.

9. "The Reminiscences of William Adams Delano," unpublished oral memoir, Columbia University, New York, 1972, 48.

10. Delano designed a house in Syosset, Long Island, for Paul Mellon's sister, Mrs. David Bruce, which he "had visited frequently and . . . admired." Letter from Paul Mellon to the author, 22 July 1985.

11. Warren Susman, "The Culture of The Thirties," in *Culture As History: The Transformation of American Society in the Twentieth Century,* New York, Pantheon, 1984, 150–183. Susman argues that "it is not too extreme to propose that it was during the Thirties that the idea of culture was domesticated, with important consequences. Americans then began thinking in terms of patterns of behavior and belief, values and life-styles, symbols and meanings. It was during this period that we find, for the first time, frequent reference to an 'American Way of Life'" (154).

12. Ferdinand Lundberg, *America's Sixty Families,* New York, Vanguard, 1937. Lundberg estimated the Mellon family fortune to be between $450 million and $1 billion in 1937.

13. "Lake Forest, Illinois," *House and Garden* 5, no. 6 (June 1904): 275.

14. For a treatment of the social and historical issues related to the upper class during this era, see Dixon Wecter, *The Saga of American Society,* New York, Scribner's, 1937; Robert H. Wiebe, *The Search for Order, 1877–1920,* New York, Hill and Wang, 1967; T. J. Jackson Lears, *No Place of Grace,* New York, Pantheon, 1981; Allan Trachtenberg, *The Incorporation of America,* New York, 1983.

15. Herbert Gans, *Popular Culture and High Culture: An Analysis of the Evolution of Taste,* New York, Basic Books, 1974.

16. *House and Garden* was founded in 1901, as was *Country Life in America,* which ran until 1942; *American Homes and Gardens* ran from 1905 to 1915, *Arts and Decoration* from 1910 to 1942; *Antiques* was founded in 1922, and *Town and Country* in 1846.

17. See, for instance, E. P. Powell, "The American Country House," *House and Garden* 8, no. 5 (December 1905): 221; Horace B. Mann, "Style in the Country House," *American Architect* 107, no. 2055 (12 May 1915): 294; Fiske Kimball, "American Country House," *Architectural Record* (hereafter cited as *AR*) 46, no. 4 (October 1919): 291–349.

18. E. Digby Baltzell, *The Protestant Establishment,* New York, Random House, 1969, 110.

19. Ibid.

20. Listed in Rexford Guy Tugwell, Thomas Munro, and Roy E. Stryker, *American Economic Life and the Means of Its Improvement,* New York, Harcourt, Brace, 1925, 98: Henry Ford, $550 million; John D. Rockefeller, $500 million; Percy Rockefeller, J. B. Duke, and George F. Baker, $100 million each. Family wealth: Guggenheims, $200 million; Vanderbilts, $75 million; Astors, $100 million; Mellons, $75 million.

21. Lundberg, *Sixty Families,* 1937.

22. Cited in Desmond and Croly, *Stately Homes,* 31.

23. These compounds and estates are described in detail by Lundberg, 420–432. The Pratt, DuPont, and Rockefeller families owned the largest compounds of individual houses. Lattingtown, Long Island, was incorporated as a village by Aldred, George F. Baker, J. P. Morgan, Harvey D. Gibson, S. Parker Gilbert, Clarence H. Mackay, and William D. Guthrie so that they could impose their own property taxes (430).

24. Kenneth Jackson, *Crabgrass Frontier: The Suburbanization of the United States,* New York, Oxford University Press, 1985, 97–99; Baltzell, *The Protestant Establishment,* 212–227; J. C. Furnas, *The Americans: A Social History of the United States, 1587–1940,* New York, Putnam's, 1969, 815–817.

25. James, *The American Scene,* 322–323.

26. Baltzell, *The Protestant Establishment,* 213.

27. Ibid., 114–115.

28. "The country estates exhibit various special features. Some are grouped by families; some represent self-incorporated villages established to reduce taxes for a number of families; and others are units in an international chain of residences." Lundberg, *Sixty Families,* 428–429.

29. James, *The American Scene,* 166.

30. Desmond and Croly, *Stately Homes,* 36.

31. Kimball, "The American Country House," *AR* 46, no. 4 (October 1919): 293.

32. Thorstein Veblen, *Theory of the Leisure Class,* 1899, reprint, New York, Viking, 1931. See especially "Pecuniary Canons of Taste," 115–166. Veblen discusses several issues related to the desire for country estates, large houses, a rustic and archaic life, and the emulation of aristocratic codes of behavior and dress. "The leisure class lives by the industrial community rather than in it" (246).

33. For a social analysis of earlier manor houses and country estates, see Roger Kennedy, *Architecture, Men, Women and Money in America, 1600–1860,* New York, Random House, 1985.

34. Kimball, "American Country House," 293.

35. Dept. of Commerce, Bureau of the Census, *Historical Statistics of the United States,* 2 vols., Washington, D.C., 1975, table A43–72.

36. Dept. of Commerce, Bureau of the Census, *Abstract of the Fourteenth Census, 1920,* Washington, D.C., 1923, table 18, 87–89.

37. See Kenneth Jackson, "A Nation of Suburbs," *Chicago History* 13, no. 2 (Summer 1984): 6–25; and Baltzell, *The Protestant Establishment,* 109–129. As Baltzell says, "The prosperity of this new urban-corporate world was largely built upon the blood and sweat of the men, and the tears of the women, who came to this country in such large numbers from the peasant villages of Southern and Eastern Europe" (111). He argues that the "social defense of caste" mandated a "quest for homogeneity" in such institutions as the elite suburb, the country house, the summer resort, and the country club.

38. The period literature is filled with contradictory labels. Even the *American Country Houses of To-Day* series includes examples that vary widely in type, location, social purpose, and lot size, from houses now thought to be suburban to resort cottages.

39. Peter T. Schmitt, *Back To Nature: The Arcadian Myth in Urban America, 1900–1930,* New York, Oxford University Press, 1969.

40. Kimball, "American Country House," 310.

41. Bruce Price, "The Suburban House," *Scribner's Magazine,* 8, no. 1 (July 1890): 5–19. See also, in the same issue, Donald G. Mitchell, "The Country House," 314–335.

42. Powell, "The American Country House," 221.

43. See, for instance, "The Point of View," editorial in *AR* 9 (1900): 394–395.

44. See "Comfort," in Tugwell et al., *American Economic Life.*

45. For a treatment of the problems of definition, see Richard Guy Wilson, "Picturesque Ambiguities: The Country House Tradition in America," in Bedford, ed., *The Long Island Country House, 1870–1930,* Southampton, N. Y., Parrish Art Gallery, 13–36.

46. Michael A. Tomlan, "Architectural Press, U.S.," in *Wiley Encyclopedia of Architecture: Design, Engineering and Construction,* ed. Joseph A. Wilkes and Robert T. Packard, vol. 1, John Wiley, New York, 1988, 269.

47. Thomas Bender, *New York Intellect: A History of Intellectual Life in New York City, from 1750 to the Beginnings of Our Own Time,* Baltimore, Johns Hopkins University Press, 1987, 222.

48. David Levy, *Herbert Croly of the New Republic,* Princeton, Princeton University Press, 1985, 3–13, 46–72.

49. The first issue appeared in July 1891, under the editorship of Harry W. Desmond. Both journals were owned by the F. W. Dodge Corporation, directed by Clinton Sweet. Croly wrote for the *Record and Guide* during the late 1880s before moving to the sister publication. See Levy, *Herbert Croly,* 72–85.

50. *American Builder* (1868–95) was the first sustained architectural periodical in the United States. From 1874 to 1876 an important transitional journal appeared, *The New York Sketch Book of Architecture,* to which both Charles McKim and Montgomery Schuyler contributed. *American Architect and Building News* (*AABN*) began publication in 1876 and remained the leading professional periodical until *Record* rose to preeminence after 1900. The *AABN* absorbed several other journals during its period of publication and changed its title accordingly. Other important professional periodicals included the *Architectural Review* (Boston) (1891–1921), *Scientific American Building*

Monthly (1885–1905), *Architecture and Building* (1882–1932), and *Brickbuilder* (1892–1916).

51. For an incisive analysis of Croly's views on the role of the critic in American society and of the metropolitan intellectual, see Bender, *New York Intellect,* 222–228.

52. Croly reviewed this book in the *Architectural Record,* in one of his finest pieces on the nature of the American country house and its site planning. He felt that the book did not fully define the type and did so himself by distinguishing large estates (of up to five hundred acres) from villas (on three or four acres of suburban land). He pointed out that country houses were built by wealthy men who wished to have a place within two hours of their city businesses, in order to connect their families to the tradition of the manor house or plantation. He recognized that this connection was merely ornamental and speculated that this was one reason why the early stately homes seemed to have little real sense of belonging to their place. He called for a new awareness of garden design and its relationship to landscape, which would be fulfilled by the school of early twentieth-century landscape gardeners of whom Platt was the father. See "The American Country Estate," *AR* 18 (July 1905): 1–7.

53. Joy Wheeler Dow, *American Renaissance: A Review of Domestic Architecture,* New York, Comstock, 1904.

54. Barr Ferree, *American Estates and Gardens,* New York, Munn, 1904. For a discussion of Veblen's cultural influence, see Henry Steele Commager, *The American Mind,* New Haven, Yale University Press, 1950, 227–246.

55. "A dwelling derives its fairest chance of beauty from the congruity with which it expresses a certain definite and distinguished kind of life—whether of a class or of an individual." Desmond and Croly, *Stately Homes,* 351.

56. Croly, "Rich Men and Their Houses," *AR* 12 (June 1902): 27–32.

57. Ibid., 29. This quote is paralleled by one from Dow's book, as follows: "[The home] must presuppose, by subtle architectonic expression, both in itself and its surroundings, that its owner possessed, once upon a time, two good parents, four grandparents, . . . that bienseance and family order have flourished in his life from time immemorial. . . and that he has inherited heirlooms, plates, portraits, miniatures, pictures, rare volumes, diaries, letters and state archives to link him up properly in historical succession and progression. We are covetous of our niche in history. We want to belong somewhere and to something." *American Renaissance,* 18.

58. Croly, "What Is Indigenous Architecture," *AR* 21 (June 1907): 440.

59. Croly, "Recent Works of John Russell Pope," *AR* 29, no. 6 (June 1911): 444.

60. Desmond and Croly, *Stately Homes,* 86.

61. Ibid., 117.

62. Ibid., 132.

63. By architect and client: Biltmore (Asheville, North Carolina, 1892–95), Richard Morris Hunt for George Washington Vanderbilt; Whitehall (Palm Beach, Florida, 1902), Carrère and Hastings for Henry Morrison Flagler; The Breakers (Newport, Rhode Island, 1895), Richard Morris Hunt for Cornelius Vanderbilt II; Harbour Hill (Roslyn, Long Island, 1906), Stanford White for Clarence Mackay; Blairsden (Bernardsville, New Jersey, 1898), Carrère and Hastings for C. Ledyard Blair; Georgian Court (Lakewood, New Jersey, 1899), Bruce Price for George Gould.

64. Levy, *Herbert Croly,* 79.

65. For a history of the colony, see Keith Morgan, "Charles Platt's Houses and Gardens in Cornish, New Hampshire," *Antiques* 122 (July 1982): 117–129.

66. Croly, "The Architectural Work of Charles A. Platt," *AR* 15 (March 1904): 181–244.

67. Keith Morgan, *Charles A. Platt: The Artist as Architect,* Cambridge, MIT Press, 1985, 76–77.

68. Croly, *The Promise of American Life,* New York, Macmillan, 1909, 444–445.

69. *Record* had just opened an office in Chicago and would offer increasing coverage of western and midwestern architecture in the coming years. See Tomlan, "Architectural Press," *Wiley Encyclopedia of Architecture,* vol. 1, 272.

70. See the following articles by Croly: "The New Use of Old Forms," *AR* 17 (April 1905): 271–293; "The Recent Works of John Russell Pope," *AR* 29 (June 1911): 441–511; "Houses by Myron Hunt and Elmer Grey," *AR* 20 (October 1906): 281–295; "Recent Work of Mr. Howard Shaw," *AR* 22 (December 1907): 421–452; "The Recent Work of Howard Shaw," with C. Matlack Price, *AR* 33 (April 1913): 285–307; "A Distinctive Type: Five Recent Country Houses by Albro and Lindeberg," *AR* 32 (October 1912): 285–306.

71. Croly [Arthur C. David, pseud.] "The Architecture of Ideas," *AR* 15 (April 1904): 361–384. It is interesting to note Croly's use of a pseudonym in this confrontational article.

72. George W. Maher, "A Plea for an Indigenous Art," *AR* 21 (June 1907): 431.

73. Croly, "What Is Indigenous Architecture," 434–437.

74. Croly, "New Phases of American Domestic Architecture," *AR* 26 (November 1909): 390–311. The article surveyed a number of recent houses and singled out John D. Rockefeller's Kykuit (Delano and Aldrich, 1907) and Edward H. Harriman's Arden House (Carrère and Hastings, 1909) as examples of large estates with less emphasis on grand and overblown eclecticism.

2 Gentlemen Architects

Epigraphs: Marianna Griswold van Rensselaer, "Architecture as a Profession," *Chautauqua Magazine* (1887), quoted in Russell Lynes, *The Tastemakers,* New York, Harper and Row, 1954, 81; Robert Herrick, *The Common Lot,* New York, Macmillan, 1913.

1. Morgan, *Charles A. Platt,* from "A Memoir by Geoffrey Platt," 200.

2. See Baker, *Richard Morris Hunt,* esp. pp. 450–461, on Hunt's influence. Baker concedes that Hunt founded no school and had no direct followers, but that he had an immense influence on the profession and was almost universally respected as a champion for his fellow architects. Many of the artistic and social values he espoused—which were conservative in nature and oriented toward the past—were passed on to the next two generations. On the immense impact of the W. K. Vanderbilt house, see pp. 274–286.

3. Dow, *American Renaissance,* 1904.

4. David Chase, "Superb Privacies: The Later Domestic Commissions of Richard Morris Hunt," in Susan R. Stein, ed., *The Architecture of Richard Morris Hunt,* Chicago, University of Chicago Press, 1986, 151–171.

5. Croly, "The Architect in Recent Fiction," *AR* 17 (February 1905): 137–139.

6. Paul R. Baker, "Richard Morris Hunt: An Introduction," in Stein, *The Architecture of Richard Morris Hunt,* 3. Quoting Charles Follen McKim in a letter of 21 April 1909 to Lawrence Grant White, McKim Papers, Library of Congress.

7. Croly, "The Architect in Recent Fiction," 137–139.

8. Robert Grant, *Unleavened Bread,* 1900, reprint, Ridgewood, New Jersey, Gregg Press, 1967, 38. Grant (1852–1940) was a Harvard-educated, Boston-bred lawyer and judge who achieved popular success as a novelist and poet. This book, his most acclaimed, turns on the theme of the acquisition of wealth without a sense of underlying moral values—also one of Croly's favorite subjects in his criticism of the upper class.

9. For an analysis of these novels as portrayals of social changes at the turn of the century, see Stow Persons, *The Decline of American Gentility,* New York, Columbia University Press, 1973, 96–103; and Leland Roth, *McKim, Mead and White, Architects,* New York, Harper and Row, 1983, 60–61.

10. William Dean Howells, *The Rise of Silas Lapham,* New York, Houghton-Mifflin, 1885, reprint, Riverside Literature Series Edition 200, (1957), 158.

11. The bibliography on McKim, Mead and White is extensive. See, for instance, Roth, *McKim, Mead and White, Architects;* and Richard Guy Wilson, *McKim, Mead and White, Architects,* New York, Rizzoli, 1983.

12. Howard Van Doren Shaw microfilm collection, no. 1980–81, Art Institute of Chicago, item 7, undated notes for speech. Shaw lists McKim and Albert Kahn as the most important architects of their generation.

13. Curtis Channing Blake, "The Architecture of Carrère and Hastings," Ph.D. diss., Columbia University, 1976, 17.

14. Letter of 20 September 1926 to Charles Moore, in Moore, *The Life and Times of Charles Follen McKim,* New York, Houghton Mifflin, 1929, 151.

15. For a study of White's patrons in particular, see Lawrence Wodehouse, *White of McKim, Mead and White,* New York, Garland, 1988.

16. Blake, "The Architecture of Carrère and Hastings," Ph.D. diss., Columbia University, chapter 1, 1–13.

17. The firm published their resort achievements in *Florida: The American Riviera,* New York, Gillis Bros. and Turnure, 1887.

18. Blake, *Carrère and Hastings,* 11–17. See T. Hastings, "The Influence of Life in the Development of an Architectural Style," *American Architect* (6 July 1913): 29–30.

19. Blake, *Carrère and Hastings,* 131, 132, lists the names in the log and analyzes these country house client connections.

20. John Taylor Boyd, "The Relations of Owner and Architect," quoting the New York architect Julius Gregory in an interview, *Arts and Decoration* 33, no. 5 (September 1930): 49.

21. MIT began classes in 1868 under William Robert Ware's leadership; Illinois, a land grant college, initiated its program under the Chicago architect James Bellangee in January 1870; Cornell started an architectural curriculum in 1871 under Charles Babcock. See Turpin C. Bannister, *The Architect at Mid-Century: Report of the A.I.A. Commission for the Survey of Education and Registration,* Washington, D.C., 1954, 96–97.

22. Ibid., 98–100. This influential institution, founded by alumni of the Ecole in 1894, had 1,100 students in 1913, its peak year, and dominated educational philosophy in the United States until the mid-1920s, according to Bannister. See also A. D. F. Hamlin, "The Influence of the Ecole des Beaux-Arts On Our Architectural Education," *AR* 23 (April 1908): 241–247.

23. For a discussion of the rise of the architectural profession in America during the nineteenth century and an interpretation of the American architect as businessman, see Andrew Saint, *The Image of the Architect,* New Haven, Yale University Press, 1983, chapter 4, 72–95.

24. The best scholarly treatment of an individual university program is found in Richard Oliver, ed., *The Making of An Architect, 1881–1981,* New York, Rizzoli, 1981. The book treats the hundred-year history of the architectural program at Columbia University, probably the most influential one for the generations discussed in this study.

25. Bannister, *The Architect at Mid-Century,* 97–98.

26. For a short biography see Herbert C. Wise, *The Brick-builder* 24, no. 12 (December 1915): 316. Day wrote an introduction to the book *Inexpensive Homes of Individuality,* New York, McBride, 1911.

27. Sandra L. Tatman and Roger W. Moss, eds., *Biographical Dictionary of Philadelphia Architects, 1700–1930,* Boston, G.K. Hall, 1985, 192.

28. Thomas Hastings, "Principles of Architectural Composition," in *Six Lectures on Architecture,* The Scannon Lectures of 1915, Art Institute of Chicago, Chicago, 1917, 73.

29. Julien Gaudet, *Éléments et théorie d'architecture,* vol. 1, Paris, Aulanier, 1901–04, 128, 130.

30. For a case study in the Beaux-Arts education of an architect of this generation, see Joan Draper, "The Ecole des Beaux-Arts and the Architectural Profession in the United States: The Case of John Galen Howard," in *The Architect, Chapters in the History of the Profession,* ed. Spiro Kostof, New York, Oxford University Press, 1977, 209–237.

31. Hastings, "Composition," 71.

32. The Ecole course and its history are extensively profiled in Richard Chaffee, "The Teaching of Architecture at the Ecole des Beaux Arts," in A. Drexler, ed., *The Architecture of the Ecole des Beaux Arts,* New York, MIT Press, 1977, 61–110.

33. John Harbeson, *The Study of Architectural Design,* New York, Pencil Points Press, 1927, 27.

34. For complete listings of the libraries of two noted eclectic specialists, see William B. O'Neal and Christopher Weeks, *The Work of William Lawrence Bottomley in Richmond,* Charlottesville, 1985, appendix 2, 243–247; and Richard Pratt, *David Adler,* New York, M. Evans, 1977.

35. For a study of such patronage patterns in Philadelphia, see George Thomas, "Architectural Patronage and Social Stratification in Philadelphia Between 1840 and 1920," in William W. Cutler III and Howard Gillette, Jr., eds., *The Divided Metropolis, Social and Spatial Dimensions of Philadelphia, 1800–1975,* Westport, Conn., Greenwood Press, 1980, 85–123. Thomas looks at old and new money society in the city and compares the careers of eight architects, including Theophilus Chandler, Cope and Stewardson, and Horace Trumbauer. His conclusions suggest a direct linkage between "establishment" social groups and architects of the same class or social stratum. See also Wayne Andrews, "Horace Trumbauer," *Dictionary of American Biography,* 2d suppl., New York, Scribner's, 1967.

36. Croly, "Recent Works of John Russell Pope," 442.

37. See *Architectural League of New York, Yearbook,* 1925.

38. On the T-Square Club, see: William R. Mitchell, "The T-Square Club, Philadelphia, 1883–1938," Master's thesis, University of Delaware, 1967; George E. Thomas, "William L. Price, Builder of Men and Buildings," Ph.D. diss., University of Pennsylvania, 1975, 63–66; "Two Decades of Club History," in *T-Square Club Catalogue,* 1903–04.

39. Albert Kelsey, ed., *The Architectural Annual,* 2d ed., published under the auspices of the Architectural League of America (ALA), Philadelphia, 1900, Directory of Schools, AIA organizations, and ALA organizations, 262–292. The ALA, formed in 1899, briefly competed with the AIA as a national organization for architects.

40. See, for instance, Elliot C. Brown Company, Inc., *Country Estates Executed by the Elliot C. Brown Company, Incorporated,* New York, 1914; and *Country Homes Constructed by the Elliot C. Brown Company, Incorporated,* New York, 1928.

41. He was the author of *Comments on Virginia Brickwork before 1800,* Boston, 1957, and numerous articles on other subjects.

42. See Myra Tolmach Davis, *Sketches in Iron: Samuel Yellin,* Washington, D.C., 1971.

43. Among the books produced during this era on the subject of representation were Harold Van Buren Magonigle's *Architectural Rendering in Wash,* Arthur Guptill's books on sketching, Eugene Clute's *Drafting Room Practice,* and Phillip Knobloch's *Good Practice in Construction.* See bibliography.

44. Exceptions to this included extremely successful firms like those of Dwight James Baum, John Russell Pope, and Horace Trumbauer, who could handle more than the typical half dozen commissions a year. As they became more established, Trumbauer and Pope increasingly depended on their key associates—Julian Abele and Otto Eggers—to handle the design of many commissions. On office organization and practice, see, for instance, H. Van Buren Magonigle, "Office Principles, Policies and Practice," *Pencil Points* 6, no. 12 (December 1925), 43–48. This is an office handbook, called "The Boss's Bible," for employees, containing procedures, philosophies of design, methods, and many entertaining and useful aphorisms on the architect's character and professional conduct. See also Julien Gaudet, "The Architect's Profession," *Pencil Points* 7, no. 7 (July 1926): 391–393, excerpted from *Éléments et théorie;* and Parker Morse Hooper, "Office Procedure: Office Manual of John Russell Pope," *AR* 69 (February 1931): 177–182; (March 1931): 261–272; (April 1931): 359–362.

45. See Delano, "Reminiscences," Columbia University Oral History Project, 1972, 18. The building was on 38th Street in Murray Hill. Delano lived only two blocks away.

46. Roger Caye, "The Office and Apartments of a Philadelphia Architect," *AR* 34, no. 7 (July 1913): 78–88.

47. Dow, *American Renaissance,* 20.

48. *Webster's Third New International Dictionary,* Merriam-Webster, Springfield, 1981, 719.

49. Wilson Eyre, "Talk on Design," typescript, 5 pages, Avery Architectural Archives, box F108, C33, p. 3.

50. Hastings, "Composition," 83.

51. Letter from Katherine Mackay to Stanford White, undated (c. 1899), in connection with Harbour Hill, collection of the New York Historical Society.

52. See J. Modaunt Crook, *The Dilemma of Style,* Chicago, University of Chicago Press, 1987; Richard Guy Wilson and Diane H. Pilgrim, *The American Renaissance,* New York, Pantheon, 1979; and Richard Longstreth, "Academic Eclecticism in America," *Winterthur Portfolio* (Spring 1982): 55–82, for a discussion of the differences between early, mid, and late nineteenth-century eclecticism.

53. Unquestionably these two architects were among the leaders in the profession nationally, but residential design was not their specialty. They have therefore not been profiled here. Cram and Goodhue, who were in partnership for some years, have been adequately treated in recent biographies. See Richard Oliver, *Bertram Grosvenor Goodhue,* Cambridge, MIT Press, 1983; and Douglas Sand Tucci, *Ralph Adams Cram: American Medievalist,* Boston, Boston Public Library, 1975.

54. Ralph Adams Cram, "A New Influence in the Architecture of Philadelphia," *AR* 15, no. 2 (February 1904): 93–121. Also Alfred Branam, Jr., *Newport's Favorite Architects,* Long Island City, New York, Classical America, 1976; Henry Hope Reed, "Trumbauer, Horace," *Macmillan Dictionary of Architects,* vol. 3, 230.

55. Tatman and Moss, *Biographical Dictionary,* 799–800.

56. This role of atelier assistant was an extremely important one in establishing a mentor relationship between McKim and Pope, as well as between Hastings and Delano. See Moore, *The Life and Times of Charles Follen McKim,* 150–151, for Pope's recollections on the Columbia ateliers.

57. For biographical information, see Richard Chaffee, "John Russell Pope," *Macmillan Dictionary of Architects,* New York, 1982, 4: 451; Deborah Nevins, *Between Traditions and Modernism,* New York, National Academy of Design, 1980, 17–18; "Pope, John Russell," *National Cyclopedia of American Biography,* 1940, vol. 28, 120–121; and the forthcoming dissertation by Steven M. Bedford, "The Architecture of John Russell Pope," Columbia University.

58. "Bonnycrest [sic], the Residence of Stuart Duncan at Newport, R.I.," *Country Life (America)* 37 (November 1919): 28–29.

59. Joseph Hudnut, "The Last of the Romans: Comment on the Building of the National Gallery of Art," *Magazine of Art* 34 (April 1941): 169–173.

60. Delano, "Reminiscences," 1–4.

61. Ibid., 10–11.

62. William Lawrence Bottomley, "A Selection from the Works of Delano and Aldrich," *AR* 54, no. 1 (July 1923): 4.

63. Royal Cortissoz, introduction, in Delano and Aldrich, *Portraits of Ten Country Houses,* New York, Doubleday, Page, 1924, xii–xiii.

64. Delano, "Reminiscences," 31. For a history of the house, see Robert B. King, *Raising a Fallen Treasure: The Otto H. Kahn Home, Huntington, Long Island,* Middleville, New York, privately printed, 1985.

65. For a treatment of Delano's early Long Island country house work, see my "William Adams Delano and the Muttontown enclave," *Antiques* 132, no. 2 (August 1987): 316–327; and the forthcoming "Domestic Portraits: The Early Long Island Country Houses of Delano and Aldrich," in *Building Long Island,* Hofstra University and Long Island Studies Institute, 1990.

66. Alfred Morton Githens, "Wilson Eyre, Jr., His Work," in Kelsey, ed., *The Architectural Annual,* 2d ed., 1900, 121.

67. Wilson Eyre, "The Development of American Dwelling Architecture during the Past Thirty Years," *Arch. Review* 22 (November 1917): 241.

68. For examples of English work of the same period, see Gavin Stamp and André Goulancourt, *The English House,* Chicago, University of Chicago Press, 1986, 87–171.

69. Eyre, "Talk on Design," p. 4.

70. John Harbeson, "Wilson Eyre, October 30, 1858–October 23, 1944," typescript, 3 pages, Wilson Eyre Collection, Avery Architectural Archives, box F108, C33. See published version, in *AIA Journal* (March 1946): 129–133.

71. The office books of McKim, Mead and White indicate that Albro worked for the firm from January 1895 through March 31, 1906; Lindeberg, listed as "Henry C.," was on the rolls from February 1901 through 31 March 1906. See Moore, *The Life and Times of Charles Follen McKim,* 333–334.

72. James A. Stillman (1871–1944) was one of four children of James J. Stillman (1850–1918), expatriate Texan, founder and president of National City Bank, and a major client of McKim, Mead and White. Lindeberg, it is said, took his first commission "out of the office" to start his career. The son married the infamous Anne U. Potter ("Fifi"), who later left him to marry Harold F. McCormick (1898–1973). McCormick was not only the roommate of Mrs. Stillman's son at Princeton, but also the son of Harold F. McCormick (m. Edith Rockefeller, 1872–1923) of Platt's Villa Turicum in Lake Forest—part of the large farm equipment family. The branches of the family tree became even more entangled in society's network when James A. Stillman's two sisters married two Rockefeller brothers, William G. and Percy A. The choice of the Pocantico site was conditioned by this, and later the estate passed into Rockefeller control, only to be partially destroyed and resold.

73. See Horace Allison, "English Cottage Types in America," *Country Life in America* 20 (1 October 1911): 39–42; *American Architect* 94 (14 October 1908) for ancillary buildings; "A Thatched Palace," *AR* 28 (October 1910): 315–328; and A. H. Forbes, "The Work of Albro and Lindeberg, *Architecture* 26 (15 November 1912): 207.

74. Cortissoz, introduction; and Harrie T. Lindeberg, "The Return of Reason in Architecture," *AR* 74 (October 1933): 252–256, 261–313. Reprinted in Lindeberg, *Domestic Architecture of Harrie T. Lindeberg,* New York, W. Helburn, 1940, 273–278.

75. See Lindeberg, *Domestic Architecture,* 275. For biographical data on Lindeberg, see Gavin Townsend, "The Tudor House in America: 1890–1930," Ph.D. diss., University of California at Santa Barbara, 1986, 257–258; *Who's Who in America* 16 (1930–31): 1374; Russell Sturgis, *A Dictionary of Architecture and Building,* 3 vols., New York, Macmillan, 1901, vol. 3; *Who Was Who in America* 3 (1951–60): 520. Townsend points out that Lindeberg maintained a partnership in the firm of Mann, McNeille and Lindeberg until around 1906. In 1914 he terminated his practice with Albro and designed many of his best houses on his own. He was married three times, in 1906, 1914, and 1937—coincidentally the same years in which he made transitions in his practice. See Townsend, 280.

76. Harrie T. Lindeberg, "Thatched Roof Effects with Shingles," *Brickbuilder* 18, no. 7 (July 1909): 134.

77. J. Lovell Little, "The Modern English Plaster House," in Henry Saylor, ed., *Architectural Style for Country Houses,* New York, R. M. McBride, 22.

78. Ibid.

79. Harrie T. Lindeberg, "The Home of the Future: The New Domestic Architecture in the East," *Craftsman* 29 (1916): 675.

80. Lindeberg was admired by most of the leading critics of his day, including Croly, C. Matlack Price (for whom he was a hero), Cortissoz, Henry Saylor, and Samuel Howe, who extensively featured his work in the 1915 volume of *American Country Houses of To-Day.*

81. Russell Whitehead, "Harrie T. Lindeberg's Contribution to American Domestic Architecture," *AR* 55, no. 4 (April 1924): 310.

82. Ibid., 341.

83. Thomas Tallmadge, "Howard Van Doren Shaw," *AR* 60, no. 1 (July 1926): 71.

84. These are contained in the Burnham Library of the Art Institute of Chicago.

85. Leonard Eaton, *Two Chicago Architects and Their Clients: Frank Lloyd Wright and Howard Van Doren Shaw,* Cambridge, MIT Press, 1969.

86. Tallmadge, "Howard Van Doren Shaw," 73.

87. Herbert Croly and C. Matlack Price, "The Recent Work of Howard Shaw," *AR* 33, no. 4 (April 1913): 289–291.

88. Tallmadge, 71.

89. Frances Wells Shaw, "Concerning Howard Shaw in His Home," typescript, 1926, Shaw Collection, Art Institute of Chicago, 7.

90. Shaw died on May 6, 1926, just after being awarded the AIA Gold Medal, which was presented posthumously to his widow.

91. See Morgan, "Charles A. Platt's Houses and Gardens in Cornish, New Hampshire," 117–129.

92. See Alan Emmet, "Faulkner Farm: An Italian Garden in Massachusetts," *Journal of Garden History* 6, no. 2 (1986): 162–178.

93. John Taylor Boyd, "Colonial Homes of Great Dignity" (part 16 of "The Home as the American Architect Sees It"), *Arts and Decoration* 35, no. 6 (October 1931): 21.

94. Morgan, *Charles A. Platt,* 24–62.

95. See bibliography and Morgan, *Charles A. Platt,* 122.

96. Herbert Croly, "The Architectural Work of Charles A. Platt," *AR* 15, no. 3 (March 1904): 234, 181.

97. See the excellent analysis of the house and grounds in Morgan, *Charles A. Platt,* 86–93. A more extensive coverage in photos, plan, and site plan appears in *Monograph of the Work of Charles A. Platt,* New York, Architectural Book Publishing Company, 1913, plates 1–10.

98. Croly, "The Architectural Works of Charles A. Platt," 242.

99. See Morgan, "List of Buildings, Gardens and Projects," in *Charles A. Platt.*

100. Boyd, "Colonial Home," 24.

3 The Architecture of Country Houses

Epigraphs: Augusta Patterson, *American Homes of To-Day,* New York, Macmillan, 1924, 21; Arthur C. Holden, *American Country Houses of To-Day,* New York, Architectural Book Publishing, 1930, iii.

1. Half a dozen books on the new country house, previously cited, appeared in the years from 1904 to 1913, such as Ferree, *American Estates and Gardens;* Desmond and Croly, *Stately Homes;* Croly, *Houses for Town or Country;* Hooper, *The Country House;* John C. Baker, ed., *American Country Homes and Their Gardens,* Philadelphia, John C. Winston, 1906; and Day, ed., *American Country Houses of To-Day* (1912).

2. Bertram Goodhue, "The Modern Architectural Problem," *Craftsman* 8 (June 1905): 332–333.

3. Frank Miles Day, "On the Choice of Style in Building a House," *House and Garden* 9, no. 2 (February 1906): 57.

4. Horace B. Mann, "Style in the Country House," *AABN* 107, no. 2055 (12 May 1915): 293–297.

5. A. D. F. Hamlin, *A Textbook of the History of Architecture,* New York, Longmans Green, 1898, xxiv; quoted in H. W. Desmond and H. W. Frohne, *Building a Home,* New York, Baker and Taylor, 1908, 40.

6. Sturgis, *A Dictionary of Architecture and Building,* vol. 3, col. 671.

7. George L. Hersey, *High Victorian Gothic,* Baltimore, Johns Hopkins University Press, 1972; and Crook, *The Dilemma of Style,* especially 13–42.

8. See Saylor, "The Best Twelve Country Houses in America," *Country Life in America* (March 1914): 46–49. This is the introduction to this important series.

9. Patterson, *American Homes of To-Day,* 192.

10. John Taylor Boyd, "What Style for the Country House?" *Arts and Decoration* 15, no. 6 (October 1921): 354.

11. C. Matlack Price, introduction, *The Work of Dwight James Baum,* New York, Helburn, 1927, unpaginated.

12. The book was published in two editions, 1912 and 1919, by the R. M. McBride Company, as part of its country house series.

13. Wallis, "The Colonial House," in Saylor, *Architectural Style,* 19–20.

14. Saylor, *Architectural Style,* 27.

15. Dow, *American Renaissance,* 144.

16. Ralph Adams Cram, "The Influence of the French School on American Architecture," address given at the Thirty-third Annual Convention of the American Institute of Architects, Pittsburgh, 14 November 1899; *American Architect and Building News* (hereafter cited as *AABN*) 66 (25 November 1899): 66.

17. Berwind was a rags-to-riches millionaire whose father, a German immigrant craftsman, had worked in a Philadelphia piano factory. After leaving the navy and Annapolis, Berwind made his fortune in Pennsylvania coal. Though dour and driven as a capitalist, he and his wife were among Newport's and New York's most lavish

entertainers. They needed a house that would match their extravagant style.

18. Vincent Scully and Antoinette Downing, *The Architectural Heritage of Newport, Rhode Island, 1640–1915,* New York, C. N. Potter, 1967, 173–174.

19. Patterson, *American Homes of To-Day,* 39.

20. Herbert Langford Warren, "The Influence of France on American Architecture," *AABN* 66 (25 November 1899): 67.

21. Cret was not known for domestic work. The three houses in question, all built in 1926, were for: Theodore C. Shaeffer, Haverford, Pennsylvania; C. H. McCormick, Harrisburg, Pennsylvania; and Clarence H. Geist, Villanova, Pennsylvania. Presumably like most architects he deferred to his clients' tastes. See Theodore B. White, *Paul Philippe Cret, Architect and Teacher,* Philadelphia, 1973.

22. See, for instance, Frank J. Forster, *Provincial Architecture of Northern France,* New York, 1931; Forster, "Norman-English Influence in Country Houses," *Architectural Forum* (hereafter cited as *Arch. Forum*) 44 (March 1926): 139–146; Leigh French, Jr., "The American Country House in the French Provincial Style," *Arch. Forum* 49, no. 3 (September 1928): 353–360.

23. Edith Wharton, *The House of Mirth,* New York, Scribner's, 1905, 160.

24. For a statistical profile of the popular styles over a several-year period published in *Architectural Record,* see A. Lawrence Kocher, "The American Country House," *AR* 58, no. 5 (November 1925): 401–512. Townsend, "The Tudor House in America," has made a graph of this data in his chapter 1.

25. Townsend, "The Tudor House in America," chapter 12, 237–253.

26. Wilson Eyre, "My Ideal for the Country Home," *Country Life in America* 24 (May 1913): 35–36.

27. Jackson, *The Half-Timber House,* 21, 23, respectively.

28. Ibid., 22.

29. For a discussion of the prairie school and Tudor, see Townsend, "The Tudor House," 198–210. The author correctly points out that Spencer, Wright and Maher were mainly building for middle-class patrons who sought novelty in design, not for the key builders of large country estates. They could thus afford to be more experimental in their Tudor work.

30. For a discussion of the Arts and Crafts movement and domestic architecture, see essay by Richard Guy Wilson, "American Arts and Crafts Architecture: Radical though Dedicated to the Cause Conservative," in Kaplan, ed., *The Art That is Life,* Boston, Museum of Fine Arts, 1987, 101–131.

31. "Conservatism in Design: Notes on Some Recent Work by Aymar Embury II," *AR* 32, no. 4 (October 1912): 329.

32. See Alan Axelrod, ed., *The Colonial Revival in America,* New York, Norton, 1985, for articles on the broader influence of this movement in American culture.

33. Roth, *America Builds,* 245; from *Century* 32 (May, June, July, 1886).

34. For a listing and analysis of their development, see Dixon Wecter, *The Saga of American Society,* 397–399.

35. William B. Rhoads, *The Colonial Revival,* New York, Garland, 1977, quoting Robert Andrews, "The Changing Styles of Country Houses," *Arch. Review* 2 (1904): 439.

36. Joseph Everett Chandler, *The Colonial House,* New York, McBride Nast, 1916, 34.

37. On the confusion in definitions, see, for instance, "English 'Georgian' Architecture: The Source of the American 'Colonial' Style," *AR* 10, no. 2 (October 1899): 97–108; R. Brown, Jr., and Robert Jackson, "Old Colonial vs. Old English Houses," *AABN* 17 (3 January 1885): 3–4.

38. Ralph Adams Cram, ed., *American Country Houses of To-Day*, New York, Architectural Book Publishing, 1913, iii.

39. William R. Ware and Charles S. Keefe, eds., *The Georgian Period*, 6 vols., New York, 1923. The articles were originally serialized in *American Architect and Building News*. See also Frank E. Wallis, "The Colonial Renaissance," *White Pine Series* 2, no. 1 (February 1916); and Wallis, *Old Colonial Architecture and Furniture*, Boston, 1887.

40. For an examination of its later stages, see David Gebhard, "The American Colonial Revival in the 1930s," *Winterthur Portfolio* 22, nos. 2–3 (Summer–Autumn 1987): 109–148.

41. Patterson, *American Homes of To-day*, 59.

42. See David Gebhard, "Architectural Imagery, the Mission, and California," *Harvard Architecture Review* 1 (1980): 137–145.

43. Felix Rey, "A Tribute to the Mission Style," *Architect and Engineer* 1 (October 1924): 77.

44. Quoted in Karen J. Weitze, *California's Mission Revival*, Los Angeles, Hennessey and Ingalls, 1984, 79.

45. Longstreth suggests that the plan was inspired by Spanish military outposts, an odd model for a house. He also points out that the building was commissioned by William Randolph Hearst, without his mother's consent, and that it was he who initiated the revival of the hacienda in California. See *On the Edge of the World*, 279–285, for a complete analysis of this extraordinary house.

46. The Phelan house was designed by William Curlett and Son, with C. E. Gottschalk. See B. J. S. Cahill, "The Country Home of the Hon. James D. Phelan," *The Architect and Engineer* 38, no. 2 (September 1914): 46–57.

47. For a discussion of resort culture and the development of Santa Barbara, see David F. Myrick, *Montecito and Santa Barbara*, vol. 1, Glendale, Trans Anglo, 1987.

48. See Carrère and Hastings, *The American Riviera*, New York, Gillis Bros. and Turnure, 1887.

49. Rexford Newcomb, *The Spanish House for America*, Philadelphia, Lippincott, 1927, 13.

50. R. W. Sexton, *Spanish Influence on American Architecture and Decoration*, New York, Brentano's, 1927, 9.

51. See the books of Rexford Newcomb, R. W. Sexton, Bottomley, Van Pelt, Ayres, and Stapley, in the bibliography.

52. John Taylor Boyd, "Country Houses of Southern California" (interview with Reginald Johnson, part 7 of "The Home as the American Architect Sees It"), *Arts and Decoration* 32, no. 5 (March 1930): 53.

53. Typical of the interest in Hispanic things was Ralph Adams Cram's 1924 series on Spanish architecture for *The American Architect*, based on his travels in that country during the winter of 1920; see R. A. Cram, "Domestic Architecture in Spain," *AABN* 125, no. 2444 (23 April 1924). Cram went to Spain on the insistence of his colleagues, to see its medieval architecture, lest he be too prejudiced toward the French and English Gothic cathedrals. His family set out for Seville in 1920: "My wife could stand it no longer and declared that whether I liked it or not, we were going to Spain for the proximate winter." Cram, *My Life in Architecture*, New York, 1936, 139. He was surprised and pleased by what he discovered and used Hispanic sources in several commissions, including the Sewall house in Houston.

54. Sexton, *Spanish Influence*, 14.

55. On the general trend toward simplification, anti-Victorian attitudes, and informal ways of living, see Clifford Clark, Jr., *The American Family Home, 1800–1960*, Chapel Hill, University of North Carolina Press, 1986, 135–170.

56. On "the simple life" as it was known in England at this time, see Gavin Stamp and André Goulancourt, *The English House, 1860–1914*, 33–38.

57. According to David Handlin, in *The American Home: Architecture and Society, 1815–1915*, Boston, Little Brown, 1979, the influential treatises on this form were widely read in America: Robert Kerr, *The Gentleman's House*, London, J. Murray, 1864; and J. J. Stevenson, *House Architecture*, 2 vols., London, Macmillan, 1880. H. H. Richardson owned a copy of both books.

58. Written under the pseudonym William Herbert. See Croly in bibliography.

59. On the uses and concept of various room types during this period, see L. Eugene Robinson, *Domestic Architecture*, New York, Macmillan, 1917, 58–65; and Hooper, *The Country House*, Garden City, Doubleday Page, 1904–05, chapters 7–10, 136–183. Most writers agreed that the living room had taken the place of several traditional formal rooms in the Victorian house—the parlor, drawing room, reception room, morning room, and even library in some cases.

60. A. J. Downing, *The Architecture of Country Houses*, New York, 1850, reprint, New York, Dover, 1969, sec. 9, 257–270; quoted in William H. Pierson, *American Buildings and Their Architects*, New York, Anchor, 1976, vol. 2, 352–353. Downing, America's first proponent and analyst of the gentleman's country house, would have grouped this example under the heading of villa; "the most refined home of America—the home of its most leisurely and educated class of citizens. Nature and art both lend it their happiest influence." He further defined this rural dwelling as "the country house of a person of competence or wealth sufficient to build or maintain it with some taste and elegance," requiring "the care of at least three or more servants."

61. Marianna Griswold van Rensselaer, "American Country Dwellings," in Roth, *America Builds*, 249. Originally in *Century* 32 (May, June, July 1886).

62. On the development, concept, and purpose of the living room, Clark is again authoritative. This room seems to develop almost concurrently in middle- and upper-class dwellings, between 1890 and 1900. See *The American Family Home*, 144–145, 163. Both Frank Lloyd Wright and Gustav Stickley were early advocates of its position as the life center of the comfortable house.

63. Hooper, *The Country House*, 149.

64. Wilson Eyre, "Brochure Article," dated 17 March 1908, Wilson Eyre Collection, Avery Architectural Archives, Columbia University, 3. He also advocated a deemphasis in the importance of the library (associated with masculine authority over the family) and reception room (associated often with the entertainment of women in the home) in the country house: "The better arrangement," he argued, "is to have a small study for writing and books and keep the large room [living room] for general use. In the country one does not usually have formal guests or need a reception room."

65. Ibid., 2.

66. On the significance of the porch, see Handlin, *The American Home*, 349–350. See also Marianna van Rensselaer, *Art Out of Doors*, New York, Scribner's, 1903, 123–135; and Robert C. Spencer, Jr., "Planning the Home: A Chapter on Porches," *House Beautiful* 17 (1905): 26–27.

67. Croly [Herbert], *Houses for Town or Country*, 179.

68. The most important advances were the introduction of city sewerage systems in the 1870s; the development of the washdown, washout, and siphonic jet toilet and watercloset with gravity cistern from 1875 onward; and the manufacture of elaborate porcelain tub, toilet, and sink shapes by the Mott works at the end of the century. By 1914 the bathroom had reached its modern configuration and dimensions. See Gail Casky Winkler, introduction, in *The Well-Appointed Bath*, Washington, D.C., Preservation Press, 1989: 11–25.

69. Mary Cable, *Top Drawer: American High Society from the Gilded Age to the Roaring Twenties*, New York, Atheneum, 1984, 86; citing Phillips, *The Reign of Gilt*, New York, James Pott, 1905. See also Charles Snell, *Vanderbilt Mansion*, Washington, D.C., National Parks Service, 1960, 21.

70. Desmond and Croly, *Stately Homes*, 510.

71. Frank Miles Day, writing in 1911, found the reasons for the compact service accommodations in American houses elsewhere, pointing to the high wages paid to domestics in this country, as compared to England, and the shortage of good help. Whereas 50 percent or more of the typical ground floor of an English house was given over to service zones, Day found only 25 to 30 percent of the ground floor similarly occupied in American country houses. See Day, *American Country Houses of To-Day*, 1912, iv.

72. Daniel E. Sutherland, *Americans and Their Servants*, Baton Rouge, LSU Press, 1981, 183. Sutherland provides the best analysis of the architectural ramifications of the servant question, especially in chapters 5, 6, and 10.

73. Roland Wood, quoting Katherine Fullerton Gerould, in *Arts and Decoration* (March 1920): 337.

74. Edith M. Jones, "The House That Will Keep Servants," *Country Life in America* 37 (March 1920): 50. Jones points to nine essentials in planning an ideal service wing: "Size, exposure, ventilation, lighting, sanitary condition, radiation, hot water, work groupings, and circulation."

75. Ibid., 51.

76. Sutherland, *Americans and Their Servants*, 114–120. See also Louis Griswold, "The Way to Solve the Servant Question," *Century* 54, no. 4 (February 1898): 636; Jones, "Servants," 50–51; and Carole Owens, *The Berkshire Cottages*, Englewood Cliffs, 1984, 85–100.

77. Sutherland, *Americans and Their Servants*, 192–199.

78. For discussion and illustrations of kitchens and their equipment in country houses, see Eugene Robinson, *Domestic Architecture*, 70–80; Hooper, *The Country House*, 166–181; and Elizabeth C. Condit, "The Service Equipment of the Country House," *Arch. Forum* 49, no. 3 (September 1928): 453–458.

79. J. B. Jackson, "The Domestication of the Garage," in *The Necessity for Ruins and Other Topics*, Springfield, University of Massachusetts Press, 1980, 103–111.

80. Kenneth K. Stowell, "Architects' Check List for Country Houses," *Arch. Forum* 49, no. 9 (September 1928): 467–469.

81. "The House That Works I and II," *Fortune* 12 (October 1935): 59–67, 94–100.

82. Patterson, *American Homes of To-day*, 227.

83. See, for instance, Harold D. Eberlein, "Designing the Dependencies," *House and Garden* (October 1926): 95–97, 162.

84. Van Rensselaer, *Art Out of Doors*, 1903, 3.

85. Patterson, *American Homes of To-day*, chapters 12 and 13 on the garden, 285.

86. Frederick Squires, *The Hollow Tile House*, New York, Comstock, 1913. This book illustrates all of the above houses and provides a comprehensive treatment of hollow tile construction systems as well as a short history of the material's use. See pp. 23, 58, and 184.

87. Oswald C. Herring, *Concrete and Stucco Houses*, New York, McBride Nast, 1912, xv.

88. On the history of reinforced concrete in the U.S., see Carl W. Condit, *American Building*, Chicago, University of Chicago Press, 1968, 168–176, 240–250. Several reinforcing systems were in use by 1910, including the Ransome system, the Kahn-Edison system, and the Turner system of flat slab construction. Condit considers the period between 1910 and 1930 the great age of experimentation in American concrete design.

89. Thomas R. Aidala, *Hearst Castle, San Simeon,* New York, Harrison House, 1981, 99.

90. On Mercer's work and his house, see Claire Gilbride Fox, "Henry Chapman Mercer: Tilemaker, Collector and Builder Extraordinary," *Antiques* (October 1973): 678–685.

91. For a discussion of structural systems in country houses, particularly steel, see Tyler Stewart Rogers, "New Structural Features of the Country House," *Arch. Forum* 49, no. 3 (September 1928): 417–422. Rogers cites five major types of structural framing: wood balloon frame, masonry bearing wall, reinforced concrete, heavy structural steel fireproofed and veneered, and lightweight steel stud construction (new in the late 1920s).

92. Pope was intent upon getting the precise look of the English models, even going so far as to provide his builders with photographs of the originals. See John Russell Pope, "Working Photographs: Notes on a Series of Hand Camera Photographs by John Russell Pope, FAIA, for Use as Adjuncts to Specifications and Working Drawings," *AABN* 125, no. 2440 (27 February 1924): 197–202, with approximately 20 plates from his English travels.

93. See Charles Thomas Davis, *A Practical Treatise on the Manufacture of Bricks, Tiles and Terracotta,* Philadelphia, 1895.

94. Such as Nathaniel Lloyd, *A History of English Brickwork,* London, 1925.

95. These were among the largest and most successful country house builders. The Brown Company published two lavish brochures of its work, in 1914 and 1928 (see bibliography). The Howell firm boasted that it constructed for all of the leading New York residential architects, such as Lindeberg, Platt et al. See *Architectural League of New York Yearbook,* 1932, 133. Ballinger built many of the noted houses of Wilson Eyre and Mellor, Meigs and Howe, including the Newbold farm, the Jeffords country estate, and the McCracken house.

96. Memorandum from historian Charles B. Snell to the Department of the Interior, 14 October 1954, 6 pages, concerning interview with Clermont. Norcross was probably the largest construction firm in the U.S. at this time, though competition was beginning to mount. Founded after the Civil War by James A. and Oscar W. Norcross, it built, among other buildings, the 42nd Street Library in New York, the Albany Railroad Depot, and many of Richardson's buildings.

97. Desmond and Frohne, *Building a Home,* 31. The book presents a table comparing land costs in various cities and rural areas, construction systems, average lot frontage, cubic foot costs, and total costs. A caveat below indicates that "the cost of labor and materials has increased so much of late that these figures are perhaps 25% too low."

98. Robinson, *Domestic Architecture,* 334–338.

99. *Arch. Forum* 49, no. 3 (September 1928): 324–400.

4 Stately Homes

Epigraph: Wecter, *The Saga of American Society,* 108.

1. Most notably Herbert Croly and Barr Ferree. The term was most recently used to describe houses of this era by Russell Lynes, in a chapter of his book on American culture and art, *The Tastemakers,* New York, Harper and Row, 1954.

2. See Jay E. Cantor, "A Monument to Trade: A. T. Stewart and the Rise of the Millionaire's Mansion in New York," *Winterthur Portfolio* 10 (1975): 165–194.

3. Describing the New York town house of the fictitious Bry family, in which a fancy dress ball is held; in *The House of Mirth,* 131.

4. Lynes was one of the first authors to look to Hunt as the father of the stately home and to offer an explanation of the social currents of the 1890s. "There were no books of etiquette to which the rich could apply for instructions on how princes should live in this country, and so [wealthy capitalists] turned to the only models available to them — to the standards of European elegance, and with the aid of architects they adapted those external trappings to their own extremely rigid, refined, and on the whole boring mode of life," he argued in 1949. Lynes, *The Tastemakers,* 137–138. See all of chapter 8, "Stately Homes," 121ff.

5. This point has been well demonstrated in Richard Guy Wilson, "Edith and Ogden: Writing, Decoration, and Architecture," in Pauline Metcalf, ed., *Ogden Codman and the Decoration of Houses,* Boston, Boston Atheneum, 1988, 133–184.

6. Peabody and Stearns, of Boston, were the architects. The house was begun in 1886 and built in a series of accretions until 1900. According to Carole Owens, the cost was over $230,000. Owens, *Berkshire Cottages,* 163.

7. Florence Adele Sloane, *Maverick in Mauve: The Diary of a Romantic Age,* with commentary by Louis Auchincloss, Garden City, Doubleday, 1983. The diary covers the years from January 1, 1893, to August 12, 1896.

8. Apparently, the Ogden Mills mansion in Barrytown served as Wharton's actual model for Bellomont. She was a frequent visitor there in her youth, just as Adele Sloane was at the Shepherd house.

9. Sloane, *Maverick in Mauve,* 77. Elm Court, Lenox, Sunday, 4 June 1893.

10. Wharton, *House of Mirth,* 132.

11. Obituary, *New York Times,* Thursday, 30 June 1938. Vanderbilt was born on 2 February 1856, and died at Hyde Park.

12. "A Social Sensation: Frederick W. Vanderbilt's Marriage," *New York Tribune,* 18 February 1879. The couple were married in the Windsor Hotel in New York on Tuesday, 17 December 1878, and Frederick's father was not told for over a week. Louise's former husband was the son of Frederick's father's sister, showing how inbred were the relations of society in the age of the moguls.

13. Estimates differ — this one is from Snell, *Vanderbilt Mansion.* According to office records, the cost of the house alone was $521,466. Total cost of the landscape improvements and other buildings may have been near $2.5 million, according to Leland Roth (*A Monograph of the Work of McKim, Mead and White, 1879–1915,* 1914–15, reprint, New York, DaCapo, 1977, 64). Roth (*The Architecture of McKim, Mead and White, 1870–1920: A Building List,* New York, Garland, 1978, entry no. 864, p. 156) lists different figures: house, $427,057; interiors, $94,409; pavilion, $42,377.

14. Snell, *Vanderbilt Mansion,* 2. More complete information is contained in Snell's Historical Handbook, "Vanderbilt Mansion National Historic Site," typescript, 100 pages, 3 February 1955, courtesy of the National Parks Service.

15. Obituary, *New York Times,* 22 August 1926. Oral history information from Vanderbilt Mansion National Historic Site, courtesy of the National Parks Service, U.S. Department of the Interior.

16. Hyde Park estate, called by Walter Creese "the most remarkable on the river" during the early nineteenth century, has a complex history. Hosack purchased the land, including the plateau upon which the house now stands, from the son of his former partner, Samuel Bard, in 1832. A Federal house built by Bard on the plateau was enlarged in 1829 by the architect Martin E. Thompson of New York. This house burned in 1845, to be replaced by the more neoclassical Langdon mansion. The landscape on the estate was also extensively cultivated and designed as early as the 1820s. Between 1827 and 1828 the French landscape designer André Parmentier is said to have worked on the grounds, executing one of the earliest picturesque gardens on the Hudson. See Walter Creese, *The Crowning of the American Landscape,* Princeton, Princeton University Press, 1985, 54–59.

17. In a letter to Charles McKim of February 1896, William R. Mead described the Vanderbilt predicament: "Fred Vanderbilt's job has met a serious delay, but he has acted very nicely about it and I think on the whole is glad that it has turned out so. When we came to tear the old house apart, it was found to be in as bad a condition as the annex — no strength to the mortar, walls out of plumb, etc., etc.; in fact, so bad that it seemed foolish to attempt to build anything on it. . . . Vanderbilt hesitated on the ground that if he had not thought there was something to save in the old building he would not have built on those lines. As matters stand now, we are rearranging the center on virtually the same lines but with certain changes in plan, and keeping the exterior just as you left it. There has been a good deal of a fight to do this, because when it was found the old house had to come down Mrs. Vanderbilt kicked over the traces and was disposed to build an English house as she called it. We have, however, used your name pretty freely as being much interested in this design and likely to be very much disappointed if anything happened to it." McKim was at this time on a trip up the Nile with Henry White. Moore, *Life and Times of Charles Follen McKim,* 268–269.

18. For recent photo coverage of the house, see John Zukowsky and Robbe Pierce Stimson, *Hudson River Villas,* New York, Rizzoli, 1985, 156–160. Working drawings are in the McKim, Mead and White Collection, New York Historical Society, tube no. 409a.

19. Charles Snell, "Travels of Mr. and Mrs. Frederick Vanderbilt 1891–1926," folder 5a, Vanderbilt Mansion National Historic Site Records.

20. See Girouard, *The Victorian Country House,* 27–37.

21. Oral history interview with Alfred Martin, former Vanderbilt butler (1909–38), 5 March 1949. Courtesy of Vanderbilt Mansion National Historic Site.

22. Katherine Boyd Menz and Donald McTernan, "Decorating for the Frederick Vanderbilts," *Nineteenth Century* (Winter 1977): 44–49. Though the basic architecture of the ground floor formal rooms was McKim's, evidence suggests that these decorators played a large role in the eventual look of the interiors. Glaezner, a "decorative furnisher" with offices in New York and Paris, bought pieces for clients, such as those from Sormani, Piorer and Rémon, used for this house. His drawings survive for the lobby, den, Gold Room, and the master's bedroom. Codman designed Mrs. Vanderbilt's bedroom, probably on referral from her brother-in-law, Cornelius, for whom he had recently done rooms in The Breakers.

23. Alfred Martin, interview, 9. Referring to the priceless Troy tapestries in the dining room, he recalled: "I don't think [Mr. Vanderbilt] was interested in that sort of thing. It was there for the purpose of decorating his room and . . . that is all it amounted to."

24. Ferree, *American Estates and Gardens,* 33.

25. Lawrence Wodehouse, "Stanford White and the Mackays: A Case Study in Architect-Client Relationships," *Winterthur Portfolio* 11 (1976): 216–217.

26. Ibid., 213–215.

27. Roth, "Notes on the Plates," *Monograph of the Work of McKim, Mead and White,* 67. The house was destroyed in 1945. See plates 166–170.

28. Ferree, *American Estates and Gardens,* 33.

29. Letter of 27 July 1899, Katherine Mackay to Stanford White, Newport. New York Historical Society.

30. Letter of 3 November 1902, Mackay to White. New York Historical Society.

31. Letter of 24 February 1903, Clarence Mackay to Stanford White. New York Historical Society.

32. Wodehouse, "Stanford White and the Mackays," 216–228. The author argues that "in the instance of Harbour Hill, and perhaps in the instances of other private commissions by wealthy clients, the clients took an individualistic pride in arranging details and in providing informed criticism—sometimes too much criticism" (216).

33. For another extensive discussion of the architect-client relationship, see Lawrence Wodehouse, *White of McKim, Mead and White,* New York, Garland, 1988, 33–42.

34. For coverage of the estate, see Baker, ed., *American Country Homes,* 160–169; *AABN* 66 (25 November 1899), plate 1248, and (16 December 1899), plate 1351; *A Pride of Palaces: Lenox Summer Cottages 1883–1933,* Lenox Library Association, 1981, 41–52 (Edwin Hale Lincoln photographs).

35. Bellefontaine's gardens and estate plan were famous during its time. It was featured as the opening house in volume 2 of *House and Garden* in January 1902.

36. For information and lore on the house, much of it apocryphal, see Owens, *The Berkshire Cottages,* 160–162. The Lenox Library contains files on Bellefontaine and many other Lenox estates.

37. Tuxedo Park was founded in 1885 by the tobacco king Pierre Lorillard (it was here that the tuxedo purportedly originated). Originally planned as a seven-thousand-acre private hunting reserve and club for Lorillard and his friends, and consciously intended to snub the opulence of Newport, it eventually became a year-round community, only thirty-five miles by train from New York. Designed by Ernest Bowditch, the Olmstedian landscape architect, the enclave was intended to support only modest shingled cottages around the picturesque mountain lake. Bruce Price was retained by Lorillard to design the first cottages, which were among his most compelling and influential domestic works. He also designed the first clubhouse, located at the center of the park on the lakeshore. See Townsend, "Tudor House," 113–114; Samuel Graybill, "Bruce Price, American Architect, 1845–1903," Ph.D. diss., Yale University, 1957, chapter 4; George M. Rushmore, *The World With a Fence Around It: Tuxedo Park—The Early Days,* New York, 1957; Samuel Swift, "Community Life in Tuxedo Park," *House and Garden* 8 (August 1905): 67–71; Emily Post, "Tuxedo Park, An American Rural Community," *Century Magazine* 72 (October 1911): 795–805.

38. Ferree, *American Estates and Gardens,* 124.

39. Obituary, *New York Times,* 14 April 1915, 13, col. 5.

40. Townsend, *Tudor House,* 76–78.

41. Ibid., 75.

42. "Poor, Henry William, financier," *National Cyclopedia of American Biography,* vol. 16, 33–34. Much of the above information can also be found in this source. Poor died in New York City on April 13, 1915.

43. Ferree, *American Estates and Gardens,* 124.

44. *AR* 21 (January 1907): 36.

45. See Aidala, *Hearst Castle,* 39–111.

46. Porter Garnett, *Stately Homes of California,* Boston, Little Brown, 1915 40–41.

47. See Alson Clark, "Myron Hunt in Southern California," in Clark, ed., *Myron Hunt, 1868–1952,* Pasadena, Baxter Art Gallery, 1984, 22–55.

48. Virginia Historical Society Manuscript, VHS-MSS1W412bb/Fa2. See also *A Description of Virginia House, in Henrico County, near Richmond, Virginia,* Richmond, Virginia, Historical Society, 1947. The house is currently open to the public as part of the society's collections.

49. Aslet, *Last Country Houses,* 183–212.

50. James T. Maher, *The Twilight of Splendor,* Boston, Little Brown, 1975, 197, and entire chapter on Vizcaya, 159–214.

51. Ibid., 159–178. A complete and detailed description of the roles of Chalfin, Hoffman, Suarez, and Deering in the design and construction of the estate can be found here, including Chalfin's bitter feelings about credit and authorship.

52. Chalfin, quoted in John Barrington Bayley, "The Villa Vizcaya," in *Classical America,* no. 3 (1973): 71. Quotes taken from *Arch. Review* (July 1917).

53. Marcus Binney, "Villa Vizcaya, Flordia - I," *Country Life* (UK) (10 January 1980): 73; from Chalfin's description in the *Miami Herald,* 1934.

54. Chalfin, "The Gardens at Vizcaya," *Arch. Review* (July 1917): 123.

55. After two years of preliminary planning and site work, construction on the house began in May 1914. See Kathryn Chapman Harwood, *The Lives of Vizcaya,* Miami, Banyan, 1985, chapters 1–4.

56. Chalfin, "The Gardens at Vizcaya," 123.

57. The idea of a home or domicile as a representation of the self in psychological and sociological terms has been convincingly demonstrated by Claire Cooper. See her "The House as Symbol of Self," in Lang et al., eds., *Designing for Human Behavior,* Stroudsburg, Penn., Dowden, Hutchinston and Ross, 1974, 130–146.

58. T. J. Jackson Lears, *No Place of Grace: Antimodernism and the Transformation of American Culture 1880–1920,* New York, 1981.

59. Desmond and Croly, *Stately Homes,* 408.

5 Country Places

Epigraph: "What This Magazine Stands For," editorial, *Country Life in America* 1 (November 1901–April 1902): 24–25. The editorial goes on to proclaim: "The interest in country life is various. . . . Some [want] to get away from the city, some [want] nature for nature's sake, some [are] farmers. Spread out a map of North America. Note the mere dots that represent cities; contrast the immense expanses of the country."

1. Newton, *Design On the Land,* Cambridge, Harvard University Press, 1971, 427–446.

2. Like the term *country house, country place* is not precisely defined in the popular literature, but it appears often in descriptions of country houses around 1900 to describe estates that are clearly not suburban but that also do not conform to the gigantic dimensions of some stately home properties (ranging in the hundreds, even thousands of acres). I have used the term somewhat loosely here, to describe houses that partook of the general arcadian philosophy of the house and garden movement. For a peculiar, capitalistic slant on the concept, see Joseph Dillaway Sawyer, *How to Make a Country Place,* New York, O. Judd, 1914.

3. Peter T. Schmitt, *Back To Nature: The Arcadian Myth in Urban America,* New York, Oxford University Press, 1969, 16–19.

4. The house was reputedly a duplicate of Shakespeare's dwelling at Stratford-on-Avon.

5. Doubleday Page, the publisher of *Country Life in America,* had its headquarters in Garden City, Long Island. It was more than a business for its owners, who saw themselves as prophets of country living and gardening. Frank Nelson Doubleday married Neltje de Graaf (1865–1918) in 1886, and the two were tireless advocates of the pastoral way of life. Using her pen name, Neltje Blanchan, Mrs. Doubleday published several popular books on native plants, garden cultivation, and horticulture. The press sponsored many books on gardening, house building, leisure activities, sports, architecture, and general memoirs on country living.

6. Frances Kinsley Hutchinson, *Wychwood: The History of An Idea,* Chicago, A. C. McClurg, 1928, 164, 235. Three vols. published as one: *Our Country Home* (1907), *Our Country Life* (1912), *Our Final Aim* (1928).

7. Ibid., 162.

8. Mrs. Hutchinson was guided by the ideas of Charles Sprague Sargent, the noted horticulturist, in planning her seventy-acre country place. She conceived one of the earliest and most influential wild gardens in America there, as well as a wildlife refuge and conservation area for native plants. The grounds of the house were laid out with the professional design assistance of the Olmsted Brothers. Mrs. Hutchinson went on to found the Lake Geneva Garden Club and the Gardeners' and Foremen's Association. She deeded the estate to the University of Chicago in 1932, stipulating that it could not be sold for twenty-five years. Unfortunately, at the end of that period, after careful maintenance by the university, the estate was sold and the house heavily altered.

9. See Louise de Koven Bowen, *Baymeath* (privately printed), Chicago, Ralph F. Seymour, 1944–45, 137 pages, 15 illustrations. See also abridged excerpts in *Yankee Magazine* (September 1974): 101–110; C. William Chilman, "Baymeath and the Bar Harbor That Was," *New England Galaxy* (Summer 1972): 10–20; Dalton Wylie, "Lessons from a Seaside Estate," *Country Life in America* (July 1907): 308–318.

10. Bowen, *Baymeath,* 33.

11. Caroline T. Trambell, "Ida M. Tarbell and Her Farm," *Country Life in America* 29, no. 1 (November 1915): 19.

12. For an excellent treatment of her life there, see R. W. B. Lewis, *Edith Wharton, A Biography,* New York, Harper and Row, 1975, chapter 9, 135–156.

13. Information on the construction and design of The Mount courtesy of Scott Marshall, assistant director, Edith Wharton Restorations. Mr. Marshall's history of the house is contained in chapters of a Historic Structures Report prepared by Mesick, Cohen and Waite, Architects, of Albany. I am grateful to him for providing me with a draft of these sections.

14. See Wharton and Codman, *The Decoration of Houses,* New York, Scribner's, 1897. For an analysis of the relationship between the two, see Richard Guy Wilson, "Edith and Ogden: Writing, Decoration, and Architecture," in Metcalf, ed., *Ogden Codman and the Decoration of Houses,* 133–184. There is an extensive treatment of The Mount's design in this essay as well, including the initial plan studies made by Codman before he was replaced as architect.

15. Edith Wharton, *A Backward Glance,* New York, D. Appleton-Century, 1934, 149, 143.

16. John Baptiste Fisher, "A Jaunt to Wychwood, Lake Geneva, Wisconsin," *AR* 17, no. 2 (February 1905): 127.

17. This is particularly evident in the survey published in Boston's *Arch. Review* 11 (1904): 1–122. Among the many informal houses featured are Howard Shaw's Ragdale; Wilson Eyre's house for Thomas Shields Clarke in Lenox, Massachusetts; Bernard Maybeck's extraordinary Sierra Camp for Phoebe Hearst in Siskiyou County, California; John Calvin Stevens' shingled house for Mrs. Henry St. John Smith, Bellefield, in Maine; and Charles Platt's Cabot house in Hyde Park, Massachusetts.

18. *National Cyclopedia of American Biography,* vol. 21, 396–397. Collier was the leader of the Lincoln Farm Association, which raised funds for the purchase of Lincoln's birthplace at Hodgenville, Kentucky. He commissioned John Russell Pope to design a classical memorial there to house the famous log cabin.

19. Patterson, *American Homes of To-Day,* 61.

20. Barr Ferree, "Notable American Homes: 'Hill-Stead,' the Estate of Alfred Atmore Pope, Esq., Farmington, Conn.," *American Homes and Gardens* (February 1910): 45.

21. For a discussion of the conditions of the founding of the Hill-Stead museum and the subsequent lawsuits involving its operations, see Nancy LaRoche, "The Hill-Stead Museum," *Art News* 4 (December 1975): 70–71.

22. On the collection, see Helen Hall, "Alfred and Ada Pope as Collectors," *Antiques* 134, no. 4 (October 1987): 862–863.

23. On Pope's life, see *Who's Who in America,* 1909, 752; 1910–11, 1531. Originally in business with his father and brothers, Alton Pope and Sons, woolen manufacturers, he joined the Cleveland iron firm as secretary/treasurer in 1869. He became president of Cleveland Malleable Iron in 1877 and consolidated several midwestern iron firms into the National Malleable Castings Company.

24. Emeny Brooks, *Theodate Pope Riddle and the Founding of Avon Old Farms* (privately printed), 1973, 6; quoted in Judith Paine, *Theodate Pope Riddle,* New York, Theodore Roosevelt Birthplace, 1979, 3.

25. See Paine, above, 4; and archives, Hill-Stead Museum, letter of December 1893 to A. Marquand of the Princeton faculty about studying. She appears to have been at Princeton during the spring of 1895 and spring of 1896.

26. Telegram, no. 527, dated 3 August 1898, from Alfred Pope to Theodate, Hill-Stead archives.

27. Letter, no. 539, dated 5 September 1898, Innsbruck, AAP to TP, Hill-Stead archives.

28. The letter, in the McKim, Mead and White collection of the New York Historical Society, reads as follows:

McKim, Mead and White   Farmington, Connecticut

Dear Sirs,

We are considering building a country home in this town and want plans to look at. It is my father who persuaded Mr. J. H. Whittemore of Naugatuck, Conn. to have his house planned by you and as a result all the other buildings he has since put up. (This is simply an aside, as an introduction).

Do you think you would better send some one up to see the site or can you work to good advantage after my description of the location which I will give you.

We are very accustomed to seeing plans and know at a glance if they have had much *thought* spent on them. The location is a knoll with the land sloping away in a valley to the *west* which the house will face. The drive to the house is from the South. The house is to be frame — one very large living room very [large] dining [room] also a study and bedroom and little sitting room — the two last connected, then pantrys [sic] kitchen scullery and laundry *all* on ground floor. Do what you can for nice guest rooms up stairs besides servants rooms have two guest rooms with baths connecting also a general bath room and one connected with first floor bed room. Now the important thing to be born in mind is not to make a *pretty* looking drawing — that does not take with us at all — we want a beautifully planned house in thoroughly good style and *self*-contained and dignified. Will you furnish plans according to this *not an elevation* at present and then furnish working plans and a man to oversee it but have it built by Hartford builders?

And please — what time you have spent on this preliminary plan have the man spend in thought and not in lines with fancy lead coloring. We know all that.

Sincerely, Theodate Pope

29. It has been assumed that Stanford White was the partner in charge of the commission, yet nothing in the correspondence indicates this. William Rutherford Mead appears to have handled the early negotiations with the Popes, after which Egerton Swartwout, one of White's assistants, was put in charge. Except in rare cases in which a conflict develops, Theodate acted as liaison between the architects and her father throughout the design and production of working drawings, which occured between August 1898 and February 1900. She also acted as an on-site superintendent, for which the architects reduced their fee from the traditional 10 percent to 3½ percent of the construction cost. Leland Roth, the leading McKim, Mead and White scholar, was the first to attribute the job to White, although he has recently questioned the attribution. His assessment of the reasons behind the firm's decision to go ahead with the job under such unusual circumstances were spelled out in a letter to Katherine Warwick, shared with the author. He points out that the firm had gone through a difficult recession and needed the commission and that they did not want to turn down Alfred Pope because he was a close friend of one of their biggest clients, John Howard Whittemore of Naugatuck, for whom they designed virtually an entire town. Letter from Leland Roth to Katherine Warwick, 24 April 1988, Hill-Stead archives.

30. Letter from TP to Swartwout, 13 October 1898, New York Historical Society.

31. "C. F. McKim (?), on Colonial Architecture," in Roth, *America Builds,* 232.

32. For the best treatment to date of the development of Colonial Revival houses, see Rhoads, *The Colonial Revival,* especially chapter 3, "The Colonial Revival House to 1885," 48–76, and chapter 5, "The Georgian Revival After 1885," 82–104. On the Breese house and other Long Island work of McKim, Mead and White, see Steven Bedford, *The Long Island Country House, 1870–1930,* Southampton, Parrish Art Museum, 1988, 55–63.

33. Theodate Pope, diaries for 1901–02, Hill-Stead archives. The house was first published in the *Arch. Review* in 1903, showing the porch. Later, in *AR* 20, no. 2 (August 1906): 122–129, the house was extensively documented. There are thus no photographs of the building without the porch addition.

34. James, *The American Scene,* 45–46.

35. Eyre's project list records work on the Pepper estate during the years 1887 (residence), 1893 (alterations), 1895 (barns and sheds), 1898 (alterations), 1899 (stables), 1901 (alterations), 1902 (alterations), and 1904 (second house).

36. For a published memoir of the trip, see "From Liverpool to London," *Arch. Review* (Boston) 4 (January 1896): 3–5; see also typescripts, cited below, n. 42.

37. Baltzell, *Philadelphia Gentlemen,* 75, 93, 168–171.

38. For a biography of John W. Pepper and a genealogy of the Pepper family, see Thomas Lynch Montgomery, *Encyclopedia of Pennsylvania Biography,* 1923, vol. 14, 210–212. The son of Frederick Seckel Pepper (1814–1891, one of eight children of George Pepper and Mary Catherine Seckel), John Pepper was born on June 24, 1852. Educated in Philadelphia schools, he entered business with his uncle, William Lowber, in 1868, eventually becoming vice president of the Sharpless Dyewood Extract Company, a producer of dyes. Pepper retired from business in 1906 to devote himself to philanthropy and to his estate. He married twice, first to cousin Emily A. Lowber, in 1879, and after her death to Henrietta Dallas Bache, great granddaughter of Benjamin Franklin, in 1910. Listed in the *Blue Book* of 1918, Pepper held memberships in the Acorn, Rittenhouse, Raquet, Huntington Valley Country, Germantown Cricket, and Philadelphia Country Clubs. He was a director of the Insurance Company of North America and a vestryman in the churches of St. James the Less, St. Luke's in Philadelphia, and the Church of Our Savior in Jenkintown.

39. Julian Millard, "The Work of Wilson Eyre," *AR* 14 (1903): 290: "In an attempt to be eccentric the plan has become awkward especially in the hall and dining-room. . . . The exterior is an outgrowth of the plan, but, while the various parts are well designed and the whole excites a lively interest, the architectural effect is disappointing."

40. A note on the back of one of Eyre's drawings of the first house, probably written by Louisa Eyre, calls it "the one Wilson did not like," indicating that the architect came to share his critics' opinions of the earlier version. Eyre Collection, Avery Architectural Archives, Columbia University.

41. Millard, "The Work of Wilson Eyre," 292.

42. Typescript (5 pages) of an article by Wilson Eyre, "Some months ago I took a delightful sketching trip to England," in Wilson Eyre Collection, Avery Architectural Archives, Columbia University, manuscript box F108, C33, folder no. 6, p. 4. Preceding quote from p. 5.

43. Saylor, "The Best Twelve Country Houses in America: Fairacres, The Home of John W. Pepper at Jenkintown, Pa.," *Country Life in America* 28 (September 1915): 27.

44. Frederick Wallick, "'Fairacres' and Some Other Recent Country Houses by Wilson Eyre," *International Studio* 40, no. 158 (April 1910): 29–34 and plates; "Alterations and Additions to Country House for Mr. John W. Pepper, Jenkintown, Pa.," *AR* (October 1918): 410–418. See also *AABN* 93, no. 1684 (April 1908), for floor plans; "The Residence of J. W. Pepper, Jenkintown," *House and Garden* (November 1906); and "Country House That Will Become a Museum," *Arts and Decoration* (November 1932). The house was then presented to the Museum of the City of Philadelphia by Henrietta Sands Merrick. It no longer stands.

45. The house still stands in relatively unaltered condition, recently sold by the estate of Chapman's son, Chanler Armstrong Chapman. See John Zukowsky and Robbe Pierce Stimson, *Hudson River Villas,* New York, Rizzoli, 186–187.

46. Chapman's major books include *Emerson and Other Essays* (1883), *Causes and Consequences* (1898), and *Practical Agitation* (1900). See *Who's Who in America,* 1910–11, vol. 6, 344.

47. Melvin Bernstein, "John Jay Chapman and the Insurgent Individual," in H. Goldberg, ed., *American Radicals,* New York, Monthly Review Press, 1957, 21–35.

48. John Jay Chapman, *Causes and Consequences,* New York, 1898, 64.

49. *Arch. Review* 15 (January 1908): 10; "The House of Mr. John J. Chapman at Barrytown, N.Y.," *AR* 24, no. 9 (September 1908): 207–217.

50. Morgan, *Charles A. Platt,* 97–100.

51. "Residence of John Jay Chapman, Esq.," *Arch. Review* 15 (January 1908): 10.

52. On Bartlett's life, see *Who's Who in America,* 1901–02, 64. He was born in Stratford, New York, in 1844 and went to Chicago to seek his fortune at age nineteen. He made his way up in the business world by hard work, first entering the employ of Tuttle, Hibbard and Co. and later becoming a partner in several firms. He was president of the Commercial Club of Chicago (which commissioned the famous 1909 Burnham/Bennett plan) and a trustee of the University of Chicago. This or any of his many club affiliations would have brought him into contact with Howard Shaw.

53. Leonard K. Eaton, *Two Chicago Architects and Their Clients,* Cambridge, MIT Press, 1969, 160. Eaton's book does not profile the Bartlett houses but extensively analyzes the connections between Shaw's education, beliefs, and social affiliations and those of his major clients—the Swifts, Ryersons, Marks, Vincents, et al.

54. Saylor, "The Best Twelve Country Houses in America: The House in the Woods, The Home of A.C. Bartlett, Esq., Lake Geneva, Wis.," *Country Life in America* (March 1916). The other houses in the series were: McKim, Mead and White's estate for James Breese; Charles Platt's The Manor House for John T. Pratt in Glen Cove, Long Island; Charles Klauder's own house in Mt. Airy, Pennsylvania; Electus Litchfield's own place in New Canaan, Connecticut; the John W. Pepper house in Jenkintown, Pennsylvania, by Eyre and McIlvaine; El Fureidis, by Bertram Goodhue in Montecito, California; Francis T. Underhill's own house in Santa Barbara; the Truman Newberry house in Grosse Pointe Farms, Michigan; Eastover, Platt's Palmer house in New London, Connecticut; Albro and Lindeberg's Foxhollow Farm in Rhinebeck, New York; and (surely for honorific reasons) George Washington's Mount Vernon.

55. Samuel Howe, ed., *American Country Houses of To-Day,* New York, Architectural Book Publishing, 1915, 49.

56. Geneva Lake Land Conservancy, *Lake Geneva Historic Survey,* 1984, including report on the Snake Road Historic district, in which both Wychwood and House in the Woods are located. Courtesy of the State Historical Society of Wisconsin.

57. For a more detailed account of this development, upon which this is based, see my "William Adams Delano and the Muttontown Enclave," *Antiques* (August 1987): 316–327.

58. This house, like the others in the enclave, was published in Delano and Aldrich, *Portraits of Ten Country Houses,* Garden City, Doubleday Page, 1924, plates 44–49. Photos appear in *American Architect* 1081, no. 2063 (7 July 1915).

59. See for instance the W. G. Borland House in Mount Kisco (Howe, *American Country Houses of To-Day,* 1915, 21–25), the W. Osgood Field House in Lenox, Massachusetts (232–233), and the C. B. Alexander House in Bernardsville, New Jersey (27–33).

60. William Adams Delano, text of address given upon receipt of the AIA Gold Medal, dated 30 March 1953. Avery Architectural Archives, Columbia University.

61. Delano and Aldrich, *Portraits of Ten Country Houses,* xii.

62. Farrand worked on Delano's house from 1921 on, after the basic site plan had been made. Her association with the firm extended to other major projects, the most important of which was the Willard Straight estate (1914–32). Diana Balmori, Diane Kustial McGuire, and Eleanor McPeck, ed., *Beatrix Farrand's American Landscapes: Her Gardens and Campuses,* Sagaponack, New York, Sagapress, 1985, 197–201.

63. For his own remembrances of country life at Muttontown, see "Reminiscences of William Adams Delano," Columbia Oral History Project, 1972, 23–26.

64. Not to be confused with the elder Egerton (1839–1916), friend of Edith Wharton and father of Bronson and Egerton, Jr. (1862–1926). The younger was also an attorney and member of his brother's firm. See *National Cyclopedia of American Biography,* vol. 38, 569, for his life and career.

65. Samuel Howe, "The Country House of Mr. E. L. Winthrop, Jr.," *Town and Country* (14 November 1914): 16–17. See also Howe, *American Country Houses of To-Day,* 1915, 240–245; *Architecture* 41, no. 4 (April 1920): plate 56.

66. The standard interpretation of Wright's antiurban views is given in Morton and Lucia White, *The Intellectual Versus*

the City, New York, Oxford University Press, 1977, 189–199. The authors argue that FLW was the most "irascible, bombastic critic of the American city," and the architectural counterpart of "Dewey in philosophy, Jane Addams in social work, and Robert Park in urban sociology."

67. "Prairie Architecture," in E. J. Kaufmann and Ben Raeburn, ed., *Frank Lloyd Wright: Writings and Buildings,* Cleveland, Meriden Books, 1960, 38–55; excerpted and reprinted from his *Modern Architecture,* 1931.

68. These client relationships are analyzed, and this point is made in Eaton, *Two Chicago Architects and Their Clients.* See also Joseph Connors, *The Robie House of Frank Lloyd Wright,* Chicago, University of Chicago Press, 1984, and Morrison Hechscher and Elizabeth Miller, *An Architect and His Client, Frank Lloyd Wright and Francis W. Little,* New York, Metropolitan Museum of Art, 1973. There is more material on Wright's client relationships than on those of any other American architect.

69. The story of Wright's celebrated and controversial affair and its tragic aftermath is recounted and evenhandedly analyzed in Robert C. Twombly, *Frank Lloyd Wright: His Life and His Architecture,* New York, John Wiley, 1979, 119–143. Twombly points out that Taliesin was both open and closed, environment-embracing and fortresslike, and that Wright "attempted to maximize contact with nature—to him benign and inspirational— [while] also looking to minimize contact with a suspicious and critical world" (135).

70. See Creese, *The Crowning of the American Landscape,* chapter 8.

71. For a concise clarification and analysis of Wright's planning, see H. Allen Brooks, "Frank Lloyd Wright and the Destruction of the Box," *Journal of the Society of Architectural Historians* (hereafter cited as *JSAH*) 38, no. 1 (March 1979): 7–14.

72. Wright's relationship to nature was brilliantly analyzed by Neil Levine and Kathryn Smith in their lectures at the 1986 conference on Fallingwater at the Buell Center for the Study of American Architecture at Columbia University.

73. Taliesin was published in *AR* 33 (January 1913): 45–54; *Western Architect* 19 (February 1913): n.p.; and P. B. Wright's article on the country house in the Midwest in *AR* 38 (October 1915): 385–421. Wright's own extensive comments on it, excerpted from *An Autobiography,* 1932, can be found in Kaufmann and Raeburn, *Frank Lloyd Wright,* 172–181.

74. Walter Creese carefully analyzes the development of the various buildings on the site and illustrates several site plans showing the estate at various stages of its life. He also mentions the original approach to the house and the sweeping entrance drives (*Crowning,* 241–263).

75. Dates for all Wright projects are taken from William Allin Storrer, *The Architecture of Frank Lloyd Wright,* 2nd ed., Cambridge, MIT Press, 1982. See entries 172, 182, 218 for the Taliesin houses. Only the living quarters of Taliesin I were destroyed in the first fire.

76. For an excellent history of this house, see Kathryn Smith, "Frank Lloyd Wright, Hollyhock House and Olive Hill, 1914–24," *JSAH* 38, no. 1 (March 1979): 15–33. Smith points out that although there was no direct relationship between the plans of the two houses, the Olive Hill artistic complex and Taliesin had much in common programmatically, philosophically, and conceptually.

77. "Van Beuren, Michael Murray, Stockbroker," *National Cyclopedia of American Biography,* vol. 39, 499. Van Beuren, a Republican and Episcopalian, was a member of the Union, Brook, Turf and Field, Raquet and Tennis, and Westminster Kennel Clubs. He served as a leader of

a number of Newport clubs, including the Newport Casino, Clambake, Reading Room, and Country Clubs. He was also active on the Newport Town Council and on the Rhode Island State Board of Roads.

78. Colin Carroll, "Newport's Classic Home," *Arts and Decoration* 45 (October 1936): 16.

79. Jeanne Marie Teutonico, "Marian Cruger Coffin: The Long Island Estates. A Study of the Early Work of a Pioneering Woman in American Landscape Architecture," Master's thesis in historic preservation, Columbia University, 1983. This and much of the following material comes from chapter 4, on Hillwood, 67–85.

80. The house was published first in *AR* 52 (December 1922): 492–494. See also Liisa and Donald Sclare, *Beaux-Arts Estates,* New York, Viking, 1979, 138–143.

81. Teutonico, "Coffin," 74.

82. The firm, Field, Glore and Co., was founded with Charles F. Glore and Pierce C. Ward. Field divorced Evelyn Marshall in 1930 and immediately married Audrey James Coats, the English goddaughter of Edward VII. Evelyn, significantly, married the noted garden designer Diego Suarez and built a fine country house in nearby Syosset.

83. Daniel P. Higgins, "Business and Management in the Practice of Architecture," *AABN* 133, no. 2543 (20 April 1928): 491–567. Caumsett was featured in two previous volumes of the magazine: 130 (30 August 1926): 171–173; and 131 (20 January 1927): winter cottage photos. See also *Monograph of the Work of John Russell Pope,* New York, Helburn, 1937, vol. 3, plates 51–75.

84. "Editorial Comment," *AABN* 133 (20 April 1928): 503. The editor stresses the history of the place, noting that it was first a favorite camping ground of the Matinecock, Massapeaque, and Secatogne tribes. Two British forts were located on Lloyd's Neck, as was a 1712 manor house, at one time occupied by Benjamin Thompson, Count Rumford. "Tradition, legend and history give Loyd Neck a romantic background which we are glad to see has evidently been considered and perpetuated in the design of the Estate of Mrs. Field."

85. John Trebbel, *The Marshall Fields: A Study in Wealth,* New York, Dutton, 1947, 170–185 and ff. See also *National Cyclopedia of American Biography,* vol. G, 1943–46, 85–86.

86. See Julius and Jacqueline Sadler, *American Stables: An Architectural Tour,* New York, New York Graphic Society, 1981.

87. Patterson, *American Homes of To-Day,* 112. See all of chapter 6 for several of Pope's houses, including the Field estate.

88. Howe, *American Country Houses of To-Day,* 1915, 317.

6 Regional Traditions

Epigraphs: John Gaw Meem, "Old Forms for New Buildings," *The American Architect* 145 (November 1934): 20; David Gebhard, *George Washington Smith, 1876–1930: The Spanish Colonial Revival in California,* Santa Barbara, The Art Gallery, University of California at Santa Barbara, 1964, 1. See also Gebhard, "The Spanish Colonial Revival in Southern California (1895–1930)," *JSAH* 26, no. 2 (May 1967): 131–147.

1. Cf. H. Allen Brooks, *The Prairie School,* Toronto, University of Toronto Press, 1972; and Longstreth, *On the Edge of the World.*

2. Anne Rowe, "Regionalism and Popular Culture," in M. Thos. Inge, ed., *Handbook of American Popular Culture,* vol. 3, Westport, Ct., Greenwood Press, 1981, 413–427.

3. "Antiques Speaks for Itself," *Antiques, A Magazine for Collectors and Others Who Find Interest in Times Past and in the Articles for Daily Use and Adornment Devised by the Forefathers* 1, no. 1 (January 1922): 7–9.

4. Jackson, *Crabgrass Frontier,* 175. The author argues that the most significant factors in the suburban boom between the wars were the automobile and municipal annexation. See chapters 8–10.

5. Both were instrumental in the creation of the Mission Revival. Jackson's novel *Ramona* (1884) became a beacon for Anglo-Hispanicism; Lummis' editorship of *The Land of Sunshine* and the founding of the Landmark Club in Los Angeles in 1894 were crucial to the growth of the Spanish Colonial myth. See Gebhard, "Architectural Imagery," 137–145; and Kevin Starr, *Inventing the Dream: California Through the Progressive Era,* New York, Oxford University Press, 1985, 31–98.

6. Among the dozens of articles emphasizing regional country house living, see "An Early Connecticut Farmhouse Undergoes a Second Regeneration," *House and Garden* (April 1930): 111–113; "The Classical Style in Syracuse, New York" [the Greek Revival W. L. Sporburg house by Dwight James Baum], *House and Garden* (November 1929): 115–117; "Reviving the Greek Revival" [Neel Reid's Mimosa Hall], *House and Garden* (January 1925): 47–49; Erna Ferguson, "Adobe or Not Adobe: The Southwest Has Its Own Architecture," *Country Life in America* (January 1931): 65–66; "Ancient Architecture in Santa Fe, New Mexico," *AABN* 125, no. 2445 (7 May 1924): 421–424; "In the Vernacular of Pennsylvania" [J. R. Pope, T. H. Carstairs house, Ardmore, Pa.], and "An Adobe House of the Southwest" [for Samuel Hamilton], *House and Garden* (April 1925); "Ranch Estate of Thomas H. Ince, Beverly Hills, Calif." [Roy Seldon Price, architect], *AABN* 125, no. 2448 (18 June 1924); and "Canterbury Farms, The Warrenton, Virginia Estate of Mrs. Albert E. Pierce" [Walcott and Work, architects], *Country Life in America* 69 (March 1936): 39–41.

7. Meem, "Old Forms," 13.

8. William Lawrence Bottomley, "The American Country House," *AR* 48 (November 1920): 259.

9. He illustrated and analyzed the following houses, among others: Mellor, Meigs and Howe's Caspar Morris house—representing the English type; George Washington Smith's Casa Dracaena, built for himself in 1916 in Montecito—the Andalusian type; M. H. Baillie-Scott's unusual Henry B. Binse house in Short Hills, New Jersey—the Arts and Crafts type; Willis Polk's Charles D. Blaney estate in Saratoga, California—the Mission type; John Russell Pope's Andrew V. Stout house in Red Bank, New Jersey—the Georgian Colonial type; and Reginald Johnson's T. R. Coffin house in San Marino, California—another variant of Spanish Colonial. See above, 295–360.

10. Richard Cheek brought this information to my attention.

11. It is now being reprinted. See William C. Davis, "Historical Introduction to the Series," *Architectural Treasures of Early America,* Harrisburg, Pa., 1987, vol. 1, 5–7.

12. Lewis E. Crook, Jr., ed., *Southern Architecture Illustrated,* Atlanta, American Institute of Architects, 1931. Introduction by Dwight James Baum. Atlanta supported two architectural journals during this period: *Southern Architect and Building News,* published from 1927 through 1932, and *Southern Architectural Review,* published from March 1936 through May 1938.

13. Cf. American Institute of Architects, *Residential Architecture in Southern California,* Los Angeles, 1939; and H. Philip Staats, *California Architecture in Santa Barbara,* New York, Architectural Book Publishing Co., 1929.

14. Arthur Ingersoll Meigs, *An American Country House: The Property of Arthur E. Newbold, Jr., Laverock, Pa.,* New York, Architectural Book Publishing, 1925. The farm is discussed by Edward Teitelman in "Philadelphia Tradition, Architectural Images of Farm and Forefathers,

1919–1931," a paper presented at the Thirty-eighth Annual Meeting of the Society of Architectural Historians in Pittsburgh, April 1985. See also *T-Square Club Annual,* 1929; and G. H. Edgell, *American Architecture of To-Day,* New York, Scribner's, 1928, 116, 47–55.

15. "Walter Mellor," biography by "C.M.P.," *Brickbuilder* 24, no. 8 (August 1915): 208.

16. Owen Wister, preface, *Monograph of the Works of Mellor, Meigs and Howe,* New York, Architectural Book Publishing, 1923, unpaginated.

17. Howe seceded from the firm in 1928, taking with him the prestigious Philadelphia Savings Fund Society building, which he executed in an International Style idiom with William Lescaze in 1929. For a comprehensive discussion and interpretation of Howe's work with the firm, see Robert A. M. Stern, *George Howe: Toward A Modern American Architecture,* New Haven, Yale University Press, 1975, 30–54.

18. Chandler (1845–1928) was educated at Harvard and in Paris at the Atelier of Vaudremer. Of old New England ancestry, he was a great patrician clubman, with memberships in the Radnor Hunt Club, Union League, Sons of the Revolution, and Society of Mayflower Ancestors. He was connected through his mother's family to the DuPonts of Delaware and worked on alterations to Winterthur among other commissions for the family. See Tatman and Moss, *Biographical Dictionary of Philadelphia Architects,* 139–143.

19. Tatman and Moss, *Biographical Dictionary,* 524–527. See also the entry for George Howe (1886–1955), 394–396.

20. Francis Salisbury McIlhenny (born in Georgia in 1873) was one of the city's most prominent attorneys and a director of a number of major corporations. He received his B.A. (1895) and LL. B. (1898) from the University of Pennsylvania and was admitted to the Pennsylvania bar in 1898. He served as a state senator from 1907 to 1915. See *Who's Who in America,* 1920–21, p. 1914.

21. Sandra Lee Tatman, "A Study of the Work of Mellor, Meigs and Howe," Master's thesis, University of Oregon, 1977, 51; see also 1–10, 34–60. The study also contains a relatively complete bibliography and a catalogue of works.

22. *Monograph of the Works of Mellor, Meigs and Howe,* 33; reprinted from *Arch. Forum* (October 1919).

23. The best coverage of this house is found in the Mellor, Meigs and Howe *Monograph,* 1–13. See also *Arts and Decoration* 12, no. 6 (April 1920): 400–401; *Arch. Forum* 31, no. 4 (October 1919): 122.

24. Among the illustrious members of this Philadelphia family were Cadwalader Morris (1741–95), a merchant and member of the Continental Congress; Anthony Morris (1654–1721), mayor of Philadelphia from 1703 to 1704; and the physician Caspar Morris (1805–84), the founder of several major hospitals and a noted member of the medical profession in America.

25. See Tatman and Moss, *Biographical Dictionary,* 629–632. I am indebted to George E. Thomas, Price's biographer, for information on Price's country house work.

26. For biographical and interpretive information, see Tatman and Moss, *Biographical Dictionary,* 304–307, 514–517. See also Daniel C. Williamson, "The Architecture of Robert Rodes McGoodwin," unpublished essay, 1977, Atheneum of Philadelphia; Gilchrist papers and drawings, Architectural Archives, University of Pennsylvania.

27. Lewis Mumford, "The Architecture of Escape," *The New Republic* 43 (12 August 1925): 321–322.

28. Kevin Starr, *Americans and the California Dream, 1850–1915,* New York, Oxford University Press, 1973, esp. 365–414; and Starr's sequel, *Inventing the Dream.*

29. See Harold Kirker, *California's Architectural Frontier,* Salt

Lake City, Peregrine Smith, 1986 (reprint of 1960 edition).

30. Saylor, "The Best Twelve Country Houses," pt. 4, *Country Life in America* 28 (October 1915): 29–31. Though most observers saw Spanish influence in the house, Saylor described its style as "indefinite," while admitting its exoticism and allure.

31. Oliver, *Bertram Grosvenor Goodhue,* 40–42. As the author points out, Goodhue was a fanciful inventor of architectural images, illustrating places he had never even seen in magnificently evocative renderings. Particularly interesting were his three travel articles on imaginary historical places: St. Kavin's Church, Traumburg, Bohemia; Monteventoso, Italy; and Villa Fosca, Italy (written during 1897–99). The drawings became important sources for his later architectural designs. Goodhue, *A Book of Architectural and Decorative Drawings by Bertram Grosvenor Goodhue,* New York, Architectural Book Publishing, 1914.

32. Goodhue, *A Book of Architectural and Decorative Drawings,* 89–97.

33. The house was extensively published in its time. See Day, *American Country Houses of To-Day,* 1912, 52–58; *Arch. Review* (Boston) 10 (September 1903): 139–140; *House and Garden* 4 (September 1903): 97–103; Montgomery Schuyler, "Works of Cram, Goodhue and Ferguson," *AR* 29 (January 1911): 14–16; and "El Fuereidas [sic]," *Sunset Magazine* 32 (May 1914): 1060–1063.

34. Clark, *Myron Hunt.* Hunt was a successful Arts and Crafts architect in Chicago from 1896 to 1903, when his wife's ill health forced him to move his family to Pasadena. Practicing with Grey, formerly of Milwaukee, who also came to California for health reasons, he quickly became one of the leaders of the California regionalist movement.

35. For a history of its development as a resort and information on estates and country places, see Myrick, *Montecito and Santa Barbara.*

36. The Montecito Land Company developed the hills around that village in the 1880s, buying and subdividing some four hundred acres of land. See David Gebhard and Robert Winter, *A Guide to Architecture in Los Angeles and Southern California,* Salt Lake City, Peregrine Smith, 1977, 560–561; and Myrick, above, 81–104.

37. Gebhard, *George Washington Smith,* 1–2.

38. John Taylor Boyd, "Houses Showing a Distinguished Simplicity," *Arts and Decoration* 33, no. 6 (October 1930): 57.

39. As David Gebhard has pointed out in his seminal analysis of Smith's work, the paintings of Cézanne and Gauguin, primitive and folk art forms, and a general admiration for the abstract simplicity of modern art were at the heart of Smith's architecture. *George Washington Smith,* 1–6.

40. Ibid.

41. David Gebhard, "Casa del Herrero, the George F. Steedman house, Montecito, California," *Antiques* (August 1986): 280–283. In the same issue, see also David C. Streatfield, "The Garden at Casa del Herrero," 284–289.

42. On the gardens and their development, see Streatfield, above, 284–289. Stevens' original plan was extensively altered by both the Steedmans and the two other landscape architects over the years.

43. *AR* 60 (November 1926): 471–474. The house was also illustrated in the compendium of Santa Barbara architecture: Staats, *California Architecture in Santa Barbara.*

44. See *Arch. Forum* 56 (April 1932): 361–366; for Hanson's own description of the gardens, see A. E. Hanson, *An Arcadian Landscape,* Los Angeles, Hennessey and Ingalls, 1985, 69–83.

45. Boyd, "Houses Showing Distinguished Simplicity," 59.

46. This and the above information on the Bryces' travels are courtesy of their grandson, Marc Appleton, who has a complete file on the estate. The author wishes to thank Mr. Appleton for his comments, analysis, and photos concerning this as well as other Smith projects. Florestal was sold upon Mrs. Bryce's death in the early 1980s; a second house was constructed on the site, and the original house severely altered.

47. Neff designed houses for, among others, Douglas Fairbanks, Jr., Groucho Marx, Frederick March, King Vidor, and Amelita Galli-Curci. See Alson Clark and Wallace Neff, Jr., ed., *Wallace Neff: Architect of California's Golden Age,* Santa Barbara, Capra Press, 1986.

48. David Gebhard, Lauren Bricker, and David Bricker, *A Catalogue of the Architectural Drawing Collection,* University of California at Santa Barbara, 1983, 145; see also Lauren Weiss Bricker, "The Residential Architecture of Roland E. Coate, Jr.," Master's thesis, University of California at Santa Barbara, 1983.

49. It nevertheless confused some observers. See "Spain of the Moors Finds a Renaissance in California," *House and Garden* (January 1930): 93–95.

50. See Longstreth, *On the Edge of the World.*

51. "A Ranch in the Hills of California, Belonging to King C. Gillette, Esq.," *Country Life in America* 59 (December 1930): 43–45.

52. Ibid., 44.

53. See "Kemper Campbell Ranch," (California) *Architect and Engineer* (October 1946): 21–25, for photos and information on construction. The date of initial construction is from a typescript by Elliot Welsh on the work of John Byers, p. 54, courtesy of Marc Appleton. See also Gebhard, Bricker, and Bricker, *Architectural Drawing Collection.*

54. Slim Barnard, "Scouts Visit Ghost Town, Guest Ranch," *Los Angeles Examiner,* 7 January 1951, sec. 3, pp. 9–10, cols. 7–8. See also "Rustic Holiday," *Los Angeles Times,* 26 May 1946, 13–14. The Campbell ranch was cited in these two articles as a "true example" of the California ranch house from the "early days of the Southland." This information is courtesy of Marc Appleton.

55. John Byers, "At Home on the Desert," *California Arts and Architecture* 52 (October 1937): 16–17.

56. See Atlee B. Ayres, *Mexican Architecture, Ecclesiastical, Civil, Domestic,* New York, Helburn, 1926. He also published "The Earliest Mission Buildings of San Antonio," *AABN* 126, no. 27 (August 1924): 171–178.

57. On the latter, see "A House of Distinction in San Antonio," *House and Garden* 56 (August 1929): 89–91.

58. For a treatment of the firm's work, see John C. Ferguson, "The Country Houses of Atlee B. and Robert M. Ayres," *Cite* (Spring 1986): 18–20.

59. Bainbridge Bunting, *John Gaw Meem: Southwestern Architect,* Albuquerque, University of New Mexico Press, 1983, 3–21.

60. Ibid., 44–49.

61. See Meem, "Old Forms for New Buildings," 14, for plans and photos of this house.

62. Ibid., 10.

63. Fiske Kimball, "Recent Architecture in the South," *AR* 55 (March 1924): 212.

64. For histories of these movements, see Charles F. Hosmer, Jr., *Presence of the Past,* New York, Putnam, 1965.

65. Wilson, "Picturesque Ambiguities: The Country House Tradition in America," in Bedford, ed., *The Long Island Country House,* 19–21.

66. W. Duncan Lee, "The Renascence of Carter's Grove, on the James River, Virginia, Now the Home of Mr. and Mrs. Archibald M. McRea," *Architecture* 67, no. 4 (April 1933): 207–210.

67. See Crook, *Southern Architecture Illustrated,* 42–44.

68. See William B. O'Neal and Christopher Weeks, *The Work of William Lawrence Bottomley in Richmond,* Charlottesville, University Press of Virginia, 1985, for excellent treatments of many of these houses.

69. Ibid., 190–215.

70. Both Bottomley and Delano worked on restorations of plantations. Delanos commissions in Virginia included the refurbishment of Victorian Staunton Hill for Mr. and Mrs. David Bruce; alterations to Mirador for Mr. and Mrs. Ronald F. Tree of Chicago; a house near Charlottesville for General Edwin W. Watson, a military aide to Roosevelt; and another, nearby, for the Martford family, owners of the A & P food chain. Information from Delano's "Reminiscences," Oral History Project, Columbia University.

71. For a history of this garden, see Catharine M. Howett, "A Southern Lady's Legacy: The Italian 'Terraces' of La Grange, Georgia," *Journal of Garden History* 2, no. 4 (1982), 343–360.

72. Earl S. Draper, "The Gardens at Hills and Dales," *House Beautiful* (May 1932): 372–378, 416. Draper says that the Ferrell house burned, an assertion not confirmed by the above source.

73. Reid (1885–1926) graduated from Columbia's architectural program in 1906 and worked for the New York office of Murphy and Dana before setting up practice in 1909. Shutze, who died in 1977, attended the architectural school of the Georgia Institute of Technology in 1912, went to Columbia for two years, won the Prix de Rome in 1915, and subsequently worked in New York for F. Burrall Hoffman and Mott Schmidt, before joining the Atlanta office in 1919.

74. See James H. Grady, *The Architecture of Neel Reid in Georgia,* Athens, University of Georgia Press, 1973; Catharine M. Howett, "The Residential Architecture of Neel Reid," *Georgia Journal* 2, no. 2 (February/March): 21–27; and William R. Mitchell, Jr., *Landmark Homes of Georgia, 1733–1983,* Atlanta, 1983, 162–169.

75. The story was related in its proper version by Mrs. Alice Callaway in a conversation with the author at Hills and Dales in August 1988. He apologizes for any inconsistencies in the retelling.

76. For an overview of Shutze's work with a focus on the Swan House, see Henry Hope Reed, "America's Greatest Living Classical Architect: Philip Trammell Schutze of Atlanta, Georgia," *Classical America* 4 (1977): 5–46. Shutze's papers and drawings are in the collection of the Atlanta Historical Society.

77. Staub's architecture and career are extensively documented and analyzed in Howard Barnstone, *The Architecture of John F. Staub,* Austin, University of Texas Press, 1977. He designed a wider variety of suburban country houses than nearly any of his third-generation competitors and must be considered one of the major domestic architects of his generation.

78. For a brief, vivid biography of this great Texas lady, see David F. Warren, "Ima Hogg and Bayou Bend: A History," *Bulletin of the Museum of Fine Arts* (Houston) 12, no. 1 (Fall 1988): 2–12.

79. Barnstone, *The Architecture of John F. Staub,* 107. From an interview with the architect and Miss Hogg recorded shortly before her death.

80. For a history of the gardens, see David F. Warren, "Bayou Bend: The Plan and History of the Gardens," *Bulletin of the Museum of Fine Arts* (Houston) 12, no. 2 (Winter–Spring 1989), entire issue. Additional documentation on the house is available in Barnstone, *The Architecture of John F. Staub,* 106–113. Contemporaneous publications include: Crook, ed., *Southern Architecture Illustrated,* 33–38; *Southern Architect and Building News* 57 (November 1931): 14–20. See also Peter C. Papademetriou, *Houston: An Architectural Guide,* Houston, American Institute of Architects, 1975.

81. Information courtesy of Samuel Wilson, Jr., FAIA, Koch's partner and biographer. On Koch's life and work, see *Who's Who in America,* 1964–65.

82. C. Matlack Price, introduction, in Baum, *The Work of Dwight James Baum, Architect,* New York, Helburn, 1927, unpaginated.

83. See Eileen M. Michels, *Encounter with Artists, Number Nine: Edwin Hugh Lundie, F.A.I.A. (1886–1972),* St. Paul, Minneapolis Museum of Art, 1972; also David Gebhard and Tom Martinson, *A Guide to the Architecture of Minnesota,* Minneapolis, University of Minnesota Press, 1977, 132, 133, 391ff; S. E. Ellis, *Picturesque Lake Minnetonka,* Minneapolis, 1906; reprinted in 1974 by the Excelsior-Lake Minnetonka Historical Society.

84. See Janssen in biographies. See also James D. Van Trump and Arthur Ziegler, Jr., *Landmark Architecture of Allegheny County, Pennsylvania,* Pittsburgh, 1967, 15, 191. Janssen's finest country house was probably Latourelle (1924–25), the Edgar Kaufmann house in Fox Chapel.

85. For an interview with Dominick, see Boyd, "Variety and Elegance Dominate These Houses," *Arts and Decoration* 34, no. 2 (December 1930): 43–45, 101–102. Dominick's complete office records, papers, and drawings are in the collection of the Department of Prints and Drawings, Library of Congress.

7 Modernist Experiments

Epigraphs: Meigs, *An American Country House,* x; F. R. S. Yorke, *The Modern House,* London, Architectural Press, 1934, 18; "The House That Works: I" *Fortune* 12 (October 1935): 59.

1. *Arch. Forum* 53 (July–September 1930): "Modernist and Traditionalist," remarks by Howe, Walker et al., 49–50; Rynwood, 51–86; Adolph Glassgold, "House of William Stix Wasserman, Esq.," 230–232, first version with renderings by Lescaze.

2. See *Arch. Forum* 60 (March 1934): 185–186, for first presentation of the Mandel house; *Forum* 63 (August 1935): 79–89, for final presentation; *Forum* 62 (March 1935): 195–205, for presentation of the revised version of Square Shadows.

3. For an entertaining discussion of modernist "conspicuous austerity" versus domestic comfort, see Witold Rybczynski, *Home: A Short History of an Idea,* New York, Viking, 1986, 195–230.

4. Yorke, an architect, was a founding member of the experimental Modern Architecture Research Group (MARS) in Britain and a one-time associate of Marcel Breuer.

5. Yorke, *Modern House,* 14.

6. James Ford and Katharine Morrow Ford. *The Modern House in America,* New York, Architectural Book Publishing, 1940, 8.

7. The author of "The House That Works" maintained that there were around fifty, with no more than a dozen on the eastern seaboard.

8. Frederic Arden Pawley, "The Country House Room by Room: A Check List with Suggestions," *Arch. Forum* 58 (March 1933): 194–204.

9. "Modern Architectural," *Architecture* 58, no. 4 (October 1928): 209.

10. John Taylor Boyd, an open-minded critic, queried several leading eclectics about modernism in his series of interviews in *Arts and Decoration.* George Washington Smith thought Le Corbusier "a tonic" and was impressed with the freshness of European work, whereas both Chester Aldrich and Arthur Meigs were rather antimodernist, as might be expected.

11. *House and Garden* changed its point of view during the 1930s, but also aimed its marketing more at the middle class. *Fortune* was the most receptive to modernism. *Country Life in America* remained conservative to the end, as did *Town and Country.*

12. William Jordy, *American Buildings and Their Architects,* vol. 5, *The Impact of European Modernism in the Mid-Twentieth Century,* Garden City, Anchor Press, 1972, 174–175.

13. Robert Stern points this out in *George Howe.*

14. CBS radio interview, "The Modern House: The Architect's Point of View," 18 December 1939; quoted in Stern, *George Howe,* 170.

15. From 1928 to 1933, residential construction dropped by a staggering 95 percent, while expenditures on home repairs fell by 90 percent. Jackson, *Crabgrass Frontier,* 193.

16. "The Modern House," *Fortune* 12 (October 1935): 59–67.

17. See Harriet S. Gillespie, "A Modernistic House on the Atlantic Beach," *Arts and Decoration* 32, no. 1 (January 1930): 52.

18. *Fortune* profiled Mandel as so thorough a modernist that he even designed a tombstone in the style. His interest came about as a result of a visit to the Exposition des Arts Décoratifs of 1925 in Paris, while on a summer vacation from Dartmouth. He inherited his wealth from the Mandel Brothers department store fortune of Chicago. See "Modern Owners," *Fortune* 12 (October 1935): 28.

19. For a description of the house, clients, and program see Thomas S. Hines, *Richard Neutra and the Search for Modern Architecture,* New York, Oxford, 1982, 151–158.

20. The house was extensively published, in Yorke (150–152); and in "Aluminaire: A House for Contemporary Life," *Shelter* 2, no. 5 (May 1932): 58. Originally designed for the Architectural and Allied Arts exposition of the Architectural League of New York in 1931, it was reerected in Syosset, Long Island, as a country retreat.

21. As pointed out by Stern, *George Howe,* 107–108. The house was constructed on a thirty-acre tract, at the top of a hill facing south, and cost $50,000.

22. Yorke, *Modern House,* 150.

23. William Lescaze, "The Future American Country House," *AR* 64, no. 11 (November 1928): 418.

24. For an incisive critique of the use of technics as symbolic imagery in modernism, see Alan Colquhoun, "Symbolic and Literal Aspects of Technology," in *Essays in Architectural Criticism,* Cambridge, MIT Press, 1981, 26–30.

25. See, for instance, Wills' delightful *Houses for Good Living,* New York, Architectural Book Publishing, 1940. In it he said, "Country living has four facets—a) The quiet spaciousness of a small village. b) A rural cottage on a road outside the corporate limits. c) A farm group for the genuinely bucolic. d) A country estate with its dependencies, lying within ample grounds" (7). He nevertheless suggested that suburban life was preferable for the majority of Americans.

26. Robert A. M. Stern, *Raymond M. Hood,* Institute for Architecture and Urban Studies, New York, Rizzoli International, 1982, 22–23. See also Fay Hines, "Steel for the Private Life of a Business Man: Office Building Structure in a Country House," *Arts and Decoration* 43, no. 11 (November 1935): 18–20; "Living Room and Fireplace," *AABN* 142, no. 2611 (September 1932): 36–37; Allene Talmey, "Man Against the Sky," *The New Yorker* 7, no. 8 (11 April 1931).

27. "Forward House," *Arch. Forum* 55, no. 10 (October 1933): 282. See also R. H. Macy and Company, *The Forward House,* New York, 1933, 11–14.

28. Letter from William S. Wasserman to Robert Stern, 8 January 1974, quoted in Stern, *George Howe,* 162–163. Information on the history of the house, used here, can be found in Stern, 162–169.

29. "Modern Owners," 28, 34.

30. These innovations, and their dual significance, are pointed out by Stern, in *George Howe,* cited above. The stair was almost unique, the only other one of the type being in Antonin Raymond's Kawasaki house (1933) in Tokyo.

31. A fine synopsis of the story of the most published of Wright's houses can be found in Donald Hoffman, *Frank Lloyd Wright's Fallingwater: The House and Its History,* New York, Dover, 1978.

32. Frank Lloyd Wright, *An Autobiography,* New York, Duell, Sloan, and Pearce, 1943, 475.

33. See Jonathan Lipman, *Frank Lloyd Wright's Johnson Wax Buildings,* New York, Rizzoli, 1986, for an excellent history of the project.

34. Biographical material courtesy of S. C. Johnson and Son, Inc.

35. Wright, *An Autobiography,* 477, 474–475.

36. Though Wright suggested that the first "zoned" house was his own Coonley house of 1909. Ibid., 476.

37. Ibid., 475.

38. "Mr. Wright and the Johnsons of Racine, Wis.," *AIA Journal* (January 1979), courtesy of the Johnson Wax Company. Text of a speech given at a meeting of the AIA by Samuel Johnson.

39. "The 'last of the prairie houses' it shall be, so I thought—though I don't know why." *An Autobiography,* 477.

40. This point has been made by Thomas Hines in his excellent book, cited above.

8 Domestic Eclecticism

Epigraph: Mumford, "The Architecture of Escape," 321.

1. See Aslet, *The Last Country Houses,* chapter 1. The author argues that there were essentially two types: the social house built for status and class solidarity, and the romantic country house built for sentiment and historical association.

2. This point is made definitively by Richard Guy Wilson, *The American Renaissance,* New York, Pantheon, 1979, chapter 1.

3. James, *The American Scene,* 11.

4. Ibid.

5. For an illustration of this argument, see *Western Ranch Houses by Cliff May,* Menlo Park, California, Sunset Magazine, 1958, 13–14.

Epilogue

1. Nancy A. Ruhling, "Manors for the Masses," *Historic Preservation* 38, no. 1 (February 1986): 50–55. See also Robert B. King, *Raising a Fallen Treasure: The Otto H. Kahn Home, Huntington, Long Island,* Middleville, New York, 1985, 100ff.

2. See Erica Abeel, "Magnificent Obsession: A House in the Country," *New York Times Magazine* (19 April 1987): 20–30.

Bibliography

Abbreviations

AABN   *American Architect and Building News* and *The American Architect*

A and D   *Arts and Decoration*

Arch. Forum   *The Architectural Forum*

Arch. Review   *The Architectural Review* (Boston)

AR   *Architectural Record*

CLA   *Country Life in America*

JSAH   *Journal of the Society of Architectural Historians* (U.S.)

Books

Aidala, Thomas R. *Hearst Castle, San Simeon.* New York, Harrison House, 1981.

Albro, Lewis Colt, and Harrie T. Lindeberg. *Domestic Architecture.* New York, privately printed, 1912.

Algoud, Henri. *Le mobilier provençal.* Paris, C. Massin, 1928.

Allen, Lewis F. *Rural Architecture.* New York, 1852.

Allingham, Helen, and Dick Stewart. *The Cottage Homes of England.* London, E. Arnold, 1909.

American Country Houses of To-Day. 8 vols. New York, Architectural Book Publishing, 1912–35 (Editors: Frank Miles Day, 1912; Ralph Adams Cram, 1913; Samuel Howe, 1915; Aymar Embury II, 1917; Bernard Wells Close, 1922; Alfred Hopkins, 1927; R. W. Sexton, 1930; Lewis A. Coffin, 1935).

American Institute of Architects, Southern California Chapter. *Residential Architecture in Southern California.* Los Angeles, 1939.

American Society of Landscape Architects (J. Hayden Twiss, ed.). *ASLA Yearbook.* 1931–34.

Ammen, Daniel. *Country Homes and Their Improvement.* Washington, D.C., J. Shillington, 1885.

Amory, Cleveland. *The Last Resorts.* New York, Harper and Brothers, 1952.

——. *Who Killed Society?* New York, Harper and Brothers, 1960.

Andrews, Wayne. *The Vanderbilt Legend.* New York, Harcourt, Brace, 1941.

Architectural Forum. *Forward House, 1933.* New York, R. H. Macy, 1938.

Architectural League of New York. *Yearbook.* 1925.

——. *Yearbook.* 1932.

Architectural Review (Boston). *Country Houses.* Boston, 1904.

Architecture of Southern California: A Selection of Photographs, Plans, and Scale Details from the Work of Wallace Neff, F.A.I.A. Chicago, Rand McNally, 1964.

Arnold, Charles Dudley. *Country Architecture in France and England, Fifteenth and Sixteenth Centuries.* Buffalo, Arnold, 1896.

Arnott, James A., and John Wilson, *The Petit Trianon, Versailles.* London, Batsford, 1908.

Artistic Houses. New York, printed for subscribers by D. Appleton, 1883–84.

Aslet, Clive. *The Last Country Houses.* New Haven, Yale University Press, 1982.

Axelrod, Alan, ed. *The Colonial Revival in America.* New York, Norton in association with the Winterthur Museum, 1985.

Ayres, Atlee B. *Mexican Architecture: Ecclesiastical, Civil, Domestic.* New York, Helburn, 1926.

Bacon, Mardges. *Ernest Flagg, Jr.* American Monographs Series. Cambridge, MIT Press and the Architectural History Foundation, 1985.

Badel, E. *Nancy: Architecture, Beaux-arts, Monuments.* Paris, Armand Guérinet, [1890s].

Bailey, Liberty Hyde. *Report of the Commission on Country Life.* Introduction by Theodore Roosevelt. New York, Sturgis and Walton, 1911.

Baker, John C., ed. *American Country Homes and Their Gardens.* Philadelphia, John C. Winston, 1906.

Baker, Paul R. *Richard Morris Hunt.* Cambridge, Mass., MIT Press, 1983.

Baldwin, Charles C. *Stanford White.* New York, 1931.

Baldwin, William. *Billy Baldwin Remembers.* New York, Condé Nast, 1974.

Ballinger, R. M. *The Illustrated Guide to the Houses of America.* New York, 1971.

Balmori, Diana, Diane Kustial McGuire, and Eleanor McPeck. *Beatrix Farrand's American Landscapes: Her Gardens and Campuses.* Sagaponack, New York, Sagapress, 1985.

Baltzell, E. Digby. *Philadelphia Gentlemen.* Glencoe, Illinois, Free Press, 1958.

——. *The Protestant Establishment.* New York, Random House, 1964.

Bannister, Turpin C. *The Architect at Mid-Century: Report of the A.I.A. Commission for the Survey of Education and Registration.* Washington, D.C., 1954.

Barnstone, Howard. *The Architecture of John F. Staub.* Austin, University of Texas Press, 1977.

Barry, William E. *Pen Sketches of Old Houses.* Boston, n.d.

Baum, Dwight James. *The Work of Dwight James Baum, Architect.* Foreword by Harvey Wiley Corbett. New York, Helburn, 1927.

Baxter, Sylvester. *Spanish-Colonial Architecture in Mexico.* 10 vols. Boston, J. B. Millet, 1901.

Bedford, Stephen M., ed. *The Long Island Country House, 1870–1930.* Southampton, New York, Parrish Art Gallery, 1988.

Beer, Thomas. *The Mauve Decade: American Life at the End of the Nineteenth Century.* 1926. Reprint. New York, Vintage, 1961.

Berg, Donald J., ed. *Modern American Dwellings, 1897: A Sampler of Nineteenth-Century Rural Homes and Gardens.* New York, Antiquity Reprints, 1982.

Blanchan, Neltjie. *Nature's Garden.* New York, Doubleday, Page, 1900.

The Book of One Hundred Homes. 1906. Reprint. St. Paul, Minnesota, Brown-Blodgett, 1942.

A Book of Pictures in Roland Park, Baltimore, Maryland. Baltimore, N. T. A. Munder, 1912.

Bossom, Alfred C. *An Architectural Pilgrimage in Old Mexico.* New York, Scribner's, 1924.

Bottomley, M. E. *The Art of Home Landscape.* New York, A. T. DeLaMare, 1935.

Bottomley, William Lawrence. *Spanish Details.* New York, Helburn, 1924.

Boutelle, Sara Holmes. *Julia Morgan, Architect.* New York, Abbeville Press, 1988.

Bowen, Louise de Koven. *Baymeath.* Chicago, Ralph F. Seymour, 1944–45.

Branam, Alfred, Jr. *Newport's Favorite Architects.* New York, Classical America, 1976.

Brehme, Hugo. *Picturesque Mexico: The Country, the People and the Architecture.* London, Jarrolds, 1925.

Bremner, Robert H., ed. *American Social History since 1860.* New York, Appleton-Century-Crofts, 1971.

Briggs, Martin S. *The Homes of the Pilgrim Fathers in England and America, 1620–1685.* London, Oxford University Press, 1932.

Brimo, René. *L'évolution du goût aux Etats-Unis d'après l'histoire des collections.* Paris, J. Fortune, 1938.

Brooks, H. Allen. *The Prairie School: Frank Lloyd Wright and His Midwest Contemporaries.* Toronto, University of Toronto Press, 1972.

Brown, Erica. *Sixty Years of Interior Design: The World of McMillen.* New York, Viking Press, 1982

Brown, Glenn. *Brief Description and History of the Octagon House.* Washington, D.C., 1903.

Bullock, John. *The American Cottage Builder.* New York, Stringer and Townsend, 1854.

Bunting, Bainbridge. *John Gaw Meem, Southwestern Architect.* Albuquerque, University of New Mexico Press, 1983.

Byne, Arthur, and Mildred Stapley Byne. *Provincial Houses of Spain.* New York, Helburn, 1925.

——. *Spanish Architecture of the Sixteenth Century.* New York, Putnam's, 1915.

——. *Spanish Gardens and Patios.* London, Lippincott, 1924.

——. *Spanish Interiors and Furniture.* 3 vols. New York, 1921.

——. *Spanish Ironwork.* New York, Hispanic Society of America, 1915.

Cable, Mary. *Top Drawer: American High Society from the Gilded Age to the Roaring Twenties.* New York, Atheneum, 1984.

Calvert, Albert Frederick. *Spain: An Historical and Descriptive Account of Its Architecture, Landscape, and Arts.* 2 vols. New York, 1924.

Campen, Richard N. *Ohio: An Architectural Portrait.* Chagrin Falls, Ohio, 1973.

Capen, Oliver Bronson. *Country Homes of Famous Americans.* New York, Doubleday, Page, 1905.

Carrère, John, and Thomas Hastings. *Florida, The American Riviera.* New York, Gillis Brothers and Turnure, 1887.

Cautley, Marjorie Sewell. *Garden Design: The Principles of Abstract Design as Applied to Landscape Composition.* New York, Dodd, Mead, 1935.

Chamberlain, Nathan Henry. *A Paper on New England Architecture.* Boston, Crosby, Nichols, 1858.

Chandler, Joseph Everett. *The Colonial House.* 1916. 2d ed. New York, McBride, 1924.

Charles, C. J. *Elizabethan Interiors.* London, Newnes, 1911.

Chase, David. "Superb Privacies: The Later Domestic Commissions of Richard Morris Hunt." In *The Architecture of Richard Morris Hunt,* edited by Susan R. Stein, 151–171. Chicago, University of Chicago Press, 1986.

Chestnut Hill: An Architectural History. Philadelphia, Willard S. Detweiler, Jr., Inc., in association with Chestnut Hill Historical Society, 1969.

Clairborne, Herbert A. *Comments on Virginia Brickwork before 1800.* Boston, 1957.

Clark, Alson, ed. *Myron Hunt, 1868–1952: The Search for a Regional Architecture.* Los Angeles, Hennesey and Ingalls, 1984.

Clark, Alson, and Wallace Neff, Jr., eds. *Wallace Neff: Architect of California's Golden Age.* Santa Barbara, Capra Press, 1986.

Clark, Clifford Edward, Jr. *The American Family Home, 1800–1960.* Chapel Hill, University of North Carolina Press, 1986.

Clark, Robert Judson. *The Arts and Crafts Movement in America, 1876–1916.* Princeton, 1972.

Clarke, Thomas Hutchings. *Domestic Architecture of the Reigns of Queen Elizabeth and James the First.* London, Priestley and Weale, 1833.

Clute, Eugene. *Drafting Room Practice.* New York, Pencil Points Press, 1928.

Codman, Florence. *The Clever Young Boston Architect.* Augusta, Maine, 1970.

Coffin, Lewis A., Jr., Henry M. Polhemus, and Addison F. Worthington. *Small French Buildings.* 1901. Reprint. New York, Scribner's, 1921.

Coffin, Marian Cruger. *Trees and Shrubs for Landscape Effects.* New York, 1940.

Cohn, Jan. *The Palace or the Poorhouse: The American House as a Cultural Symbol.* East Lansing, Michigan State University Press, 1979.

Commager, Henry Steele. *The American Mind.* New Haven, Yale University Press, 1950.

Comstock, William Phillips. *The Housing Book.* New York, 1919.

Concrete Country Residences. 2d ed. New York, Atlas Portland Cement Company, 1907.

Cook, Clarence. *The House Beautiful.* New York, Scribner, Armstrong, 1878.

Cooper, Claire. "The House as Symbol of Self." In *Designing for Human Behavior: Architecture and the Behavioral Sciences,* edited by Jon T. Lang, Charles Burnette, Walter Moleski, and David Vachon, 130–146. Stroudsburg, Pennsylvania, Dowden, Hutchinson and Ross, 1974.

Corner, James M., and E. E. Soderholtz. *Examples of Domestic Colonial Architecture in Maryland and Virginia.* Boston, Boston Architectural Club, 1892.

———. *Examples of Domestic Colonial Architecture in New England.* Boston, Boston Architectural Club, 1891.

Country Estates Executed by the Elliot C. Brown Company, Incorporated. New York, DeVinne Press, 1914.

Country Homes Constructed by the Elliot C. Brown Company, Incorporated. New York, Elliot C. Brown Co., 1928.

Crain, Marion. *Gardens in America.* New York, Macmillan, 1932.

Cram, Ralph Adams. *Farm Houses, Manor Houses, Minor Châteaux, and Small Churches from the Eleventh to the Sixteenth Centuries in Normandy, Brittany, and Other Parts of France.* New York, Architectural Book Publishing, 1917.

Cram, Ralph Adams, Thomas Hastings, and Claude Bragdon. *Six Lectures on Architecture.* Chicago, University of Chicago Press, 1917.

Creese, Walter. *The Crowning of the American Landscape: Eight Great Spaces and Their Buildings.* Princeton, Princeton University Press, 1985.

Croly, Herbert D. [William Herbert, pseud.]. *Houses for Town or Country.* New York, Duffield, 1907.

———. *The Promise of American Life.* New York, Macmillan, 1909.

Crook, J. Mordaunt. *The Dilemma of Style.* Chicago, University of Chicago Press, 1987.

Crook, Lewis E., Jr., ed. *Southern Architecture Illustrated.* Atlanta, American Institute of Architects, 1931.

Curl, Donald. *Mizener's Florida.* Cambridge, MIT Press and the Architectural History Foundation, 1984.

Curtis, Nathanial C. *Architectural Composition.* Cleveland, Janson, 1923.

Cutler, William W., III, and Howard Gillette, Jr., eds. *The Divided Metropolis: Social and Spatial Dimensions of Philadelphia, 1800–1975.* Westport, Connecticut, Greenwood Press, 1980.

Daniels, E. A. *Facts and Fancies and Repetitions about Dark Harbor by One of the Very Oldest Cottagers, 1890–1932.* Cambridge, Mass., privately printed, 1935.

Davie, W. Galsworthy. *Old Cottages and Farmhouses in Surrey.* London, Batsford, 1908.

———. *Old Cottages, Farmhouses, and Other Stone Buildings in the Cotswold District.* London, Batsford, 1905.

Davie, W. Galsworthy, and E. Guy Dawber. *Old Cottages and Farmhouses in Kent and Sussex.* London, Batsford, 1905.

Davie, W. Galsworthy, and L. A. Shuffrey. *The English Fireplace.* London, Batsford, 1912.

Davie, W. Galsworthy, and Henry Tanner. *Old English Doorways: Examples from Tudor Times to the End of the Eighteenth Century.* London, 1903.

Davis, Myra Tolmach. *Sketches in Iron: Samuel Yellin, American Master of Wrought Iron, 1885–1940.* Washington, D.C., 1971.

Dean, Ruth. *The Liveable House: Its Garden.* New York, 1917.

Delano, William A., and Chester Aldrich. *Portraits of Ten Country Houses.* Introduction by Royal Cortissoz. Garden City, New York, Doubleday, Page, 1924.

Desmond, Harry W., and Herbert D. Croly. *Stately Homes in America: From Colonial Times to the Present Day.* New York, D. Appleton, 1903.

Desmond, Harry W., and H. W. Frohne. *Building a Home.* New York, Baker and Taylor, 1908.

Detached Dwellings: Country and Suburban. New York, Swetland, 1909. 2d ed. American Architect, New York, 1911.

De Wolfe, Elsie. *The House in Good Taste.* New York, Century Company, 1915.

Ditchfield, Peter Harrison. *The Charm of the English Village.* London, Batsford, 1908.

———. *The Cottages and Village Life of Rural England.* London, 1912.

———. *The Manor Houses of England.* London, Batsford, 1910.

———. *Picturesque English Cottages and Their Doorway Gardens.* Philadelphia, J. C. Winston, 1905.

Dow, Joy Wheeler. *American Renaissance: A Review of Domestic Architecture.* New York, W. T. Comstock, 1904.

Downing, A. J. *The Architecture of Country Houses.* New York, 1850. Reprint. New York, Dover, 1969.

Drake, Samuel Adams. *Our Colonial Homes.* Boston, Lee and Shepard, 1894.

Draper, Joan. "The Ecole des Beaux-Arts and the Architectural Profession in the United States: The Case of John Galen Howard." In *The Architect: Chapters in the History of the Profession,* edited by Spiro Kostof, 209–237. New York, Oxford University Press, 1977.

Drexler, Arthur, ed. *The Architecture of the Ecole des Beaux-Arts.* New York, Museum of Modern Art, 1977.

Dudden, Faye E. *Serving Women: Household Service in Nineteenth-Century America.* Middletown, Connecticut, Wesleyan University Press, 1983.

Eaton, Leonard K. *Landscape Artist in America: The Life and Work of Jens Jensen.* Cambridge, MIT Press, 1969.

———. *Two Chicago Architects and Their Clients: Frank Lloyd Wright and Howard Van Doren Shaw.* Cambridge, MIT Press, 1969.

Eberlein, Harold D. *The Architecture of Colonial America.* 1915. Reprint. London, Johnson, 1968.

———. *Spanish Interiors.* New York, 1925.

Eberlein, Harold D., and Cortland Hubbard. *The Practical Book of Garden Structure and Design.* New York, Lippincott, 1937.

Eberlein, Harold D., and Roger W. Ramsdell. *Small Manor Houses and Farmsteads in France.* Philadelphia, Lippincott, 1926.

Edgell, George Harold. *American Architecture of To-Day.* New York, Scribner's, 1928.

Elder-Duncan, J. H. *Country Cottages.* London, 1906.

Ellis, S. E. *Picturesque Lake Minnetonka.* Minneapolis, 1906. Reprint. Excelsior-Lake Minnetonka Historical Society, 1974.

Elwood, P. H., Jr., ec. *American Landscape Architecture.* New York, Architectural Book Publishing, 1924.

Embury, Aymar, II. *Country Houses.* Garden City, New York, Doubleday, Page, 1914.

———. *The Dutch Colonial House.* New York, McBride, Nast, 1913.

———. *Early American Churches.* Doubleday, Page, 1914.

———. *The Liveable House: Its Plan and Design.* Moffat, Yard, 1917.

———. *One Hundred Country Houses: Modern American Examples.* New York, Century Company, 1909.

Ferree, Barr. *American Estates and Gardens.* New York, Munn, 1904.

Fisher, Richard B. *Syrie Maugham.* London, Duckworth, 1978.

Flagg, Ernest. *Small Houses: Their Economic Design and Construction.* New York, Scribner's, 1922.

Folsom, Merrill. *Great American Mansions and Their Stories.* New York, Hastings House, 1963.

Ford, James, and Katharine Morrow Ford. *The Modern House in America.* New York, Architectural Book Publishing, 1940.

Forster, Frank J. *Country Houses: The Work of Frank J. Forster.* New York, Helburn, 1931.

———. *Provincial Architecture of Northern France.* New York, Ludowici-Celadon, 1931.

Foster, William D. *Cottages, Manoirs, and Other Minor Buildings of Normandy and Brittany.* New York, Architectural Book Publishing, 1926.

French, Leigh, Jr. *Colonial Interiors.* New York, Helburn, 1923.

———. *The Smaller Houses and Gardens of Versailles from 1680 to 1815.* New York, Pencil Points Press, 1926.

French, Lillie Hamilton. *The House Dignified.* New York, G. P. Putnam, 1908.

Furnas, J. C. *The Americans: A Social History of the United States, 1587–1940.* New York, G. P. Putnam, 1969.

Gannon, Thomas. *Newport Mansions: The Gilded Age.* Photographs by Richard Cheek. Dublin, New Hampshire, Foremost, 1982.

Gans, Herbert. *Popular Culture and High Culture: An Analysis of the Evolution of Taste.* New York, Basic Books, 1974.

Gardner, E. C. *Homes and How to Make Them.* Boston, Osgood, 1874.

Garner, Thomas, and Arthur Stratton. *The Domestic Architecture of England during the Tudor Period.* London, Batsford, 1911.

Garnett, Porter. *Stately Homes of California.* Introduction by Bruce Porter. Boston, Little, Brown, 1915.

Gaudet, Julien. *Eléments et théorie d'architecture.* 4 vols. Paris, Aulanier, 1901–04.

Gebhard, David. *George Washington Smith.* Santa Barbara, The Art Museum, University of California at Santa Barbara, 1964.

Gebhard, David, Lauren Bricker, and David Bricker. *A Catalogue of the Architectural Drawing Collection.* 2 vols. Santa Barbara, The Art Museum, University of California at Santa Barbara, 1983.

Gebhard, David, and Tom Martinson. *A Guide to the Architecture of Minnesota.* Minneapolis, University of Minnesota Press, 1977.

Gebhard, David, and Harriet Von Breton. *Architecture in California, 1868–1968.* Santa Barbara, 1968.

Gebhard, David, and Robert Winter. *A Guide to Architecture in Los Angeles and Southern California.* Salt Lake City, Peregrine Smith, 1977.

Gibson, Louis H. *Beautiful Houses.* New York, Cravell, 1895.

———. *Convenient Houses.* New York, Cravell, 1889.

Girouard, Mark. *The Victorian Country House.* Rev. ed.

New Haven, Yale University Press, 1979.

Goldsmith, Margaret Olthof. *Designs for Outdoor Living.* New York, G. W. Stewart, 1941.

Goodhue, Bertram. *A Book of Architectural and Decorative Drawings by Bertram Grosvenor Goodhue.* New York, Architectural Book Publishing, 1914.

Goodnow, Ruby Ross. *The Honest House.* New York, Goodnow, 1914.

Goodwin, Philip Lippincott. *Rooftrees: The Architectural History of an American Family.* Philadelphia, Lippincott, 1933.

Goodwin, Philip Lippincott, and Henry O. Milliken. *French Provincial Architecture.* New York, 1924.

Gotch, John Alfred. *Architecture of the Renaissance in England.* London, Batsford, 1891.

———. *A Complete Account, Illustrated by Measured Drawings, of the Buildings Erected in Northamptonshire by Sir Thomas Tresham between the Years 1575 and 1605.* London, Northampton, Taylor, 1883.

———. *Early Renaissance Architecture in England.* London, Batsford, 1901.

———. *The Old Halls and Manor-Houses of Northamptonshire.* London, Batsford, 1936.

Gowans, Alan. *The Comfortable House: North American Suburban Architecture.* Cambridge, MIT Press, 1987.

———. *Images of American Living.* New York, Harper and Row, 1976.

Grady, H. James. *The Architecture of Neel Reid in Georgia.* Athens, University of Georgia Press, 1973.

Granger, Alfred Hoyt. *Charles Follen McKim: A Study of His Life and Work.* Boston, Houghton Mifflin, 1913.

Grant, Robert. *Unleavened Bread.* 1900. Reprint. Ridgewood, New Jersey, Gregg Press, 1967.

Gray, David. *Thomas Hastings, Architect.* Cambridge, Mass., Houghton Mifflin, 1933.

Gray, Greta. *House and Home: A Manual and Textbook of Practical House Planning.* Philadelphia, Lippincott, 1935.

Halsey, R. T. H., and Charles O. Cornelius. *A Handbook of the American Wing, Metropolitan Museum of Art.* 4th ed. New York, The Museum, 1928.

Hamlin, A. D. F. *A Textbook of the History of Architecture.* New York, Longmans Green, 1898.

Hamlin, Talbot. *The American Spirit in Architecture.* New Haven, Yale University Press, 1926.

Handlin, David. *The American Home: Architecture and Society, 1815–1915.* Boston, Little Brown, 1979.

Hanson, A. E. *An Arcadian Landscape: The California Gardens of A. E. Hanson.* Edited by David Gebhard and Sheila Lynde. Los Angeles, Hennessey and Ingalls, 1985.

Harbeson, John. *The Study of Architectural Design.* New York, Pencil Points Press, 1927.

Harwood, Kathryn Chapman. The *Lives of Vizcaya.* Miami, Banyan Books, 1985.

Havemeyer, Louisine. *Sixteen to Sixty.* New York, privately printed, 1961.

Hayden, Dolores. *The Grand Domestic Revolution.* Cambridge, MIT Press, 1984.

Hayward, Arthur H. *Colonial Lighting.* Boston, Brimmer, 1923.

Hechscher, Morrison, and Elizabeth Miller. *An Architect and His Client: Frank Lloyd Wright and Francis W. Little.* New York, Metropolitan Museum of Art, 1973.

Hefner, Robert J., ed. *East Hampton's Heritage: An Illustrated Architectural Record.* Essays by Clay Lancaster and Robert A. M. Stern. New York, Norton, 1982.

Herring, Oswald C. *Concrete and Stucco Houses.* New York, McBride Nast, 1912.

Hersey, George L. *High Victorian Gothic.* Baltimore, Johns Hopkins University Press, 1972.

Hielscher, Kurt. *Picturesque Spain.* New York, Brentano's, 1922.

Hill, Frederick P. *Charles Follen McKim: The Man.* Francestown, New Hampshire, 1950.

Hines, Thomas S. *Richard Neutra and the Search for Modern Architecture.* New York, Oxford University Press, 1982.

Hitchcock, Henry-Russell. *American Architectural Books.* Minneapolis, University of Minnesota Press, 1962.

———. *In the Nature of Materials, 1887–1941: The Buildings of Frank Lloyd Wright.* New York, Duell, Sloan and Pierce, 1942.

Hofstadter, Richard. *The Age of Reform: From Bryan to FDR.* New York: Vintage, 1955.

Hollister, Paul M. *Famous Colonial Houses.* Philadelphia, McKay, 1921.

Holloway, Edward Stratton. *American Furniture and Decoration: Colonial and Federal.* Philadelphia, Lippincott, 1928.

Holly, Henry Hudson. *Country Seats: Containing Lithographic Designs for Cottages, Villas, Mansions, Etc.* New York, Appleton, 1866.

———. *Modern Dwellings in Town and Country: Adapted to American Wants and Climate.* New York, Harper, 1878.

Holme, Charles, ed. *Old English Country Cottages.* London, The Studio, 1906.

———. *Old English Mansions.* London, The Studio, 1915.

———. *The Village Homes of England.* London, 1912.

Homes in City and Country (articles by Russell Sturgis, J. W. Root, Bruce Price, Donald W. Mitchell, Samuel Parsons, Jr., and W. W. Linn). New York, Century Company, 1893.

Hooper, Charles Edward. *The Country House: A Practical Manual of the Planning and Construction of the American Country Home and Its Surroundings.* New York, Doubleday, Page, 1905.

Hopkins, Alfred. *Planning for Sunshine and Fresh Air.* New York, Architectural Book Publishing, 1931.

Horowitz, Helen Lefkowitz. *Culture and the City.* Lexington, Kentucky, University of Kentucky Press, 1976.

Hosmer, Charles F., Jr. *Presence of the Past: A History of the Preservation Movement in the United States before Williamsburg.* New York, G. P. Putnam, 1965.

The Housing Book. New York, W. T. Comstock, 1919.

Howells, John Mead. *Lost Examples of Colonial Architecture.* New York, Helburn, 1931.

Howells, William Dean. *The Rise of Silas Lapham.* 1884. Reprint. New York, Rinehart, 1939.

Hutchinson, Frances. *Wychwood: The History of an Idea. Our Country Home; Our Country Life; Our Final Aim.* Chicago, A. C. McClurg, 1928.

Hutchinson, Martha B. *The Spirit of the Garden.* Boston, Atlantic Monthly, 1923.

Isham, Norman, and Albert F. Brown. *Early Rhode Island Houses.* Providence, Preston and Rounds, 1895.

Jackson, Allen. *The Half-Timber House.* New York, McBride, 1912.

Jackson, J. B. *The Necessity for Ruins, and Other Topics.* Amherst, University of Massachusetts Press, 1980.

Jackson, Kenneth. *Crabgrass Frontier: The Suburbanization of the United States.* New York, Oxford University Press, 1985.

James, Henry. *The American Scene.* Edited by Leon Edel. Bloomington, University of Indiana Press, 1968.

Jensen, Jens. *Siftings.* Chicago, R. F. Seymour, 1939.

Jones, Sydney. *The Village Homes of England.* London, The Studio, 1912.

Jordain, Margaret. *English Decoration and Furniture of the Early Renaissance.* London, 1924.

———. *English Decorative Plasterwork of the Renaissance.*

London, 1926.

———. *The Work of William Kent.* New York, 1948.

Jordy, William. *American Buildings and Their Architects.* Vol. 5, *The Impact of European Modernism in the Mid-Twentieth Century.* Garden City, Anchor Press, 1972.

Kaplan, Wendy, ed. *The Art That Is Life: The Arts and Crafts Movement in America, 1875–1920.* Boston, Little, Brown in association with the Museum of Fine Arts, 1987.

Kaufmann, E. J., Jr., and Ben Raeburn, eds. *Frank Lloyd Wright: Writings and Buildings.* Cleveland, Meriden Books, 1960.

Keefe, Charles S. *The American Home.* New York, U.P.C. Book Company, 1922.

Kelley, J. Frederick. *The Early Domestic Architecture of Connecticut.* 1924. Reprint. New York, Dover, 1963.

Kelsey, Albert, ed. *The Architectural Annual.* Philadelphia, Architectural League of America, 1900.

Kennedy, Rogert G. *Architecture, Men, Women, and Money in America, 1600–1860.* New York, Random House, 1985.

Kerr, Robert. *The Gentleman's House.* London, J. Murray, 1864.

Kidney, Walter C. The *Architecture of Choice: Eclecticism in America, 1880–1930.* New York, Braziller, 1974.

Kimball, Sydney Fiske. *Domestic Architecture of the American Colonies and the Early Republic.* New York, Scribner's, 1922.

———. *Thomas Jefferson, Architect.* 1916. Reprint. Cambridge, Mass., Riverside, 1966.

King, Robert B. *Raising a Fallen Treasure: The Otto H. Kahn Home, Huntington, Long Island.* Middleville, New York, privately printed, 1985.

King, Willford Isbell. *Wealth and Income of the People of the United States.* New York, Macmillan. 1915.

Kirker, Harold. *California's Architectural Frontier.* 1960. Reprint. Salt Lake City, Peregrine Smith, 1986.

Knobloch, Phillip. *Good Practice in Construction.* 2 vols. New York, Pencil Points Press, 1923.

Kostof, Spiro, ed. *The Architect: Chapters in the History of the Profession.* New York, Oxford University Press, 1977.

La Beaume, Louis, and William Booth Papin. *The Picturesque Architecture of Mexico.* New York, Architectural Book Publishing, 1915.

Lears, T. J. Jackson. *No Place of Grace. Antimodernism and the Transformation of American Culture, 1880–1920.* New York, Pantheon, 1981.

Le Clerc, Léon. *Le mobilier normand.* Paris, 1924.

Le Corbusier. *Oeuvre complète.* Vol. 2, 1929–1934. 1938. Reprint. Zurich, Editions d'Architecture, 1973.

LeMoyne, Louis Valcoulon. *Country Residences in Europe and America.* 2d ed. New York, G. P. Putnam's Sons, 1921.

Levy, David. *Herbert Croly of the New Republic.* Princeton, Princeton University Press, 1985.

Lewis, Arnold. *American Country Houses of the Gilded Age* (reprint of Sheldon's *Artist Country Seats*). New York, Dover, 1982.

Lindeberg, Harrie T. *Domestic Architecture of H. T. Lindeberg.* Introduction by Royal Cortissoz. New York, Helburn, 1940.

Lloyd, Nathaniel. *A History of English Brickwork.* London, Montgomery, 1928.

———. *A History of the English House from Primitive Times to the Victorian Period.* New York, Helburn, 1931.

Lockwood, Luke Vincent. *Colonial Furniture in America.* Vol. 1. New York, Scribner's, 1901.

Longstreth, Richard. *Julia Morgan, Architect.* Berkeley, Berkeley Architectural Heritage Association, 1977.

———. *On the Edge of the World: Four Architects in San Francisco at the Turn of the Century.* Cambridge, MIT Press and the Architectural History Foundation, 1984.

Lowell, Guy, ed. *American Gardens*. Boston, Bates and Guild, 1902.

Lucie-Smith, Edward, and Celestine Dars. *How the Rich Lived*. New York, Two Continents, 1976.

Lundberg, Ferdinand. *America's Sixty Families*. New York, Vanguard, 1937.

Lynes, Russell. *The Domesticated Americans*. New York, Harper and Row, 1963.

———. *The Tastemakers*. New York, Harper and Row, 1954.

Lyon, Irving W. *The Colonial Furniture of New England*. Boston, Houghton Mifflin, 1891.

Maass, John. *The Victorian Home in America*. New York, Hawthorn, 1972.

McCarthy, Muriel Quest. *David R. Williams, Pioneer Architect*. Dallas, Southern Methodist University Press, 1984.

McClelland, Nancy. *Historic Wall-Papers*. Philadelphia, Lippincott, 1924.

McCormick, Harriet Hammond. *Landscape Art Past and Present*. New York, Scribner's, 1923.

McGoodwin, Robert. The *Work of Robert Rodes McGoodwin, 1910–40*. Philadelphia, W. F. Fell, 1942.

McGuire, Diana K., and Lois Fern, eds. *Beatrix Jones Farrand: Fifty Years of American Landscape Architecture*. Washington, D.C., Dumbarton Oaks Trustees for Harvard University, 1982.

Magonigle, Harold Van Buren. *Architectural Rendering in Wash*. New York, Scribner's, 1921.

Maher, James T. *The Twilight of Splendor: Chronicles of the Age of American Palaces*. Boston, Little, Brown, 1975.

Mann, William. *Fads and Fancies of Representative Americans at the Beginning of the Twentieth Century: Being a Portrayal of Their Tastes, Diversions, and Achievements*. New York, Town Topics, 1905.

Manning, Warren H., and William A. Lambeth. *Thomas Jefferson as an Architect and a Designer of Landscapes*. Boston, Houghton Mifflin, 1913.

Mays, Victor. *Pathway to a Village: A History of Bronxville*. Bronxville, New York, 1961.

Meigs, Arthur Ingersoll. *An American Country House: The Property of Arthur E. Newbold, Jr., Laverock, Pa*. New York, Architectural Book Publishing, 1925.

Messent, Claude. *The Old Cottages and Farm-Houses of Norfolk*. London, Hunt, 1928.

Metcalf, Pauline. *Ogden Codman and the Decoration of Houses*. Boston, Boston Atheneum, 1988.

Metcalf, Pauline, and Valencia Libby, eds. *The House and Garden*. Roslyn, New York, Nassau County Museum of Fine Arts, 1986.

Michels, Eileen M. *Encounter with Artists, Number Nine: Edwin Hugh Lundie, F.A.I.A., 1886–1972*. St. Paul, Minneapolis Museum of Art, 1972.

Miller, Lillian B. *Patrons and Patriotism*. Chicago, University of Chicago Press, 1966.

Mitchell, Donald G. *American Land and Letters*. 2 vols. New York, 1897–99.

———. *Out of Town Places*. New York, 1884.

———. *Rural Studies*. New York, Scribner's, 1867.

Mitchell, William R., Jr. *Landmark Homes of Georgia, 1733–1983*. Atlanta, 1984.

———. *Lewis Edmund Crook, Jr., Architect, 1898–1967*. Atlanta, 1985.

Monograph of the Work of John Russell Pope. 3 vols. New York, Helburn, 1937.

Monograph of the Work of McKim, Mead and White, 1879–1915. New York, Architectural Book Publishing, 1915. Reprint. New York, Arno, 1977.

Monograph of the Work of Mellor, Meigs and Howe. New York, Architectural Book Publishing, 1923.

Moore, Charles Herbert. *The Life and Times of Charles Follem McKim*. Boston, Houghton Mifflin, 1929.

Morgan, Keith. *Charles A. Platt: The Artist as Architect*. Cambridge, MIT Press and the Architectural History Foundation, 1985.

Morison, Samuel Eliot. *The Story of Mount Desert Island*. Boston, Little, Brown, 1960.

Morse, Frances Clary. *Furniture of the Olden Time*. New York, Macmillan, 1902.

Moulin, Gabriel. *Gabriel Moulin's San Francisco Peninsula: Town and Country Homes, 1910–30*. San Francisco, Windgate Press, 1985.

Mumford, Lewis. *The Brown Decades*. 1931. 2d ed. New York, Dover, 1955.

Myrick, David F. *Montecito and Santa Barbara: From Farms to Estates*. Vol. 1. Glendale, California, Trans Anglo Books, 1987.

Nash, Joseph. *The Mansions of England in the Olden Time*. 4 vols. London, Lean, 1838–49.

Neville, Ralph. *Old Cottage and Domestic Architecture in South-West Surrey*. 2d ed. London, Guildford, Billing, 1891.

Nevins, Allan. *The Emergence of Modern America*. New York, 1927.

Nevins, Deborah. *Between Traditions and Modernism*. New York, National Academy of Design, 1980.

Newcomb, Rexford. *Architecture in Old Kentucky*. Urbana, University of Illinois Press, 1953.

———. *A Brief History of Rural Architecture in the United States*. Vol. 7. Washington, D.C., 1932.

———. *The Colonial and Federal House: How to Build an Authentic Colonial House*. Philadelphia, Lippincott, 1933.

———. *Franciscan Mission Architecture of Alta, California*. 1916. Reprint. New York, Dover, 1973.

———. *Mediterranean Domestic Architecture in the United States*. Cleveland, J. H. Jansen, 1928.

———. *Old Mission Churches and Historic Houses of California*. London, 1925.

———. *Spanish Colonial Architecture in the United States*. New York, J. J. Augustin, 1937.

———. *The Spanish House for America: Its Design, Furnishing, and Garden*. Philadelphia, Lippincott, 1927.

Newsom, Samuel, and Joseph C. Newsom. *Picturesque Californian Homes*. 1885. Reprint. San Francisco, Hennessey and Ingalls, 1978.

Newton, Ernest, *A Book of Country Houses*, London, Batsford, 1903.

Newton, Norman T. *Design on the Land: The Development of Landscape Architecture*. Cambridge, Harvard University Press, 1971.

Northend, Mary H. *Colonial Homes and Their Furnishings*. Boston, Little, Brown, 1912.

Noted Long Island Homes. Babylon, New York, E. W. Howell, 1933.

Nutting, Wallace. *Furniture Treasury (Mostly of American Origin), 1620–1720*. 3 vols. Framingham, Mass., Old America, 1928–33.

———. *Virginia Beautiful*. Framingham, Mass., Old America, 1935.

———. *Wallace Nutting Pictures: Expansible Catalog*. Framingham, Mass., 1915.

O'Connor, Harvey. *The Astors*. New York, Knopf, 1941.

Oliver, Richard. *Bertram Grosvenor Goodhue*. Cambridge, MIT Press and the Architectural History Foundation, 1983.

Oliver, Richard, ed. *The Making of an Architect, 1881–1981*. New York, Rizzoli, 1981.

O'Neal, William B., and Christopher Weeks. *The Work of William Lawrence Bottomley in Richmond*. Charlottesville, University Press of Virginia, 1985.

Osborne, Charles Francis. *Country Homes and Gardens of Moderate Cost*. Philadelphia, J. C. Winston, 1907.

———. *Notes on the Art of House Planning*. New York, 1888.

Ould, E. A. *Old Cottages, Farm Houses, and Other Half-Timber Buildings in Schropshire, Herefordshire, and Cheshire*. London, Batsford, 1904.

Owens, Carole. *The Berkshire Cottages*. Englewood Cliffs, New Jersey, 1984.

Paine, Judith. *Theodate Pope Riddle: Her Life and Work*. New York, Theodore Roosevelt Birthplace, 1979.

Patterson, Augusta Owen. *American Homes of To-Day: Their Architectural Style, Their Environment, Their Characteristics*. New York, Macmillan, 1924.

Paul, M. Rea, and K. J. Bowman. *Color in Colonial Times*. New York, 1932.

Peabody, Henrietta C. *Outside the House Beautiful: A Collection of Exterior Views Showing the Surroundings of the Home*. Boston, Atlantic Monthly Press, 1923.

Peabody, Robert Swain. *An Architect's Sketch Book*. Boston, Houghton Mifflin, 1912.

Persons, Stow. *The Decline of American Gentility*. New York, Columbia University Press, 1973.

Pfnor, Rudolphe. *Architecture, décoration et ameublement, l'époque Louis XVI*. Paris, A. Morel, 1865.

Pierson, William Harvey. *American Buildings and Their Architects*. Vol. 1. Garden City, New York, Anchor, 1976.

Placek, Adolph K., ed. *Macmillan Dictionary of Architects*. 4 vols. New York, Macmillan, 1982.

Platt, Charles. *Monograph of the Work of Charles A. Platt*. New York, Architectural Book Publishing, 1913. 2d ed., rev. and enl. 1925.

Powell, Edward Payson. *The Country Home*. New York, McClure, Phillipe, 1904.

Pratt, Richard. *David Adler*. New York, M. Evans, 1970.

Prentice, A. N. *Renaissance Architecture and Ornament in Spain*. London, Batsford, 1893.

Price, Bruce. *Modern Architectural Practice: No. 1, A Large Country House*. New York, Comstock, 1887.

A Pride of Palaces: Lenox Summer Cottages, 1883–1933. Lenox, Mass., Lenox Library Association, 1981.

Reed, Henry Hope., ed. *Mott B. Schmidt: An Architectural Portrait*. Katonah, New York, 1980.

Rehmann, Elsa. *Garden Making*. Boston, Houghton Mifflin, 1926.

Reilly, Charles. *McKim, Mead and White*. London, Ernest Benn, 1924.

Rhoads, William B. *The Colonial Revival*. New York, Garland, 1977.

Richardson, Charles James. *Fragments and Details of Architecture, Decoration, and Furniture of the Elizabethan Period*. London, 1841. Reprint. New York, Helburn, [1910s].

———. *Studies of Old English Mansions*. 4 vols. London, 1841–48.

Robinson, Albert G. *Old New England Doorways*. New York, Scribner's, 1928.

Robinson, L. Eugene. *Domestic Architecture*. New York, Macmillan, 1917.

Robinson, Peter Frederick. *Domestic Architecture of the Tudor Style*. London, privately printed, 1837.

Rosenthal, Louis Conrad. *Cottages, Farmhouses, and Other Minor Buildings in England of the Sixteenth, Seventeenth, and Eighteenth Centuries*. London, 1923.

Roth, Leland M. *The Architecture of McKim, Mead and White, 1870–1920: A Building List*. New York, Garland, 1978.

———. *McKim, Mead and White, Architects*. New York, Harper and Row, 1983.

———. "McKim, Mead and White Reappraised."

Introductory essay and notes on the plates to *A Monograph of the Work of McKim, Mead and White, 1879–1915.* New York, Architectural Book Publishing, 1915. Reprint. New York, DaCapo, 1977.

———. *America Builds.* New York, Harper and Row, 1983.

Rudge, William Edwin. *Beauty in Gardens: A Tribute.* New York, privately printed, 1928.

Rumler, E. *Le style Empire.* Vols. 1–3. Paris, n.d.

———. *Le style Louis XV.* Paris, 1914.

Rushmore, George M. *The World with a Fence around It: Tuxedo Park—The Early Days.* New York, 1957.

Ruskin, John. *The Seven Lamps of Architecture.* New York, Farrar, Straus and Giroux, 1984.

Rybczynski, Witold. *Home: A Short History of an Idea.* New York, Viking, 1986.

Rykwert, Joseph. *The First Moderns.* Cambridge, MIT Press, 1980.

Sadler, Julius T., and Jacqueline Sadler. *American Stables: An Architectural Tour.* New York, New York Graphic Society, 1981.

Saint, Andrew. *The Image of the Architect.* New Haven, Yale University Press, 1983.

Saint-Sauveur [Hector, pseud.]. *Châteaux de France.* Paris, C. Massin, 1912–13.

Sale, Edith Tunis. *Colonial Interiors.* 2d ser. New York, Helburn, 1930.

Salmon, Lucy Maynard. *Domestic Service.* New York, Macmillan, 1901.

Savage, Charles. *The Architecture of the Private Streets of St. Louis.* Columbia, University of Missouri Press, 1987.

Sawyer, Joseph Dillaway. *How to Make a Country Place.* New York, O. Judd, 1914.

Saylor, Henry Hodgman. *Architectural Style for Country Houses.* New York, R. M. McBride, 1912. Reprint. 1919.

Schmitt, Peter T. *Back to Nature: The Arcadian Myth in Urban America, 1900–30.* New York, Oxford University Press, 1969.

Schuyler, Montgomery. *American Architecture.* New York, 1892.

Sclare, Liisa, and Donald Sclare. *Beaux-Arts Estates: A Guide to the Architecture of Long Island.* New York, Viking, 1979.

Scott, Frank J. *The Art of Beautifying Suburban Home Grounds.* New York, Appleton, 1870.

Scully, Vincent, Jr. "American Houses: Thomas Jefferson to Frank Lloyd Wright." In *The Rise of an American Architecture,* edited by Edgar Kaufmann, Jr., 163–209. New York, 1970.

Scully, Vincent, and Antoinette Downing. *The Architectural Heritage of Newport, Rhode Island, 1640–1915.* New York, C. N. Potter, 1967.

Seale, William. *The Tasteful Interlude.* New York, Praeger, 1975.

Sexton, R. W. *Interior Architecture.* New York, Architectural Book Publishing, 1927.

———. *Spanish Influence on American Architecture and Decoration.* New York, Architectural Book Publishing, 1927.

Shackleton, Robert, and Elizabeth Shackleton. *The Quest of the Colonial.* New York, Century, 1906.

Sheldon, George William, ed. *Artistic Country Seats: Types of Recent American Villa and Cottage Architecture, with Instances of Country Club Houses.* 4 vols. 1887. Reprint. New York, DaCapo Press, 1979.

Shelton, Louise. *Beautiful Gardens in America.* New York, Scribner's, 1915. 2d ed. 1924.

Shoppell, Robert W. *Modern Houses, Beautiful Homes.* New York, Co-operative Building Plan Assoc., 1887.

Simons, Albert, and Samuel Lapham. *The Octagon Library of Early American Architecture: Charleston, South Carolina.* New York, American Institute of Architects Press, 1927.

Sloane, Florence Adele. *Maverick in Mauve: Diary of a Romantic Age.* Garden City, New York, Doubleday, 1983.

Small, Tunstall. *Mouldings of the Tudor Period.* London, Architectural Press, 1930.

Smith, Jane S. *Elsie de Wolfe: A Life in the High Style.* New York, Atheneum, 1982.

Snell, Charles W. *Vanderbilt Mansion.* Washington, D.C., National Parks Service, 1960.

Sonn, Albert H. *Early American Wrought Iron.* 3 vols. New York, Scribner's, 1928.

Soule, Winsor. *Spanish Farmhouses and Minor Public Buildings.* New York, Architectural Book Publishing, 1924.

Squires, Frederick. *The Hollow Tile House.* New York, Comstock, 1913.

Staats, H. Philip. *California Architecture in Santa Barbara.* New York, Architectural Book Publishing, 1929.

Stamp, Gavin, and André Goulancourt. *The English House, 1860–1914.* Chicago, University of Chicago Press, 1986.

Starr, Kevin. *Americans and the California Dream, 1850–1915.* New York, Oxford University Press, 1973.

———. *Inventing the Dream: California through the Progressive Era.* New York, Oxford University Press, 1985.

Stein, Susan R., ed. *The Architecture of Richard Morris Hunt.* Chicago, University of Chicago Press, 1986.

Stern, Robert A. M. *George Howe: Toward a Modern American Architecture.* New Haven, Yale University Press, 1975.

———. *Raymond M. Hood.* Catalogue 15, New York, Institute for Architecture and Urban Studies. New York, Rizzoli, 1982.

Stevens, John Calvin, and Albert Winslow Cobb. *Examples of American Domestic Architecture.* New York, Comstock, 1889.

Stevenson, J. J. *House Architecture.* 2 vols. London, Macmillan, 1880.

Stilgoe, John R. *Metropolitan Corridor: Railroads and the American Scene.* New Haven, Yale University Press, 1983.

Stokes, Anson Phelps. *Stokes Records: Notes Regarding the Ancestry and Life of the Anson Phelps and Helen Louisa Stokes.* New York, 1910.

Stoney, Samuel Gaillard. *Plantations of the Carolina Low Country.* Edited by Albert Simmons and Samuel Lapham. Charleston, Carolina Art Association, 1938.

Storrer, William Allin. *The Architecture of Frank Lloyd Wright: A Complete Catalogue.* 2d ed. Cambridge, MIT Press, 1982.

Surdam, Charles Edward, and W. G. Osgoodby. *Beautiful Homes of Morris County and Northern New Jersey.* Morristown, New Jersey, Pierson and Surdam, 1910.

Susman, Warren. *Culture as History: The Transformation of American Society in the Twentieth Century.* New York, Pantheon, 1984.

Sutherland, Daniel E. *Americans and Their Servants: Domestic Service in the United States from 1800 to 1920.* Baton Rouge, LSU Press, 1981.

Tarbell, Ida. *Florida Architecture of Addison Mizner.* New York, Helburn, 1928.

Tatman, Sandra L., and Roger W. Moss, eds. *Biographical Dictionary of Philadelphia Architects, 1700–1930.* Boston, G. K. Hall, 1985.

Taylor, Henry. *Old Halls in Lancashire and Cheshire.* Manchester, Cornish, 1884.

Tebbel, John William. *The Marshall Fields.* New York, E. P. Dutton, 1947.

Teitelman, Edward, and Betsy Fahlman. "Wilson Eyre and the Colonial Revival in Philadelphia." In *The Colonial Revival in America,* edited by Alan Axelrod. New York, Norton in association with the Winterthur Museum, 1985.

Thaxter, Celia. *An Island Garden.* 1894. Reprint. Boston, Houghton Mifflin, 1988.

Throop, Lucy Abbott. *Furnishing the Home of Good Taste.* New York, McBride Nast, 1912.

Tipping, H. Avray. *English Homes, Period 3: Late Tudor and Early Stuart, 1558–1649.* London, 1922.

———. *English Homes, Period 2: Early Tudor, 1485–1558.* London, 1924.

———. *In English Homes.* 3 vols. London, 1904–09.

———. *Old English Furniture.* London, 1928.

———. *English Homes of the Early Renaissance: Elizabethan and Jacobean Houses and Gardens.* 1912. Reprint. New York, Scribner's, 1972.

Tischler, William, ed. *American Landscape Architecture: Designers and Places.* Washington, D.C., Preservation Press, 1989.

Todd, Sereno Edwards. *Country Homes, or Winning Solid Wealth.* Philadelphia, Hubbard Brothers, 1888.

———. *Todd's Country Homes and How to Save Money.* Hartford, Hartford Publishing, 1870.

Tomlan, Michael A. "Architectural Press, U.S." In *The Wiley Encyclopedia of Architecture: Design, Engineering, and Construction,* vol. 1, edited by Joseph A. Wilkes and Robert T. Packard, 269. New York, John Wiley and Sons, 1988.

Trachtenberg, Allan. *The Incorporation of America.* New York, Hill and Wang, 1982.

Trebbel, John. *The Marshall Fields: A Study in Wealth.* New York, E. P. Dutton, 1947.

Tucci, Douglas Sand. *Ralph Adams Cram: American Medievalist.* Boston, Boston Public Library, 1975.

Tweed, Katharine, ed. *The Finest Rooms by America's Great Decorators.* Introduction by Russell Lynes. New York, Viking, 1964.

Twombly, Robert C. *Frank Lloyd Wright: His Life and Architecture.* New York, John Wiley and Sons, 1979.

U.S. Bureau of the Census. *Abstract of the Fourteenth Census, 1920.* Washington, D.C., Government Printing Office, 1923.

———. *Historical Statistics of the United States, Colonial Times to 1970.* 2 vols. Washington, D.C., Government Printing Office, 1975.

Vacquier, Jules Felix. *Les vieux hôtels de Paris: Le faubourg Saint-Germain.* Vol. 2. Paris, 1910

Van der Bent, J. T. *The Planning of Apartment Houses and Country Homes.* New York, Brentano's, 1917.

Vanderbilt, Cornelius, IV. *Farewell to Fifth Avenue.* New York, Simon and Schuster, 1935.

Vanderbilt Mansion. Photographs by Richard Cheek. Little Compton, Rhode Island, Fort Church Publishers with the Hyde Park Historical Association, 1988.

Van Pelt, Garrett, Jr. *Old Architecture of Southern Mexico.* Cleveland, Jansen, 1926.

Van Pelt, John. *A Discussion of Composition.* New York, Macmillan, 1902.

———. *Masterpieces of Spanish Architecture: Romanesque and Allied Styles.* Vol. 4. New York, Pencil Points Press, 1925.

Van Rensselaer, Marianna Griswold. *The Art of Gardening.* New York, 1903.

———. *Art Out of Doors: Hints on Good Taste in Gardening.* New York, Scribner's, 1893. Reprint. 1904.

Van Trump, James D., and Arthur Ziegler, Jr. *Landmark Architecture of Allegheny County, Pennsylvania.*

Pittsburgh, Pittsburgh History and Landmark Foundation, 1967.

Veblen, Thorstein. *Theory of the Leisure Class.* 1899. Reprint. New York, Viking, 1931.

Verey, Rosemary, and Ellen Samuels. *The American Woman's Garden.* Boston, Little, Brown, 1984.

Vogel, F. Rud. *Das amerikanische Haus.* Berlin, Ernst Wasmuth, 1910.

Wagner, E. D. *The Arts and Decoration Book of Successful Houses.* New York, 1940.

Wallace, Philip B., and M. Luther Miller. *Colonial Houses.* New York, Bonanza, 1931.

Wallis, Frank E. *Old Colonial Architecture and Furniture.* Boston, Polley, 1887.

Ware, William R., and Charles S. Keefe, eds. *The Georgian Period.* 6 vols. New York, U.P.C. Book Co., 1923.

Waterman, Thomas Tileston, and John A. Barrows. *Domestic Colonial Architecture of Tidewater Virginia.* 1932. Reprint. New York, Dover, 1969.

————. *Mansions of Virginia, 1706–1776.* Chapel Hill, North Carolina, 1946.

Wecter, Dixon. *The Saga of American Society.* New York, Scribner's, 1937.

Weitze, Karen J. *California's Mission Revival.* Los Angeles, Hennessey and Ingalls, 1984.

The Well-Appointed Bath. Introduction by Gail Caskey Winkler. Washington, D.C., Preservation Press, 1989.

Wharton, Edith. *The Age of Innocence.* New York, Scribner's, 1920.

————. *A Backward Glance.* New York, D. Appleton Century, 1934.

————. *The House of Mirth.* New York, Scribner's, 1905.

Wharton, Edith, and Ogden Codman. *The Decoration of Houses.* New York, Scribner's, 1897.

Wheeler, Gervase. *Rural Homes, or Sketches of Houses Suited to American Country Life with Original Plans, Designs, Etc.* 9 issues. New York, Scribner's, 1851–68.

————. *Homes for the People in Suburb and Country, Etc.* 6 issues. New York, Scribner's, 1855–68.

Whitaker, Charles Harris, ed. *Bertram Grosvenor Goodhue: Architect and Master of Many Arts.* New York, American Institute of Architects, 1925.

White, Morton, and Lucia White. *The Intellectual Versus the City.* 1962. Reprint. New York, Oxford University Press, 1977.

White, Theodore B. *Paul Philippe Cret, Architect and Teacher.* Philadelphia, Art Alliance Press, 1973.

Whitehead, Russell F., Frank C. Brown, and Lisa J. Mullins. *Architectural Treasures of Early America.* Harrisburg, Pennsylvania, National Historical Society, 1987.

Whittlesey, Austin. *The Minor Ecclesiastical, Domestic, and Garden Architecture of Southern Spain.* New York, Architectural Book Publishing, 1917.

————. *The Renaissance Architecture of Central and Northern Spain.* New York, Architectural Book Publishing, 1920.

Wiebe, Robert H. *The Search for Order, 1877–1920.* New York, Hill and Wang, 1967.

Williams, Leonard. *The Arts and Crafts of Older Spain.* 3 vols. Chicago, McClung, 1908.

Wills, Royal Barry. *Houses for Good Living.* New York, Architectural Book Publishing, 1940.

Wilson, Richard Guy. *The A.I.A. Gold Medal.* New York, McGraw-Hill, 1984.

————. *McKim, Mead and White, Architects.* New York, Rizzoli, 1983.

Wilson, Richard Guy, Dianne H. Pilgrim, and Dikran Tashjian. *The Machine Age in America, 1918–41.* New York, Abrams in association with the Brooklyn Museum, 1986.

Wilson, Richard Guy, and Dianne H. Pilgrim, eds. *The American Renaissance, 1876–1917.* New York, Pantheon in association with the Brooklyn Museum, 1979.

Wise, Herbert C., and Ferdinand Beidleman. *Colonial Architecture for Those about to Build.* Philadelphia, Lippincott, 1913.

Withey, Henry F., and Elsie Rathburn Withey. *Biographical Dictionary of American Architects (Deceased).* Los Angeles, New Age Press, 1956.

Wodehouse, Lawrence. *White of McKim, Mead and White.* New York, Garland, 1988.

Wodehouse, Lawrence, ed. *American Architects from the Civil War to the First World War.* Vol. 3. Detroit, Gale Research Series, 1976.

————. *American Architects from the First World War to the Present.* Vol. 4. Detroit, Gale Research Series, 1977.

Woodward, George Evertson. *Woodward's Country Homes.* 8 issues. 1865–[1870s]. Reprint. Watkins Glen, New York, American Life Foundation, 1970.

The Work of Cram and Ferguson, Architects. New York, Pencil Points Press, 1929.

Wright, Frank Lloyd. *An Autobiography.* New York, Duell, Sloan, and Pearce, 1943.

Wright, Gwendolyn. *Moralism and the Model Home.* Chicago, University of Chicago Press, 1980.

Wright, Richardson. *House and Garden: Second Book of Houses.* New York, Condé Nast, 1925.

Yerbury, F. R. *Lesser Known Architecture of Spain.* New York, Helburn, 1926.

Yorke, F. R. S. *The Modern House.* London, Architectural Press, 1934.

Zaitevsky, Cynthia. *The Architecture of William Ralph Emerson.* Cambridge, Mass., Fogg Art Museum, 1969.

Zukowsky, John, and Robbe Pierce Stimson. *Hudson River Villas.* New York, Rizzoli, 1985.

Journals

Abeel, Erica, "Magnificent Obsession: A House in the Country," *New York Times Magazine* (19 April 1987): 20–30.

Adams, Rayne, "Edmund B. Gilchrist," *Architecture* 64 (September 1931): 127–132.

————, "Frank Forster," *Architecture* 63 (June 1931): 329–334.

Allen, Gerald, and Mark Hewitt, "Biltmore," *Via 6,* Journal of the Graduate School of Fine Arts, University of Pennsylvania (1983): 130–141.

Allison, Horace, "English Cottage Types in America," *CLA* (1 October 1911): 39–42.

"Aluminaire: A House for Contemporary Life," *Shelter* 2 (May 1932): 58.

Andrews, Robert S., "The Changing Styles of Country Houses," *Arch. Review* 2 (1904): 1–4.

Andrews, Wayne, "Random Reflections on the Colonial Revival," *Journal of the Archives of American Art* (April 1964): 1–4.

"*Antiques* Speaks for Itself," *Antiques* (1 January 1922): 7–9.

"The Architect's Library," *AR* 63 (January 1978): 90, 91.

"An Argument for Simplicity in Household Furnishings," *Craftsman* (October 1901): iii.

Aslet, Clive, "America's 'Winter Newport': Jekyll Island, Georgia," *Country Life* (UK) (27 September 1984): 834–37.

————, "Changing Enthusiasms," *Country Life* (UK) (4 October 1984): 947–950.

"Awbury, Whitemarsh, Pa.," *House and Garden* (July 1901): 18–22.

Ayres, Atlee B., "The Earliest Mission Buildings of San Antonio," *AABN* 126 (August 1924): 171–178.

Bach, Richard F., "Books on Colonial Architecture," *AR* 39 (February 1916): 185–189.

Baum, D. J., "The Forum Studies of Architectural Precedents," *Arch. Forum* 46 (May 1927): 437.

Bayley, John Barrington, "The Villa Vizcaya," *Classical America* 3 (1973): 71.

Binney, Marcus, "Villa Vizcaya, Florida: 1," *Country Life* (UK) (10 January 1980): 71–74.

Blackall, Clarence, "Fifty Years Ago," *AABN* (5 January 1926): 7–9.

"Bonnycrest, the Residence of Stuart Duncan at Newport, R.I.," *CLA* 37 (November 1919): 28–29.

Bottomley, Harriet, "An Architect's Country House," *AR* 37 (January 1915): 49–63.

Bottomley, William Lawrence, "The American Country House," *AR* 48 (October 1920): 258–368.

————, "The Design of the Country House," *AR* 49 (October 1921): 243–273.

————, "A Selection from the Works of Delano and Aldrich," *AR* 54 (July 1923): 3–71.

Bowman, Lewis, "A Criticism of Reproductions of the Early English Manner," *Arch. Forum* 45 (November 1926): 293–296.

Boyd, John Taylor, "The Home as the American Architect Sees It" (series of sixteen interviews with leading country house architects, including Lindeberg, Aldrich, Wright, Bottomley, Gregory, Baum, Bullard, G. W. Smith, Reginald Johnson, Meigs, Mizener, Platt, Forster, Atterbury, Bowman, Dominick), *A and D* 31–35 (September 1929–October 1931).

————, "Houses Showing a Distinguished Simplicity," *A and D* 33 (October 1930): 57.

————, "Philadelphia House Architecture," *AR* 42 (September 1917): 287–288.

————, "The Relations of Owner and Architect," *A and D* 33 (September 1930): 47.

————, "Variety and Elegance Dominate These Houses," *A and D* 34 (December 1930): 43–45, 101–102.

————, "What Style for the Country House? A Logical Discussion of an Old Question," *A and D* 15 (October 1921): 354.

Brooks, H. Allen, "Frank Lloyd Wright and the Destruction of the Box," *JSAH* 38 (March 1979): 7–14.

Brown, Frank Chouteau, "The Designing of Homes," *Craftsman* (May 1908): 189–200.

————, "The English Derived Treatment of the Small American Dwelling," *AABN* (24 August 1910): 57–63.

————, "The Relation between English and American Domestic Architecture," *Brickbuilder* (July 1906): 138–144; (August 1906): 158–163.

Brown, Robert, Jr., and Robert Jackson, "Old Colonial vs. Old English Houses," *AABN* (3 January 1885): 3–4.

Bryant, H. Stafford, "Two Twentieth-Century Domestic Architects in the South: Neel Reid and William L. Bottomley," *Classical America* 1 (1972): 30–36.

Byers, John, "At Home on the Desert," *California Arts and Architecture* 52 (October 1937): 16–17.

Cahill, B. J. S., "The Country Home of the Honorable James D. Phelan," *Architect and Engineer* 38 (September 1914): 46–57.

Cantor, Jay E., "A Monument to Trade: A. T. Stewart and the Rise of the Millionaire's Mansion in New York," *Winterthur Portfolio* 10 (1975): 165–194.

Carroll, Colin, "Newport's Classic Home: M. M. Van Beuren House," *A and D* 45 (October 1936): 12–16.

Caye, Roger, "The Office and Apartments of a Philadelphia Architect," *AR* 34 (July 1913): 78–88.

Chase, David, "The Beginnings of the Landscape Tradition in America," *Historic Preservation* 25 (January–March 1973): 34–41.

Chilman, C. William, "Baymeath and the Bar Harbor That Was," *New England Galaxy* (Summer 1972).

"Colonial Architecture in the West," *AR* 20 (October 1906): 341–346.

Colton, Arthur Willis, "The Work of William Lawrence Bottomley," *AR* 50 (November–December 1921): 338–357, 418–441.

"Common Brick House Competition," *Arch. Forum* 54 (January 1931): 81–82.

Condit, Elizabeth C., "The Service Equipment of the Country House," *Arch. Forum* 49 (September 1928): 453–458.

"Conservatism in Design: Notes on Some Recent Work by Aymar Embury II," *AR* 32 (October 1912): 329.

"Country Houses Designed by Aymar Embury Which Express the Modern American Spirit in Home Architecture," *Craftsman* (November 1909): 164–172.

Cram, Ralph Adams, "The Influence of the French School on American Architecture," *AABN* (25 November 1899): 66.

———, "A New Influence in the Architecture of Philadelphia," *AR* 15 (February 1904): 93–121.

———, "The Work of Messrs. Frank Miles Day and Brother," *AR* 15 (May 1904): 397–421.

Croly, Herbert, "American Architecture of Today," *AR* 14 (December 1903): 413–435.

———, "The American Country Estate," *AR* 18 (July 1905): 1–7.

———, "American Country Life and Art," *AR* 12 (January 1902): 112–114.

———, "The Architect in Recent Fiction," *AR* 17 (February 1905): 137–139.

———, "Architect of Residences in San Francisco," *AR* 20 (July 1906): 47–62.

———, "An Architectural Oasis," *AR* 19 (February 1906): 135–144.

———, "The Architectural Work of Charles A. Platt," *AR* 15 (March 1904): 181–244.

———[Arthur C. David, pseud.], "The Architecture of Ideas," *AR* 15 (April 1904): 361–384.

———, "The Country House in California," *AR* 34 (December 1913): 483–519.

———, "A Distinctive Type: Five Recent Country Houses by Albro and Lindeberg," *AR* 32 (October 1912): 285–306.

———, "Houses by Howard Shaw," *AR* 19 (February 1906): 104–122.

———, "Houses by Myron Hunt and Elmer Grey," *AR* 20 (October 1906): 281–295.

———, "How to Get a Well Designed House," *AR* 25 (April 1909): 221–234.

———, "Lay-Out of a Large Estate," *AR* 16 (December 1904): 531–555.

———, "The New Architecture," *AR* 28 (December 1910): 388–403.

———[Arthur C. David, pseud.], "New Phases of American Domestic Architecture," *AR* 26 (November 1909): 309–312.

———, "The New Use of Old Forms," *AR* 17 (April 1905): 271–293.

———, "Recent Work of Mr. Howard Shaw, *AR* 22 (December 1907): 421–452.

———, "The Recent Works of John Russell Pope," *AR* 29 (June 1911): 441–511.

———, "Rich Men and Their Houses," *AR* 12 (May 1902): 29–30.

———, "Stuart Duncan Residence at Newport," *AR* 38 (May 1907): 288–309.

———, "What Is Indigenous Architecture?" *AR* 21 (May 1907): 434–442.

———, "The Work of Parker, Thomas, and Rice," *AR* 34 (August 1913): 96–167.

Croly, Herbert, and C. Matlack Price, "The Recent Work of Howard Shaw," *AR* 33 (April 1913): 285–307.

Day, Frank Miles, "On the Choice of Style in Building a House," *House and Garden* 9 (February 1906): 57–65.

Desmond, H. W., "By Way of Introduction," *AR* 1 (July–September 1891): 6.

Duell, Prentice, ' Some Recent Works of Marston and Van Pelt," *AR* 52 (July 1922): 16–38.

Duncan, Frances. "The Gardens of Cornish," *Century* 71 (May 1906): 1–17.

Eberlein, Harold D., "The Anglo-American Country House," *AR* 34 (October 1913): 354–365.

———, "Cotswold Influence in America," *CLA* 40 (June 1921): 58–61.

———, "Examples of the Work of Mellor and Meigs," *AR* 39 (March 1916): 212–246.

———, "Five Phases of the American Country House," *AR* 36 (October 1914): 274–341.

———, "The Gallic Trend in Domestic Architecture," *House and Garden* 42 (November 1922): 54–55, 102.

———, "Philadelphia and Its Residential Development," *AR* 39 (January 1916): 24–39.

"Editorial Comment," *AABN* (20 April 1928): 503.

"El Fuereidas [sic]," *Sunset Magazine* 32 (May 1914): 1060–1063.

Embury, Aymar, II, "Current Tendencies in Country House Design in the East," *AR* 52 (October 1922): 251–283.

Emmet, Alan, "Faulkner Farm: An Italian Garden in Massachusetts," *Journal of Garden History* 6, no. 2 (1986): 162–178.

"English 'Georgian' Architecture: The Source of the American 'Colonial' Style," *AR* 10 (October 1899): 97–108.

Eyre, Wilson, "The Development of American Dwelling Architecture during the Past Thirty Years," *Arch. Review* 22 (November 1917): 241.

———, "My Ideal for the Country Home," *CLA* 24 (May 1913): 35–36.

Fairbanks, Jonathan L., "The Architectural Development of Winterthur House," *Winterthur Portfolio* 1 (1964): 80–105.

Ferguson, John C., "The Country Houses of Atlee B. and Robert M. Ayres," *CITE, the Architecture and Design Review of Houston* (Spring 1986): 18–20.

Ferree, Barr, "Artistic Domestic Architecture in America," *New England Magazine* (June 1895): 451–466.

———, "Notable American Homes: 'Hill-Stead,' the Estate of Alfred Atmore Pope, Esq., Farmington, Conn.," *American Homes and Gardens* (February 1910): 45–47.

Fisher, John Baptiste, "A Jaunt to Wychwood, Lake Geneva, Wisconsin," *AR* 17 (February 1905): 127.

Fleming, E. M., "The History of the Winterthur Estate," *Winterthur Portfolio* 1 (1964): 9–51.

Forbes, A. H., "The Work of Albro and Lindeberg," *Architecture* 26 (1912): 206–240.

Forster, Frank J., "Impressions of an Architect's Visit to Normandy," *AABN* (5 June 1927): 755–760; (20 July 1927): 119–125.

———, "Norman-English Influence in Country Houses," *Arch. Forum* 44 (March 1926): 139–146.

———, "True Sources of Country House Design," *Garden and Home Builder* 45 (August 1927): 558–559, 595; 46 (September 1927): 33–34, 104–105; 47 (October 1927): 156–157, 177.

———, "Use of English and French Types for American Country Houses," *Arch. Forum* 49 (September 1928): 361–366.

French, Leigh, Jr., "The American Country House in the French Provincial Style," *Arch. Forum* 49 (September 1928): 353–360.

"A French Village, Chestnut Hill, Pa.," *AABN* (20 April 1929): 499–509.

Gade, John A., "Long Island Country Places Designed by McKim, Mead and White: The Orchard at Southampton," *House and Garden* 3 (March 1903): 117–126.

———, "Successful Country Houses: Examples of American Domestic Architecture from Every Part of the Country with a Frank Discussion of Each Case by an Experienced Architect," *CLA* 4 (October 1903): 397–405.

Gebhard, David, "The American Colonial Revival in the 1930s," *Winterthur Portfolio* 22 (Summer–Autumn 1987): 109–148.

———, "Architectural Imagery: The Mission and California," *Harvard Architecture Review* 1 (1980): 137–145.

———, "Casa del Herrero: The George F. Steedman House, Montecito, California," *Antiques* (August 1986): 280–283.

———, "C. F. A. Voysey: To and from America," *JSAH* 30 (December 1971): 304–307.

———, "The Spanish Colonial Revival in Southern California, 1885–1930," *JSAH* 26 (May 1967): 131–147.

Gillespie, Harriet S., "A Modernistic House on the Atlantic Beach," *A and D* (January 1930): 52.

Grady, James, "A Question of Style: Houses in Atlanta, 1885–1900," *Perspecta* 15 (1975): 18–34.

Greene, Nathaniel Coit, "The Most Inspiring Estate in New England," *New England Magazine* 38 (April 1908): 136–143.

Gregory, Julius, "On the Charm and Character of the English Cottage," *Arch. Forum* 44 (March 1926): 147–152.

Grey, Elmer, "Some Country House Architecture in the Far West," *AR* 52 (October 1922): 308–344.

Griswold, Louis, "The Way to Solve the Servant Question," *Century* 54 (February 1898): 636.

Hamlin, A. D. F., "The American Country House," *AR* 42 (October 1917): 292–391.

———, "The American Country House: With Particular Reference to Types Developed or Improved during the War," *AR* 44 (October 1918): 274–379.

———, "Twenty-Five Years of American Architecture," *AR* 40 (July 1916): 12.

Hastings, Thomas, "The Influence of Life in the Development of an Architectural Style," *AABN* (6 July 1913): 29–30.

Hawley, Sherwin, "Good Taste in Country Houses," *CLA* 10 (October 1906): 610–624.

Hawthorne, Hildegarde, "A Garden of the Imagination: Mrs. Gardner's at 'Green Hills,' near Boston," *Century Magazine* 80 (July 1910): 446–452.

Hersey, George L., "J. C. Loudon and Architectural Associationism," *Arch. Review* (London) 144 (August 1968): 89–92.

Hewitt, Mark A., 'Hill-Stead, Farmington, Connecticut: The Making of a Colonial Revival Country House," *Antiques* 134 (October 1988): 848–861.

———, "William Adams Delano and the Muttontown Enclave," *Antiques* 132 (August 1987): 316–327.

Higgins, Daniel P., "Business and Management in the Practice of Architecture," *AABN* (20 April 1928): 491–502.

Hines, Fay, "Steel for the Private Life of a Business Man: Office Building Structure in a Country House," *A and D* 43 (November 1935): 18–20.

Hitchcock, Henry-Russell, "Frank Lloyd Wright and the 'Academic Tradition,'" *Journal of the Warburg and Courtauld Institutes* 7 (1944): 46–63.

Holden, Wheaton, "The Peabody Touch: Peabody and Stearns of Boston, 1870–1917," *JSAH* 32 (March 1973): 114–131.

"House of James Waldron Gillespie, Montecito, California," *House and Garden* 4 (September 1903): 97–103.

"House of William Stix Wasserman, Esq.," *Arch. Forum* 53 (July–September 1930): 230–232; 62 (March 1935): 195–205.

"Houses Designed by H. T. Lindeberg," *AR* (October 1933): 261–288.

"The House That Works: 1, 2," *Fortune* 12 (October 1935): 59–67, 94–100.

Howe, Samuel, "The Country House of Mr. E. L. Winthrop, Jr.," *Town and Country* (14 November 1914).

———, "One Source of Color Values [Louis C. Tiffany gardens]," *House and Garden* 10 (September 1906): 105–113.

Howett, Catherine M., "The Residential Architecture of Neel Reid," *Georgia Journal* 2 (February–March 1982): 21–27.

———, "A Southern Lady's Legacy: The Italian 'Terraces' of La Grange, Georgia," *Journal of Garden History* 2, no. 4 (1982): 343–360.

"How *House and Garden* Began," *House and Garden* 50, no. 1 (1926): 60–71.

Hudnut, Joseph, "The Last of the Romans: Comment on the Building of the National Gallery of Art," *Magazine of Art* 34 (April 1941): 169–173.

Jackson, Kenneth, "A Nation of Suburbs," *Chicago History* 13 (Summer 1984): 6–25.

Jones, Edith M., "The House That Will Keep Servants," *CLA* 37 (March 1920): 50–51.

Kaufmann, Edgar, Jr., "At Home with L. C. Tiffany," *Interiors* 117 (December 1947); 112–125, 183.

"Kemper Campbell Ranch," *Architect and Engineer* (October 1946): 21–25.

Kocher, A. Lawrence, "The American Country House," *AR* 58 (November 1925): 401–512.

Koehl, William, "Domestic Architecture of To-Day," *Architect and Engineer* (July 1913): 63–75.

Kimball, Fiske, "The American Country House," *AR* 46 (October 1919): 291–400.

———, "Recent Architecture in the South," *AR* 55 (March 1924): 212.

"Lake Forest, Illinois," *House and Garden* 5 (June 1904): 275.

Landau, Sarah Bradford, "Richard Morris Hunt: The Continental Picturesque and the 'Stick Style,'" *JSAH* 42 (October 1983): 272–289.

Lane, Jonathan, "The Period House in the 1920s," *JSAH* 20 (December 1961): 169–178.

LaRoche, Nancy, "The Hill-Stead Museum: A Victory for the Muses," *Art News* 4 (December 1975): 70–71.

Lee, W. Duncan, "The Renascence of Carter's Grove, on the James River, Virginia, Now the Home of Mr. and Mrs. Archibald M. McRea," *Architecture* 67 (April 1933): 207–210.

Lescaze, William, "The Future American Country House," *AR* 64 (November 1928): 417–428.

Lindeberg, Harrie T., "The Design and Plan of the Country House," *AABN* (12 April 1911): 133–137.

———, "The Home of the Future: The New Domestic Architecture in the East," *Craftsman* 29 (1916): 675.

———, "The Return of Reason in Architecture," *AR* 74 (October 1933): 252–256.

Litchfield, Electus D., "Country House Architecture in the East," *AR* 38 (October 1915): 453–488.

Longstreth, Richard, "Academic Eclecticism in America," *Winterthur Portfolio* (Spring 1982): 55–82.

———, "Julia Morgan: Some Introductory Notes," *Perspecta* 15 (1975): 74–86.

McCabe, L. R., "Darlington, a Jacobean Manor in New Jersey," *AR* 32 (October 1912): 496–509.

MacDonald, Kenneth, Jr., "Residence Design," *Architect and Engineer* 42 (November 1915): 44–47.

Magonigle, Harold Van Buren, "Office Principles, Policies, and Practice," *Pencil Points* 6 (December 1925): 43–48.

Maher, George W., "Obituary," *A.I.A. Journal* 14 (1926): 504; and *AABN* 130 (October–December 1926): 323.

———, "A Plea for an Indigenous Art," *AR* 21 (June 1907): 431.

Mann, Horace B., "Style in the Country House," *AABN* (12 May 1915): 293–297.

Meeks, Carroll L. V., "Creative Eclecticism," *JSAH* 13, no. 4 (1953): 17.

———, "Picturesque Eclecticism," *Art Bulletin* 32 (September 1950): 226–235.

Meem, John Gaw, "Old Forms for New Buildings," *AABN* (November 1934): 10–12.

Menz, Katherine Boyd, and Donald McTernan, "Decorating for the Frederick Vanderbilts," *Nineteenth Century* 3 (Winter 1977): 44–50.

Metcalf, Pauline, "Ogden Codman, Jr., and 'The Grange,'" *Old Time New England* 71, no. 258 (1981): 68–84.

Millard, Julian, "The Work of Wilson Eyre," *AR* 14 (1903): 279–320.

Miller, Wilhelm, "Have We Progressed in Gardening?" *CLA* (15 April 1912).

Mitchell, Donald G., "The Country House," *Scribner's Magazine* 8 (July 1890): 314–335.

"Modern Owners," *Fortune* 12 (October 1935): 28, 34.

Morgan, Keith N., "Charles A. Platt's Houses and Gardens in Cornish, New Hampshire," *Antiques* 122 (July 1982): 117–129.

Mullgardt, Louis Christian, "Country House Architecture on the Pacific Coast," *AR* 38 (October 1915): 423–451.

Mumford, Lewis, "The Architecture of Escape," *New Republic* (12 August 1925): 321–322.

Nevins, Deborah, "Poet's Garden, Painter's Eye," *House and Garden* (August 1984): 92–96.

———, "The Triumph of Flora: Women and the American Landscape, 1890–1915," *Antiques* 127 (April 1985): 904–922.

"A New Influence in the Architecture of Philadelphia," *AR* 15 (February 1904): 92–121.

Nicholas, Dorothy, "A Great American Garden," *CLA* 79 (April 1941): 24–27, 53.

Nolan, Thomas, "Recent Suburban Architecture in Philadelphia and Vicinity," *AR* 19 (March 1906): 166–193.

Ochsner, Jeffrey Karl, "H. H. Richardson's Frank William Andrews House," *JSAH* 43 (March 1984): 20–32.

O'Neal, William B., "Town and Country, Garden and Field," *Arts in Virginia* 4 (Fall 1963): 18–25.

Pawley, Frederic Arden, "The Country House Room by Room: A Checklist with Suggestions," *Arch. Forum* (March 1933): 194–204.

Post, Emily, "Tuxedo Park: An American Rural Community," *Century* 72 (October 1911): 795–805.

Powell, Edward Payson, "The American Country House," *House and Garden* 8 (December 1905): 221.

Price, Bruce, "The Suburban House," *Scribner's Magazine* 8 (July 1890): 5–19.

Price, C. Matlack, "Building American Houses of Fieldstone," *Craftsman* 22 (1912): 407–416.

———, "The Country House in Good Taste," *A and D* 23 (October 1925): 42–44, 95.

———, "The Development of a National Architecture: The Pennsylvania Type," *A and D* 3 (September 1913): 363–366.

———, "The New Spirit in Country House Design as Expressed by the Work of Harrie T. Lindeberg," *House Beautiful* 57 (February 1925): 128–132.

———, "The True Spirit of the American Country House," *A and D* 12 (January 1920): 156–159.

Reed, Henry Hope, "America's Greatest Living Classical Architect: Philip Trammell Shutze of Atlanta, Georgia," *Classical America* 4 (1977): 5–46.

"Residence of John Jay Chapman, Esq., Barrytown, New York: Charles A. Platt, Architect," *Arch. Review* 15 (January 1908): 10, and plates.

Rey, Felix, "A Tribute to the Mission Style," *Architect and Engineer* (October 1924): 77.

Rogers, Tyler Stewart, "New Structural Features of the Country House," *Arch. Forum* 49, no. 3 (1928): 417–422.

Root, Ralph Rainey, "Country Place Types of the Middle West," *AR* 55 (January 1924): 1–32.

Riley, Phil, "Elizabethan Houses in America," *CLA* 20 (August 1911): 46.

Rudd, William J., "George W. Maher," *Prairie School Review* 1 (First Quarter 1964): 5–13.

Saylor, Henry Hodgman, "The Best Twelve Country Houses in America," parts 1–12, *CLA* (May 1915–April 1916).

Schmidt, Mott B., "Constructing the Curved Stairway," *Arch. Forum* 39 (1923): 37–40.

Schuyler, Montgomery, "Recent American Country Houses," *AR* 32 (October 1912): 271–274.

———, "Works of Cram, Goodhue and Ferguson," *AR* 29 (January 1911): 14–16.

Scully, Vincent, Jr., "Romantic Rationalism and the Expression of Structure in Wood: Downing, Wheeler, Gardner, and the 'Stick Style,' 1840–76," *Art Bulletin* 35 (1953): 121–142.

Smith, Kathryn, "Frank Lloyd Wright, Hollyhock House, and Olive Hill, 1914–24," *JSAH* 38 (March 1979): 15–33.

Spalding, Melvin Pratt, "Are We Losing Our Early English Precedents?" *AABN* (5 March 1929): 281–286.

Spencer, Robert C., Jr., "American Farmhouses," *Brickbuilder* 9 (September 1900): 179–186.

Stowell, Kenneth Kingsley, "Architects' Check List for Country Houses," *Arch. Forum* 49 (September 1928): 467–469.

———, "Design for Living," *Arch. Forum* 58 (March 1933): 173–176.

Streatfield, David C., "Echoes of England and Italy 'On the Edge of the World': Green Gables and Charles Green," *Journal of Garden History* 2, no. 4 (1982): 377–398.

———, "The Garden at Casa del Herrero," *Antiques* 130 (August 1986): 286–293.

Sturgis, D. N. B., "American Residences of Today," *AR* 16 (October 1904): 297–405.

Swift, Samuel, "Community Life in Tuxedo Park," *House and Garden* 8 (August 1905): 67–71.

Tallmadge, Thomas E., "Country House Architecture in

the Middle West," *AR* 52 (October 1922): 285–307.

Tatum, George B., "The Emergence of an American School of Landscape Design," *Historic Preservation* 25 (April–June 1973): 34–41.

"A Thatched Place," *AR* (October 1910): 315–328.

Thompson, Winfield M., "The Hunnewell Estate," *New England Magazine* 25 (October 1901): 151–167.

Trambell, Caroline T., "Ida M. Tarbell and Her Farm," *CLA* 29 (November 1915): 19.

Trowbridge, Charles, "The Spirit of the American Country House," *A and D* 9 (July 1918): 158–160.

Van Rensselaer, Marianna, "American Country Dwellings," *Century* (May 1886): 18–19.

———, "Architecture as a Profession," *Chautauqua Magazine* (1887).

Wack, Henry Wellington, "Taxiing Back and Forth from the Country Estate," *A and D* 34 (November 1930): 47–50.

Wallick, Frederick, "'Fairacres' and Some Other Recent Country Houses by Wilson Eyre," *International Studio* 40 (April 1910): 29–34 and plates.

Wallis, Frank E., "The Colonial Renaissance," *White Pine Series* 2 (February 1916).

"Walter Mellor," *Brickbuilder* 24 (1915): 208.

Warren, David F., "Ima Hogg and Bayou Bend: A History," *Bulletin of the Museum of Fine Arts* (Houston) 12 (Fall 1988).

Warren, Herbert Langford, "The Influence of France on American Architecture," *AABN* (25 November 1899): 67.

"What This Magazine Stands For," *CLA* I (November 1901): 24–25.

White, Elizabeth C., "Gardening as a Hobby," *CLA* 27 (March 1915).

Whitehead, Russell F., "The American Country House," *AR* 54 (November 1923): 393–489.

———, "Current Country House Architecture: The Pendulum of Design Swings," *AR* 56 (November 1924): 385–488.

———, "Harrie T. Lindeberg's Contribution to American Domestic Architecture," *AABN* 146 (April 1935): 33–48.

Wight, Peter B., "Country House Architecture in the Middle West," *AR* 38 (October 1915): 387–421.

Wilson, Richard Guy, "The Early Work of Charles F. McKim: Country House Commissions," *Winterthur Portfolio* 11 (1976): 234–267.

Wise, Herbert C., "Frank Miles Day," *Brickbuilder* 24 (December 1915): 316.

Wodehouse, Lawrence, "Stanford White and the Mackeys: A Case Study in Architect-Client Relationships," *Winterthur Portfolio* 11 (1976): 213–233.

"Women in Horticulture," *House and Garden* 47 (March 1925): 64.

Wylie, Dalton, "Lessons from a Seaside Estate: Beautiful Baymeath Where Inland Flowers Are Made to Grow at the Edge of the Salt Sea," *CLA* (July 1907): 308–318.

Ziegler, Carl A., "The Architect and the More Pretentious House," *AABN* (5 April 1928): 422–432.

Unpublished Sources

Bedford, Steven M.. "The Architecture of John Russell Pope," Ph.D. diss., Columbia University, forthcoming.

Blake, Curtis Channing, "The Architecture of Carrère and Hastings," Ph.D. diss., Columbia University, 1976.

Bricker, Lauren Weiss, "The Residential Architecture of Roland E. Coat, Jr.," Master's thesis, University of California at Santa Barbara, 1983.

Daniel, Anne Minor, "The Early Architecture of Ralph Adams Cram," Ph.D. diss., University of North Carolina at Chapel Hill, 1978.

Delano, William Adams, "The Reminiscences of William Adams Delano," Columbia University, 1972.

Graybill, Samuel, "Bruce Price, American Architect, 1845–1903," Ph.D. diss., Yale University, 1957.

Greenberg, Allan, and Mark Hewitt, "Town and Country Georgian: The Architecture of Mott B. Schmidt, 1889–1977," 1983.

Heintzelman, Patricia Lawson, "The Life and Work of Frank Miles Day," Ph.D. diss., University of Delaware, 1980.

Holden, Wheaton, "Robert Swain Peabody of Peabody and Stearns in Boston: The Early Years, 1870–86," Ph.D. diss., Boston University, 1969.

Hood, Davyd Foard, "William Lawrence Bottomley in Virginia: The 'Neo-Georgian' Houses in Richmond," Master's thesis, University of Virginia, 1975.

Lake Geneva Land Conservancy, *Lake Geneva Historic Survey,* State Historical Society of Wisconsin, 1984.

Metcalf, Pauline, "Ogden Codman, Jr., Architect, Decorator: Elegance without Excess," Master's thesis, Columbia University, 1978.

Mitchell, William R., "The T-Square Club, Philadelphia, 1883–1938," Master's thesis, University of Delaware, 1967.

Shaw, Howard Van Doren, collection of papers and drawings, microfilm no. 1980–1, Burnham Library, Art Institute of Chicago.

Tatman, Sandra, "A Study of the Work of Mellor, Meigs and Howe," Master's thesis, University of Oregon, 1977.

Teutonico, Jeanne Marie, "Marian Cruger Coffin: The Long Island Estates," Master's thesis, Columbia University, 1983.

Thomas, George E., "William L. Price: Builder of Men and Buildings," Ph.D. diss., University of Pennsylvania, 1975.

Tomlan, M. A., "Popular and Professional American Architectural Literature in the Late Nineteenth Century," Ph.D. diss., Cornell University, 1983.

Townsend, Gavin, "The Tudor House in America, 1890–1930," Ph.D. diss., University of California at Santa Barbara, 1986.

Walton, Elizabeth, "The Building Art of Wilson Eyre: A Study of 'Queen Anne Motifs' in American Architecture," Master's thesis, Pennsylvania State University, 1962.

Williamson, Daniel C., "The Architecture of Robert Rodes McGoodwin," Atheneum of Philadelphia, 1977.

Collections

Art Institute of Chicago, Burnham Library.

Chicago Historical Society.

Columbia University, Avery Architectural Archives, New York.

Cornell University, Ellen Biddle Shipman Collection.

Gottscho Schleissner Collection, Long Island City, New York.

Hagley Museum and Library, Wilmington, Delaware.

Historical Society of Palm Beach, West Palm Beach, Florida.

Hofstra University, Long Island Studies Institute, Nassau County, New York.

Lenox Library, Lenox, Massachusetts.

Library of Congress, Prints and Drawings Collection.

Museum of the City of New York.

New York Historical Society.

Society for the Preservation of New England Antiquities, Boston, Massachusetts.

Syracuse University, Architectural Drawings Collection, George Arents Research Library.

University of California at Santa Barbara, Architectural Drawing Collection, University Art Museum.

University of Pennsylvania, Architectural Archives.

University of Texas at Austin, Architectural Drawings Collection.

Index